T0178076

Lecture Notes in Artificial Intelligence 13416

Subseries of Lecture Notes in Computer Science

More information about this subseries at https://link.springer.com/bookseries/1244

Georg Gottlob · Daniela Inclezan ·
Marco Maratea (Eds.)

Logic Programming and Nonmonotonic Reasoning

16th International Conference, LPNMR 2022
Genova, Italy, September 5–9, 2022
Proceedings

 Springer

Editors
Georg Gottlob ⓘ
University of Oxford
Oxford, UK

Daniela Inclezan ⓘ
Miami University
Oxford, OH, USA

Marco Maratea ⓘ
University of Genoa
Genoa, Italy

ISSN 0302-9743   ISSN 1611-3349 (electronic)
Lecture Notes in Artificial Intelligence
ISBN 978-3-031-15706-6   ISBN 978-3-031-15707-3 (eBook)
https://doi.org/10.1007/978-3-031-15707-3

LNCS Sublibrary: SL7 – Artificial Intelligence

This Springer imprint is published by the registered company Springer Nature Switzerland AG
The registered company address is: Gewerbestrasse 11, 6330 Cham, Switzerland

Preface

This volume contains the papers presented at the 16th International Conference on Logic Programming and Non-monotonic Reasoning (LPNMR 2022) held during September 5–9, 2022, in Genova Nervi, Italy.

LPNMR 2022 was the sixteenth in the series of international meetings on logic programming and non-monotonic reasoning. LPNMR is a forum for exchanging ideas on declarative logic programming, non-monotonic reasoning, and knowledge representation. The aim of the conference is to facilitate interactions between researchers and practitioners interested in the design and implementation of logic-based programming languages and database systems, and those working in knowledge representation and non-monotonic reasoning. LPNMR strives to encompass theoretical and experimental studies that have led or will lead to advances in declarative programming and knowledge representation, as well as their use in practical applications. The past editions of LPNMR were held in Washington, D.C., USA (1991), Lisbon, Portugal (1993), Lexington, Kentucky, USA (1995), Dagstuhl, Germany (1997), El Paso, Texas, USA (1999), Vienna, Austria (2001), Fort Lauderdale, Florida, USA (2004), Diamante, Italy (2005), Tempe, Arizona, USA (2007), Potsdam, Germany (2009), Vancouver, Canada (2011), Coruña, Spain (2013), Lexington, Kentucky, USA (2015), Espoo, Finland (2017), and Philadelphia, USA (2019).

LPNMR 2022 received 57 submissions. Every submission was reviewed by at least three Program Committee members. In total, 34 papers were accepted as regular long papers, and five as short papers. Thus, 39 of the 57 papers were accepted. The scientific program also included four invited talks by Nicola Leone, University of Calabria, Italy; Sheila McIlraith, University of Toronto, Canada; Alessandra Russo, Imperial College London, UK; and Stefan Woltran, TU Wien, Austria. Moreover, the program was completed by three thematic invited tutorials by Stefania Costantini, University of L'Aquila, Italy; Viviana Mascardi, University of Genoa, Italy; and Andreas Pieris, University of Edinburgh, UK.

Springer sponsored the best technical paper award, while the Italian Association for Logic Programming (GULP) sponsored for the best student paper award. These awards were granted during the conference, followed by the selection of papers to have their long versions invited for Rapid Publication Track to the Artificial Intelligence Journal and to the journal of Theory and Practice of Logic Programming.

Three workshops were co-located with LPNMR 2022: the 4th International Workshop on the Resurgence of Datalog in Academia and Industry (DATALOG 2.0), the First International Workshop on HYbrid Models for Coupling Deductive and Inductive ReAsoning (HYDRA 2022), and the 29th RCRA Workshop on Experimental Evaluation of Algorithms for Solving Problems with Combinatorial Explosion (RCRA 2022). A Doctoral Consortium (DC) was also part of the program. We thank the workshop and DC organizers for their efforts.

We would like to express our warmest thanks and acknowledgments to those who played an important role in the organization of LPNMR 2022: the Program Committee and additional reviewers for their fair and thorough evaluations of submitted papers; Viviana Mascardi for coordinating the workshops, Martin Gebser for organizing the Doctoral Consortium, Jessica Zengari for advertising the conference and its workshops through a number of channels, and the members of the Local Organizing Committee (Angelo Ferrando, Matteo Cardellini, and Marco Mochi) and the other volunteer members for working hard towards the success of the event.

The LPNMR 2022 conference received support from several organizations. We gratefully acknowledge the DIBRIS Department of the University of Genoa, the National Science Foundation, the Artificial Intelligence Journal, the Italian Association for Logic Programming (GULP), Springer, the Association for Logic Programming, Potassco Solutions, SurgiQ, DLVSystem, the Royal Society (supporting G. Gottlob by Project RAISON DATA No. RP\R1\201074), and the Alan Turing Institute.

The conference was managed with the help of EasyChair.

September 2022

Georg Gottlob
Daniela Inclezan
Marco Maratea

Organization

General Chair

Georg Gottlob   University of Oxford, UK

Program Committee Chairs

Daniela Inclezan   Miami University, USA
Marco Maratea   University of Genoa, Italy

Workshop Chair

Viviana Mascardi   University of Genoa, Italy

Doctoral Consortium Chair

Martin Gebser   University of Klagenfurt, Austria

Publicity Chair

Jessica Zangari   University of Calabria, Italy

Local Organization

Angelo Ferrando   University of Genoa, Italy
Matteo Cardellini   University of Genoa, Italy
Marco Mochi   University of Genoa, Italy

Program Committee

Marco Alviano   University of Calabria, Italy
Chitta Baral   Arizona State University, USA
Marcello Balduccini   Saint Joseph's University, USA
Francesco Calimeri   University of Calabria, Italy
Marina De Vos   University of Bath, UK
Carmine Dodaro   University of Calabria, Italy
Agostino Dovier   University of Udine, Italy
Thomas Eiter   TU Wien, Austria
Esra Erdem   Sabanci University, Turkey
Wolfgang Feber   University of Klagenfurt, Austria
Johannes K. Fichte   TU Wien, Austria
Paul Fodor   Stony Brook University, USA

Gerhard Friedrich	University of Klagenfurt, Austria
Sarah Alice Gaggl	TU Dresden, Germany
Martin Gebser	University of Klagenfurt, Austria
Michael Gelfond	Texas Tech University, USA
Gopal Gupta	University of Texas at Dallas, USA
Katsumi Inoue	National Institute of Informatics, Japan
Tomi Janhunen	Tampere University, Finland
Gabriele Kern-Isberner	TU Dortmund, Germany
Matthias Knorr	Universidade Nova de Lisboa, Portugal
Emily LeBlanc	Drexel University, USA
João Leite	Universidade Nova de Lisboa, Portugal
Vladimir Lifschitz	University of Texas at Austin, USA
Enrico Pontelli	New Mexico State University, USA
Francesco Ricca	University of Calabria, Italy
Alessandra Russo	Imperial College London, UK
Orkunt Sabuncu	TED University, Turkey
Chiaki Sakama	Wakayama University, Japan
Torsten Schaub	University of Potsdam, Germany
Guillermo R. Simari	Universidad del Sur in Bahia Blanca, Argentina
Theresa Swift	Universidade Nova de Lisboa, Portugal
Daniele Theseider Dupré	Università del Piemonte Orientale, Italy
Matthias Thimm	FernUniversität in Hagen, Germany
Hans Tompits	TU Wien, Austria
Mirek Truszczynski	University of Kentucky, USA
Johannes P. Wallner	Graz University of Technology, Austria
Kewen Wang	Griffith University, Australia
Stefan Woltran	TU Wien, Austria
Jia-Huai You	University of Alberta, Canada

Additional Reviewers

Ramsha Ali
George Baryannis
Sotiris Batsakis
Arvid Becker
Michael Bernreiter
Elise Böhl
Martin Diller
Dragan Doder
Mohammed El-Kholany
Tobias Geibinger
Susana Hahn
Markus Hecher
Antonio Ielo
Rafael Kiesel

Giovanni Melissari
Johannes Oetsch
Henry Otunuya
Kristian Reale
Dominik Rusovac
Elmer Salazar
Emanuel Sallinger
Patrik Schneider
Kenneth Skiba
Klaus Strauch
Alice Tarzariol
Sarat Chandra Varanasi
Zhiqiang Zhuang

Sponsors and Collaborators

Alan Turing Institute
Artificial Intelligence Journal, Elsevier
Association for Logic Programming (ALP)
DIBRIS, University of Genoa
DLVSystem
Gruppo Utenti Logic Programming (GULP)
Italian Association for Artificial Intelligence (AI*IA)
National Science Foundation (NSF)
Potassco Solutions
Royal Society
Springer
SurgiQ
Theory and Practice of Logic Programming, Cambridge University Press

Abstracts of Invited Talks

DLV Evolution from Datalog to Ontology and Stream Reasoning

N. Leone, M. Alviano, F. Calimeri, C. Dodaro, G. Ianni, M. Manna,
E. Mastria, M.C. Morelli, F. Pacenza, S. Perri, K. Reale, F. Ricca,
G. Terracina, and J. Zangari

University of Calabria, Italy
{n.leone, m.alviano, f.calimeri, c.dodaro, g.ianni,
m.manna, e.mastria, m.c.morelli, f.pacenza, s.perri,
k.reale, f.ricca, g.terracina, j.zangari}@unical.it

Abstract. DLV has been one of the first solid and reliable integrated systems for Answer Set Programming (ASP). DLV has significantly contributed both in spreading the use of ASP and in fostering AI-based technological transfer activities. This paper overviews the history and the recent evolution of the system, which enable effective reasoning on ontologies and streams of data, and the development of new applications.

Keywords: Answer set programming · Ontologies · Stream reasoning

The DLV System

DLV [27] has been one of the first solid and reliable integrated ASP systems. Its project started a few years after the first definition of answer set semantics [21]. It has always been, since the beginning, a suitable tool for applications in academic and real-world scenarios, and significantly contributed both in spreading the use of ASP and in fostering AI-based technological transfer activities [2, 19, 23]. After years of incremental updates, a brand new version has been released, namely DLV-2 [4], a modern ASP system featuring efficient evaluation techniques, proper development tools, versatility, and interoperability. The project firstly focussed on developing separate solutions for *grounding* and *solving*, releasing the I-DLV grounder [13] and the WASP solver [5]; later on, the two systems have been integrated in a monolithic, yet slender body. As for the input language, DLV-2 was born fully compliant with the ASP-Core-2 standard language; in addition, it offers additional constructs and tools for further enhancing usability in real-world contexts [2, 23]. Historically, one of the most distinctive traits of DLV is a full-fledged deductive-database system nature; nevertheless, it has been steadily maintained and properly updated beyond this scope to handle an increasing number of real-world and industrial applications. Actually, the development of industrial applications of DLV started around 2010, with the first success story being the development of a team-building system [23]. The number of DLV-based industrial applications is constantly growing, among latest we mention: a system querying

DBpedia in natural language [17], a tool for rescheduling of nurse shifts in hospitals [6], a decision support system for the diagnosis of headache disorders [16], and a system for compliance-checking of electric panels [8]. Recently, DLV has been empowered with tools and extensions to handle large scale reasoning with Datalog, run on smart devices, and connect to big data systems [26, 28]. Nonetheless, some of the most compelling challenges consist of empowering DLV with means for ontological reasoning, and stream reasoning.

DLV for Ontological Reasoning

Since 2012, DLV has been actively supporting *Ontology-Based Query Answering* (OBQA) [10], where a query $q(\mathbf{x})$ is evaluated over a *knowledge base* consisting of an extensional *dataset D* paired with an *ontology Σ*. In this context, Description Logics (DLs) [1] and Datalog$^{\pm}$ [10] have been recognized as the two main formalisms to specify ontologies. Unfortunately, in both cases, OBQA is generally undecidable [9]. To overcome this limitation, a number of classes of ontologies that guarantee the decidability of query answering have been proposed with the aim of offering a good balance between computational complexity and expressiveness. Since DLV natively deals with plain Datalog, it can deal with Linear [11], Guarded [9] and Sticky [12], which are Datalog rewritable under conjunctive queries, namely the ontology and the query can be rewritten, independently from datasets, into an equivalent Datalog program. Analogously, since DLV natively supports function symbols and value invention in a controlled way, it directly supports Weakly–Acyclic, which admits canonical models of finite size. In 2012, DLV started supporting Shy, which encompasses and generalizes plain Datalog, Linear and DL-Lite$_R$. In particular, DLV$^\exists$ [25]—the branch of DLV supporting Shy—implements a fixed-point operator called *parsimonious chase* and it is still considered a top system over these classes [7]. Subsequently, a new branch of DLV, called OWL2DLV [3], has been developed with the aim of evaluating SPARQL queries over very large OWL 2 knowledge bases. In particular, OWL2DLV supports Horn-$\mathcal{SHIQ}$ and a large fragment of $\mathcal{EL}$++. Moreover, OWL2DLV incorporates novel optimizations sensibly reducing memory consumption and a server-like behavior to support multiple query scenarios. The high potential of OWL2DLV for large-scale reasoning is outlined by the results of an experiment on data-intensive benchmarks, and confirmed by the direct interest of a major international industrial player, which has stimulated and partially supported this work. More recently, DaR-Ling [20]—a Datalog rewriter for DLP ontologies under SPARQL queries—enriched the DLV suite for OBQA to deal with the *sameAs* and to support concrete datatypes. Finally, by exploiting a novel algorithm designed for the so called *dyadic existential rules* [22], it is now possible to exploit DLV$^\exists$ to deal also with Ward ontologies.

DLV for Stream Reasoning

DLV has been empowered with Stream Reasoning capabilities, which are nowadays a key requirement for deploying effective applications in several real-world domains, such as IoT, Smart Cities, Emergency Management. Stream Reasoning (SR) [18] consists in the application of inference techniques to highly dynamic data streams, and ASP is generally acknowledged as a particularly attractive basis for it. In this view, a new incarnation of DLV has been released, namely *I-DLV-sr* [15], that features a language ad-hoc conceived for easily modeling SR tasks along with robust performance and high scalability. In fact, the input language consists in normal (i.e., non-disjunctive) stratified ASP programs featuring *streaming* literals in rule bodies, over the operators: *in*, *always*, *count*, *at least*, and *at most*; recursion involving streaming literals is allowed. The system takes advantage from *Apache Flink* for efficiently processing data streams and from incremental evaluation techniques [14, 24] to efficiently scale over real-world application domains. *I-DLV-sr* proved to be effectively usable over real-world SR domains; nevertheless, being under steady development, it has been significantly improving over time with respect of stability, performance and language features; for instance, inspired by applications in the smart city domain, new constructs have been recently introduced that further ease the modeling of reasoning tasks and enable new functionalities, such as external sources of computation, trigger rules, means for explicitly refer to time, generalized streaming atoms.

Conclusion

DLV is one of the first solid and reliable integrated ASP systems. We reported on the development of DLV, mentioned some of the latest applications, and focused on some recent enhancements for reasoning on ontologies and streams of data.

References

1. The Description Logic Handbook: Theory, Implementation, and Applications. Cambridge University Press (2003)
2. Adrian, W.T., et al.: The ASP system DLV: advancements and applications. KI. **32**, 177–179 (2018). https://doi.org/10.1007/s13218-018-0533-0
3. Allocca, C., et al.: Large-scale reasoning on expressive horn ontologies. In: Datalog. CEUR Workshop Proceedings, vol. 2368, pp. 10–21. CEUR-WS.org (2019)
4. Alviano, M., et al.: The ASP system DLV2. In: Balduccini, M., Janhunen, T. (eds.) LPNMR 2017. LNCS, vol. 10377, pp. 215–221. Springer, Cham (2017). https://doi.org/10.1007/978-3-319-61660-5_19
5. Alviano, M., Dodaro, C., Leone, N., Ricca, F.: Advances in WASP. In: Calimeri, F., Ianni, G., Truszczynski, M. (eds.) LPNMR 2015. LNCS, vol. 9345, pp. 40–54. Springer, Cham (2015). https://doi.org/10.1007/978-3-319-23264-5_5
6. Alviano, M., Dodaro, C., Maratea, M.: Nurse (re)scheduling via answer set programming. Intelligenza Artificiale **12**(2), 109–124 (2018)
7. Baldazzi, T., Bellomarini, L., Favorito, M., Sallinger, E.: On the relationship between shy and warded datalog+/− (2022)
8. Barbara, V., et al.: Neural-symbolic approach to compliance of electric panels. In: Proceedings of the of CILC 22
9. Calì, A., Gottlob, G., Kifer, M.: Taming the infinite chase: query answering under expressive relational constraints. J. Artif. Intell. Res. **48**, 115–174 (2013)

10. Calì, A., Gottlob, G., Lukasiewicz, T.: Tractable query answering over ontologies with datalog+/−. In: Description Logics. CEUR Workshop Proceedings, vol. 477. CEUR-WS.org (2009)
11. Calì, A., Gottlob, G., Lukasiewicz, T.: A general datalog-based framework for tractable query answering over ontologies. J. Web Semant. **14**, 57–83 (2012)
12. Calì, A., Gottlob, G., Pieris, A.: Towards more expressive ontology languages: the query answering problem. Artif. Intell. **193**, 87–128 (2012)
13. Calimeri, F., Fuscà, D., Perri, S., Zangari, J.: I-DLV: the new intelligent grounder of DLV. IA **11**(1), 5–20 (2017)
14. Calimeri, F., Ianni, G., Pacenza, F., Perri, S., Zangari, J.: Incremental answer set programming with overgrounding. TPLP **19**(5-6), 957–973 (2019)
15. Calimeri, F., Manna, M., Mastria, E., Morelli, M.C., Perri, S., Zangari, J.: I-dlv-sr: A stream reasoning system based on I-DLV. TPLP **21**(5), 610–628 (2021)
16. Costabile, R., Catalano, G., Cuteri, B., Morelli, M.C., Leone, N., Manna, M.: A logic-based decision support system for the diagnosis of headache disorders according to the ICHD-3 international classification. TPLP **20**(6), 864–879 (2020)
17. Cuteri, B., Reale, K., Ricca, F.: A logic-based question answering system for cultural heritage. In: Calimeri, F., Leone, N., Manna, M. (eds.) JELIA 2019. LNCS, vol. 11468, pp. 526–541. Springer, Cham (2019). https://doi.org/10.1007/978-3-030-19570-0_35
18. Dell'Aglio, D., Valle, E.D., van Harmelen, F., Bernstein, A.: Stream reasoning: a survey and outlook. Data Sci. **1**(1–2), 59–83 (2017)
19. Erdem, E., Gelfond, M., Leone, N.: Applications of answer set programming. AI Mag. **37**(3), 53–68 (2016)
20. Fiorentino, A., Zangari, J., Manna, M.: Darling: a datalog rewriter for OWL 2 RL ontological reasoning under SPARQL queries. TPLP **20**(6), 958–973 (2020)
21. Gelfond, M., Lifschitz, V.: Classical negation in logic programs and disjunctive databases. NGC **9**(3/4), 365–386 (1991)
22. Gottlob, G., Manna, M., Marte, C.: Dyadic existential rules. In: Datalog 2.0. (2022, paper under review)
23. Grasso, G., Leone, N., Ricca, F.: Answer set programming: language, applications and development tools. In: Faber, W., Lembo, D. (eds.) RR 2013. LNCS, vol. 7994, pp. 19–34. Springer, Heidelberg (2013). https://doi.org/10.1007/978-3-642-39666-3_3
24. Ianni, G., Pacenza, F., Zangari, J.: Incremental maintenance of overgrounded logic programs with tailored simplifications. TPLP **20**(5), 719–734 (2020)
25. Leone, N., Manna, M., Terracina, G., Veltri, P.: Fast query answering over existential rules. ACM Trans. Comput. Log. **20**(2), 12:1–12:48 (2019)
26. Leone, N., Perri, S., Ricca, F., Veltri, P., Zangari, J.: First steps towards reasoning on big data with DLV. In: Bergamaschi, S., Noia, T.D., Maurino, A. (eds.) Proceedings of the SEBD 2018. CEUR Workshop Proceedings, vol. 2161. CEUR-WS.org (2018)
27. Leone, N., et al.: The DLV system for knowledge representation and reasoning. ACM Trans. Comput. Log. **7**(3), 499–562 (2006)
28. Reale, K., Calimeri, F., Leone, N., Ricca, F.: Smart devices and large scale reasoning via ASP: tools and applications. In: Cheney, J., Perri, S. (eds.) PADL 2022. LNCS, vol. 13165, pp. 154–161. Springer, Cham. https://doi.org/10.1007/978-3-030-94479-7_1

Reward Machines: Formal Languages and Automata for Reinforcement Learning

Sheila McIlraith

University of Toronto, Toronto, Canada
sheila@cs.toronto.edu

Reinforcement Learning (RL) is proving to be a powerful technique for building sequential decision making systems in cases where the complexity of the underlying environment is difficult to model. Two challenges that face RL are reward specification and sample complexity. Specification of a reward function – a mapping from state to numeric value – can be challenging, particularly when reward-worthy behaviour is complex and temporally extended. Further, when reward is sparse, it can require millions of exploratory episodes for an RL agent to converge to a reasonable quality policy. In this talk I'll show how formal languages and automata can be used to represent complex non-Markovian reward functions. I'll present the notion of a Reward Machine, an automata-based structure that provides a normal form representation for reward functions, exposing function structure in a manner that greatly expedites learning. Finally, I'll also show how these machines can be generated via symbolic planning or learned from data, solving (deep) RL problems that otherwise could not be solved.

Logic-Based Machine Learning: Recent Advances and Their Role in Neuro-Symbolic AI

Alessandra Russo, Mark Law, Daniel Cunnington, Daniel
Furelos-Blanco, and Krysia Broda

Department of Computing, Imperial College London
{a.russo, mark.law09, d.cunnington20,
d.furelos-blanco18, k.broda}@imperial.ac.uk

Abstract. Over the last two decades there has been a growing interest in logic-based machine learning, where the goal is to learn a logic program, called a *hypothesis*, that together with a given background knowledge explains a set of examples. Although logic-based machine learning has traditionally addressed the task of learning definite logic programs (with no negation), our logic-based machine learning approaches have extended this field to a wider class of formalisms for knowledge representation, captured by the answer set programming (ASP) semantics. The ASP formalism is truly declarative and due to its non-monotonicity it is particularly well suited to commonsense reasoning. It allows constructs such as choice rules, hard and weak constraints, and support for default inference and default assumptions. Choice rules and weak constraints are particularly useful for modelling human preferences, as the choice rules can represent the choices available to the user, and the weak constraints can specify which choices a human prefers. In the recent years we have made fundamental contributions to the field of logic-based machine learning by extending it to the learning of the full class of ASP programs and the first part of this talk provides an introduction to these results and to the general field of learning under the answer set semantics, referred here as *learning from answer sets* (LAS).

To be applicable to real-world problems, LAS has to be tolerant to noise in the data, scalable over large search spaces, amenable to user-defined domain-specific optimisation criteria and capable of learning interpretable knowledge from structured and unstructured data. The second part of this talk shows how these problems are addressed by our recently proposed FastLAS approach for learning Answer Set Programs, which is targeted at solving restricted versions of observational and non-observational predicate learning from answer sets tasks. The advanced features of our family of LAS systems have made it possible to solve a variety of real-world problems in a manner that is data efficient, scalable and robust to noise. LAS can be combined with statistical learning methods to realise neuro-symbolic solutions that perform both fast, low-level prediction from unstructured data, and high-level logic-based learning of interpretable knowledge. The talk concludes with presenting two such neuro-symbolic solutions for respectively solving image classification problems in the presence of distribution shifts, and discovering sub-goal structures for reinforcement learning agents.

Non-monotonic Logic-Based Machine Learning

Over the last decade we have witnessed a growing interest in Machine Learning. In recent years Deep Learning has been demonstrated to achieve high-levels of accuracy in data analytics, signal and information processing tasks, bringing transformative impact in domains such as facial, image, speech recognition, and natural language processing. They have best performance on computational tasks that involve large quantities of data and for which the labelling process and feature extraction would be difficult to handle. However, they suffer from two main drawbacks, which are crucial in the context of cognitive computing. They are not capable of supporting AI solutions that are good at more than one task. They are very effective when applied to single specific tasks, but applying the same technology from one task to another within the same class of problems would often require retraining, causing the system to possibly *forget* how to solve a previously learned task. Secondly, and most importantly, they are *not transparent*. Operating primarily as black boxes, deep learning approaches are not amenable to human inspection and human feedbacks, and the learned models are not explainable, leaving the humans agnostic of the cognitive and learning process performed by the system. This lack of transparency hinders human comprehension, auditing of the learned outcomes, and human active engagement into the learning and reasoning processes performed by the AI systems. This has become an increasingly important issue in view of the recent General Data Protection Regulation (GDPR) which requires actions taken as a result of a prediction from a learned model to be justified.

There has been a growing interest in logic-based machine learning approaches whose learned models are explainable and human interpretable. The goal of these approaches is the automated acquisition of knowledge (expressed as a logic program) from given (labelled) examples and existing background knowledge. One of the main advantage of these machine learning approaches is that the learned knowledge can be easily expressed into plain English and explained to a human user, so facilitating a closer interaction between humans and the machine. Logic-based machine learning has traditionally addressed the task of learning knowledge expressible in a very limited form [14] (definite clauses). Our logic-based machine learning systems [1, 2, 7] have extended this field to a wider class of formalisms for knowledge representation, captured by the answer set programming (ASP) semantics [4]. This ASP formalism is truly declarative, and due to its non-monotonicity it is particularly well suited to common-sense reasoning It allows constructs such as choice rules, hard and weak constraints, and support for default inference and default assumptions. Choice rules and weak constraints are particularly useful for modelling human preferences, as the choice rules can represent the choices available to the user, and the weak constraints can specify which choices a human prefers. In the recent years we have made fundamental contributions to the field of logic-based machine learning by extending it to the learning of the full class of ASP programs [5]. Early approaches to learning ASP programs can mostly be divided into two categories: *brave* learners aim to learn a program such that at least one answer set covers the examples; on the other hand, *cautious* learners aim to find a program which covers the examples in all answer sets. Most of the early

ASP-based ILP systems were brave. In [7], we showed that some ASP programs cannot be learned using either the brave or the cautious settings, and in fact a combination of *both* brave and cautious semantics is needed. This has the original motivation for the *Learning from Answer Sets* family of frameworks [8–11] which we have developed since then and have been shown to be able to learn any ASP program.

One of the main features of our LAS framework is the ability to support non-monotonic learning. Non-monotonicity permits incremental learning, allowing the machine to periodically revise rules and knowledge learnt, as examples of user behaviours are continuously observed. The non-monotonicity property is particularly relevant in pervasive computing, where systems are expected to autonomously adapt to changes in user context and behaviour, whilst operating seamlessly with minimal user intervention. We have used our non-monotonic LAS systems in mobile privacy [13], where devices learn and revise user's models from sensory input and user actions (e.g. user's actions on mobile devices), and in security [3], where anomaly detection policies are learned from historical data using domain-specific function for scoring candidate rules to guide the learning process towards the best policies. In both applications, the declarative representation of the learned programs make them explainable to human users, and providing way for users to understand and amend what has been learnt.

Often, many alternative solutions can be learned to explain given set of examples, and most logic-based learning systems employ a bias towards shorter solutions, based on Occam's razor (the solution with the fewest assumptions is the most likely). Choosing the shortest hypothesis may lead to very general hypotheses being learned from relatively few examples. While this can be a huge advantage of logic-based machine learning over other machine learning approaches that need larger quantities of data, learning such general rules without sufficient quantities of data to justify them may not be desirable in every application domain. For example, in access control, wrongly allowing access to a resource may be far more dangerous than wrongly denying access. So, learning a more general hypothesis, representing a more permissive policy, would be more dangerous than a specific hypothesis, representing a more conservative policy. Equally, for access control where the need for resources is time critical, wrongly denying access could be more dangerous than wrongly allowing access. When learning such policies, and choosing between alternative hypotheses, it would be useful to specify whether the search should be biased towards more or less general hypotheses. In [6], we have proposed a logic-based machine learning system, called FastLAS, targeted at solving a restricted version of the context-dependent learning from answer sets tasks that require only observational predicate learning. This system has two main advantages: it allows for domain-specific scoring function for hypotheses which generalises the standard Occam's razor approach, where hypotheses with the lowest number of literals are normally assumed to be preferred; and it is specifically designed to be scalable with respect to the hypothesis space. Its restriction to observational predicate learning has been lifted in [12], where the FastNonOPL system is proposed to solve non observational predicate learning from answer set tasks, whilst preserving scalability is a challenging open problem.

References

1. Athakravi, D., Corapi, D., Broda, K., Russo, A.: Learning through hypothesis refinement using answer set programming. In: Zaverucha, G., Santos Costa, V., Paes, A. (eds.) ILP 2013. LNCS, vol. 8812, pp. 31–46. Springer, Heidelberg (2014). https://doi.org/10.1007/978-3-662-44923-3_3
2. Corapi, D., Russo, A., Lupu, E.: Inductive logic programming in answer set programming. In: Muggleton, S.H., Tamaddoni-Nezhad, A., Lisi, F.A. (eds.) ILP 2011. LNCS, vol. 7207, pp. 91–97. Springer, Heidelberg (2012). https://doi.org/10.1007/978-3-642-31951-8_12
3. Drozdov, A., Law, M., Lobo, J., Russo, A., Don, M.W.: Online symbolic learning of policies for explainable security. In: 3rd IEEE International Conference on Trust, Privacy and Security in Intelligent Systems and Applications, TPS-ISA 2021, Atlanta, GA, USA, 13–15 December 2021, pp. 269–278 (2021)
4. Gelfond, M., Lifschitz, V.: The stable model semantics for logic programming. In: ICLP/SLP, vol. 88, pp. 1070–1080 (1988)
5. Law, M.: Inductive learning of answer set programs. Ph.D. thesis, Imperial College London, UK (2018). https://ethos.bl.uk/OrderDetails.do?uin=uk.bl.ethos.762179
6. Law, M., Russo, A., Bertino, E., Broda, K., Lobo, J.: Fastlas: scalable inductive logic programming incorporating domain-specific optimisation criteria. In: The Thirty-Fourth AAAI Conference on Artificial Intelligence, AAAI 2020, The Thirty-Second Innovative Applications of Artificial Intelligence Conference, IAAI 2020, The Tenth AAAI Symposium on Educational Advances in Artificial Intelligence, EAAI 2020, New York, NY, USA, 7–12 February 2020, pp. 2877–2885 (2020)
7. Law, M., Russo, A., Broda, K.: Inductive learning of answer set programs. In: Logics in Artificial Intelligence - 14th European Conference, JELIA 2014, Funchal, Madeira, Portugal, 24–26 September 2014, Proceedings, pp. 311–325 (2014)
8. Law, M., Russo, A., Broda, K.: Learning weak constraints in answer set programming. Theory Pract. Logic Program. 15(4–5), 511–525 (2015)
9. Law, M., Russo, A., Broda, K.: Iterative learning of answer set programs from context-dependent examples. Theory Pract. Logic Program. (2016)
10. Law, M., Russo, A., Broda, K.: The complexity and generality of learning answer set programs. Artif. Intell. 259, 110–146 (2018). https://doi.org/10.1016/j.artint.2018.03.005
11. Law, M., Russo, A., Broda, K.: The ILASP system for inductive learning of answer set programs. CoRR abs/2005.00904 (2020). https://arxiv.org/abs/2005.00904
12. Law, M., Russo, A., Broda, K., Bertino, E.: Scalable non-observational predicate learning in ASP. In: Proceedings of the Thirtieth International Joint Conference on Artificial Intelligence, IJCAI 2021, Virtual Event/Montreal, Canada, 19–27 August 2021, pp. 1936–1943 (2021)
13. Markitanis, A., Corapi, D., Russo, A., Lupu, E.: Learning user behaviours in real mobile domains. In: Latest Advances in Inductive Logic Programming. Imperial College Press (ILP 2011 Post-proceeding)
14. Muggleton, S.: Inverse entailment and progol. New Gener. Comput. 13(3–4), 245–286 (1995)

Abstract Argumentation with Focus on Argument Claims – An Overview[1]

Michael Bernreiter, Wolfgang Dvořák, Anna Rapberger,
and Stefan Woltran

TU Wien, Institute of Logic and Computation, Austria
{mbernrei,dvorak,arapberg,woltran}@dbai.tuwien.ac.at

Abstract. Abstract argumentation frameworks are among the best researched formalisms in the last two decades. They can be used to model discourses, provide a common ground for several nonmonotonic logics, and are employed to define semantics for more advanced argumentation formalisms. In the latter two domains, it is not the abstract argument's name, but the claim the argument represents, which should be in the focus of reasoning tasks. In this context, the fact that different arguments can represent the same claim leads to certain intricacies when it comes to the actual definition of semantics and in terms of computational aspects. In this talk, we give an overview on recent results in this direction. Those include the relation between argumentation and logic programming semantics, as well as a complexity analysis of acceptance problems in terms of claims and the effect of preferences in this setting.

Keywords: Argumentation Semantics · Claim-based Reasoning · Computational Complexity · Preferences

A Claim-Based Perspective on Logic Programming

Computational argumentation is a vibrant research area in AI [1, 2]; it is concerned with conflict resolution of inconsistent information and the justification of *defeasible statements (claims)* through logical or evidence-based reasoning. The *abstract* representation of conflicting information, significantly shaped by Dung [6], is among the most prominent approaches in this context. In his *abstract argumentation frameworks (AFs)*, each argument is treated as an abstract entity while an attack relation encodes (asymmetric) conflicts between them. Acceptance of arguments is evaluated with respect to *argumentation semantics*. In recent years, the acceptance of *claims* received increasing attention [3, 9]. *Claim-augmented argumentation frameworks (CAFs)* [9] extend Dung's model by assigning each argument its own claim, allowing for systematic study of structural and relational properties of claim acceptance. Formally, a CAF is a triple (A, R, cl) consisting of a set of arguments A, a set of directed attacks

---

[1] Supported by WWTF through project ICT19-065, and FWF through projects P30168 and W1255-N23.

$R{\subseteq}A \times A$ between arguments, and a claim-function cl assigning a claim to each argument. They can be represented as directed labeled graphs (cf. Example 1).

Argumentation and logic programming are closely related [5, 6, 13]. The correspondence of stable model semantics with stable semantics in AFs is probably the most fundamental example [6], but also other logic programming semantics admit equivalent argumentation semantics [13]. With CAFs, the correspondence is particularly close: when identifying *atoms* in a given logic program (LP) P with *claims* of arguments constructed from rules in P we obtain a natural correspondence between LP semantics and AF semantics in terms of claims.

Example 1 (adapted from [5]). Consider the following logic program P:

$r_0 :a \leftarrow \text{not } d$ $r_2 :b \leftarrow \text{not } a$ $r_4 :e \leftarrow \text{not } e$
$r_1 :d \leftarrow \text{not } a$ $r_3 :c \leftarrow \text{not } a, \text{not } b$ $r_5 :e \leftarrow \text{not } a, \text{not } e$

When we interpret each rule r_i as an argument x_i with claim $head(r_i)$ and consider attacks between arguments x_i and x_j if the claim of x_i appears negated in the body of the rule r_j corresponding to x_j, we obtain the following CAF $\mathcal{F}$:

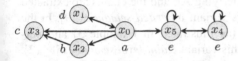

P returns $\emptyset$, $\{a\}$, and $\{d, b\}$ under *p-stable model semantics* (where one allows for undecided atoms). The complete[2] argument-sets of $\mathcal{F}$ in turn are $\emptyset$, $\{x_0\}$, and $\{x_1, x_2\}$. Inspecting the claims of these sets, $\mathcal{F}$ thus yields the same outcome as P. This is not a coincidence: as shown in [5], complete semantics correspond to p-stable model semantics when extracting the claims of the arguments.   ◇

Hence the representation as CAF establishes the connection between the two paradigms without detours, i.e., no additional steps or mappings are needed. Moreover, with CAFs, it is possible to capture semantics that make direct use of the claims. This advantage becomes apparent when we consider semantics that take *false* atoms into account: *L-stable semantics* [10] minimizes the set of undecided atoms in a p-stable model. *Semi-stable semantics* can be seen as their AF counter-part: here, the set of arguments which are neither accepted (i.e., contained in a complete extension) nor attacked is minimized. However, when evaluating our LP P under L-stable model semantics and its corresponding CAF $\mathcal{F}$ under semi-stable semantics we observe an undesired discrepancy.

Example 2 (Example 1 ctd.). The L-stable models of P are $\{a\}$ (atoms b, c, d are false) and $\{d, b\}$ (here, a, c are false). We obtain the single semi-stable extension $\{x_0\}$ in $\mathcal{F}$ (x_0 attacks all remaining arguments except x_4, minimizing undecided arguments), hence $\{a\}$ is the only semi-stable claim-set of $\mathcal{F}$.   ◇

---

[2] A set of arguments E is complete if it is conflict-free, defends itself, and contains all arguments it defends (E defends a if each attacker b of a is counter-attacked).

With CAFs, it is possible to define argumentation semantics such that they mimic the behavior of performing maximization on conclusion-level and minimize the set of undecided *claims* instead. For this, it is crucial to consider the *defeated claims* of an extension: intuitively, a claim is defeated iff all arguments carrying this claim are attacked. We illustrate the idea on our example.

Example 3 (Example 1 ctd.). We model L-stable semantics by maximizing accepted and defeated claims of complete sets: The set $\{x_0\}$ defeats claims b, c, d; claim e is not defeated because x_0 does not attack all occurrences of e. The set of accepted and defeated claims w.r.t. the extension $\{x_0\}$ (the *claim-range* of $\{x_0\}$) is thus given by $\{a, b, c, d\}$. Note that we obtain the same claim-range for the complete set $\{x_1, x_2\}$, which provides us with two semi-stable extensions under this evaluation method. Now, $\mathcal{F}$ yields the same outcome as P when evaluated under L-stable semantics.   ◇

Advances in Claim-Based Reasoning in a Nutshell

Claim-Based Semantics. We sketched two different evaluation methods for CAFs, taking into account different aspects of claim-based reasoning: In the first method, semantics are evaluated with respect to the underlying AF and the claims are extracted in the final step of the evaluation. We call this variant *inherited semantics* [9]. In the second method, we considered claim-defeat (as illustrated in Example 3) and performed maximization on claim-level. We call this variant *claim-level semantics* [8, 12]. Both variants capture claim-based reasoning in different aspects. While inherited semantics are well-suited to investigate justification in structured argumentation, claim-level semantics capture reasoning in conclusion-oriented formalisms. In the talk, we will review a detailed comparison between these two variants, cf. [8].

Well-formed CAFs. Observe that in CAFs obtained from LPs (cf. Example 5), any two arguments with the same claim attack the same arguments, i.e., if x and y have the same claim then x attacks the argument z iff y attacks z. This behavior is common to many instantiations of CAFs, and gives rise to the important class of well-formed CAFs. Formally, a CAF (A, R, cl) is well-formed iff for all $x, y \in A$ with $cl(x) = cl(y)$ we have $\{z \mid (x, z) \in R\} = \{z \mid (y, z) \in R\}$. As mentioned, well-formed CAFs capture LP-instantiations. Moreover, well-formed CAFs have benefits over general CAFs with regards to semantic properties and computational complexity. We furthermore note that the inherited and claim-based versions of prominent (e.g., stable) semantics coincide on well-formed CAFs [8].

Preferences in Claim-Based Reasoning. While well-formed CAFs are a natural sub-class of CAFs, they fail to account for a notion common to many formalisms instantiated into AFs, namely preferences. Specifically, in the course of the instantiation process, it often occurs that one argument x is considered stronger than (or: preferred to) another argument y ($x \succ y$). If there is an attack violating this preference, i.e., $(y, x) \in R$, then this is called a critical attack. This notion of preference in terms of argument strength leads to a generalization of well-formed CAFs to so-called Preference-based CAFs (PCAFs) [4]. Formally, a PCAF is given as $(A, R, cl, \succ)$ where (A, R, cl) is a well-formed CAF and $\succ$ is an asymmetric preference relation over A.

Preferences are then resolved via so-called preference-reductions which transform PCAFs into CAFs. The literature [11] describes several such reductions for AFs: a prominent method is to delete critical attacks; further approaches revert critical attacks or delete them only if there is also an attack from the stronger to the weaker argument, Finally a combination of the latter two is often considered. These four reductions give rise to four new CAF-classes being strictly located between well-formed CAFs and general CAFs. Also, only some of these classes preserve certain benefits of well-formed CAFs while others exhibit the same behavior as general CAFs.

Complexity Results. In the talk, we finally review complexity results obtained for CAFs and PCAFs [4, 7, 9]. It has been shown that the verification problem (testing whether a given claim set is an extension for a given CAF/PCAF) can have higher complexity for CAFs than for AFs, while this gap does not show up for most semantics when restricting ourselves to well-formed CAFs. Interestingly, for PCAFs this effect depends on the chosen reduction.

References

1. Atkinson, K., et al.: Towards artificial argumentation. AI Mag. **38**(3), 25–36 (2017)
2. Baroni, P., Gabbay, D.M., Giacomin, M.: Handbook of Formal Argumentation. College Publications (2018)
3. Baroni, P., Riveret, R.: Enclling systems. J. Artif. Intell. Res. **66**, 793–860 (2019)
4. Bernreiter, M., Dvořák, W., Rapberger, A., Woltran, S.: The effect of preferences in abstract argumentation under a claim-centric view. CoRR (2022). https://doi.org/10.48550/arXiv.2204.13305, accepted for publication at NMR'22
5. Caminada, M., Sá, S., Alcântara, J., Dvořák, W.: On the equivalence between logic programming semantics and argumentation semantics. Int. J. Approx. Reas. **58**, 87–111 (2015)
6. Dung, P.M.: On the acceptability of arguments and its fundamental role in nonmonotonic reasoning, logic programming and n-person games. Artif. Intell. **77**(2), 321–358 (1995)
7. Dvořák, W., Greßler, A., Rapberger, A., Woltran, S.: The complexity landscape of claim-augmented argumentation frameworks. In: AAAI, pp. 6296–6303 (2021)
8. Dvořák, W., Rapberger, A., Woltran, S.: Argumentation semantics under a claim-centric view: Properties, expressiveness and relation to SETAFs. In: KR, pp. 341–350 (2020)
9. Dvořák, W., Woltran, S.: Complexity of abstract argumentation under a claim-centric view. Artif. Intell. **285**, 103290 (2020)
10. Eiter, T., Leone, N., Saccà, D.: On the partial semantics for disjunctive deductive databases. Ann. Math. Artif. Intell. **19**(1–2), 59–96 (1997). https://doi.org/10.1023/A:1018947420290
11. Kaci, S., van der Torre, L.W.N., Vesic, S., Villata, S.: Preference in abstract argumentation. In: Handbook of Formal Argumentation, vol. 2, pp. 211–248. College Publications (2021)
12. Rapberger, A.: Defining argumentation semantics under a claim-centric view. In: STAIRS-ECAI. CEUR Workshop Proceedings, vol. 2655. CEUR-WS.org (2020)
13. Wu, Y., Caminada, M., Gabbay, D.M.: Complete extensions in argumentation coincide with 3-valued stable models in logic programming. Studia Logica **93**(2–3), 383–403 (2009)

Contents

Systems

Applications

xxx   Contents

Technical Contributions

Syntactic ASP Forgetting with Forks

Felicidad Aguado[1] , Pedro Cabalar[1(⊠)] , Jorge Fandinno[2] ,
David Pearce[3] , Gilberto Pérez[1] , and Concepción Vidal[1]

[1] University of Corunna, Corunna, Spain
{felicidad.aguado,cabalar,gperez,concepcion.vidalm}@udc.es
[2] University of Nebraska at Omaha, Omaha, NE, USA
jfandinno@unomaha.edu
[3] Universidad Politécnica de Madrid, Madrid, Spain
david.pearce@upm.es

Abstract. In this paper, we present a syntactic transformation, called
the *unfolding* operator, that allows forgetting an atom in a logic program
(under ASP semantics). The main advantage of unfolding is that, unlike
other syntactic operators, it is always applicable and guarantees strong
persistence, that is, the result preserves the same stable models with
respect to any context where the forgotten atom does not occur. The
price for its completeness is that the result is an expression that may
contain the fork operator. Yet, we illustrate how, in some cases, the
application of fork properties may allow us to reduce the fork to a logic
program, even in conditions that could not be treated before using the
syntactic methods in the literature.

Keywords: Answer Set Programming · Equilibrium Logic ·
Forgetting · Strong Persistence · Strong Equivalence · Forks

1 Introduction

A common representational technique in Answer Set Programming [13,15] (ASP)
is the use of auxiliary atoms. Their introduction in a program may be due to
many different reasons, for instance, looking for a simpler reading, providing
new constructions (choice rules, aggregates, transitive closure, etc.) or reducing
the corresponding ground program. When a program (or program fragment)
Π for signature $\mathcal{AT}$ uses auxiliary atoms $A \subseteq \mathcal{AT}$, they do not have a relevant
meaning outside Π. Accordingly, they are usually removed[1] from the final stable
models, so the latter only use atoms in $V = \mathcal{AT} \setminus A$, that is, the relevant or
public vocabulary that encodes the solutions to our problem in mind. Thus, when
seen from outside, Π becomes a black box that hides internal atoms from A and
provides solutions in terms of public atoms from V. A reasonable question is
whether we can transform these black boxes into white boxes, that is, whether
we can reformulate some program Π exclusively in terms of public atoms V,

---

[1] Most ASP solvers allow hiding the extension of some chosen predicates.

© The Author(s), under exclusive license to Springer Nature Switzerland AG 2022
G. Gottlob et al. (Eds.): LPNMR 2022, LNAI 13416, pp. 3–15, 2022.
https://doi.org/10.1007/978-3-031-15707-3_1

forgetting the auxiliary ones in A. A *forgetting operator* $f(\Pi, A) = \Pi'$ transforms a logic program Π into a new program Π' that does not contain atoms in A but has a *similar* behaviour on the public atoms V. Of course, the key point here is the definition of similarity between Π and Π' (relative to V) something that gave rise to different alternative forgetting operators, further classified in families, depending on the properties they satisfy – see [9] for an overview. From all this wide spectrum, however, when our purpose is forgetting auxiliary atoms, similarity can only be understood as *preserving the same knowledge* for public atoms in V, and this can be formalised as a very specific property. In particular, both programs Π and $\Pi' = f(\Pi, A)$ should not only produce the same stable models (projected on V) but also keep doing so even if we add a new piece of program Δ without atoms in A. This property, known as *strong persistence*, was introduced in [12] but, later on, [10] proved that it is not always possible to forget A in an arbitrary program Π under strong persistence. Moreover, [10] also provided a semantic condition, called Ω, on the models of Π in the logic of Here-and-There (HT) [11] (the monotonic basis of *Equilibrium Logic* [16]) so that atoms A are forgettable in Π iff Ω does not hold. When this happens, their approach can be used to construct $f(\Pi, A)$ from the HT models using, for instance, the method from [5,7]. Going one step further in this model-based orientation for forgetting, [1] overcame the limitation of unforgettable sets of atoms at the price of introducing a new type of disjunction, called *fork* and represented as '|'. To this aim, [1] defined an HT-based denotational semantics for forks.

Semantic-based forgetting is useful when we are interested in obtaining a compact representation. For instance, the method from [7] allows obtaining a minimal logic program from a set of HT-countermodels. However, this is done at a high computational cost (similar to Boolean function minimisation techniques). When combined with the Ω-condition or, similarly, with the use of HT-denotations, this method becomes practically unfeasible without the use of a computer. This may become a problem, for instance, when we try to prove properties of some new use of auxiliary atoms in a given setting, since one would expect a human-readable proof rather than resorting to a computer-based exhaustive exploration of models. On the other hand, semantic forgetting may easily produce results that look substantially different from the original program, even when this is not necessary. For example, if we apply an empty forgetting $f(\Pi, \emptyset)$ strictly under this method, we will usually obtain a different program Π', strongly equivalent to Π, but built up from countermodels of the latter, possibly having a very different syntactic look.

An alternative and in some sense complementary orientation for forgetting is the use of *syntactic transformations*. [12] introduced the first syntactic forgetting operator, f_{as}, that satisfied strong persistence. This operator forgot a single atom $A = \{a\}$ at a time and was applicable, under some conditions, to non-disjunctive logic programs. More recently, [4] presented a more general syntactic operator f_{sp}, also for a single atom $A = \{a\}$, that can be applied to any arbitrary logic program and satisfies strong persistence when the atom can be forgotten (i.e. the Ω condition does not hold). Moreover, Berthold et al. [4] also provided three syntactic sufficient conditions (that they call *a-forgettable*) under which Ω does not hold, and so, under which $\mathbf{f}_{sp}$ is strongly persistent. Perhaps the main difficulty of $\mathbf{f}_{sp}$ comes from its complex definition: it involves 10 different types of rule-matching that further deal with multiple partitions of Π (using a construction called *as-dual*). As a result, even though it offers full generality when the atom is forgettable, its application by hand does not seem very practical, requiring too many steps and a careful reading of the transformations.

In this paper, we provide a general syntactic operator, called *unfolding*, that is always applicable and allows forgetting an atom in a program, although it produces a result that may combine forks and arbitrary propositional formulas. We also discuss some examples in which a fork can be removed in favour of a formula, something that allows one to obtain a standard program (since formulas can always be reduced to that form [6]). We show examples where sufficient syntactic conditions identified so far are not applicable, whereas our method can still safely be applied to obtain a correct result, relying on properties of forks. Unfolding relies on another syntactic operator for forgetting a single atom, $\mathbf{f}_c$, based on the *cut rule* from a sequent calculus and is close to the application of $\mathbf{f}_{sp}$ from [4]. This operator produces a propositional formula without forks, but is only applicable under some sufficient syntactic conditions.

The rest of the paper is organised as follows. Section 2 contains a background with definitions and results from HT, stable models and the semantics of forks. Section 3 presents the cut transformation that produces a propositional formula. Then, Sect. 4 introduces the unfolding, which makes use of the cut and produces a fork in the general case. Finally, Sect. 5 concludes the paper.

2   Background

We begin by recalling some basic definitions and results related to the logic of HT. Let $\mathcal{AT}$ be a finite set of atoms called the *alphabet* or *vocabulary*. A *(propositional) formula* φ is defined using the grammar:

$$\varphi ::= \bot \mid p \mid \varphi \wedge \varphi \mid \varphi \vee \varphi \mid \varphi \rightarrow \varphi$$

where p is an atom $p \in \mathcal{AT}$. We define the *language* $\mathcal{L}_{\mathcal{AT}}$ as the set of all propositional formulas that can be formed over alphabet $\mathcal{AT}$. We use Greek letters φ, ψ, γ and their variants to stand for formulas. Implication $\varphi \rightarrow \psi$ will be sometimes reversed as $\psi \leftarrow \varphi$. We also define the derived operators $\neg\varphi \overset{\text{def}}{=} (\varphi \rightarrow \bot)$, $\top \overset{\text{def}}{=} \neg\bot$ and $\varphi \leftrightarrow \psi \overset{\text{def}}{=} (\varphi \rightarrow \psi) \wedge (\varphi \leftarrow \psi)$. We use letters p, q, a, b for representing atoms in $\mathcal{AT}$, but normally use a for an auxiliary atom to be forgotten. A *theory* Γ is a finite[2] set of formulas that can be also understood as their conjunction. When a theory consists of a single formula $\Gamma = \{\varphi\}$ we will

---

[2] As we will see, the cut operator support is a conjunction built from a finite set of rules that is sometimes negated. Generalising to infinite theories would require infinitary Boolean connectives.

frequently omit the brackets. Given any theory Γ, we write $\Gamma[\gamma/\varphi]$ to denote
the uniform substitution of all occurrences of subformula γ in Γ by formula φ.
An *extended disjunctive rule* r is an implication of the form:

$$p_1 \wedge \cdots \wedge p_m \wedge \neg p_{m+1} \wedge \cdots \wedge \neg p_n \wedge \neg\neg p_{n+1} \wedge \cdots \wedge \neg\neg p_k \rightarrow p_{k+1} \vee \cdots \vee p_h$$

where all p_i above are atoms in $\mathcal{AT}$ and $0 \leq m \leq n \leq k \leq h$. The antecedent and
consequent of a rule r are respectively called the *body* and the *head*. We define
the sets of atoms $Hd(r) \stackrel{\text{def}}{=} \{p_{k+1}, \ldots, p_h\}$, $Bd^+(r) \stackrel{\text{def}}{=} \{p_1, \ldots, p_m\}$, $Bd^-(r) \stackrel{\text{def}}{=}$
$\{p_{m+1}, \ldots, p_n\}$, $Bd^{--}(r) \stackrel{\text{def}}{=} \{p_{n+1}, \ldots, p_k\}$ and $Bd(r) \stackrel{\text{def}}{=} Bd^+(r) \cup Bd^-(r) \cup$
$Bd^{--}(r)$. We say that r is an *extended normal rule* if $|Hd(r)| \leq 1$. A rule with
$Hd(r) = \emptyset$ is called a *constraint*. A normal rule with $Bd(r) = \emptyset$ and $|Hd(r)| = 1$
is called a *fact*. Given some atom a, a rule r is said to contain an *a-choice* if
$a \in Bd^{--}(r) \cap Hd(r)$, that is, the rule has the form $\varphi \wedge \neg\neg a \rightarrow \psi \vee a$. A
program is a finite set of rules, sometimes represented as their conjunction. We
say that program Π belongs to a syntactic category if all its rules belong to
that category. For instance, Π is an extended normal program if all its rules
are extended normal. We will usually refer to the most general class, extended
disjunctive logic programs, just as logic programs for short.

A *classical interpretation* T is a set of atoms $T \subseteq \mathcal{AT}$. We write $T \models \varphi$ to
stand for the usual classical satisfaction of a formula φ. An HT-*interpretation* is
a pair $\langle H, T \rangle$ (respectively called "here" and "there") of sets of atoms $H \subseteq T \subseteq$
$\mathcal{AT}$; it is said to be *total* when $H = T$. The fact that an interpretation $\langle H, T \rangle$
satisfies a formula φ, written $\langle H, T \rangle \models \varphi$, is recursively defined as follows:

- $\langle H, T \rangle \not\models \bot$
- $\langle H, T \rangle \models p$ iff $p \in H$
- $\langle H, T \rangle \models \varphi \wedge \psi$ iff $\langle H, T \rangle \models \varphi$ and $\langle H, T \rangle \models \psi$
- $\langle H, T \rangle \models \varphi \vee \psi$ iff $\langle H, T \rangle \models \varphi$ or $\langle H, T \rangle \models \psi$
- $\langle H, T \rangle \models \varphi \rightarrow \psi$ iff both (i) $T \models \varphi \rightarrow \psi$ and (ii) $\langle H, T \rangle \not\models \varphi$ or $\langle H, T \rangle \models \psi$

An HT-interpretation $\langle H, T \rangle$ is a *model* of a theory Γ if $\langle H, T \rangle \models \varphi$ for all
$\varphi \in \Gamma$. Two formulas (or theories) φ and ψ are HT-equivalent, written $\varphi \equiv \psi$, if
they have the same HT-models. The logic of HT satisfies the law of substitution
of logical equivalents so, in particular:

$$\Pi \wedge a \equiv \Pi \wedge (a \leftrightarrow \top) \equiv \Pi[a/\top] \wedge a \tag{1}$$

$$\Pi \wedge \neg a \equiv \Pi \wedge (a \leftrightarrow \bot) \equiv \Pi[a/\bot] \wedge \neg a \tag{2}$$

$$\Pi \wedge \neg\neg a \equiv \Pi \wedge (\neg a \leftrightarrow \bot) \equiv \Pi[\neg a/\bot] \wedge \neg\neg a \tag{3}$$

A total interpretation $\langle T, T \rangle$ is an *equilibrium model* of a formula φ iff $\langle T, T \rangle \models \varphi$
and there is no $H \subset T$ such that $\langle H, T \rangle \models \varphi$. If so, we say that T is a *stable
model* of φ. We write $SM(\varphi)$ to stand for the set of stable models of φ and
$SM_V(\varphi) \stackrel{\text{def}}{=} \{T \cap V \mid T \in SM(\varphi)\}$ for their projection onto some vocabulary V.

In [1], we extended logic programs to include a new construct '$|$' we called
fork and whose intuitive meaning is that the stable models of two logic programs
$\Pi_1 \mid \Pi_2$ correspond to the union of stable models from Π_1 and Π_2 in any context

Π', that is $SM((\Pi_1 \mid \Pi_2) \wedge \Pi') = SM(\Pi_1 \wedge \Pi') \cup SM(\Pi_2 \wedge \Pi')$. Using this construct, we studied the property of projective strong equivalence (PSE) for forks: two forks satisfy PSE for a vocabulary V iff they yield the same stable models projected on V for any context over V. We also provided a semantic characterisation of PSE that allowed us to prove that it is always possible to forget (under strong persistence) an auxiliary atom in a fork, something proved to be false in standard HT. We recall now some definitions from [1] and [3].

Definition 1. *Given $T \subseteq \mathcal{AT}$, a T-support $\mathcal{H}$ is a set of subsets of T, that is $\mathcal{H} \subseteq 2^T$, satisfying that $\mathcal{H} \neq \emptyset$ iff $T \in \mathcal{H}$.*

To increase readability, we write a support as a sequence of interpretations between square brackets. For instance, possible supports for $T = \{a,b\}$ are $[\{a,b\}\ \{a\}]$, $[\{a,b\}\ \{b\}\ \emptyset]$ or the empty support $[\ ]$. Given a propositional formula φ and $T \subseteq \mathcal{AT}$, the set of HT-models $\{H \subseteq T \mid \langle H,T \rangle \models \varphi\}$ forms a T-support we denote as $[\![\varphi]\!]^T$.

For any T-support $\mathcal{H}$ and set of atoms V, we write $\mathcal{H}_V$ to stand for $\{H \cap V \mid H \in \mathcal{H}\}$. We say that a T-support $\mathcal{H}$ is V-*feasible* iff there is no $H \subset T$ in $\mathcal{H}$ satisfying that $H \cap V = T \cap V$. The name comes from the fact that, if this condition does not hold for some $\mathcal{H} = [\![\varphi]\!]^T$ with $T \subseteq V$, then T cannot be stable for any formula $\varphi \wedge \psi$ with $\psi \in \mathcal{L}(V)$ because $\langle H,T \rangle \models \varphi \wedge \psi$ and $H \subset T$.

We can define an order relation $\preceq$ between T-supports by saying that, given two T-supports, $\mathcal{H}$ and $\mathcal{H}'$, $\mathcal{H} \preceq \mathcal{H}'$ iff either $\mathcal{H} = [\ ]$ or $[\ ] \neq \mathcal{H}' \subseteq \mathcal{H}$. It is clear that $[\ ]$ and $[T]$ are the bottom and top elements, respectively, in the class of all T-supports. Given a T-support $\mathcal{H}$, we define its complementary support $\overline{\mathcal{H}}$ as:

$$\overline{\mathcal{H}} \overset{\text{def}}{=} \begin{cases} [\ ] & \text{if } \mathcal{H} = 2^T \\ [T] \cup \{H \subseteq T \mid H \notin \mathcal{H}\} & \text{otherwise} \end{cases}$$

We also consider the *ideal* of $\mathcal{H}$ defined as $\downarrow\mathcal{H} = \{\mathcal{H}' \mid \mathcal{H}' \preceq \mathcal{H}\} \setminus \{[\ ]\}$. Note that, the empty support $[\ ]$ is not included in the ideal, so $\downarrow[\ ] = \emptyset$. If Δ is any set of supports:

$$\downarrow\Delta \overset{\text{def}}{=} \bigcup_{\mathcal{H} \in \Delta} \downarrow\mathcal{H} = \bigcup_{\mathcal{H} \in \Delta} \{\mathcal{H}' \preceq \mathcal{H} \mid \mathcal{H}' \neq [\ ]\}$$

Definition 2. *A T-view Δ is a set of T-supports that is $\preceq$-closed, i.e., $\downarrow\Delta = \Delta$.*

A fork is defined using the grammar:

$$F ::= \ \bot \ \mid \ p \ \mid \ (F \mid F) \ \mid \ F \wedge F \ \mid \ \varphi \vee \varphi \ \mid \ \varphi \to F$$

where φ is a propositional formula and $p \in \mathcal{AT}$ is an atom. We write $\mathcal{L}_{\mathcal{AT}}$ to stand for the language formed by all forks for signature $\mathcal{AT}$. Given a fork $(F \mid G)$, we say that F and G are its left and right *branches*, respectively.

We provide next the semantics of forks in terms of T-*denotations*. To this aim, we will use a weaker version of the membership relation, $\hat{\in}$, defined as follows. Given a T-view Δ, we write $\mathcal{H} \hat{\in} \Delta$ iff $\mathcal{H} \in \Delta$ or both $\mathcal{H} = [\ ]$ and $\Delta = \emptyset$.

Definition 3 (*T*-denotation of a fork). *Let $\mathcal{AT}$ be a propositional signature and $T \subseteq \mathcal{AT}$ a set of atoms. The T-denotation of a fork F, written $\langle\!\langle\, F\,\rangle\!\rangle^T$, is a T-view recursively defined as follows:*

$$\langle\!\langle\, \bot\,\rangle\!\rangle^T \stackrel{\text{def}}{=} \emptyset$$

$$\langle\!\langle\, p\,\rangle\!\rangle^T \stackrel{\text{def}}{=} \downarrow[\![\, p\,]\!]^T \quad \text{for any atom } p$$

$$\langle\!\langle\, F \wedge G\,\rangle\!\rangle^T \stackrel{\text{def}}{=} \downarrow\{\, \mathcal{H} \cap \mathcal{H}' \mid \mathcal{H} \in \langle\!\langle\, F\,\rangle\!\rangle^T \text{ and } \mathcal{H}' \in \langle\!\langle\, G\,\rangle\!\rangle^T \,\}$$

$$\langle\!\langle\, \varphi \vee \psi\,\rangle\!\rangle^T \stackrel{\text{def}}{=} \downarrow\{\, \mathcal{H} \cup \mathcal{H}' \mid \mathcal{H} \,\hat{\in}\, \langle\!\langle\, \varphi\,\rangle\!\rangle^T \text{ and } \mathcal{H}' \,\hat{\in}\, \langle\!\langle\, \psi\,\rangle\!\rangle^T \,\}$$

$$\langle\!\langle\, \varphi \to F\,\rangle\!\rangle^T \stackrel{\text{def}}{=} \begin{cases} \{2^T\} & \text{if } [\![\, \varphi\,]\!]^T = [\,] \\ \downarrow\{\, \overline{[\![\, \varphi\,]\!]^T} \cup \mathcal{H} \mid \mathcal{H} \in \langle\!\langle\, F\,\rangle\!\rangle^T \,\} & \text{otherwise} \end{cases}$$

$$\langle\!\langle\, F \mid G\,\rangle\!\rangle^T \stackrel{\text{def}}{=} \langle\!\langle\, F\,\rangle\!\rangle^T \cup \langle\!\langle\, G\,\rangle\!\rangle^T$$

If F is a fork and $T \subseteq V \subseteq \mathcal{AT}$, we can define the T-view:

$$\langle\!\langle\, F\,\rangle\!\rangle^T_V \stackrel{\text{def}}{=} \downarrow\{\, \mathcal{H}_{|V} \mid \mathcal{H} \in \langle\!\langle\, F\,\rangle\!\rangle^Z \text{ s.t. } Z \cap V = T \text{ and } \mathcal{H} \text{ is } V\text{-feasible} \,\}$$

Definition 4 (Projective Strong Equivalence). *Let F and G be forks and $V \subseteq \mathcal{AT}$ a set of atoms. We say that F and G are V-strongly equivalent, in symbols $F \cong_V G$, if for any fork L in $\mathcal{L}_V$, $SM_V(F \wedge L) = SM_V(G \wedge L)$. When $V = \mathcal{AT}$ we write $F \cong G$ dropping the V subindex and simply saying that F and G are strongly equivalent.*

The properties listed in the following theorem were proved in [1].

Theorem 1. *Let F and G be arbitrary forks, and φ and ψ propositional formulas all of them for signature $\mathcal{AT}$, and let $V \subseteq \mathcal{AT}$. Then:*

(i) *$F \cong_V G$ iff $\langle\!\langle\, F\,\rangle\!\rangle^T_V = \langle\!\langle\, G\,\rangle\!\rangle^T_V$, for every $T \subseteq V$*
(ii) *$F \cong G$ iff $\langle\!\langle\, F\,\rangle\!\rangle^T = \langle\!\langle\, G\,\rangle\!\rangle^T$, for every $T \subseteq \mathcal{AT}$*
(iii) *$\langle\!\langle\, \varphi\,\rangle\!\rangle^T = \downarrow[\![\, \varphi\,]\!]^T$ for every $T \subseteq \mathcal{AT}$*
(iv) *$\varphi \cong \psi$ iff $[\![\, \varphi\,]\!]^T = [\![\, \psi\,]\!]^T$, for every $T \subseteq \mathcal{AT}$, iff $\varphi \equiv \psi$ in HT.*
(v) *The set of atoms $\mathcal{AT} \setminus V$ can be forgotten in F as a strongly persistent propositional formula[3] iff for each $T \subseteq V$, $\langle\!\langle\, F\,\rangle\!\rangle^T_V$ has a unique maximal support.* □

Proposition 1. *For every pair α and β of propositional formulas:*

$$(\top \mid \alpha) \cong (\neg\alpha \mid \alpha) \cong \neg\neg\alpha \to \alpha \cong \alpha \vee \neg\alpha \tag{4}$$

$$(\bot \mid \alpha) \cong \alpha \tag{5}$$

$$(\neg\alpha \mid \neg\neg\alpha) \cong \top \tag{6}$$

$$(\alpha \wedge \neg\beta \mid \alpha \wedge \neg\neg\beta) \cong \alpha \tag{7}$$

Proposition 2. *Let F, F', G and G' be forks for some signature $\mathcal{AT}$ and let $V \subseteq \mathcal{AT}$. If $F \cong_V F'$ and $G \cong_V G'$ then $(F \mid G) \cong_V (F' \mid G')$.* □

---

[3] This is, therefore, equivalent to not satisfying the Ω condition from [10].

3   The Cut Operator

Given any program Π, let us define the syntactic transformation $behead^a(\Pi)$ as the result of removing all rules with $a \in Hd(r) \cap Bd^+(r)$ and all head occurrences of a from rules where $a \in Hd(r) \cap Bd^-(r)$. Intuitively, $behead^a(\Pi)$ removes from Π all rules that, having a in the head, do not provide a support for a. In fact, rules with $a \in Hd(r) \cap Bd^+(r)$ are tautological, whereas rules of the form $\varphi \wedge \neg a \to a \vee \psi$ are strongly equivalent to $\varphi \wedge \neg a \to \psi$. As a result:

Proposition 3. *For any logic program* $\Pi \colon \Pi \cong behead^a(\Pi)$. □

The cut operator is defined in terms of the well-known *cut inference rule* from the sequent calculus which, when rephrased for program rules, amounts to:

$$\frac{\varphi \wedge a \to \psi \qquad \varphi' \to a \vee \psi'}{\varphi \wedge \varphi' \to \psi \vee \psi'} \tag{CUT}$$

where φ, φ' are conjunctions of elements that can be an atom a, its negation $\neg a$ or its double negation $\neg\neg a$, and ψ' and ψ are disjunctions of atoms. If r and r' stand for $\varphi \wedge a \to \psi$ and $\varphi' \to a \vee \psi'$ respectively, then we denote $Cut(a, r, r')$ to stand for the resulting implication $\varphi \wedge \varphi' \to \psi \vee \psi'$.

Example 1 (Example 9 from [4]). Let Π_1 be the program:

$$a \to l \tag{8}$$
$$\neg a \to v \tag{9}$$
$$s \to a \tag{10}$$
$$r \to a \vee u \tag{11}$$

Then, $Cut(a, (8), (11)) = (r \to t \vee u)$ is the result of the cut application:

$$\frac{\top \wedge a \to t \qquad r \to a \vee u}{\top \wedge r \to t \vee u}$$

In this program we can also perform a second cut through atom a corresponding to $Cut(a, (8), (10)) = (s \to t)$. □

Given a rule r with $a \in Bd^+(r)$, we define the formula:

$$NES(\Pi, a, r) \stackrel{\text{def}}{=} \bigwedge\{\, Cut(a, r, r') \mid r' \in \Pi,\ a \in Hd(r') \,\}$$

that is, $NES(\Pi, a, r)$ collects the conjunction of all possible cuts in Π for a given atom a and a selected rule r with a in the positive body. For instance, in our example program Π_1 for rule (8) we get:

$$NES(\Pi_1, a, (8)) = (r \to t \vee u) \wedge (s \to t). \tag{12}$$

When $r = \neg a = (\top \wedge a \to \bot)$ we can observe that:

$$NES(\Pi, a, \neg a) = \bigwedge\{(\top \wedge \varphi' \to \bot \vee \psi') \mid (\varphi' \to a \vee \psi') \in \Pi\}$$
$$= \bigwedge\{(\varphi' \to \psi') \mid (\varphi' \to a \vee \psi') \in \Pi\}$$

That is, we just take the rules with a in the head, but after removing a from that head. As an example, $NES(\Pi_1, a, \neg a) = (s \rightarrow \bot) \wedge (r \rightarrow u) = \neg s \wedge (r \rightarrow u)$. Note that, since a was the only head atom in (10), after removing it, we obtained an empty head $\bot$ leading to $(s \rightarrow \bot)$.

An interesting relation emerges from the negation of NES that can be connected with the so-called *external support* from [8]. In particular, we can use de Morgan and the HT equivalence $\neg(\varphi' \rightarrow \psi') \equiv \neg\neg\varphi' \wedge \neg\psi'$ to conclude:

$$\neg NES(\Pi, a, \neg a) = \neg\neg \bigvee \{(\varphi' \wedge \neg\psi') \mid (\varphi' \rightarrow a \vee \psi') \in \Pi\} = \neg\neg ES_\Pi(a)$$

where $ES_\Pi(a)$ corresponds to the external support[4] $ES_\Pi(Y)$ from [8] for any set of atoms Y, but applied here to $Y = \{a\}$. In the example:

$$\neg NES(\Pi_1, a, \neg a) = \neg(\neg s \wedge (r \rightarrow u)) \equiv \neg\neg s \vee (\neg\neg r \wedge \neg u) \qquad (13)$$

Definition 5 (Cut operator $\mathbf{f}_c$). *Let Π be a logic program for alphabet $\mathcal{AT}$ and let $a \in \mathcal{AT}$. Then $\mathbf{f}_c(\Pi, a)$ is defined as the result of:*

(i)   Remove atom 'a' from non-supporting heads obtaining $\Pi' = behead^a(\Pi)$;
(ii) Replace each rule $r \in \Pi'$ with $a \in B^+(r)$ by $NES(\Pi', a, r)$.
(iii) From the result, remove every rule r with $Hd(r) = \{a\}$;
(iv) Finally, replace the remaining occurrences of 'a' by $\neg NES(\Pi', a, \neg a)$. □

Example 2 (Example 1 continued). Step (i) has no effect, since $behead^a(\Pi_1) = \Pi_1$. For step (ii) , the only rule with a in the positive body is (8) and so, the latter is replaced by (12). Step (iii) removes rule (10) and, finally, Step (iv) replaces a by (13) in rules (9) and (11). Finally, $\mathbf{f}_c(\Pi_1, a)$ becomes to the conjunction of:

$$(s \rightarrow t) \wedge (r \rightarrow t \vee u) \qquad (14)$$
$$\neg(\neg\neg s \vee (\neg\neg r \wedge \neg u)) \rightarrow v \qquad (15)$$
$$r \rightarrow \neg\neg s \vee (\neg\neg r \wedge \neg u) \vee u \qquad (16)$$

Now, by simple HT transformations [6], it is easy to see that the antecedent of (15) amounts to $\neg s \wedge (\neg r \vee \neg\neg u))$, so (15) can be replaced by the two rules (17) and (18) below, whereas (16) is equivalent to the conjunction of (19) below that stems from $r \rightarrow \neg\neg s \vee \neg u \vee u$, plus the rule $r \rightarrow \neg\neg s \vee \neg\neg r \vee u$ that is tautological and can be removed.

$$\neg s \wedge \neg r \rightarrow v \qquad (17)$$
$$\neg s \wedge \neg\neg u \rightarrow v \qquad (18)$$
$$r \wedge \neg s \wedge \neg\neg u \rightarrow u \qquad (19)$$

To sum up, $\mathbf{f}_c(\Pi_1, a)$ is strongly equivalent to program (14) $\wedge$ (17) $\wedge$ (18) $\wedge$ (19). □

---

[4] In fact, [2] presented a more limited forgetting operator $\mathbf{f}_{es}$ based on the external support.

The program we obtained above is the same one obtained with the f_{sp} operator in [4] although the process to achieve it, is slightly different. This is because, in general, $f_c(\Pi, a)$ takes a logic program Π but produces a *propositional formula* where a has been forgotten, whereas f_{sp} produces the logic program in a direct way. Although, at a first sight, this could be seen as a limitation of f_c, the truth is that it is not an important restriction, since there exist well-known syntactic methods [6,14] to transform a propositional formula[5] into a (strongly equivalent) logic program under the logic of HT. Moreover, in the case of f_{sp}, directly producing a logic program comes with the cost of a more complex transformation, with ten different cases and the combinatorial construction of a so-called *as-dual* set of rules generated from multiple partitions of the original program[6]. We suggest that well-known logical rules such as de Morgan or distributivity (many of them still valid in intuitionistic logic) are far easier to learn and apply than the f_{sp} transformation when performing syntactic transformations by hand. On the other hand, we may sometimes be interested in keeping the propositional formula representation inside HT (for instance, for studying strong equivalence or the relation to other constructions) rather than being forced to unfold the formula into a logic program, possibly leading to a combinatorial explosion due to distributivity.

As happened with f_{sp}, the main restriction of f_c is that it does not always guarantee strong persistence. Note that this was expected, given the already commented result on the impossibility of arbitrary forgetting by just produc ing an HT formula. To check whether forgetting a in Π is possible, we can use semantic conditions like Theorem 1(v) or the Ω-condition, but these imply inspecting the models of Π. If we want to keep the method at a purely syntactic level, however, we can at best enumerate sufficient conditions for forgettability. For instance, [4] proved that a can be forgotten under strong persistence in any program Π that satisfies any of the following syntactic conditions:

Definition 6 (Definition 4 from [4]). *An extended logic program Π is a-forgettable if, at least one of the following conditions is satisfied:*

1. *Π contains the fact 'a' as a rule.*
2. *Π does not contain a-choices.*
3. *All rules in Π in which a occurs are a-choices.*

It is not difficult to see that Condition 2 above is equivalent to requiring that atom a does not occur in $NES(\Pi, a, \neg a)$, since the only possibility for a to occur in that formula is that there is a rule in Π of the form $\neg\neg a \wedge \varphi \rightarrow a \vee \psi$. In fact, as we prove below, Definition 6 is a quite general, sufficient syntactic condition for the applicability of f_c.

---

[5] In most cases, after unfolding f_c as a logic program, we usually obtain not only a result strongly equivalent to f_{sp} but also the same or a very close syntactic representation.

[6] In fact, the as-dual set from [4] can be seen as an effect of the (CUT) rule. Moreover, our use of the latter was inspired by this as-dual construction.

Theorem 2. *Let Π be a logic program for signature $\mathcal{AT}$, let $V \subseteq \mathcal{AT}$ and $a \in \mathcal{AT} \setminus V$ and let $\Pi' = behead^a(\Pi)$. If Π' is a-forgettable, then: $\Pi \cong_V \mathbf{f}_c(\Pi, a)$.* $\quad\square$

In our example, it is easy to see that this condition is satisfied because $behead^a(\Pi_1) = \Pi_1$ and this program does not contain a-choices.

4   Forgetting into Forks: The *Unfolding* Operator

As we have seen, syntactic forgetting is limited to a family of transformation operators whose applicability can be analysed in terms of sufficient syntactic conditions. This method is incomplete in the sense that forgetting a in Π may be possible, but still the syntactic conditions we use for applicability may not be satisfied. Consider the following example.

Example 3. Take the following logic program Π_3:

$$\neg\neg a \to a \tag{20}$$

$$\neg a \to b \tag{21}$$

$$a \to c \tag{22}$$

$$b \to c \tag{23}$$

$$c \to b \tag{24}$$

This program does not fit into the a-forgettable syntactic form, but in fact we can forget a under strong persistence to obtain $b \wedge c$, as we will see later. $\square$

If we look for a complete forgetting method, one interesting possibility is allowing the result to contain the fork operator. As proved in [1], forgettability as a fork is always guaranteed: that is, it is always possible to forget any atom if we allow the result to be in the general form of a fork. The method provided in [1] to obtain such a fork, however, was based on synthesis from the fork denotation, which deals with sets of sets of HT models. We propose next an always applicable syntactic method to obtain a fork as the result of forgetting any atom.

   In the context of propositional logic, forgetting an atom a in a formula φ corresponds to the quantified Boolean formula $\exists a\ \varphi$ which, in turn, is equivalent to the unfolding $\varphi[a/\bot] \vee \varphi[a/\top]$. In the case of Equilibrium Logic, we will apply a similar unfolding but, instead of disjunction, we will use the fork connective, and rather than $\bot$ and $\top$ we will have to divide the cases into $\neg a$ and $\neg\neg a$, since $(\neg a \mid \neg\neg a) \equiv \top$. More precisely, using (6) and (7) from Proposition 1 we can build the chain of equivalences $\Pi \cong \Pi \wedge \top \cong \Pi \wedge (\neg a \mid \neg\neg a) \cong (\Pi \wedge \neg a \mid \Pi \wedge \neg\neg a)$. Then, by Proposition 2, we separate the task of forgetting a in Π into forgetting a in each one of these two branches, leading to:

Definition 7 (Unfolding operator, $\mathbf{f}_|$). *For any logic program Π and atom a we define:* $\mathbf{f}_|(\Pi, a) \overset{\text{def}}{=} (\ \mathbf{f}_c(\Pi \wedge \neg a, a) \mid \mathbf{f}_c(\Pi \wedge \neg\neg a, a)\ )$ $\quad\square$

Theorem 3. *Let Π be a logic program for signature $\mathcal{AT}$, let $V \subseteq \mathcal{AT}$ and $a \in \mathcal{AT} \setminus V$. Then, $\Pi \cong_V \mathbf{f}_|(\Pi, a)$.* $\quad\square$

Corollary 1. *If $a \notin V$ and Π is a-forgettable then* $\mathbf{f}_|(\Pi, a) \cong_V \mathbf{f}_c(\Pi, a)$, *and so,* $\mathbf{f}_|(\Pi, a) \cong \mathbf{f}_c(\Pi, a)$.   □

Using (2) and (3), it is easy to prove:

Theorem 4. *For any logic program Π and atom a:*

$$\mathbf{f}_|(\Pi, a) \cong (\ \mathbf{f}_c(\Pi[a/\bot] \wedge \neg a, a)\ |\ \mathbf{f}_c(\Pi[\neg a/\bot] \wedge \neg\neg a, a)\ )$$
$$\cong (\ \Pi[a/\bot]\ |\ \mathbf{f}_c(\Pi[\neg a/\bot] \wedge \neg\neg a, a)\ )$$

This theorem provides a simpler application of the unfolding operator: the left branch, for instance, is now the result of replacing a by $\bot$. The right branch applies the cut operator, but introducing a prior step: we add the formula $\neg\neg a$ and replace all occurrences of $\neg a$ by $\bot$. It is easy to see that, in this previous step, any occurrence of a in the scope of negation is removed in favour of truth constants[7]. This means that the result has no a-choices since a will only occur in the scope of negation in the rule $\neg\neg a = (\neg a \to \bot)$. Therefore, the use of $\mathbf{f}_c$ in $\mathbf{f}_|$ is always applicable. Moreover, in many cases, we can use elementary HT transformations to simplify the programs $\Pi[a/\bot]$ and $\Pi[\neg a/\bot] \wedge \neg\neg a$, to look for a simpler application of $\mathbf{f}_c$, or to apply properties about the obtained fork.

As an illustration, consider again forgetting a in Π_3 and let us use the transformation in Theorem 4. We can observe that $\Pi_3[a/\bot]$ replaces (20), (21) and (22) respectively by $(\neg\neg\bot \to \bot)$ (a tautology), $(\neg\bot \to b) \equiv b$ and $(\bot \to c)$ (again, a tautology), leaving (23)-(24) untouched. To sum up, $\Pi_3[a/\bot] = b \wedge (b \to c) \wedge (c \to b) \equiv (b \wedge c)$. On the other hand, $\Pi_3[\neg a/\bot]$ replaces (20) and (21) respectively by $(\neg\bot \to a) \equiv a$ and $(\bot \to b)$ (a tautology), so that $\Pi_3[\neg a/\bot] \wedge \neg\neg a$ amounts to the formula $a \wedge (a \to b) \wedge (b \to c) \wedge (c \to b) \wedge \neg\neg a$ which is equivalent to $a \wedge b \wedge c$ and, trivially, $\mathbf{f}_c(a \wedge b \wedge c, a) = (b \wedge c)$. Putting everything together, we get $\mathbf{f}_|(\Pi_3, a) \cong (b \wedge c\ |\ b \wedge c) \cong (b \wedge c)$ since forks satisfy the idempotence property for '|' – see (11) from Proposition 12 in [1]. In this way, we have *syntactically* proved that a was indeed forgettable in Π_3 leading to $b \wedge c$ even though this program was not a-forgettable. We claim that the $\mathbf{f}_|$ operator plus the use of properties about forks (like the idempotence used above) opens a wider range of syntactic conditions under which forks can be reduced into formulas, and so, under which an atom can be forgotten in ASP.

An important advantage of the unfolding operator is that, since it is always applicable, it can be used to forget a set of atoms by forgetting them one by one. We illustrate this with another example.

Example 4. Suppose we want to forget atoms $\{a, b\}$ in the program $\Pi_{twoatoms} \overset{\text{def}}{=}$ (20) $\wedge$ (21) $\wedge$ (22) where we simply removed (23) and (24) from Π_3.

This program is not a-forgettable, but nevertheless let us assume that we start forgetting a with the application of the unfolding $\mathbf{f}_|(\Pi_4, a)$. For the left hand

---

[7] Truth constants can be removed using trivial HT simplifications.

side, we get that $\Pi_4[a/\bot] \equiv (\neg\neg\bot \to a) \land (\neg\bot \to b) \land (\bot \to c) \equiv b$ as we had seen before. Similarly, for the right hand side:

$$\Pi_4[\neg a/\bot] \land \neg\neg a = (\neg\bot \to a) \land (\bot \to b) \land (a \to c) \land \neg\neg a \cong a \land c$$

so the application of $\mathtt{f}_c$ becomes trivially $\mathtt{f}_c(a \land c, a) = c$ and the final result amounts to $\mathtt{f}_|(\Pi_4, a) = (b \mid c)$ that is, a fork of two atoms, which as discussed in [1], is (possibly the simplest case of) a fork that *cannot be reduced to a formula*. Still, we can use Proposition 2 to continue forgetting b in each of the two branches of $(b \mid c)$. As none of them contains b-choices, we can just apply $\mathtt{f}_c$ to obtain the fork $(\mathtt{f}_c(b,b) \mid \mathtt{f}_c(b,c)) = (\top \mid c)$ which, by (4), is equivalent to the formula $(\neg\neg c \to c)$. We end up with one more example.

Example 5. Suppose we want to forget q in the following program Π_5:

$$\neg\neg q \to q \qquad q \to u \qquad q \to s \qquad \neg q \to t$$

Although this program is not q-forgettable, it was included as Example 7 in [4] to illustrate the application of operator $\mathtt{f}_{sp}$. If we use $\mathtt{f}_|(\Pi_5, q)$, it is very easy to see that $\Pi_5[q/\bot] \cong t$ whereas $\Pi_5[\neg q/\bot] \land \neg\neg q \cong q \land u \land s$ so that we get $\mathtt{f}_|(\Pi_5, q) = (t \mid \mathtt{f}_c(q \land u \land s, q)) = (t \mid (u \land s))$. This fork *cannot* be represented as a formula, since t and $u \land s$ have no logical relation and the fork is homomorphic to $(b \mid c)$ obtained before. In other words, atom q cannot be forgotten in Π_5 as a formula, and so, $\mathtt{f}_{sp}(\Pi_5, q)$ from [4] does not satisfy strong persistence.

5   Conclusions

We have presented a syntactic transformation, we called *unfolding*, that is always applicable on any logic program and allows forgetting an atom (under strong persistence), producing an expression that may combine the fork operator and propositional formulas. Unfolding relies on another syntactic transformation, we called the *cut* operator (close to $\mathtt{f}_{sp}$ from [4]), that can be applied on any program that does not contain choice rules for the forgotten atom and, unlike unfolding, it returns a propositional formula without forks. Although, in general, the forks we obtain by unfolding cannot be reduced to propositional formulas, we have also illustrated how the use of general properties of forks makes this possible sometimes, even in conditions where previous syntactic methods were not known to be applicable. Future work will be focused on extending the syntactic conditions under which forks can be reduced to formulas – we claim that this is an analogous situation to finding conditions under which second order quantifiers can be removed in second order logic. We will also study the extension of the unfolding operator to sets of atoms, instead of proceeding one by one.

Acknowledgements. We want to thank the anonymous reviewers for their suggestions that helped to improve this paper. Partially funded by Xunta de Galicia and the European Union, grants CITIC (ED431G 2019/01) and GPC ED431B 2022/33, and by the Spanish Ministry of Science and Innovation (grant PID2020-116201GB-I00).

References

1. Aguado, F., Cabalar, P., Fandinno, J., Pearce, D., Pérez, G., Vidal, C.: Forgetting auxiliary atoms in forks. Artif. Intell. **275**, 575–601 (2019)
2. Aguado, F., Cabalar, P., Fandinno, J., Pérez, G., Vidal, C.: A logic program transformation for strongly persistent forgetting - extended abstract. In: Proc. of the 37th International Conference on Logic Programming (ICLP 2021), Porto, Portugal (virtual event). Electronic Proceedings in Theoretical Computer Science (EPTCS), vol. 345, pp. 11–13 (2021)
3. Aguado, F., Cabalar, P., Pearce, D., Pérez, G., Vidal, C.: A denotational semantics for equilibrium logic. Theory Pract. Logic Program. **15**(4–5), 620–634 (2015)
4. Berthold, M., Gonçalves, R., Knorr, M., Leite, J.: A syntactic operator for forgetting that satisfies strong persistence. Theory Pract. Logic Program. **19**(5–6), 1038–1055 (2019)
5. Cabalar, P., Ferraris, P.: Propositional theories are strongly equivalent to logic programs. Theory Pract. Logic Program. **7**(6), 745–759 (2007)
6. Cabalar, P., Pearce, D., Valverde, A.: Reducing propositional theories in equilibrium logic to logic programs. In: Bento, C., Cardoso, A., Dias, G. (eds.) EPIA 2005. LNCS (LNAI), vol. 3808, pp. 4–17. Springer, Heidelberg (2005). https://doi.org/10.1007/11595014_2
7. Cabalar, P., Pearce, D., Valverde, A.: Minimal logic programs. In: Dahl, V., Niemelä, I. (eds.) ICLP 2007. LNCS, vol. 4670, pp. 104–118. Springer, Heidelberg (2007). https://doi.org/10.1007/978-3-540-74610-2_8
8. Ferraris, P., Lee, J., Lifschitz, V.: A generalization of the Lin-Zhao theorem. Ann. Math. Artif Intell. **47**(1–2), 79–101 (2006)
9. Gonçalves, R., Knorr, M., Leite, J.: The ultimate guide to forgetting in answer set programming. In: KR, pp. 135–144. AAAI Press (2016)
10. Gonçalves, R., Knorr, M., Leite, J.: You can't always forget what you want: on the limits of forgetting in answer set programming. In: Kaminka, G.A., et al. (eds.) Proceedings of 22nd European Conference on Artificial Intelligence (ECAI 2016). Frontiers in Artificial Intelligence and Applications, vol. 285, pp. 957–965. IOS Press (2016)
11. Heyting, A.: Die formalen Regeln der intuitionistischen Logik. In: Sitzungsberichte der Preussischen Akademie der Wissenschaften, pp. 42–56. Deutsche Akademie der Wissenschaften zu Berlin (1930), reprint in Logik-Texte: Kommentierte Auswahl zur Geschichte der Modernen Logik, Akademie-Verlag (1986)
12. Knorr, M., Alferes, J.J.: Preserving strong equivalence while forgetting. In: Fermé, E., Leite, J. (eds.) JELIA 2014. LNCS (LNAI), vol. 8761, pp. 412–425. Springer, Cham (2014). https://doi.org/10.1007/978-3-319-11558-0_29
13. Marek, V., Truszczyński, M.: Stable models and an alternative logic programming paradigm. In: The Logic Programming Paradigm: a 25-Year Perspective, pp. 169–181. Springer-Verlag (1999). https://doi.org/10.1007/978-3-642-60085-2_17
14. Mints, G.: Cut-free formulations for a quantified logic of here and there. Ann. Pure Appl. Logic **162**(3), 237–242 (2010)
15. Niemelä, I.: Logic programs with stable model semantics as a constraint programming paradigm. Ann. Math. Artif. Intell. **25**, 241–273 (1999)
16. Pearce, D.: A new logical characterisation of stable models and answer sets. In: Dix, J., Pereira, L.M., Przymusinski, T.C. (eds.) NMELP 1996. LNCS, vol. 1216, pp. 57–70. Springer, Heidelberg (1997). https://doi.org/10.1007/BFb0023801

Modal Logic S5 in Answer Set Programming with Lazy Creation of Worlds

Mario Alviano[1(✉)], Sotiris Batsakis[2,3], and George Baryannis[3]

[1] University of Calabria, Rende, Italy
alviano@mat.unical.it
[2] Technical University of Crete, Chania, Crete, Greece
sbatsakis@isc.tuc.gr
[3] School of Computing and Engineering, University of Huddersfield, Huddersfield, UK
g.bargiannis@hud.ac.uk

Abstract. Modal logic S5 is used extensively for representing knowledge that includes statements about necessity and possibility, owing to its simplicity in handling chained modal operators. Significant research effort has been devoted in developing efficient reasoning mechanisms over complex S5 formulas, resulting in various solvers taking advantage of the boolean satisfiability problem (SAT). Among them, the most performant solver implements a heuristic for identifying worlds that can be merged, hence reducing the size of SAT instances to be checked. Recently, Answer Set Programming (ASP) has also been considered, and different ASP encodings were proposed and tested, reaching state-of-the-art performance. In particular, a heuristic for identifying the propositional atoms that are relevant in every world resulted in a performance gain in previous experiments. This work addresses the open question of whether the aforementioned two heuristics can be combined, as well as possibly enabling lazy instantiation of the resulting encodings, and what their potential impact is on the performance of the ASP-based solver. Experiments show that lazy creation of worlds provides some further performance gain to the ASP-based solver on the tested instances.

Keywords: Modal Logic · S5 · Answer Set Programming

1 Introduction

Modal logics extend standard logic-based languages to include the ability to express modalities qualifying truth statements, and have numerous applications, among them legal reasoning [4], linguistics [15] and multi-agent systems [13]. S5 is one of the most well-known and studied syntax systems, while Kripke semantics [11] is the commonly accepted model-theoretic approach to defining modal logic semantics. The defining characteristic of S5 is that it allows simplifying complex sequences of modal operators by retaining only the last one in the sequence and pruning all the rest. Kripke semantics interprets formulas as true or false in a set of possible worlds and defines an accessibility relation that can link pairs of these worlds, meaning that if a formula is true in one world then it is possibly true in all other worlds that lead to it. While, in

© The Author(s), under exclusive license to Springer Nature Switzerland AG 2022
G. Gottlob et al. (Eds.): LPNMR 2022, LNAI 13416, pp. 16–28, 2022.
https://doi.org/10.1007/978-3-031-15707-3_2

general, the accessibility relation can be any binary relation, each modal logic syntax system restricts its definition. In the case of S5, the accessibility relation is an equivalence relation, satisfying all three of the reflexive, symmetric and transitive properties.

S5 satisfiability is an NP-complete problem [12], and it has been addressed by adopting techniques like resolution [16], tableau [9] and propositional satisfiability (SAT). Solvers relying on SAT have shown great potential, but their need for Skolemisation to represent truth values in different possible worlds may lead to long formulas. State-of-the-art solvers use different methods to attack such an issue, with S52SAT [6] reducing the number of possible worlds that need to be explored to find a model and using structural caching techniques, and S5CHEETAH [10] using formula normalisation and optimising conflicts between modalised literals through the use of graphs.

Recently, a novel S5 solver named S5PY [1] was designed and implemented based on Answer Set Programming (ASP) [5, 14]. ASP was considered due to its close relationship with SAT and the readability and configurability afforded by ASP encodings due to their logic programming nature [2, 3]. The most efficient algorithm implemented by S5PY is based on a heuristic for identifying the propositional atoms that are relevant in every world. Whether such a heuristic can be combined with the heuristic employed by S5CHEETAH to merge non-conflictual worlds remains an open question, which is addressed in this work. Additionally, we report on a lazy algorithm for the incremental instantiation of the ASP encoding used by S5PY, where worlds associated with modalised literals are not immediately introduced but delayed until required.

The main contributions of this paper can be summarised as follows:

- The heuristic implemented by S5CHEETAH using graph colouring to identify non-conflictual worlds is integrated in S5PY. The main differences between the way such a heuristic is implemented in S5CHEETAH and S5PY are discussed in Sect. 6.
- The most efficient encoding of S5PY presented in [1] is redesigned so that lazy instantiation can be enabled, as well as the heuristic using graph colouring. In this way, the underlying ASP system is not obliged to eagerly materialise all propositional atoms and rules before starting the search for an answer set, and in fact it may complete its computational task without materialising worlds associated with false modalised literals.
- An empirical evaluation of four different configurations of S5PY is reported, showing that some small performance gain is achieved by lazy creation of worlds, while merging worlds introduces overhead to the implemented solver.

2   Background

S5 extends propositional logic with the modal operators $\Box$ for encoding *necessity* and $\Diamond$ for encoding *possibility*. The language is defined by the grammar

$$\phi := p \mid \neg\phi \mid \phi \wedge \phi \mid \phi \vee \phi \mid \Box\phi \mid \Diamond\phi \qquad (1)$$

where p is a *propositional atom* among those of a fixed countably infinite set $\mathscr{A}$. Moreover, logical connectives for implication and equivalence are used as syntactic sugar with the usual meaning, i.e. $\phi \to \psi := \neg\phi \vee \psi$ and $\phi \leftrightarrow \psi := (\phi \to \psi) \wedge (\psi \to \phi)$, for every pair of formulas ϕ and ψ. The *complement* of a propositional literal is defined as usual, i.e. $\overline{p} = \neg p$ and $\overline{\neg p} = p$ for all $p \in \mathscr{A}$, and the notation is naturally extended to sets of propositional literals.

The semantics of S5 formulas is given by *Kripke structures*, that is, non-empty sets of *worlds* connected by an accessibility relation; the accessibility relation can be assumed to be total for S5 formulas [7], so for the purposes of this paper only the set of worlds will be used, and actually worlds will be represented in a list so to associate the i-th $\Diamond$-literal with the world in position i. A *world* is an interpretation of propositional logic, that is, a function I assigning a truth value of either 0 (false) or 1 (true) to every propositional atom in $\mathscr{A}$. Interpretations are usually represented by the sets of propositional atoms that are assigned a value of true.

Let **I** be the list $[I_0, \ldots, I_n]$ of worlds, for some $n \geq 0$, and let $0 \leq i \leq n$. The *satisfiability relation* $\models$ for S5 formulas is defined as follows: $(\mathbf{I}, i) \models p$ iff $I_i(p) = 1$; $(\mathbf{I}, i) \models \neg\phi$ iff $(\mathbf{I}, i) \not\models \phi$; $(\mathbf{I}, i) \models \phi \wedge \psi$ iff $(\mathbf{I}, i) \models \phi$ and $(\mathbf{I}, i) \models \psi$; $(\mathbf{I}, i) \models \phi \vee \psi$ iff $(\mathbf{I}, i) \models \phi$ or $(\mathbf{I}, i) \models \psi$; $(\mathbf{I}, i) \models \Box\phi$ iff $(\mathbf{I}, j) \models \phi$ for all $j \in [0..n]$; $(\mathbf{I}, i) \models \Diamond\phi$ iff $(\mathbf{I}, j) \models \phi$ for some $j \in [0..n]$. The *satisfiability problem* associated with S5 is the following: given an S5 formula ϕ, is there a list $\mathbf{I} = [I_0, \ldots, I_n]$ (for some $n \geq 0$) such that $(\mathbf{I}, 0) \models \phi$?

Every S5 formula ψ can be transformed into an equi-satisfiable *S5 normal form (S5-NF)* formula [1,10], defined as follows. A *propositional literal* ℓ is either a propositional atom or its negation. A $\Box$-*literal* has the form $\Box(\ell_1 \vee \cdots \vee \ell_n)$, where $n \geq 1$ and $\ell_1, \ldots, \ell_n$ are propositional literals. A $\Diamond$-*literal* has the form $\Diamond(\ell_1 \wedge \cdots \wedge \ell_n)$, where $n \geq 1$ and $\ell_1, \ldots, \ell_n$ are propositional literals. An *S5-literal* is a propositional literal, a $\Box$-literal, or a $\Diamond$-literal. A disjunction of S5-literals is called an *S5-clause*. A formula ϕ is in S5-NF if ϕ is a conjunction of S5-clauses. Let $atoms(\phi)$ and $lits(\phi)$ denote the sets of propositional atoms and literals occurring in ϕ, respectively.

3 S5 Satisfiability Checking Encodings

S5 satisfiability can be expressed in monadic first-order logic, and eventually reduced to SAT by applying Skolemisation and Herbrand expansion, optimising the Tseitin-like transformation by enabling only worlds associated with true $\Diamond$-literals not already witnessed by world 0 [1]. The resulting encoding can be improved by means of some properties related to an overestimate of the literals involved in unit propagation [1,10]. In this section, we first review such encodings by adopting a uniform notation, and then show how they can be combined in a new encoding.

Let ϕ be an S5-NF formula, and let us fix an enumeration $\Box\psi_1^\Box, \ldots, \Box\psi_m^\Box, \Diamond\psi_1^\Diamond, \ldots, \Diamond\psi_n^\Diamond$ of its $\Box$- and $\Diamond$-literals, for some $m \geq 0$ and $n \geq 0$. Let $\psi(x)$ denote the monadic first-order formula obtained from ψ by adding argument x to all propositional atoms occurring in ψ. The following propositional atoms are used:

- $p(i)$, representing truth of atom p in world i, for $i \in [0..n]$;
- b_i, representing truth of $\Box\psi_i^\Box$, for $i \in [1..m]$;
- d_j, representing truth of $\Diamond\psi_j^\Diamond$, for $j \in [1..n]$;
- $implied_j$, representing that $\Diamond\psi_j^\Diamond$ is witnessed by world 0, for $j \in [1..n]$.

The *basic encoding* of ϕ, denoted $basic(\phi)$, comprises the following formulas:

1. $b_i \rightarrow \psi_i^{\square}(0)$, and $b_i \wedge d_j \wedge \neg implied_j \rightarrow \psi_i^{\square}(j)$, for all $i \in [1..m]$ and $j \in [1..n]$;
2. $implied_j \leftrightarrow \psi_j^{\Diamond}(0)$, $implied_j \rightarrow d_j$, and $d_j \wedge \neg implied_j \rightarrow \psi_j^{\Diamond}(j)$ for all $j \in [1..n]$;

where any remaining propositional atom p (i.e. those not under the scope of any modal) is replaced by $p(0)$. Intuitively, formulas in the first group enforce that clauses in $\square$-literals are satisfied in all worlds associated with *true-and-not-implied* $\Diamond$-literals, and formulas in the second group define implied $\Diamond$-literals as those witnessed by world 0 and impose the satisfaction of true-and-not-implied $\Diamond$-literals in their worlds.

Example 1 (Running example). Let ϕ be $\square(p \vee q) \wedge \Diamond p \wedge \Diamond \neg p \wedge \Diamond \neg q$. Clauses in $basic(\phi)$ encode the following formulas:

$$b_1 \wedge d_1 \wedge d_2 \wedge d_3 \qquad b_1 \rightarrow p(0) \vee q(0) \qquad b_1 \wedge d_1 \wedge \neg implied_1 \rightarrow p(1) \vee q(1)$$
$$b_1 \wedge d_2 \wedge \neg implied_2 \rightarrow p(2) \vee q(2) \qquad b_1 \wedge d_3 \wedge \neg implied_3 \rightarrow p(3) \vee q(3)$$
$$implied_1 \leftrightarrow p(0) \qquad implied_1 \rightarrow d_1 \qquad d_1 \wedge \neg implied_1 \rightarrow p(1)$$
$$implied_2 \leftrightarrow \neg p(0) \qquad implied_2 \rightarrow d_2 \qquad d_2 \wedge implied_2 \rightarrow \neg p(2)$$
$$implied_3 \leftrightarrow \neg q(0) \qquad implied_3 \rightarrow d_3 \qquad d_2 \wedge \neg implied_3 \rightarrow \neg q(3)$$

Formula ϕ is satisfied by $\mathbf{I} = [\{p\}, \{p,q\}, \{q\}, \{p\}]$, and the associated model of $basic(\phi)$ is $I = \{b_1, d_1, d_2, d_3, p(0), p(1), q(1), q(2), p(3)\}$. ∎

Proposition 1. *For every S5 NF formula ϕ, $basic(\phi)$ is equi-satisfiable to ϕ.*

Proof. By combining Proposition 3.1 and Theorem 3.1 in [1]. □

The basic encoding can be improved thanks to a property that can be checked by computing an overestimate of the literals involved in unit propagation starting from those in $\Diamond$-literals. Formally, for a set L of literals

$$UP(L) := L \cup \bigcup \left\{ lits(\psi_i^{\square}) \setminus \{\bar{\ell}\} \mid \ell \in L, \ i \in [1..m], \bar{\ell} \in lits(\psi_i^{\square}) \right\} \qquad (2)$$

$$B_j := \left\{ i \in [1..m] \mid \overline{UP \Uparrow lits(\psi_j^{\Diamond})} \cap lits(\psi_i^{\square}) \neq \emptyset \right\} \qquad (3)$$

Intuitively, $UP(L)$ is the set of literals that may be used to satisfy every $\psi_i^{\square}$ affected by the assignment of L, $UP \Uparrow lits(\psi_j^{\Diamond})$ is the set of literals reached in this way from the literals in $\psi_j^{\Diamond}$, and B_j represents the set of $\square$-literals involved in this computation. The *reach encoding* of ϕ, denoted $reach(\phi)$, is obtained from $basic(\phi)$ by removing formulas encoding $b_i \wedge d_j \wedge \neg implied_j \rightarrow \psi_i^{\square}(j)$, for all $i \in [1..m]$ and $j \in [1..n]$ such that $i \notin B_j$ (i.e. the truth of $\square \psi_i^{\square}$ in the world associated with $\Diamond \psi_j^{\Diamond}$ can be witnessed by world 0).

Example 2 (Continuing Example 1). To construct $reach(\phi)$, we have to compute sets B_1, B_2 and B_3, respectively associated with $\Diamond$-literals $\Diamond p$, $\Diamond \neg p$ and $\Diamond \neg q$. Let us first determine the sets of reached literals from $\{p\}$, $\{\neg p\}$ and $\{\neg q\}$ according to (2): $UP(\{p\}) = \{p\}$, as $\bar{p} \notin lits(p \vee q)$; $UP(\{\neg p\}) = \{\neg p, q\}$, as $\overline{\neg p} \in lits(p \vee q)$ and

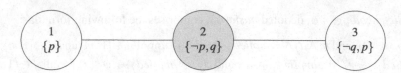

Fig. 1. Diamond conflict graph of formula ϕ from Examples 1–3, with graph colouring

therefore literals in $lits(p \vee q) \setminus \{\overline{\neg p}\} = \{q\}$ are added to $UP(\{\neg p\})$; $UP(\{\neg p, q\}) = \{\neg p, q\}$, as $\overline{q} \notin lits(p \vee q)$ and therefore no other literal is added to $UP(\{\neg p, q\})$; $UP(\{\neg q\}) = \{\neg q, p\}$, as $\overline{\neg q} \in lits(p \vee q)$ and therefore literals in $lits(p \vee q) \setminus \{\overline{\neg q}\} = \{p\}$ are added to $UP(\{\neg q\})$; $UP(\{\neg q, p\}) = \{\neg q, p\}$, as $\overline{p} \notin lits(p \vee q)$ and therefore no other literal is added to $UP(\{\neg q, p\})$. Hence, we have that $UP \Uparrow lits(\{p\}) = \{p\}$, $UP \Uparrow lits(\{\neg p\}) = \{\neg p, q\}$ and $UP \Uparrow lits(\{\neg q\}) = \{\neg q, p\}$. Now using (3), $B_1 = \emptyset$ and $B_2 = B_3 = \{1\}$, that is, $\Diamond p$ does not interact with the $\square$-literal, while $\Diamond \neg p$ and $\Diamond \neg q$ interact with the $\square$-literal. Accordingly, $reach(\phi)$ is obtained from $basic(\phi)$ by removing clauses encoding $b_1 \wedge d_1 \wedge \neg implied_1 \to p(1) \vee q(1)$. In fact, such a formula can be satisfied by assigning to $q(1)$ the same truth value of $q(0)$. For example, if I is a model of $reach(\phi)$ such that $I(q(0)) = 1$, then $I \cup \{q(1)\}$ is a model of $basic(\phi)$; similarly, if I is a model of $reach(\phi)$ such that $I(q(0)) = 0$, then $I \setminus \{q(1)\}$ is a model of $basic(\phi)$. ∎

Proposition 2. *For every S5-NF formula ϕ, $reach(\phi)$ is equi-satisfiable to $basic(\phi)$.*

Proof. Shown in [1] as Theorem 3.2.

Alternatively, the basic encoding can be improved by merging some "non-conflictual" worlds, an idea first introduced in [10] and revised here. Formally, the *diamond conflict graph* of ϕ, denoted $\mathcal{G}_\phi$, has vertex set $[1..n]$, and edge set $\{ij \mid \exists \ell \in lits(\psi_i^\Diamond) \text{ such that } \bar{\ell} \in UP \Uparrow lits(\psi_j^\Diamond)\}$. Let $colour : [1..n] \to [1..n]$ be a *graph colouring* of $\mathcal{G}_\phi$, that is, $colour$ is such that $colour(i) \neq colour(j)$ holds for all edges ij in $\mathcal{G}_\phi$. The *basic-merge encoding* of ϕ wrt. $colour$, denoted $basic(\phi, colour)$, is obtained from $basic(\phi)$ by replacing

1. $b_i \wedge d_j \wedge \neg implied_j \to \psi_i^\square(j)$ with $b_i \wedge d_j \wedge \neg implied_j \to \psi_i^\square(colour(j))$, for all $i \in [1..m]$ and $j \in [1..n]$;
2. $d_j \wedge \neg implied_j \to \psi_j^\Diamond(j)$ with $d_j \wedge \neg implied_j \to \psi_j^\Diamond(colour(j))$, for all $j \in [1..n]$.

(Note that the basic encoding is a special case of the basic-merge encoding in which *colour* is the *identity function* $id : i \mapsto i$.) Essentially, the idea underlying the basic-merge encoding is that $\Diamond$-literals whose propositional literals cannot produce any conflict via unit propagation can share the same world.

Example 3 (Continuing Example 2). The diamond conflict graph $\mathcal{G}_\phi$ of ϕ is shown in Fig. 1, where vertices are also annotated with the reached literals. The figure also shows the graph colouring $colour = \{1 \mapsto 1, 2 \mapsto 2, 3 \mapsto 1\}$, where colour 1 is white and colour 2 is gray. It turns out that the first and third $\Diamond$-literals can share the same world, and therefore the following formulas of $basic(\phi)$

$$b_1 \wedge d_3 \wedge \neg implied_3 \to p(3) \vee q(3) \qquad d_2 \wedge \neg implied_3 \to \neg q(3)$$

are replaced by

$$b_1 \wedge d_3 \wedge \neg implied_3 \rightarrow p(1) \vee q(1) \qquad d_2 \wedge \neg implied_3 \rightarrow \neg q(1)$$

to obtain $basic(\phi, colour)$. Note that if I is a model of $basic(\phi)$, then it must satisfy $I(p(1)) = 1$ and $I(q(3)) = 0$ because of the $\Diamond$-literals. Moreover, $I(p(3)) = 1$ because of the $\Box$-literal. Hence, worlds 1 needs p, and worlds 3 needs p and $\neg q$. A model of $basic(\phi, colour$ is then obtained from I by merging worlds 1 and 3 as follows: $(I \cup \{p(1)\}) \setminus \{q(1), p(3), q(3)\}$. ∎

Proposition 3. *For every S5-NF formula ϕ and every graph colouring colour of $\mathcal{G}_\phi$, $basic(\phi, colour)$ is equi-satisfiable to $basic(\phi)$.*

Proof. Let $I \models basic(\phi, colour)$. Hence, the following is a model of $basic(\phi)$:

$$\{b_i \in I \mid i \in [1..m]\} \cup \{d_j \in I \mid j \in [1..n]\} \cup \{implied_j \in I \mid j \in [1..n]\}$$
$$\cup \{p(0) \mid p(0) \in I\} \quad \cup \{p(j) \mid j \in [1..n], \, p(colour(j)) \in I\}.$$

Essentially, multiple copies of the shared worlds are introduced.

Let $I \models basic(\phi)$. For every colour $i \in [1..n]$, let us define the following set of non-conflictual literals: $L_i := \{\ell \in UP \Uparrow lits(\psi_j^\Diamond) \mid j \in [1..n], \, colour(j) = i, \, I(d_j) = I(\ell) = 1\}$. Hence, the following is a model of $basic(\phi, colour)$:

$$\{b_i \in I \mid i \in [1..m]\} \cup \{d_j \in I \mid j \in [1..n]\} \cup \{implied_j \in I \mid j \in [1..n]\}$$
$$\cup \{p(0) \mid p(0) \in I\} \quad \cup \{p(colour(j)) \mid j \in [1..n], \, p \subset L_{colour(j)}\}.$$

Essentially, multiple worlds are merged according to the given graph colouring. □

A new encoding, denoted $reach(\phi, colour)$ and called *reach-merge encoding* of ϕ w.r.t. *colour*, can be obtained by combining the ideas presented in [1] and [10]. It comprises all formulas of $basic(\phi, colour)$ but those of the form $b_i \wedge d_j \wedge \neg implied_j \rightarrow \psi_i^\Box(colour(j))$, for all $i \in [1..m]$ and $j \in [1..n]$ such that $i \notin B_j$ (i.e. the truth of $\Box\psi_i^\Box$ in the world associated with $\Diamond\psi_j^\Diamond$ can be witnessed by world 0). Also note that the reach encoding is a special case of the reach-merge encoding in which *colour* is the identity function *id*.

Example 4 (Continuing Example 3). The reach-merge encoding of ϕ w.r.t. *colour* is obtained from $basic(\phi, colour)$ by removing formula $b_1 \wedge d_3 \wedge \neg implied_3 \rightarrow p(1) \vee q(1)$, similar to how $reach(\phi)$ is obtained from $basic(\phi)$. ∎

Lemma 1. *For every S5-NF formula ϕ and every graph colouring colour of $\mathcal{G}_\phi$, $reach(\phi, colour)$ is equi-satisfiable to $basic(\phi, colour)$.*

Proof. The construction is aligned to the proof of Theorem 3.2 in [1]. $I \models basic(\phi, colour)$ implies $I \models reach(\phi, colour)$ because $reach(\phi, colour) \subseteq basic(\phi, colour)$. As for the other direction, let $I \models reach(\phi, colour)$ be such that $I \models b_i \wedge d_j \wedge \neg implied_j \wedge \neg\psi_i^\Box(colour(j))$ for some $i \in [1..m]$ and $j \in [1..n]$ such that $i \notin B_j$—otherwise $I \models basic(\phi, colour)$. Since $b_i \rightarrow \psi_i^\Box(0)$ belongs to $reach(\phi, colour)$, we have that $I \models \psi_i^\Box(0)$, and we can copy a portion of world 0 into world *colour*(j) to construct a model I' for *reach*(ϕ, *colour*) such that $I' \models \psi_i^\square(colour(j))$: $L = atoms(\psi_i^\square(colour(j))) \setminus atoms(\psi_j^\lozenge(colour(j)))$; $I' = I \setminus \{p(colour(j)) \in L\} \cup \{p(colour(j)) \in L \mid p(0) \in I\}$. By reiterating the process, we end up with a model of *basic*(ϕ, *colour*). □

Theorem 1. *For every S5-NF formula ϕ and every graph colouring colour of $\mathcal{G}_\phi$, reach*(ϕ, *colour*) *is equi-satisfiable to ϕ.*

Proof. By combining Lemma 1, Proposition 3 and Proposition 1. □

We conclude this section by observing that both *basic*(ϕ, *colour*) and *reach*(ϕ, *colour*) merge worlds, and not $\lozenge$-literals. Actually, the fact that two worlds are merged does not immediately imply that the associated $\lozenge$-literals can be jointly satisfied in that world, but instead that those satisfied in a Kripke structure can also be satisfied in a single world. The following example clarifies this fact.

Example 5. Consider the S5-formula $\phi := \square p \wedge (\lozenge q \vee \lozenge \neg p)$, which can be satisfied by $\mathbf{I} = [\{p\}, \{p, q\}]$. The two $\lozenge$-literals are non-conflictual, and therefore *colour* $= \{1 \mapsto 1, 2 \mapsto 1\}$ is a graph colouring of $\mathcal{G}_\phi$. The model of *basic*(ϕ, *colour*) and *reach*(ϕ, *colour*) associated with $\mathbf{I}$ is $\{b_1, d_1, p(0), p(1), q(1)\}$, and reflect the fact that the worlds of $\lozenge q$ and $\lozenge \neg p$ can be merged. On the other hand, note that $\lozenge \neg p$ is not satisfied by $\mathbf{I}$, and in fact merging the two $\lozenge$-literals would result into $\square p \wedge (\lozenge q \wedge \neg p)$, an unsatisfiable formula. ∎

4   Implementation in Answer Set Programming

This section presents an ASP implementation of the propositional theory *reach*(ϕ, *colour*) introduced in the previous section. As already observed, *colour* can also be the identity function *id* (for example, in case one does not want to afford for the computation of a graph colouring). Moreover, many formulas associated with world *colour*(j) in *reach*(ϕ, *colour*) are vacuously true if atom d_j is false, that is, if the associated $\lozenge$-literal is assumed false. Based on this observation, an incremental instantiation strategy is introduced, materialising such formulas only after d_j is assigned true for the first time.

The S5-NF formula ϕ and the graph colouring *colour* are encoded by the following facts, denoted $\Pi_{re}(\phi, colour)$ and called the *relational encoding* of ϕ:

- atom(p), for every propositional atom p occurring in ϕ;
- box(b), pos_box(b,p_i), and neg_box(b,p_j), for every $\square$-literal of ϕ of the form $\square(p_1 \vee \cdots \vee p_m \vee \neg p\_m+1 \vee \cdots \vee \neg p_n)$, with $n \geq 1$ and $n \geq m \geq 0$, and all $i \in [1..m]$ and $j \in [m+1..n]$, where b is an identifier for the $\square$-literal;
- diamond(d), pos_diamond(d,p_i), and neg_diamond(d,p_j), for every $\lozenge$-literal of ϕ of the form $\lozenge(p_1 \wedge \cdots \wedge p_m \wedge \neg p\_m+1 \wedge \cdots \wedge \neg p_n)$, with $n \geq 1$ and $n \geq m \geq 0$, and all $i \in [1..m]$ and $j \in [m+1..n]$, where d is an identifier for the $\lozenge$-literal;
- clause(c), pos_clause(c,lit$_i$), and neg_clause(c,p_j), for every S5-clause of ϕ of the form $\ell_1 \vee \cdots \vee \ell_m \vee \neg p\_m+1 \vee \cdots \vee \neg p_n$, with $n \geq 1$ and $n \geq m \geq 0$, and all $i \in [1..m]$ and $j \in [m+1..n]$, where c is an identifier for the S5-clause and each lit$_i$ is the identifier of the associated S5-literal ℓ_i;

- lrl(p_i,s_i,p_j,s_j), where p_i and p_j are propositional atoms, and s_i,s_j belong to {pos,neg}, to encode the *reach* relation introduced in Sect. 3 for literals occurring in some $\Diamond$-literal of ϕ—essentially, set $UP(L)$ in (2);
- lrb(p_j,s_j,b_i), where p_j is a propositional atom, s_j belongs to {pos,neg}, and $i \in [1..m]$, to encode the *reach* relation introduced in Sect. 3 for $\Box$-literals reached by the associated $\Diamond$-literals—essentially, sets B_j in (3);
- diamond_world(d,w), where d is the identifier of a $\Diamond$-literal, and w the associated world—essentially, $colour(\text{d}) = \text{w}$.

Example 6 (Continuing Example 4). Let ϕ be $\Box(p \vee q) \wedge \Diamond p \wedge \Diamond \neg p \wedge \Diamond \neg q$, and *colour* be $\{1 \mapsto 1, 2 \mapsto 2, 3 \mapsto 1\}$. Program $\Pi_{re}(\phi, colour)$ contains the following facts:

```
box(b1).          pos_box(b1,p).      pos_box(b1,q).   atom(p).  atom(q).
diamond(d1).      pos_diamond(d1,p).  clause(c1).      pos_clause(c1,b1).
diamond(d2).      neg_diamond(d1,p).  clause(c2).      pos_clause(c2,d1).
diamond(d3).      neg_diamond(d1,q).  clause(c3).      pos_clause(c2,d2).
                                      clause(c4).      pos_clause(c2,d3).
lrl(p,pos, p,pos).
lrl(p,neg, p,neg).    lrl(p,neg, q,pos).    lrb(p,neg, b1).
lrl(q,neg, q,neg).    lrl(q,neg, p,pos).    lrb(q,neg, b1).
diamond_world(d1,1).  diamond_world(d2,2).  diamond_world(d3,1).
```

Note that replacing *colour* with *id* results in the same set of facts, with the exception of diamond_world(d3,1), which would be replaced by diamond_world(d3,3). ∎

In order to possibly enable a progressive instantiation of the ASP program, two sets of rules are used, where the first set is processed once, and the second set is processed at most once for each world associated with some $\Diamond$-literals of ϕ. The following atoms are defined in these sets of rules:

- true(X), to guess true atoms in world 0, true $\Box$-literals, and true $\Diamond$-literals;
- true(W,X), to guess true atoms in each world (different from 0);
- dra(D,Y), to determine atoms reached by $\Diamond$-literals;
- drb(D,B), to determine $\Box$-literals reached by $\Diamond$-literals;
- world_need_atom(W,X), to determine if atoms in a world can be ignored because all associated $\Diamond$-literals are false;
- active_box_in_world(B,W), to determine if a $\Box$-literals is reached by some true-and-not-implied $\Diamond$-literals associated with world W.

Let Π_{base} be the following set of rules:

```
r1 :   {true(X)} :- box(X).
r2 :   {true(X)} :- diamond(X).
r3 :   {true(X)} :- atom(X).
r4 :   dra(D,Y) :- pos_diamond(D,X); lrl(X,pos,Y,_).
r5 :   dra(D,Y) :- neg_diamond(D,X); lrl(X,neg,Y,_).
r6 :   drb(D,B) :- pos_diamond(D,X); lrb(X,pos,B).
r7 :   drb(D,B) :- neg_diamond(D,X); lrb(X,neg,B).
r8 :     :- clause(C); not true(X) : pos_clause(C,X);
                        true(X) : neg_clause(C,X).
```

r_9 :   :- box(B), true(B); not true(X) : pos_box(B,X);
                          true(X) : neg_box(B,X).
r_{10} :   implied(D) :- diamond(D);   true(X) : pos_diamond(D,X);
                          not true(X) : neg_diamond(D,X).
r_{11} :   :- diamond(D), implied(D), not true(D).
r_{12} :   true_not_implied(D) :- diamond(D), true(D), not implied(D).

Let $\Pi_w(world)$ be the following set of rules parameterized by constant *world*:

r_{13} :   {true(X,W)} :- W = world; diamond_world(D,W);
              diamond_reach_atom(D,X).
r_{14} :   :- W = world; diamond(D), true_not_implied(D);
              diamond_world(D,W); pos_diamond(D,X); not true(X,W).
r_{15} :   :- W = world; diamond(D), true_not_implied(D);
              diamond_world(D,W); neg_diamond(D,X);   true(X,W).
r_{16} :   world_need_atom(W,X) :- W = world; diamond_world(D,W);
              diamond_reach_atom(D,X); true(D)_not_implied(D).
r_{17} :   :- W = world; true(X,W); not world_need_atom(W,X).
r_{18} :   active_box_in_world(B,W) :- W = world;
              diamond_world(D,W), drb(D,B);
              box(B), true(B), diamond(D), true_not_implied(D).
r_{19} :   :- W = world; active_box_in_world(B,W);
              not true(X,W) : pos_box(B,X); true(X,W) : neg_box(B,X).

The above programs can be combined in several ways. Let *colour* be a graph colour-ing of $\mathscr{G}_\phi$ obtained by a greedy algorithm which considers the vertices in descending order according to their degrees, and assigns to each vertex the smallest available colour in this order [17]. For an ASP program Π, let Search(Π) return a stable model I of Π if any, or otherwise $\bot$. We define the following four algorithms for S5 satisfiability checking:

A1. Search($\Pi_{re}(\phi, id) \cup \Pi_{base} \cup \bigcup_{i \in [1..n]} \Pi_w(i)$)—no merge, no lazy;
A2. Search($\Pi_{re}(\phi, colour) \cup \Pi_{base} \cup \bigcup_{i \in [1..n]} \Pi_w(i)$)—merge, no lazy;
A3. SearchWithLazyWorlds(ϕ, id)—no merge, lazy;
A4. SearchWithLazyWorlds($\phi, colour$)—merge, lazy;

where SearchWithLazyWorlds is shown as Algorithm 1 and is characterised by the incremental instantiation of the rules in $\Pi_w(world)$.

5 Evaluation

The ASP encodings presented in Sect. 4 have been implemented into the solver S5PY [1]. The solver is written in Python and uses CLINGO version 5.4.0 [8] to search for answer sets. This section reports on an empirical comparison between the algorithms discussed in the previous section. S5PY and pointers to benchmark files are provided at http://www.mat.unical.it/~alviano/LPNMR2022-s5py.zip. The experiments were run on an Intel Xeon 2.4 GHz with 16 GB of memory. Time and memory were limited to 300 s and 15 GB, as in [1]. For each instance solved within these limits, we measured both execution time and memory usage.

Algorithm 1. SearchWithLazyWorlds(ψ: S5-NF formula, *colour*: a graph colouring of $\mathcal{G}_\phi$)

---

1   $\Pi := \Pi_{re}(\phi, colour) \cup \Pi_{base};$ $W := \emptyset;$
2   **loop**
3      $I := \text{Search}(\Pi);$
4   **if** $I = \bot$ **then return** $\bot;$
5      $W' := \{w \mid \exists d \text{ s.t. } \texttt{diamond\_world}(d,w) \text{ and } \texttt{true}(d) \text{ are true in } I\} \setminus W;$
6   **if** $W' = \emptyset$ **then return** $I;$
7      $\Pi := \Pi \cup \bigcup_{world \in W'} \Pi_w(world);$ $W := W \cup W';$

The first algorithm (A1—no merge, no lazy) is essentially the reach encoding with no incremental instantiation, the most performant algorithm presented in [1], which is therefore our baseline for comparing how the other techniques discussed in this paper affect the computation of S5PY. As reported in Fig. 2, the baseline on the number of solved instances is already over 99%, but a small performance gain is provided by the lazy creation of worlds (2 new solved instances, as well as an improvement of around 0.4 s and 14 MiB on average, when A1 is replaced by A3). On the other hand, the heuristic based on the merging of non-conflictual worlds introduces a significant overhead (A2 has 44 timeouts more than A1), which is only minimally compensated by the lazy creation of worlds (A4 solves 8 instances more than A2). Figure 2 also shows a cactus plot of the running time of the tested algorithms, confirming that the lazy creation of worlds provides a minimal but consistent performance gain (A1 vs A3; A2 vs A4).

Figure 3 shows scatter plots comparing the running time of the tested algorithms on each tested instance. A point above the diagonal (dotted red line) means that the algorithm on axis x is faster than the algorithm on axis y. It can be observed that the first two plots (A1 vs A2 and A3 vs A4) evidence the fact that the performance of S5PY deteriorates when non-conflictual worlds are merged. On the other hand, the other two plots (A1 vs A3 and A2 vs A4) witness the small performance gain ascribable to the lazy creation of worlds.

6   Related Work

Directly related work in literature includes the research on the SAT-based S5CHEETAH solver [10] and the original version of the ASP-based solver S5PY [1]. The algorithm that is implemented by S5CHEETAH estimates an upper bound on possible worlds by applying the *graph colourability heuristic*, which is used for identifying non interacting worlds that can be essentially merged. In this work we adapt such an heuristic to S5PY, using the same greedy algorithm for computing graph colouring in polynomial time [17], but differently from S5CHEETAH we associate worlds with $\Diamond$-literals rather than S5-clauses. The argument in favour of associating worlds with S5-clauses is that in this way some $\Diamond$-literals are possibly grouped if they occur under the scope of the same disjunction connective. On the other hand, literals can be combined to form exponentially many clauses, which is the argument in favour of our choice.

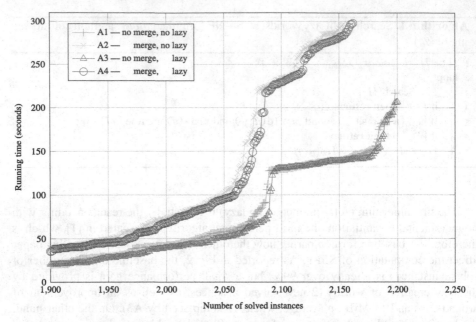

Fig. 2. Number of solved instances within a time budget (cactus plot), and overall statistics on 2214 instances (no memory out recorded).

Example 7. Consider the formula $(p \lor \Diamond q) \land (\neg p \lor \Diamond q)$. Even if there is only one $\Diamond$-literal, namely $\Diamond q$, there are two different clauses containing some $\Diamond$-literal. In such a case, it is preferable to associate worlds with $\Diamond$-literals, as it is done by S5PY. ∎

According to the experiment reported in [1], the original version of the S5PY solver introduced several encodings to address S5 satisfiability checking via ASP, and reached a comparable performance with S5CHEETAH. In particular, the most efficient encoding is the one relying on the reachability relation associated with unit propagation and used to define the reach encoding in Sect. 3. Such an encoding is now the default strategy used by S5PY, while the other encodings presented in [1] are no longer considered because of their minimal or negative impact on computation. Additionally, the new version of S5PY presented in this work can take advantage of incremental instantiation as implemented by CLINGO.

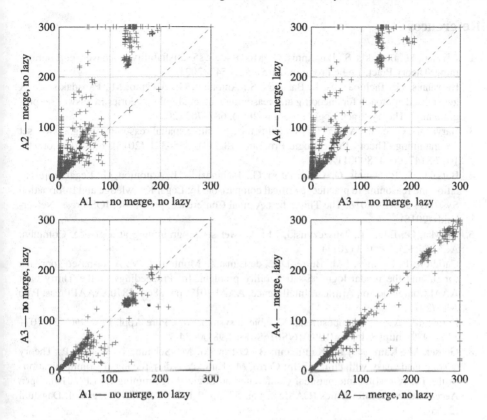

Fig. 3. Instance by instance comparison on execution time (in seconds; timeouts normalised to the limit): Impact of the merging of worlds (top) and the lazy creation of worlds (bottom).

7   Conclusion

This work confirms that ASP is an ideal language for implementing a solver for modal logic S5, and that the good performance achieved by S5PY is mainly ascribable to the reachability relation used to optimise its knowledge compilation algorithm. We have also shown how such a reachability relation can be combined with the graph colourability heuristic implemented by S5CHEETAH, and how the resulting encodings can be incrementally instantiated. Our experiments report no significant gain when combining the two heuristics. This is not necessarily considered a negative result, since the baseline on the number of solved instances is already over 99% and because lazy creation of worlds provides some further performance gain to the original ASP-based solver.

In the future, we intend to further investigate the potential positive impact of incremental instantiation. For instance, we can employ the search heuristic of CLINGO in order to falsify $\Diamond$-literals with the aim of reducing the number of worlds to be actually materialised. We also intend, to explore whether improvements can be made to the graph colourability heuristic to mitigate the overhead it introduces and the increased implementation complexity which negatively affects the performance of S5PY.

28   M. Alviano et al.

References

1. Alviano, M., Batsakis, S., Baryannis, G.: Modal logic s5 satisfiability in answer set programming. Theory Pract. Logic Program. **21**(5), 527–542 (2021)
2. Baryannis, G., Tachmazidis, I., Batsakis, S., Antoniou, G., Alviano, M., Papadakis, E.: A generalised approach for encoding and reasoning with qualitative theories in answer set programming. Theory Pract. Logic Program. **20**(5), 687–702 (2020)
3. Baryannis, G., et al.: A trajectory calculus for qualitative spatial reasoning using answer set programming. Theory Pract. Logic Program. **18**(3–4), 355–371 (2018). https://doi.org/10. 1017/S147106841800011X
4. Batsakis, S., Baryannis, G., Governatori, G., Tachmazidis, I., Antoniou, G.: Legal representation and reasoning in practice: a critical comparison. In: Legal Knowledge and Information Systems - JURIX 2018: The Thirty-first Annual Conference, pp. 31–40. IOS Press, Netherlands (2018)
5. Brewka, G., Eiter, T., Truszczyński, M.: Answer set programming at a glance. Commun. ACM **54**(12), 92–103 (2011)
6. Caridroit, T., Lagniez, J.M., Berre, D.L., de Lima, T., Montmirail, V.: A sat-based approach for solving the modal logic s5-satisfiability problem. In: Proceedings of the Thirty-First AAAI Conference on Artificial Intelligence, AAAI 2017, pp. 3864–3870. AAAI Press, Palo Alto (2017)
7. Fitting, M.: A simple propositional S5 tableau system. Ann. Pure Appl. Log. **96**(1–3), 107–115 (1999). https://doi.org/10.1016/S0168-0072(98)00034-7
8. Gebser, M., Kaminski, R., Kaufmann, B., Ostrowski, M., Schaub, T., Wanko, P.: Theory solving made easy with clingo 5. In: Carro, M., King, A. (eds.) Technical Communications of the Thirty-second International Conference on Logic Programming (ICLP 2016). Open Access Series in Informatics (OASIcs), vol. 52, pp. 2:1–2:15. Schloss Dagstuhl, Dagstuhl (2016)
9. Goré, R.: Tableau methods for modal and temporal logics. In: D'Agostino, M., Gabbay, D.M., Hähnle, R., Posegga, J. (eds.) Handbook Tableau Methods, pp. 297–396. Springer, Netherlands (1999). https://doi.org/10.1007/978-94-017-1754-0_6
10. Huang, P., Liu, M., Wang, P., Zhang, W., Ma, F., Zhang, J.: Solving the satisfiability problem of modal logic S5 guided by graph coloring. In: Kraus, S. (ed.) Proceedings of the Twenty-Eighth International Joint Conference on Artificial Intelligence, IJCAI 2019. pp. 1093–1100. ijcai.org, California (2019)
11. Kripke, S.A.: A completeness theorem in modal logic. J. Symbolic Logic **24**(1), 1–14 (1959)
12. Ladner, R.E.: The computational complexity of provability in systems of modal propositional logic. SIAM J. Comput. **6**(3), 467–480 (1977)
13. Liau, C.J.: Belief, information acquisition, and trust in multi-agent systems-a modal logic formulation. Artif. Intell. **149**(1), 31–60 (2003)
14. Lifschitz, V.: Answer set programming. Springer, Berlin (2019). https://doi.org/10.1007/978-3-030-24658-7
15. Moss, L.S., Tiede, H.J.: 19 applications of modal logic in linguistics. In: Blackburn, P., Van Benthem, J., Wolter, F. (eds.) Handbook of Modal Logic, Studies in Logic and Practical Reasoning, vol. 3, pp. 1031–1076. Elsevier, Amsterdam (2007)
16. Nalon, C., Hustadt, U., Dixon, C.: Ksp: A resolution-based prover for multimodal k, abridged report. In: IJCAI, California, vol. 17, pp. 4919–4923 (2017), ijcai.org
17. Welsh, D.J.A., Powell, M.B.: An upper bound for the chromatic number of a graph and its application to timetabling problems. Comput. J. **10**(1), 85–86 (1967). https://doi.org/10. 1093/comjnl/10.1.85

Enumeration of Minimal Models and MUSes in WASP

Mario Alviano[1], Carmine Dodaro[1(✉)], Salvatore Fiorentino[1],
Alessandro Previti[2], and Francesco Ricca[3]

[1] Department of Mathematics and Computer Science, Arcavacata, Italy
{mario.alviano,carmine.dodaro,francesco.ricca}@unical.it,
fiorentinosalvatore65@gmail.com
[2] Ericsson Research, Stockholm, Sweden
alessandro.previti@ericsson.com
[3] University of Calabria, Arcavacata, Italy

Abstract. Several AI problems can be conveniently modelled in ASP, and many of them require to enumerate solutions characterized by an optimality property that can be expressed in terms of subset-minimality with respect to some objective atoms. In this context, solutions are often either (i) answer sets or (ii) sets of atoms that enforce the absence of answer sets on the ASP program at hand—such sets are referred to as minimal unsatisfiable subsets (MUSes). In both cases, the required enumeration task is currently not supported by state-of-the-art ASP solvers.

Keywords: Answer Set Programming · Enumeration · Minimal models · MUS

1 Introduction

Answer Set Programming (ASP) [7] is a well-known formalism for Knowledge Representation and Reasoning (KRR) developed in the areas of logic programming and non-monotonic reasoning. ASP became popular because it combines two important features for a KRR formalism: high knowledge-modeling power and efficient implementations [16]. These features made ASP a convenient choice for modeling and solving several industrial and academic problems, and also made it attractive for companies [12].

The classic idea of problem solving in ASP is to write a logic program in such a way that the solution of the problem to be solved correspond to its answer sets (or stable models). Thus, ASP implementations were primarily focused on the computation of the answer sets of logic programs provided as input [16].

This work is partially supported by the Italian Ministry of Research under PRIN project "exPlaInable kNowledge-aware PrOcess INTelligence" (PINPOINT), CUP H23C22000280006.

G. Gottlob et al. (Eds.): LPNMR 2022, LNAI 13416, pp. 29–42, 2022.
https://doi.org/10.1007/978-3-031-15707-3_3

As a matter of fact, besides answer set computation, there are several other tasks that are very important from both the theoretical and practical perspective [16], such as the computation of brave and cautious consequences (i.e., atoms that are true in some (resp. all) answer sets) [3] or the computation of some form of optimal and preferred answer sets [6,21]. Thus, the implementations of these computational tasks have found stable place in state of the art ASP solvers.

In the last few years, the development of ASP-based solutions for AI problems of various nature, such as the debugging of ASP programs [10,20] and paracoherent semantics [5], suggests there is the need for supporting additional tasks in ASP solvers. In particular, the above-mentioned solutions are based on the tasks of enumerating solutions characterized by an optimality property that can be expressed in terms of subset-minimality with respect to some objective atoms. In this context, solutions are often either (i) answer sets or (ii) sets of atoms that enforce the absence of answer sets on the ASP program at hand (such sets are referred to as minimal unsatisfiable subsets (MUSes) [18,20]). In both cases, the required enumeration task is not currently supported by state-of-the-art ASP solvers, like CLASP [15] and WASP [2].

In this paper, we fill the gap by proposing several algorithms to enumerate subset-minimal answer sets and MUSes, which we also implement on top of WASP. Eventually, we report the results of an experimental analysis on several hard benchmarks showing that WASP configured with the proposed algorithms is competitive with state-of-the-art approaches.

2   Preliminaries

This section introduces syntax and semantics of ASP programs, where the syntax is properly simplified to ease the presentation.

Let $\mathcal{A}$ be a set of *atoms*. An *atomic formula* is either an atom, or the connective $\bot$. A *literal* is an atomic formula possibly preceded by the *default negation* symbol $\sim$. For a literal ℓ, let $\bar{\ell}$ denote the *complement* of ℓ, that is, $\bar{p} = \sim p$ and $\overline{\sim p} = p$ for all $p \in \mathcal{A} \cup \{\bot\}$; for a set L of literals, let $\overline{L}$ be $\{\bar{\ell} \mid \ell \in L\}$. Let $\top$ be a compact representation of $\sim\bot$.

A *rule* is of one of the following forms:

$$p_1 \vee \cdots \vee p_m \leftarrow \ell_1, \ldots, \ell_n \tag{1}$$

$$\{p_1, \ldots, p_m\} \geq b \leftarrow \top \tag{2}$$

where $m \geq 1$, $n \geq 0$, $p_1, \ldots, p_m$ are atomic formulas, $\ell_1, \ldots, \ell_n$ are distinct literals, and b is a non-negative integer. For a rule r, let $H(r)$ denote the set $\{p_1, \ldots, p_m\} \cap \mathcal{A}$ of *head atoms* (note that $H(r)$ is a set of atoms, so $\bot \notin H(r)$ even if $p_i = \bot$ for some $i \in [1..m]$). For a rule r of the form (1), called *disjunctive rule*, let $B(r)$ denote the set $\{\ell_1, \ldots, \ell_n\}$ of *body literals*. For a rule r of the form (2), called *choice rule*, let $bound(r)$ denote the *bound* b.

Algorithm 1: Minimal Models Enumeration

    Input : A program Π, a set of objective atoms O
    Output: Stable models of Π that are subset-minimal w.r.t. O.

1 **loop**
2     $I := \text{ComputeMinStableModel}(\Pi, O)$;
3   **if** $I = \bot$ **then return**;
4     $\text{Enumerate}(\Pi, (O \cap I) \cup \overline{(O \setminus I)})$;
5     $\Pi := \Pi \cup \{\bot \leftarrow O \cap I\}$;

A *program* Π is a finite set of rules. Let $atoms(\Pi)$, $rules(\Pi)$, and $rules^{\#}(\Pi)$ denote respectively the set of atoms occurring in Π, the set of disjunctive rules in Π, and the set of choice rules in Π. For an atom $p \in \mathcal{A}$, let $heads(p) := \{r \mid p \in H(r)\}$ be the set of rules where p appears in the head.

An *interpretation* I for a program Π is a set of atoms such that $I \subseteq atoms(\Pi)$; intuitively, atoms in I are true, those in $atoms(\Pi) \setminus I$ are false. Relation $\models$ is inductively defined as follows. For an atomic formula $p \in \mathcal{A} \cup \{\bot\}$, $I \models p$ if $p \in I$, and $I \models \sim p$ if $p \notin I$—hence, $I \not\models \bot$, and $I \models \top$; for a disjunctive rule r, $I \models B(r)$ if $I \models \ell$ for all $\ell \in B(r)$, $I \models H(r)$ if $I \models p$ for some $p \in H(r)$, and $I \models r$ if $I \models H(r)$ whenever $I \models B(r)$; for a choice rule r, $I \models r$ if $|\{p \in H(r) \mid I \models p\}| \geq bound(r)$; for a program Π, $I \vdash \Pi$ if $I \vdash r$ for all $r \in \Pi$. For any expression π, if $I \models \pi$, we say that I is a *model* of π.

Π^I denotes the *reduct* of a program Π with respect to an interpretation I. For each disjunctive rule r of Π such that $I \models B(r)$, Π^I contains a rule r^I of the form (1) with $H(r^I) = H(r)$, and $B(r^I) = B(r) \cap \mathcal{A}$; and for each choice rule r of Π, Π^I contains a rule of the form $p \leftarrow \top$ for every true head atom, i.e., for every $p \in H(r) \cap I$. An interpretation I is a *stable model* of a program Π if $I \models \Pi$ and there is no $J \subset I$ such that $J \models \Pi^I$. Let $SM(\Pi)$ denote the set of stable models of Π. A program Π is said to be *incoherent* if $SM(\Pi) = \emptyset$.

3   Enumeration of Minimal Stable Models

This section introduces the algorithms for the enumeration of minimal models. In the following, we assume the reader to be familiar with the stable model search algorithm (CDCL) implemented by modern ASP solvers [2,15]. Moreover, ComputeStableModel(Π,A) denotes a call to such an algorithm, where Π is a propositional program, and a set A of literals, called *assumption literals* (or *assumptions*). The output of the algorithm is a pair $(I, \emptyset)$, where I is a stable model of Π such that $I \models \ell$ for all $\ell \in A$, if such an I exists. Otherwise, the algorithm returns as output a set $(\bot, C)$, where $C \subseteq A$ is such that $SM(\Pi \cup \{\bot \leftarrow \overline{\ell} \mid \ell \in C\}) = \emptyset$; such a set C is called an *unsatisfiable core* of Π with respect to A. We will also use a slightly different version of ComputeStableModel, called ComputeStableModel*, which returns as output (I, B) where I is a stable model and B is the set of branching literals used to compute I; or $(\bot, \emptyset)$ if the program

---

Function. Enumerate(Π, S)

```
1  A := [...S, ⊥];     F := ∅; // initialize assumptions and flipped literals
2  loop
3      while A ≠ [] and top(A) ∈ F do
4          F := F \ {pop(A)};                  // remove flipped assumptions
5      if A = [...S] then return;              // no assumptions to flip
6      push(A, top(A)); F := F ∪ top(A);       // flip top assumption
7      (I, B) := ComputeStableModel*(Π, A);    // search I ∈ SM(Π) s.t.
       A ⊆ I
8      if I ≠ ⊥ then                           // found I using branching literals B
9          print I;
10         for ℓ ∈ B \ A do push(A, ℓ);  // extend A with new elements in B
```

---

does not admit stable models. Algorithm 1 provides a common skeleton shared by several algorithms for enumerating minimal models w.r.t. a set of objective atoms O. These algorithms take as input a program Π and a set of atoms O, and print as output all stable models of Π that are subset-minimal w.r.t. O. The algorithms take advantage of the function ComputeMinStableModel, whose input is a program Π and a set O of objective atoms, and whose output is a minimal stable model of Π w.r.t. O. The idea of the algorithm is to iteratively call ComputeMinStableModel to compute one minimal stable model, say I. If such a model does not exist, the algorithm terminates. Otherwise, the algorithm enumerates all stable models where objective atoms are fixed w.r.t. I by calling function Enumerate. In particular, function Enumerate takes advantage of literal assumptions to perform chronological backtracking on the branching literals used to find a minimal stable model as proposed by Alviano and Dodaro in [1]. Note that ...S denotes the expansion of S, so that $[...S, \perp]$ is the list comprising the elements of S and terminated by $\perp$. After the enumeration, Π is extended with a new rule, called *block-up*, which ensures that enumerated minimal models are not found again in subsequent iterations.

Example 1. Let $O = \{o_1, o_2\}$ be the set of objective atoms and let Π_1 be the following program:

$$r_1 : p_1 \vee p_2 \leftarrow \qquad r_2 : p_3 \leftarrow \sim p_4 \qquad r_3 : p_4 \leftarrow \sim p_3$$
$$r_4 : \{p_5, p_6\} \geq 1 \leftarrow \top \qquad r_5 : \perp \leftarrow p_5, p_6 \qquad r_6 : o_1 \leftarrow p_1$$
$$r_7 : o_2 \leftarrow p_2 \qquad r_8 : o_1 \leftarrow p_3 \qquad r_9 : o_2 \leftarrow p_4$$

Then, $SM(\Pi_1)$ is $\{I_1 = \{o_1, o_2, p_1, p_4, p_6\}, I_2 = \{o_1, o_2, p_1, p_4, p_5\}, I_3 = \{o_1, p_1, p_3, p_5\}, I_4 = \{o_1, p_1, p_3, p_6\}, I_5 = \{o_1, o_2, p_2, p_3, p_6\}, I_6 = \{o_2, p_2, p_4, p_6\}, I_7 = \{o_1, o_2, p_2, p_3, p_5\}$, and $I_8 = \{o_2, p_2, p_4, p_5\}$ $\}$. ComputeMinStableModel(Π_1, O) returns a stable model between $\{I_3, I_4, I_6, I_8\}$, say I_3. The subsequent call to Enumerate($\Pi_1, \{o_1, \sim o_2\}$) enumerates and prints each stable model M such that $o_1 \in M$ and $o_2 \notin M$, thus I_3 and I_4. After the enumeration Π is extended

---

Function. Opt(Π, O)

```
1  A := [];                        // stack of assumptions, also used as a set
2  loop
3  |   while O \ (A ∪ Ā) ≠ ∅ do
4  |   |   A.push(~ OneOf(O \ (A ∪ Ā)));
5  |   |   Propagate(Π, A);
6  |   (I, C) := ComputeStableModel(Π, A);
7  |   if I ≠ ⊥ then return I;
8  |   if C = ∅ then return ⊥;
9  |   while C ⊄ A do A.pop();                      // restore consistency
```

---

with $\perp \leftarrow o_1$. The next call to ComputeMinStableModel(Π_1, O) returns a stable model between $\{I_6, I_8\}$, say I_6. The next call to Enumerate(Π_1, $\{\sim o_1, o_2\}$) enumerates and prints each stable model M such that $o_2 \in M$ and $o_1 \notin M$, thus both I_6 and I_8. Then, Π is extended with $\perp \leftarrow o_2$. Thus, the subsequent call ComputeMinStableModel(Π_1, O) returns $\perp$ and the algorithm terminates. ◁

Algorithm 1 is actually a meta-algorithm that can be instantiated in several ways by using different versions of the function ComputeMinStableModel. Several alternatives are presented in the following, i.e., Opt is based on the techniques implemented by Dodaro and Previti in [11], One is based on the MaxSAT algorithm proposed by Alviano et al. in [4], and Minimize and Split are extensions of the algorithms proposed by Amendola et al. in [5].

Opt. The idea of this strategy is to force the branching heuristic of the solver to select $\overline{p}$ for each p in the set of objective literals O, before any other unassigned literal. In this way, the stable model search is driven to falsify as many atoms in O as possible. When all atoms in O are assigned, standard stable model search procedure is applied. Therefore, whenever a stable model is found, it is guaranteed to be minimal w.r.t. O. Otherwise, if the partial assignment cannot be extended to a stable model, then a conflict involving some objective atoms is detected, and the assignment of some atom in O is then flipped. Therefore, the procedure is repeated with a different assignment for the objective atoms.

Function Opt reports such a strategy. In particular, Opt takes advantage of a stack A of assumption literals, initially empty (line 1), that is populated with $\overline{O}$ (line 4). After each insertion, *propagate*(Π, A) is used to extend A with (unit) implied literals, if possible; otherwise, in case of conflict, Π is extended by the learning procedure, some literal in A is flipped, and propagation is repeated. When all atoms in O occur in A, a stable model extending A is searched (line 6). If such a stable model is found, it is returned (line 7). Otherwise, ComputeStable-Model returns an unsatisfiable core C. If C is empty, then the inconsistency of Π does not depend on A and thus the algorithm terminates returning $\perp$ (line 8).

Function. One(Π, O)

---

1 $S := \overline{O}$; $A := atoms(\Pi)$;
2 **loop**
3 | $(I, C) :=$ ComputeStableModel(Π, S);
4 | **if** $I \neq \bot$ **then return** $I \cap A$;
5 | **if** $C = \emptyset$ **then return** $\bot$;
6 | Let $p'_1, \ldots, p'_n$ be $|C| - 1$ fresh atoms;
7 | $S := (S \setminus C) \cup \{\sim p'_1, \ldots, \sim p'_n\}$;
8 | $\Pi := \Pi \cup \{C \cup \{p'_1, \ldots, p'_n\} \geq n \leftarrow \top\} \cup \{\bot \leftarrow p'_i, \sim p'_{i-1} \mid i \in [2..n]\}$;

Function. Minimize(Π, O)

---

1 $(I, C) :=$ ComputeStableModel(Π, $\emptyset$);
2 **if** $I = \bot$ **then return** $\bot$;
3 $S := O \setminus I$;
4 Let $P := p', p_{o_1}, \ldots, p_{o_n}$ be $|O| + 1$ fresh atoms where $o_1, \ldots, o_n \in O$;
5 $R := \{\leftarrow p', \sim p_{o_1}, \ldots, \sim p_{o_n}\} \cup \{\leftarrow o_1, p_{o_1}\} \cup \ldots \cup \{\leftarrow o_n, p_{o_n}\}$;
6 $\Pi := (\Pi \setminus \{\leftarrow p \mid p \in P\}) \cup \{\{p', p_{o_1}, \ldots, p_{o_n}\} \geq 0 \leftarrow \top\}$;
7 **loop**
8 | $(I, C) :=$ ComputeStableModel($\Pi \cup R$, $\{p'\} \cup \overline{S} \cup \{\sim p_o \mid o \in S\}$);
9 | **if** $I = \bot$ **then** $\Pi := \Pi \cup \{\leftarrow p \mid p \in P\}$;   **return** $O \setminus S$;
10 | $S := O \setminus I$;

Otherwise, some literals in A are removed so to not incur again in the returned unsatisfiable core (line 9).

One. Cardinality-minimal models are special cases of subset-minimal models. Therefore, in this section, we employ a state-of-the-art algorithm, namely One, to compute a cardinality-minimal model. In more detail, function One takes as input a coherent program Π and a set O of objective atoms, and returns a minimal stable model of Π with respect to O. Then, One keeps a set S of *soft literals* to be maximized, initially set to the complements of the atoms in O (line 1). At each step of computation, a stable model of Π subject to the assumptions S is searched (line 3), and eventually returned (line 4). When the search fails, instead, an unsatisfiable core C is computed. If C is empty, then function ComputeStableModel terminates returning $\bot$, since Π does not admit stable models (line 5). Otherwise, soft literals in C are replaced by fresh literals $p_1, \ldots, p_n$ (line 6), and the program is extended with a choice rule enforcing the satisfaction of at least n literals among those in $C \cup \{p_1, \ldots, p_n\}$ (line 8). Since the next stable model search is forced to assign false to the fresh atoms, the rule drives the search to a stable model containing at least n literals among those in the unsatisfiable core. Additionally, constraints of the form $\bot \leftarrow p_i, \sim p_{i-1}$ are added to the program to eliminate symmetric solutions.

Function. Split(Π, O)

1   $(I, C) :=$ ComputeStableModel(Π, $\emptyset$);
2   **if** $I = \bot$ **then return** $\bot$;
3   $S := O \cap I$; $T := \emptyset$;
4   **loop**
5   **if** $S \setminus T = \emptyset$ **then return** T;
6     $o :=$ OneOf($S \setminus T$);
7     $(I, C) :=$ ComputeStableModel(Π, $\{\sim o\} \cup \overline{(O \setminus S)}$);
8   **if** $I \neq \bot$ **then** $S := S \cap I$;
9   **else** $T := T \cup \{o\}$;

Minimize. The idea of this strategy is to build a minimal model by iteratively removing at least one literal from a minimal stable model candidate until there are no further literals to remove. In particular, function Minimize first computes a stable model of Π, say I (line 1). If such a stable model does not exist, the algorithm terminates returning $\bot$. Otherwise, all objective literals that are false w.r.t. I are stored in a set S. Then, the algorithm creates a set of fresh atoms, namely P, containing one fresh atom, say p', for each objective literal in O, where such fresh atoms are used to ensure the correctness of the enumeration. Then, it creates a set of rules and add them to P. Intuitively, such rules enforce that (i) when p' is true then at least one of the other atoms in P is true; and (ii) when an atom $p_o \in P \setminus \{p'\}$ is true then the atom $o \in O$ is false (line 4). It is important to remark here that the creation of P and R is done only once in the actual implementation. Then, the algorithm performs a stable model search enforcing that at least one of the objective literals that are not in S is falsified. If such a model exists, say I, then S is updated by adding the objective literals that are false w.r.t. I. If such a model does not exists, then all literals in $O \setminus S$ are necessarily in a minimal model, since none of them can be removed, and the algorithm terminates returning it. Moreover, an additional rule $\leftarrow p$ is added for each atom in P. In this way, the enumeration of the minimal models is not affected by the rules R added in Π.

Split. The idea of this strategy is to build a minimal model by removing, one by one, all unnecessary literals from a minimal stable model candidate. In particular, function Split first computes a stable model of Π, say I (line 1). If such a stable model does not exist, the algorithm terminates returning $\bot$. Otherwise, all objective literals that are true w.r.t. I are stored in S. Moreover, a set of necessarily true literals, namely T, is created. If there are no more literals in S to test then the algorithm terminates returning T (line 5). Otherwise, a literal in S that is not in T is selected, say o. Then, a stable model I is searched, where I must falsify o and all the literals in $O \setminus S$ (line 7). If such an I exists, then all false literals w.r.t. I are removed from S. Otherwise, o must be necessarily true and is added to T. The algorithm then loops until there are no further literals in S to test.

Algorithm 2: MUS Enumeration

Input : A program Π, a set of atoms $O \mid \forall o \in O, heads(o) = \{\{o\} \geq 0 \leftarrow \top\}$
Output: MUSes of Π w.r.t. O.

1 $\Pi_s := \{O \geq 0 \leftarrow \top\}$;   // $atoms(\Pi_s) = O$
2 **loop**
3     $I := \mathrm{Opt}(\Pi_s, \overline{O})$;   // Minimal models of Π_s w.r.t. $\overline{O}$
4   **if** $I = \bot$ **then** **return**;
5     $(I', C) := \mathrm{ComputeStableModel}(\Pi, I)$;
6   **if** $I' \neq \bot$ **then** $\Pi_s := \Pi_s \cup \{\bot \leftarrow \overline{(O \setminus I)}\}$;
7   **else**
8        $M := \mathrm{Minimize}(\Pi, C)$;   // where $M \subseteq C \subseteq I$
9        $\mathrm{Print}(M)$;   // M is a MUS
10       $\Pi_s := \Pi_s \cup \{\bot \leftarrow M\}$;

---

4   Enumeration of MUSes

In this section, we present the algorithm for enumerating Minimal Unsatisfiable Subsets (MUSes) of a given program.

Definition 1 (Minimal Unsatisfiable Subset—MUS). *Let Π be a program, and $O \subseteq atoms(\Pi)$ be a set of objective atoms. A set $U \subseteq O$ is an* unsatisfiable subset *for Π w.r.t. O if*

$$\Pi \cup \{O \geq 0 \leftarrow \top\} \cup \{\bot \leftarrow \sim o \mid o \in U\} \tag{3}$$

is incoherent, that is, the program extended with a free choice of objective atoms is incoherent after forcing truth of atoms in U. A minimal unsatisfiable subset *for Π w.r.t. O is an unsatisfiable subset $U \subseteq O$ for Π w.r.t. O such that there is no $U' \subset U$ being an unsatisfiable subset for Π w.r.t. O.*

An important property of Definition 1 is that unsatisfiable subsets are monotone. More specifically, given a program Π and a set of objective atoms O, if $U \subseteq O$ is an unsatisfiable subset, then $U \subseteq U' \subseteq O$ implies that U' is also an unsatisfiable subset.

Equipped with the definition of MUS, we are now able to present an algorithm for their enumeration, reported as Algorithm 2, which represents a slight adaptation of the algorithm emax proposed by Mencía and João Marques-Silva in [20] to enumerate MSISes.

The algorithm takes as input a program Π and a set of objective atoms O, and prints as output all MUSes of Π w.r.t. O. Then, the algorithm takes advantage of another program, namely Π_s, initialized with a choice rule for each atom in O, thus $atoms(\Pi_s) = O$, which is used later on to block the sets of printed MUSes. Then, the algorithm computes a subset-minimal model I of φ w.r.t. $\overline{O}$ using function Opt described in Sect. 3. ComputeStableModel is then called trying to find a stable model $I' \supseteq I$. If such a stable model exists then Π_s is extended with a new constraint enforcing that at least one of the objective atoms that are not included in I is flipped (line 6). Otherwise, ComputeStableModel(Π, I) returns $(\bot, C)$, and C is minimized (line 8; e.g., by using the algorithm QUICKXPLAIN [17]). Note that since I contains only atoms, the notion of unsatisfiable core returned by the solver corresponds to the one of Unsatisfiable Set of Definition 1. Therefore, minimizing C coincides with computing a MUS M, that is later on printed. Moreover, a novel constraint is added to Π_s enforcing that M is not found in future searches (line 10).

5 Experiments

The algorithms for minimal stable models and MUSes enumeration given in Sects. 3 and 4 have been implemented in WASP [2], an ASP solver implementing non-chronological backtracking and handling assumption literals. Binaries, source code, and instructions to reproduce the experiments can be found at https://www.mat.unical.it/~dodaso/research/enumeration/. In the experiments, time and memory were limited to 5 min and 10 GB, respectively.

Benchmarks. The analysis was executed on a set of incoherent instances proposed in the literature. In particular, concerning minimal stable models enumeration, we used the benchmarks in the folder decisional and optimization used by Amendola et al. in [5] and available at https://doi.org/10.5281/zenodo.3963790. In the following we will omit the benchmarks graph colouring, stable marriage, and system synthesis since all tested solvers could not find even the first model. This experiment concerns the computational task of enumerating paracoherent answer sets using the semistable semantics [5]. In particular, for each incoherent instance we applied the rewriting technique proposed by Amendola et al. in [5], then minimal stable models w.r.t. the atoms of the form $gap(\cdot)$ correspond to the paracoherent answer sets. Concerning MUSes, we used all the benchmarks proposed in [20]. This experiment investigates the problem of explaining the inconsistency of ASP programs, where an ASP encoding is assumed to be correct and we are interested in enumerating all the (minimal) sets of facts leading to the inconsistency. In particular, to compute MUSes as defined in this paper, we converted each fact of the form $p \leftarrow$ in a rule of the form $p \leftarrow aux_p$ and a choice rule of the form $\{aux_p\} \geq 0 \leftarrow \top$, where aux_p is a fresh atom not appearing in the program. Then, we considered as the set of objective atoms all the atoms of the form aux_p.

Solvers. Concerning minimal stable model enumeration, the performance of the algorithms is compared in terms of computed solutions with the state-of-the-art tool ASPRIN (v. 3.1.1) [6]. Concerning MUSes enumeration, we employed the tool presented in [20] configured with the algorithm emax, and referred in the following as EMAX. In the following, OPT, ONE, MIN, SPLIT refer to WASP employing the algorithm based on the functions Opt, One, Minimize, and Split, respectively; and WASP-MUS refer to WASP configured for enumerating MUSes.

Table 1. Total sum of enumerated minimal models. Best results are in bold.

Benchmark	ASPRIN	ONE	OPT	MIN	SPLIT
KnightTour	0	**2 490**	1 846	0	0
MinimalDiagn	0	**27 901**	27 107	0	23 784
QualSpatReas	0	9 923	18 158	**20 987**	12 895
Visit-all	**729 220**	407 840	333 190	295 465	438 113
ADF	**27 297 528**	1 597 652	1 918 437	1 925 346	1 678 899
Bayes	719 768	13 222 883	**13 884 518**	9 001 178	10 311 603
ConMaxStillLife	20 740	0	**2 171 561**	775 825	89 670
CrossingMin	18 549 858	27 152 665	35 604 656	31 421 298	**42 338 833**
Markov	781	574 447	**590 658**	308 196	423 655
MaxClique	25	0	**42 740**	261	66
SteinerTree	976	339 666	442 201	**554 410**	290 106
Supertree	131 027	0	603 937	**630 603**	336 975
TSP	11 338	1 041 987	662 644	**1 746 535**	890 064
VideoStreaming	811	45 046	50 482	48 261	**50 752**

Table 2. Number of different solved instances by each solver with a limit to the number of models to enumerate set to 10, 10^3, and 10^4. Best results are in bold.

	Max 10 models					Max 10^3 models					Max 10^4 models				
Benchmark	ASPRIN	ONE	OPT	MIN	SPLIT	ASPRIN	ONE	OPT	MIN	SPLIT	ASPRIN	ONE	OPT	MIN	SPLIT
KnightTour	0	**2**	1	0	0	0	**2**	1	0	0	0	0	0	0	0
MinimalDiagn	0	**64**	62	0	63	0	**3**	**3**	0	**3**	0	0	0	0	0
QualSpatReas	0	19	30	**38**	26	0	0	0	0	0	0	0	0	0	0
Visit-all	**5**	**5**	**5**	4	**5**	**5**	**5**	**5**	4	**5**	**5**	3	4	3	3
ADF	**196**	143	191	166	145	**194**	142	191	164	143	**178**	76	75	75	74
Bayes	54	**60**	**60**	**60**	**60**	26	**60**	**60**	**60**	**60**	13	**60**	**60**	59	58
ConMaxStillLife	**120**	0	**120**	105	**120**	0	0	**117**	103	33	0	0	**101**	28	0
CrossingMin	85	76	**85**	**85**	**85**	**85**	77	**85**	**85**	**85**	**85**	74	**85**	**85**	**85**
Markov	11	**50**	**50**	48	42	0	**50**	49	33	15	0	16	**17**	7	5
MaxClique	0	0	**136**	1	0	0	0	**12**	0	0	0	0	0	0	0
SteinerTree	25	21	44	**49**	**49**	2	21	34	**45**	32	2	18	21	**27**	20
Supertree	24	0	20	**58**	41	24	0	20	**53**	25	3	0	17	**21**	11
TSP	70	47	61	**72**	67	2	44	47	**63**	34	2	**31**	20	30	23
VideoStreaming	8	**43**	**43**	**43**	**43**	0	**39**	**39**	**39**	**39**	0	0	0	0	0

Enumeration of Minimal Stable Models. Results are shown in Table 1, where we report, for each tested solver and for each benchmark, the total sum of enumerated minimal stable models. The best performance overall is obtained by SPLIT, which enumerated the greatest number of minimal stable models, followed by OPT that obtained a similar performance. It is interesting to compare the performance of ASPRIN with the one of OPT, since they employ the same technique for computing a single minimal stable model. In this case, OPT outperforms ASPRIN in all the domains but Visit-all and ADF, where the latter is much faster than all

Table 3. Total sum of enumerated MUSes, solved instances, and wins for each solver. Best results are in bold.

Benchmark	#	Sum of enumerated MUSes		Number of solved		Number of wins	
		EMAX	WASP-MUS	EMAX	WASP-MUS	EMAX	WASP-MUS
GracefulGraphs	120	153	**401**	60	60	4	**33**
KnightTour	120	**7570**	5273	41	36	31	**43**
Solitaire	120	**976**	510	**34**	24	**31**	0

WASP-based alternatives. To obtain a clearer picture of the results, we conducted an additional analysis. In particular, we executed the solvers with different limits on the number of minimal stable models to enumerate. Results are reported in Table 2, where for each tested solver and for each benchmark, we report the sum of solved instances within the budget. In this case, it is possible to observe that the performance difference between the tested solvers is reduced when the limit is set to 10 models. In particular, ASPRIN and OPT obtained similar performance on benchmarks of the optimization setting. Interestingly, the performance of ASPRIN deteriorates when the limit is set to 10^3. Indeed, overall it solves 598 instances when the limit is set to 10 and 338 instances when the limit is set to 10^3, with a percentage loss equal to 77%, whereas algorithms implemented in WASP report a lower percentage loss that are 20%, 37%, 12%, and 57% for ONE, OPT, MIN, and SPLIT, respectively. This performance can be explained by the fact that ASPRIN adds exponentially many blocking constraints to avoid the enumeration of the same minimal models (see Sect. 6), whereas function Enumerate described in Sect. 3 requires no additional space. A similar result was observed by Alviano and Dodaro in [1].

Enumeration of MUSes. Results are shown in Table 1, where we report, for each tested solver and for each benchmark, the total sum of enumerated muses, the number of solved instances (i.e., where all MUSes have been computed), and the number of wins (where an instance is counted as a win for a solver if it enumerates more MUSes than the other one). In this case, the two solvers obtain similar performance overall, since EMAX outperforms WASP-MUS in terms of enumerated MUSes in KnightTour and Solitaire, whereas WASP-MUS outperforms EMAX in GracefulGraphs. Interestingly, if we consider the number of wins, WASP-MUS outperforms EMAX on both GracefulGraphs and KnightTour, whereas EMAX is much faster on instances of Solitaire.

6 Related Work

The computational task of enumerating stable models was widely studied in the context of ASP. Modern solvers, like CLASP [15] and WASP [2], support two strategies. The first one is based on blocking constraints, where the idea is to add a single constraint for each enumerated stable model, whose drawback is that in the worst case the number of introduced constraints is exponential in the size of the input program. The second (polyspace) strategy [1,14] is similar to the one proposed in function Enumerate, whose idea is to combine chronological backtracking on the branching literals of the latest printed answer set with the non-chronological backtracking implemented in the solver. We adopted such a strategy for the enumeration of minimal models, whereas the tool ASPRIN [6] is instead based on blocking constraints, and as shown in the experiments (see Sect. 5), this strategy quickly deteriorates the performance of the solver. Moreover, enumeration strategies were also studied in presence of weak constraints, e.g., Pajunen and Janhunen [21] proposed the enumeration of stable models ordered by their optimality costs.

Algorithm 1 captures a family of strategies that basically differ on how a minimal model is computed. In particular, the algorithm Opt adapts the OPTSAT algorithm [9] and extends it in the way suggested by Dodaro and Previti in [11], that uses a novel heuristic for the implementation of the function *OneOf*. The ASP system CLINGO also supports the computation of a minimal model with an algorithm similar to Opt by using the `#heuristic` directive [13] and the command line option `-heuristic=domain`. Moreover, using the command line option `-enum-mode=domRec`, CLINGO introduces a blocking clause after each minimal model found. This is similar to the execution of Algorithm 1 with the function Opt but without calling the function Enumerate. Algorithm One is instead based on the MaxSAT algorithm One [4]. Algorithms Minimize and Split extend the algorithms proposed by Amendola et al. in [5].

MUSes are widely studied in the context of propositional satisfiability [18,19]. The algorithm proposed in Sect. 4 represents a native implementation of the one proposed by Mencía and Marques-Silva in [20]. Concerning ASP, different definitions of MUSes have been proposed. In particular, Brewka et al. in [8] introduced the notion of strong inconsistency, showing that it plays a similar role as MUS in propositional satisfiability. Similarly, Dodaro et al. in [10] introduced the notion of a (minimal) reason of incoherence.

7   Conclusions

Enumeration of subset-minimal solutions w.r.t. set of objective atoms can be efficiently implemented in modern ASP solvers. In this paper, we provide the description of a meta-algorithm for enumerating stable models that are subset-minimal w.r.t. a set of objective atoms. Such an algorithm efficiently combines several techniques presented in the literature and can be easily instantiated in multiple ways by updating one of its components. Moreover, we provided the first native implementation of an existing algorithm for enumerating MUSes in the ASP solver WASP.

References

1. Alviano, M., Dodaro, C.: Model enumeration via assumption literals. Fundam. Informaticae **167**(1–2), 31–58 (2019)

2. Alviano, M., Dodaro, C., Leone, N., Ricca, F.: Advances in WASP. In: Calimeri, F., Ianni, G., Truszczynski, M. (eds.) LPNMR 2015. LNCS (LNAI), vol. 9345, pp. 40–54. Springer, Cham (2015). https://doi.org/10.1007/978-3-319-23264-5_5

3. Alviano, M., Dodaro, C., Ricca, F.: Anytime computation of cautious consequences in answer set programming. Theory Pract. Log. Program. **14**(4–5), 755–770 (2014). https://doi.org/10.1017/S1471068414000325

4. Alviano, M., Dodaro, C., Ricca, F.: A maxsat algorithm using cardinality constraints of bounded size. In: Proceedings of IJCAI, pp. 2677–2683. AAAI Press (2015). http://ijcai.org/Abstract/15/379

5. Amendola, G., Dodaro, C., Faber, W., Ricca, F.: Paracoherent answer set computation. Artif. Intell. **299**, 103519 (2021). https://doi.org/10.1016/j.artint.2021.103519

6. Brewka, G., Delgrande, J.P., Romero, J., Schaub, T.: Asprin: Customizing answer set preferences without a headache. In: Proceedings of AAAI. pp. 1467–1474. AAAI Press (2015). http://www.aaai.org/ocs/index.php/AAAI/AAAI15/paper/view/9535

7. Brewka, G., Eiter, T., Truszczynski, M.: Answer set programming at a glance. Commun. ACM **54**(12), 92–103 (2011). https://doi.org/10.1145/2043174.2043195

8. Brewka, G., Thimm, M., Ulbricht, M.: Strong inconsistency. Artif. Intell. **267**, 78–117 (2019). https://doi.org/10.1016/j.artint.2018.11.002

9. Di Rosa, E., Giunchiglia, E., Maratea, M.: Solving satisfiability problems with preferences. Constraints An Int. J. **15**(4), 485–515 (2010). https://doi.org/10.1007/s10601-010-9095-y

10. Dodaro, C., Gasteiger, P., Reale, K., Ricca, F., Schekotihin, K.: Debugging nonground ASP programs: Technique and graphical tools. Theory Pract. Log. Program. **19**(2), 290–316 (2019). https://doi.org/10.1017/S1471068418000492

11. Dodaro, C., Previti, A.: Minipref: A tool for preferences in SAT (short paper). In: Proceedings of RCRA. CEUR Workshop Proceedings, vol. 2538. CEUR-WS.org (2019)

12. Erdem, E., Gelfond, M., Leone, N.: Applications of answer set programming. AI Mag. **37**(3), 53–68 (2016). https://doi.org/10.1609/aimag.v37i3.2678

13. Gebser, M., Kaminski, R., Kaufmann, B., Ostrowski, M., Schaub, T., Wanko, P.: Theory solving made easy with clingo 5. In: Proceedings of ICLP (TC). OASICS, vol. 52, pp. 2:1–2:15. Schloss Dagstuhl - Leibniz-Zentrum für Informatik (2016)

14. Gebser, M., Kaufmann, B., Neumann, A., Schaub, T.: Conflict-driven answer set enumeration. In: Baral, C., Brewka, G., Schlipf, J. (eds.) LPNMR 2007. LNCS (LNAI), vol. 4483, pp. 136–148. Springer, Heidelberg (2007). https://doi.org/10.1007/978-3-540-72200-7_13

15. Gebser, M., Kaufmann, B., Schaub, T.: Conflict-driven answer set solving: from theory to practice. Artif. Intell. **187**, 52–89 (2012). https://doi.org/10.1016/j.artint.2012.04.001

16. Gebser, M., Leone, N., Maratea, M., Perri, S., Ricca, F., Schaub, T.: Evaluation techniques and systems for answer set programming: a survey. In: Proceedings of IJCAI, pp. 5450–5456. ijcai.org (2018). https://doi.org/10.24963/ijcai.2018/769

17. Junker, U.: QUICKXPLAIN: preferred explanations and relaxations for over-constrained problems. In: Proceedings of AAAI, pp. 167–172. AAAI Press/The MIT Press (2004). http://www.aaai.org/Library/AAAI/2004/aaai04-027.php

18. Liffiton, M.H., Previti, A., Malik, A., Marques-Silva, J.: Fast, flexible MUS enumeration. Constraints **21**(2), 223–250 (2015). https://doi.org/10.1007/s10601-015-9183-0

19. Marques-Silva, J., Janota, M., Mencía, C.: Minimal sets on propositional formulae. problems and reductions. Artif. Intell. **252**, 22–50 (2017)
20. Mencía, C., Marques-Silva, J.: Reasoning about strong inconsistency in ASP. In: Pulina, L., Seidl, M. (eds.) SAT 2020. LNCS, vol. 12178, pp. 332–342. Springer, Cham (2020). https://doi.org/10.1007/978-3-030-51825-7_24
21. Pajunen, J., Janhunen, T.: Solution enumeration by optimality in answer set programming. Theory Pract. Log. Program. **21**(6), 750–767 (2021)

Statistical Statements in Probabilistic Logic Programming

Damiano Azzolini[1](✉)(iD), Elena Bellodi[2](iD), and Fabrizio Riguzzi[1](iD)

[1] Dipartimento di Matematica e Informatica, Università di Ferrara,
Via Saragat 1, 44122 Ferrara, Italy
{damiano.azzolini,fabrizio.riguzzi}@unife.it
[2] Dipartimento di Ingegneria, Università di Ferrara,
Via Saragat 1, 44122 Ferrara, Italy
elena.bellodi@unife.it

Abstract. Probabilistic Logic Programs under the distribution semantics (PLPDS) do not allow statistical probabilistic statements of the form "90% of birds fly", which were defined "Type 1" statements by Halpern. In this paper, we add this kind of statements to PLPDS and introduce the PASTA ("Probabilistic Answer set programming for STAtistical probabilities") language. We translate programs in our new formalism into probabilistic answer set programs under the credal semantics. This approach differs from previous proposals, such as the one based on "probabilistic conditionals" as, instead of choosing a single model by making the maximum entropy assumption, we take into consideration all models and we assign probability intervals to queries. In this way we refrain from making assumptions and we obtain a more neutral framework. We also propose an inference algorithm and compare it with an existing solver for probabilistic answer set programs on a number of programs of increasing size, showing that our solution is faster and can deal with larger instances.

Keywords: Probabilistic Logic Programming · Statistical statements · Statistical Relational Artificial Intelligence

1 Introduction

Probabilistic Logic Programming (PLP) [19] extends Logic Programming (LP) by considering various probabilistic constructs. ProbLog [8] is an example of a PLP language based on the distribution semantics (PLPDS) [20]. This semantics assumes that every program has a two-valued well-founded model [24].

In giving a semantics to First-Order knowledge bases, Halpern [13] distinguishes statistical statements from statements about degrees of belief, and presents two examples: "the probability that a randomly chosen bird flies is 0.9" and "the probability that Tweety (a particular bird) flies is 0.9". The first statement captures statistical information about the world while the second captures a degree of belief. The first type of statement is called "Type 1" while the latter "Type 2". The first statement can be read as "90% of the population of birds flies".

The original version of this chapter was revised: this chapter was previously published non-open access. The correction to this chapter is available at
https://doi.org/10.1007/978-3-031-15707-3_40

G. Gottlob et al. (Eds.): LPNMR 2022, LNAI 13416, pp. 43–55, 2022.
https://doi.org/10.1007/978-3-031-15707-3_4

The distribution semantics allows statements stating that, if a specific x is a bird, then x flies with probability 0.9 (or it does not with probability 0.1). In fact, the semantics of general rules of the form `0.9::flies(X) :- bird(X).` is given by the set of its ground instantiations of the form `0.9::flies(x) :- bird(x).`, which has the just described meaning. In this paper, we aim at adding to PLPDS the possibility of expressing "Type 1" statements, exploiting for this purpose Probabilistic Answer Set Programming.

Answer Set Programming (ASP) [5] is a powerful rule-based language for knowledge representation and reasoning. An extension to ASP that manages uncertain data is Probabilistic Answer Set Programming (PASP). The credal semantics [6] assigns a probability range to every query to probabilistic answer set programs - instead of a sharp value as in PLPDS - where lower and upper probability bounds are computed by analyzing the stable models of every world.

"Type 1" statements are called "probabilistic conditionals" in [15], where they are given a semantics in terms of the principle of maximum entropy: the unique model with maximum entropy is chosen. Instead of selecting only one model, we keep all models at the cost of inferring a probability interval instead of a sharp probability. We think this is of interest because it avoids making the rather strong maximum entropy assumption.

We propose a new language, called PASTA for "Probabilistic Answer set programming for STAtistical probabilities", where we exploit the credal semantics to take into account "Type 1" statements in PLPDS. In particular, probabilistic conditionals are converted into an ASP rule plus two constraints: the rule characterizes the elements of the domain while the constraints inject the statistical information on the possible stable models of every world. To perform exact inference under this semantics we developed an algorithm, taking the same name of the language, which returns lower and upper bounds for the probability of queries, and compared it with PASOCS [23]. The results show that, if we preprocess the input program into a form that allows reasoning about its structure, it is possible to obtain better performance on every program we tested.

The paper is structured as follows: in Sect. 2 we review the basic knowledge relative to ASP, PLPDS, the credal semantics, and probabilistic conditionals. In Sect. 3 we describe the PASTA language. In Sect. 4 we introduce an algorithm to perform exact inference on PASTA programs, that is experimentally tested in Sect. 5. Section 6 surveys related work and Sect. 7 concludes the paper.

2   Background

2.1   Answer Set Programming

We expect the reader to be familiar with the basic concepts of Logic Programming and First-Order Logic. We consider here also *aggregate atoms* [1] of the form $g_0 \diamond_0 \# f\{e_1; \ldots; e_n\} \diamond_1 g_1$, where f is an aggregate function symbol, $\diamond_0$ and $\diamond_1$ are arithmetic comparison operators, and g_0 and g_1 are constants or variables called *guards*; each e_i is an expression of the form $t_1, \ldots, t_l : F$, where F is a conjunction of literals and $t_1, \ldots, t_l$, with $l > 0$, are terms whose variables appear in F. $g_0 \diamond_0$ or $g_1 \diamond_1$ or even both can be omitted. Moreover, $\diamond_0$ and $\diamond_1$ can be omitted as well and, if omitted, are considered equivalent to $\leq$. A *disjunctive rule* (or simply *rule*) is an expression of the form

$$H_1 \vee \cdots \vee H_m \leftarrow B_1, \ldots, B_n$$

where each H_i is an atom and each B_i is a literal. $H_1 \vee \cdots \vee H_m$ is the *head* of the rule and $B_1, \ldots, B_n$ is the body. We will usually replace $\vee$ with ; and $\leftarrow$ with :- when describing actual code. We consider only *safe* rules, where all variables occur in a positive literal in the body. If $m = 0$ and $n > 0$, the rule is an *integrity constraint*. Facts can also be defined through a range with the notation f(a..b), where both a and b are integers. A rule is *ground* when it does not contain variables. A *program*, also called *knowledge base*, is a finite set of rules. Given an answer set program $\mathcal{P}$, we define its *Herbrand base* (denoted with $B_\mathcal{P}$) as the set of all ground atoms that can be constructed using the symbols in the program. An *interpretation* I for $\mathcal{P}$ is a set such that $I \subset B_\mathcal{P}$. An interpretation I *satisfies* a ground rule if at least one head atom is true in I when the body is true in I. If an interpretation satisfies all the groundings of all the rules of a program it is called a *model*. Given a ground program $\mathcal{P}_g$ and an interpretation I we call *reduct* [10] of $\mathcal{P}_g$ with respect to I the program obtained by removing from $\mathcal{P}_g$ the rules in which a literal in the body is false in I. An interpretation I is an *answer set* (also called *stable model*) for $\mathcal{P}$ if I is a minimal model (under set inclusion) of the reduct of $\mathcal{P}_g$. We denote with $AS(\mathcal{P})$ the set of all the answer sets of a program $\mathcal{P}$. Sometimes, not all the elements of an answer set are needed, so we can project the computed solution into a set of atoms. That is, we would like to compute the *projective solutions* [12] given a set of ground atoms V, represented by the set $AS_V(\mathcal{P}) = \{A \cap V \mid A \in AS(\mathcal{P})\}$. An atom a is a *brave consequence* of a program $\mathcal{P}$ if $\exists A \in AS(\mathcal{P})$ such that $a \in A$. We denote the set containing all the brave consequences with $BC(\mathcal{P})$. Similarly, a is a *cautious consequence* if $\forall A \in AS(\mathcal{P})$, $a \in A$, and we denote the set containing all the cautious consequences with $CC(\mathcal{P})$.

Example 1 (Bird). Consider the following answer set program $\mathcal{P}$:

```
bird(1..4).
fly(X) ; not_fly(X):- bird(X).
:- #count{X:fly(X),bird(X)} = FB,
   #count{X:bird(X)} = B, 10*FB < 6*B.
```

The first line states that there are 4 birds, indexed with 1, 2, 3, and 4. The disjunctive rule states that a bird X can fly or not fly. In the constraint, the first aggregate counts the flying birds and assigns this value to FB, while the second aggregate counts the birds and assigns the result to B. Overall, the constraint imposes that at least 60% of the birds fly (we converted the values into integers since ASP cannot easily manage floating point numbers). This program has 5 answer sets, $BC(\mathcal{P}) = $ {b(1) b(2) b(3) b(4) f(1) nf(1) f(2) nf(2) f(3) nf(3) f(4) nf(4)}, $CC(\mathcal{P}) = $ {b(1) b(2) b(3) b(4)}, and $AS_V(\mathcal{P}) = $ {{b(1) b(2) b(3) b(4)}} where b/1 stands for bird/1, f/1 for fly/1, nf/1 for not_fly/1 and $V = $ {b(1), b(2), b(3), b(4)}.

2.2 Probabilistic Logic Programming

In LP, a large body of work has appeared for allowing probabilistic reasoning. One of the most widespread approaches is the distribution semantics (DS) [20] according to which a probabilistic logic program defines a probability distribution over normal logic programs called *worlds*. The DS underlies many languages such as ProbLog [8]. Following the ProbLog syntax, probabilistic facts take the form $\Pi :: f.$ where f is a fact and $\Pi \in]0, 1]$. For example, with 0.9::fly(tweety). we are stating that the probability that tweety flies is 0.9, i.e., we believe in the truth of fly(tweety) with probability 0.9. This is a "Type 2" statement.

An *atomic choice* indicates whether a grounding $f\theta$, where θ is a substitution, for a probabilistic fact $\Pi :: f$ is selected for a world or not, and it is represented with the triple (f, θ, k) where k can be 1 (fact selected) or 0 (fact not selected). A *composite choice* is a consistent set of atomic choices, i.e., only one choice can be made for a single ground probabilistic fact. The probability of a composite choice κ can be computed with the formula:

$$P(\kappa) = \prod_{(f_i,\theta,1)\in\kappa} \Pi_i \cdot \prod_{(f_i,\theta,0)\in\kappa} (1 - \Pi_i) \tag{1}$$

If a composite choice contains one atomic choice for every grounding of each probabilistic fact, it is called a *total* composite choice or *selection*, and it is usually indicated with σ. Every selection identifies a normal logic program w called *world* composed of the rules of the program and the probabilistic facts that correspond to atomic choices with $k = 1$. Finally, the probability of a *query* q (a ground literal or a conjunction of ground literals) is computed as the sum of the probabilities of the worlds where the query is true:

$$P(q) = \sum_{w\models q} P(w) \tag{2}$$

where $P(w)$ is given by the probability of the corresponding selection (computed with Eq. 1).

2.3 Credal Semantics

The DS considers only programs where each world has a two-valued well-founded model [24]. However, in the case of answer set programs, this often does not hold. When logic programs are not stratified, they may have none or several stable models, in which case the well-founded model is not two-valued. If the program has multiple stable models, there are various available semantics: here we focus on the *credal* semantics [6,7]. Under this semantics, every query q is described by a lower and an upper probability, denoted respectively with $\underline{P}(q)$ and $\overline{P}(q)$, with the intuitive meaning that $P(q)$ lies in the range $[\underline{P}(q), \overline{P}(q)]$. If every world has exactly one stable model, $\overline{P}(q) = \underline{P}(q)$ and the credal semantics coincides with the DS. A world w contributes to the upper probability if the query is true in at least one of its stable models and to the lower probability if the query is true in all its stable models. In formulas,

$$\overline{P}(q) = \sum_{w_i | \exists m \in AS(w_i),\ m \models q} P(w_i), \quad \underline{P}(q) = \sum_{w_i | \forall m \in AS(w_i),\ m \models q} P(w_i) \tag{3}$$

[6] also suggested an algorithm to compute the probability of q given evidence e (conditional probability). In this case, the upper conditional probability is given by

$$\overline{P}(q \mid e) = \frac{\overline{P}(q, e)}{\overline{P}(q, e) + \underline{P}(\neg q, e)} \tag{4}$$

If $\overline{P}(q, e) + \underline{P}(\neg q, e) = 0$ and $\overline{P}(\neg q, e) > 0$, $\overline{P}(q \mid e) = 0$. If both $\overline{P}(q, e)$ and $\overline{P}(\neg q, e)$ are 0, this value is undefined. The formula for the lower conditional probability is

$$\underline{P}(q \mid e) = \frac{\underline{P}(q, e)}{\underline{P}(q, e) + \overline{P}(\neg q, e)} \tag{5}$$

If $\underline{P}(q, e) + \overline{P}(\neg q, e) = 0$ and $\overline{P}(q, e) > 0$, $\underline{P}(q \mid e) = 1$. As before, if both $\overline{P}(q, e)$ and $\overline{P}(\neg q, e)$ are 0, this value is undefined.

2.4 Probabilistic Conditionals

Following [15], a probabilistic conditional is a formula of the form $K = (C \mid A)[\Pi]$ where C and A are First-Order formulas and $\Pi \in [0, 1]$. The intuitive meaning is: the number of individuals that satisfy C is $100 \cdot \Pi$ percent of the individuals that satisfy A.

Example 2 (Bird conditional). Consider the following example, inspired by [25]:

```
bird(1)
(fly(X) | bird(X))[0.6]
```

The second statement says that, out of all the birds, 60% fly.

In this setting, [21] define a possible world w as an interpretation. Let Ω be the set of all possible worlds. A *probabilistic interpretation* P is a probability distribution over Ω, i.e., a function $P : \Omega \to [0, 1]$. Given a conjunction of ground literals q, $P(q) = \sum_{w \models q} P(w)$. The aggregating semantics states that a probability distribution P over interpretations is a *model of a First-Order formula* if and only if $w \not\models F \implies P(w) = 0\ \forall w$, and is a *model of a conditional* $K = (C \mid A)[\Pi]$ if and only if

$$\frac{\sum_{(C_i | A_i) \in G(K)} P(A_i, C_i)}{\sum_{(C_i | A_i) \in G(K)} P(A_i)} = \Pi \tag{6}$$

where $G(K)$ is the set containing all the ground instances of a conditional K. A probabilistic interpretation is a model for a knowledge base if it models all the formulas and all the conditionals. According to [18, 25], the semantics of a knowledge base composed of probabilistic conditionals is given by the model with the highest entropy. The maximum entropy (MaxEnt) distribution for a knowledge base $\mathcal{K}$ is defined as:

$$P^{MaxEnt} = \arg\max_{P \models \mathcal{K}} - \sum_{w_i} P(w_i) \cdot log(P(w_i))$$

With this formulation, it is possible to assign a sharp probability value to every query. In this paper, we follow a different approach and we consider probabilistic conditionals as statistical "Type 1" statements [13], interpreting them under the credal semantics.

3   Probabilistic Answer Set Programming for Statistical Probabilities (PASTA)

A probabilistic conditional expresses statistical information about the world of interest, but we would like to avoid selecting a model making the maximum entropy assumption. We would rather consider all possible models and derive lower and upper bounds on the probability of queries using the credal semantics. Here, we consider "Type 1"/probabilistic conditionals of the form

$$(C \mid A)[\Pi_l, \Pi_u].$$

with a lower (Π_l) and an upper (Π_u) bound, with the intuitive meaning that the fraction of As that are also Cs is between Π_l and Π_u. Note that Π_l and Π_u can be vacuous, i.e., they can be respectively 0 and 1. We follow an approach based on the DS, so here worlds are ground programs. The meaning of the statement above is that the models of a world where the constraint

$$\Pi_l \leq \frac{\#count\{\mathbf{X} : C(\mathbf{X}), A(\mathbf{X})\}}{\#count\{\mathbf{X} : A(\mathbf{X})\}} \leq \Pi_u \tag{7}$$

does not hold should be excluded, where $\mathbf{X}$ is the vector of variables appearing in C and A.

We consider a program as being composed of regular rules, probabilistic facts, and conditionals of the previously described form, and we assign a semantics to it by translating it into a probabilistic answer set program. We call this language PASTA (Probabilistic Answer set programming for STAtistical probabilities). Probabilistic facts and rules appear unmodified in the probabilistic answer set program. The conditional $(C \mid A)[\Pi_l, \Pi_u]$ is transformed into three answer set rules. The first is a disjunctive rule of the form `C;not_C:-A`. We require this rule to be safe. Then, we introduce two integrity constraints that mimic Eq. 7 through aggregates: we count all the ground atoms that satisfy A (call this value ND) and A and C (call this value NN) and we impose that NN must be greater than or equal to $100 \cdot \Pi_l$ percent of ND and smaller than or equal to $100 \cdot \Pi_u$ percent of ND. The constraints are not generated if the bounds are vacuous. The conditional `(fly(X) | bird(X))[0.6]` of Example 2 is transformed into the rule and the constraint shown in Example 1. Finally, the probability interval of a query from a PASTA program is the probability interval of the query computed from the transformed probabilistic answer set program.

Example 3 (Bird probabilistic). Consider the program

```
0.4::bird(1..4).
(fly(X)|bird(X))[0.6].
```

This program is transformed into a probabilistic answer set program including four probabilistic facts, the rule, and the constraint from Example 1. There is only one constraint since the upper bound is vacuous. Consider the query $q =$ fly(1). There are $2^4 = 16$ possible worlds. The query is false if bird(1) is false, so we can consider only $2^3 = 8$ worlds. There is 1 world with 4 birds, and it has 5 models. The query is true only in 4 of them, so we have a contribution of 0.4^4 to the upper probability. There are 3 worlds with 3 birds: these have 4 models each and the query is true in only three of them, so we have a contribution of $3 \cdot (0.4^3 \cdot (1 - 0.4))$ to the upper probability. There are 3 worlds with 2 birds: these have only one model and the query is true in it, so we have a contribution to both lower and upper probabilities of $3 \cdot (0.4^2 \cdot (1-0.4)^2)$. Finally, there is only 1 world with 1 bird, it has only 1 model and the query is true in it, so we have a contribution to both lower and upper probabilities of $0.4 \cdot (1 - 0.4)^3$. Overall, for the query fly(1) we get 0.2592 for the lower and 0.4 for the upper probability, so the probability lies in the range $[0.2592, 0.4]$. Similarly, by applying Formulas 4 and 5, the probability of the same query given evidence $e =$ fly(2) is in the range $[0.144, 0.44247]$ since $\underline{P}(q, e) = 0.0576$, $\overline{P}(q, e) = 0.16$, $\underline{P}(\neg q, e) = 0.2016$, and $\overline{P}(\neg q, e) = 0.3424$.

4   Inference in PASTA

By rewriting probabilistic conditionals as ASP rules, computing the probability of a query requires performing inference in PASP. To the best of our knowledge, the only system that allows (exact) inference in probabilistic answer set programs with aggregates is PASOCS [23], an implementation of the algorithm presented in [6]. The algorithm computes the probability of a query by generating all possible worlds (2^n, where n is the number of ground probabilistic facts in the program). For each world, it computes the brave and cautious consequences (there is no need to compute all the answer sets). If the query is present in the brave consequences of a world, that world contributes to the upper probability. If the query is also present in the cautious consequences, that world also contributes to the lower probability. Despite its simplicity, this algorithm relies on the generation of all the possible worlds and does not take advantage of the structure of a program. For example, in Example 3, with query fly(1), the probabilistic fact bird(1) must be true to get a contribution to the lower or upper probability, and so we can avoid generating the worlds where this fact is not present. Moreover, for both conditional and unconditional queries, we do not need to generate all the possible models for every world, we just need to check whether there is at least one model that satisfies the required constraints. To accommodate these ideas, we propose Algorithm 1, that we call PASTA like the language.

Consider first the problem of computing the probability of a query q (without evidence). We generate a non-probabilistic answer set program as follows. Every certain rule is kept unchanged. Every conditional is converted into three ASP rules as described in Sect. 3. Every ground probabilistic fact of the form P::f is converted into two rules of the form f(P1):- f. not_f(1-P1):- not f. where P1 is P $\cdot 10^n$ (since ASP cannot manage floating point numbers). The atom f is then defined by a rule of the form 0{f}1. Function CONVERTPROBFACTSAND-CONDITIONALS performs these conversions. Let us call the resulting program $PASP_p$. We then add to $PASP_p$ a constraint (line 4) imposing that the query must be true, represented with :- not query. (for Example 3 it becomes :- not fly(1).). We are not interested in all possible solutions, but only in the cautious consequences projected over the ground probabilistic facts, since we want to extract the probabilistic facts that are true in every answer set. These will constitute the *minimal* set of probabilistic facts. Function COMPUTEMINI-MALSET computes this set. These facts can be set to true since they are always present in the answer sets when the query is true, and so when there is a contribution to the probabilities. In the worst case, the resulting set will be empty. If we consider Example 3 and query fly(1), the only atom (already converted as described before with $n = 3$) in this set will be bird(1,400), so the corresponding probabilistic fact must be always true. After this step, we add to $PASP_p$ one integrity constraint for every element in the minimal set of probabilistic facts, to set them to true. Note that now $PASP_p$ does not contain the constraint imposed on the query in the previous step. For Example 3 and query fly(1), we add :- not bird(1,400). to the program (line 9). Moreover, we add two more rules that indicate whether a model contains or not the query (line 11). For Example 3 and query fly(1) these are: q:- fly(1). nq:- not fly(1). Finally, we project the answer sets [12] to the probabilistic facts and atoms q and nq, since we need to consider only the truth values of the probabilistic facts to compute the probability of a world (line 13). The probabilistic facts present in the projected answer sets identify a world. Given an answer set, its probability (the probability of the world it represents) is given by the product of the probabilities of the probabilistic facts in it. Function COMPUTECONTRIBUTION (line 18) computes the probability of every world and counts the models, the models where the query is true, the models where the query is false, the models where the query and evidence are true, and the models where the query is false and the evidence is true. For a query without evidence, the number of models where the query is true and the number of models where the query is false will only be either 0 or 1. To get the lower and upper probabilities, we apply Formulas 3. If we consider again Example 3 with query fly(1), two of the possible projective solutions are:

```
b(1,400) b(2,400) b(3,400) b(4,400) nq
b(1,400) b(2,400) b(3,400) b(4,400) q
```

where, for the sake of brevity, b/2 stands for bird/2. These two solutions show that the world with 4 birds has at least one model where the query is true and at least one model where the query is false, so it only contributes to the upper probability with $0.4 \cdot 0.4 \cdot 0.4 \cdot 0.4 = 0.0256$. Here, we also see the improvement given by computing the projective solutions: we only need to know whether the query is true or false in some models of a world, and not the exact number of models in which the query is true. For example, as shown in Example 1, the world with 4 birds has 5 models: 4 where the query is true and 1 where the query is false. However, to compute the probability bounds, it is not necessary to know the exact number: at most two stable models (one with the query true and one with the query false) for each world are needed instead of five. A difference with [23] is that PASOCS computes both brave and cautious consequences for every world, while PASTA computes projective solutions only once.

Consider now a conditional query. As before, we need to identify the minimal subset of probabilistic facts. However, we now add a constraint forcing the evidence (ev) to true instead of the query (line 6). We then add two more rules of the form e:- ev. and ne:- not ev. (line 15) and project the solutions also on the e and ne atoms (line 16). Finally, we analyse the resulting answer sets to compute the values that contribute to the lower (lp) and upper (up) probability, as described in Formulas 4 and 5.

5   Experiments

We implemented Algorithm 1 with Python3 using clingo [11] to compute answer sets.[1] We performed a series of experiments to compare PASTA with PASOCS [23]. For PASOCS, we use the single threaded mode and select exact inference. For PASTA, the execution time includes both the computation of the minimal set of probabilistic facts and the computation of the projective solutions. Usually, the time required for the first operation is negligible with respect to the computation of the probability. We selected three different programs described in [25]. The first program, brd, is {(fly(X) | bird(X))[0.8,1],0.1::fly(1)} with an increasing number of probabilistic facts bird/1 with an associated probability of 0.5. The goal is to compute the probability of the query fly(1). The second program, mky, represents the pair of conditionals {(f(X) | h(X)) [0.2,1],(f(X,Y) | h(Y),r(X,Y))[0.9,1]}, with an increasing number of probabilistic facts h/1 and r/2, both with an associated probability of 0.5. The distribution of the facts r/2 follows a Barabási-Albert model, i.e., a graph, generated with the Python networkx package with parameter m_0 (representing the number of edges to attach from a new node to existing nodes) set to 3 and an increasing number of nodes. We randomly selected half of the total number of nodes to generate the h/1 facts. The query is f(0),f(0,1). The third program, smk, represents the conditional {(smokes(Y) | smokes(X),friend(X,Y))[0.4,1]} with an increasing number of probabilistic facts friend/2 with an associated probability of 0.5, following the Barabási-Albert model. The query is smokes(I), where I is a random node. For both mky and smk, the results are averaged over 10 different programs, to make

---

[1] Source code and programs available at: https://github.com/damianoazzolini/pasta.

Algorithm 1. Function COMPUTEPROBABILITYBOUNDS: computation of the probability bounds of a query *query* given evidence *ev* in a PASTA program $\mathcal{P}$.

```
1: function COMPUTEPROBABILITYBOUNDS(query, ev, P)
2:     probFacts, PASP_p ← CONVERTPROBFACTSANDCONDITIONALS(P)
3:     if ev is undefined then
4:         minSet ← COMPUTEMINIMALSET(PASP_p ∪ {:- not query.})
5:     else
6:         minSet ← COMPUTEMINIMALSET(PASP_p ∪ {:- not ev.})
7:     end if
8:     for all a ∈ minSet do                                    ▷ a represents a probabilistic fact
9:         PASP_p ← PASP_p ∪ {:- not a.}
10:    end for
11:    PASP_p^q ← PASP_p ∪ {q:- query., nq:- not query.}
12:    if ev is undefined then
13:        AS ← PROJECTSOLUTIONS(PASP_p^q, probFacts, q ∪ nq)
14:    else
15:        PASP_p^{qe} ← PASP_p^q ∪ {e:- ev., ne:- not ev.}
16:        AS ← PROJECTSOLUTIONS(PASP_p^{qe}, probFacts, q ∪ nq ∪ e ∪ ne)
17:    end if
18:    worldsList ← COMPUTECONTRIBUTION(AS)
19:    lp ← 0, up ← 0
20:    for all w ∈ worldsList do                                ▷ Loop through answer sets
21:        if ev is undefined then
22:            if w.modelQueryCounter > 0 then
23:                up ← up + P(w)
24:                if w.modelNotQueryCounter == 0 then
25:                    lp ← lp + P(w)
26:                end if
27:            end if
28:        else
29:            up_{qe} ← 0, lp_{qe} ← 0, up_{nqe} ← 0, lp_{nqe} ← 0
30:            if w.modelQueryEvCounter > 0 then
31:                up_{qe} ← up_{qe} + P(w)
32:                if w.modelQueryEvCounter = w.models then
33:                    lp_{qe} ← lp_{qe} + P(w)
34:                end if
35:            end if
36:            if w.modelNotQueryEvCounter > 0 then
37:                up_{nqe} ← up_{nqe} + P(w)
38:                if w.modelNotQueryEvCounter = w.models then
39:                    lp_{nqe} ← lp_{nqe} + P(w)
40:                end if
41:            end if
42:        end if
43:    end for
44:    if ev is not undefined then
45:        if up_{qe} + lp_{nqe} == 0 and up_{nqe} > 0 then
46:            lp ← 0, up ← 0
47:        else if lp_{qe} + up_{nqe} == 0 and up_{qe} > 0 then
48:            lp ← 1, up ← 1
49:        else
50:            lp ← \frac{lp_{qe}}{lp_{qe}+up_{nqe}}, up ← \frac{up_{qe}}{up_{qe}+lp_{nqe}}
51:        end if
52:    end if
53:    return lp, up
54: end function
```

them more representative since the graph generation is not deterministic, and thus some instances can be easier to query. For all the three programs, the minimal set of probabilistic facts is empty, so the PASOCS and PASTA work on the same set of worlds. Inference times are shown in Fig. 1a. PASOCS on mky returned an inter-

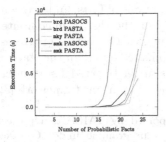

(a) Inference times for the brd, mky, and smk experiments.

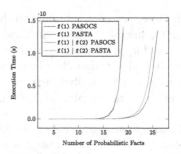

(b) Inference times for the bird experiments.

Fig. 1. Results for the experiments.

nal error of the solver while parsing the program. In a second experiment, bird, we modify the brd program by removing 0.1::fly(1), and we ask two queries: fly(1), and fly(1) given that fly(2) has been observed. For these two experiments, the minimal set of probabilistic facts contains bird(1). Results are shown in Fig. 1b. Overall, with our solution we can manage a larger number of probabilistic facts. Moreover, the introduction of the minimal set of probabilistic facts gives a substantial improvement, as shown in Fig. 1b. However, both PASOCS and PASTA rely on the generation of all the worlds, which increase in an exponential way.

6   Related Work

There are several PASP systems such as P-log [4], LPMLN [16], PrASP [17], and SMProbLog [22]: these aim at finding sharp probability values. We compare PASTA only with PASOCS [23] since, to the best of our knowledge, it is the only system that performs inference on probabilistic answer set programs with aggregates under the credal semantics. The solver proposed in [9] allows counting the answer sets of a given program, so, in principle, may be applied to perform inference in PASTA programs, however, aggregates are not allowed. The solution proposed in [2] adopts ASP techniques to perform inference in probabilistic logic programs but it is still focused on the computation of a sharp probability value. Statistical statements are considered also by [14] where a semantics is given by resorting to cross entropy minimization. Similarly to the case of [25], we differ because we do not select a specific model but we consider all the models consistent with the statements and we compare lower and upper bounds.

7   Conclusions

In this paper, we considered probabilistic conditionals as statistical statements - "Type 1" statements according to Halpern's definition - and interpreted them under the credal semantics of probabilistic answer set programs. Our approach, called PASTA, includes both a language and an inference algorithm: the language is given a semantics by converting a probabilistic conditional into three

ASP rules, one corresponding to the possible combinations of facts, and two con-straints, one for the lower and one for the upper bound; the algorithm computes lower and upper probability values for conditional queries. On various programs, PASTA is able to handle a larger number of probabilistic facts than the state of the art solver for probabilistic answer set programs under the credal semantics. As future work, we plan to introduce abductive reasoning in this framework [3].

Acknowledgements. This research was partly supported by TAILOR, a project funded by EU Horizon 2020 research and innovation programme under GA No. 952215. Damiano Azzolini was supported by IndAM - GNCS Project with code CUP_E55F22000270001.

References

1. Alviano, M., Faber, W.: Aggregates in answer set programming. KI-Künstliche Intelligenz **32**(2), 119–124 (2018)
2. Aziz, R.A., Chu, G., Muise, C.J., Stuckey, P.J.: Stable model counting and its application in probabilistic logic programming. In: Bonet, B., Koenig, S. (eds.) Proceedings of the Twenty-Ninth AAAI Conference on Artificial Intelligence, pp. 3468–3474. AAAI Press (2015)
3. Azzolini, D., Bellodi, E., Ferilli, S., Riguzzi, F., Zese, R.: Abduction with probabilis-tic logic programming under the distribution semantics. Int. J. Approx. Reason. **142**, 41–63 (2022)
4. Baral, C., Gelfond, M., Rushton, N.: Probabilistic reasoning with answer sets. Theor. Pract. Log. Prog. **9**(1), 57–144 (2009)
5. Brewka, G., Eiter, T., Truszczyński, M.: Answer set programming at a glance. Commun. ACM **54**(12), 92–103 (2011)
6. Cozman, F.G., Mauá, D.D.: On the semantics and complexity of probabilistic logic programs. J. Artif. Intell. Res. **60**, 221–262 (2017)
7. Cozman, F.G., Mauá, D.D.: The joy of probabilistic answer set programming: semantics, complexity, expressivity, inference. Int. J. Approx. Reason. **125**, 218–239 (2020)
8. De Raedt, L., Kimmig, A., Toivonen, H.: ProbLog: a probabilistic Prolog and its application in link discovery. In: Veloso, M.M. (ed.) IJCAI 2007, vol. 7, pp. 2462–2467. AAAI Press/IJCAI (2007)
9. Eiter, T., Hecher, M., Kiesel, R.: Treewidth-aware cycle breaking for algebraic answer set counting. In: Bienvenu, M., Lakemeyer, G., Erdem, E. (eds.) Proceed-ings of the 18th International Conference on Principles of Knowledge Representa-tion and Reasoning, KR 2021, pp. 269–279 (2021)
10. Faber, W., Leone, N., Pfeifer, G.: Recursive aggregates in disjunctive logic pro-grams: semantics and complexity. In: Alferes, J.J., Leite, J. (eds.) JELIA 2004. LNCS (LNAI), vol. 3229, pp. 200–212. Springer, Heidelberg (2004). https://doi.org/10.1007/978-3-540-30227-8_19
11. Gebser, M., Kaminski, R., Kaufmann, B., Schaub, T.: Multi-shot asp solving with clingo. Theory Pract. Logic Program. **19**(1), 27–82 (2019)
12. Gebser, M., Kaufmann, B., Schaub, T.: Solution enumeration for projected Boolean search problems. In: van Hoeve, W.-J., Hooker, J.N. (eds.) CPAIOR 2009. LNCS, vol. 5547, pp. 71–86. Springer, Heidelberg (2009). https://doi.org/10.1007/978-3-642-01929-6_7

13. Halpern, J.Y.: An analysis of first-order logics of probability. Artif. Intell. **46**(3), 311–350 (1990)
14. Jaeger, M.: Probabilistic reasoning in terminological logics. In: Doyle, J., Sandewall, E., Torasso, P. (eds.) 4th International Conference on Principles of Knowledge Representation and Reasoning, pp. 305–316. Morgan Kaufmann (1994)
15. Kern-Isberner, G., Thimm, M.: Novel semantical approaches to relational probabilistic conditionals. In: Proceedings of the Twelfth International Conference on Principles of Knowledge Representation and Reasoning, pp. 382–392. AAAI Press (2010)
16. Lee, J., Wang, Y.: A probabilistic extension of the stable model semantics. In: AAAI Spring Symposia (2015)
17. Nickles, M.: A tool for probabilistic reasoning based on logic programming and first-order theories under stable model semantics. In: Michael, L., Kakas, A. (eds.) JELIA 2016. LNCS (LNAI), vol. 10021, pp. 369–384. Springer, Cham (2016). https://doi.org/10.1007/978-3-319-48758-8_24
18. Paris, J.B.: The Uncertain Reasoner's Companion: A Mathematical Perspective. Cambridge Tracts in Theoretical Computer Science. Cambridge University Press (1995)
19. Riguzzi, F.: Foundations of Probabilistic Logic Programming: Languages, Semantics, Inference and Learning. River Publishers, Gistrup (2018)
20. Sato, T.: A statistical learning method for logic programs with distribution semantics. In: Sterling, L. (ed.) ICLP 1995, pp. 715–729. MIT Press (1995)
21. Thimm, M., Kern-Isberner, G.: On probabilistic inference in relational conditional logics. Logic J. IGPL **20**(5), 872–908 (2012)
22. Totis, P., Kimmig, A., Raedt, L.D.: SMProbLog: stable model semantics in ProbLog and its applications in argumentation. ArXiv arXiv:2110.01990 (2021)
23. Tuckey, D., Russo, A., Broda, K.: PASOCS: a parallel approximate solver for probabilistic logic programs under the credal semantics. ArXiv arXiv:2105.10908 (2021)
24. Van Gelder, A., Ross, K.A., Schlipf, J.S.: The well-founded semantics for general logic programs. J. ACM **38**(3), 620–650 (1991)
25. Wilhelm, M., Kern-Isberner, G., Finthammer, M., Beierle, C.: Integrating typed model counting into first-order maximum entropy computations and the connection to Markov logic networks. In: Barták, R., Brawner, K.W. (eds.) Proceedings of the Thirty-Second International Florida Artificial Intelligence Research Society Conference, pp. 494–499. AAAI Press (2019)

A Comparative Study of Three Neural-Symbolic Approaches to Inductive Logic Programming

Davide Beretta[1], Stefania Monica[2], and Federico Bergenti[1(✉)]

[1] Dipartimento di Scienze Matematiche, Fisiche e Informatiche,
Università degli Studi di Parma, 43124 Parma, Italy
{davide.beretta,federico.bergenti}@unipr.it
[2] Dipartimento di Scienze e Metodi dell'Ingegneria,
Università degli Studi di Modena e Reggio Emilia, 42122 Reggio Emilia, Italy
stefania.monica@unimore.it

Abstract. An interesting feature that traditional approaches to inductive logic programming are missing is the ability to treat noisy and non-logical data. Neural-symbolic approaches to inductive logic programming have been recently proposed to combine the advantages of inductive logic programming, in terms of interpretability and generalization capability, with the characteristic capacity of deep learning to treat noisy and non-logical data. This paper concisely surveys and briefly compares three promising neural-symbolic approaches to inductive logic programming that have been proposed in the last five years. The considered approaches use Datalog dialects to represent background knowledge, and they are capable of producing reusable logical rules from noisy and non-logical data. Therefore, they provide an effective means to combine logical reasoning with state-of-the-art machine learning.

Keywords: Neural-symbolic learning · Inductive logic programming · Machine learning · Artificial intelligence

1 Introduction

Inductive logic programming (*ILP*) (e.g., [6]) has been studied for more than thirty years with the major goal of delivering effective algorithms to induce logical rules from data. State-of-the-art ILP algorithms now provide advanced features, like recursive rules, that were considered as huge obstacles a few years ago. Despite these progresses, ILP algorithms are typically not able to cope with noisy and non-logical data like sounds, images, and videos. Moreover, the background knowledge that ILP algorithms process is normally expressed as facts and rules that do not contempt uncertainty. On the other hand, deep learning is very good at treating noisy and erroneous data, but its limitations with respect to explainability and interpretability are evident. Therefore, ILP and deep learning can be considered as complementary, and the literature is

G. Gottlob et al. (Eds.): LPNMR 2022, LNAI 13416, pp. 56–61, 2022.
https://doi.org/10.1007/978-3-031-15707-3_5

witnessing several attempts at combining them in the so-called *neural-symbolic approaches to ILP* (e.g., [11]).

The major contribution of this paper is to briefly survey three promising neural-symbolic approaches to ILP that have been proposed in the last five years, paying particular attention to the reusability of the learned rules. Actually, the discussed approaches generate logical rules written in Datalog dialects, so that generated rules are immediately reusable.

Note that this paper is not a comprehensive survey of the literature on neural-symbolic ILP, rather it is intended to briefly compare the features of the three discussed algorithms in terms of reusability, interpretability, and related characteristics. Interested readers are invited to consult recent surveys on neural-symbolic approaches (e.g., [1,4,10,11]) for a wider overview of the subject.

2   Studied Neural-Symbolic Algorithms for ILP

This section briefly discusses three of the most relevant neural-symbolic approaches to ILP that have been considered in the literature in the last five years. The selection of the approaches to take into consideration started from recent surveys on ILP and neural-symbolic algorithms [1,2,4,10,11], and then it was extended by considering (possibly indirect) references taken from the mentioned surveys. Only the techniques designed to learn logical rules expressed in a Datalog dialect were finally selected for inclusion in this paper.

δILP [5] is a neural-symbolic approach to ILP in which rules are generated using a program template before being tested against training data. In order to effectively treat noisy and erroneous data, δILP uses a continuous relaxation of the truth value of each rule, and it associates each pair of rules with a weight that represents the probability of the pair to be part of the induced program. In order to choose the correct value for the weights associated with the pairs of rules, δILP trains a deep neural network to predict the truth values of random atoms from the training set. The supervised training of this neural network requires the expected truth values of positive and negative examples, and these values are obtained by performing a predetermined number of forward chaining steps followed by the application of the generated rules to background facts.

dNL-ILP [8,9] associates a membership weight with each atom that can be part of the generated formulae. In addition, it defines a specific neural network, whose nodes implement fuzzy operators, to model generated formulae, which are expressed in a, conjunctive or disjunctive, normal form. For each generated formula, dNL-ILP generates a list that contains the atoms that can be part of the formula. The algorithm then performs a predetermined number of forward chaining steps to continuously update the values $X_p^t[e]$, which are computed using the expected truth value of all the substitutions that would produce the atom e. At each forward chaining step, dNL-ILP updates the membership weights, and, at the end of the training, dNL-ILP uses the obtained membership weights to extract the learned formulae from the network. Finally, note that dNL-ILP is genuinely different from δILP because dNL-ILP associates weights with atoms while δILP associates weights with rules.

Unlike δILP and dNL-ILP, Meta$_{\text{Abd}}$ [3] works only on images. Meta$_{\text{Abd}}$ tries to map non-logical data to symbolic input and, at the same time, it induces a set of rules that defines the target predicate. Meta$_{\text{Abd}}$ is composed of two modules: the perception module and the reasoning module. The perception module performs the mapping between the sub-symbolic input x and the symbolic input z. The perception module is a neural network with parameters θ that estimates the conditional probability $P(z|x,\theta)$. The reasoning module comprises the reasoner H, which is expressed as a set of rules used to infer the output symbol y, provided that z is available together with sufficient background knowledge. The goal of Meta$_{\text{Abd}}$ is to learn θ and H simultaneously from training data.

3   A Comparison Based on Four Characteristics

This section compares the discussed algorithms using four characteristics: the type of representation used for the data in the training set and in the background knowledge, the language bias that is (possibly implicitly) enforced to guide the generation of the rules, if recursion is allowed in the induced rules, and if predicates can be invented during the generation of the rules. Table 1 summarizes the proposed comparison among the three studied algorithms using these characteristics, as detailed in the remaining of this section.

3.1   Representation of Data

The representations of the background knowledge and of the training examples play important roles in the considered learning tasks. Normally, ILP algorithms assume that the background knowledge is provided in terms of a set of facts and logical rules, while the training examples are represented as a set of facts used to define the target predicate. Unfortunately, these representations cannot be used to adequately treat noisy and erroneous data, and they must be reconsidered in the scope of neural-symbolic approaches to ILP.

The training examples are provided in different forms to the three studied algorithms: both δILP and dNL-ILP define target predicates using sets of facts, while Meta$_{\text{Abd}}$ requires a training set composed of images. However, all the studied algorithms allow mislabelled examples because they all minimize an error function instead of trying to satisfy a strict constraint, which is what traditional ILP algorithms do. Finally, it is worth noting that δILP was coupled with a perception module implemented using a neural network trained to recognize handwritten numbers [5]. δILP was then tested together with this perception module, but the results were not considered satisfactory [5]. This negative result suggests that a finer integration between a perception module and a neural-symbolic algorithm, like the integration proposed by Meta$_{\text{Abd}}$, is needed to reach a satisfactory performance.

The background knowledge is provided in different forms to the three studied algorithms: both δILP and dNL-ILP define initial predicates as sets of facts, while Meta$_{\text{Abd}}$ represents the background knowledge as a set of clauses. The

Table 1. Summary of the features that characterize surveyed algorithms, where the representation of data is detailed for the background knowledge (BK column) and for the training set (Dataset column).

Algorithm	BK	Dataset	Language bias	Recursion	Predicate invention
δILP	Facts	Facts	Templates and constraints	Yes	Partially
dNL-ILP	Facts	Facts	Templates	Yes	Partially
Meta$_{Abd}$	Rules	Images	Meta-rules	Yes	Yes

representation adopted by Meta$_{Abd}$ is advantageous because it does not require to manually specify the set of ground atoms that define the initial predicates. In particular, the use of clauses allows to treat large, or even infinite, domains. Actually, the description of the background knowledge in terms of facts makes the learning process impractical when the number of domain elements is large. From the perspective of noisy background knowledge, both δILP and dNL-ILP assign a value in $[0, 1]$ to background facts, while Meta$_{Abd}$ assumes that the background knowledge is free from uncertainty. This limitation of Meta$_{Abd}$ is problematic because background knowledge is often uncertain.

3.2 Language Bias

The induction of rules requires searching in a large search space. In order to guide the search, ILP algorithms normally employ a language bias, which is typically defined as a set of restrictions that partially define accepted solutions.

δILP assumes several restrictions on the generation of rules, as follows:

1. Constants are not allowed;
2. A predicate can be defined only by two rules;
3. Predicates of arity higher than three are not allowed;
4. Each rule must contain exactly two atoms in its body;
5. Each variable that appears in the head of a rule must appear also in its body;
6. Two rules cannot differ only in the order of the atoms in their bodies; and
7. An atom cannot be used in the head and the body of the same rule.

These restrictions on the generation of rules, combined with a program template, allow δILP to effectively learn from data. However, this approach is not sufficiently scalable because the number of weights grows quickly as the difficulty of the learning task increases.

dNL-ILP is more flexible, and it only requires a few parameters to define the search space for the generation of rules. Rules are generated by specifying the target and the auxiliary predicates in terms of the name and the arity of each predicate together with the number of variables in the body of each rule. Note that dNL-ILP is more scalable than δILP because the number of required weights is smaller.

Finally, Meta$_{Abd}$ follows a different approach than δILP and dNL-ILP because it uses meta-rules to define the structure of the generated rules. The adoption of meta-rules allows domain experts to use their domain knowledge to improve the learning process. However, it is rarely possible to accurately foresee the structure of the searched rules, which makes meta-rules impractical for many real-world applications.

3.3 Recursion

The execution of an unlimited number of deductions using a finite logic program requires learning recursive rules. Recursion allows generalizing from a small number of examples because it allows defining a general rule instead of learning a separate rule for each specific situation. δILP and dNL-ILP support recursion by design because they generate all the possible rules, including recursive rules. On the contrary, Meta$_{Abd}$ follows a different approach, and it uses meta-rules to provide for recursion. Meta-rules represent predicate symbols with generic predicate names, and therefore recursion is not specified explicitly, but the algorithm tries to correctly associate the predicate names in the meta-rule with the predicate names defined as part of the learning task.

3.4 Predicate Invention

In many real-world problems, it is difficult, or even impossible, to provide an appropriate background knowledge. Therefore, predicate invention is useful to automatically generate new predicates and extend the background knowledge without the explicit intervention of domain experts. Predicate invention is a major challenge in ILP, and most of the ordinary algorithms do not support it. δILP and dNL-ILP support predicate invention only partially because they require domain experts to manually specify the name and the arity of each auxiliary predicate. However, it is often very difficult, or even impossible, to foresee the structure of a possible solution for many real-world learning tasks. This makes the use δILP and dNL-ILP impractical from the perspective of predicate invention. On the contrary, Meta$_{Abd}$ is an extension of the MIL interpreter [7], which natively supports predicate invention. Meta$_{Abd}$ uses meta-rules to prune the search space and to invent new predicates whenever necessary. Therefore, invented predicates are coherently defined using meta-rules.

4 Open Challenges and Conclusion

This paper surveys three relevant neural-symbolic approaches to ILP focusing specifically on approaches that produce rules in a Datalog dialect and that appeared in the literature in the last five years. In summary, from the perspective of the studied features, it is worth noting that the studied approaches do not satisfactory support predicate invention. Moreover, the language biases used to guide the generation of rules impose too many restrictions, or they require the domain experts to inject too much domain knowledge. In addition, it is worth recalling that Meta$_{Abd}$ represents the background knowledge as a set of rules, while the other studied algorithms require that the background knowledge is represented in terms of ground atoms only. Therefore, Meta$_{Abd}$ is capable of handling infinite domains, unlike δILP and dNL-ILP. On the other hand, Meta$_{Abd}$ does not support noisy background knowledge, which is instead supported by the two other algorithms. None of the discussed algorithms support both infinite domains and noisy background knowledge, and it would be interesting to further investigate in this direction to support both these features.

The proposed comparison suggests that several improvements to the studied algorithms are possible. Actually, many problems remain to be tackled, like, for example, well-maintained implementations, standard benchmarks, reasonable constraints and domain knowledge requirements for induction of rules, and a satisfactory support of infinite domains and noisy background knowledge. Nonetheless, the works discussed in this paper witness that neural-symbolic ILP has the potential to overcome the limitations of traditional ILP, allowing to produce reusable solutions to real-world problems.

References

1. Calegari, R., Ciatto, G., Omicini, A.: On the integration of symbolic and subsymbolic techniques for XAI: a survey. Intelligenza Artificiale **14**(1), 7–32 (2020)
2. Cropper, A., Dumančić, S., Evans, R., Muggleton, S.H.: Inductive logic programming at 30. Mach. Learn. **111**, 147–172 (2022). https://doi.org/10.1007/s10994-021-06089-1
3. Dai, W.Z., Muggleton, S.: Abductive knowledge induction from raw data. In: Proceedings of the 30th International Joint Conference on Artificial Intelligence (IJCAI 2021), pp. 1845–1851. International Joint Conferences on Artificial Intelligence Organization (2021)
4. De Raedt, L., Dumančić, S., Manhaeve, R., Marra, G.: From statistical relational to neural-symbolic artificial intelligence. In: Proceedings of the 29th International Joint Conference on Artificial Intelligence (IJCAI 2020), pp. 4943–4950. International Joint Conferences on Artificial Intelligence Organization (2021)
5. Evans, R., Grefenstette, E.: Learning explanatory rules from noisy data. J. Artif. Intell. Res. **61**, 1–64 (2018)
6. Muggleton, S.: Inductive logic programming. New Gener. Comput. **8**(4), 295–318 (1991)
7. Muggleton, S.H., Lin, D., Tamaddoni-Nezhad, A.: Meta-interpretive learning of higher-order dyadic datalog: predicate invention revisited. Mach. Learn. **100**(1), 49–73 (2015)
8. Payani, A., Fekri, F.: Inductive logic programming via differentiable deep neural logic networks. arXiv preprint arXiv:1906.03523 (2019)
9. Payani, A., Fekri, F.: Learning algorithms via neural logic networks. arXiv preprint arXiv:1904.01554 (2019)
10. Sarker, M.K., Zhou, L., Eberhart, A., Hitzler, P.: Neuro-symbolic artificial intelligence: current trends. arXiv preprint arXiv:2105.05330 (2021)
11. Yu, D., Yang, B., Liu, D., Wang, H.: A survey on neural-symbolic systems. arXiv preprint arXiv:2111.08164 (2021)

A Definition of Sceptical Semantics in the Constellations Approach

Stefano Bistarelli and Francesco Santini[(✉)]

Dipartimento di Matematica e Informatica, Università degli Studi di Perugia,
Perugia, Italy
{stefano.bistarelli,francesco.santini}@unipg.it

Abstract. We propose a different way to compute sceptical semantics
in the constellations approach: we define the grounded, ideal, and eager
extension of a *Probabilistic Argumentation Framework* by merging the
subsets with the maximal probability of complete, preferred, semi-stable
extensions respectively. Differently from the original work (i.e., [19]), the
extension we propose is unique, as the principle of scepticism usually
demands. This definition maintains some well-known properties, as set-
inclusion among the three semantics. Moreover, we advance a quantitative relaxation of these semantics with the purpose to mitigate scepticism
in case the result corresponds to empty-set, which is not very informative.

1 Introduction

Abstract Argumentation is a high-level language describing conflicting information, which can be simply represented by a set of arguments and a binary
attack-relationship. Argumentation is "abstract" because the conflict between
two arguments is not formally motivated, and the internal structure of an argument is not specified. Such an abstraction can be used to capture general properties of a debate, but it also fostered the enrichment of frameworks with additional
information (e.g., probabilities).

In *uncertain reasoning* we can distinguish *qualitative* and *quantitative*
approaches. The former ones focus on issues such as defeasibility, and default
assumptions: computational models of argumentations are an example. The latter ones focus on the problem of quantifying the acceptance status of statements:
an example is probabilistic reasoning. Probabilistic Argumentation frameworks
(*PrAFs* for short) combine them by bringing together the qualitative view of
argumentation and the probability values associated with arguments and attacks.
The two main approaches on PrAFs in the literature consist in the *constellations*
and *epistemic* approaches (see Sect. 3).

The authors are members of the INdAM Research group GNCS and of Consorzio CINI.
This work has been partially supported by: project RACRA - funded by "Ricerca
di Base 2018–2019" (Univeristy of Perugia), project DopUP - "REGIONE UMBRIA
PSR" 2014–2020.

G. Gottlob et al. (Eds.): LPNMR 2022, LNAI 13416, pp. 62–74, 2022.
https://doi.org/10.1007/978-3-031-15707-3_6

In this paper we focus on the former: values determine the likelihood of arguments and attacks to be part of a framework, thus generating different frameworks with a different existence probability.

As advanced in several works in the related literature (e.g., [2,13]), the idea behind the grounded semantics in Abstract Argumentation is to accept only the arguments that must be accepted and to reject only the arguments that one cannot avoid to reject. This leads to the definition of the most *sceptical* (or *least committed*) semantics among those based on complete extensions. The ideal [14] and eager [10] semantics have been defined as less sceptical positions, since the grounded extension is a subset of the ideal extension, which is a subset of the grounded one [10]. In case of a sceptical approach, the existence of more than one possible argumentative position is often dealt with by taking the intersection of different extensions. For instance, the ideal semantics uses the intersection of all the preferred extensions in its definition. Even the grounded extension, though originally defined as the *least fixed-point* of a framework *characteristic function* [13], also corresponds to the intersection of complete extensions.

In this paper we propose a different way to compute sceptical extensions of a PrAF in the constellations approach [17,19]: hence we focus on the grounded, ideal, and eager semantics. The main goal is to propose a single extension for the whole set of frameworks induced from a given PrAF. On the contrary, in [19] all the most frequent subsets of arguments that belong to a grounded extension in induced frameworks are equally-good candidates.

A simple example is any PrAF where both $P(a) = P(b) = 1$, and a, b are not attacked: they are present in all the induced frameworks and they always belong to the grounded extension. Hence, either $\{a\}$ or $\{b\}$ have the same (highest possible) probability 1 to satisfy the grounded semantics.

To obtain unicity, we consider the probability of the intersection of the events *i)* a set of arguments is a subset of a complete/preferred/semi-stable extension in an induced framework, and *ii)* that framework is induced by the considered PrAF. Then, sceptical semantics can be seen as the union of argument-sets maximising the probability of these two events: by taking maximum-probability positions we realise scepticism in PrAFs.

With such an approach, we show that the sceptical extensions of a PrAF correspond to the intersection of their equivalents obtained on all the induced frameworks. As introduced before, this intersection operation is also often used in non-probabilistic frameworks to define classical sceptical semantics. By having characterised the intersection of possible frameworks in a quantitative (probabilistic) way, we end up with the opportunity of relaxing scepticism by taking less-than-maximal-probability sets. Therefore, the proposed approach offers a way to quantitatively relax scepticism, as classical ideal and eager semantics do in a qualitatively way with respect to the grounded extension instead. Being the grounded extension the intersection of all the complete extensions from all the induced frameworks, a (uninformative) result of empty-set is thus very likely.

The paper is organised as follows: Sect. 2 introduces the necessary background about semantics and PrAFs defined with the constellations approach.

Section 4 redefines the grounded semantics in PrAFs, with related formal results and examples, while in Sect. 5 we extend former results to the ideal and eager semantics. Section 3 summarises some of the related work about PrAFs, and finally Sect. 6 wraps up the paper with final conclusions and future work.

2 The Constellations Approach

An *Abstract Argumentation Framework* (AF, for short) [13] is a tuple $\mathcal{F} = (A, R)$ where A is a set of arguments and R is the attack relation $R \subseteq A \times A$.

A set $E \subseteq A$ is *conflict-free* (in $\mathcal{F}$) if and only if there are no $a, b \in E$ with $a \rightarrow b$ (i.e., "a attacks b"). E is *admissible* (i.e., $E \in \mathbf{ad}(\mathcal{F})$) if and only if it is conflict-free and each $a \in E$ is defended by E, i.e., E attacks any attacker of a. Finally, the *range* of E in $\mathcal{F}$, i.e., $E_{\mathcal{F}}^+$, collects the same E and the set of arguments attacked by E: $E_{\mathcal{F}}^+ = E \cup \{a \in A \mid \exists b \in E : b \rightarrow a\}$. Argumentation semantics determine sets of jointly acceptable arguments, called *extensions*, by mapping each $\mathcal{F} = (A, R)$ to a set $\sigma(\mathcal{F}) \subseteq 2^A$, where 2^A is the power-set of A, and σ parametrically stands for any of the considered semantics. The extensions under complete, preferred, semi-stable, grounded, ideal and eager semantics are respectively defined as follows. Given $\mathcal{F} = (A, R)$ and a set $E \subseteq A$,

- $E \in \mathbf{co}(\mathcal{F})$ if and only if E is admissible in $\mathcal{F}$ and if $a \in A$ is defended by E in $\mathcal{F}$ then $a \in E$,
- $E \in \mathbf{pr}(\mathcal{F})$ if and only if $E \in \mathbf{co}(\mathcal{F})$ and there is no $E' \in \mathbf{co}(\mathcal{F})$ s.t. $E' \supset E$,
- $E \in \mathbf{sst}(\mathcal{F})$ if and only if $E \in \mathbf{co}(\mathcal{F})$ and there is no $E' \in \mathbf{co}(\mathcal{F})$ s.t. $E_{\mathcal{F}}'^+ \supset E_{\mathcal{F}}^+$,
- $E \in \mathbf{gr}(\mathcal{F})$ if and only if $E \in \mathbf{co}(\mathcal{F})$ and there is no $E' \in \mathbf{co}(\mathcal{F})$ s.t. $E' \subset E$,
- $E \in \mathbf{id}(\mathcal{F})$ if and only if E is admissible, $E \subseteq \bigcap \mathbf{pr}(\mathcal{F})$ and there is no admissible $E' \subseteq \bigcap \mathbf{pr}(\mathcal{F})$ s.t. $E' \supset E$,
- $E \in \mathbf{eg}(\mathcal{F})$ if and only if E is admissible, $E \subseteq \bigcap \mathbf{sst}(\mathcal{F})$ and there is no admissible $E' \subseteq \bigcap \mathbf{sst}(\mathcal{F})$ s.t. $E' \supset E$.

A *Probabilistic Argumentation Framework* (*PrAF*) [19] represents the set of all AFs that can potentially be induced from it. A PrAF is a Dung's framework where both arguments (A_p) and attacks (R_p) are associated with their likelihood of existence: i.e., $P_{A_p} : A_p \rightarrow (0, 1]$, and $P_{R_p} : R_p \rightarrow (0, 1]$: hence, $\mathcal{F}_p = (A_p, R_p, P_{A_p}, P_{R_p})$. An induced AF includes all the arguments and attacks with a likelihood of 1, as well as further components as specified by Definition 1.

Definition 1 (Inducing an AF [19]). *A Dung abstract framework $\mathcal{F} = (A, R)$ is induced from a $\mathcal{F}_p = (A_p, R_p, P_{A_p}, P_{R_p})$ if and only if the remainder holds:* i) $A \subseteq A_p$, ii) $R \subseteq (R_p \cap (A \times A))$, iii) $\forall a \in A_p$ *such that* $P_{A_p}(a) = 1$, *then* $a \in A$, iv) $\forall (a_i, a_j) \in R_p$ *such that* $P_{R_p}(a_i, a_j) = 1$ *and* $a_i, a_j \in A$, *then* $(a_i, a_j) \in R$. *We write* $\mathbb{I}(\mathcal{F}_p)$ *to represent the set of all AFs that can be induced from a* $\mathcal{F}_p$.

Therefore, arguments and attacks with a likelihood of 1 must be present in all the induced frameworks whenever possible (i.e., an attack also needs incident arguments to be present), while not-completely certain components can appear or not in an induced framework. The probability of an induced AF is computed as the joint probability of all the independent variables:

Definition 2 (Probability of induced $\mathcal{F}$ [19]). *With $\mathcal{F}_p = (A_p, R_p, P_{A_p}, P_{R_p})$, the probability of $\mathcal{F} = (A, R) \in \mathbb{I}(\mathcal{F}_p)$ is:*

$$P_{\mathcal{F}_p}^{\mathbb{I}}(\mathcal{F}) = \prod_{a_i \in A} P_{A_p}(a_i) \prod_{a_i \in (A_p \setminus A)} (1 - P_{A_p}(a_i))$$

$$\prod_{(a_i, a_j) \in R} P_{R_p}((a_i, a_j)) \prod_{(a_i, a_j) \in (R_p \setminus R) \ s.t. \ a_i, b_j \in A} (1 - P_{R_p}((a_i, a_j)))$$

The set of possible worlds induced by a PrAF sums up to a probability of 1.

Proposition 1 [19]. *The sum of all the probability values of all the frameworks that can be induced from a $\mathcal{F}_p = (A_p, R_p, P_{A_p}, P_{R_p})$ is 1:*

$$\sum_{\mathcal{F}_i \in \mathbb{I}(\mathcal{F}_p)} P_{\mathcal{F}_p}^{\mathbb{I}}(\mathcal{F}_i) = 1$$

Definition 3 computes the likelihood of a set E of arguments being "consistent" with respect a given argumentation semantics σ.

Definition 3 (Extension probability [19]). *Given a $\mathcal{F}_p = (A_p, R_p, P_{A_p}, P_{R_p})$, the probability that a given set of arguments $B \subseteq P_{A_p}$ satisfies a semantics σ is (function ξ is discussed in the following paragraph):*

$$P_\sigma(B, \mathcal{F}_p) = \sum_{\mathcal{F}_i \in \mathbb{I}(\mathcal{F}_p)} P_{\mathcal{F}_p}^{\mathbb{I}}(\mathcal{F}_i) \text{ where } \xi^\sigma(\mathcal{F}_i, B) = true$$

In [19] function $\xi^\sigma(\mathcal{F}_i, B)$ is said to return true if and only if the set of arguments B is deemed "consistent" using semantics σ when evaluated over a framework $\mathcal{F}_i$ induced from $\mathcal{F}_p$. For instance, we can consider ξ to return true if and only if $B \in \sigma(\mathcal{F}_i)$, that is if and only if B is an extension in $\mathcal{F}_i$ according to semantics σ, or if B is just a subset of a σ extension, as proposed in [19].

Example 1. In Fig. 1 we show an example of PrAF. Such a relatively small graph induces thirteen different frameworks: $\mathcal{F}_1 = (\{a, e\}, \{\})$, $\mathcal{F}_2 = (\{a, b, e\}, \{(a, b)\})$, $\mathcal{F}_3 = (\{a, c, e\}, \{\})$, $\mathcal{F}_4 = (\{a, b, c, e\}, \{(a, b)\})$, $\mathcal{F}_5 = (\{a, b, c, e\}, \{(a, b), (c, b)\})$, $\mathcal{F}_6 = (\{a, d, e\}, \{(d, e)\})$, $\mathcal{F}_7 = (\{a, b, d, e\}, \{(a, b), (d, e)\})$, $\mathcal{F}_8 = (\{a, c, d, e\}, \{(d, c), (d, e)\})$, $\mathcal{F}_9 = (\{a, c, d, e\}, \{(c, d), (d, c), (d, e)\})$, $\mathcal{F}_{10} = (\{a, b, c, d, e\}, \{(a, b), (d, c), (d, e)\})$, $\mathcal{F}_{11} = (\{a, b, c, d, e\}, \{(a, b), (c, b), (d, c), (d, e)\})$, $\mathcal{F}_{12} = (\{a, b, c, d, e\}, \{(a, b), (c, d), (d, c), (d, e)\})$, $\mathcal{F}_{13} = (\{a, b, c, d, e\}, \{(a, b), (c, b), (c, d), (d, c), (d, e)\})$, whose probabilities are $[0.09, 0.06, 0.21, 0.056, 0.084, 0.09, 0.06, 0.147, 0.063, 0.0392, 0.0588, 0.0168, 0.0252]$. These values clearly sum up to 1.

3   Related Work

In the literature there exist two main approaches to probabilistic argumentation: the constellations [19] and the epistemic approaches [22]. A third approach is proposed in [20]: in that case, the probability distribution over labellings [9] gives

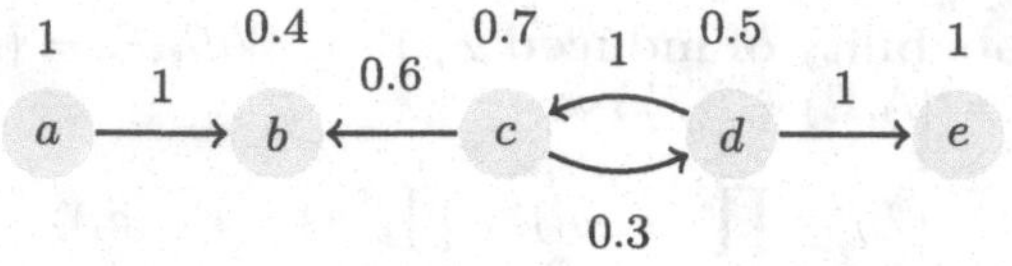

Fig. 1. An example of PrAF.

a form of probabilistic argumentation that overlaps with both the constellations and epistemic approaches.

In the constellations approach, the uncertainty resides in the topology of the considered AF: probability values label arguments and attacks. The authors of [15] provided the first proposal to extend abstract argumentation with a probability distribution over sets of arguments which they use with a version of assumption-based argumentation in which a subset of the rules are probabilistic rules. In [19] a probability distribution over the sub-graphs of the argument graph is introduced, and this can then be used to give a probability assignment for a set of arguments being an admissible set or extension of the argument graph. In [12] the authors characterise the different semantics from the approach of [19] in terms of probabilistic logic with the purpose of providing an uniform logical formalisation and also pave the way for future implementations. Complexity aspects related to computing the probability that a set of arguments is an extension according to a given semantics are instead presented in [16].

In the epistemic approach instead, the topology of a graph is fixed, but the more likely an agent is to believe in an argument, the less likely it is to believe in an argument attacking it. This reminds other related approached such as *ranking-based semantics* [1] and *weighted argumentation frameworks* [5,6,8]. For instance, in [3] the authors cast epistemic probabilities in the context of de Finetti's theory of subjective probability, and they analyse and revise the relevant rationality properties in relation with de Finetti's notion of coherence. However, most of the work in this directions is authored by M. Thimm [22] and A. Hunter [17]. In the first work, the author proposes a probabilistic approach assigning probabilities or degrees of belief to individual arguments. The presented semantics generalise the classical notions of semantics [13]. In the second work, the author starts from considering logic-based argumentation with uncertain arguments, but ends showing how this formalisation relates to uncertainty of abstract arguments. The two authors join their efforts in [18].

Some more related references concern the use of frameworks whose topology is not completely expressed, similarly to the constellations approach. For example, the work in [11] introduced the notion of *Partial Argumentation Framework* (*PAF*), which are defined by a set of arguments, an attack relation $\rightarrow \subseteq (A \times A)$ specifying attacks *known to exist*, and an *ignorance relation* $ign \subseteq (A \times A)$ specifying attacks whose existence is not known. This reflects the fact that some agents may ignore arguments pointed out by other agents, as well as how such arguments interact with her own ones: the goal of the authors is to merge different frameworks together, and thus not all the agents are assumed to share the same global set of arguments. *Incomplete Argumentation Frameworks* (*IAF*) further generalise PAFs, since they can represent uncertainty about the existence of individual arguments, uncertainty about the existence of individual attacks, or both simultaneously [4].

4   The Grounded Semantics of a PrAF

In [19] the authors suggests $\xi^{\mathbf{gr}}(\mathcal{F}_i, B)$ to return "true" when the set of arguments B is a subset of the grounded extension of $\mathcal{F}_i$ (see Definition 3). However, this choice for ξ leads to some issues related to the non-uniqueness of the grounded extension, which is indeed a desirable result being it also defined as a *unique*-status or *single-status* semantics in Dung's frameworks [2]. For example, the PrAF in Fig. 1 has two alternative choices for the grounded extension: $P_{\mathbf{gr}}(\emptyset, \mathcal{F}_p) = P_{\mathbf{gr}}(\{a\}, \mathcal{F}_p) = 1$.

This is the main motivation that moved us towards a different definition of the grounded semantics, with the purpose to have one single result (with the maximal probability), together with the need to connect its characteristic of scepticism to probabilistic frameworks: the grounded extension minimises the overall uncertainty and includes only the least questionable arguments present in complete extensions. In order to rephrase this characteristic into probabilistic frameworks, the grounded extension should include the arguments that are *most likely* included in the complete extensions of all the possible induced frameworks.

To accomplish this, we were inspired by the *law of total probability* to compute the average probability of an event U on the probability space defined by the events $\{V_n : n = 1, 2, \ldots, n\}$, which are a finite or countably infinite partition of such sample space: $P(U) = \sum_i P(U \cap V_i) = \sum_i P(U \mid V_i) \cdot P(V_i)$.

In our specific case, $P(V_i)$ describes the probability of $\mathcal{F}_i$ to be an induced framework of $\mathcal{F}_p$, that is $P^{\mathbb{I}}_{\mathcal{F}_p}(\mathcal{F}_i)$. Such a probability value is weighted by $P(U \mid V_i)$, which in our case is not really a probability but the frequency of a subset B to appear in the complete extensions of $\mathcal{F}_i$ instead.

Definition 4 (Probability B is a subset of a complete extension in $\mathcal{F}_p$).
Given $\mathcal{F}_p = (\mathsf{A}_p, \mathsf{R}_p, P_{\mathsf{A}_p}, P_{\mathsf{R}_p})$, the probability of $B \in \mathsf{A}_p$ to be a subset of the complete extensions in $\mathcal{F}_p$ is computed as:

$$P(B)^{\mathbf{co}}_{\mathcal{F}_p} = \sum_{\mathcal{F}_i \in \mathbb{I}(\mathcal{F}_p)} (|E \in \mathbf{co}(\mathcal{F}_i)| \; s.t. \; B \subseteq E) \, / \, |\mathbf{co}(\mathcal{F}_i)| \cdot P^{\mathbb{I}}_{\mathcal{F}_p}(\mathcal{F}_i)$$

For example, if B is a subset of half of the complete extensions in an induced $\mathcal{F}_i$ and $P^{\mathbb{I}}_{\mathcal{F}_p}(\mathcal{F}_i) = 0.25$, then the contribution of $\mathcal{F}_i$ to $P(B)^{\mathbf{co}}_{\mathcal{F}_p}$ is $0.5 \cdot 0.25 = 0.125$. To compute the total contribution one has to consider all the $\mathcal{F}_i$.

It is now possible to define the grounded semantics of a PrAF as the union of the subsets of maximal-probability, with probability as defined in Definition 4.

Definition 5 (Grounded semantics). *Given* $\mathcal{F}_p = (A_p, R_p, PA_p, PR_p)$, *a family of sets* S, *the grounded extension is defined as the union* $\bigcup$ *of subsets of maximal* $P(B)_{\mathcal{F}_p}^{co}$:

$$\mathbf{gr}(\mathcal{F}_p) = \bigcup\{B \mid P(B)_{\mathcal{F}_p}^{co} \text{ is maximal}\} \tag{1}$$

Example 2. Given the PrAF in Fig. 1, the thirteen induced frameworks has the following sets of complete extensions: $\mathbf{co}(\mathcal{F}_1) = \{\{a,e\}\}$, $\mathbf{co}(\mathcal{F}_2) = \{\{a,e\}\}$, $\mathbf{co}(\mathcal{F}_3) = \{\{a,c,e\}\}$, $\mathbf{co}(\mathcal{F}_4) = \{\{a,c,e\}\}$, $\mathbf{co}(\mathcal{F}_5) = \{\{a,c,e\}\}$, $\mathbf{co}(\mathcal{F}_6) = \{\{a,d\}\}$, $\mathbf{co}(\mathcal{F}_7) = \{\{a,d\}\}$, $\mathbf{co}(\mathcal{F}_8) = \{\{a,d\}\}$, $\mathbf{co}(\mathcal{F}_9) = \{\{a\},\{a,d\},\{a,c,e\}\}$, $\mathbf{co}(\mathcal{F}_{10}) = \{\{a,d\}\}$, $\mathbf{co}(\mathcal{F}_{11}) = \{\{a,d\}\}$, and $\mathbf{co}(\mathcal{F}_{12}) = \{\{a\},\{a,d\},\{a,c,e\}\}$, and $\mathbf{co}(\mathcal{F}_{13}) = \{\{a\},\{a,d\},\{a,c,e\}\}$. There exist ten possible subsets of complete extensions in $\mathcal{F}_p$, that is $\emptyset, \{a\}, \{c\}, \{d\}, \{e\}, \{a,c\}, \{a,d\}, \{a,e\}, \{c,e\}, \{a, c, e\}$, whose probability as defined in Definition 4 are respectively defined by the array $[1, 1, 0.385, 0.43, 0.535, 0.385, 0.43, 0.535, 0.385, 0.385]$. Hence, as stated by Definition 5, $\mathbf{gr}(\mathcal{F}_p) = \emptyset \cup \{a\} = \{a\}$, since both $\emptyset$ and $\{a\}$ have a probability of 1.

The next remark explains why it is possible to replace "maximal probability" with $P(B)_{\mathcal{F}_p}^{co} = 1$ in Definition 5 without changing the result.

Remark 1. Note that the probability of empty-set is always maximal, since it is trivially a subset of any $E \in \mathbf{co}(\mathcal{F}_i)$: as a consequence, empty-set will always be considered with a probability of 1 in the union of sets in Eq. 1. For the same reason, any subset B with a probability strictly less than 1 will never be considered to be part of the grounded extension. Therefore, maximal and equal to 1 probabilities will be interchangeably used in the rest of the paper.

The grounded semantics always results in a single extension.

Proposition 2 (Unicity). *The grounded extension in* $\mathcal{F}_p = (A_p, R_p, PA_p, PR_p)$ *is unique.*

Proof. It straightforwardly follows from the fact that the grounded extension is defined as the union of some sets of arguments.

In addition, when from $\mathcal{F}_p$ it is possible to induce a single framework, i.e., $|\mathbb{I}(\mathcal{F}_p)| = 1$, then the grounded semantics corresponds to its classical definition given by P. M. Dung in [13]. This allows to reconnect to classical abstract argumentation in case of no uncertainty in the framework topology.

Theorem 1 (Correspondence with Dung). *Given* $\mathcal{F}_p = (A_p, R_p, PA_p, PR_p)$ *such that* $\mathbb{I}(\mathcal{F}_p) = \{\mathcal{F}\}$, *then* $\mathbf{gr}(\mathcal{F}_p) = \mathbf{gr}(\mathcal{F})$.

Proof. Since we only have one induced framework $\mathcal{F}$ by hypothesis, whose probability is 1 according to Proposition 1, then $P(B)_{\mathcal{F}_p}^{co} = \sum_{\mathcal{F}_i \in \mathbb{I}(\mathcal{F}_p)}(|E \in \mathbf{co}(\mathcal{F}_i)| \, s.t. \, B \subseteq E) / |\mathbf{co}(\mathcal{F}_i)| \cdot P_{\mathcal{F}_p}^{\mathbb{I}}(\mathcal{F}_i) = (|E \in \mathbf{co}(\mathcal{F})| \, s.t. \, B \subseteq E) / |\mathbf{co}(\mathcal{F})|$. Since $\mathbf{gr}(\mathcal{F})$ is defined as the intersection of all the complete extensions in $\mathcal{F}$, then we have that $P(\mathbf{gr}(\mathcal{F}))_{\mathcal{F}_p}^{co}$ is 1, while for any $B \neq \emptyset$ and $B \neq \mathbf{gr}(\mathcal{F})$, $P(B)_{\mathcal{F}_p}^{co} < 1$. From Definition 5 we obtain $\mathbf{gr}(\mathcal{F}_p) = \mathbf{gr}(\mathcal{F})$.

Example 3. If we consider a PrAF $\mathcal{F}_p$ s.t. $A_p = \{a, b, c, d\}$, $R_p = \{(a, b), (b, c), (c, d)\}$, $P_{A_p} = \{1, 1, 1, 1\}$, $P_{R_p} = \{1, 1, 1\}$, we have a single induced framework whose complete extension is $\{a, c\}$. Hence, its subsets are $\{\emptyset, \{c\}, \{a\}, \{a, c\}\}$ with probabilities $[1.0, 1.0, 1.0, 1.0]$. The union of all these maximal-probability subsets is equivalent to $\mathbf{gr}(\mathcal{F}_p) = \{a, c\}$.

Theorem 2 states that the definition of grounded extension given in Definition 5 adheres to the principle often used to enforce scepticism in Abstract Argumentation: as introduced in Sect. 1, the intersection of different extensions leads to only those arguments that are taken in all of them, thus eliminating uncertainty. Also in the case of PrAFs, the grounded extension of each induced $\mathcal{F}_i$ is the intersection of complete extensions, while the grounded extension of the entire $\mathcal{F}_p$ is the intersection of all the different grounded extensions for each $\mathcal{F}_i$.

Theorem 2 (Intersection of grounded ext.s). *Being* $\mathcal{F}_p = (A_p, R_p, P_{A_p}, P_{R_p})$ *any PrAF, then the grounded extension defined in Definition 5 corresponds to:*

$$\mathbf{gr}(\mathcal{F}_p) = \bigcap_{\mathcal{F}_i \in \mathbb{I}(\mathcal{F}_p)} \mathbf{gr}(\mathcal{F}_i)$$

Proof. Given any $a \in A_p$, if $\forall \mathcal{F}_i \in \mathbb{I}(\mathcal{F}_p)$ (except the empty framework, if it exists) $a \in \mathbf{gr}(\mathcal{F}_i)$ then $P(\{a\})_{\mathcal{F}_p}^{co}$, since a is included in any complete extension of each $\mathcal{F}_i$. According to Definition 3.2 we have that $\bigcup_a \{a\} = \mathbf{gr}(\mathcal{F}_p)$, because all these sets have maximal probability. On the contrary, if $\exists \mathcal{F}_i \in \mathbb{I}(\mathcal{F}_p).a \notin \mathbf{gr}(\mathcal{F}_i)$ then $P(\{a\})_{\mathcal{F}_p}^{co}$ is not maximal (i.e., it has a probability strictly lower than 1).

Note that from Theorem 2 we directly derive that $\mathbf{gr}(\mathcal{F}_p)$ is conflict-free in $\mathcal{F}_p$, even if it make little sense to check it in a PrAF, since an attack may or may not exist depending on the induced framework.

Corollary 1 underlines the scepticism behind the definition of grounded semantics given in Definition 5. If an induced framework such that its grounded extension is empty-set exists, or equivalently empty-set is a complete extension of that framework, then the grounded extension of the whole PrAF is empty-set as well.

Corollary 1 (Empty-set dominance). *If* $\exists \mathcal{F}_i \in \mathbb{I}(\mathcal{F}_p)$ *s.t.* $\emptyset \in \mathbf{co}(\mathcal{F}_i)$, *then* $\mathbf{gr}(\mathcal{F}_p) = \emptyset$.

Proof. We have that $P(\emptyset)_{\mathcal{F}_p}^{co} = 1$ for any $\mathcal{F}_i \in \mathbb{I}(\mathcal{F}_p)$. If $\emptyset \in \mathbf{co}(\mathcal{F}_i)$, then $\forall B \neq \emptyset$ we have that $B \not\subseteq (E = \emptyset)$. For this reason, $P(B)_{\mathcal{F}_p}^{co} < 1$ for any $B \neq \emptyset$. Since Definition 3.2 aggregates maximal-probability subsets only, then $\mathbf{gr}(\mathcal{F}_p)$ corresponds to the union of empty-set only.

In the definition of the grounded semantics for probabilistic frameworks we tried to stick to the principle of scepticism, according to which empty-set is clearly the most sceptical position to be taken. In the next example we recap the previous formal results.

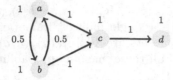

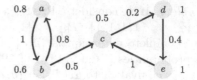

Fig. 2. An example of PrAF.   Fig. 3. A second example of PrAF.

Example 4. In Fig. 2 we show an example of a PrAF that induces the four frameworks represented in Fig. 4. These frameworks respectively have $\mathbf{co}(\mathcal{F}_1) = \{\{a, b, d\}\}$, $\mathbf{co}(\mathcal{F}_2) = \{\{a, d\}\}$, $\mathbf{co}(\mathcal{F}_3) = \{\{b, d\}\}$, $\mathbf{co}(\mathcal{F}_3) = \{\emptyset, \{a, d\}, \{b, d\}\}$. Thus, subsets of complete extensions are $\emptyset$, $\{a\}$, $\{b\}$, $\{d\}$, $\{a, b\}$, $\{a, d\}$, $\{b, d\}$, $\{a, b, d\}$ and their probability is $[1, 0.583, 0.583, 0.916, 0.25, 0.583, 0.583, 0.25]$. The four grounded extensions are $\mathbf{gr}(\mathcal{F}_1) = \{a, b, d\}$, $\mathbf{gr}(\mathcal{F}_2) = \{a, d\}$, $\mathbf{gr}(\mathcal{F}_3) = \{b, d\}$, and $\mathbf{gr}(\mathcal{F}_4) = \emptyset$. The intersection of all the grounded extensions from the four frameworks is $\emptyset$.

Because of the aforementioned motivations, having defined the grounded extension of a PrAF as the intersection of the grounded extensions of each induced framework, the probability for a framework to be empty-set is clearly high. This result is clearly not very informative, and it is a possible drawback of being too much sceptical. However, by having defined a quantitative approach to the definition of the grounded semantics, we can also think of relaxing scepticism by imposing a lower threshold on probability when merging the subsets as suggested in Definition 4, instead of taking the most probable subsets.

Definition 6 (t-relaxed grounded semantics). *Given* $\mathcal{F}_p = (A_p, R_p, PA_p, P_{R_p})$, *a family of sets* S, $t \in [0, 1]$, *the t-relaxed grounded extension is defined as the union of subsets whose* $P(B \subseteq (E \in \mathbf{co}(\mathcal{F}_p)))$ *is greater-equal than* t:

$$\overset{t}{\mathbf{gr}}(\mathcal{F}_p) = \bigcup\{B \mid P(B)_{\mathcal{F}_p}^{\mathbf{co}} \geq t\} \tag{2}$$

Example 5. If we set $t = 0.9$, the t-grounded extension of the PrAF in Fig. 2 is $\{d\}$, since the probability of this subset is 0.916, and $\emptyset \cup \{d\} = \{d\}$.

Clearly, $\overset{1}{\mathbf{gr}}(\mathcal{F}_p)$ corresponds to $\mathbf{gr}(\mathcal{F}_p)$ in Definition 5.

5   Further Sceptical Semantics

There are two other sceptical semantics in the literature, which share the unique-statusness with the grounded: the ideal and eager semantics. Both **eg** and **id** have been designed to relax scepticism of the former one: $\mathbf{gr}(\mathcal{F}) \subseteq \mathbf{id}(\mathcal{F}) \subseteq \mathbf{eg}(\mathcal{F})$ [10].

Because of their importance and closeness to the grounded semantics, in the following of this section we provide a probabilistic definition of these two semantics, in the style of what proposed in Sect. 4.

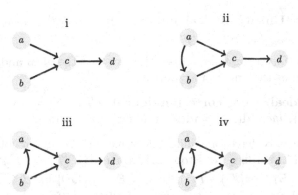

Fig. 4. The four frameworks induced by the PrAF in Fig 2.

Definition 7 (Probability of id and eg). *Given* $\mathcal{F}_p = (A_p, R_p, P_{A_p}, P_{R_p})$, *the probability of* $B \in A_p$ *to be a subset of the preferred/semi-stable extensions in* $\mathcal{F}_p$, *are respectively computed as:*

$$P(B)_{\mathcal{F}_p}^{\mathbf{pr}} = \sum_{\mathcal{F}_i \in \mathbb{I}(\mathcal{F}_p)} (|E \in \mathbf{pr}(\mathcal{F}_i)| \ s.t. \ B \subseteq E) \, / \, |\mathbf{pr}(\mathcal{F}_i)| \cdot P_{\mathcal{F}_p}^{\mathbb{I}}(\mathcal{F}_i) \qquad (3)$$

$$P(B)_{\mathcal{F}_p}^{\mathbf{sst}} = \sum_{\mathcal{F}_i \in \mathbb{I}(\mathcal{F}_p)} (|E \in \mathbf{sst}(\mathcal{F}_i)| \ s.t. \ B \subseteq E) \, / \, |\mathbf{sst}(\mathcal{F}_i)| \cdot P_{\mathcal{F}_p}^{\mathbb{I}}(\mathcal{F}_i) \qquad (4)$$

In Definition 8 we use Eq. 3 and Eq. 4 to propose a definition of respectively ideal and eager semantics in PrAFs.

Definition 8 (Ideal/eager semantics). *Given* $\mathcal{F}_p = (A_p, R_p, P_{A_p}, P_{R_p})$, *the ideal/eager extensions are defined as the union of maximal-probability subsets, as defined in Eq. 3 and Eq. 4 respectively:*

$$\mathbf{id}(\mathcal{F}_p) = \bigcup \{B \mid P(B)_{\mathcal{F}_p}^{\mathbf{pr}} \ is \ maximal\}, \quad \mathbf{eg}(\mathcal{F}_p) = \bigcup \{B \mid P(B)_{\mathcal{F}_p}^{\mathbf{sst}} \ is \ maximal\}$$

Example 6. The grounded, ideal, and eager extensions in Fig. 2 are $\emptyset$. The grounded extension in Fig. 2b is $\emptyset$, while the ideal and the eager ones are $\{a\}$: in this case, the induced frameworks are $\mathcal{F}_1 = (\{a, b\}, \{(a, b), (b, a), (b, b)\})$ and $\mathcal{F}_2 = (\{a, b\}, \{(a, b), (b, b)\})$. Thus, subsets of complete extensions are $\emptyset$ and $\{a\}$, with probability of 1 and 0.5.

Remark 2. As in Remark 1, empty-set is always contained in every preferred and semi-stable extension, and thus $P(\emptyset)_{\mathcal{F}_p}^{\mathbf{pr}} = P(\emptyset)_{\mathcal{F}_p}^{\mathbf{sst}} = 1$ for any possible $\mathcal{F}_p$. For this reason, requiring maximal probability or a probability value equal to 1 is equivalent in Definition 8. Both the ideal and eager extensions will always be made of only subsets B with a probability of 1.

In case of a single induced framework from $\mathcal{F}_p$, the ideal and eager extensions correspond to their classical definition in [14] and [10] respectively.

Proposition 3 (Unicity of ideal and eager). *The ideal and eager extensions in* $\mathcal{F}_p = (A_p, R_p, P_{A_p}, P_{R_p})$ *are unique.*

Proof. It straightforwardly follows from the fact that the ideal and eager extensions are defined as the union of argument sets.

Theorem 3 (Ideal/eager correspondence). *Given* $\mathcal{F}_p = (A_p, R_p, P_{A_p}, P_{R_p})$ *s.t.* $\mathbb{I}(\mathcal{F}_p) = \{\mathcal{F}\}$, *then* $\mathbf{id}(\mathcal{F}_p) = \mathbf{id}(\mathcal{F})$ *and* $\mathbf{eg}(\mathcal{F}_p) = \mathbf{eg}(\mathcal{F})$.

Proof. Since we only have one induced framework $\mathcal{F}$ by hypothesis, whose probability is 1 according to Prop. 2.1, then $P(B)^{\mathbf{pr}}_{\mathcal{F}_p} = \sum_{\mathcal{F}_i \in \mathbb{I}(\mathcal{F}_p)}(|E \in \mathbf{pr}(\mathcal{F}_i)|\, s.t.\, B \subseteq E)\,/\,|\mathbf{pr}(\mathcal{F}_i)| \cdot P^{\mathbb{I}}_{\mathcal{F}_p}(\mathcal{F}_i) = (|E \in \mathbf{pr}(\mathcal{F})|\, s.t.\, B \subseteq E)\,/\,|\mathbf{pr}(\mathcal{F})|$. Since $\mathbf{id}(\mathcal{F})$ is defined as the intersection of all the preferred extensions in $\mathcal{F}$, then we have that $P(\mathbf{id}(\mathcal{F}))^{\mathbf{pr}}_{\mathcal{F}_p}$ is 1, while for any $B \neq \emptyset$ and $B \neq \mathbf{id}(\mathcal{F})$, $P(B)^{\mathbf{pr}}_{\mathcal{F}_p} < 1$. From Definition 3.2 we obtain $\mathbf{id}(\mathcal{F}_p) = \mathbf{id}(\mathcal{F})$. Similar considerations hold for the eager semantics, with respect to semi-stable extensions.

Even for these two sceptical semantics we can prove that they can be both obtained by intersecting all the respectively ideal/eager extensions on all the induced frameworks, as Theorem 2 shows for the grounded semantics.

Theorem 4. (Intersection of extensions). *Being* $\mathcal{F}_p = (A_p, R_p, P_{A_p}, P_{R_p})$ *any PrAF, then the ideal and eager extensions respectively correspond to:*

$$\mathbf{id}(\mathcal{F}_p) = \bigcap_{\mathcal{F}_i \in \mathbb{I}(\mathcal{F}_p)} \mathbf{id}(F_i) \qquad \mathbf{eg}(\mathcal{F}_p) = \bigcap_{\mathcal{F}_i \in \mathbb{I}(\mathcal{F}_p)} \mathbf{eg}(F_i)$$

Proof. The proof follows the same approach adopted in Theorem 2.

From Theorem 3, in case of a single induced framework $\mathcal{F}$ we straightforwardly inherit the result that $\mathbf{gr}(\mathcal{F}_p) \subseteq \mathbf{id}(\mathcal{F}_p) \subseteq \mathbf{eg}(\mathcal{F}_p)$ from previous works [10,14]. The following theorem extends this result to more than one induced framework, that is, to all possible PrAFs.

Theorem 5 (Sceptical semantics inclusion). *The subset inclusion* $\mathbf{gr}(\mathcal{F}_p) \subseteq \mathbf{id}(\mathcal{F}_p) \subseteq \mathbf{eg}(\mathcal{F}_p)$ *holds for any PrAF* $\mathcal{F}_p$.

Proof. Since for each $\mathcal{F}_i \in \mathbb{I}(\mathcal{F}_p)$ it holds that $\mathbf{gr}(\mathcal{F}_i) \subseteq \mathbf{id}(\mathcal{F}_i) \subseteq \mathbf{eg}(\mathcal{F}_i)$ from Theorem 1 and Theorem 3, then from Theorem 4 the intersection of all $\mathbf{gr}(\mathcal{F}_i)/\mathbf{id}(\mathcal{F}_i)$ is included in the intersection of respectively $\mathbf{id}(\mathcal{F}_i)/\mathbf{eg}(\mathcal{F}_i)$.

It is then possible to relax the ideal and eager extensions as shown for the grounded extension in Definition 6 (similar motivations in mitigating scepticism).

Definition 9 (t-relaxed ideal and eager). *Given* $\mathcal{F}_p = (A_p, R_p, P_{A_p}, P_{R_p})$ *and* $t \in [0, 1]$, *the t-relaxed ideal/eager extension is defined as the union of subsets whose* $P(B)^{\mathbf{pr}}_{\mathcal{F}_p}/P(B)^{\mathbf{sst}}_{\mathcal{F}_p}$ *is greater-equal than t:*

$$\overset{t}{\mathbf{id}}(\mathcal{F}_p) = \bigcup \{B \mid P(B)^{\mathbf{pr}}_{\mathcal{F}_p} \geq t\} \qquad \overset{t}{\mathbf{eg}}(\mathcal{F}_p) = \bigcup \{B \mid P(B)^{\mathbf{pr}}_{\mathcal{F}_p} \geq t\}$$

Example 7. The PrAF in Fig. 3 induces 42 different frameworks (which we do not report here for the sake of conciseness); $\mathbf{eg}(\mathcal{F}_p) = \emptyset$, while $\overset{0.601}{\mathbf{eg}}(\mathcal{F}_p)$ is $\{a, d\}$, which happens to be the eager extension if we consider the same framework in the classical Dung's setting. Moreover, $\overset{0.6}{\mathbf{eg}}(\mathcal{F}_p) = \{a, d, e\}$, since $P(\{d\})^{\mathbf{sst}}_{\mathcal{F}_p} = 0.97008$, $P(\{a\})^{\mathbf{sst}}_{\mathcal{F}_p} = 0.60416$, and $P(\{e\})^{\mathbf{sst}}_{\mathcal{F}_p} = 0.6$.

Clearly, by increasing the threshold it is possible to progressively include more arguments.

Proposition 4. *For any $\mathcal{F}_p = (A_p, R_p, P_{A_p}, P_{R_p})$ and thresholds $t_1, t_2 \in [0, 1]$, if $t_2 < t_1$ then $\overset{t_1}{\mathbf{gr}}(\mathcal{F}_p) \subseteq \overset{t_2}{\mathbf{gr}}(\mathcal{F}_p)$, $\overset{t_1}{\mathbf{id}}(\mathcal{F}_p) \subseteq \overset{t_2}{\mathbf{id}}(\mathcal{F}_p)$, and $\overset{t_1}{\mathbf{eg}}(\mathcal{F}_p) \subseteq \overset{t_2}{\mathbf{eg}}(\mathcal{F}_p)$.*

6 Conclusions and Future Work

In this paper we have provided a probabilistic view of sceptical semantics in the constellations approach, since we have focused on the grounded, ideal, and eager extensions. The purpose was to compute clear and single solutions for these semantics, as it happens in Dung's frameworks. To achieve this, we have computed how frequently subsets of arguments appear in complete, preferred, and semi-stable extensions by considering all the induced frameworks. Then, by merging maximal-probability subsets among them we enforce the idea of scepticism in PrAFs. Such a quantitative approach reconnects to the qualitative one often used in argumentation, that is the intersection of different alternatives. However, by using probability values we now also have a quantitative means to relax scepticism, besides using the ideal and eager semantics proposed in Sect. 5. The presented framework has been implemented with a Python script that calls the Docker container of ConArg [7] to enumerate complete, preferred and semi-stable extensions on all the induced frameworks.

In the future we plan to enrich the paper with a definition of more credulous semantics, for example the preferred and stable ones, while still satisfying classical implications among semantics. We will also investigate similarities and differences w.r.t. *standard epistemic extensions* [18], which are directly related to Dung's semantics. Finally, the presented framework can be equipped with a more fine-grained probabilistic logic that explicitly takes epistemic uncertainty and belief (and disbelief as well) into account: i.e., *subjective logic* [21].

References

1. Amgoud, L., Ben-Naim, J., Doder, D., Vesic, S.: Acceptability semantics for weighted argumentation frameworks. In: Proceedings of the Twenty-Sixth International Joint Conference on Artificial Intelligence, pp. 56–62. ijcai.org (2017)
2. Baroni, P., Caminada, M., Giacomin, M.: An introduction to argumentation semantics. Knowl. Eng. Rev. **26**(4), 365–410 (2011)
3. Baroni, P., Giacomin, M., Vicig, P.: On rationality conditions for epistemic probabilities in abstract argumentation. In: Computational Models of Argument - Proceedings of COMMA, FAIA, vol. 266, pp. 121–132. IOS Press (2014)

4. Baumeister, D., Neugebauer, D., Rothe, J.: Collective acceptability in abstract argumentation. FLAP **8**(6), 1503–1542 (2021)
5. Bistarelli, S., Rossi, F., Santini, F.: ConArg: a tool for classical and weighted argumentation. In: Computational Models of Argument - Proceedings of COMMA, FAIA, vol. 287, pp. 463–464. IOS Press (2016)
6. Bistarelli, S., Rossi, F., Santini, F.: A ConArg-based library for abstract argumentation. In: 29th IEEE International Conference on Tools with Artificial Intelligence, ICTAI, pp. 374–381. IEEE Computer Society (2017)
7. Bistarelli, S., Rossi, F., Santini, F.: ConArgLib: an argumentation library with support to search strategies and parallel search. J. Exp. Theor. Artif. Intell. **33**(6), 891–918 (2021)
8. Bistarelli, S., Santini, F.: Weighted argumentation. FLAP **8**(6), 1589–1622 (2021)
9. Caminada, M.: On the issue of reinstatement in argumentation. In: Fisher, M., van der Hoek, W., Konev, B., Lisitsa, A. (eds.) JELIA 2006. LNCS (LNAI), vol. 4160, pp. 111–123. Springer, Heidelberg (2006). https://doi.org/10.1007/11853886_11
10. Caminada, M.: Comparing two unique extension semantics for formal argumentation: ideal and eager. In: Belgian-Dutch Conference on Artificial Intelligence (BNAIC), pp. 81–87 (2007)
11. Coste-Marquis, S., Devred, C., Konieczny, S., Lagasquie-Schiex, M., Marquis, P.: On the merging of Dung's argumentation systems. Artif. Intell. **171**(10–15), 730–753 (2007)
12. Doder, D., Woltran, S.: Probabilistic argumentation frameworks – a logical approach. In: Straccia, U., Calì, A. (eds.) SUM 2014. LNCS (LNAI), vol. 8720, pp. 134–147. Springer, Cham (2014). https://doi.org/10.1007/978-3-319-11508-5_12
13. Dung, P.M.: On the acceptability of arguments and its fundamental role in non-monotonic reasoning, logic programming and n-person games. Artif. Intell. **77**(2), 321–357 (1995)
14. Dung, P.M., Mancarella, P., Toni, F.: Computing ideal sceptical argumentation. Artif. Intell. **171**(10–15), 642–674 (2007)
15. Dung, P.M., Thang, P.M.: Towards (probabilistic) argumentation for jury-based dispute resolution. In: Computational Models of Argument: Proceedings of COMMA, FAIA, vol. 216, pp. 171–182. IOS Press (2010)
16. Fazzinga, B., Flesca, S., Parisi, F.: On the complexity of probabilistic abstract argumentation frameworks. ACM Trans. Comput. Log. **16**(3), 22:1–22:39 (2015)
17. Hunter, A.: A probabilistic approach to modelling uncertain logical arguments. Int. J. Approx. Reason. **54**(1), 47–81 (2013)
18. Hunter, A., Thimm, M.: Probabilistic reasoning with abstract argumentation frameworks. J. Artif. Intell. Res. **59**, 565–611 (2017)
19. Li, H., Oren, N., Norman, T.J.: Probabilistic argumentation frameworks. In: Modgil, S., Oren, N., Toni, F. (eds.) TAFA 2011. LNCS (LNAI), vol. 7132, pp. 1–16. Springer, Heidelberg (2012). https://doi.org/10.1007/978-3-642-29184-5_1
20. Riveret, R., Governatori, G.: On learning attacks in probabilistic abstract argumentation. In: Proceedings of the 2016 International Conference on Autonomous Agents & Multiagent Systems, pp. 653–661. ACM (2016)
21. Santini, F., Jøsang, A., Pini, M.S.: Are my arguments trustworthy? Abstract argumentation with subjective logic. In: 21st International Conference on Information Fusion, FUSION, pp. 1982–1989. IEEE (2018)
22. Thimm, M.: A probabilistic semantics for abstract argumentation. In: ECAI - 20th European Conference on Artificial Intelligence, FAIA, vol. 242, pp. 750–755. IOS Press (2012)

SHACL: A Description Logic in Disguise

Bart Bogaerts[1] , Maxime Jakubowski[1,2](✉) , and Jan Van den Bussche[2]

[1] Vrije Universiteit Brussel, Brussels, Belgium
{bart.bogaerts,maxime.jakubowski}@vub.be
[2] Universiteit Hasselt, Hasselt, Belgium
{maxime.jakubowski,jan.vandenbussche}@uhasselt.be

Abstract. SHACL is a W3C-proposed language for expressing structural constraints on RDF graphs. In recent years, SHACL's popularity has risen quickly. This rise in popularity comes with questions related to its place in the semantic web, particularly about its relation to OWL (the de facto standard for expressing ontological information on the web) and description logics (which form the formal foundations of OWL). We answer these questions by arguing that *SHACL is in fact a description logic*. On the one hand, our answer is surprisingly simple, some might even say obvious. But, on the other hand, our answer is also controversial. By resolving this issue once and for all, we establish the field of description logics as the solid formal foundations of SHACL.

Keywords: Shapes · SHACL · Description Logics · Ontologies

1 Introduction

The Resource Description Framework (RDF [20]) is a standard format for publishing data on the web. RDF represents information in the form of directed graphs, where labeled edges indicate properties of nodes. To facilitate more effective access and exchange, it is important for a consumer of an RDF graph to know what properties to expect, or, more generally, to be able to rely on certain structural constraints that the graph is guaranteed to satisfy. We therefore need a declarative language in which such constraints can be expressed formally.

Two prominent proposals in this vein have been ShEx [8] and SHACL [23]. In both approaches, a formula expressing the presence (or absence) of certain properties of a node (or its neighbors) is referred to as a "shape". In this paper, we adopt the elegant formalization of shapes in SHACL proposed by Corman, Reutter and Savkovic [9]. That work has revealed a striking similarity between *shapes* and *concept expressions*, familiar from description logics (DLs) [5].

The similarity between SHACL and DLs runs even deeper when we account for *named shapes* and *targeting*, which is the actual mechanism to express constraints on an RDF graph using shapes. A *shape schema* is essentially a finite list of shapes, where each shape ϕ_s is given a name s and additionally associated with a target query q_s. The shape–name combinations in a shape schema specify, in DL terminology, an *acyclyc TBox* consisting of all the formulas

$$s \equiv \phi_s.$$

Given an RDF graph G, this acyclic TBox determines a unique interpretation of sets of nodes to shape names s. We then say that G *conforms* to the schema if for each query q_s, each node v returned by q_s on G satisfies s in the extension of G.

Now interestingly, the types of target queries q considered for this purpose in SHACL as well as in ShEx, actually correspond to simple cases of shapes ϕ_{q_s} and the actual integrity constraint thus becomes

$$\phi_{q_s} \sqsubseteq s.$$

As such, in description logic terminology, a shape schema consists of two parts: an acyclic TBox (defining the shapes in terms of the given input graph) and a general TBox (containing the actual integrity constraints).

2   The Wedge

Despite the strong similarity between SHACL and DLs, and despite the fact that in a couple of papers, SHACL has been formalized in a way that is extremely similar to description logics [3,9,14], this connection is not recognized in the community. In fact, some important stakeholders in SHACL recently even wrote the following in a blog post explaining why they use SHACL, rather than OWL:

> OWL was inspired by and designed to exploit 20+ years of research in Description Logics (DL). This is a field of mathematics that made a lot of scientific progress right before creation of OWL. I have no intention of belittling accomplishments of researchers in this field. However, there is little connection between this research and the practical data modeling needs of the common real world software systems.   —   [19]

thereby suggesting that SHACL and DLs are two completely separated worlds and as such contradicting the introductory paragraphs of this paper. On top of that, SHACL is presented by some stakeholders [25] as an alternative to the Web ontology language OWL [16], which is based on the description logic SROIQ [10].

This naturally begs the question: which misunderstanding is it that drives this wedge between communities? How can we explain this discrepancy from a mathematical perspective (thereby patently ignoring strategic, economic, social, and other aspects that play a role).

3   SHACL, OWL, and Description Logics

Our answer is that there are two important differences between OWL and SHACL that deserve attention. These differences, however, do not contradict the central thesis of this paper, which is that *SHACL is a description logic*.

1. The first difference is that **in SHACL, the data graph (implicitly) represents a first-order interpretation, while in OWL, it represents a first-order theory (an ABox)**. Of course, viewing the same syntactic structure (an RDF graph) as an interpretation is very different from viewing it as a theory. While this is a discrepancy between OWL and SHACL, theories as well as interpretations exist in the world of description logic and as such, this view is perfectly compatible with our central thesis. There is, however, one caveat with this claim that deserves some attention, and that is highlighted by the use of the world "implicitly". Namely, to the best of our knowledge, it is never mentioned that the data graph simply represents a standard first-order interpretation, and it has not been made formal what *exactly* the interpretation is that is associated to a graph. Instead, SHACL's language features are typically evaluated *directly* on the data graph. There are several reasons why we believe it is important to make this translation of a graph into an interpretation *explicit*.
   - This translation makes *the assumptions SHACL makes about the data* explicit. For instance, it is often informally stated that "SHACL uses closed-world assumptions" [13]; we will make this statement more precise: SHACL uses closed-world assumptions with respect to the relations, but open-world assumptions on the domain.
   - Once the graph is eliminated, we are in familiar territory. In the field of description logics a plethora of language features have been studied. It now becomes clear how to add them to SHACL, if desired. The 20+ years of research mentioned in [19] suddenly become directly applicable to SHACL.
2. The second difference, which closely relates to the first, is that **OWL and SHACL have a different (default) inference task**: the standard inference task at hand in OWL is *deduction*, while in SHACL, the main task is validation of RDF graphs against shape schemas. In logical terminology, this is evaluating whether a given interpretation satisfies a theory (TBox), i.e., this is the task of *model checking*.
   Of course, the fact that a different inference task is typically associated with these languages does not mean that their logical foundations are substantially different. Furthermore, recently, other researchers [14,17,18] have started to investigate tasks such as *satisfiability* and *containment* (which are among the tasks typically studied in DLs) for SHACL, making it all the more obvious that the field of description logics has something to offer for studying properties of SHACL.

In the next section, we develop our formalization of SHACL, building on the work mentioned above. Our formalization differs form existing formalizations of

SHACL in a couple of small but important ways. First, as we mentioned, we explicitly make use of a first-order interpretation, rather than a graph, thereby indeed showing that SHACL is in fact a description logic. Second, the semantics for SHACL we develop would be called a "natural" semantics in database theory [1]: variables always range over the universe of all possible nodes. The use of the natural semantics avoids an anomaly that crops up in the definitions of Andreşel et al. [3], where an "active-domain" semantics is adopted instead, in which variables range only over the set of nodes actually occurring in the input graph. Unfortunately, such a semantics does not work well with constants. The problem is that a constant mentioned in a shape may or may not actually occur in the input graph. As a result, the semantics adopted by Andreşel et al. violates familiar logic laws like De Morgan's law. This is troublesome, since automated tools (and humans!) that generate and manipulate logic formulas may reasonably and unwittingly assume these laws to hold. Also other research papers (see Remark 4) contain flaws related to not taking into account nodes that *do not* occur in the graph. This highlights the importance of taking a logical perspective on SHACL.

A minor caveat with the natural semantics is that decidability of validation is no longer totally obvious, since the universe of nodes is infinite. A solution to this problem is well-known from relational databases [1, Theorem 5.6.1]. Using an application of solving the first-order theory of equality, one can reduce, over finite graphs, an infinite domain to a finite domain, by adding symbolic constants [4,11]. It turns out that in our case, just a single extra constant suffices.

In this paper, we will not give a complete syntactic translation of SHACL shapes to logical expressions. In fact, such a translation has already been developed by Corman et al. [9], and was later extended to account for all SHACL features by Jakubowski [12]. Instead, we show very precisely how the data graph at hand can be viewed as an interpretation, and that after this small but crucial step, we are on familiar grounds and know well how to evaluate expressions.

As already mentioned before, our formalization of SHACL differs in a couple of ways from existing work. These design choices are grounded in true SHACL: with each of them we will provide actual SHACL specifications that prove that SHACL validators indeed behave in the way we expected. All our examples have been tested on three SHACL implementations: Apache Jena SHACL[1] (using their Java library) TopBraid SHACL[2] (using their Java library as well as their online playground), and Zazuko[3] (using their online playground). The raw files encoding our examples (SHACL specifications and the corresponding graphs) are available online.[4]

All our SHACL examples will assume the following prefixes are defined:

```
@prefix ex: <http://www.example.org/> .
@prefix sh: <http://www.w3.org/ns/shacl#> .
```

---

[1] https://jena.apache.org/documentation/shacl/index.html.
[2] https://shacl.org/playground/.
[3] https://shacl-playground.zazuko.com/.
[4] https://vub-my.sharepoint.com/:f:/g/personal/bart_bogaerts_vub_be/
Eicv10DwSnVEnT0BWNwEW8QBFuQjYTbwYYct1WYrkoefKQ?e=XhE8o0.

4   SHACL: The Logical Perspective

In this section of the paper we begin with the formal development. We define shapes, shape schemas, and validation. Our point of departure is the treatment by Andreşel et al. [3], which we adapt and extend to our purposes.

From the outset we assume three disjoint, infinite universes N, S, and P of *node names*, *shape names*, and *property names*, respectively.[5]

We define *path expressions* E and *shapes* ϕ by the following grammar:

$$E ::= p \mid p^- \mid E \cup E \mid E \circ E \mid E^* \mid E?$$
$$\phi ::= \top \mid s \mid \{c\} \mid \phi \wedge \phi \mid \phi \vee \phi \mid \neg\phi \mid \geq_n E.\phi \mid eq(p, E) \mid disj(p, E) \mid closed(Q)$$

where p, s, and c stand for property names, shape names, and node names, respectively, n stands for nonzero natural numbers, and Q stands for finite sets of property names. In description logic terminology, a node name c is a *constant*, a shape name is a *concept name* and a property name is a *role name*.

As we will formalize below, every property/role name evaluates to a binary relation, as does each path expression. In the path expressions, p^- represents the inverse relation of p, $E \circ E$ represents composition of binary relations, E^* the reflexive-transitive closure of E and $E?$ the reflexive closure of E. As we will see, shapes (which represent unary predicates) will evaluate to a subset of the domain. The three last expressions are probably the least familiar. Equality ($eq(p, E)$) means that there are outgoing p-edges (edges labeled p) exactly to those nodes for which there is a path satisfying the expression E (defined below). Disjointness ($disj(p, E)$) means that there are *no* outgoing p-edges to which there is also a path satisfying E. For instance in the graph in Fig. 1, $eq(p, p^*)$ would evaluate to $\{c\}$, since c is the only node that has direct outgoing p-edge to all nodes that are reachable using only p-edges, and $disj(p, p^-)$ would evaluate to $\{d\}$ since d is the only node that has no symmetric p-edges. Closedness is also a typical SHACL feature: $closed(Q)$ represents that there are no outgoing edges about any predicates other than those in Q. In our example figure $closed(\{p\})$ would evaluate to $\{a, b, c, d\}$ and $closed(\{q\})$ to the empty set.

Remark 1. Andreşel et al. [3] also have the construct $\forall E.\phi$, which can be omitted (at least for theoretical purposes) as it is equivalent to $\neg \geq_1 E.\neg\phi$. In our semantics, the same applies to $\phi_1 \wedge \phi_2$ and $\phi_1 \vee \phi_2$, of which we need only one as the other is then expressible via De Morgan's laws. However, here we keep both for the sake of our later Remark 3. In addition to the constructors of Andreşel et al. [3], we also have $E?$, *disj*, and *closed*, corresponding to SHACL features that were not included there.   □

---

[5] In practice, node names, shape names, and property names are IRIs [20], hence the disjointness assumption does not hold. However, this assumption is only made for simplicity of notation.

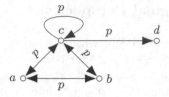

Fig. 1. An example graph to illustrate language features of SHACL.

Table 1. Semantics of a path expression E in an interpretation I over Σ.

E	$\llbracket E \rrbracket^I$
p^-	$\{(a,b) \mid (b,a) \in \llbracket p \rrbracket^I\}$
$E_1 \cup E_2$	$\llbracket E_1 \rrbracket^I \cup \llbracket E_2 \rrbracket^I$
$E_1 \circ E_2$	$\{(a,b) \mid \exists c : (a,c) \in \llbracket E_1 \rrbracket^I \wedge (c,b) \in \llbracket E_2 \rrbracket^I\}$
E^*	the reflexive-transitive closure of $\llbracket E \rrbracket^I$
$E?$	$\llbracket E \rrbracket^I \cup \{(a,a) \mid a \in \Delta^I\}$

A *vocabulary* Σ is a subset of $N \cup S \cup P$. A path expression or shape is said to be *over* Σ if it only uses symbols from Σ.

On the most general logical level, shapes are evaluated in *interpretations*. We recall the familiar definition: An interpretation I over Σ consists of

1. a set Δ^I, called the *domain* of I;
2. for each constant $c \in \Sigma$, an element $\llbracket c \rrbracket^I \in \Delta^I$;
3. for each shape name $s \in \Sigma$, a subset $\llbracket s \rrbracket^I$ of Δ^I; and
4. for each property name $p \in \Sigma$, a binary relation $\llbracket p \rrbracket^I$ on Δ^I.

On any interpretation I as above, every path expression E over Σ evaluates to a binary relation $\llbracket E \rrbracket^I$ on Δ^I, and every shape ϕ over Σ evaluates to a subset of Δ^I, as defined in Tables 1 and 2.

As argued above, we define a *shape schema* $\mathcal{S}$ over Σ as a tuple (D, T), where

- D is an *acyclic TBox* [5], i.e., a finite set of expressions of the form $s \equiv \phi_s$ with s a shape name in Σ and ϕ_s a shape over Σ and where
  1. each s occurs exactly once as the left-hand-side of such an expression and
  2. the transitive closure of the relation $\{(s,t) \mid t \text{ occurs in } \phi_s\}$ is acyclic.
- T is a TBox, i.e., a finite set of statements of the form $\phi_1 \sqsubseteq \phi_2$, with ϕ_1 and ϕ_2 shapes.

If $\mathcal{S} = (D, T)$ is a shape schema over Σ and I an interpretation over $\Sigma \setminus \mathcal{S}$, then there is a unique interpretation $I \diamond D$ that agrees with I outside of $\mathcal{S}$ and that satisfies D, i.e., such that for every expression $s \equiv \phi_s \in D$, $\llbracket s \rrbracket^{I \diamond D} = \llbracket \phi_s \rrbracket^{I \diamond D}$. We say that I *conforms to* $\mathcal{S}$, denoted by $I \models \mathcal{S}$, if $\llbracket \phi_1 \rrbracket^{I \diamond D}$ is a subset of $\llbracket \phi_2 \rrbracket^{I \diamond D}$, for every statement $\phi_1 \sqsubseteq \phi_2$ in T. In other words, I conforms to $\mathcal{S}$ if there exists an interpretation that satisfies $D \cup T$ that coincides with I on $N \cup P$.

Table 2. Semantics of a shape ϕ in an interpretation I over Σ. For a set X, we use $\sharp X$ to denote its cardinality. For a binary relation R and an element a, we use $R(a)$ to denote the set $\{b \mid (a, b) \in R\}$.

ϕ	$[\![\phi]\!]^I$
$\top$	Δ^I
$\{c\}$	$\{c^I\}$
$\phi_1 \wedge \phi_2$	$[\![\phi_1]\!]^I \cap [\![\phi_2]\!]^I$
$\phi_1 \vee \phi_2$	$[\![\phi_1]\!]^I \cup [\![\phi_2]\!]^I$
$\neg\phi_1$	$\Delta^I \setminus [\![\phi_1]\!]^I$
$\geq_n E.\phi_1$	$\{a \in \Delta^I \mid \sharp([\![\phi_1]\!]^I \cap [\![E]\!]^I(a)) \geq n\}$
$eq(p, E)$	$\{a \in \Delta^I \mid [\![p]\!]^I(a) = [\![E]\!]^I(a)\}$
$disj(p, E)$	$\{a \in \Delta^I \mid [\![p]\!]^I(a) \cap [\![E]\!]^I(a) = \emptyset\}$
$closed(Q)$	$\{a \mid [\![p]\!]^I(a) = \emptyset \text{ for every } p \in \Sigma \setminus Q\}$

Remark 2. In real SHACL, a shape schema is called a "shapes graph". There are some notable differences between shapes graphs and our shape schemas.

First, we take abstraction of some features of real SHACL, such as checking data types like numbers and strings.

Second, in real SHACL, the left-hand side of an inclusion statement in T is called a "target" and is actually restricted to shapes of the following forms: a constant ("node target"); $\exists r.\{c\}$ ("class-based target", where r is 'rdf:type'); $\exists r.\top$ ("subjects-of target"); or $\exists r^-.\top$ ("objects-of target"). Our claims remain valid if this syntactic restriction imposed.

Third, in real SHACL not every shape name needs to occur in the left-hand side of a defining rule. The default that is taken in real SHACL is that shapes without a definition are *always satisfied*. On the logical level, this means that for every shape s name that has no explicit definition, a definition $s \equiv \top$ is implicitly assumed. The example that illustrates that our chosen default indeed corresponds to actual SHACL.   ☐

Example 1. The following SHACL shape `ex:MyShape` states that all nodes with an `ex:r`-edge must conform to the `ex:NoDef` and `ex:AlsoNoDef` shapes which we do not define.

```
ex:MyShape a sh:NodeShape ;
    sh:and ( ex:NoDef ex:AlsoNoDef ) .
ex:MyShape sh:targetSubjectsOf ex:r .
```

In our formal notation, this shapes graph corresponds to the shape schema

$$\text{ex:MyShape} \equiv \text{ex:NoDef} \wedge \text{ex:AlsoNoDef}$$

$$\exists\text{ex:r}.\top \sqsubseteq \text{ex:MyShape}$$

where the first line is the definition of `ex:MyShape`, and the second line its target.

When validating a graph containing only the triple `ex:a ex:r ex:b` (as we will show later, this corresponds to an interpretation in which the property name `ex:r` has the interpretation $\{(\texttt{ex:a}, \texttt{ex:b})\}$ and the interpretation of all other property names is empty), and thus targeting the node `ex:a`, it validates without violation. This supports our observation that **shapes without an explicit definition are assumed to be satisfied by all nodes (i.e., are interpreted as** $\top$**)**.

To further strengthen this claim, if instead we consider the SHACL shapes graph

```
ex:MyShape a sh:NodeShape ;
    sh:not ex:NoDef .
ex:MyShape sh:targetSubjectsOf ex:r .
```

i.e., the shape schema

$$\texttt{ex:MyShape} \equiv \neg\texttt{ex:NoDef}$$
$$\exists\texttt{ex:r}.\top \sqsubseteq \texttt{ex:MyShape}$$

validation on the same graph yields the validation error that "node `ex:a` does not satisfy `ex:MyShape` since it has shape `ex:NoDef`". □

5 From Graphs to Interpretations

Up to this point, we have discussed the logical semantics of SHACL, i.e., how to evaluate a SHACL expression in a standard first-order interpretation. However, in practice, SHACL is not evaluated on interpretations but on RDF graphs. In this section, we show precisely and unambiguously how to go from a graph to a logical interpretation (in such a way that the actual SHACL semantics coincides with what we described above). A *graph* is a finite set of *facts*, where a fact is of the form $p(a, b)$, with p a property name and a and b node names. We refer to the node names appearing in a graph G simply as the *nodes* of G; the set of nodes of G is denoted by N_G. A pair (a, b) with $p(a, b) \in G$ is referred to as an *edge*, or a p-*edge*, in G. The set of p-edges in G is denoted by $[\![p]\!]^G$ (this set might be empty).

We want to be able to evaluate *any* shape on *any* graph (independently of the vocabulary the shape is over). Thereto, we will unambiguously associate, to any given graph G, an interpretation I over $N \cup P$ as follows:

- Δ^I equals N (the universe of all node names).
- $[\![c]\!]^I$ equals c itself, for every node name c.
- $[\![p]\!]^I$ equals $[\![p]\!]^G$, for every property name p.

If I is the interpretation associated to G, we use $[\![E]\!]^G$ and $[\![\phi]\!]^G$ to mean $[\![E]\!]^I$ and $[\![\phi]\!]^I$, respectively.

RDF also has a model-theoretic semantics [21]. These semantics reflect the view of an RDF graph as a basic ontology or logical theory, as opposed to the view of an RDF graph as an interpretation. Since the latter view is the one followed by SHACL, it is thus remarkable that SHACL effectively ignores the W3C-recommended semantics of RDF.

Remark 3. Andreşel et al. [3] define $[\![\phi]\!]^G$ a bit differently. For a constant c, they define $[\![\{c\}]\!]^G = \{c\}$ like we do. For all other constructs, however, they define $[\![\phi]\!]^G$ to be $[\![\phi]\!]^I$, but with the domain of I taken to be N_G, rather than N. In that approach, if $c \notin N_G$, $[\![\neg\neg\{c\}]\!]^G$ would be empty rather than $\{c\}$ as one would expect. For another illustration, still assuming $c \notin N_G$, $[\![\neg(\neg\phi \wedge \neg\{c\})]\!]^G$ would be $[\![\phi]\!]^G$ rather than $[\![\phi]\!]^G \cup \{c\}$, so De Morgan's law would fail. The next examples shows that actual SHACL implementations indeed coincide with our semantics.   □

Example 2. The following SHACL shape ex:MyShape states that it cannot be so that the node ex:MyNode is different from itself (i.e., that it must be equal to itself, but specified with a double negation).

```
ex:MyShape a sh:NodeShape ;
    sh:not [ sh:not [ sh:hasValue ex:MyNode ] ] .
ex:MyShape sh:targetNode ex:MyNode .
```

In our formal notation, this shapes graph corresponds to the shape schema

$$\text{ex:MyShape} \equiv \neg\neg\{\text{ex:MyNode}\}$$
$$\{\text{ex:MyNode}\} \sqsubseteq \text{ex:MyShape}$$

Clearly, this shape should validate every graph, also graphs in which the node ex:MyNode is not present and it indeed does so in all SHACL implementations we tested. This supports our **choice of the natural semantics**, rather than the active domain semantics of [3]. Indeed, in that semantics, this shape will never validate any graph because the right-hand side of the inclusion will be evaluated to be the empty set.   □

Example 3. Another example in the same vein as the previous, to show that the **natural semantics** correctly formalizes is the one where [3]'s semantics does not respect the De Morgan's laws, as follows:

```
ex:MyShape a sh:NodeShape ;
    sh:not [
        sh:and (
            [ sh:not [
                sh:path ex:r ;
                sh:minCount 1 ] ]
            [ sh:not [ sh:hasValue ex:MyNode ] ] ) ] .
ex:MyShape sh:targetNode ex:MyNode .
```

This shapes graph corresponds to the shape schema

$$ex{:}MyShape \equiv \neg(\neg\exists ex{:}r.\top \wedge \neg\{ex{:}MyNode\})$$
$$\{ex{:}MyNode\} \sqsubseteq ex{:}MyShape$$

In the formalism of Andreşel et al. [3], this schema does not validate on graphs that do not mention the node ex:MyNode, but in our formalism (and all SHACL implementations), it does validate.   □

Remark 4. The use of active domain semantics has also introduced some errors in previous work. For instance [14, Theorem 1] is factually incorrect. The problem originates with the notion of *faithful assignment* introduced by Corman et al. [9] and adopted by Leinberger et al. This notion is defined in an active-domain fashion, only considering nodes actually appearing in the graph. For a concrete counterexample to that theorem, consider a single shape named s defined as $\exists r.\top$, with target $\{b\}$. In our terminology, this means that

$$D = \{s \equiv \exists r.\top\}, \text{ and}$$
$$T = \{\{b\} \sqsubseteq s\}.$$

On a graph G in which b does not appear, we can assign $\{s\}$ to all nodes from G with an outgoing r-edge (meaning that all these nodes satisfy s and no other shape (names)), and assign the empty set to all other nodes (meaning that all other nodes do not satisfy any shape). According to the definition, this is a faithful assignment. However, the inclusion $\{b\} \sqsubseteq s$ is not satisfied in the interpretation they construct from this assignment, thus violating their Theorem 1.   □

The bug in [14], as well as the violation of De Morgan's laws will only occur in corner cases where the shape schema mentions nodes that not occur in the graph. After personal communications, Leinberger et al. [14] included an errata section where they suggest to fix this by demanding that (in order to conform) the target queries do not mention any nodes not in the graph. While technically, this indeed resolves the issue (under that condition, Theorem 1 indeed holds), this solution in itself has weaknesses as well. Indeed, shape schemas are designed to validate graphs not known at design-time, and it should be possible to check conformance of *any* graph with respect to *any* shape schema. As the following example shows, it makes sense that a graph should conform to a schema in case a certain node does *not* occur in the graph (or does not occur in a certain context), and that— contrary to the existing SHACL formalizations—the natural semantics indeed coincides with the behaviour of SHACL validators in such cases.

Example 4. Consider a schema with $D = \emptyset$ and T consisting of a single inclusion

$$\{MarcoMaratea\} \sqsubseteq \neg\exists(author \circ venue).\{LPNMR22\},$$

which states that Marco Maratea (one of the LPNMR PC chairs) does not author any LPNMR paper. If Marco Maratea does not occur in the list of of accepted papers, this list should clearly[6] conform to this schema. This example can be translated into actual SHACL as follows:

```
ex:NotAnAuthor a sh:NodeShape ;
    sh:not [
        a sh:PropertyShape ;
        sh:path (ex:author ex:venue) ;
        sh:qualifiedValueShape [ sh:hasValue ex:LPNMR22 ] ;
        sh:qualifiedMinCount 1 ] .
ex:NotAnAuthor sh:targetNode ex:MarcoMaratea .
```

where we simply give the name ex:NotAnAuthor to the shape that holds for all nodes that do not author any LPNMR paper and subsequently enforce that Marco Maratea satisfy this shape. We see that indeed, in accordance with our proposed semantics, graphs without a node ex:MarcoMaratea validate with respect to this SHACL specification. The fix in the erratum of Leinberger et al. [14], on the other hand, specifies that this does not validate.   □

The definition of I makes —completely independent of the actual language features of SHACL—a couple of assumptions explicit. First of all, SHACL uses unique names assumptions (UNA): each constant is interpreted in I as a different domain element. Secondly, if $p(a, b)$ does not occur in the graph, it is assumed to be *false*. However, if a node c does not occur anywhere in the graph, it is not assumed to not exist: the domain of I is infinite! Rephrasing this: SHACL makes the Closed World Assumption (CWA) on predicates, but not on objects.

Effective Evaluation. Since the interpretation defined from a graph has the infinite domain N, it is not immediately clear that shapes can be effectively evaluated over graphs. As indicated above, however, we can reduce to a finite interpretation. Let $\Sigma \subseteq N \cup P$ be a finite vocabulary, let ϕ be a shape over Σ, and let G be a graph. From G we define the interpretation $I_\star$ over Σ just like I above, except that the domain of $I_\star$ is not N but rather

$$N_G \cup (\Sigma \cap N) \cup \{\star\},$$

where $\star$ is an element not in N. We use $[\![\phi]\!]^G_\star$ to denote $[\![\phi]\!]^{I_\star}$ and find:

Theorem 1. *For every $x \in N_G \cup (\Sigma \cap N)$, we have $x \in [\![\phi]\!]^G$ if and only if $x \in [\![\phi]\!]^G_\star$. For all other node names x, we have $x \in [\![\phi]\!]^G$ if and only if $\star \in [\![\phi]\!]^G_\star$. Hence, I conforms to S if and only if $I_\star$ does.*

Theorem 1 shows that conformance can be performed by finite model checking, but other tasks typically studied in DLs are not decidable; this can be shown with a small modification of the proof of undecidability of the description logic $\mathcal{ALRC}$, as detailed by Schmidt-Schauß [22].

---

[6] Technically, the standard is slightly ambiguous with respect to nodes not occurring in the data graph.

Theorem 2. *Consistency of a shape schema (i.e., the question whether or not some I conforms to S) is undecidable.*

Following description logic traditions, decidable fragments of SHACL have been studied already; for instance Leinberger et al. [14] disallow equality, disjointness, and closedness in shapes, as well as union and Kleene star in path expressions.

6   Related Work and Conclusion

Formal investigations of SHACL have started only relatively recently. We already mentioned the important and influential works by Corman et al. [9] and by Andreşel et al. [3], which formed the starting point for the present paper. The focus of these papers is mainly on the extending the semantics to *recursive* SHACL schemas, which are not present in the standard yet, and which we also do not consider in the current paper.

The connection between SHACL and description logics has also been observed by several other groups of researchers [2,14,17,18]. There, the focus is on typical reasoning tasks from DLs applied to shapes, and on reductions of these tasks to decidable description logics or decidable fragments of first-order logic. In its most general form, this cannot work (see Theorem 2), but the addressed works impose restrictions on the allowed shape expressions.

Next to shapes, other proposals for adding integrity constraints to the semantic web have been proposed, for instance by integrating them in OWL ontologies [15,24]. There, the entire ontology is viewed as an incomplete database.

None of the discussed works takes the explicit viewpoint that a data graph represents a standard first-order interpretation or that SHACL validation is model checking. We took this viewpoint and in doing so formalized precisely how SHACL relates to the field of description logics. There are (at least) three reasons why this formalization is important. First, it establishes a bridge between two communities, thereby allowing to exploit the many years of research in DLs also for studying SHACL. Second, our formalization of SHACL clearly separates two orthogonal concerns:

1. *Which information does a data graph represent?* This is handled in the translation of a graph into its *natural interpretation.*
2. *What is the semantics of language constructs?* This is handled purely in the well-studied logical setting.

Third, as we showed above, our formalization corresponds closer to actual SHACL than existing formalizations, respects well-known laws (such as De Morgan's) and avoids issues with nodes not occurring in the graph requiring special treatment. As such, we believe that by rooting SHACL in the logical setting, we have devised solid foundations for future studies and extensions of the language. We already build on the logical foundations of the current paper in our work on extending the semantics to *recursive* shape schemas [6], as well as in an analysis of the primitivity of the different language features of SHACL [7].

References

1. Abiteboul, S., Hull, R., Vianu, V.: Foundations of Databases. Addison-Wesley (1995)
2. Ahmetaj, S., David, R., Ortiz, M., Polleres, A., Shehu, B., Simkus, M.: Reasoning about explanations for non-validation in SHACL. In: Proceedings of KR, pp. 12–21. IJCAI Organization (2021)
3. Andreşel, M., Corman, J., Ortiz, M., Reutter, J., Savkovic, O., Simkus, M.: Stable model semantics for recursive SHACL. In: Proceedings of WWW, pp. 1570–1580 (2020)
4. Aylamazyan, A., Gilula, M., Stolboushkin, A., Schwartz, G.: Reduction of the relational model with infinite domains to the case of finite domains. Dokl. Akad. Nauk SSSR **286**(2), 308–311 (1986). (in Russian)
5. Baader, F., Calvanese, D., McGuiness, D., Nardi, D., Patel-Schneider, P. (eds.): The Description Logic Handbook. Cambridge University Press (2003)
6. Bogaerts, B., Jakubowski, M.: Fixpoint semantics for recursive SHACL. In: Formisano, A., Liu, Y., et al. (eds.) Proceedings ICLP. Electronic Proceedings in Theoretical Computer Science, vol. 345, pp. 41–47 (2021)
7. Bogaerts, B., Jakubowski, M., Van den Bussche, J.: Expressiveness of SHACL features. In: Olteanu, D., Vortmeier, N. (eds.) Proceedings of ICDT, vol. 220, pp. 15:1–15:16. Schloss Dagstuhl-Leibniz-Zentrum für Informatik (2022)
8. Boneva, I., Gayo, J.L., Prud'hommeaux, E.: Semantics and validation of shape schemas for RDF. In: Proceedings of ISWC, pp. 104–120 (2017)
9. Corman, J., Reutter, J., Savkovic, O.: Semantics and validation of recursive SHACL. In: Proceedings of ISWC, pp. 318–336 (2018). Extended version, technical report KRDB18-01
10. Horrocks, I., Kutz, O., Sattler, U.: The even more irresistible SROIQ. In: Proceedings of KR, pp. 57–67 (2016)
11. Hull, R., Su, J.: Domain independence and the relational calculus. Acta Informatica **31**, 513–524 (1994)
12. Jakubowski, M.: Formalization of SHACL. https://www.mjakubowski.info/files/shacl.pdf. Accessed 16 Jun 2021
13. Knublauch, H.: SHACL and OWL compared. https://spinrdf.org/shacl-and-owl.html. Accessed 16 Jun 2021
14. Leinberger, M., Seifer, P., Rienstra, T., Lämmel, R., Staab, S.: Deciding SHACL shape containment through description logics reasoning. In: Pan, J.Z., et al. (eds.) ISWC 2020. LNCS, vol. 12506, pp. 366–383. Springer, Cham (2020). https://doi.org/10.1007/978-3-030-62419-4_21
15. Motik, B., Horrocks, I., Sattler, U.: Bridging the gap between OWL and relational databases. J. Web Semant. **7**(2), 74–89 (2009)
16. OWL 2 Web ontology language: Structural specification and functional-style syntax. W3C Recommendation (December 2012)
17. Pareti, P., Konstantinidis, G., Mogavero, F., Norman, T.J.: SHACL satisfiability and containment. In: Proceedings of ISWC, pp. 474–493 (2020)
18. Pareti, P., Konstantinidis, G., Mogavero, F.: Satisfiability and containment of recursive SHACL. J. Web Semant. (2022). https://doi.org/10.1016/j.websem.2022.100721, https://arxiv.org/abs/2108.13063
19. Polikoff, I.: Why I don't use OWL anymore - Top Quadrant blog. https://www.topquadrant.com/owl-blog/. Accessed 04 Jun 2021
20. RDF 1.1 primer. W3C Working Group Note, June 2014

21. RDF 1.1 semantics. W3C Recommendation, February 2014
22. Schmidt-Schauß, M.: Subsumption in KL-ONE is undecidable. In: Proceedings of KR, pp. 421–431 (1989)
23. Shapes constraint language (SHACL). W3C Recommendation, July 2017
24. Tao, J., Sirin, E., Bao, J., McGuinness, D.L.: Integrity constraints in OWL. In: Proceedings of AAAI (2010)
25. TopQuadrant: An overview of SHACL: a new W3C standard for data validation and modeling (2017). Webinar slides. https://www.topquadrant.com/an-overview-of-shacl/

Tunas - Fishing for Diverse Answer Sets: A Multi-shot Trade up Strategy

Elisa Böhl[✉][iD] and Sarah Alice Gaggl[iD]

Logic Programming and Argumentation Group, TU Dresden, Dresden, Germany
{elisa.boehl,sarah.gaggl}@tu-dresden.de

Abstract. Answer set programming (ASP) solvers have advanced in recent years, with a variety of different specialisation and overall development. Thus, even more complex and detailed programs can be solved. A side effect of this development are growing solution spaces and the problem of how to find those answer sets one is interested in. One general approach is to give an overview in form of a small number of highly diverse answer sets. By choosing a favourite and repeating the process, the user is able to leap through the solution space. But finding highly diverse answer sets is computationally expensive. In this paper we introduce a new approach called *Tunas* for *Trade Up Navigation for Answer Sets* to find diverse answer sets by reworking existing solution collections. The core idea is to collect diverse answer sets one after another by iteratively solving and updating the program. Once no more answer sets can be added to the collection, the program is allowed to trade answer sets from the collection for different answer sets, as long as the collection grows and stays diverse. Elaboration of the approach is possible in three variations, which we implemented and compared to established methods in an empirical evaluation. The evaluation shows that the Tunas approach is competitive with existing methods, and that efficiency of the approach is highly connected to the underlying logic program.

Keywords: multi-shot answer set programming · navigation · diverse answer sets

1 Introduction

Answer set programming (ASP) is a rising declarative programming paradigm based on logic programming and non-monotonic reasoning [12]. ASP is particularly well suited to model and solve combinatorial search problems such as scheduling [1,22], planning [8,11], and product configuration [24,25]. Over the last decade ASP solvers such as clingo [16], WASP [4] and dlv [2] have been improved and further developed to solve and enumerate answer sets faster [17], allow for more control over the grounding and solving process [14] and even enhanced with theory reasoning capabilities [21].

Due to these developments ASP finds more and more it's way into industrial applications [10,19]. Which reveals the issue that for real world applications the

G. Gottlob et al. (Eds.): LPNMR 2022, LNAI 13416, pp. 89–102, 2022.
https://doi.org/10.1007/978-3-031-15707-3_8

solution space can be extremely large. Recently Fichte et al. [13] introduced a framework that allows to navigate the solution space by introducing weights on atoms that occur in some but not all answer sets. Another way to tackle this problem is to search for optimal solutions by formulating preferences [5,6] or optimisation criteria [3,15]. However, the user might not have a particular preference in mind. For example consider the product configuration domain, where the producer models the product to configure in terms of ASP. This kind of combinatorial problem usually allows for many combinations of parts of the product, together with a rather low number of constraints, leading to a combinatorial explosion of solutions (answer sets). For the potential customer it is not possible to inspect all (possibly several million) configurations. Therefore, it would be beneficial to be able to provide a small collection of highly diverse configurations, such that the customer obtains an overview on the different characteristics of the potential products. Eiter et al. [9] introduced several approaches how to compute similar and diverse answer sets, ranging from post processing enumerations over parallel solving to iterative solving. The approaches diverge in behaviour, so is the parallel solving complete but becomes infeasible quickly while the fast iterative solving often leads to suboptimal results.

In this work we revisit four problems formulated in [9] and propose a novel approach for computing diverse answer sets based on reworking collections of solutions. The main idea is to trade solutions from a collection is allowed as long as the collection grows. Therefore the approach works iteratively, improving the result stepwise and thus can be interrupted at *anytime*. For our approach we introduce the corresponding problem and analyse its complexity by forming a many-one hierarchy. Furthermore we lay out three different elaborations to implement the core functionality. We compare our approach with the methods based on Eiter et al. [9] in an empirical evaluation, showing that the novel Tunas approach is competitive. Also the implementations of the iterative approaches benefit from the multi-shot functionality within the `clingo` solver, by updating existing logic programs instead of re-grounding and solving from scratch. Therefore a re-evaluation of the established methods using state-of-the art solvers and wrappers is of interest as well.

2   Preliminaries

2.1   Multi-shot Answer Set Programming

A (disjunctive) program $\mathcal{P}$ in ASP is a set of rules r of the form:

$$a_1; \ldots; a_m :- a_{m+1}, \ldots, a_n, \text{ not } a_{n+1}, \ldots, \text{ not } a_o.$$

where each *atom* a_i is of the form $p(t_1, \ldots, t_k)$, p is a *predicate* symbol of *arity* k and $t_1, \ldots, t_k$ are *terms* built using constants and variables. For $k = 0$ $p()$ abbreviates to p. A *naf* (negation as failure) *literal* is of the form a or *not* a for an atom a. A rule is called *fact* if $m = o = 1$, *normal* if $m = 1$ and *integrity constraint* if $m = 0$. Each rule can be split into a *head* $h(r) = \{a_1, \ldots, a_m\}$ and a *body* $B(r) = \{a_{m+1}, \ldots, not\ a_o\}$, which divides into a positive part $B^+(r) = \{a_{m+1}, \ldots, a_n\}$ and a negative part $B^-(r) = \{a_{n+1}, \ldots, a_o\}$. A term, atom, rule or program is said to be *ground* if it does not contain variables. For a program $\mathcal{P}$ its *ground instance* $Grd(\mathcal{P})$ is the set of all ground rules obtained by substituting all variables in each rule with ground terms. Let M be a set of ground atoms, for a ground rule r we say that $M \models r$ iff $M \cap h(r) \neq \emptyset$ whenever $B^+(r) \subseteq M$ and $B^-(r) \cap M = \emptyset$. M is a *model* of $\mathcal{P}$ if $M \models r$ for each $r \in \mathcal{P}$. M is a *stable model* (also called *answer set*) iff M is a $\subseteq$-minimal model satisfying the Gelfond-Lifschitz *reduct* of $\mathcal{P}$ w.r.t. M. The reduct is defined as $\mathcal{P}^M = \{h(r) \leftarrow B^+(r) | M \cap B^-(r) = \emptyset, r \in \mathcal{P}\}$ [18].

For the solver `clingo` several meta-statements are available, such as the `#show` directive to selectively include (and rename) atoms in the output. The *multi-shot* [14] feature within `clingo` allows altering and rerunning logic programs by defining parametrised subprograms. Subprograms are identified by a name sp and arity k and require a list of arguments $(p_1, \ldots, p_k)$. Within the logic program, the subprogram $sp(p_1, \ldots, p_k)$ starts after the directive `#program` $sp(p_1, \ldots, p_k)$. and ends before the next subprogram. If not declared the first block is attached to *base/0*. Usually the multi-shot program is handled by a wrapper script, communicating with the grounder and solver through a control object. Subprograms can be altered dynamically, allowing for flexible implementation at runtime. Truth values of atoms can be pre-assigned for each solve call via *assumptions* or *external* atoms. If used, assumptions need to be declared explicitly for each solve call, while external values are set persistently.

2.2 Diverse Solutions

Problems. The umbrella term *similar/diverse* covers a bouquet of problems focusing mainly around four decision problems [9]. In our work we target the diverse problem and therefore omit the (symmetric) *similar* co-problem. For convenience, the problems are often referenced by their short notation (Γ). The term "$\mathcal{P}$ and Δ for P" abbreviates "an ASP program $\mathcal{P}$ that formulates a computational problem P and a distance measure Δ that maps a set of solutions for P to a nonnegative integer". The complexity class is added to each problem.

(1) $\Gamma_{\mathcal{P}\Delta}^{nk}$ - *n k*-DIVERSE SOLUTIONS: Given $\mathcal{P}$ and Δ for P and two nonnegative integers n and k, decide whether a set S of n solutions for P exists such that $\Delta(S) \geqslant k$. (Complexity: NP-complete)

(2) $\Gamma_{\mathcal{P}\Delta}^{+1}$ - *k*-DISTANT SOLUTION: Given $\mathcal{P}$ and Δ for P, a set S of solutions for P, and a nonnegative integer k, decide whether some solution s ($s \notin S$) for P exists such that $\Delta(S \cup \{s\}) \geqslant k$. (Complexity: NP-complete)

(3) $\Gamma_{\mathcal{P}\Delta}^{k\uparrow}$ - *n*-MOST DIVERSE SOLUTIONS: Given $\mathcal{P}$ and Δ for P and a nonnegative integer n, find a set S of n solutions for P with the maximum distance $\Delta(S)$. (Complexity: FNP//log-complete)

(4) $\Gamma_{\mathcal{P}\Delta}^{n\uparrow}$ - MAXIMAL *n k*-DIVERSE SOLUTIONS: Given $\mathcal{P}$ and Δ for P and a nonnegative integer k, find a $\subseteq$-maximal set S of at most n solutions for P s.t. $\Delta(S) \geqslant k$. (Complexity: FP^{NP}-complete; FNP//log-complete if k is bounded)

$\Gamma_{\mathcal{P}\Delta}^{nk}$ addresses the core problem: finding a set S of n solutions for a given program for which the distance measure is larger than k. The distance measure Δ is a function which maps a set of solutions to a non-negative integer. In practice Δ is usually monotone ($\Delta(S) \geqslant \Delta(S \cup S')$ for any sets S, S' of solutions) and can be customised. A default implementation is the minimum of the hamming distance for any pair of solutions within the collection. $\Gamma_{\mathcal{P}\Delta}^{+1}$ asks for *one* solution which is at least k-distant to each element of a provided solution set (*collection*). Therefore $\Gamma_{\mathcal{P}\Delta}^{+1}$ can be utilised to semi-decide $\Gamma_{\mathcal{P}\Delta}^{nk}$. The other two problems target maximising k ($\Gamma_{\mathcal{P}\Delta}^{k\uparrow}$) and n ($\Gamma_{\mathcal{P}\Delta}^{n\bar{1}1}$) and can be decided by repeatedly solving $\Gamma_{\mathcal{P}\Delta}^{nk}$ for increasing k (resp. n).

Related Work. In [9] the following approaches targeting $\Gamma_{\mathcal{P}\Delta}^{nk}$ were introduced.

Offline solves $\Gamma_{\mathcal{P}\Delta}^{nk}$ directly by collecting some or all answer sets and picking diverse answer sets in a detached process, which in principle solves the NP-complete $k - clique$ problem for a potentially exponential input. Since solutions are generated in vaguely sorted order, restricting the output size will impact the outcome drastically. Therefore Offline faces heavy drawbacks and will not be covered in our evaluation.

Online1 is based on manipulating the original logic program to solve n copies of the problem at the same time while satisfying constraints on the distance measure, targeting $\Gamma_{\mathcal{P}\Delta}^{nk}$ in a single shot. Online1 is a complete approach.

Online2 tries to solve the main problem $\Gamma_{\mathcal{P}\Delta}^{nk}$ by repeatedly solving $\Gamma_{\mathcal{P}\Delta}^{+1}$. The program generates a solution and wrapper script adds it to the program, forcing the next solution to be diverse to the collected solutions. This process repeats until the collection has the desired quantity or the program becomes unsatisfiable. Additional to the original program and a wrapper script, this approach requires a method to add distance constraints. Online2 semi-decides $\Gamma_{\mathcal{P}\Delta}^{nk}$.

Online3 works similar to Online2 but the functionality is embedded into the solver instead of a script. [9] presented clasp-nk, a branch-development of clasp 1.1.3 which included hard-coding a distance calculation for one freely selectable predicate. Since this solver is not competitive with current generation solvers, we did not include Online3 despite showing comparable results to Online2.

Further Related Work. Romero et al. [23] propose a multi-shot framework for computing diverse *preferred* answer sets for *asprin*. The paper presents three advanced diversification techniques for programs with preferences, which are generalised methods based on [9], partly utilising preferences into the solving process. Since Romero et al. are using preferences, the methods are not directly empirical comparable to our work.

3   Iterative Reworking Strategies

So far there exist four problems and two promising approaches. The parallel approach (Online1) lifts the original program to solve $\Gamma_{\mathcal{P}\Delta}^{nk}$, while the iterative

---

[1] $\Gamma_{\mathcal{P}\Delta}^{n\bar{1}}$ asks for $\subseteq$-maximal sets and restricts the maximal value to bound output size.

approach (Online2) collects solutions by repeatedly solving and updating the logic program. Once the program becomes unsatisfiable, the diverse collection is subset-maximal and can not grow in any further. In our iterative reworking strategy, we aim to surpass this subset-maximal boundary by trading $m \geq 0$ solutions from a given collection S for at least $m + 1$ new solutions. This novel approach does not target any of the introduced problems directly, therefore we define and analyse the corresponding problem before introducing the actual approach.

3.1 Problem Definition and Complexity

Based on the notations from Sect. 2.2 we describe a new problem, which introduces the possibility of replacing at most m solutions from a given collection S with at least $m + 1$ solutions to form an improved diverse collection S'.

(5) $\Gamma_{\mathcal{P}\Delta}^{\leq m}$ - m-DIFFERENT k-DISTANT SET: Given $\mathcal{P}$ and Δ for P, a set S of solutions for P, two nonnegative integer k and m with $m \leqslant |S|$, decide if a set S' of solutions for P exists s.t. $|S'| > |S|$, $|S \backslash S'| \leqslant m$ and $\Delta(S') \geqslant k$.

In other words: we try to expand the given, potentially empty collection S of solutions by exchanging up to m solutions for a greater number of solutions. It is valid to exchange less than m solutions as long as the collection grows. While sharing similarities with $1_{\mathcal{P}\Delta}^{nk}$ and $\Gamma_{\mathcal{P}\Delta}^{+1}$, $\Gamma_{\mathcal{P}\Delta}^{\leq m}$ introduces a new parameter m, creating $|S| + 1$ possible sub-problems for a given set S of solutions. For convenience we will write "$\Gamma_{\mathcal{P}\Delta}^{\leq m}$ with $m = t$" as $\Gamma_{\mathcal{P}\Delta}^{\leq t}$ for any non-negative integer t. We will proceed to show equality of $\Gamma_{\mathcal{P}\Delta}^{+1}$ and $\Gamma_{\mathcal{P}\Delta}^{\leq 0}$ (Lemma 1) as well as interchangeability of $\Gamma_{\mathcal{P}\Delta}^{nk}$ and $\Gamma_{\mathcal{P}\Delta}^{\leq n-1}$ (Lemma 2). We will furthermore establish a hierarchy within $\Gamma_{\mathcal{P}\Delta}^{\leq m}$ (Lemma 3) to show NP-completeness (Theorem 1). For the proofs we assume Δ to be monotone ($\Delta(S) \geqslant \Delta(S \cup S')$ for any sets S, S' of solutions).

Lemma 1. $\Gamma_{\mathcal{P}\Delta}^{+1}(S, k)$ iff $\Gamma_{\mathcal{P}\Delta}^{\leq 0}(S, k)$.

Proof. $\Gamma_{\mathcal{P}\Delta}^{+1}(S, k) \Rightarrow \Gamma_{\mathcal{P}\Delta}^{\leq 0}(S, k)$: if there exists a solution s s.t. $\Delta(S \cup \{s\}) \geqslant k$ then the set $S' = S \cup \{s\}$ satisfies $|S'| > |S|$, $|S \backslash S'| \leqslant 0$ and $\Delta(S') \geqslant k$.
$\Gamma_{\mathcal{P}\Delta}^{\leq 0}(S, k) \Rightarrow \Gamma_{\mathcal{P}\Delta}^{+1}(S, k)$: if there exists a set of solutions S' s.t. $|S'| > |S|$, $|S \backslash S'| \leqslant 0$ and $\Delta(S') \geqslant k$ then $S \subset S'$ and for all $s \in (S' \backslash S)$: $\Delta(S \cup \{s\}) \geqslant k$. □

Lemma 2. $\Gamma_{\mathcal{P}\Delta}^{nk}(n, k)$ and $\Gamma_{\mathcal{P}\Delta}^{\leq n-1}(S, k)$ are interchangeable for $|S| = n - 1$.

Proof. $\Gamma_{\mathcal{P}\Delta}^{nk}(n, k) \Rightarrow \Gamma_{\mathcal{P}\Delta}^{\leq n-1}(S, k)$ with $|S| = n-1$: if there exists a set of solutions S' s.t. $|S'| = n$ and $\Delta(S') \geqslant k$ then for any possible set S of solutions with $|S| = n - 1$: $|S'| > |S|$, $|S \backslash S'| \leqslant n - 1$ and $\Delta(S') \geqslant k$.[2]
$\Gamma_{\mathcal{P}\Delta}^{\leq n-1}(S, k) \Rightarrow \Gamma_{\mathcal{P}\Delta}^{nk}(n, k)$: given a set S of at least $n-1$ solutions, if there exists a set S' of solutions s.t. $|S'| > |S| \geqslant n - 1$ and $\Delta(S') \geqslant k$ then there exists $S'' \subseteq S'$ where $|S''| = n$ and $\Delta(S'') \geqslant k$. □

We covered complexity for $\Gamma_{\mathcal{P}\Delta}^{\leq m}(S, k)$ for $m = 0$ and $m = |S|$, for the remaining $0 < m < |S|$ we can build a hierarchy using a poly-time many-one-reduction.

---

[2] This implication even holds if S and S' share elements ($S \cap S' \neq \emptyset$) or if $\Delta(S) < k$.

Lemma 3. $\Gamma_{\mathcal{PA}}^{\leq m}(S, k) \leq_p \Gamma_{\mathcal{PA}}^{\leq m+1}(S, k)$ *(poly-time many-one-reduction)*

Proof. $\Gamma_{\mathcal{PA}}^{\leq m}(S, k)$ has the problem instance $(\mathcal{P}, \Delta, S, k)$ which we will convert to $(\mathcal{P}^{\pm}, \Delta^{\pm}, S^{\pm}, k^{\pm})$ for $\Gamma_{\mathcal{P}^{\pm}, \Delta^{\pm}}^{\leq m+1}(S^{\pm}, k^{\pm})$ by introducing two artificial, unique solutions ϵ^+ and ϵ^-. The program $\mathcal{P}$ is altered to accept ϵ^+ and ϵ^-, forming $\mathcal{P}^{\pm}$. $\Delta^{\pm}$ is derived from Δ by adding distance information for ϵ^- and ϵ^+: ϵ^- has distance 0 to any solution and ϵ^+ has distance $k + 1$ to any original solution. To avoid loopholes regarding $k = 0$, the distance value for each original solution pair is increased by 1 for $\Delta^{\pm}$, therefore k has to be updated as well $(k^{\pm} = k + 1)$. The "negative" solution ϵ^- is added to the initial solution set $S^{\pm} = S \cup \{\epsilon^-\}$, whereas the "positive" solution ϵ^+ remains as potential solution to compensate for the forced selection of ϵ^-. Both instances return the same value for their problem:

$\Gamma_{\mathcal{PA}}^{\leq m}(S, k) \Rightarrow \Gamma_{\mathcal{P}^{\pm}\Delta^{\pm}}^{\leq m+1}(S^{\pm}, k^{\pm})$: if there is a solution set S' for s.t. $|S'| > |S|$, $|S \backslash S'| \leq m$ and $\Delta(S') \geq k$ with $\epsilon^-, \epsilon^+ \notin (S \cup S')$ then the solution set $S^{\pm'} = S' \cup \{\epsilon^+\}$ satisfies all criteria for $\Gamma_{\mathcal{P}^{\pm}\Delta^{\pm}}^{\leq m+1}(S \cup \{\epsilon^-\}, k + 1)$: $|S^{\pm'}| > |S \cup \{\epsilon^-\}|$, $|(S \cup \{\epsilon^-\}) \backslash S^{\pm'}| \leq m + 1$ and $\Delta^{\pm}(S^{\pm'}) \geq k + 1$.

$\Gamma_{\mathcal{P}^{\pm}\Delta^{\pm}}^{\leq m+1}(S^{\pm}, k^{\pm}) \Rightarrow \Gamma_{\mathcal{PA}}^{\leq m}(S, k)$: if there is a solution set $S^{\pm'}$ such that $|S^{\pm'}| > |S \cup \{\epsilon^-\}|$, $|(S \cup \{\epsilon^-\}) \backslash S^{\pm'}| \leq m + 1$ and $\Delta^{\pm}(S^{\pm'}) \geq k + 1$ (implying $\epsilon^-, \epsilon^+ \notin S$ and $\epsilon^- \notin S^{\pm'}$) then $S' = S^{\pm'} \backslash \{\epsilon^+\}$ satisfies $|S'| > |S|$, $|S \backslash S'| \leq m$ and $\Delta(S') \geq k$. This implication holds for both cases $\epsilon^+ \in S^{\pm'}$ and $\epsilon^+ \notin S^{\pm'}$.

$\square$

Theorem 1. *Problem* $\Gamma_{\mathcal{PA}}^{\leq m}$ *- m-DIFFERENT k-DISTANT SET is NP-complete.*

Proof. As proven in Lemma 3 there exists a hierarchy within $\Gamma_{\mathcal{PA}}^{\leq m}$ where $\Gamma_{\mathcal{PA}}^{\leq m} \leq_p \Gamma_{\mathcal{PA}}^{\leq m+1}$. Since the problem for the lowest m $(m = 0)$ corresponds to the NP-complete problem $\Gamma_{\mathcal{PA}}^{+1}$ (Lemma 1), all problems are NP-hard. And since the top-most problem $(m = |S|)$ corresponds to the NP-complete problem $\Gamma_{\mathcal{PA}}^{nk}$(Lemma 2) all problems in the hierarchy lie within NP. Since lower and upper bound are NP-complete, all problems in $\Gamma_{\mathcal{PA}}^{\leq m}$ are NP-complete as well. $\square$

3.2 Reworking Methods

The *Trade Up Navigation for Answer Sets* (short *Tunas*) approach is a framework that allows to solve $\Gamma_{\mathcal{PA}}^{nk}$ by iteratively solving $\Gamma_{\mathcal{PA}}^{\leq m}$. The core idea is to remove up to m solutions from a collection to gain a larger collection, therefore improving the result. Since $\Gamma_{\mathcal{PA}}^{\leq m}$ is easier to compute than $\Gamma_{\mathcal{PA}}^{\leq m+1}$, the approach begins with $m = 0$ and ends at a given maximal value $m = M$. Like this, building an initial collection equals Online2. Only when the program becomes unsatisfiable, the actual reworking process starts working. An outline of the general implementation can be seen in Algorithm 1. The different implementations of the core function *replaceM(ctl, m, pool, idx)*, which provides deletion candidates and new solutions, are explained afterwards.

Some notes to the general framework: The logic program itself is handled by the control structure *ctl* which allows for grounding and solving as well as for additional functionality such as managing external atoms. The wrapper script uses indices to reference solutions, the set *pool* holds all indices from the current

---

Algorithm 1: Tunas Framework

Input: A fitting multi-shot logic program P, minimum distance measure K,
number of solutions N, maximum Number M of deletion candidates, set
Init of subprograms to ground initially, implementation of *replaceM*

1 $ctl.load(P)$
2 $ctl.ground(Init)$ // **ground original program**
3 $idx \leftarrow 1$
4 $pool \leftarrow \{\}$
5 **do** :
6   **for** $m \leftarrow 0$ **to** M :
7           $(delS, newS, idx) \leftarrow replaceM(ctl, m, pool, idx)$ // **core function**
8   **if** $newS \neq \emptyset$:
9   **for** $del \in delS$:
10                  $ctl.release\_external(\text{visible}(del))$ // **remove from collection**
11              $pool \leftarrow (\, pool \setminus delS\,) \cup newS$
12   **break**
13 **while** $(|pool| \leq N)$ **and** $(newS \neq \emptyset)$

---

collection. The basic framework consists mainly of two loops: one to enlarge the collection and one to escalate the current m up to the maximum M. A core function is called (line **7**) to solve the current problem which returns indices of deletion candidates ($delS$) and indices of new solutions ($newS$) to be added to the collection. If a solution for the current m was found, the deletion is made permanent by releasing corresponding atoms (line **10**) and updating the set *pool* which represents the collection. Also the current escalation of m is disrupted to start over from 0.

Since the basic framework is explained, let us have a detailed look into the possible implementations of *replaceM*. Each implemtation requires a base program in the form of subprogram calls (*Init*, line **2**).

TunasMND. implements generating multiple (M) solutions and nondeterministic (ND) choosing of deletion candidates. In other words: the logic program guesses the deletion candidates and generates all new solutions in a single call. An outline of the wrapper functionality can be seen in Algorithm 2 implementing *replaceM* from the framework in Algorithm 1. The initial program (see *Init* from Algorithm 2) contains the subprogram names of the modified original program. For TunasMND this is comparable to Online1 to compute up to $M + 1$ diverse solutions.

The amount m of deletion candidates (and consequently $m + 1$ new solutions) is predetermined by the wrapper and passed onto the logic program via an assumption over a corresponding predicate (*line* **1**). An internal mechanism induces the temporary concealment of exactly m solutions. If successful, their indices can be extracted from the model (*line* **8**). Also the model contains $m + 1$ new solutions. The #show directive (*line* **2**) within the logic program is used to distinguish between solution defining atoms (*goal atoms*) and auxiliary atoms.

Algorithm 2: TunasMND - *replaceM*(*ctl, m, pool, idx*) : (*delS, newS, idx*)

Input: A control structure *ctl* which handles the current logic program, a
        number $m \geqslant 0$ of deletion candidates, a set *pool* of indices representing
        established solutions, the next solution index *idx*
Output: A set of indices referencing to deletion candidates, a set of indices
        referencing to new solutions, the next solution index

1 **if** $mdl \leftarrow ctl.solve(assumption = \{(\mathsf{chooseNum}(m), true)\})$:
2 $\quad\quad grnd \leftarrow \{p(idx+i, t_1, ..., t_k) : p(i, t_1, ..., t_k) \in mdl \wedge \#show(p(i, t_1, ..., t_k)) \in Init\}$
3 $\quad\quad registerPredicates(ctl, grnd)$
4 $\quad\quad ctl.ground(grnd)$
5 $\quad\quad$ **for** $i \leftarrow 0$ **to** m :
6 $\quad\quad\quad\quad ctl.ground(\{itDistM(idx + i)\})$
7 $\quad\quad\quad\quad ctl.assign\_external(\mathsf{visible}(idx + i), true)$
8 $\quad\quad$ **return**($\{i : \mathsf{choose}(i) \in mdl\}, \{idx, ..., idx+m\}, idx+m+1$)
9 **return**($\emptyset, \emptyset, idx$)

Since generated solutions proceed to become collected solutions, their index is updated before grounding them back into the logic program (*line* **2**).

For multi-shot programs, adding atoms to a program is possible by defining sub-programs which contain the atoms. We implemented the function *registerPredicates* to construct and register those subprograms automatically, allowing flexible and dynamic handling of heterogenous goal atoms. Afterwards the distance constraints for the new solutions are grounded (*line* **6**), which become active, when setting the corresponding external atom to *true* (*line* **7**).

If successful the set of indices for the deletion candidates and the newly generated solutions are returned (*line* **8**). Otherwise empty sets are returned.

TunasMIT implements generating multiple (M) solutions and iterative (IT) choosing of deletion candidates: all new solutions are generated at once, while the deletion candidates are provided by the wrapper. In comparison to TunasMND, two mayor changes are required: disabling the choosing mechanism and handling the deletion candidates before solving. The candidates are selected by iterating over all combinations of size m from the set *pool*. The current set of deletion candidates is temporarily excluded from the collection by setting the corresponding external key predicate (visible/1) to *false* before solving the current program. If no solution could be found, the deletion candidates are made visible again and the wrapper continues with the next combination of m deletion candidates.

We will use *TunasM* to address TunasMIT and TunasMND at once.

TunasS implements the single (S) generating, iterative choosing (IT) approach. The underlying logic program is an extension of the logic program for Online2 - in fact Online2 and TunasS are equivalent for $M = 0$. In comparison to TunasMIT the solve call is embedded into another loop because each solve call generates only one instead of $m + 1$ solutions. The currently generated solution streak is held in limbo until either all $m + 1$ solutions could be computed or the program becomes unsatisfiable, resulting in the deletion of the current streak.

We left out the single solving (S), nondeterministic choosing (ND) approach due to contradiction in progression: The (ongoing) suggestion of deletion candidates requires the program to stay unaltered in case the generating part fails and different deletion candidates need to be derived. Yet at the same time the program needs to be updated and solved to generate solutions. Splitting the program into two separate programs boils down to TunasS.

4 Experimental Evaluation

To show feasibility of our approach, we compare it with the established methods Online1 and Online2. The evaluation focuses around solving $\Gamma_{\mathcal{PA}}^{k\uparrow}$- n-MOST DIVERSE SOLUTIONS, which combines highest complexity along with highest relevance for applications. We analyse the behaviour of the approaches regarding the following questions: **Q1**: Is the Tunas approach competitive with existing methods in terms of solving the problem $\Gamma_{\mathcal{PA}}^{k\uparrow}$? **Q2**: How do the approaches perform in time? **Q3**: How reliable are the methods?

Software: We implemented our approaches along with Online1 and a multishot version of Online2. Online1 was extended to maximise for k to solve $\Gamma_{\mathcal{PA}}^{k\uparrow}$. The other approaches required repetitive solving $\Gamma_{\mathcal{PA}}^{nk}(n, k)$ for increasing k since they only semi-decide $\Gamma_{\mathcal{PA}}^{nk}(n, k)$: if $\Gamma_{\mathcal{PA}}^{nk}(n, k)$ was satisfied, k is incremented. This repeats infinitely but can be interrupted at any time (timeout).

Setup and Hardware: Our environment is a virtual machine (Debian 5.10.46, 64Bit, Intel Xeon Gold, 3 GHz, clingo 5.5, python 3.8.8). We tested for $n \in \{3, 5, 10, 15, 25\}$, timeout at 300 s sharp. Each configuration was repeated 20 times. We use random generated seeds (random frequency: 10%). The test-setup including all data is available for download [7].

Test instances: We used 5 instances for our evaluation: (**I1**) Phylogenesis (ancestry tress for languages) and (**I2**) blocks-world (planing problem) from [9] (**I3**) PC configurator (configuration problem) from [20] (with 2 instead of the default 10 hardware instances) (**I4**) an encoding of stable extensions and (**I5**) preferred extensions, both for the same argumentation framework (AF) instance [13]. I1 uses a custom distance (nodal), all other use hamming distance. The first three instances have a vast search space ($>10^9$ answer sets). The AF instances **I4** and **I5** share an identical and comparatively small solution space (7696 answer sets), but the problem classes differ in complexity.

The average maximal k for **I3**, **I4** and **I5** are listed in Table 1. For **I1** and **I2** all approaches reached the maximal k, and thus they will not be discussed further here. We ordered the methods from non-deterministic to iterative, where each Tunas method is evaluated for $M \in \{1, 2\}$. The entries can be ranked for

Table 1. maximal k for $\Gamma_{\mathcal{PA}}^{k\uparrow}(n)$ for 3 instances, average over 20 runs. For Tunas numbers outside (resp. inside) of brackets reference to $M = 1$ (resp. $M = 2$). * marks a proven maximal value by Online1, best results are bold.

PC I3	$n = 3$		$n = 5$		$n = 10$		$n = 15$		$n = 25$	
Online1	**46.5**		37.7		29.3		23.7		9.3	
TunasMND	42.5	(43.2)	39.5	**(40.0)**	36.2	(36.3)	33.8	(33.9)	23.4	(22.3)
TunasMIT	42.0	(43.0)	39.8	(39.6)	36.4	(36.1)	**34.0**	**(34.0)**	30.6	(30.9)
TunasS	41.9	(42.0)	39.8	(39.7)	**36.5**	(36.4)	**34.0**	**(34.0)**	**31.1**	(30.9)
Online2	42.0		39.8		36.2		33.9		30.9	
AF stable I4	$n = 3$		$n = 5$		$n = 10$		$n = 15$		$n = 25$	
Online1	**81.0***		**63.0**		47.9		40.9		34.3	
TunasMND	**81.0**	**(81.0)**	61.8	(61.7)	48.8	(48.3)	42.0	(42.0)	**36.0**	(35.5)
TunasMIT	**81.0**	**(81.0)**	61.7	(62.2)	48.4	**(48.9)**	42.2	(42.3)	**36.0**	(35.9)
TunasS	**81.0**	**(81.0)**	61.6	(62.1)	48.4	(48.8)	42.3	**(43.0)**	**36.0**	(35.9)
Online2	75.1		58.6		46.4		41.0		35.0	
AF pref. I5	$n = 3$		$n = 5$		$n = 10$		$n = 15$		$n = 25$	
Online1	54.9		35.1		23.2		15.1		5.1	
TunasMND	77.6	(73.7)	54.0	(54.1)	43.5	(43.9)	37.9	(37.7)	31.4	(31.1)
TunasMIT	**77.8**	(73.2)	54.5	(54.4)	43.2	(43.9)	37.9	(37.6)	31.2	(30.9)
TunasS	70.7	(72.2)	55.4	(55.9)	44.3	(44.0)	38.1	(38.1)	31.9	(31.4)
Online2	71.9		**56.7**		**45.0**		**39.1**		**33.1**	

each instance and n, for example for **I4** and $n = 5$, Online1 has the highest value (63.0), whereas the Online2 has the lowest value (58.6), implying better results from Online1 than Online2 for this setting.

In general we observe that Online1 performs best for smaller n, which is not surprising since the size of the problem encoding is related to n. For **I3** all iterative methods perform on the same level (except TunasMND for $n = 25$). Notably is the lead for Online1 for $n = 3$, which results from low chances to guess a solution which can form a diverse collection of size 3. A closer look at the data reveals that **I3** has no repeating attempts, implying high time cost for returning unsatisfiable. This explains the equal performance of the iterative methods, since all Tunas methods start with $m = 0$ and are unable to progress to $m = 1$.

The upper bounds of k for **I4** and **I5** are identical since they share an identical solution space, but belong to different complexity classes. Online1 shows good results for **I4**, even leading for $n \leq 5$ but performs worst for **I5**. Online2 performs unexpected sub-optimal for **I4** but leads for **I5**. For **I4** all Tunas methods perform at similar levels. For **I5** TunasS performs slightly better than TunasM with exception for $n = 3$ where TunasM outperforms all other methods. To better

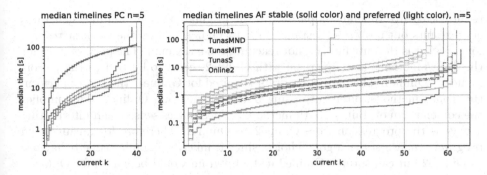

Fig. 1. Median timelines of current k for 20 runs, $n = 5$. Tunas methods: solid lines for $M = 2$, striped lines for $M = 1$. The right figure includes AF stable (solid colors) and AF preferred (light colors).

understand the results, the median[3] run time can be seen in Fig. 1 for $n = 5$. The maximal value on the x-axis for each curve corresponds to the data in Table 1 while the y-axis reflects the median time to reach the corresponding k. The optimal curves are wide and flat: large k values for low execution times. The plot visualises also different results for different timeouts. For Example with $timeout = 10$ s TunasS has a larger k for both AF instances as Online2, implying better performance for this timeout. Timelines for TunasS and Online2 progress similar, while TunasM requires more time for larger M. In contrast to the iterative methods, Online1 has unsteady escalation times. One interesting curve is Online2 for **I4**: at around $k = 56$ Online2 struggles to keep the pace, implying lower probability of satisfying $\Gamma_{\mathcal{P}\Delta}^{nk}(n, k)$. This effect can be seen for the Tunas methods as well but for higher k. The curves for **I3** (PC, $n = 5$) hint an explanation to the performance drop of TunasMND for $n = 25$: since TunasMND progresses significantly slower it is expected to be the first to suffer a performance decline for increased difficulty or lower timeout.

Now, let us answer the question. **Q1**: None of the evaluated methods is superior, all methods lead at least once for maximal k. The outcome depends highly on the instance, n and the timeout. **Q2**: Online1 is fastest for lower n. Also it is the only terminating approach, since the other approaches are allowed to start over. Online2 is the fastest method, providing good results in a short amount of time. TunasS behaves similar as Online2: in most cases they are comparable in speed and performance. Depending on instance, n and timeout one performs better than the other. The TunasM methods proceed comparatively slow but perform surprisingly good in some cases, such as **I5** for $n = 3$. The value of M seems to have no major impact for TunasS, but for TunasM; the performance differs most for $n = 3$. Also a higher M is often related to higher computation time, which is important for low timeouts. **Q3**: Online1 is suited for smaller n but can not guarantee providing any result, since grounding and solving may

---

[3] Not all timelines cover the same k due to the time limit, distorting the mean value. The median is robust against those outliers by setting missing data to the time limit.

require excessive time in comparison to the original problem. Online2 generates good results but not for all instances: for **I4** Online2 shows the weakest results, for $n = 3$ it is the only method not reaching the maximum. The performance for the Tunas methods in comparison with Online2 seems to be tied to the performance of Online1: The more a program is suited for Online1, the better perform the Tunas methods, often surpassing both, Online1 and Online2. This implies the combination of traits of both methods, which makes sense when interpreting Tunas as the progression from Online2 to Online1. Therefore for an unknown program, TunasS states a good choice, since it inherits a similar time behaviour as Online2 but can surpass Online2 if the program would be suited for Online1.

5   Conclusion and Future Work

We presented a novel and competitive approach to compute diverse answer sets of logic programs based on reworking methods. To characterise the base mechanism, we introduced a new problem related to the approach and prove NP-completeness. Basic analysis of the approach leads to three elaborations, which we implemented along with two methods from Eiter et al. [9] (as multi-shot variant). Our empirical evaluation to find n-MOST DIVERSE SOLUTIONS reveals no superior method, since problem instance, number n of solutions and timeout highly influence the performance. However the Tunas methods show promising results, especially for large solution spaces and typical NP problems.

For future work, we believe investigating the connection of facet counting weights [13] and diverse answer sets is a promising direction. Furthermore, the extension to preferred logic programs would be of interest [23].

Acknowledgements. This work was partly supported by Deutsche Forschungsgemeinschaft (DFG) in project 389792660 (TRR 248, Center for Perspicuous Systems), and by the Bundesministerium für Bildung und Forschung (BMBF) in project 01IS20056_NAVAS.

References

1. Abels, D., Jordi, J., Ostrowski, M., Schaub, T., Toletti, A., Wanko, P.: Train scheduling with hybrid answer set programming. TPLP **21**(3), 317–347 (2021)
2. Alviano, M., et al.: The ASP System DLV2. In: Balduccini, M., Janhunen, T. (eds.) LPNMR 2017. LNCS (LNAI), vol. 10377, pp. 215–221. Springer, Cham (2017). https://doi.org/10.1007/978-3-319-61660-5_19
3. Alviano, M., Dodaro, C.: Anytime answer set optimization via unsatisfiable core shrinking. TPLP **16**(5–6), 533–551 (2016)
4. Alviano, M., Dodaro, C., Faber, W., Leone, N., Ricca, F.: WASP: a native ASP solver based on constraint learning. In: Cabalar, P., Son, T.C. (eds.) LPNMR 2013. LNCS (LNAI), vol. 8148, pp. 54–66. Springer, Heidelberg (2013). https://doi.org/10.1007/978-3-642-40564-8_6
5. Alviano, M., Romero, J., Schaub, T.: Preference relations by approximation. In: Thielscher, M., Toni, F., Wolter, F. (eds.) Proceedings of KR 2018, pp. 2–11. AAAI Press (2018)

6. Brewka, G., Delgrande, J.P., Romero, J., Schaub, T.: asprin: Customizing answer set preferences without a headache. In: Bonet, B., Koenig, S. (eds.) Proceedings of AAAI 2015, pp. 1467–1474. AAAI Press (2015)
7. Böhl, E., Gaggl, S.A.: Tunas - Fishing for diverse Answer Sets: a Multi- Shot Trade up Strategy (Tool & Experiments), June 2022. https://doi.org/10.5281/zenodo.6762554
8. Dimopoulos, Y., Nebel, B., Koehler, J.: Encoding planning problems in nonmonotonic logic programs. In: Steel, S., Alami, R. (eds.) ECP 1997. LNCS, vol. 1348, pp. 169–181. Springer, Heidelberg (1997). https://doi.org/10.1007/3-540-63912-8_84
9. Eiter, T., Erdem, E., Erdogan, H., Fink, M.: Finding similar/diverse solutions in answer set programming. Theory Pract. Log. Program. 13(3), 303–359 (2013)
10. Eiter, T., Falkner, A.A., Schneider, P., Schüller, P.: Asp-based signal plan adjustments for traffic flow optimization. In: Giacomo, G.D., et al. (eds.) Proceedings of ECAI 2020, FAIA, vol. 325, pp. 3026–3033. IOS Press (2020)
11. Erdem, E., Lifschitz, V.: Transformations of logic programs related to causality and planning. In: Gelfond, M., Leone, N., Pfeifer, G. (eds.) LPNMR 1999. LNCS (LNAI), vol. 1730, pp. 107–116. Springer, Heidelberg (1999). https://doi.org/10.1007/3-540-46767-X_8
12. Faber, W.: An introduction to answer set programming and some of its extensions. In: Manna, M., Pieris, A. (eds.) Reasoning Web 2020. LNCS, vol. 12258, pp. 149–185. Springer, Cham (2020). https://doi.org/10.1007/978-3-030-60067-9_6
13. Fichte, J.K., Gaggl, S.A., Rusovac, D.: Rushing and strolling among answer sets - navigation made easy. In: Proceedings of AAAI 2022 (2022)
14. Gebser, M., Kaminski, R., Kaufmann, B., Schaub, T.: Multi-shot asp solving with clingo. TPLP 19(1), 27–82 (2019)
15. Gebser, M., Kaminski, R., Schaub, T.: Complex optimization in answer set programming. TPLP 11(4–5), 821–839 (2011)
16. Gebser, M., Kaufmann, B., Kaminski, R., Ostrowski, M., Schaub, T., Schneider, M.: Potassco: the potsdam answer set solving collection. AI Commun. 24(2), 107–124 (2011)
17. Gebser, M., Maratea, M., Ricca, F.: The seventh answer set programming competition: design and results. TPLP 20(2), 176–204 (2020)
18. Gelfond, M., Lifschitz, V.: The stable model semantics for logic programming. In: Kowalski, R., Bowen, Kenneth (eds.) Proceedings of International Logic Programming Conference and Symposium, pp. 1070–1080. MIT Press (1988)
19. Gençay, E., Schüller, P., Erdem, E.: Applications of non-monotonic reasoning to automotive product configuration using answer set programming. J. Intell. Manuf. 30(3), 1407–1422 (2017). https://doi.org/10.1007/s10845-017-1333-3
20. Gorczyca, P.: Configuration Problem ASP Encoding Generator (2020). https://doi.org/10.5281/zenodo.5777217
21. Janhunen, T., Kaminski, R., Ostrowski, M., Schellhorn, S., Wanko, P., Schaub, T.: Clingo goes linear constraints over reals and integers. TPLP 17(5–6), 872–888 (2017)
22. Kahraman, M.K., Erdem, E.: Personalized course schedule planning using answer set programming. In: Alferes, J.J., Johansson, M. (eds.) PADL 2019. LNCS, vol. 11372, pp. 37–45. Springer, Cham (2019). https://doi.org/10.1007/978-3-030-05998-9_3
23. Romero, J., Schaub, T., Wanko, P.: Computing diverse optimal stable models. In: Carro, M., King, A., Saeedloei, N., Vos, M.D. (eds.) TC of ICLP 2016. OASIcs, vol. 52, pp. 3:1–3:14. Schloss Dagstuhl-Leibniz-Zentrum fuer Informatik (2016)

24. Soininen, T., Niemelä, I.: Developing a declarative rule language for applications in product configuration. In: Gupta, G. (ed.) PADL 1999. LNCS, vol. 1551, pp. 305–319. Springer, Heidelberg (1998). https://doi.org/10.1007/3-540-49201-1_21
25. Soininen, T., Niemelä, I., Tiihonen, J., Sulonen, R.: Representing configuration knowledge with weight constraint rules. In: Provetti, A., Son, T.C. (eds.) Proceedings of ASP 2001 (2001)

Emotional Reasoning in an Action Language for Emotion-Aware Planning

Andreas Brännström$^{(\boxtimes)}$ and Juan Carlos Nieves

Department of Computing Science, Umeå University, 901 87 Umeå, Sweden
{andreasb,jcnieves}@cs.umu.se

Abstract. This paper introduces formal models for emotional reasoning, expressing emotional states and emotional causality, using action reasoning and transition systems. A general framework is defined, comprised of two main components: 1) a model for emotions based on the Appraisal theory of Emotion (AE), and 2) a model for emotional change based on Hedonic Emotion Regulation (HER). A particular transition system is modelled in which states correspond to human emotional states and transitions correspond to restrictive (safe) ways to influence emotions while reducing negative emotional side-effects. The introduced emotional reasoning can be applied to guide a software agent's actions for dealing with emotions while estimating and planning future interactions with humans.

Keywords: Emotional reasoning · Human-aware planning · Action languages · Appraisal theory

1 Introduction

An aim in the area of Human-Agent Interaction (HAI) is to develop interactive cognitive systems that are *human-aware*, providing a proactive and personalized interaction. Human-Aware Planning (HAP) [11] regards a scenario where an intelligent system is situated in an environment populated by humans, in which the system must plan its actions by meeting the requirements of human plans and goals. In order for a software agent to execute suitable actions in interactions with humans, the agent must consider the mental states of its human interlocutors in its internal reasoning and decision-making. This is an ability, referred to as Theory of Mind (ToM) [12], to infer another agent's beliefs, such as emotions, motivations, goals and intentions. We need to develop dynamic ways for systems to compute a ToM of their users, making systems aware of human mental properties and their causes. "Emotions" play a fundamental role in human behavior and interactions [2]. By providing a system mathematical computational models for emotional reasoning [9] when planning its actions, interaction capabilities of an agent can be greatly improved. The software agent must be aware of what emotions that are present in the mind of the human and what emotions that can be triggered, in each state of the interaction.

© The Author(s), under exclusive license to Springer Nature Switzerland AG 2022
G. Gottlob et al. (Eds.): LPNMR 2022, LNAI 13416, pp. 103–116, 2022.
https://doi.org/10.1007/978-3-031-15707-3_9

Challenges when building *emotion-aware* [4] interactive systems include to provide capabilities of: 1) backward reasoning, e.g., recognizing and reasoning about causes of emotions, 2) context reasoning, e.g., evaluating timely and appropriate emotional states, 3) forward reasoning, e.g., predicting the effects of their actions on emotions of humans, and 4) action reasoning for adapting their behaviors accordingly, promoting appropriate emotions while avoiding unintended emotional side-effects. To achieve such capabilities, intelligent systems require models that capture explanations to why and how emotions arise and change. Previous approaches to computational emotional reasoning [1,9,12,14] mainly focus on recognizing emotional context, e.g., by simulating emotional behavior [12] or to model expected human behavior in response to emotions [9], and do not capture explanations for emotional change as state transitions. In order to predict the effects of an agent's actions on emotions of humans, the agent needs a way to reason backward and forward using models that specify how human emotions are caused and change, in terms of states and transitions. Given the challenges of emotional reasoning in the setting of HAI, the following research question arises:—How to track emotional states of human agents in a goal-oriented interaction between humans and software agents?

We introduce a methodology to model emotional state transitions by formalizing two emotion theories, the Appraisal theory of Emotion (AE) [6] and Hedonic Emotion Regulation (HER) [17], capturing links between human emotions and their underlying beliefs, using transition systems and action reasoning [7]. To this end, a set of action specifications is introduced, C_{AE}, that captures transitions between human emotions. The proposed emotional reasoning framework regards two main components: 1) a model for emotion representation, following the psychological theory of AE, through which a set of 16 basic human emotions is explained, and 2) a model for emotional change, following the theory of HER, aiming to increase positive emotion and decrease negative emotion.

This paper is organized as follows. In Sect. 2, the state-of-the-art in emotional reasoning is presented. In Sect. 3, the theoretical (computational and psychological) background is presented. In Sect. 4, syntax and semantics of the proposed emotional framework reasoning are presented. Finally, in Sect. 5 and 6, the paper is concluded by discussing potential applications, limitations, and directions for future work.

2   Related Work

There is a diverse body of research related to the ideas presented in the present work. In the area of affective agents and computational theory of mind [1,12], agent models have been developed to reason about emotion and behavior. For instance, agents based on Partially Observable Markov Decision Processes (POMDP) [12] have been used to (similar to the present study) model appraisal and emotion. Their models show potential in simulating human emotional behavior. They have, however, lacked to capture human emotional change to deliberate about emotion regulation, future interactions and emotional effects of actions.

A variety of Emotion BDI (Belief, Desire, Intention) frameworks [9,14,15] have been introduced. These approaches have aimed, e.g., to model behaviors which are expected from agents under the influence of emotions [14], or to provide modular generic interfaces for emotional agents [9] to enable emotion theory-based models as filters for emotional reasoning. While these works define generic architectures for emotional agents, they need to be coupled with emotion theory-based models to enable reasoning about emotional change, and human-aware reasoning to avoid unintended emotional side-effects in their interactions.

3   Theoretical Background

This section presents the emotion theories of AE and HER, the theoretical base of the proposed emotional reasoning framework. The section then presents action reasoning languages and transition systems, serving as a platform on which emotional reasoning is formalized and characterized.

3.1   Emotion Theories: AE and HER

AE [6] proposes that emotions are caused by an appraisal of a situation in terms of 1) being consistent or inconsistent with needs, 2) being consistent or inconsistent with goals, 3) the accountability of a situation, which can be the environment, others, or oneself, and 4) as being easy or difficult to control. According to AE, the difference between goal consistency and need consistency determines negative, stable and positive emotions. More intense negative emotions (e.g., Anger or Fear) arise when the need consistency is greater than the goal consistency, while less intense negative emotions can arise when both the need consistency and goal consistency are low. On the other hand, positive emotions (e.g., Joy or Liking) arise when the goal consistency is greater than the need consistency, or when both are high. By ranking consistency values as Low < Undecided < High and by looking at the difference between need and goal consistency, positive and negative emotions can be distinguished.

HER [17] is a theory for regulating emotions, guided by the goals to 1) increase positive emotion and 2) decrease negative emotion. According to HER, both of these emotion regulation goals are associated with improved well-being, where decreasing of negative emotion has been most effective [13]. The principles of HER can be applied in the framework of AE to reason about emotional change.

3.2   Action Reasoning and Transition Systems

A transition system is a directed graph, whose nodes correspond to states (configurations of variables) and edges correspond to valid transitions between states. A transition system has an initial state (the current observation) and a set of goal states (which it aims to reach). Action reasoning [7] regards logical descriptions of actions that result in transitions between states. As a platform for our emotional reasoning specification, we build on the action language $\mathcal{C}_{TAID}$ [5]. The alphabet of $\mathcal{C}_{TAID}$ consists of two nonempty disjoint sets of symbols $\mathbf{F}$ and $\mathbf{A}$. They are called the set of fluents $\mathbf{F}$ and the set of actions $\mathbf{A}$. A *fluent* expresses a property of an object in a world, and forms part of the description of states of the world. A *fluent literal* is a fluent or a fluent preceded by $\neg$. A *state* σ is a collection of fluents. A fluent f holds in a state σ if $f \in \sigma$. A fluent literal $\neg f$ holds in σ if $f \notin \sigma$.

4   Emotional Reasoning

The contribution of the paper starts in this section, which presents an emotional reasoning specification, $\mathcal{C}_{AE}$. Components of AE are formalized as a particular transition system, called an emotion decision-graph (EDG), to reason about emotional states and (safe) emotional change to reduce unintended emotional side-effects. The EDG specifies transitions between emotional states (in terms of HER), which serve as safety restrictions for emotion-influencing actions.

Recall that AE defines emotions as a composition of an individual's appraisal of a situation, in terms of consistency with needs, consistency with goals, accountability and control potential. By following this definition of emotional causes, we specify states with emotion fluents and values of the following form:

- need_consistency(ne), $ne \in \{\text{low} = l, \text{high} = h, \text{undecided} = u\}$,
- goal_consistency(go), $go \in \{\text{low} = l, \text{high} = h, \text{undecided} = u\}$,
- accountability(ac), $ac \in \{\text{environment} = e, \text{others} = o, \text{self} = s, \text{undecided} = u\}$,
- control_potential(co), $co \in \{\text{low} = l, \text{high} = h, \text{undecided} = u\}$

By defining a set of emotions following AE in this way, and by utilizing principles of hedonic emotion regulation, we can specify preferable (safe) transitions between emotional states. In the following subsection, we specify an EDG to reason about emotional transitions.

4.1   Emotion Decision-Graph (EDG)

Following AE, 16 emotional states are specified, one for each basic emotion explained by AE theory, i.e., {Anger, Dislike, Disgust, Sadness, Hope, Frustration, Fear, Distress, Joy, Liking, Pride, Surprise, Relief, Regret, Shame, Guilt}. We can model these states and transitions as a graph, an EDG, that represents a prioritized focus of emotional change given a recognized emotional state (see Fig. 1).

Definition 1. *An emotion decision-graph EDG is a transition system that is a tuple of the form $EDG = (E, Act, T, O)$ where E is a non-empty set of states such that each state contains emotion fluents in terms of AE, Act is a set of actions, $T \subseteq E \times E$ is a non-empty set of transition relations between emotional states, O is a set of initial observations.*

The emotion decision-graph is formalized by the semantics of the action language specification $\mathcal{C}_{AE}$, serving as restrictions for safe emotional change, presented in the following section.

Anger	Hope	Joy	Relief
ne:h go:l ac:o co:h	ne:u go:h ac:e co:l	ne:h go:h ac:e co:u	ne:h go:h ac:e co:u

Dislike	Frustration	Liking	Regret
ne:u go:l ac:o co:l	ne:h go:l ac:e co:h	ne:u go:h ac:o co:u	ne:u go:l ac:s co:l

Disgust	Fear	Pride	Shame
ne:l go:l ac:e co:h	ne:u go:l ac:e co:l	ne:u go:h ac:s co:u	ne:l go:l ac:s co:h

Sadness	Distress	Surprise	Guilt
ne:h go:l ac:e co:l	ne:l go:l ac:e co:l	ne:u go:u ac:e co:u	ne:h go:h ac:s co:h

Fig. 1. Emotional states following Appraisal theory of Emotion [6].

4.2 Action Language Specifications

$\mathcal{C}_{AE}$ is comprised of sets of symbols to represent emotional appraisals, which define an emotion-aware alphabet as follows:

Definition 2 (Emotion-aware alphabet). *Let* **A** *be a non-empty set of actions and* **F** *be a non-empty set of fluents.*

- $\mathbf{F} = \mathbf{F}^E \cup \mathbf{F}^H$ *such that* $\mathbf{F}^E$ *is a non-empty set of fluent literals describing observable items in an environment and* $\mathbf{F}^H$ *is a non-empty set of fluent literals describing the emotional-states of humans.* $\mathbf{F}^E$ *and* $\mathbf{F}^H$ *are pairwise disjoint.*
- $\mathbf{F}^H = \mathbf{F}^N \cup \mathbf{F}^G \cup \mathbf{F}^A \cup \mathbf{F}^C$ *such that* $\mathbf{F}^N, \mathbf{F}^G, \mathbf{F}^A$ *and* $\mathbf{F}^C$ *are non-empty pairwise disjoint sets of fluent literals describing a human agent's need consistency, goal consistency, accountability and control potential, respectively.*
- $\mathbf{A} = \mathbf{A}^E \cup \mathbf{A}^H$ *such that* $\mathbf{A}^E$ *is a non-empty set of actions that can be performed by a software agent and* $\mathbf{A}^H$ *is non-empty set of actions that can be performed by a human agent.* $\mathbf{A}^E$ *and* $\mathbf{A}^H$ *are pairwise disjoint.*

Definition 3 (Emotion fluent). *An emotion fluent is a predicate f(X, Y, Z) of arity 3 such that* $X \in \{ne, go, ac, co\}$, $Y \in \{l, h, u, e, o, s\}$ *and* $Z \in \mathbb{N} \cup \{0\}$. *An emotion fluent f(X, Y, Z) is well-formed if the following conditions hold true:*

1. *if* $X \in ne, go, co$, *then* $Y \in \{l, h, u\}$
2. *if* $X = ac$, *then* $Y \in \{e, o, s, u\}$

where ne represents need consistency, go represents goal consistency, ac represents accountability and co represents control potential; l represents low, h represents high, u represents undecided, e represents environment, o represents other and s represents self; and Z represents a point in time.

$\mathcal{C}_{AE}$ defines a set of static and dynamic causal laws of actions. These laws specify emotional influences, either as effects of actions or as indirect causal effects. Laws for emotional change work by influencing appraisal of a situation in the human agent while complying with the constraints of the EDG.

Definition 4 (Emotion-aware domain description language). *An emotion-aware domain description language $D^{ae}(\mathbf{A}, \mathbf{F})$ consists of static and dynamic causal laws of the following form:*

$\mathcal{C}_{TAID}$ domain description language:

$$(a \textbf{ causes } f_1, \ldots, f_n \textbf{ if } g_1, \ldots g_m) \tag{1}$$
$$(f_1, \ldots, f_n \textbf{ if } g_1, \ldots g_m) \tag{2}$$
$$(f_1, \ldots, f_n \textbf{ triggers } a) \tag{3}$$
$$(f_1, \ldots, f_n \textbf{ allows } a) \tag{4}$$
$$(f_1, \ldots, f_n \textbf{ inhibits } a) \tag{5}$$
$$(\textbf{noconcurrency } a_1, \ldots, a_n) \tag{6}$$
$$(\textbf{default } g) \tag{7}$$

$\mathcal{C}_{AE}$ emotional reasoning extension:

$$(a \textbf{ influences need consistency } f \textbf{ if } f_1, \ldots f_n) \tag{8}$$
$$(a \textbf{ influences goal consistency } f \textbf{ if } f_1, \ldots f_n) \tag{9}$$
$$(a \textbf{ influences accountability } f \textbf{ if } f_1, \ldots f_n) \tag{10}$$
$$(a \textbf{ influences control potential } f \textbf{ if } f_1, \ldots f_n) \tag{11}$$
$$(f_1, \ldots, f_n \textbf{ influences need consistency } f) \tag{12}$$
$$(f_1, \ldots, f_n \textbf{ influences goal consistency } f) \tag{13}$$
$$(f_1, \ldots, f_n \textbf{ influences accountability } f) \tag{14}$$
$$(f_1, \ldots, f_n \textbf{ influences control potential } f) \tag{15}$$
$$(f_1, \ldots, f_n \textbf{ intervenes action tendency } a) \tag{16}$$
$$(f_1, \ldots, f_n \textbf{ facilitates action tendency } a) \tag{17}$$

where $a \in \mathbf{A}$ and $a_i \in \mathbf{A}$ $(0 \leq i \leq n)$ and $f_j \in \mathbf{F}$, $(0 \leq j \leq n)$ and $g_j \in \mathbf{F}$, $(0 \leq j \leq n)$, and $f \in \mathbf{F}$ is a well-formed emotion fluent.

The semantics of $\mathcal{C}_{AE}$ is characterized by the constraints of the EDG, captured by the definition of emotional state, specified through a set of static causal laws. In this way, we can restrict states and state-transitions to comply with safe emotional change.

Definition 5 (Emotional state). *An emotional state $s \in S$ of the domain description $D^{ae}(\mathbf{A}, \mathbf{F})$ is an interpretation over F such that*

1. *for every static causal law $(f_1, \ldots, f_n \textbf{ if } g_1, \ldots g_m) \in D^{ae}(\mathbf{A}, \mathbf{F})$, we have $\{f_1, \ldots, f_n\} \subseteq s$ whenever $\{g_1, \ldots g_m\} \subseteq s$.*
2. *for every static causal law $(f_1, \ldots, f_n \textbf{ influences need consistency } f) \in D^{ae}(\mathbf{A}, \mathbf{F})$, we have $\{f\} \subset s$ whenever $\{f_1, \ldots, f_n\} \subseteq s$, and $f \in F^N$.*
3. *for every static causal law $(f_1, \ldots, f_n \textbf{ influences goal consistency } f) \in D^{ae}(\mathbf{A}, \mathbf{F})$, we have $\{f\} \subset s$ whenever $\{f_1, \ldots, f_n\} \subseteq s$, and $f \in F^G$.*
4. *for every static causal law $(f_1, \ldots, f_n \textbf{ influences accountability } f) \in D^{ae}(\mathbf{A}, \mathbf{F})$, we have $\{f\} \subset s$ whenever $\{f_1, \ldots, f_n\} \subseteq s$, and $f \in F^A$.*
5. *for every static causal law $(f_1, \ldots, f_n \textbf{ influences control potential } f) \in D^{ae}(\mathbf{A}, \mathbf{F})$, we have $\{f\} \subset s$ whenever $\{f_1, \ldots, f_n\} \subseteq s$, and $f \in F^C$.*

S denotes all the possible states of $D^{ae}(\mathbf{A}, \mathbf{F})$.

The general definition of emotional state captures a fully connected EDG transition system. For any particular application, we need to define an EDG that, based on application specific interaction goals and relevant theories for emotion regulation, avoids unintended emotional states. Here, we define a safe emotional state that follows principles of HER. Note that this specifies an EDG with a subset of transitions (in the fully connected graph) that is considered safe/valid.

Definition 6 (Safe emotional state). *A safe emotional state* $s \in S$ *of the domain description* $D^{ae}(\mathbf{A}, \mathbf{F})$ *is an emotional state following principles of hedonic emotion regulation, where s is an interpretation over F such that*

1. *for every static causal law* $(f_1, \ldots, f_n \text{ if } g_1, \ldots g_m) \in D^{ae}(\mathbf{A}, \mathbf{F})$, *we have* $\{f_1, \ldots, f_n\} \subseteq s$ *whenever* $\{g_1, \ldots g_m\} \subseteq s$.
2. *for every static causal law* $(f_1, \ldots, f_n$ **influences need consistency** $f) \in D^{ae}(\mathbf{A}, \mathbf{F})$, *we have* $\{f\} \subset s$ *whenever* $\{f_1, \ldots, f_n\} \subseteq s$, *and* $(f \in F^N \wedge f(ne, high, \_) \in s \wedge \exists f_i \in F^N (1 \leq i \leq n) \wedge f_i(ne, low, \_) \in s \wedge \exists f_j \in F^G (1 < j \leq n) \wedge f_j(go, high, \_) \in s) \vee (f \in F^N \wedge f(ne, undecided, \_) \in s \wedge \exists f_i \in F^N (1 < i \leq n) \wedge f_i(ne, low, \_) \in s \wedge \exists f_j \in F^G (1 \leq j \leq n) \wedge f_j(go, high, \_) \in s)$.
3. *for every static causal law* $(f_1, \ldots, f_n$ **influences goal consistency** $f) \in D^{ae}(\mathbf{A}, \mathbf{F})$, *we have* $\{f\} \subset s$ *whenever* $\{f_1, \ldots, f_n\} \subseteq s$, *and* $(f \in F^G \wedge f(go, high, \_) \in s)$.
4. *for every static causal law* $(f_1, \ldots, f_n$ **influences accountability** $f) \in D^{ae}(\mathbf{A}, \mathbf{F})$, *we have* $\{f\} \subset s$ *whenever* $\{f_1, \ldots, f_n\} \subseteq s$, *and* $(f \in F^A \wedge f(ac, other, \_) \in s \wedge (\exists f_j \in F^G (1 \leq j \leq n) \wedge f_j(go, high, \_) \in s)) \vee (f \in F^A \wedge f(ac, environment, \_) \in s \wedge (\exists f_j \in F^G (1 \leq j \leq n) \wedge f_j(go, high, \_) \in s)) \vee (f \in F^A \wedge f(ac, self, \_) \in s \wedge (\exists f_j \in F^G (1 \leq j \leq n) \wedge f_j(go, high, \_) \in s))$.
5. *for every static causal law* $(f_1, \ldots, f_n$ **influences control potential** $f) \in D^{ae}(\mathbf{A}, \mathbf{F})$, *we have* $\{f\} \subset s$ *whenever* $\{f_1, \ldots, f_n\} \subseteq s$, *and* $((f \in F^C \wedge f(co, high, \_) \in s \vee f(co, undecided, \_) \in s) \wedge (\exists f_j \in F^G (1 \leq j \leq n) \wedge f_j(go, high, \_) \in s)) \vee (f \in F^C \wedge f(co, high, \_) \in s \wedge (\exists f_i \in F^N (1 \leq i \leq n) \wedge (f_i(ne, low, \_) \in s \vee f_i(ne, undecided, \_) \in s) \wedge (\exists f_j \in F^G (1 \leq j \leq n) \wedge f_j(go, low, \_) \in s) \wedge (\exists f_k \in F^A (1 \leq k \leq n) \wedge f_k(ac, environment, \_) \in s)))$.

S denotes all the possible safe emotional states of $D^{ae}(\mathbf{A}, \mathbf{F})$.

Definition 7. *Let $D^{ae}(\mathbf{A}, \mathbf{F})$ be a domain description and s a state of $D^{ae}(\mathbf{A}, \mathbf{F})$.*

1. *An inhibition rule* $(f_1, \ldots, f_n$ **inhibits** $a)$ *is active in s, if $s \models f_1, \ldots, f_n$, otherwise, passive. The set $A_I(s)$ is the set of actions for which there exists at least one active inhibition rule in s (as in C_{TAID} [5]).*

2. *A triggering rule* $(f_1, \ldots, f_n$ **triggers** $a)$ *is active in* s, *if* $s \models f_1, \ldots, f_n$ *and all inhibition rules of action* a *are passive in* s, *otherwise, the triggering rule is passive in* s. *The set* $A_T(s)$ *is the set of actions for which there exists at least one active triggering rule in* s. *The set* $\overline{A}_T(s)$ *is the set of actions for which there exists at least one triggering rule and all triggering rules are passive in* s *(as in* $\mathcal{C}_{TAID}$ *[5]).*

3. *An allowance rule* $(f_1, \ldots, f_n$ **allows** $a)$ *is active in* s, *if* $s \models f_1, \ldots, f_n$ *and all inhibition rules of action* a *are passive in* s, *otherwise, the allowance rule is passive in* s. *The set* $A_A(s)$ *is the set of actions for which there exists at least one active allowance rule in* s. *The set* $\overline{A}_A(s)$ *is the set of actions for which there exists at least one allowance rule and all allowance rules are passive in* s *(as in* $\mathcal{C}_{TAID}$ *[5]).*

4. *A facilitating rule* $(f_1, \ldots, f_n$ **facilitates action tendency** $a)$ *is active in* s, *if* $a \in \mathbf{A}^H$ *and* $s \models f_1, \ldots, f_n$ *and all inhibition rules and intervening rules of action* a *are passive in* s, *otherwise, the facilitating rule is passive in* s. *The set* $A_{FAC}(s)$ *is the set of actions for which there exists at least one active facilitating rule in* s. *The set* $\overline{A}_{FAC}(s)$ *is the set of actions for which there exists at least one facilitating rule and all facilitating rules are passive in* s.

5. *An intervening rule* $(f_1, \ldots, f_n$ **intervenes action tendency** $a)$ *is active in* s, *if* $a \in \mathbf{A}^H$ *and* $s \models f_1, \ldots, f_n$ *and all inhibition rules and facilitating rules of action* a *are passive in* s, *otherwise, the intervening rule is passive in* s. *The set* $A_{INT}(s)$ *is the set of actions for which there exists at least one active intervening rule in* s. *The set* $\overline{A}_{INT}(s)$ *is the set of actions for which there exists at least one intervening rule and all intervening rules are passive in* s.

6. *A dynamic causal law* $(a$ causes $f_1, \ldots, f_n$ if $g_1, \ldots, g_n$ $)$ *is applicable in* s, *if* $s \models g_1, \ldots, g_n$.

7. *A static causal law* $(f_1, \ldots, f_n$ if $g_1, \ldots, g_n$ $)$ *is applicable in* s, *if* $s \models g_1, \ldots, g_n$.

8. *A dynamic causal law* $(a$ **influences need consistency** f if $f_1, \ldots, f_n$ $)$ *is applicable in* s, *if* $s \models f_1, \ldots, f_n$, *and* $f \in F^N$, *and* $\exists f_i \in F^N (1 \leq i \leq n)$, *and* $\exists f_j \in F^G (1 \leq j \leq n)$, *and* $\exists f_k \in F^A (1 \leq k \leq n)$, *and* $\exists f_m \in F^C (1 \leq m \leq n)$.

9. *A dynamic causal law* $(a$ **influences goal consistency** f if $f_1, \ldots, f_n$ $)$ *is applicable in* s, *if* $s \models f_1, \ldots, f_n$, *and* $f \in F^G$, *and* $\exists f_i \in F^N (1 \leq i \leq n)$, *and* $\exists f_j \in F^G (1 \leq j \leq n)$, *and* $\exists f_k \in F^A (1 \leq k \leq n)$, *and* $\exists f_m \in F^C (1 \leq m \leq n)$.

10. *A dynamic causal law* $(a$ **influences accountability** f if $f_1, \ldots, f_n$ $)$ *is applicable in* s, *if* $s \models f_1, \ldots, f_n$, *and* $f \in F^A$, *and* $\exists f_i \in F^N (1 \leq i \leq n)$, *and* $\exists f_j \in F^G (1 \leq j \leq n)$, *and* $\exists f_k \in F^A (1 \leq k \leq n)$, *and* $\exists f_m \in F^C (1 \leq m \leq n)$.

11. *A dynamic causal law* $(a$ **influences control potential** f if $f_1, \ldots, f_n$ $)$ *is applicable in* s, *if* $s \models f_1, \ldots, f_n$, *and* $f \in F^C$, *and* $\exists f_i \in F^N (1 \leq i \leq n)$, *and* $\exists f_j \in F^G (1 \leq j \leq n)$, *and* $\exists f_k \in F^A (1 \leq k \leq n)$, *and* $\exists f_m \in F^C (1 \leq m \leq n)$.

12. *A static causal law* $(f_1, \ldots, f_n$ ***influences need consistency*** $f)$ *is applicable in* s, *if* $s \models f_1, \ldots, f_n$, *and* $f \in F^N$, *and* $\exists f_i \in F^N (1 \leq i \leq n)$, *and* $\exists f_j \in F^G (1 \leq j \leq n)$, *and* $\exists f_k \in F^A (1 \leq k \leq n)$, *and* $\exists f_m \in F^C (1 \leq m \leq n)$.
13. *A static causal law* $(f_1, \ldots, f_n$ ***influences goal consistency*** $f)$ *is applicable in* s, *if* $s \models f_1, \ldots, f_n$, *and* $f \in F^G$, *and* $\exists f_i \in F^N (1 \leq i \leq n)$, *and* $\exists f_j \in F^G (1 \leq j \leq n)$, *and* $\exists f_k \in F^A (1 \leq k \leq n)$, *and* $\exists f_m \in F^C (1 \leq m \leq n)$.
14. *A static causal law* $(f_1, \ldots, f_n$ ***influences accountability*** $f)$ *is applicable in* s, *if* $s \models f_1, \ldots, f_n$, *and* $f \in F^A$, *and* $\exists f_i \in F^N (1 \leq i \leq n)$, *and* $\exists f_j \in F^G (1 \leq j \leq n)$, *and* $\exists f_k \in F^A (1 \leq k \leq n)$, *and* $\exists f_m \in F^C (1 \leq m \leq n)$.
15. *A static causal law* $(f_1, \ldots, f_n$ ***influences control potential*** $f)$ *is applicable in* s, *if* $s \models f_1, \ldots, f_n$, *and* $f \in F^C$, *and* $\exists f_i \in F^N (1 \leq i \leq n)$, *and* $\exists f_j \in F^G (1 \leq j \leq n)$, *and* $\exists f_k \in F^A (1 \leq k \leq n)$, *and* $\exists f_m \in F^C (1 \leq m \leq n)$.

Definition 8 (Trajectory). *Let* $D^{ae}(\mathbf{A}, \mathbf{F})$ *be a domain description. A trajectory* $\langle s_0, A_1, s_1, A_2, \ldots, A_n, s_n \rangle$ *of* $D^{ae}(\mathbf{A}, \mathbf{F})$ *is a sequence of sets of actions* $A_i \subseteq A$ *and states* s_i *of* $D^{ae}(\mathbf{A}, \mathbf{F})$ *satisfying the following conditions for* $0 \leq i < n$:

1. $(s_i, A, s_{i+1}) \in S \times 2^A \backslash \{\} \times S$
2. $A_T(s_i) \subseteq A_{i+1}$
3. $A_{FAC}(s_i) \subseteq A_{i+1}$
4. $A_{INT}(s_i) \subseteq A_{i+1}$
5. $\overline{A}_T(s_i) \cap A_{i+1} = \emptyset$
6. $\overline{A}_A(s_i) \cap A_{i+1} = \emptyset$
7. $A_I(s_i) \cap A_{i+1} = \emptyset$
8. $\overline{A}_{FAC}(s_i) \cap A_{i+1} = \emptyset$
9. $\overline{A}_{INT}(s_i) \cap A_{i+1} = \emptyset$
10. $|A_i \cap B| \leq 1$ *for all* (*noconcurrency* B) $\in D^{ae}(\mathbf{A}, \mathbf{F})$.

Definition 9 (Action Observation Language). *The action observation language of* $\mathcal{C}_{AE}$ *(similar to* $\mathcal{C}_{TAID}$) *consists of expressions of the following form:*

$$(f \textbf{ at } t_i) \quad (a \textbf{ occurs\_at } t_i) \quad (8)$$

where $f \in \mathbf{F}$, a *is an action and* t_i *is a point of time.*

Definition 10 (Action Theory). *Let* D *be a domain description and* O *be a set of observations. The pair* (D, O) *is called an action theory.*

Definition 11 (Trajectory Model). *Let* (D, O) *be an action theory. A trajectory* $\langle s_0, A_1, s_1, A_2, \ldots, A_n, s_n \rangle$ *of* D *is a trajectory model of* (D, O), *if it satisfies all observations of* O *in the following way:*

1. *if* $(f \textit{ at } t) \in O$, *then* $f \in s_t$
2. *if* $(a \textit{ occurs\_at } t) \in O$, *then* $a \in A_{t+1}$.

Definition 12 (Action Query Language). *The action query language of $\mathcal{C}_{AE}$ regards assertions about executing sequences of actions with expressions that constitute trajectories. A query is of the following form:* $(f_1, \ldots, f_n$ **after** A_i **occurs_at** $t_i, \ldots, A_m$ **occurs_at** $t_m)$ *where* $f_1, \ldots, f_n$ *are fluent literals* $\in \mathbf{F}$, $A_i, \ldots, A_m$ *are subsets of* $\mathbf{A}$, *and* $t_i, \ldots, t_m$ *are points in time.*

We can observe that actions in a trajectory model can be actions executed by a rational agent, to influence appraisals of the situation, or action tendencies estimated to be executed by the human agent. Adjustments of appraisal must be done in a controlled and safe way to reduce unintended emotional side-effects. In the next section, we present a proof for safe emotional change.

4.3 Proving Safe Emotional Change

We present a theorem and prove that trajectories generated by $\mathcal{C}_{AE}$ preserve a safety property in terms of avoiding unintended emotional side-effects. An invariance property is defined by following principles of hedonic emotion regulation, called an Emotional Invariant (EI), a state predicate which is preserved by the state conditions of the EDG. This is proven using the invariance principle [8]. To support readability of the proof, we define an emotion labeling.

Definition 13 (Emotion labeling). *For any trajectory* $\langle s_0, A_1, s_1, A_2, \ldots, A_n, s_n \rangle$ *of* $D^{ae}(\mathbf{A}, \mathbf{F})$, *there is a transition emotion labeling* $\langle E_O, \ldots, E_n \rangle$ *such that* $Labeling(s_i) = E_i$ $(0 \leq i \leq n)$, *and* $E_i = [V_N, V_G, V_A, V_C, i]$, *where* V_N, V_G, V_A, V_C *are values of well-formed emotion fluents* $e_N, e_G, e_A, e_C \in s_i$, *representing need consistency, goal consistency, accountability and control potential, respectively.*

Theorem 1 (Safe emotional change). *Let* $(D^{ae}, O_{initial})$ *be an action theory such that* $O_{initial}$ *are the fluent observations of the initial state, i.e., the fluents of the situation/interaction and the fluents of the estimated emotional state of the human agent. Let Q be a query according to Definition 12 and let*

$$A_Q = \{(a \ occurs\_at \ t_i) \mid a \in A_i, 1 \leq i \leq m\}.$$

If there is a trajectory model $M = \langle s_0, A_1, s_1, A_2, \ldots, A_n, s_m \rangle$ *where* $A_i \subseteq \mathbf{A}$ $(0 \leq i \leq m)$ *of* $\mathcal{C}_{AE}$ $(D^{ae}, O_{initial} \cup A_Q)$, *then all states* $s \in M$ *at the time points* $0 \leq t \leq m$ *preserve a state predicate EI, where the goal consistency is equal or higher than the need consistency, denoted according to Definition 6 as* $[V_N, V_G, V_A, V_C, t] \wedge V_N \leq V_G$ *and where* $V_N, V_G \in \{low, undecided, high\}$ *are ranked as* $low < undecided < high$ *(following the intuition of AE in Sect. 3).*

Proof. We must show that EI holds in each state condition (Definition 6) of the EDG. We do this by showing that an initial observation holds, which we specify as [undecided, undecided, undecided, undecided, 0] $\wedge V_N \leq V_G$. We then show that any transition from time step t to t+1 preserves EI, such that

$[V_N, V_G, V_A, V_C, t] \land V_N \leq V_G$ implies $[V_N', V_G', V_A', V_C', t+1] \land V_N' \leq V_G'$.

Looking at each transition rule, we can observe that

- it is clear that the emotional invariant $[V_N, V_G, V_A, V_C, t] \land V_N \leq V_G$ holds in the initial observation [undecided, undecided, undecided, undecided, 0] $\land$ undecided $\leq$ undecided.
- for every static causal law $(f_1, \ldots, f_n$ **influences need consistency** $f) \in D^{ae}(\mathbf{A}, \mathbf{F})$, only changes of V_N to high or undecided are permitted, and require that V_G is high. It is clear that $undecided \lor high \leq high$ preserves EI in a transition from t to t+1.
- for every static causal law $(f_1, \ldots, f_n$ **influences goal consistency** $f) \in D^{ae}(\mathbf{A}, \mathbf{F})$, only changes of V_G to high are permitted. It is clear that a condition $V_N \leq high$ preserves EI in a transition from t to t+1.
- for every static causal law $(f_1, \ldots, f_n$ **influences accountability** $f) \in D^{ae}(\mathbf{A}, \mathbf{F})$, no changes regard either V_N or V_G, which preserves EI in a transition from t to t+1.
- for every static causal law $(f_1, \ldots, f_n$ **influences control potential** $f) \in D^{ae}(\mathbf{A}, \mathbf{F})$, no changes regard either V_N or V_G, which preserves EI in a transition from t to t+1.

We can conclude, by looking at an initial observation, and all state conditions in any transition from time step t to t+1, that the emotional invariant is preserved in the EDG according to hedonic emotion regulation, and show that the system avoids unintended emotional side-effects.

4.4 Example Scenario: Backward Reasoning

Backward reasoning is a process of searching past states in the interaction to reason about why a certain emotional state was reached. In the case of AE, this is explained by changes in appraisal of a situation. For instance, in the past trajectory:

$\langle s_0 : \{Frustration[h, l, e, h, 0]\},$
$A_1 : \{Influence\_accountability(o)\},$
$s_1 : \{Anger[h, l, o, h, 1]\}\rangle$

In this example, the agent looks one state backward (s_0) to find that the emotional state of frustration led to the emotional state of anger in the initial state (s_1). In addition, the agent can find that the state of anger was promoted due to a change of accountability from *environment* (e) to *other* (o). Such inferences can be taken in consideration when planning future interactions.

4.5 Example Scenario: Forward Reasoning

Forward reasoning is a process of planning future interactions by considering emotional change in response to actions that adapt the human agent's appraisal.

This is a process of generating a set of alternative trajectories for reaching the goal of the interaction while reasoning about emotions in each state of the interaction. For instance, an alternative trajectory can be:

$\langle\ s_0 : \{Anger[h, l, o, h, 0]\},$

$A_1 : \{Influence\_accountability(e)\},$

$s_1 : \{Frustration[h, l, e, h, 1]\},$

$A_2 : \{Influence\_need(u),\ Influence\_goal(h),\ Influence\_control(l)\},$

$s_2 : \{Hope[u, h, e, l, 2]\},$

$A_3 : \{Influence\_need(h),\ Influence\_control(u)\},$

$s_3 : \{Joy[h, h, e, u, 3]\}\rangle.$

In this example, starting in an emotional state of anger, the agent plans an interaction while managing the human agent's emotions to decrease frustration and maintain a pleasurable interaction. Following the specified transition system for safe emotional change (Definition 6), the agent filters alternative trajectories and selects actions to avoid negative emotional side-effects.

5   Discussion

In this paper, we introduce *emotion-aware planning*. Emotional reasoning has been formalized in a structure called $\mathcal{C}_{AE}$, in terms of action reasoning and transition systems, formalizing the emotion theories of AE and HER. This constitutes computational models for emotions and emotional change, which can provide emotion-aware planning and decision-making in human-agent interactions.

An emotional state, to be captured by an agent, needs a representation of the emotion. Through a set of variables, recognized by an aggregation of the appraisal theory of emotion, abstractions of emotions are given. The emotion decision graph (transition system) is a representation, and we expect human emotions to be represented there. In that respect, the agent creates a theory of the mind of the human as an abstraction based on appraisal theory of emotion. This is one of the main contributions of this paper; We take psychological (emotion) theories and transform them into tangible, computational and multi-dimensional models of emotion.

Limitations of the proposed framework can be inherited from the appraisal theory of emotion, where emotions are solely based on appraisal [6]. This can limit the expressiveness of the model, not accounting for other components of emotions which are not related to human conscious reasoning. There are many other emotion theories that can be applied to model emotional states. For instance, emotions can be defined in terms of Arousal and Valence [10]. However, the chosen theory is particularly interesting for the current work due to its way of capturing emotional causes.

6   Conclusion and Future Work

The proposed framework for emotional reasoning enables a software agent to acquire a particular theory of the mind of the human to deal with emotions in interaction. The formal specifications assure that generated plans comply with safe emotional change. The main contribution of this paper is a framework to enable: 1) backward reasoning, by modelling causes to emotions; 2) context reasoning, to infer emotional states; 3) forward reasoning, by modelling emotional change in terms of state transitions; and 4) emotion-aware planning, to plan an agent's actions to be in balance with emotions in each state of the interaction, aiming to avoid unintended emotional side-effects.

The specified EDG filters trajectories by capturing principles of AE and HER, aiming to reduce negative emotions and increase positive emotions. However, depending on the goal of the interaction (such as stress-management, coaching or therapy), different emotion regulation theories are suitable. In a generalization of the framework, we can replace AE and HER for other emotion theories (such as the Two-Factor Theory of Emotion [3] or the Cognitive-Mediational Theory [16]). In this way, the proposed emotional reasoning framework can provide a modular tool for integrating, evaluating and comparing different emotion theories (by analyzing filtered trajectories). This is a focus for future work.

Acknowledgements. This work was partially funded by the Knut and Alice Wallenberg Foundation. We thank the anonymous reviewers for their valuable and useful comments.

References

1. Belkaid, M., Sabouret, N.: A logical model of theory of mind for virtual agents in the context of job interview simulation. arXiv preprint arXiv:1402.5043 (2014)
2. Blanchette, I.: Emotion and Reasoning. Psychology Press (2013)
3. Cornelius, R.R.: Gregorio Marañon's two-factor theory of emotion. Pers. Soc. Psychol. Bull. **17**(1), 65–69 (1991)
4. Di Lascio, E.: Emotion-aware systems for promoting human well-being. In: Proceedings of the 2018 ACM International Joint Conference and 2018 International Symposium on Pervasive and Ubiquitous Computing and Wearable Computers, pp. 529–534 (2018)
5. Dworschak, S., Grell, S., Nikiforova, V., Schaub, T., Selbig, J.: Modeling biological networks by action languages via answer set programming. Constraints **13**(1), 21–65 (2008)
6. Ellsworth, P.C.: Appraisal theory: old and new questions. Emot. Rev. **5**(2), 125–131 (2013)
7. Gelfond, M., Lifschitz, V.: Action languages. Comput. Inf. Sci. **3**(16) (1998)
8. Hansen, M.N., Schmidt, E.M.: Algorithms and data structures: transition systems. Datalogisk Institut, Aarhus Universitet (2003)
9. Jiang, H., Vidal, J.M., Huhns, M.N.: EBDI: an architecture for emotional agents. In: Proceedings of the 6th International Joint Conference on Autonomous Agents and Multiagent Systems, pp. 1–3 (2007)
10. Knez, I., Hygge, S.: The circumplex structure of affect: a Swedish version. Scand. J. Psychol. **42**(5), 389–398 (2001)
11. Leonetti, M., Iocchi, L., Cohn, A.G., Nardi, D.: Adaptive human-aware task planning. In: ICAPS Workshop on Planning and Robotics (PlanRob) (2019)

12. Ong, D.C., Zaki, J., Goodman, N.D.: Computational models of emotion inference in theory of mind: a review and roadmap. Top. Cogn. Sci. **11**(2), 338–357 (2019)
13. Ortner, C.N., Corno, D., Fung, T.Y., Rapinda, K.: The roles of hedonic and eudaimonic motives in emotion regulation. Pers. Individ. Differ. **120**, 209–212 (2018)
14. Pereira, D., Oliveira, E., Moreira, N.: Formal modelling of emotions in BDI agents. In: Sadri, F., Satoh, K. (eds.) CLIMA 2007. LNCS (LNAI), vol. 5056, pp. 62–81. Springer, Heidelberg (2008). https://doi.org/10.1007/978-3-540-88833-8_4
15. Sánchez-López, Y., Cerezo, E.: Designing emotional BDI agents: good practices and open questions. Knowl. Eng. Rev. **34**, E26 (2019)
16. Schulz, M.S., Lazarus, R.S.: Regulating emotion in adolescence: a cognitive-mediational conceptualization (2012)
17. Zaki, J.: Integrating empathy and interpersonal emotion regulation. Annu. Rev. Psychol. **71**, 517–540 (2020)

Metric Temporal Answer Set Programming over Timed Traces

Pedro Cabalar[1], Martín Diéguez[2], Torsten Schaub[3(✉)], and Anna Schuhmann[3]

[1] University of Corunna, Coruña, Spain
[2] LERIA, Université d'Angers, Angers, France
[3] University of Potsdam, Potsdam, Germany
torsten@cs.uni-potsdam.de

Abstract. In temporal extensions of Answer Set Programming (ASP) based on linear-time, the behavior of dynamic systems is captured by sequences of states. While this representation reflects their relative order, it abstracts away the specific times associated with each state. In many applications, however, timing constraints are important like, for instance, when planning and scheduling go hand in hand. We address this by developing a metric extension of linear-time temporal equilibrium logic, in which temporal operators are constrained by intervals over natural numbers. The resulting Metric Equilibrium Logic provides the foundation of an ASP-based approach for specifying qualitative and quantitative dynamic constraints. To this end, we define a translation of metric formulas into monadic first-order formulas and give a correspondence between their models in Metric Equilibrium Logic and Monadic Quantified Equilibrium Logic, respectively. Interestingly, our translation provides a blue print for implementation in terms of ASP modulo difference constraints.

1 Introduction

Reasoning about action and change, or more generally about dynamic systems, is not only central to knowledge representation and reasoning but at the heart of computer science [14]. In practice, this often requires both qualitative as well as quantitative dynamic constraints. For instance, when planning and scheduling at once, actions may have durations and their effects may need to meet deadlines.

Over the last years, we addressed qualitative dynamic constraints by combining traditional approaches, like Dynamic and Linear Temporal Logic (DL [16] and LTL [26]), with the base logic of Answer Set Programming (ASP [21]), namely, the logic of Here-and-There (HT [17]) and its non-monotonic extension, called Equilibrium Logic [24]. This resulted in non-monotonic linear dynamic and temporal equilibrium logics (DEL [5,8] and TEL [1,11]) that gave rise to the temporal ASP system *telingo* [7,10] extending the ASP system *clingo* [15].

Another commonality of dynamic and temporal logics is that they abstract from specific time points when capturing temporal relationships. For instance,

---

An extended abstract of this paper appeared in [12].

© The Author(s), under exclusive license to Springer Nature Switzerland AG 2022
G. Gottlob et al. (Eds.): LPNMR 2022, LNAI 13416, pp. 117–130, 2022.
https://doi.org/10.1007/978-3-031-15707-3_10

in temporal logic, we can use the formula $\Box(use \rightarrow \Diamond clean)$ to express that a machine has to be eventually cleaned after being used. Nothing can be said about the delay between using and cleaning the machine.

A key design decision was to base both logics, TEL and DEL, on the same linear-time semantics. We continued to maintain the same linear-time semantics, embodied by sequences of states, when elaborating upon a first "light-weight" metric temporal extension of HT [9]. The "light-weightiness" is due to treating time as a state counter by identifying the next time with the next state. For instance, this allows us to refine our example by stating that, if the machine is used, it has to be cleaned within the next 3 states, viz. $\Box(use \rightarrow \Diamond_{[1..3]} clean)$. Although this permits the restriction of temporal operators to subsequences of states, no fine-grained timing constraints are expressible.

In this paper, we address this by associating each state with its *time*, as done in Metric Temporal Logic (MTL [20]). This allows us to measure time differences between events. For instance, in our example, we may thus express that whenever the machine is used, it has to be cleaned within 60 to 120 time units, by writing:

$$\Box(use \rightarrow \Diamond_{[60..120]} clean) \,.$$

Unlike the non-metric version, this stipulates that once *use* is true in a state, *clean* must be true in some future state whose associated time is at least 60 and at most 120 time units after the time of *use*. The choice of time domain is crucial, and might even lead to undecidability in the continuous case. We rather adapt a discrete approach that offers a sequence of snapshots of a dynamic system.

2   Metric Temporal Logic

Given $m \in \mathbb{N}$ and $n \in \mathbb{N} \cup \{\omega\}$, we let $[m..n]$ stand for the set $\{i \in \mathbb{N} \mid m \leq i \leq n\}$, $[m..n)$ for $\{i \in \mathbb{N} \mid m \leq i < n\}$, and $(m..n]$ stand for $\{i \in \mathbb{N} \mid m < i \leq n\}$.

Given a set $\mathcal{A}$ of propositional variables (called *alphabet*), a *metric formula* φ is defined by the grammar:

$$\varphi ::= p \mid \bot \mid \varphi_1 \otimes \varphi_2 \mid \bullet_{\mathcal{I}} \varphi \mid \varphi_1 \, \mathsf{S}_{\mathcal{I}} \, \varphi_2 \mid \varphi_1 \, \mathsf{T}_{\mathcal{I}} \, \varphi_2 \mid \circ_{\mathcal{I}} \varphi \mid \varphi_1 \, \mathsf{U}_{\mathcal{I}} \, \varphi_2 \mid \varphi_1 \, \mathbb{R}_{\mathcal{I}} \, \varphi_2$$

where $p \in \mathcal{A}$ is an atom and $\otimes$ is any binary Boolean connective $\otimes \in \{\rightarrow, \wedge, \vee\}$. The last six cases above correspond to temporal operators, each of them indexed by some interval $\mathcal{I}$ of the form $[m..n)$ with $m \in \mathbb{N}$ and $n \in \mathbb{N} \cup \{\omega\}$. In words, $\bullet_{\mathcal{I}}$, $\mathsf{S}_{\mathcal{I}}$, and $\mathsf{T}_{\mathcal{I}}$ are past operators called *previous*, *since*, and *trigger*, respectively; their future counterparts $\circ_{\mathcal{I}}$, $\mathsf{U}_{\mathcal{I}}$, and $\mathbb{R}_{\mathcal{I}}$ are called *next*, *until*, and *release*. We let subindex $[m..n]$ stand for $[m..n+1)$, provided $n \neq \omega$. Also, we sometimes use the subindices '$\leq n$', '$\geq m$' and 'm' as abbreviations of intervals $[0..n]$, $[m..\omega)$ and $[m..m]$, respectively. Also, whenever $\mathcal{I} = [0..\omega)$, we simply omit subindex $\mathcal{I}$.

A *metric theory* is a (possibly infinite) set of metric formulas.

We also define several common derived operators like the Boolean connectives $\top \overset{def}{=} \neg\bot$, $\neg\varphi \overset{def}{=} \varphi \rightarrow \bot$, $\varphi \leftrightarrow \psi \overset{def}{=} (\varphi \rightarrow \psi) \wedge (\psi \rightarrow \varphi)$, and the following temporal operators:

$\blacksquare_{\mathcal{I}}\varphi \stackrel{def}{=} \bot \, \mathbf{T}_{\mathcal{I}} \, \varphi$ *always before* $\square_{\mathcal{I}}\varphi \stackrel{def}{=} \bot \, \mathbb{R}_{\mathcal{I}} \, \varphi$ *always afterward*

$\blacklozenge_{\mathcal{I}}\varphi \stackrel{def}{=} \top \, \mathbf{S}_{\mathcal{I}} \, \varphi$ *eventually before* $\lozenge_{\mathcal{I}}\varphi \stackrel{def}{=} \top \, \mathbb{U}_{\mathcal{I}} \, \varphi$ *eventually afterward*

$\mathsf{I} \stackrel{def}{=} \neg \bullet \top$ *initial* $\mathbb{F} \stackrel{def}{=} \neg \circ \top$ *final*

$\widehat{\bullet}_{\mathcal{I}}\varphi \stackrel{def}{=} \bullet_{\mathcal{I}}\varphi \lor \neg\bullet_{\mathcal{I}}\top$ *weak previous* $\widehat{\circ}_{\mathcal{I}}\varphi \stackrel{def}{=} \circ_{\mathcal{I}}\varphi \lor \neg\circ_{\mathcal{I}}\top$ *weak next*

Note that *initial* and *final* are not indexed by any interval; they only depend on the state of the trace, not on the actual time that this state is mapped to. On the other hand, the weak version of *next* can no longer be defined in terms of *final*, as done in [11] with non-metric $\widehat{\circ}\varphi \equiv \circ\varphi \lor \mathbb{F}$. For the metric case $\widehat{\circ}_{\mathcal{I}}\varphi$, the disjunction $\circ_{\mathcal{I}}\varphi \lor \neg\circ_{\mathcal{I}}\top$ must be used instead, in order to keep the usual dualities among operators (the same applies to weak *previous*).

The definition of *Metric Equilibrium Logic* (MEL for short) is done in two steps. We start with the definition of a monotonic logic called *Metric logic of Here-and-There* (MHT), a temporal extension of the intermediate logic of Here-and-There [17]. We then select some models from MHT that are said to be in equilibrium, obtaining in this way a non-monotonic entailment relation.

An example of metric formulas is the modeling of traffic lights. While the light is red by default, it changes to green within less than 15 time units (say, seconds) whenever the button is pushed; and it stays green for another 30 s at most. This can be represented as follows.

$$\square(red \land green \rightarrow \bot) \tag{1}$$

$$\square(\neg green \rightarrow red) \tag{2}$$

$$\square(push \rightarrow \lozenge_{[1..15)}(\square_{\leq 30} \, green)) \tag{3}$$

Note that this example combines a default rule (2) with a metric rule (3), describing the initiation and duration period of events. This nicely illustrates the interest in non-monotonic metric representation and reasoning methods.

A *Here-and-There trace* (for short HT-*trace*) of length $\lambda \in \mathbb{N} \cup \{\omega\}$ over alphabet $\mathcal{A}$ is a sequence of pairs $(\langle H_i, T_i \rangle)_{i \in [0..\lambda)}$ with $H_i \subseteq T_i \subseteq \mathcal{A}$ for any $i \in [0..\lambda)$. For convenience, we usually represent an HT-trace as the pair $\langle \mathbf{H}, \mathbf{T} \rangle$ of traces $\mathbf{H} = (H_i)_{i \in [0..\lambda)}$ and $\mathbf{T} = (T_i)_{i \in [0..\lambda)}$. Notice that, when $\lambda = \omega$, this covers traces of infinite length. We say that $\langle \mathbf{H}, \mathbf{T} \rangle$ is *total* when $\mathbf{H} = \mathbf{T}$, that is, $H_i = T_i$ for all $i \in [0..\lambda)$.

Definition 1. *A* timed trace $(\langle \mathbf{H}, \mathbf{T} \rangle, \tau)$ *over* $(\mathbb{N}, <)$ *is a pair consisting of*

- *an HT-trace* $\langle \mathbf{H}, \mathbf{T} \rangle = (\langle H_i, T_i \rangle)_{i \in [0..\lambda)}$ *and*
- *a function* $\tau : [0..\lambda) \rightarrow \mathbb{N}$ *such that* $\tau(i) \leq \tau(i+1)$.

A timed trace of length $\lambda > 1$ *is called* strict *if* $\tau(i) < \tau(i+1)$ *for all* $i \in [0..\lambda)$ *such that* $i + 1 < \lambda$ *and* non-strict *otherwise. We assume w.l.o.g. that* $\tau(0) = 0$. $\square$

Function τ assigns, to each state index $i \in [0..\lambda)$, a time point $\tau(i) \in \mathbb{N}$ representing the number of time units (seconds, miliseconds, etc., depending on the chosen granularity) elapsed since time point $\tau(0) = 0$ chosen as the beginning of the trace. The difference to the variant of MHT presented in [9] boils down to the choice of function τ. In [9], this was the identity function on the interval $[0..\lambda)$.

Given any timed HT-trace, satisfaction of formulas is defined as follows.

Definition 2 (MHT-satisfaction). *A timed HT-trace* $\mathbf{M} = (\langle \mathbf{H}, \mathbf{T} \rangle, \tau)$ *of length* λ *over alphabet* $\mathcal{A}$ *satisfies a metric formula* φ *at step* $k \in [0..\lambda)$, *written* $\mathbf{M}, k \models \varphi$, *if the following conditions hold:*

1. $\mathbf{M}, k \not\models \bot$
2. $\mathbf{M}, k \models p$ *if* $p \in H_k$ *for any atom* $p \in \mathcal{A}$
3. $\mathbf{M}, k \models \varphi \wedge \psi$ *iff* $\mathbf{M}, k \models \varphi$ *and* $\mathbf{M}, k \models \psi$
4. $\mathbf{M}, k \models \varphi \vee \psi$ *iff* $\mathbf{M}, k \models \varphi$ *or* $\mathbf{M}, k \models \psi$
5. $\mathbf{M}, k \models \varphi \rightarrow \psi$ *iff* $\mathbf{M}', k \not\models \varphi$ *or* $\mathbf{M}', k \models \psi$, *for both* $\mathbf{M}' = \mathbf{M}$ *and* $\mathbf{M}' = (\langle \mathbf{T}, \mathbf{T} \rangle, \tau)$
6. $\mathbf{M}, k \models \bullet_{\mathcal{I}} \varphi$ *iff* $k > 0$ *and* $\mathbf{M}, k{-}1 \models \varphi$ *and* $\tau(k) - \tau(k{-}1) \in \mathcal{I}$
7. $\mathbf{M}, k \models \varphi \mathbf{S}_{\mathcal{I}} \psi$ *iff for some* $j \in [0..k]$ *with* $\tau(k) - \tau(j) \in \mathcal{I}$, *we have* $\mathbf{M}, j \models \psi$ *and* $\mathbf{M}, i \models \varphi$ *for all* $i \in (j..k]$
8. $\mathbf{M}, k \models \varphi \mathbf{T}_{\mathcal{I}} \psi$ *iff for all* $j \in [0..k]$ *with* $\tau(k) - \tau(j) \in \mathcal{I}$, *we have* $\mathbf{M}, j \models \psi$ *or* $\mathbf{M}, i \models \varphi$ *for some* $i \in (j..k]$
9. $\mathbf{M}, k \models \circ_{\mathcal{I}} \varphi$ *iff* $k + 1 < \lambda$ *and* $\mathbf{M}, k{+}1 \models \varphi$ *and* $\tau(k{+}1) - \tau(k) \in \mathcal{I}$
10. $\mathbf{M}, k \models \varphi \mathbb{U}_{\mathcal{I}} \psi$ *iff for some* $j \in [k..\lambda)$ *with* $\tau(j) - \tau(k) \in \mathcal{I}$, *we have* $\mathbf{M}, j \models \psi$ *and* $\mathbf{M}, i \models \varphi$ *for all* $i \in [k..j)$
11. $\mathbf{M}, k \models \varphi \mathbb{R}_{\mathcal{I}} \psi$ *iff for all* $j \in [k..\lambda)$ *with* $\tau(j) - \tau(k) \in \mathcal{I}$, *we have* $\mathbf{M}, j \models \psi$ *or* $\mathbf{M}, i \models \varphi$ *for some* $i \in [k..j)$ □

Satisfaction of derived operators can be easily deduced:

Proposition 1. *Let* $\mathbf{M} = (\langle \mathbf{H}, \mathbf{T} \rangle, \tau)$ *be a timed HT-trace of length* λ *over* $\mathcal{A}$. *Given the respective definitions of derived operators, we get the following satisfaction conditions:*

13. $\mathbf{M}, k \models \mathbf{I}$ *iff* $k = 0$
14. $\mathbf{M}, k \models \hat{\bullet}_{\mathcal{I}} \varphi$ *iff* $k = 0$ *or* $\mathbf{M}, k{-}1 \models \varphi$ *or* $\tau(k) - \tau(k{-}1) \notin \mathcal{I}$
15. $\mathbf{M}, k \models \blacklozenge_{\mathcal{I}} \varphi$ *iff* $\mathbf{M}, i \models \varphi$ *for some* $i \in [0..k]$ *with* $\tau(k) - \tau(i) \in \mathcal{I}$
16. $\mathbf{M}, k \models \blacksquare_{\mathcal{I}} \varphi$ *iff* $\mathbf{M}, i \models \varphi$ *for all* $i \in [0..k]$ *with* $\tau(k) - \tau(i) \in \mathcal{I}$
17. $\mathbf{M}, k \models \mathbb{F}$ *iff* $k + 1 = \lambda$
18. $\mathbf{M}, k \models \hat{\circ}_{\mathcal{I}} \varphi$ *iff* $k + 1 < \lambda$ *or* $\mathbf{M}, k{+}1 \models \varphi$ *or* $\tau(k{+}1) - \tau(k) \notin \mathcal{I}$
19. $\mathbf{M}, k \models \Diamond_{\mathcal{I}} \varphi$ *iff* $\mathbf{M}, i \models \varphi$ *for some* $i \in [k..\lambda)$ *with* $\tau(i) - \tau(k) \in \mathcal{I}$
20. $\mathbf{M}, k \models \Box_{\mathcal{I}} \varphi$ *iff* $\mathbf{M}, i \models \varphi$ *for all* $i \in [k..\lambda)$ *with* $\tau(i) - \tau(k) \in \mathcal{I}$ □

A formula φ is a *tautology* (or is valid), written $\models \varphi$, iff $\mathbf{M}, k \models \varphi$ for any timed HT-trace $\mathbf{M}$ and any $k \in [0..\lambda)$. MHT is the logic induced by the set of all such tautologies. For two formulas φ, ψ we write $\varphi \equiv \psi$, iff $\models \varphi \leftrightarrow \psi$, that is, $\mathbf{M}, k \models \varphi \leftrightarrow \psi$ for any timed HT-trace $\mathbf{M}$ of length λ and any $k \in [0..\lambda)$. A timed HT-trace $\mathbf{M}$ is an MHT *model* of a metric theory Γ if $\mathbf{M}, 0 \models \varphi$ for all $\varphi \in \Gamma$. The set of MHT models of Γ having length λ is denoted as $\mathrm{MHT}(\Gamma, \lambda)$, whereas $\mathrm{MHT}(\Gamma) \stackrel{def}{=} \bigcup_{\lambda=0}^{\omega} \mathrm{MHT}(\Gamma, \lambda)$ is the set of all MHT models of Γ of any length. We may obtain fragments of any metric logic by imposing restrictions on the timed traces used for defining tautologies and models. That is, MHT_f stands for the restriction of MHT to traces of any finite length $\lambda \in \mathbb{N}$ and MHT_ω corresponds to the restriction to traces of infinite length $\lambda = \omega$.

An interesting subset of MHT is the one formed by total timed traces $(\langle \mathbf{T}, \mathbf{T} \rangle, \tau)$. In the non-metric version of temporal HT, the restriction to total models corresponds to Linear Temporal Logic (LTL [26]). In our case, the restriction to total traces defines a metric version of LTL, that we call *Metric Temporal Logic* (MTL for short). It can be proved that MTL are those models of MHT satisfying the excluded middle axiom schema: $\Box(p \lor \neg p)$ for any atom $p \in \mathcal{A}$. We present next several properties about total traces and the relation between MHT and MTL.

Proposition 2 (Persistence). *Let $(\langle \mathbf{H}, \mathbf{T} \rangle, \tau)$ be a timed HT-trace of length λ over $\mathcal{A}$ and let φ be a metric formula over $\mathcal{A}$. Then, for any $k \in [0..\lambda)$, if $(\langle \mathbf{H}, \mathbf{T} \rangle, \tau), k \models \varphi$ then $(\langle \mathbf{T}, \mathbf{T} \rangle, \tau), k \models \varphi$.* $\square$

Thanks to Proposition 2 and a decidability result in [23], we get:

Corollary 1 (Decidability of MHT_f). *The logic of MHT_f is decidable.* $\square$

Proposition 3. *Let $(\langle \mathbf{H}, \mathbf{T} \rangle, \tau)$ be a timed HT-trace of length λ over $\mathcal{A}$ and let φ be a metric formula over $\mathcal{A}$. Then, $(\langle \mathbf{H}, \mathbf{T} \rangle, \tau), k \models \neg\varphi$ iff $(\langle \mathbf{T}, \mathbf{T} \rangle, \tau), k \not\models \varphi$.* $\square$

Proposition 4. *Let φ and ψ be metric formulas without implication (and so, without negation either). Then, $\varphi \equiv \psi$ in MTL iff $\varphi \equiv \psi$ in MHT.* $\square$

Many tautologies in MHT or its fragments have a dual version depending on the nature of the operators involved. The following pair of duality properties allows us to save space and proof effort when listing interesting valid equivalences. We define all pairs of dual connectives as follows: $\land_\mathcal{I}/\lor_\mathcal{I}$, $\top_\mathcal{I}/\bot_\mathcal{I}$, $\mathsf{U}_\mathcal{I}/\mathbb{R}_\mathcal{I}$, $\circ_\mathcal{I}/\hat{\circ}_\mathcal{I}$, $\Box_\mathcal{I}/\Diamond_\mathcal{I}$, $\mathsf{S}_\mathcal{I}/\mathsf{T}_\mathcal{I}$, $\bullet_\mathcal{I}/\hat{\bullet}_\mathcal{I}$, $\blacksquare_\mathcal{I}/\blacklozenge_\mathcal{I}$. For any formula φ without implications, we define $\delta(\varphi)$ as the result of replacing each connective by its dual operator.

Then, we get the following corollary of Proposition 4.

Corollary 2 (Boolean Duality). *Let φ and ψ be formulas without implication. Then, MHT satisfies: $\varphi \equiv \psi$ iff $\delta(\varphi) \equiv \delta(\psi)$.* $\square$

Let $\mathsf{U}_\mathcal{I}/\mathsf{S}_\mathcal{I}$, $\mathbb{R}_\mathcal{I}/\mathsf{T}_\mathcal{I}$, $\circ_\mathcal{I}/\bullet_\mathcal{I}$, $\hat{\circ}_\mathcal{I}/\hat{\bullet}_\mathcal{I}$, $\Box_\mathcal{I}/\blacksquare_\mathcal{I}$, and $\Diamond_\mathcal{I}/\blacklozenge_\mathcal{I}$ be all pairs of swapped-time connectives and $\sigma(\varphi)$ be the replacement in φ of each connective by its swapped-time version. Then, we have the following result for finite traces.

Lemma 1. *There exists a mapping ϱ on finite timed HT-traces $\mathbf{M}$ of the same length $\lambda \geq 0$ such that for any $k \in [0..\lambda)$, $\mathbf{M}, k \models \varphi$ iff $\varrho(\mathbf{M}), \lambda - 1 - k \models \sigma(\varphi)$.*

Theorem 1 (Temporal Duality Theorem). *A metric formula φ is a MHT_f-tautology iff $\sigma(\varphi)$ is a MHT_f-tautology.* $\square$

As in traditional Equilibrium Logic [24], non-monotonicity is achieved by a selection among the MHT models of a theory.

Definition 3 (Metric Equilibrium/Stable Model). *Let* $\mathfrak{S}$ *be some set of timed* HT-*traces. A total timed* HT-*trace* $(\langle \mathbf{T}, \mathbf{T} \rangle, \tau) \in \mathfrak{S}$ *is a metric equilibrium model of* $\mathfrak{S}$ *iff there is no other* $\mathbf{H} < \mathbf{T}$ *such that* $(\langle \mathbf{H}, \mathbf{T} \rangle, \tau) \in \mathfrak{S}$. *The timed trace* $(\mathbf{T}, \tau)$ *is called a metric stable model of* $\mathfrak{S}$. □

We talk about metric equilibrium (or metric stable) models of a theory Γ when $\mathfrak{S} = \text{MHT}(\Gamma)$, and we write $\text{MEL}(\Gamma, \lambda)$ and $\text{MEL}(\Gamma)$ to stand for the metric equilibrium models of $\text{MHT}(\Gamma, \lambda)$ and $\text{MHT}(\Gamma)$, respectively. *Metric Equilibrium Logic* (MEL) is the non-monotonic logic induced by the metric equilibrium models of metric theories. As before, variants MEL_f and MEL_ω refer to MEL when restricted to traces of finite and infinite length, respectively.

Proposition 5. *The set of metric equilibrium models of* Γ *can be partitioned on the trace lengths, namely,* $\bigcup_{\lambda=0}^{\omega} \text{MEL}(\Gamma, \lambda) = \text{MEL}(\Gamma)$. □

We can enforce metric models to be traces with a strict timing function τ, that is, $\tau(i) < \tau(i+1)$ for any i such that $i + 1 \in [1..\lambda]$. This can be achieved with the simple addition of the axiom $\square \neg \mathrm{o}_0 \top$. In the following, we assume that this axiom is included and consider, in this way, strict timing. For instance, a consequence of strict timing is that one-step operators become definable in terms of other connectives. For non-empty intervals $[m..n)$ with $m < n$, we get:

$$\bullet_{[m..n)}\varphi \equiv \blacksquare_{[1..m)}\bot \wedge \blacklozenge_{[h..n)}\varphi$$
$$\mathrm{o}_{[m..n)}\varphi \equiv \square_{[1..m)}\bot \wedge \Diamond_{[h..n)}\varphi \qquad \text{where } h = \max(1, m);$$

whereas for empty intervals with $m \geq n$, we obtain $\bullet_{[m..n)}\varphi \equiv \mathrm{o}_{[m..n)}\varphi \equiv \bot$.

Back to our example, suppose we have the theory Γ consisting of the formulas (1)–(3). In the example, we abbreviate subsets of the set of atoms $\{green, push, red\}$ as strings formed by their initials: For instance, pr stands for $\{push, red\}$. For readability sake, we represent traces (T_0, T_1, T_2) as $T_0 \cdot T_1 \cdot T_2$. Consider first the total models of Γ: the first two rules force one of the two atoms $green$ or red to hold at every state. Besides, we can choose adding $push$ or not, but if we do so, $green$ should hold later on according to (3). Now, for any total model $(\langle \mathbf{T}, \mathbf{T} \rangle, \tau), 0 \models \Gamma$ where $green$ or $push$ hold at some states, we can always form $\mathbf{H}$ where we remove those atoms from all the states and it is not difficult to see that $(\langle \mathbf{H}, \mathbf{T} \rangle, \tau), 0 \models \Gamma$, so $(\langle \mathbf{T}, \mathbf{T} \rangle, \tau)$ is not in equilibrium. As a consequence, metric equilibrium models of Γ have the form $(\langle \mathbf{T}, \mathbf{T} \rangle, \tau)$ being $\mathbf{T} = \langle T_i \rangle_{i \in [0..\lambda)}$ with $T_i = \{red\}$ for all $i \in [0..\lambda)$ and any arbitrary strict timing function τ. To illustrate non-monotonicity, suppose now that we have $\Gamma' = \Gamma \cup \{\mathrm{o}_5\ push\}$ and, for simplicity, consider length $\lambda = 3$ and traces of the form $T_0 \cdot T_1 \cdot T_2$. Again, it is not hard to see that total models with $green$ or $push$ in state T_0 are not in equilibrium, being the only option $T_0 = \{red\}$. The same happens for $green$ at T_1, so we get $T_1 = \{push, red\}$ as only candidate for equilibrium model. However, since $push \in T_1$, the only possibility to satisfy the consequent of (3) is having $green \in T_2$. Again, we can also see that adding *push* at that state would not be in equilibrium so that the only trace in equilibrium is $T_0 = \{red\}$, $T_1 = \{push, red\}$ and $T_2 = \{green\}$. As for the timing, $\tau(0) = 0$ is fixed, and satisfaction of formula $(\bigcirc_5 \; push)$ fixes $\tau(1) = 5$. Then, from (3) we conclude that *green* must hold at any moment starting at t between $5 + 1$ and $5 + 14$ and is kept true in all states between t and $t + 30$ time units, but as $\lambda = 2$, this means just t. To sum up, we get 14 metric equilibrium models with $\tau(0) = 0$ and $\tau(1) = 5$ fixed, but varying $\tau(2)$ between 6 and 19.

We observe next the effect of the semantics of *always* and *eventually* on truth constants. Let φ be an arbitrary metric formula and $m, n \in \mathbb{N}$. Then, $\square_{[m..n)} \bot$ means that there is no state in interval $[m..n)$ and $\lozenge_{[m..n)} \top$ means that there is at least one state in this interval. The formula $\square_{[m..n)} \top$ is a tautology, whereas $\lozenge_{[m..n)} \bot$ is unsatisfiable. The same applies to past operators $\blacklozenge_{[m..n)}$ and $\blacksquare_{[m..n)}$.

The following equivalences state that interval $\mathcal{I} = [0..0]$ makes all binary metric operators collapse into their right hand argument formula, whereas unary operators collapse to a truth constant. For metric formulas ψ and φ, we have:

$$\psi \; \mathbb{U}_0 \; \varphi \equiv \psi \; \mathbb{R}_0 \; \varphi \equiv \varphi \tag{4}$$

$$\bigcirc_0 \varphi \equiv \bullet_0 \varphi \equiv \bot \tag{5}$$

$$\widehat{\bigcirc}_0 \varphi \equiv \widehat{\bullet}_0 \varphi \equiv \top \tag{6}$$

The last two lines are precisely an effect of dealing with strict traces: For instance, $\bigcirc_0 \varphi \equiv \bot$ tells us that it is always impossible to have a successor state with the same time (the time difference is 0) as the current one, regardless of the formula φ we want to check. The next lemma allows us to unfold metric operators for single-point time intervals $[n..n]$ with $n > 0$.

Lemma 2. *For metric formulas ψ and φ and for $n > 0$, we have:*

$$\psi \; \mathbb{U}_n \; \varphi \equiv \bigvee_{i=1}^{n} \bigcirc_i (\psi \; \mathbb{U}_{n-i} \; \varphi) \tag{7} \qquad \lozenge_n \varphi \equiv \bigvee_{i=1}^{n} \bigcirc_i \lozenge_{n-i} \varphi \tag{9}$$

$$\psi \; \mathbb{R}_n \; \varphi \equiv \bigwedge_{i=1}^{n} \widehat{\bigcirc}_i (\psi \; \mathbb{R}_{n-i} \; \varphi) \tag{8} \qquad \square_n \varphi \equiv \bigwedge_{i=1}^{n} \widehat{\bigcirc}_i \square_{n-i} \varphi \tag{10}$$

The same applies for the dual past operators. □

Going one step further, we can also unfold *until* and *release* for intervals of the form $[0..n]$ with the application of the following result.

Lemma 3. *For metric formulas ψ and φ and for $n > 0$, we have:*

$$\psi \; \mathbb{U}_{\leq n} \; \varphi \equiv \varphi \vee (\psi \wedge \bigvee_{i=1}^{n} \bigcirc_i (\psi \; \mathbb{U}_{\leq (n-i)} \; \varphi)) \tag{11}$$

$$\psi \; \mathbb{R}_{\leq n} \; \varphi \equiv \varphi \wedge (\psi \vee \bigwedge_{i=1}^{n} \widehat{\bigcirc}_i (\psi \; \mathbb{R}_{\leq (n-i)} \; \varphi)) \tag{12}$$

The same applies for the dual past operators. □

Finally, the next theorem contains a pair of equivalences that, when dealing with finite intervals, can be used to recursively unfold *until* and *release* into combinations of *next* with Boolean operators (an analogous result applies for *since*, *trigger* and *previous* due to temporal duality).

Theorem 2 (Next-unfolding). *For metric formulas ψ and φ and for $m, n \in \mathbb{N}$ such that $0 < m$ and $m < n - 1$ we have:*

$$\psi \, \mathbb{U}_{[m..n)} \, \varphi \equiv \bigvee_{i=1}^{m} \bigcirc_i(\psi \, \mathbb{U}_{[m-i..n-i)} \, \varphi) \vee \bigvee_{i=m+1}^{n-1} \bigcirc_i(\psi \, \mathbb{U}_{\leq(n-1-i)} \, \varphi) \qquad (13)$$

$$\psi \, \mathbb{R}_{[m..n)} \, \varphi \equiv \bigwedge_{i=1}^{m} \widehat{\bigcirc}_i(\psi \, \mathbb{R}_{[(m-i)..(n-i))} \, \varphi) \wedge \bigwedge_{i=m+1}^{n-1} \widehat{\bigcirc}_i(\psi \, \mathbb{R}_{\leq(n-1-i)} \, \varphi) \qquad (14)$$

The same applies for the dual past operators. $\qquad\square$

As an example, consider the metric formula $p \, \mathbb{U}_{[2..4)} \, q$.

$$p \, \mathbb{U}_{[2..4)} \, q \equiv \bigvee_{i=1}^{2} \bigcirc_i(p \, \mathbb{U}_{[(2-i)..(4-i))} \, q) \vee \bigvee_{i=2+1}^{3} \bigcirc_i(p \, \mathbb{U}_{\leq(3-i)} \, q)$$

$$\equiv \bigcirc_1(p \, \mathbb{U}_{[1..3)} \, q) \vee \bigcirc_2(p \, \mathbb{U}_{\leq 1} \, q) \vee \bigcirc_3(p \, \mathbb{U}_0 \, q)$$

$$\equiv \bigcirc_1(p \, \mathbb{U}_{[1..3)} \, q) \vee \bigcirc_2(q \vee (p \wedge \bigcirc_1 q)) \vee \bigcirc_3 q$$

$$\equiv \bigcirc_1(\bigcirc_1(q \vee (p \wedge \bigcirc_1 q)) \vee \bigcirc_2 q) \vee \bigcirc_2(q \vee (p \wedge \bigcirc_1 q)) \vee \bigcirc_3 q$$

Another useful result that can be applied to unfold metric operators is the following range splitting theorem.

Theorem 3 (Range splitting). *For metric formulas ψ and φ, we have*

$$\psi \, \mathbb{U}_{[m..n)} \, \varphi \equiv (\psi \, \mathbb{U}_{[m..i)} \, \varphi) \vee (\psi \, \mathbb{U}_{[i..n)} \, \varphi) \qquad \textit{for all } i \in [m..n)$$

$$\psi \, \mathbb{R}_{[m..n)} \, \varphi \equiv (\psi \, \mathbb{R}_{[m..i)} \, \varphi) \wedge (\psi \, \mathbb{R}_{[i..n)} \, \varphi) \qquad \textit{for all } i \in [m..n)$$

The same applies for the dual past operators. $\qquad\square$

3   Translation into Monadic Quantified Here-and-There with Difference Constraints

In a similar spirit as the well-known translation of Kamp [19] from LTL to first-order logic, we consider a translation from MHT into a first-order version of HT, more precisely, a function-free fragment of the logic of Quantified Here-and-There with static domains (QHT^s in [25]). The word *static* means that the first-order domain D is fixed for both worlds, here and there. We refer to our fragment of QHT^s as *monadic QHT with difference constraints* ($QHT[\preccurlyeq_\delta]$). In this logic, the static domain is a subset $D \subseteq \mathbb{N}$ of the natural numbers containing at least the element $0 \in D$. Intuitively, D corresponds to the set of relevant time points (i.e. those associated to states) considered in each model. Note that the first state is always associated with time $0 \in D$.

The syntax of $QHT[\preccurlyeq_\delta]$ is the same as for first-order logic with several restrictions: First, there are no functions other than the 0-ary function (or constant) '0' always interpreted as the domain element 0 (when there is no ambiguity, we drop quotes around constant names). Second, all predicates are monadic except for a family of binary predicates of the form $\preccurlyeq_\delta$ with $\delta \in \mathbb{Z} \cup \{\omega\}$ where δ is understood as part of the predicate name. For simplicity, we write $x \preccurlyeq_\delta y$ instead of $\preccurlyeq_\delta (x,y)$ and $x \preccurlyeq_\delta y \preccurlyeq_{\delta'} z$ to stand for $x \preccurlyeq_\delta y \wedge y \preccurlyeq_{\delta'} z$. Unlike monadic predicates, the interpretation of $x \preccurlyeq_\delta y$ is static (it does not vary in worlds here and there) and intuitively means that the difference $x - y$ in time points is smaller or equal than δ. A first-order formula φ satisfying all these restrictions is called a *first-order metric formula* or *FOM-formula* for short. A formula is a *sentence* if it contains no free variables. For instance, we will see that the metric formula (3) can be equivalently translated into the FOM-sentence:

$$\forall x \, (x \preccurlyeq_0 0 \wedge push(x) \rightarrow \exists y \, (x \preccurlyeq_{-1} y \preccurlyeq_{14} x \wedge \forall z \, (y \preccurlyeq_0 z \preccurlyeq_{30} y \rightarrow green(z)))) \tag{15}$$

We sometimes handle *partially grounded* FOM sentences where some variables in predicate arguments have been directly replaced by elements from D. For instance, if we represent (15) as $\forall x \, \varphi(x)$, the expression $\varphi(4)$ stands for:

$$4 \preccurlyeq_0 0 \wedge push(4) \rightarrow \exists y \, (x \preccurlyeq_{-1} y \preccurlyeq_{14} x \wedge \forall z \, (y \preccurlyeq_0 z \preccurlyeq_{30} y \rightarrow green(z)))$$

and corresponds to a partially grounded FOM-sentence where the domain element 4 is used as predicate argument in atoms $4 \preccurlyeq_0 0$ and $push(4)$.

A *$QHT[\preccurlyeq_\delta]$-signature* is simply a set of monadic predicates $\mathcal{P}$. Given D as above, $Atoms(D, \mathcal{P})$ denotes the set of all ground atoms $p(n)$ for every monadic predicate $p \in \mathcal{P}$ and every $n \in D$. A $QHT[\preccurlyeq_\delta]$-interpretation for signature $\mathcal{P}$ has the form $\langle D, H, T \rangle$ where $D \subseteq \mathbb{N}$, $0 \in D$ and $H \subseteq T \subseteq Atoms(D, \mathcal{P})$.

Definition 4 ($QHT[\preccurlyeq_\delta]$-satisfaction; [25]). *A $QHT[\preccurlyeq_\delta]$-interpretation $\mathcal{M} = \langle D, H, T \rangle$ satisfies a (partially grounded) FOM-sentence φ, written $\mathcal{M} \models \varphi$, if the following conditions hold:*

1. *$\mathcal{M} \models \top$ and $\mathcal{M} \not\models \bot$*
2. *$\mathcal{M} \models p(d)$ iff $p(d) \in H$*
3. *$\mathcal{M} \models t_1 \preccurlyeq_\delta t_2$ iff $t_1 - t_2 \leq \delta$, with $t_1, t_2 \in D$*
4. *$\mathcal{M} \models \varphi \wedge \psi$ iff $\mathcal{M} \models \varphi$ and $\mathcal{M} \models \psi$*
5. *$\mathcal{M} \models \varphi \vee \psi$ iff $\mathcal{M} \models \varphi$ or $\mathcal{M} \models \psi$*
6. *$\mathcal{M} \models \varphi \rightarrow \psi$ iff $\langle D, X, T \rangle \not\models \varphi$ or $\langle D, X, T \rangle \models \psi$, for $X \in \{H, T\}$*
7. *$\mathcal{M} \models \forall x \, \varphi(x)$ iff $\mathcal{M} \models \varphi(t)$, for all $t \in D$*
8. *$\mathcal{M} \models \exists x \, \varphi(x)$ iff $\mathcal{M} \models \varphi(t)$, for some $t \in D$* □

We can read the expression $x \preccurlyeq_\delta y$ as just another way of writing the difference constraint $x - y \leq \delta$. When δ is an integer, we may see it as a lower bound $x - \delta \leq y$ for y or as an upper bound $x \leq y + \delta$ for x. For $\delta = \omega$, $x \preccurlyeq_\omega y$ is equivalent to $\top$ since it amounts to the comparison $x - y \leq \omega$. An important observation is that this difference predicate $\preccurlyeq_\delta$ satisfies the excluded middle axiom, that is, the following formula is a $QHT[\preccurlyeq_\delta]$-tautology:

$$\forall x \, \forall y \, (\, x \preccurlyeq_\delta y \vee \neg(x \preccurlyeq_\delta y) \,) \tag{16}$$

for every $\delta \in \mathbb{Z} \cup \{\omega\}$. We provide next several useful abbreviations:

$$x \prec_\delta y \overset{def}{=} \neg(y \preccurlyeq_{-\delta} x)$$
$$x \leq y \overset{def}{=} x \preccurlyeq_0 y \qquad\qquad x \neq y \overset{def}{=} \neg(x = y)$$
$$x = y \overset{def}{=} (x \leq y) \wedge (y \leq x) \qquad\qquad x < y \overset{def}{=} (x \leq y) \wedge (x \neq y)$$

For any pair $\odot$, $\oplus$ of comparison symbols, we extend the abbreviation $x \odot y \oplus z$ to stand for the conjunction $x \odot y \wedge y \oplus z$. Note that the above derived order relation $x \leq y$ captures the one used in Kamp's original translation [19] for LTL.

Equilibrium models for first-order theories are defined as in [25].

Definition 5 (Quantified Equilibrium Model; [25]). *Let φ be a first-order formula. A total $QHT[\preccurlyeq_\delta]$-interpretation $\langle D, T, T \rangle$ is a first-order equilibrium model of φ if $\langle D, T, T \rangle \models \varphi$ and there is no $H \subset T$ satisfying $\langle D, H, T \rangle \models \varphi$.* $\square$

Before presenting our translation, we need to remark that we consider non-empty intervals of the form $[m..n)$ with $m < n$.

Definition 6 (First-order encoding). *Let φ be a metric formula over $\mathcal{A}$. We define the translation $[\varphi]_x$ of φ for some time point $x \in \mathbb{N}$ as follows:*

$$[\bot]_x \overset{def}{=} \bot$$

$$[p]_x \overset{def}{=} p(x), \quad \text{for any } p \in \mathcal{A}$$

$$[\varphi \otimes \psi]_x \overset{def}{=} [\varphi]_x \otimes [\beta]_x, \quad \text{for any connective } \otimes \in \{\wedge, \vee, \rightarrow\}$$

$$[\bigcirc_{[m,n)}\psi]_x \overset{def}{=} \exists y\, (x < y \wedge (\neg \exists z\, x < z < y) \wedge x \preccurlyeq_{-m} y \prec_n x \wedge [\psi]_y)$$

$$[\widehat{\bigcirc}_{[m,n)}\psi]_x \overset{def}{=} \forall y\, (x < y \wedge (\neg \exists z\, x < z < y) \wedge x \preccurlyeq_{-m} y \prec_n x \rightarrow [\psi]_y)$$

$$[\varphi\, \mathbb{U}_{[m,n)}\, \psi]_x \overset{def}{=} \exists y\, (x \leq y \wedge x \preccurlyeq_{-m} y \prec_n x \wedge [\psi]_y \wedge \forall z\, (x \leq z < y \rightarrow [\varphi]_z))$$

$$[\varphi\, \mathbb{R}_{[m,n)}\, \psi]_x \overset{def}{=} \forall y\, ((x \leq y \wedge x \preccurlyeq_{-m} y \prec_n x) \rightarrow ([\psi]_y \vee \exists z\, (x \leq z < y \wedge [\varphi]_z)))$$

$$[\bullet_{[m,n)}\psi]_x \overset{def}{=} \exists y\, (y < x \wedge \neg \exists z\, (y < z < x) \wedge x \prec_n y \preccurlyeq_{-m} x \wedge [\psi]_y)$$

$$[\widehat{\bullet}_{[m,n)}\psi]_x \overset{def}{=} \forall y\, ((y < x \wedge \neg \exists z\, (y < z < x) \wedge x \prec_n y \preccurlyeq_{-m} x) \rightarrow [\psi]_y)$$

$$[\varphi\, \mathsf{S}_{[m,n)}\, \psi]_x \overset{def}{=} \exists y\, (y \leq x \wedge x \prec_n y \preccurlyeq_{-m} x \wedge [\psi]_y \wedge \forall (y < z < x \rightarrow [\varphi]_z))$$

$$[\varphi\, \mathsf{T}_{[m,n)}\, \psi]_x \overset{def}{=} \forall y\, ((y \leq x \wedge x \prec_n y \preccurlyeq_{-m} x) \rightarrow ([\psi]_y \vee \exists z\, (y < z \leq x \wedge [\varphi]_z)))$$

$\square$

Each quantification introduces a new variable. For instance, consider the translation of (3) at point $x = 0$. Let us denote (3) as $\square(push \rightarrow \alpha)$ where $\alpha := \Diamond_{[1..15)}(\square_{\leq 30}\, green)$. Then, if we translate the outermost operator $\square$, we get:

$$[\square(push \rightarrow \alpha)]_0$$

$$= [\bot\ \mathbb{R}_{[0..\omega)}\, (push \rightarrow \alpha)]_0$$

$$= \forall y\, ((0 \leq y \wedge 0 \preccurlyeq_{-0} y \prec_\omega 0) \rightarrow ([push \rightarrow \alpha]_y \vee \exists z\, (0 \leq z < y \wedge \bot)))$$

$$\equiv \forall y\, (0 \leq y \wedge 0 \leq y \wedge \top \rightarrow ([push]_y \rightarrow [\alpha]_y) \vee \bot)$$

$$\equiv \forall y\, (0 \leq y \wedge push(y) \rightarrow [\alpha]_y)$$

$$\equiv \forall x\, (0 \leq x \wedge push(x) \rightarrow [\alpha]_x)$$

where we renamed the quantified variable for convenience. If we proceed further, with α as $\Diamond_{[1..15)}\beta$ letting $\beta := (\Box_{\leq 30}\ green)$, we obtain:

$$
\begin{aligned}
[\alpha]_x &= [\Diamond_{[1..15)}\beta]_x \\
&= [\top\ \mathsf{U}_{[1..15)}\ \beta]_x \\
&= \exists y\ (x \leq y \wedge x \preccurlyeq_{-1} y \prec_{15} x \wedge [\beta]_y \wedge \forall z\,(x \leq z < y \to \top)) \\
&\equiv \exists y\ (x \preccurlyeq_{-1} y \prec_{15} x \wedge [\beta]_y) \equiv \exists y\ (x \preccurlyeq_{-1} y \preccurlyeq_{14} x \wedge [\beta]_y)
\end{aligned}
$$

Finally, the translation of β at y amounts to:

$$
\begin{aligned}
&[\Box_{\leq 30}\ green]_y \\
&= [\bot\ \mathsf{R}_{[0..30)}\ green]_y \\
&= \forall y'\ (\ y \leq y' \wedge y \preccurlyeq_{-0} y' \prec_{30} y \to green(y') \vee \exists z\,(y \leq z < y' \wedge \bot)\ ) \\
&\equiv \forall y'\ (\ y \leq y' \wedge y \preccurlyeq_0 y' \wedge y' \prec_{30} y \to green(y')\ ) \\
&\equiv \forall y'\ (\ y \preccurlyeq_0 y' \prec_{30} y \to green(y')\ ) \\
&\equiv \forall z\ (\ y \preccurlyeq_0 z \prec_{30} y \to green(z)\ )
\end{aligned}
$$

so that, when joining all steps together, we get the formula (15) given above.

The following model correspondence between MHT_f and $QHT[\preccurlyeq_\delta]$ interpretations can be established. Given a timed trace $(\langle\mathbf{H},\mathbf{T}\rangle,\tau)$ of length $\lambda > 0$ for signature $\mathcal{A}$, we define the first-order signature $\mathcal{P} = \{p/1 \mid p \in \mathcal{A}\}$ and a corresponding $QHT[\preccurlyeq_\delta]$ interpretation $\langle D, H, T\rangle$ where $D = \{\tau(i) \mid i \in [0..\lambda)\}$, $H = \{p(\tau(i)) \mid i \in [0..\lambda)\text{ and }p \in H_i\}$ and $T = \{p(\tau(i)) \mid i \in [0..\lambda)\text{ and }p \in T_i\}$. Under the assumption of strict semantics, the following model correspondence can be proved by structural induction.

Theorem 4. *Let* φ *be a metric temporal formula,* $(\langle\mathbf{H},\mathbf{T}\rangle,\tau)$ *a metric trace,* $\langle D, H, T\rangle$ *its corresponding* $QHT[\preccurlyeq_\delta]$ *interpretation and* $i \in [0..\lambda)$.

$$
(\langle\mathbf{H},\mathbf{T}\rangle,\tau), i \models \varphi \quad\text{iff}\quad \langle D, H, T\rangle \models [\varphi]_{\tau(i)} \tag{17}
$$

$$
(\langle\mathbf{T},\mathbf{T}\rangle,\tau), i \models \varphi \quad\text{iff}\quad \langle D, T, T\rangle \models [\varphi]_{\tau(i)} \tag{18}
$$

$\square$

4   Discussion

Seen from far, we have presented an extension of the logic of Here-and-There with qualitative and quantitative temporal constraints. More closely, our logics MHT and MEL can be seen es metric extensions of the linear-time logics THT and TEL obtained by constraining temporal operators by intervals over natural numbers. The current approach generalizes the previous metric extension of TEL from [9] by uncoupling the ordinal position i of a state in the trace from its location in the time line $\tau(i)$, which indicates now the elapsed time since the beginning of that trace. Thus, while $\Diamond_{[5..5]}\ p$ meant in [9] that p must hold exactly after 5 transitions, it means here that there must be some future state (after $n > 0$ transitions) satisfying p and located 5 time units later. As a first approach, we have considered time points as natural numbers, $\tau(i) \in \mathbb{N}$. Our choice of a discrete rather than continuous time domain is primarily motivated by our practical objective to implement the logic programming fragment of MEL on top of existing temporal ASP systems, like *telingo*, and thus to avoid undecidability.

The need for quantitative time constraints is well recognized and many metric extensions have been proposed. For instance, actions with durations are considered in [27] in an action language adapting a state-based approach. Interestingly, quantitative time constraints also gave rise to combining ASP with Constraint Solving [3]; this connection is now semantically reinforced by our translation advocating the enrichment of ASP with difference constraints. Even earlier, metric extensions of Logic Programming were proposed in [6]. As well, metric extensions of Datalog are introduced in [28] and applied to stream reasoning in [29]. An ASP-based approach to stream reasoning is elaborated in abundance in [4]. Streams can be seen as infinite traces. Hence, apart from certain dedicated concepts, like time windows, such approaches bear a close relation to metric reasoning. Detailing this relationship is an interesting topic of future research. More remotely, metric constructs were used in trace alignment [13], scheduling [22], and an extension to Golog [18].

Acknowledgments. This work was supported by MICINN, Spain, grant PID2020-116201GB-I00, Xunta de Galicia, Spain (GPC ED431B 2019/03), Région Pays de la Loire, France (EL4HC and étoiles montantes CTASP), DFG grants SCHA 550/11 and 15, Germany, and European Union COST action CA-17124.

References

1. Aguado, F., Cabalar, P., Diéguez, M., Pérez, G., Vidal, C.: Temporal equilibrium logic: a survey. J. Appl. Non-Class. Log. **23**(1–2), 2–24 (2013)
2. Balduccini, M., Lierler, Y., Woltran, S. (eds.): Proceedings of the Fifteenth International Conference on Logic Programming and Nonmonotonic Reasoning (LPNMR 2019), LNAI, vol. 11481. Springer, Cham (2019). https://doi.org/10.1007/978-3-030-20528-7
3. Baselice, S., Bonatti, P.A., Gelfond, M.: Towards an integration of answer set and constraint solving. In: Gabbrielli, M., Gupta, G. (eds.) ICLP 2005. LNCS, vol. 3668, pp. 52–66. Springer, Heidelberg (2005). https://doi.org/10.1007/11562931_7
4. Beck, H., Dao-Tran, M., Eiter, T.: LARS: a logic-based framework for analytic reasoning over streams. Artif. Intell. **261**, 16–70 (2018)
5. Bosser, A., Cabalar, P., Diéguez, M., Schaub, T.: Introducing temporal stable models for linear dynamic logic. In: Proceedings of the Sixteenth International Conference on Principles of Knowledge Representation and Reasoning (KR 2018), pp. 12–21. AAAI Press (2018)
6. Brzoska, C.: Temporal logic programming with metric and past operators. In: Fisher, M., Owens, R. (eds.) IJCAI 1993. LNCS, vol. 897, pp. 21–39. Springer, Heidelberg (1995). https://doi.org/10.1007/3-540-58976-7_2
7. Cabalar, P., Diéguez, M., Laferriere, F., Schaub, T.: Implementing dynamic answer set programming over finite traces. In: Proceedings of the Twenty-Fourth European Conference on Artificial Intelligence (ECAI 2020), pp. 656–663. IOS Press (2020)

8. Cabalar, P., Diéguez, M., Schaub, T.: Towards dynamic answer set programming over finite traces. In: [2], pp. 148–162 (2019)
9. Cabalar, P., Diéguez, M., Schaub, T., Schuhmann, A.: Towards metric temporal answer set programming. Theory Pract. Logic Program. **20**(5), 783–798 (2020)
10. Cabalar, P., Kaminski, R., Morkisch, P., Schaub, T.: telingo = ASP + Time. In: [2], pp. 256–269 (2019)
11. Cabalar, P., Kaminski, R., Schaub, T., Schuhmann, A.: Temporal answer set programming on finite traces. Theory Pract. Logic Program. **18**(3–4), 406–420 (2018)
12. Cabalar, P., Diéguez, M., Schaub, T., Schuhmann, A.: Metric temporal answer set programming over timed traces (extended abstract). In: Stream Reasoning Workshop (2021)
13. De Giacomo, G., Murano, A., Patrizi, F., Perelli, G.: Timed trace alignment with metric temporal logic over finite traces. In: Proceedings of the Eighteenth International Conference on Principles of Knowledge Representation and Reasoning (KR 2022), pp. 227–236. AAAI Press (2020)
14. Fisher, M., Gabbay, D., Vila, L. (eds.): Handbook of Temporal Reasoning in Artificial Intelligence. Elsevier Science (2005)
15. Gebser, M., Kaminski, R., Kaufmann, B., Ostrowski, M., Schaub, T., Wanko, P.: Theory solving made easy with Clingo 5. In: Technical Communications of the Thirty-Second International Conference on Logic Programming (ICLP 2016), pp. 2:1–2:15. OASIcs (2016)
16. Harel, D., Tiuryn, J., Kozen, D.: Dynamic Logic. MIT Press, Cambridge (2000)
17. Heyting, A.: Die formalen Regeln der intuitionistischen Logik. In: Sitzungsberichte der Preussischen Akademie der Wissenschaften, pp. 42 56. Deutsche Akademie der Wissenschaften zu Berlin (1930)
18. Hofmann, T., Lakemeyer, G.: A logic for specifying metric temporal constraints for Golog programs. In: Proceedings of the Eleventh Workshop on Cognitive Robotics (CogRob 2018), pp. 36–46. CEUR Workshop Proceedings (2019)
19. Kamp, J.: Tense logic and the theory of linear order. Ph.D. thesis, University of California at Los Angeles (1968)
20. Koymans, R.: Specifying real-time properties with metric temporal logic. Real-Time Syst. **2**(4), 255–299 (1990)
21. Lifschitz, V.: Answer set planning. In: Proceedings of the International Conference on Logic Programming (ICLP 1999), pp. 23–37. MIT Press (1999)
22. Luo, R., Valenzano, R., Li, Y., Beck, C., McIlraith, S.: Using metric temporal logic to specify scheduling problems. In: Proceedings of the Fifteenth International Conference on Principles of Knowledge Representation and Reasoning (KR 2016), pp. 581–584. AAAI Press (2016)
23. Ouaknine, J., Worrell, J.: On the decidability and complexity of metric temporal logic over finite words. Log. Methods Comput. Sci. **3**(1) (2007). https://doi.org/10.2168/LMCS-3(1:8)2007
24. Pearce, D.: A new logical characterisation of stable models and answer sets. In: Dix, J., Pereira, L.M., Przymusinski, T.C. (eds.) NMELP 1996. LNCS, vol. 1216, pp. 57–70. Springer, Heidelberg (1997). https://doi.org/10.1007/BFb0023801
25. Pearce, D., Valverde, A.: Quantified equilibrium logic and foundations for answer set programs. In: Garcia de la Banda, M., Pontelli, E. (eds.) ICLP 2008. LNCS, vol. 5366, pp. 546–560. Springer, Heidelberg (2008). https://doi.org/10.1007/978-3-540-89982-2_46
26. Pnueli, A.: The temporal logic of programs. In: Proceedings of the Eighteenth Symposium on Foundations of Computer Science (FOCS 1977), pp. 46–57. IEEE Computer Society Press (1977)

27. Son, T., Baral, C., Tuan, L.: Adding time and intervals to procedural and hierarchical control specifications. In: Proceedings of the Nineteenth National Conference on Artificial Intelligence (AAAI 2004), pp. 92–97. AAAI Press (2004)
28. Wałega, P., Cuenca Grau, B., Kaminski, M., Kostylev, E.: DatalogMTL: computational complexity and expressive power. In: Proceedings of the Twenty-Eighth International Joint Conference on Artificial Intelligence (IJCAI 2019), pp. 1886–1892. ijcai.org (2019)
29. Wałega, P., Kaminski, M., Cuenca Grau, B.: Reasoning over streaming data in metric temporal Datalog. In: Proceedings of the Thirty-third National Conference on Artificial Intelligence (AAAI 2019), pp. 3092–3099. AAAI Press (2019)

Epistemic Logic Programs: A Study of Some Properties

Stefania Costantini[1](✉) and Andrea Formisano[2]

[1] DISIM, Università dell'Aquila, L'Aquila, Italy
stefania.costantini@univaq.it
[2] DMIF, Università di Udine, Udine, Italy

Abstract. Epistemic Logic Programs (ELPs), extend Answer Set Programming (ASP) with epistemic operators. The semantics of such programs is provided in terms of *world views*, which are sets of belief sets. Different semantic approaches propose different characterizations of world views. Recent work has introduced semantic properties that should be met by any semantics for ELPs, like the *Epistemic Splitting Property*, that, if satisfied, allows to modularly compute world views in a bottom-up fashion, analogously to 'traditional' ASP. We analyze the possibility to change the perspective, shifting from a bottom-up to a top-down approach to splitting. Our new definition: (i) copes with concerns regarding *unfoundedness* of world views and *subjective constraint monotonicity*; (ii) is provably applicable to many of the existing semantics; (iii) operates similarly to "traditional" ASP; (iv) provably coincides with the bottom-up notion of splitting at least on the class of *Epistemically Stratified Programs* (which are, intuitively, those where the use of epistemic operators is stratified).

Keywords: Answer Set Programming · Epistemic Logic Programs · Epistemic Splitting

1 Introduction

Epistemic Logic programs (ELPs, in the following just 'programs' if not explicitly stated differently), were first introduced in [9, 12], and extend Answer Set Programs, defined under the Answer Set Semantics [11], with *epistemic operators* that are able to introspectively "look inside" a program's own semantics, which is defined in terms of its "answer sets". In fact, $\mathbf{K}A$ means that (ground) atom A is true in every answer set of the very program Π where $\mathbf{K}A$ occurs. Related operators that can be defined in terms of $\mathbf{K}$ are $\mathbf{M}A$ (not treated here), meaning that A is true in some of the answer sets of Π, and the *epistemic negation operator* $\mathbf{not}\ A$, which expresses that A *is not provably true*, meaning that A is false in at least one answer set of Π. The semantics of ELPs is provided in terms of *world views*: instead of a unique set of answer sets (a unique "world view" in the new terminology) like in Answer Set Programming (ASP), there is now a set of such sets. Each world view consistently satisfies (according to a given semantics) the epistemic expressions that appear in a given program. Many

G. Gottlob et al. (Eds.): LPNMR 2022, LNAI 13416, pp. 131–144, 2022.
https://doi.org/10.1007/978-3-031-15707-3_11

semantic approaches for ELPs have been introduced beyond the seminal work of Gelfond and Przymusinska [12], among which we mention [2,8,10,14,19,21,22]. Recent work aims to extend to Epistemic Logic Programming notions that have already been defined for ASP, and that might prove useful in ELPs as well. In particular, Cabalar et al. consider *splitting* (introduced for ASP in [17]), which allows a program to be divided into parts in a principled way: the answer sets of a given program can be computed incrementally, starting from the answer sets of the bottom part, used to simplify the top part, and then computing the answer sets of the simplified top part (such a procedure can be iterated for as many levels as the program has been divided into, i.e., the top and the bottom could be split recursively). Cabalar et al. then extend to ELPs the concept of splitting and the method of incremental calculation of the semantics (here, it is the world views that must be calculated). This by defining a notion of *Epistemic Splitting*, where top and bottom are defined w.r.t. the occurrence of epistemic operators, and a corresponding property which is fulfilled by a semantics if it allows the world views to be computed bottom up (a precise definition is seen below). Further, Cabalar et al. adapt properties of ASP to ELPs, which are implied by this property, namely the fact that adding constraints leads to reduce the number of answer sets (*Subjective Constraint Monotonicity*), and *Foundedness*, meaning that atoms composing answer sets cannot have been derived through cyclic positive dependencies. Finally, they define the class of *Epistemically Stratified Programs* that, according to [1, Theorem 2], admit a unique world view (these programs are those where, intuitively, the use of epistemic operators is stratified). In substance, Cabalar et al. establish the properties that a semantics should fulfil, and then they compare the existing semantics with respect to these properties.

In this paper, we explore a different stance: we analyze the possibility to change the perspective about how to perform a splitting, shifting from a bottom-up to a top-down approach. Our new definition: (i) copes with concerns regarding, e.g. "unfoundedness" of world views and "subjective constraint monotonicity"; (ii) is applicable to many of the existing semantics; (iii) operates similarly to splitting in "traditional" ASP; (iv) provably coincides with the bottom-up notion of splitting on a significant class of programs, including at least those which are *epistemically stratified*; (v) is compatible with ASP programming practice, where one defines a problem solution (that would constitute the top) that will be merged with a problem instance (that would constitute the bottom).

The paper is organized as follows. In Sects. 2 and 3 we recall ASP and ELPs, reporting some definitions from [1] (in the appendix, for the sake of completeness, we report at more length definitions from [1].) In Sect. 4 we introduce some observations on ELPs that lead to formulate our proposal, that we discuss in Sect. 5 where we present the proof of our main theorem, and a relevant corollary.

2   Answer Set Programming and Answer Set Semantics

One can see an answer set program (for short 'ASP program') as a set of statements that specify a problem, where each answer set represents a solution compatible with this specification. A *consistent* ASP program has one or more answer sets, while an *inconsistent* one has no answer sets, meaning that no solution could be found. Several well-developed freely available *answer set solvers* exist that compute the answer sets of a given program. Syntactically, an ASP program Π is a collection of *rules* of the form

$$A_1 | \ldots | A_g \leftarrow L_1, \ldots, L_n.$$

where each A_i, $0 \leq i \leq g$, is an atom and $|$ indicates disjunction, and the L_is, $0 \leq i \leq n$, are literals (i.e., atoms or negated atoms of the form *not A*). The left-hand side and the right-hand side of the rule are called *head* and *body*, resp. A rule with empty body is called a *fact*. Notation $A \,|\, B$ indicates disjunction, usable only in rule heads and, so, in facts. A rule with empty head (or, equivalently, with head $\perp$), of the form '$\leftarrow L_1, ..., L_n$.' or '$\perp \leftarrow L_1, ..., L_n$.', is a *constraint*, stating that literals $L_1, \ldots, L_n$ are not allowed to be simultaneously true in any answer set; the impossibility to fulfil such a requirement is one of the reasons that make a program inconsistent.

All extensions of ASP not explicitly mentioned above are not considered in this paper. We implicitly refer to the "ground" version of Π, which is obtained by replacing in all possible ways the variables occurring in Π with the constants occurring in Π itself, and is thus composed of ground atoms, i.e., atoms which contain no variables.

The answer set (or "stable model") semantics can be defined in several ways [5,16]. However, answer sets of a program Π, if any exists, are the supported minimal classical models of the program interpreted as a first-order theory in the obvious way. The original definition from [11], introduced for programs where rule heads were limited to be single atoms, was in terms of the 'GL-Operator' Γ. Given set of atoms I and program Π, $\Gamma_\Pi(I)$ is defined as the least Herbrand model of the program Π^I, namely, the Gelfond-Lifschitz reduct of Π w.r.t. I. Π^I is obtained from Π by: 1. removing all rules which contain a negative literal *not A* such that $A \in I$; and 2. removing all negative literals from the remaining rules. The fact that Π^I is a positive program ensures that a least Herbrand model exists and can be computed via the standard immediate consequence operator [18]. Then, I is an answer set whenever $\Gamma_\Pi(I) = I$.

3   Epistemic Logic Programs and Their Properties

Epistemic Logic Programs introduce into ASP programs, in the body of rules, so-called *subjective literals* (w.r.t. *objective literals*)[1]. Such new literals are constructed via the *epistemic operator* **K** (disregarding without loss of generality the other epistemic operators). An ELP program is called *objective* if no subjective literals occur therein, i.e., it is an ASP program. A constraint involving (also) subjective literals is called a *subjective constraint*, where one involving objective literals only is an *objective constraint*.

Let At be the set of atoms occurring (within either objective or subjective literals) in a given program Π, and $Atoms(r)$ be the set of atoms occurring in rule r. By some abuse of notation, we denote by $Atoms(X)$ the set of atoms occurring in X, whatever X is (a rule, a program, an expression, etc.). Let $Head(r)$ be the head of rule r and $Body_{obj}(r)$ (resp., $Body_{subj}(r)$) be the (possibly empty) set of objective (resp., subjective) literals occurring in the body of r. For simplicity, we often write $Head(r)$ and $Body_{obj}(r)$ in place of $Atoms(Head(r))$ and $Atoms(Body_{obj}(r))$, respectively, when

---

[1] Nesting of subjective literals is not considered here.

the intended meaning is clear from the context. We call *subjective rules* those rules whose body is made of subjective literals only.

Literal $\mathbf{K}A$ intuitively means that the (ground) atom A is true in every answer set of given program Π (it is a *cautious consequence* of Π). Since, as it turns out, whatever the semantic account one will choose there can be several sets of answer sets (called *world views*), the actual meaning of $\mathbf{K}A$ is that A is true in every answer set of some world view of Π. Each world view thus determines the truth value of all subjective literals in a program. There are in fact several semantic approaches to ELPs, dictating in different ways how one finds the *world views* of a given program. Although all such approaches provide the same results on some basic examples, they instead differ on others.

Formally, a semantics S is a function mapping each ELP program into sets of 'world views', i.e., sets of sets of objective literals, where if Π is an objective program, then the unique member of $S(\Pi)$ is the set of stable models of Π. Otherwise, each member of $S(\Pi)$ is a *S-world view* of Π. (We will often write "world view" in place of "S-world view" whenever mentioning the specific semantics will be irrelevant.) For a S-world view W and a literal $\mathbf{K}L$, we write $W \models \mathbf{K}L$ if L is true in all elements of W.

For instance, for program $\{a \leftarrow not\, b,\ b \leftarrow not\, a,\ e \leftarrow not\, \mathbf{K}f,\ f \leftarrow not\, \mathbf{K}e\}$, every semantics returns two world views:
$\{\{a, e\}, \{b, e\}\}$, where $\mathbf{K}e$ is true and $\mathbf{K}f$ is false, and $\{\{a, f\}, \{b, f\}\}$ where $\mathbf{K}f$ is true and $\mathbf{K}e$ is false. The presence of two answer sets in each world view is due to the cycle on objective atoms, whereas the presence of two world views is due to the cycle on subjective atoms (in general, the existence and number of world views is related to such cycles, cf., [4] for a detailed discussion).

Below we report some definitions from [1], that will be used in what follows.

Definition 1 (Epistemic splitting set). *A set of atoms $U \subseteq At$ is said to be an epistemic splitting set of a program Π if for any rule r in Π one of the following conditions hold: (i) $Atoms(r) \subseteq U$, or $\big(Body_{obj}(r) \cup Head(r)\big) \cap U = \emptyset$.*

An epistemic splitting *of Π is a pair $\langle B_U(\Pi), T_U(\Pi) \rangle$ satisfying $B_U(\Pi) \cap T_U(\Pi) = \emptyset$ and $B_U(\Pi) \cup T_U(\Pi) = \Pi$, such that all rules in $B_U(\Pi)$ satisfy (i) and all rules in $T_U(\Pi)$ satisfy (ii).*

Definition 2. *Given a semantics S, a pair $\langle W_b, W_t \rangle$ is said to be an S-solution of Π with respect to an epistemic splitting set U, if W_b is a S-world view of $B_U(\Pi)$ and W_t is a S-world view of $E_U(\Pi, W_b)$, which is a version of Π where each subjective literal L is substituted by $\top$ if $W_b \models L$ or by $\bot$ otherwise.*

Consider the following operation, that we call WBT, on sets of propositional interpretations W_b and W_t:

$$W_b \sqcup W_t = \{I_b \cup I_t | I_b \in W_b \wedge I_t \in W_t$$

As stated in [1], we have the following property:

Property 1 (Epistemic Splitting Property). A semantics S satisfies the epistemic splitting property if for any epistemic splitting set U of any program Π: W is an S-world view of Π iff there is an S-solution $\langle W_b, W_t \rangle$ of Π w.r.t. U such that $W = W_b \sqcup W_t$.

This property implies *subjective constraint monotonicity*, i.e., for any epistemic program Π and any subjective constraint r, W is a world view of $\Pi \cup \{r\}$ iff both W is a world view of Π and W satisfies r.

4 Our Observations and Proposal

The subdivision of an ELP into layers suggests that, in the upper layer, epistemic literals referring to the lower layer may be aimed at performing some kind of meta-reasoning about that layer. If the epistemic splitting property is enforced, however, meta-level reasoning is in practice prevented. This is so because if the semantics satisfies such property, then, it is the lower layer that determines the truth value of the subjective literals that connect the two layers. In fact, according to Property 1, through the simplification w.r.t. the answer sets of the lower layer, the upper layer is strongly (maybe sometimes too strongly) constrained. For instance, let us consider the program $\Pi_0 = \{a \mid b, \perp \leftarrow not\,\mathbf{K}a\}$. We can see that, while the lower level $\{a \mid b\}$, considered as a program 'per se', has the unique world view $\{\{a\}, \{b\}\}$, the overall program has no world views. In fact, in such world view $\mathbf{K}a$ does not hold, thus the constraint is violated. Notice, however, that the world view $\{\{a\}\}$ is instead accepted by some semantics, such as those defined in [10] and [19], that do not satisfy the epistemic splitting property. This world view may be seen as corresponding to an approach where the upper layer, in order to retain consistency, 'requires' the lower layer to entail a, which is absolutely feasible by choosing a over b in the disjunction. From this perspective, the knowledge modeled by the upper layer is not just used to reject potential world views of the bottom level, but, instead, can affect the way in which they are composed, by filtering out some of the answer sets. This situation is reminiscent of what actually happens for ASP: consider the plain ASP program $\{a \mid b, c \leftarrow a, \leftarrow not\,c\}$, which has unique answer set $\{a, c\}$, originating from the answer set $\{a\}$ of the lower layer $\{a \mid b\}$.

We follow (since a long time) the line, amply represented in the literature, in which meta-reasoning is aimed not only at 'observing' lower layer(s), but also at trying to influence them; this by suitably enlarging and/or restricting, as an effect of meta-rules application, the set of possible consequences of such layer(s). We discuss at length this point of view, also proposing technical solutions and several examples, in [6]. Moreover, let us notice that a common approach in modeling a problem, consists in formalizing some problem domain as the "top" part of a program. Then, such top program will be joined with a specific "bottom", representing a specific problem instance at hand, that may vary and may be, in general, unknown while defining the top. Below is an example of what we mean (over-simplified and in "skeletal form" for the sake of conciseness), taken from the realm of digital investigations, that the authors have been studying in the context of the Action COST CA17124 DIGital FORensics: evidence Analysis via intelligent Systems and Practices (DigForASP). In the example, an investigation **must** be concluded with a judgement, that can be: of innocence if in no plausible scenario (i.e., in no answer set) evidence can be found of an involvement; of demonstrable guilt if in every possible scenario the evidence of guilt can be found; of presumed innocence otherwise. Clearly, the details of each specific case (which will represent the "bottom" of the program) are added whenever needed to this general "top" part (see [4] for more examples taken from this field).

$judgement \leftarrow guilty.$ $guilty \leftarrow provably\_guilty.$
$judgement \leftarrow presumed\_innocent.$ $presumed\_innocent \leftarrow not\ provably\_guilty.$
$judgement \leftarrow innocent.$ $provably\_guilty \leftarrow \mathbf{K}\ sufficient\_evidence\_against.$
$\leftarrow not\ \mathbf{K}\ judgement.$ $innocent \leftarrow \mathbf{K}\ not\ sufficient\_evidence\_against.$

So, a study of how the semantics of any resulting overall program might be built is in order here, and in many other practical cases (think of a top part including ontological definitions). In fact, being able to compute and check a program's semantics only in dependence of each specific instance, does not seem to be elaboration-tolerant.

Therefore, we tried to understand whether the concept of splitting might be applied top-down, and how the existing semantics would behave in the new perspective. In our approach, the notion of splitting set remains the same, save for one detail concerning subjective constraints. As noticed in [1], according to the definition of splitting, subjective constraints can be placed at either level. Notice that subjective literals may either occur in a constraint directly or affect constraint's satisfaction through indirect dependencies, such as, e.g., in the program $\perp \leftarrow a.\ a \leftarrow \mathbf{K}p$ (see [7] for a formal definition of direct and indirect dependencies). Without loss of generality, we exclude here indirect dependencies concerning subjective literals involved in constraints. Moreover, notice that, as it is well-known, a constraint can be also represented as a unary odd cycle, for $\perp \leftarrow \mathbf{K}p$ it would be of the form $a \leftarrow not\ a, \mathbf{K}p$ (with a as a fresh atom), or even (as discussed in depth in [3]) as an odd cycle of any arity, of which $\mathbf{K}p$ is the unique *handle*. For the sake of simplicity, we consider constraints in their plain form, such as $\perp \leftarrow \mathbf{K}p$. For convenience concerning definitions that will be introduced later, we impose the additional condition that subjective rules satisfying condition 1 of Definition 1 and subjective constraints are put in $T_U(\Pi)$.

Let us proceed step by step towards the new definition of *Top-down Epistemic Splitting Property*. Let be given a semantics S, a program Π, and an epistemic splitting $\langle B_U(\Pi), T_U(\Pi) \rangle$ of Π, according to Definition 1. Let $F_U(\Pi)$ denote the set of all subjective literals $\mathbf{K}L_i$ occurring in $T_U(\Pi)$ (even in negative form $not\ \mathbf{K}L_i$) and referring to $B_U(\Pi)$ (in the sense that the atom involved in $\mathbf{K}L_i$ occurs in $B_U(\Pi)$ but not in $T_U(\Pi)$), together with their negations $not\ \mathbf{K}L_i$. Intuitively, subjective literals in $F_U(\Pi)$ constitute the "interface" between the top and the bottom part. Notice that $Atoms(F_U(\Pi)) \subseteq U$. Assuming $F_U(\Pi) = \{\mathbf{K}L_1, \ldots, \mathbf{K}L_z, not\ \mathbf{K}L_1, \ldots, not\ \mathbf{K}L_z\}$, let $f_U(\Pi) = \{kl_1, \ldots, kl_z, nkl_1, \ldots, nkl_z\}$ be a set of fresh atoms, and let $T'_U(\Pi)$ denote the *detached* version of $T_U(\Pi)$, namely the program made of:

- the rules obtained from rules in $T_U(\Pi)$ by substituting each occurrence of the subjective literal $\mathbf{K}L_i \in F_U(\Pi)$ or $not\ \mathbf{K}L_i \in F_U(\Pi)$ by the corresponding fresh atom $kl_i \in f_U(\Pi)$ or $nkl_i \in f_U(\Pi)$, for each $i \in \{1, \ldots, z\}$
- the facts $kl_i \mid nkl_i$, for each $i \in \{1, \ldots, z\}$.

The program $T'_U(\Pi)$ does not contain subjective literals referring to $B_U(\Pi)$, yet it may contain "local" epistemic literals. So, according to the semantics S that one wants to consider, it will have a number of world views. Notice however that, a disjunction between an epistemic literal $\mathbf{K}L$ and its negation $not\ \mathbf{K}L$ determines, as discussed in [4], two world views, one entailing $\mathbf{K}L$ and the other one entailing $not\ \mathbf{K}L$. So, each world view W of $T'_U(\Pi)$ has to be split into two world views, say W_1 and W_2, the former composed of the answer sets that contain kl_i, and the latter composed the answer sets that contain nkl_i. This splitting must be done, for each world view of $T'_U(\Pi)$, iteratively for each such disjunction, where it is easy to see that the order does not matter. Notice that, each resulting world view W'_j of the epistemic program $T'_U(\Pi)$, describes a world view W_j for $T_U(\Pi)$, that can be obtained as $W_j = \{X \setminus f_U(\Pi) \mid X \in W'_j\}$. For each of such world views W_j of $T_U(\Pi)$, Definition 3 identifies the set of subjective literals that are relevant in extending W_j to a world view of the entire Π.

Definition 3 (Epistemic Top-down Requisite Set). *Let $\langle B_U(\Pi), T_U(\Pi)\rangle$ be an epistemic splitting for a program Π, W'_j be a world view of $T'_U(\Pi)$, and $W_j = \{X \setminus f_U(\Pi) \mid X \in W'_j\}$. The set $ES_{T_U(\Pi)}(W_j) = \{KL_h \mid W'_j \models kl_h\} \cup \{not\,KL_h \mid W'_j \not\models kl_h\}$ is the* (epistemic top-down) requisite set *for W_j (w.r.t. $\langle B_U(\Pi), T_U(\Pi)\rangle$).*

Now we partition the *requisite set*, identifying two relevant subsets (technical reasons for doing so will be seen below).

Definition 4. *Given $f_U(\Pi) = \{kl_1, \ldots, kl_z, nkl_1, \ldots, nkl_z\}$ and the above definition of requisite set $ES_{T_U(\Pi)}(W_j)$, (w.r.t. an epistemic splitting $\langle B_U(\Pi), T_U(\Pi)\rangle$), let set S include those kl_i/nkl_i that occur in some constraints in $T'_U(\Pi)$. Then, we split the requisite set $ES_{T_U(\Pi)}(W_j)$ as the union of the following two (disjoint) sets:*

- *the* epistemic top-down constraint set*:*
  $EC_{T_U(\Pi)}(W_j) = (\{KL_i \mid kl_i \subset S\} \cup \{not\,KL_i \mid nkl_i \in S\}) \cap ES_{T_U(\Pi)}(W_j)$
- *the* requirement set*:* $RQ_{T_U(\Pi)}(W_j) = (\{KL_i \mid kl_i \in f_U(\Pi) \setminus S\} \cup \{not\,KL_i \mid nkl_i \in f_U(\Pi) \setminus S\}) \cap ES_{T_U(\Pi)}(W_j)$.

There is an important reason for distinguishing these two subsets. Literals in $EC_{T_U(\Pi)}(W_j)$, if not entailed in some world view of the bottom part of the program, lead to a constraint violation and so to the non-existence of some world view of Π extending W_j. Thus, $EC_{T_U(\Pi)}(W_j)$ expresses prerequisites on which epistemic literals must be entailed in a world view of $B_U(\Pi)$, so that such world view can be merged with W_j in order to obtain a world view of Π. Those in $RQ_{T_U(\Pi)}(W_j)$ instead, can be usefully exploited, as seen below, to drive the selection of which world view of the bottom can be combined with a given world view of the top.

Given a world view W of $T_U(\Pi)$, and considering literals belonging to $EC_{T_U(\Pi)}(W)$ which occur in the bodies of rules in $B_U(\Pi)$, we proceed the following simplification.

Definition 5 (Top-down Influence). *Given a world view W of $T_U(\Pi)$, and its corresponding top-down constraint set $EC_{T_U(\Pi)}(W)$, the W-tailored version $B_U^W(\Pi)$ of $B_U(\Pi)$ is obtained by substituting in $B_U(\Pi)$ all literals $KL \in EC_{T_U(\Pi)}(W)$ by L.*

The intuition behind the above definition is that, if KA is in $EC_{T_U(\Pi)}(W)$, then A must necessarily belong to every answer set of a world view of the bottom that can be possibly merged with W in order to obtain a world view of the overall program Π; so it is indifferent that in the body of rules of $B_U(\Pi)$ it occurs A rather than KA, if $KA \in EC_{T_U(\Pi)}(W)$. Substituting KA with A can however be useful, as discovered during the development of the K15 semantics [13] from G11 [10] (and as seen below in the examples), to "break" unwanted positive cycles among subjective literals, that might lead to *unfounded* world views (cf., [1, Definition 15]).

The world views of a given program Π are obtained from the world views of the top and the bottom, as in the bottom-up approach (see operation WBT)) but with two important differences: (i) top-down influence is exploited; (ii) a subset of a world view of the bottom (i.e., some of the answer sets occurring therein) may be cut out, so as to enable the merging with a 'compatible' world view of the top. Preliminarily:

Definition 6. *Given a set E of epistemic literals and a set of sets of atoms W, we say that W fulfils E iff $\forall\, \mathbf{K}L \in E, W \models L$ and $\forall\, not\,\mathbf{K}L \in E, W \not\models L$.*

Definition 7 (Candidate World View). *Given an epistemic splitting $\langle B_U(\Pi),$ $T_U(\Pi)\rangle$ for a program Π, let W_T be a world view of $T_U(\Pi)$ and let W_B be a subset of a world view of $B_U^{W_T}(\Pi)$ that fulfils $EC_{T_U(\Pi)}(W_T)$ (provided that, if such set EC is empty, W_B is the entire world view of the bottom) such that W_B fulfils $RQ_{T_U(\Pi)}(W_T)$. Then,*

$$W = W_B \sqcup W_T = \{I_b \cup I_t | I_b \in W_B \wedge I_t \in W_T\}$$

is a candidate world view *for Π (obtained from W_T and W_B).*

Note that, candidate world views are computed after applying top-down influence. It is possible that no subset of any world view of the bottom complies with the conditions posed by world views of the top. In such case, Π has no candidate world views.

We can now state a property for semantics concerning top-down epistemic splitting:

Definition 8 (Top-down Epistemic Splitting Property (TDESP)). *A semantics S satisfies* top-down epistemic splitting *if any candidate world view of Π according to Definition 7 is indeed a world view of Π under S.*

Let us experiment this methodology on some of the examples proposed in recent literature. Consider program Π_1, taken from [20]:

$$p \mid q \ \ (r1) \qquad\qquad \bot \leftarrow not\ \mathbf{K}p \ \ (C)$$

Here, $B_U(\Pi_1)$ consists of rule (r1), and $T_U(\Pi_1)$ consists of constraint (C). So, $T'_U(\Pi_1)$ is (where kp and nkp are fresh atoms):

$$kp \mid nkp \qquad\qquad \bot \leftarrow nkp$$

whose unique world view is $\{\{kp\}\}$. After cancelling kp, we obtain $W_T = \{\emptyset\}$ for $T_U(\Pi_1)$, with $ES_{T_U(\Pi_1)}(W_T) = EC_{T_U(\Pi_1)}(W_T) = \{\mathbf{K}p\}$ and $RQ_{T_U(\Pi_1)}(W_T) = \emptyset$. Regardless of the epistemic semantics S, as no subjective literals occur therein, the unique world view of $B_U(\Pi_1)$ is $\hat{W} = \{\{p\}, \{q\}\}$. Since $W_B = \{\{p\}\}$ is only subset of $\hat{W}$ fulfilling $EC_{T_U(\Pi_1)}(W_T)$ (cf. Definition 7), then it is the one selected. It is also a world view for Π_1, as the unique world view of the top part is empty. This world view violates subjective constraint monotonicity, still it is the one delivered by the semantics proposed in [19] and, as noticed in [20], by those proposed in [14,21]. In our opinion the world view $\{\{p\}\}$ captures the 'intended meaning' of the program Π_1, where the top layer "asks" the bottom layer to support, if possible, $\mathbf{K}p$ (in order not to make the overall program inconsistent).

Consider now the following program Π_2.

$$p \mid q \ (r1) \qquad \perp \leftarrow not\, \mathbf{K}p \ (C) \qquad p \leftarrow \mathbf{K}q \ (r2) \qquad q \leftarrow \mathbf{K}p \ (r3)$$

Here, $B_U(\Pi_2)$ consists of rules (r1-r3), and $T_U(\Pi_2)$ consists of constraint (C). So, $T'_U(\Pi_2)$ is (where kp and nkp are fresh atoms):

$$kp \mid nkp \qquad \perp \leftarrow nkp$$

whose unique world view is $\{\{kp\}\}$. After cancelling kp, we obtain world view $W_T = \{\emptyset\}$ for $T_U(\Pi_2)$ where $ES_{T_U(\Pi_2)}(W_T) = EC_{T_U(\Pi_2)}(W_T) = \{\mathbf{K}p\}$ and set RQ is empty. Regardless of the semantics $\mathcal{S}$, the potential world views of $B_U(\Pi_2)$ are $W_1 = \{\{p\}\}$, $W_2 = \{\{q\}\}$, $W_3 = \{\{p\},\{q\}\}$, $W_4 = \{\{p,q\}\}$. Actually, W_4 is the only one fulfilling $ES_{T_U(\Pi_2)}(W_T)$; W_1 has the problem that, having p and fulfilling $\mathbf{K}p$, (r3) might be applied thus getting q. Note that W_4 is in fact the world view returned by semantics proposed, for instance, in [13] and [19]. It is easy to see that W_4 violates foundedness. However, in our approach q is not derived via the positive cycle (extended to subjective literals), but from the $\mathbf{K}p$ "forced" by the upper layer via top-down influence, which substitutes $\mathbf{K}p$ with p in rule (r3) of $B_U(\Pi_2)$. This actually guarantees foundedness. Since the unique world view for the top is empty, then the unique world view of the overall program is indeed, according to our method, $W = W_4 = \{\{p,q\}\}$.

Let us now consider, Π_3 to be the seminal example introduced in [12], which is discussed in virtually every paper on ELP. Π_3 is epistemically stratified (see the Appendix and [1, Definition 6]). This formulation (variations have appeared over time) is from [1].

$$
\begin{array}{ll}
eligible(X) \leftarrow high(X) & (r1) \\
eligible(X) \leftarrow minority(X), fair(X) & (r2) \\
noeligible(X) \leftarrow not\, fair(X), not\, high(X) & (r3) \\
fair(mike) \mid high(mike) & (f1) \\
interview(X) \leftarrow not\, \mathbf{K}\, eligible(X), not\, \mathbf{K}\, noeligible(X) & (r4) \\
appointment(X) \leftarrow \mathbf{K}\, interview(X) & (r5)
\end{array}
$$

Since in this version of the program we have only *mike* as an individual, we may obtain the following ground abbreviated version:

$$
\begin{array}{llll}
e \leftarrow h & (r1) & ne \leftarrow not\, f, not\, h \ (r3) & in \leftarrow not\, \mathbf{K}e, not\, \mathbf{K}ne \ (r4) \\
e \leftarrow m, f & (r2) & f \mid h \qquad\qquad\quad (f1) & a \leftarrow \mathbf{K}in \qquad\qquad\quad (r5)
\end{array}
$$

Here, we consider (r5) as the top $T_U(\Pi_3)$, and (r1–r4) plus (f1) as bottom, which can be however in turn divided into the top $T1_U(\Pi_3)$ including (r4), and the bottom $B_U(\Pi_3)$, made of (r1–r3) and (f1). So, $T'_U(\Pi_3)$ is (with fresh atoms $kin, nkin$):

$$a \leftarrow kin \ (r5') \qquad kin \mid nkin$$

with two answer sets: $\{a, kin\}, \{nkin\}$. As explained in Sect. 4, $kin \mid nkin$ stands for a disjunction between the epistemic literal $\mathbf{K}in$ and its negation $not\,\mathbf{K}in$. This determines the existence of two world views, each entailing only one of these fresh atoms, i.e. epistemic literals, where atom a can however be derived only from the former. Thus, we have $W_{11} = \{\{a\}\}$ with $ES_{T_U(\Pi_3)}(W_{11}) = \{\mathbf{K}in\}$, and $W_{12} = \{\emptyset\}$ with $ES_{T_U(\Pi_3)}(W_{12}) = \{not\,\mathbf{K}in\}$. $EC_{T1_U(\Pi_3)}$ is empty for all world views, as no constraint is present in Π_3. Then, $T1'_U(\Pi_3)$ is (with $ke, nke, kne, nkne$ fresh atoms):

$$in \leftarrow nke, nkne \quad (r4') \qquad ke \mid nke \qquad kne \mid nkne.$$

By the same reasoning as above, since there are two disjunctions among fresh atoms representing epistemic literals, four world views can be found. After cancelling the fresh atoms, in fact we have $W_{21} = \{\{in\}\}$, with $ES_{T1'_U(\Pi_3)}(W_{21}) = \{not\,\mathbf{K}e, not\,\mathbf{K}ne\}$, and three empty world views $W_{22} = W_{23} = W_{24} = \{\emptyset\}$, with requisite sets $\{\mathbf{K}e, \mathbf{K}ne\}$, $\{\mathbf{K}ne, not\,\mathbf{K}e\}$, and $\{not\,\mathbf{K}ne, \mathbf{K}e\}$, respectively. Clearly, also $EC_{T1'_U(\Pi_3)}$ is empty.

Finally, $B_U(\Pi_3)$, which is made of the rules (r1–r3) and (f1), has the world view $W_3 = \{\{h, e\}, \{f\}\}$. Since the requirement set relative to world view W_{21} for the immediately upper level is satisfied in both answer sets of W_3, we can obtain an intermediate world view $W_{213} = \{\{h, e, in\}, \{f, in\}\}$ for the part of the program including (r1–r4). Considering also the top, it is easily seen that W_{213} is compliant with the requirement set of $W_{11} = \{a\}$. So, we can obtain for the overall program the unique candidate world view $W = \{\{h, e, in, a\}, \{f, in, a\}\}$, which is indeed a world view. Notice that, in fact, the world views that are part of the union, corresponding to the various sub-programs, would be the same under all known semantics for ELPs.

Assume now that, instead of $f \mid h$, the program would contain the bare fact h. Then, the world view of the bottom would be $W_3 = \{\{h, e\}\}$. This world view implies $\mathbf{K}e$, so it could be combined with a world view $\{\emptyset\}$ of the middle layer and since it also implies $not\,\mathbf{K}in$, the further combination is with world view $W_{12} = \{\emptyset\}$ of the top. So, $W_3 = \{\{h, e\}$ is the unique world view of the overall program.

5   Discussion and Conclusions

It is at this point interesting to try to assess formally which semantics (if any) satisfy the top-down epistemic splitting property. For lack of space, we examine below only the case of the semantics introduced in [13], that we call for short K15. The reason for choosing K15 however is that in [1] it is noticed that K15 slightly generalizes the semantics proposed in [10] (called G11 for short) and can be seen as a basis for the semantics proposed in [19] (called S16 for short). In particular, S16 (which considers instead of $\mathbf{K}$ the operator $not\,A$ which means $not\,\mathbf{K}A$) treats K15 world views as candidate solutions, to be pruned in a second step, where some unwanted world views are removed by maximizing what is not known. Thus, should K15 satisfy top-down epistemic splitting property, S16 would do as well, and so would G11, the latter however only for the class of programs where its world views coincide with those of K15.

Definition 9 (K15-world views). *The K15-reduct of Π with respect to a non-empty set of interpretations W is obtained by: (i) replacing by $\bot$ every subjective literal $L \in Body_{subj}(r)$ such that $W \not\models L$, and (ii) replacing all other occurrences of subjective literals of the form $\mathbf{K}L$ by L. A non-empty set of interpretations W is a K15-world view of Π iff W is the set of all stable models of the K15-reduct of Π with respect to W.*

We are able to prove the following:

Theorem 1 (K15 TDESP). *The K15 semantics satisfies the Top-down Epistemic Splitting Property. I.e., given an ELP Π, and set of sets W, where each set is composed of atoms occurring in Π, W is a K15 world view for Π if and only if it is a candidate world view for Π according to Definition 7.*

Proof. Assume an Epistemic Splitting of given program Π into two layers, top $T_U(\Pi)$ and bottom $B_U(\Pi)$ (where the reasoning below can however be iterated over a subdivision into an arbitrary number of levels). Notice that, given a K15 world view W, since each atom A that occurs in the sets composing W is derived in the part of the program including rules with head A, then W can be divided into two parts, W_T and W_B which are world views of $T_U(\Pi)$ and $B_U(\Pi)$, resp., each one composed of stable models of the K15-reduct of that part of the program.

If part. Given a K15 world view W, let Sl^T be the subjective literals occurring in $T_U(\Pi)$ which are entailed by the bottom, i.e., either of the form $\mathbf{K}A$, for which $W_B \models A$, or of the form $not\ \mathbf{K}A$, for which $W_B \not\models A$. Let such set of literals form the set $ES_{T_U(\Pi)}(W_T)$. (As mentioned, the subset of Sl^T that consists of literals involved in constraints in $T_U(\Pi)$ will form set $EC_{T_U(\Pi)}(W_T)$, and the remaining ones will form set $RQ_{T_U(\Pi)}(W_T)$.) Therefore, we can conclude that W, which is a K15 world view, is indeed a candidate world view according to Definition 7.

Only if part. Consider a candidate world view W w.r.t. the K15 semantics, obtained by combining a subset W_B of a K15 world view of $B_U(\Pi)$ with a K15 world view W_T of $T_U(\Pi)$ after top-down influence. According to Definition 7, the combination is possible only if for each epistemic literal $\mathbf{K}A \in ES_{T_U(\Pi)}(W_T)$, $W_B \models A$, and for each epistemic literal $not\ \mathbf{K}A \in ES_{T_U(\Pi)}(W_T)$, $W_B \not\models A$. If any such literal belongs to $EC_{T_U(\Pi)}(W_T)$, if this is not the case then there would be a constraint violation in $T_U(\Pi)$, so there would be no world views for $T_U(\Pi)$, and for the overall program Π. Considering a subjective literal in $RQ_{T_U(\Pi)}(W_T)$, if it were not the case that W_B entails such literal, then by definition of K15 it would have been substituted by $\bot$, so W_T would have been a different set. The top-down influence step can be disregarded, since it performs in advance on elements of $ES_{T_U(\Pi)}(W_T)$, that are required to be entailed by W_B anyway, the same transformation performed by K15, step (ii). Then, a candidate world view W obtained according to Definition 7 is a K15 world view.

In [1, Theorem 2] it is proved that, for any semantics obeying epistemic splitting, an epistemically stratified program has a unique world view. Actually, it can be seen that epistemically stratified programs admit one (and the same) world view under any semantics among those considered here: as it is well-known (see, e.g. [4,9,19]), multiple world views can arise only in consequence of negative cycles involving epistemic literals, clearly not present in such programs. So, the unique world view of an epistemically stratified program is in particular a K15 world view. Thus, we have the following.

Corollary 1. *Epistemically Stratified Programs satisfy both the Top-down and Bottom-up Epistemic Splitting Properties.*

An investigation of which other semantics might satisfy the Top-down Epistemic Splitting Property is a subject of future work. A question that may arise concerns efficiency of computing world views in a top-down fashion. If the subjective literals "connecting" adjacent layers are in small number (as it seems reasonable), then efficiency might not be a concern. Also, it remains to be seen in which kinds of applications the different approaches (top-down and bottom-up) might be most profitably exploited.

A   Epistemic Logic Programs: Useful Properties

Following [1], an (abstract) semantics S is a function mapping each program Π into sets of S-*world view* of Π, i.e., sets of sets of objective literals, where if Π is an objective program, then the unique member of $S(\Pi)$ is the set of its stable models. Drawing inspiration from the *Splitting Theorem* [17], an analogous properties is defined for ELPs:

Definition 1 (Epistemic splitting set. [1, Definition 4])
A set of atoms $U \subseteq At$ is said to be an epistemic splitting set of a program Π if for any rule r in Π one of the following conditions hold: (i) $Atoms(r) \subseteq U$; (ii) $Body_{obj}(r) \cup Head(r)) \cap U = \emptyset$. An epistemic splitting of Π is a pair $\langle B_U(\Pi), T_U(\Pi) \rangle$ satisfying $B_U(\Pi) \cap T_U(\Pi) = \emptyset$, $B_U(\Pi) \cup T_U(\Pi) = \Pi$, and also that all rules in $B_U(\Pi)$ satisfy (i) and all rules in $T_U(\Pi)$ satisfy (ii).

Intuitively, condition (ii) means that the top program $T_U(\Pi)$ may refer to atoms in U which occur as heads of rules in the bottom $B_U(\Pi)$, only through epistemic operators.

Epistemic splitting can be used, similarly to 'traditional' Lifschitz&Turner splitting, for iterative computation of world views. Indeed, Cabalar et al. [1] propose to compute first the world views of the bottom program $B_U(\Pi)$ and, for each of them, simplify the corresponding subjective literals in the top part. Given an epistemic splitting set U for Π and a set of interpretations W, they define the subjective reduct of the top with respect to W and signature U, called $E_U(\Pi, W)$. This operator, according to [1] considers all subjective literals L occurring in $T_U(\Pi)$, such that the atoms occurring in them belong to $B_U(\Pi)$. In particular, L will be substituted by $\top$ in $E_U(\Pi, W)$ if $W \models L$, and by $\bot$ otherwise. So, $E_U(\Pi, W)$ is a version of $T_U(\Pi)$ where some subjective literal, namely those referring to the bottom part of the program, have been simplified as illustrated.

Definition [1, Definition 5]
Given a semantics S, a pair $\langle W_b, W_t \rangle$ is said to be an S-solution of Π with respect to an epistemic splitting set U if W_b is a S-world view of $B_U(\Pi)$ and W_t is a S-world view of $E_U(\Pi, W_b)$.

The definition is parametric w.r.t. S, as each different semantics S will define in its own way the S-solutions for a given U and Π. So, world views of the entire program will be obtainable by suitably combining some world view of the bottom with some world view of the top, i.e., the world views of the entire program should be obtained as (where I_b and I_t are answer sets occurring respectively in W_b and W_t): $W_b \sqcup W_t = \{I_b \cup I_t | I_b \in W_b \wedge I_t \in W_t\}$. Therefore, the following property can be stated:

Property (Epistemic splitting. [1, *Property 4*])
A semantics S satisfies epistemic splitting if, for any epistemic splitting set U of any given program Π: W is an S-world view of Π iff there is an S-solution $\langle W_b, W_t \rangle$ of Π with respect to U such that $W = W_b \sqcup W_t$.

As discussed in [1], many semantics do not satisfy this property, which is satisfied only by the very first semantics of ELPs, proposed in [12] (and in some of its generalizations), and by Founded Autoepistemic Equilibrium Logic (FAEEL), defined in [2]. Epistemic splitting property implies *subjective constraint monotonicity*.

Another interesting property is *foundedness*. Again, such a notion has been extended from objective programs (see [1, Definition 15]). Intuitively, a set X of atoms is *unfounded* w.r.t. a (objective) program Π and an interpretation I, if for every $A \in X$ there is no rule of r by which A might be derived, without incurring in positive circularities and without forcing the derivation of more than one atom from the head of a disjunctive rule (see, e.g., [15] for a formal definition). For ELPs one has to consider that unfoundedness can originate also from positive dependencies on positive subjective literals, like, e.g., in the program $A \leftarrow \mathbf{K}A$. Among the existing semantics, only FAEEL satisfies foundedness.

Definition [1, *Definition 6*] *[Epistemic Stratification]*
We say that an ELP Π is epistemically stratified if we can assign an integer mapping $\lambda : At \rightarrow N$ to each atom [occurring in the program] such that:

- $\lambda(a) = \lambda(b)$ for any rule $r \in \Pi$ and atoms $a, b \in (Atoms(r) \setminus Body_{subj}(r))$, and
- $\lambda(a) > \lambda(b)$ for any pair of atoms a, b for which there is a rule $r \in \Pi$ with $a \in (Head(r) \cup Body_{obj}(r))$ and $b \in Body_{subj}(r)$.

References

1. Cabalar, P., Fandinno, J., del Cerro, L.F.: Splitting epistemic logic programs. Theory Pract. Log. Program. **21**(3), 296–316 (2021)
2. Cabalar, P., Fandinno, J., Fariñas del Cerro, L.: Splitting epistemic logic programs. In: Balduccini, M., Lierler, Y., Woltran, S. (eds.) Proceedings of LPNMR 2019. LNCS, vol. 11481, pp. 120–133. Springer, Heidelberg (2019). https://doi.org/10.1007/978-3-030-20528-7_10
3. Costantini, S.: On the existence of stable models of non-stratified logic programs. Theory Pract. Logic Program. **6**(1–2) (2006)
4. Costantini, S.: About epistemic negation and world views in epistemic logic programs. Theory Pract. Log. Program. **19**(5–6), 790–807 (2019)
5. Costantini, S., Formisano, A.: Negation as a resource: a novel view on answer set semantics. Fund. Inform. **140**(3–4), 279–305 (2015)
6. Costantini, S., Formisano, A.: Adding metalogic features to knowledge representation languages. Fundam. Informaticae **181**(1), 71–98 (2021)
7. Dix, J.: A classification theory of semantics of normal logic programs I-II. Fundamenta Informaticae **22**(3), 227–255 and 257–288 (1995)
8. Fariñas del Cerro, L., Herzig, A., Su, E.I.: Epistemic equilibrium logic. In: Yang, Q., Wooldridge, M. (eds.) Proceedings of IJCAI 2015, pp. 2964–2970. AAAI Press (2015)
9. Gelfond, M.: Logic programming and reasoning with incomplete information. Ann. Math. Artif. Intell. **12**(1–2), 89–116 (1994)

10. Gelfond, M.: New semantics for epistemic specifications. In: Delgrande, J.P., Faber, W. (eds.) LPNMR 2011. LNCS (LNAI), vol. 6645, pp. 260–265. Springer, Heidelberg (2011). https://doi.org/10.1007/978-3-642-20895-9_29

11. Gelfond, M., Lifschitz, V.: The stable model semantics for logic programming. In: Kowalski, R., Bowen, R. (eds.) Proceedings of ICLP/ILPS, pp. 1070–1080. MIT Press (1988)

12. Gelfond, M., Przymusinska, H.: Definitions in epistemic specifications. In: Nerode, A., Marek, V.W., Subrahmanian, V.S. (eds.) Proceedings of the 1st International Workshop on Logic Programming and Non-monotonic Reasoning, pp. 245–259. The MIT Press (1991)

13. Kahl, P., Watson, R., Balai, E., Gelfond, M., Zhang, Y.: The language of epistemic specifications (refined) including a prototype solver. J. Log. Comput. **30**(4), 953–989 (2015)

14. Kahl, P.T., Leclerc, A.P.: Epistemic logic programs with world view constraints. In: Palù, A.D., Tarau, P., Saeedloei, N., Fodor, P. (eds.) Technical Communications of ICLP 2018, vol. 64 of OASIcs, pp. 1:1–1:17. Schloss Dagstuhl (2018)

15. Leone, N., Rullo, P., Scarcello, F.: Disjunctive stable models: unfounded sets, fixpoint semantics, and computation. Inf. Comput. **135**(2), 69–112 (1997)

16. Lifschitz, V.: Thirteen definitions of a stable model. In: Blass, A., Dershowitz, N., Reisig, W. (eds.) Fields of Logic and Computation. LNCS, vol. 6300, pp. 488–503. Springer, Heidelberg (2010). https://doi.org/10.1007/978-3-642-15025-8_24

17. Lifschitz, V., Turner, H.: Splitting a logic program. In: Proceedings of ICLP 1994, pp. 23–37. MIT Press (1994)

18. Lloyd, J.W.: Foundations of Logic Programming. Springer, Heidelberg (1987). https://doi.org/10.1007/978-3-642-96826-6

19. Shen, Y., Eiter, T.: Evaluating epistemic negation in answer set programming. Artif. Intell. **237**, 115–135 (2016)

20. Shen, Y., Eiter, T.: Constraint monotonicity, epistemic splitting and foundedness are too strong in answer set programming. CoRR, abs/2010.00191 (2020)

21. Su, E.I.: Epistemic answer set programming. In: Calimeri, F., Leone, N., Manna, M. (eds.) JELIA 2019. LNCS (LNAI), vol. 11468, pp. 608–626. Springer, Cham (2019). https://doi.org/10.1007/978-3-030-19570-0_40

22. Truszczyński, M.: Revisiting epistemic specifications. In: Balduccini, M., Son, T.C. (eds.) Logic Programming, Knowledge Representation, and Nonmonotonic Reasoning. LNCS (LNAI), vol. 6565, pp. 315–333. Springer, Heidelberg (2011). https://doi.org/10.1007/978-3-642-20832-4_20

Deep Learning for the Generation of Heuristics in Answer Set Programming: A Case Study of Graph Coloring

Carmine Dodaro[1]([✉]) [iD], Davide Ilardi[2] [iD], Luca Oneto[2] [iD],
and Francesco Ricca[1] [iD]

[1] DeMaCS, University of Calabria, Rende, Italy
{carmine.dodaro,francesco.ricca}@unical.it
[2] DIBRIS, University of Genova, Genoa, Italy
{davide.ilardi,luca.oneto}@unige.it

Abstract. Answer Set Programming (ASP) is a well-established declarative AI formalism for knowledge representation and reasoning. ASP systems were successfully applied to both industrial and academic problems. Nonetheless, their performance can be improved by embedding domain-specific heuristics into their solving process. However, the development of domain-specific heuristics often requires both a deep knowledge of the domain at hand and a good understanding of the fundamental working principles of the ASP solvers. In this paper, we investigate the use of deep learning techniques to automatically generate domain-specific heuristics for ASP solvers targeting the well-known graph coloring problem. Empirical results show that the idea is promising: the performance of the ASP solver WASP can be improved.

Keywords: answer set programming · deep learning · heuristics · graph coloring

1 Introduction

Answer Set Programming (ASP) [5] is a well-established declarative AI formalism for knowledge representation and reasoning. ASP is a popular paradigm for solving complex problems mainly because it combines high modeling power with efficient solving technology [7]. The rich language, the intuitive semantics and the availability of efficient solvers are the key ingredients of the success of ASP on solving several industrial and academic problems [10].

Modern ASP solvers employ an extended version of the Conflict-Driven Clause Learning (CDCL) algorithm [16]. As a matter of fact, the performance of a CDCL solver heavily depends on the adoption of heuristics that drive the search for solutions. Among these, the heuristic for the selection of the branching literal (i.e., the criterion determining the literal to be assumed true at a given stage of the computation) can dramatically affect the overall performance of an implementation [8]. As default strategies, ASP implementations feature

© The Author(s), under exclusive license to Springer Nature Switzerland AG 2022
G. Gottlob et al. (Eds.): LPNMR 2022, LNAI 13416, pp. 145–158, 2022.
https://doi.org/10.1007/978-3-031-15707-3_12

very good general purpose heuristics belonging to the family of VSIDS [9]. However, they may fail to compute solutions of the hardest problems in a reasonable amount of time. Nonetheless, it is well-known that the performance of ASP solvers can be improved by embedding domain-specific heuristics into their solving process [2,8,11], and this is particularly true in the case of real-world industrial problems [24]. However, the development of domain-specific heuristics often requires both a deep knowledge of the domain at hand and a good understanding of the fundamental working principles of the ASP solvers. Thus, one might wonder whether it is possible to ease the burden of the ASP developer by leaving the task of defining proper heuristics to a machine that can learn effective heuristics from the observation of the behavior of solvers on instances from the same domain. A first positive answer to this question was provided by Balduccini in [3] who proposed the DORS framework, where the solver learns domain-specific heuristics while solving instances of a given domain [3]. The DORS framework was implemented in SMODELS, yielding interesting performance improvements. However, DORS was tailored for DPLL-style algorithms and we are not aware of any attempt to experiment with automatic learning of domain heuristics in modern solvers. Starting from the observation that the recent success of AI technology was largely propelled by the developments in deep neural networks [4], which proved to be very effective tools for solving tasks where the presence of humans was considered fundamental; we decided to investigate the use of deep learning techniques to automatically generate domain-specific heuristics for CDCL-based ASP solvers.

This paper presents our first results on employing neural networks to improve the performance of an ASP solver, and to this end, we targeted the well-known graph coloring problem as a use case. The heuristic is learned by observing the behavior of the ASP solver WASP [1] on a test set of instances randomly sampled from a population, where each sample corresponds to an ASP instance. The proposed neural network model takes inspiration from previous experiments conducted by Selsam and Bjørner in [22] and possesses a particular structure specifically designed for being invariant to permutations between literals and their negations, between literals belonging to the same rule and, finally, between rules themselves. The neural network is then trained on the test set, and the resulting model is used to alter the initial values of the heuristic counters used by WASP default heuristics so to make the most promising choices first. Empirical results show that the idea is promising: the performance of WASP can be improved by plugging-in automatically-generated neural domain heuristics.

2   Background

2.1   Graph Coloring Problem

The graph coloring problem consists of assigning colors to nodes of a graph, such that two connected nodes do not share the same color. More formally, let C be a set of colors and let $G = (N, L)$ be an undirected graph, where N is a set of natural numbers representing the nodes of G, and $L \subseteq N \times N$ be a set of links between nodes in N. The graph coloring problem consists of finding a total function $col : N \mapsto C$ such that $col(n_1) \neq col(n_2)$ for each $(n_1, n_2) \in L$. The following example shows an ASP encoding of the graph coloring problem. Note that the encoding represents a simplified version of the one used in the recent ASP Competitions [7].

Example 1 (ASP encoding of the graph coloring problem). Let C be a set of colors and $G = (N, L)$ be a graph. Let Π_G^C be the following program:

$$
\begin{aligned}
col(n, c) &\leftarrow \sim ncol(n, c) & \forall n \in N, c \in C \\
ncol(n, c) &\leftarrow col(n, c_2), c \neq c_2 & \forall n \in N, c \in C \\
ncol(n, c) &\leftarrow col(n_2, c) & \forall(n_2, n) \in L \text{ s.t. } n_2 < n, c \in C \\
colored(n) &\leftarrow col(n, c) & \forall n \in N, c \in C \\
\bot &\leftarrow \sim colored(n) & \forall n \in N
\end{aligned}
$$

If $C = \{b, g\}$ and $G = (\{1, 2\}, \{(1, 2)\})$, then Π_G^C is the following program:

r_1 :	$col(1, b) \leftarrow \sim ncol(1, b)$		r_2 :	$col(1, g) \leftarrow \sim ncol(1, g)$
r_3 :	$col(2, b) \leftarrow \sim ncol(2, b)$		r_4 :	$col(2, g) \leftarrow \sim ncol(2, g)$
r_5 :	$ncol(1, b) \leftarrow col(1, g)$		r_6 :	$ncol(1, g) \leftarrow col(1, b)$
r_7 :	$ncol(2, b) \leftarrow col(2, g)$		r_8 :	$ncol(2, g) \leftarrow col(2, b)$
r_9 :	$ncol(2, b) \leftarrow col(1, b)$		r_{10} :	$ncol(2, g) \leftarrow col(1, g)$
r_{11} :	$colored(1) \leftarrow col(1, b)$		r_{12} :	$colored(1) \leftarrow col(1, g)$
r_{13} :	$colored(2) \leftarrow col(2, b)$		r_{14} :	$colored(2) \leftarrow col(2, g)$
r_{15} :	$\bot \leftarrow \sim colored(1)$		r_{16} :	$\bot \leftarrow \sim colored(2)$

Π_G^C admits two solutions, i.e., $\{col(1, g), col(2, b), ncol(1, b), ncol(2, g), colored(1), colored(2)\}$ and $\{col(1, b), col(2, g), ncol(1, g), ncol(2, b), colored(1), colored(2)\}$ corresponding to the ones of the graph coloring problem. ◁

Moreover, in the following, an ASP program modeling the graph coloring problem is *coherent* if it admits a solution, i.e. there is a function col satisfying the requirements, otherwise it is *incoherent.*

2.2 Stable Model Search

Modern algorithms for computing stable models of a given ASP program Π employ a variant of the CDCL algorithm [16], whose idea is to build a stable model step-by-step starting from a set of literals S initially empty.

During the execution of the algorithm, some of the literals to be added in S (called branching literals) are selected according to a heuristic. Modern implementations use the MINISAT [9] heuristic (or one of its variants), whose key idea is to associate each atom to an *activity* value, that is initially set to 0. This value is incremented by a value *inc*, whenever the atom (or its corresponding literal) is used to compute a learned constraint. Then, after each learning step, the value of *inc* is multiplied by a constant greater than 1, to promote variables that occur in recently-learned constraints. When a branching literal must be selected, the heuristic chooses $\sim a$ (denoted as *negative polarity*), where a is the undefined atom with the highest activity value (ties are broken randomly).

2.3 Deep Neural Networks

Machine Learning (ML) comprises by now a huge number of algorithms to tackle several different problems [12,23]. In particular, ML algorithms observe a given data set and refine iteratively their understanding of it through measurable error's estimation. The data set is characterized by an input space $\mathcal{X} \subseteq \mathbb{R}^D$ and an output space $\mathcal{Y}$. The goal consists in determining the unknown function f, associating input and output spaces $f : \mathcal{X} \to \mathcal{Y}$. If $\mathcal{Y}$ is not empty the problem can be defined *supervised* and it determines an ease error estimation [23].

Within this context, the supervised training approach is applied to a popular ML algorithm called Deep Neural Network (DNN) [12], that can be seen as a black-box model able to extract and approximate the function f^*, governing the data set under analysis. The DNN, often called also Deep Feedforward Neural Network or Multilayer Perceptrons (MLPs), maps $y = f(\mathbf{x}; \theta)$, where $\mathbf{x}$ is the set of input features and θ the set of parameters that need to be learned in order to better approximate the function f [12]. The neural adjective takes inspiration from neuroscience, since the simplest unit of such a model (i.e., the neuron) is connected to previous and following units similarly to biological neurons [12]. The neurons are organized in layers, whose number determines the depth of the network under development [12]. The number of neurons per layer defines the width of the model and neurons belonging to the same layer act in parallel [12]. Each unit computes the weighted sum of the previous layer's outputs in addition to an optional bias value [12]. The result will be then processed by a function, also called activation function to emulate the firing activity of the biological neuron, and will be passed to the next layer or to the model's output according to its position within the network. The equation $y = \sigma(\mathbf{w}^T \mathbf{x} + b)$ summarizes the computations performed by each neuron, where $\mathbf{w}$ represents the vector of weights connecting each neuron with previous layer's ones, $\mathbf{x}$ is the vector of inputs coming from previous layer, b corresponds to the bias, σ identifies the activation function characterizing the current neuron and all its layer's neighbors and, finally, y is the neuron's output. As described above, y can be passed as input to following neurons or can be directly interpreted as the model's output. Typically, in a binary classification scenario [23] like the one proposed in this paper, the DNN is asked to determine if the given input belongs or not to a specific class. Consequently, the output space $\mathcal{Y} \in \{0,1\}$ [23]. Even though DNNs and MLPs give the human practitioners the possibility not to identify the precise function to estimate the desired non-linearity, as it can be inferred from the universal approximation theorem [15], it is still their responsibility to design the architecture and to tune properly its hyperparameters $\mathcal{H}$ through a Model Selection (MS) procedure [20]. It is fundamental to perform a reasoned MS and to choose properly the values to be assigned to the hyperparameters in order to obtain reasonable results and a good level of generalization. Thereafter, the resulting model will pass through an Error Estimation (EE) phase [20], during which its performances will be evaluated on a specific test set.

The width and the depth of the model, the activation functions of the various layers and the connections between neurons all fall into the architectural parameters to be defined. In addition to these, developers should choose the proper optimization algorithm, the size of the samples' batch to be processed before a backward propagation phase [21], the learning rate, the cost function and the regularization approach to adopt in order to guarantee a good level of generalization and to prevent under and overfitting [13].

3   Generation of Domain-Specific Heuristics in ASP

In this section, we describe the main challenges to face in order to automatically generate domain-specific heuristics, that are: finding a suitable representation of ASP instances in order to be used by deep learning algorithms, which usually operate on matrices (Sect. 3.1); generating a meaningful set of training instances (Sect. 3.2); creating a deep learning model to generate the heuristics (Sect. 3.3); embedding the heuristics into an ASP solver (Sect. 3.4).

3.1   Representation of ASP Instances

In order to create a representation of the input program that is suitable for the deep learning model, we used a variant of the matrix representation used in NeuroCore [22]. In particular, a given program Π is represented as a $|\Pi| \times 2 \cdot |atoms(\Pi) \cup \{\bot\}|$ sparse matrix denoted with letter $\mathcal{G}$, where the rows are the rules of Π and the columns are all literals occurring in Π (including $\bot$ and $\sim\!\bot$). Then, a triple $(r,\ell,-1)$ represents that the literal ℓ occurs in the head of rule r; a triple $(r,\ell,1)$ represents that the literal ℓ occurs in the body of rule r; and a triple $(r,\ell,0)$ represents that the literal ℓ does not occur in r.

Example 2. Consider again program Π_G^C of Example 1. The first row of $\mathcal{G}$ is represented by the following triples: $(r_1,col(1,b),-1)$, $(r_1,\sim\!ncol(1,b),1)$, and $(r_1,\ell,0)$ for each other literal ℓ occurring in Π_G^C. Similarly, the last row of $\mathcal{G}$ is represented by the following triples: $(r_{16},\bot,-1)$, $(r_{16},\sim\!colored(2),1)$, and $(r_{16},\ell,0)$ for each other literal ℓ occurring in Π_G^C.

3.2   Generation of the Training Set

Deep learning algorithms operate on a set of labeled examples, referred to as *training set*. In our setting, the training set is composed by a set of tuples (Π, I), where Π represents an instance of the graph coloring problem, and I is a stable model of Π. The generation of a meaningful set of training instances is a challenging problem since deep learning algorithms require huge sets of examples to be successfully trained. Moreover, instances must be *easily* solvable for the ASP solver, since it is required to compute one stable model. Note that in principle one could also enumerate a fixed number of stable models, however in our preliminary experiments we observed this was not beneficial for the solver.

Our generation strategy is as follows. Given a graph $G = (N, L)$, a set C of colors, and a positive number k; we build a set of programs $\mathcal{P}$ representing the training set, where each program in the set is a smaller portion of G. In particular, as first step, we block L and we randomly select $n\%$ of the nodes in N (with $n \in \{10, 20, 30, 40, 50\}$). For each value of n, we randomly generate k new graphs, whose corresponding programs are added to Π. Similarly, we block N and we randomly select $l\%$ of the links in L (with $l \in \{10, 20, 30, 40, 50\}$). As before, for each value of l, we randomly generate k new graphs, whose corresponding programs are added to Π. Finally, we randomly select $n\%$ of the nodes in N and $l\%$ of the links in L (with $n, l \in \{10, 20, 30, 40, 50\}$, and for each combination of n and l we randomly generate k new graphs. Hence, this strategy $35 \cdot k$ programs starting from a single input graph. In order to generate the training set, we considered all the sixty instances submitted to a recent ASP Competition [7] and we set the value of k to 100, for a total of 210 000 training instances.

3.3   Generation of the Deep Learning Model

In this section we provide the details for training a DNN model to learn the heuristic characterizing a set of graph coloring instances expressed according to the ASP formalism. After the tuning phase, the resulting model is then queried to estimate the best initial configuration to be submitted to the WASP solver to enhance the CDCL branching routine and, consequently, the solving process.

The DNN model designed in this context takes inspiration from the NeuroCore architecture proposed by Selsam and Bjørner in [22]. Despite the different targets, NeuroCore model shows distinctive characteristics that can fit this paper's needs. Recalling Sect. 3.1 and Example 2, we know that we have to deal with matrix representations. NeuroCore is able to manage problems of such matrix form thanks to its architecture, comprising three different MLPs:

$$\mathbf{R}_{\text{update}} : \mathbb{R}^{2d} \to \mathbb{R}^d, \mathbf{L}_{\text{update}} : \mathbb{R}^{3d} \to \mathbb{R}^d, \mathbf{V}_{\text{proj}} : \mathbb{R}^{2d} \to \mathbb{R}$$

where d is a fixed parameter and identifies the embedding associated with each atom and rule during model's iterations. In a nutshell, at each training step the model goes through T iterations of message passing, during which the rules' and literals' embeddings are continuously updated. The MLPs involved within these operations are $\mathbf{R}_{\text{update}}$ and $\mathbf{L}_{\text{update}}$, respectively. For the sake of clarity, the term *embedding* is usually exploited by practictioners to identify the vector exploited to translate a feature or a variable characterizing a data set in order to make the training process easier. In this context, we build a mono-dimensional vector with size d to represent each rule and each literal to be ingested by the latter MLPs. At each iteration, the output matrices of $\mathbf{L}_{\text{update}}$ and $\mathbf{R}_{\text{update}}$ are recursively combined and concatenated with the matrix $\mathcal{G}$, introduced in Sect. 3.1. These continuous combinations are necessary to guarantee the robustness of the DNN model against rules' and literals' permutations, allowed in this context. Moreover, the embedding's exploitation is crucial to manage ASP programs with different number of atoms and rules, since, in this way, the number of neurons of the different MLP's layers involved can be fixed and the only varying dimension is the number of row of the input matrices. This does not represent a problem since each program is managed singularly as a batch. Consequently, each batch represents the set of embeddings characterizing the literals or rules belonging to the same ASP program. After T iterations, $\mathbf{L}_{update}$'s output is horizontally split and the two even sub matrices, corresponding to each literal's and its negated correspondent's embeddings respectively, are vertically merged in order to build a matrix V, whose dimensions are $n_v \times 2d$ and where each row intuitively corresponds to a atom. At this point, V goes through the last MLP $\mathbf{V}_{proj}$ and $\hat{v}$ is finally obtained, which consists of a numerical score for each atom and it is finally passed to the softmax function to build a suitable probability distribution over the atoms. Concerning the embedding's size d, the number of iterations T and depth and width of the MLPs, the original values assigned by Selsam and Bjørner in [22] have been kept and are the following: 4 Iterations (T); 80 Embedding (d); 2 $\mathbf{C}_{update}$ layers; 2 $\mathbf{L}_{update}$ layers; 4 $\mathbf{V}_{proj}$ layers; 80 hidden layers neurons. The activation function exploited between each MLP's hidden layer is ReLU and the optimization algorithm adopted for training purpose is the ADAM one [17] with a constant learning rate of 10^{-4}. The considerations regarding $\mathbf{V}_{proj}$'s output layer and $\hat{v}$ interpretation need a further explanation. This paper's aim consists in determining a promising heuristic starting point for the solver's activity, which means that a value between 0 (*false*) and 1 (*true*) should be assigned to every literal of the instance under analysis. Moreover, it is fundamental to underline that literals corresponding to candidate colors for the same node are inevitably correlated and mutually exclusive. Due to this reason, the model should be able to assign a value of 1 exclusively to one of such literals in order to avoid contradictory scenarios. Consequently, $\mathbf{V}_{proj}$'s output activation function is kept linear and the softmax function is selectively applied to each group of atoms referring to the same node. Thereafter, the maximum value within each group is identified and assigned the value of 1, while 0s are assigned indistinctly to the remaining literals.

Furthermore, it is worth noting that, differently from Selsam and Bjørner's attempt in [22], the shape of the training instances, referring to the number of literals characterizing each of them, has not been fixed to a unique value. The data set considered in this context includes instances with varying sizes in the range comprised between 510 and 6032. It is feasible thanks to the NeuroCore architecture that is able to manage different shape instances through embedding representation. Nonetheless, it complicates the training process and poses important challenges to the generalization search.

3.4 Integration of the Deep Learning Model in WASP

The integration of the domain-heuristic in WASP is based on the algorithm reported as Algorithm 1. In a nutshell, the algorithm takes as input a program Π and a set of parameters (namely, k_1, k_2, k_3, h_1, and h_2, such that $0 < k_i < 1$ ($i = [1..3]$), and $h_1, h_2 \in \mathbb{N}$, $h_1 > h_2$) and returns as output a set of heuristic assignments for the atoms of the form $col(\_,\_) \in atoms(\Pi)$. Such assignments will be used later on by WASP as initial activities of the atoms. In more details, it first invokes the deep learning model to obtain the predictions

---

Algorithm 1: Integration of the heuristic

Input : A program Π, parameters k_1, k_2, k_3, h_1, and h_2
Output: A set of pairs $\mathcal{H}$

1 $\mathcal{H} := \emptyset$;
2 $(Pr, Conf) :=$ DeepLearning(Π);   // Returns predictions and confidences
3 $N := \{node \mid col(node, \_) \in atoms(\Pi)\}$;   // Nodes of the graph
4 **for** $node \in N$ **do**
5     $S := \{col(node, \_) \mid col(node, \_) \in atoms(\Pi)\}$;
6     $(first, second) :=$ ComputeAtomWithMaxConfidence(S, $Conf$);
7   **if** $Pr(first)$ *is true* **and** $Conf(first) \geq k_1$ **then**
8        $\mathcal{H} := \mathcal{H} \cup \{(first, h_1)\}$;
9        $diff := Conf(first) - Conf(second)$;
10        $sum := (\sum_{p \in S} Conf(p)) - diff$;
11   **if** $diff \leq k_2$ **and** $Conf(second) > k_3 \cdot sum$ **then**
12           $\mathcal{H} := \mathcal{H} \cup \{(second, h_2)\}$;

13 **return** $\mathcal{H}$;

(Pr) and confidences ($Conf$) for the atoms of the form $col(\_, \_)$ (line 2), where
a prediction can be either *true* (if the atom must be selected as positive) or *false*
(if the atom must be selected as negative), and a confidence is a positive (dec-
imal) number less than 1, where for a given node n the sum of the confidences
of the atoms of the form $col(n, \_)$ is equal to 1. Then, the algorithm computes
the set N of the nodes of the graph by processing the program Π (line 3; in
particular, a node n is added to the set if an atom of the form $col(n, \_)$ occurs
in Π). Later on, for each node n in N, the algorithm collects the set of atoms,
say S, of the form $col(n, \_)$ (line 5). Then, it computes the two atoms in S
associated to the highest confidences, say *first* the atom with the highest value,
and *second* the other one (line 6). At this point, if the prediction of *first* is *true*
and its confidence is greater than a given threshold (k_1), then the atom *first*
is associated to the initialization h_1 (line 8). Moreover, an additional check is
performed to provide a heuristic score also for the atom *second*. In particular, if
the difference between the confidence associated to *first* and the one associated
to *second* is less than or equal to a given threshold (k_2) and the confidence of
second is greater than a threshold (k_3) times the sum of the confidences of all
other atoms in S, then the atom *second* is associated to the initialization h_2
(line 12). Then, the default polarity of the MINISAT heuristic is set to positive
for atoms in $\mathcal{H}$. Intuitively, for each node, the atom with the highest confidence
(*first*) is used only if its confidence is greater than k_1. In this way, if the deep
learning model is not sufficiently confident about the color to assign to the node
then the heuristic is not applied to the node. Similarly, the atom with the second
highest confidence (*second*) is used only if its confidence is similar to the one of
first (i.e., their difference is smaller than k_2) and is greater than the confidence
of all other atoms multiplied by k_3. Finally, the initialization of the activities of
first and *second* to h_1 and h_2 permits the solver to select first the most promising

atoms, and then thanks to the decay of the MINISAT heuristic the activities are progressively reduced if the atoms are not used during the search.

4   Experiment

Hardware and software settings. With respect to the NeuroCore's-related model introduced in Sect. 3.3, the 210 000 instances obtained after the data generation process of 3.2 have been randomly split into training, validation and test sets. More specifically, 60% of the instances have been picked to build the training set and the remaining 40% has been equally divided between validation and test sets. The training has been performed on a NVIDIA A100 Tensor Core GPU, dividing the training samples in batches of 128 instances and applying the backward propagation algorithm in relation to the binary cross entropy (BCE) loss measured on each batch. The stopping criterion adopted to this extent has been designed to monitor the BCE loss on the validation set and to interrupt the execution in case of consecutive lack of improvements.

Then, the performance of WASP without heuristics (referred to as WASP-DEFAULT) have been compared with the ones of WASP with the domain heuristics introduced as Algorithm 1. In particular, we experimented with different values of k_1, k_2, k_3, h_1, and h_2. In the following, we report the two sets obtaining the best performance overall, where $k_1 = 0.15$, $k_2 = 0.15$, $k_3 = 1.0$, $h_1 = 10$, and $h_2 = 5$ for the first strategy and $k_1 = 0.15$, $k_2 = 0.35$, $k_3 = 1.0$, $h_1 = 10$, and $h_2 = 5$ for the second one, that are referred to as WASP-STRAT1 and WASP-STRAT2, respectively. All the variants of WASP have been executed on all the sixty instances of the graph coloring problem submitted to a recent ASP Competition [7]. Note that the training set is built on random subgraphs of the input ones used in the ASP Competition, thus the experiment is not executed on instances used during the training of the deep learning model. Time and memory limit were limited to 1200 s and 8 GB, respectively.

Results Deep Learning. Table 1 reports DNN trained model's performances measured on the test set. Recalling model's generation of Sect. 3.2, outputs can be interpreted as the confidences of the model in stating that the value of 1 can be assigned to a specific literal. The model has been evaluated in terms of TOP N accuracy, where $N \in \{1, 2, 3\}$, and it corresponds to the ratio between the predicted and expected 1s among the first N most confident estimations. Moreover, the percentage of predicted 1s for increasing confidence $C \in \{20, 30, 40, 50\}$ % is measured. As expected, the percentage accuracy increases in agreement with N and C, with approximately 80% for $N = 3$ and 70% for $C \geq 50\%$. The same confidence levels is not guaranteed for all the instances under analysis, as it is underlined by the performances measured for decreasing values of C and N. Nonetheless, it is fundamental to keep in mind the complexity of the proposed target, continuously managing graphs with different shapes.

Result on ASP Instances. Table 2 reports the results of the comparison of the different approaches implemented in WASP, where for each heuristic, we show

Table 1. DNN' EE on the test in terms of TOP N and Confidence Accuracies.

Accuracy (%)						
TOP N			Confidence $\geq C\%$			
$N = 1$	$N = 2$	$N = 3$	$C = 20$	$C = 30$	$C = 40$	$C = 50$
39.59	63.62	79.55	39.59	51.66	63.08	70.74

Table 2. Comparison of the different heuristics on ASP competition instances.

Heuristic	Coherent			Incoherent		
	#	solved	PAR10	#	solved	PAR10
WASP-DEFAULT	14	12	1744.90	24	**24**	**449.43**
WASP-STRAT1	14	13	914.97	24	20	2393.44
WASP-STRAT2	14	**14**	**82.94**	24	19	2837.65

Table 3. Comparison of the different heuristics on generated instances.

Heuristic	130 nodes			135 nodes			140 nodes		
	#	solved	PAR10	#	solved	PAR10	#	solved	PAR10
WASP-DEFAULT	60	**60**	**15.24**	89	77	1707.73	85	76	1322.17
WASP-STRAT1	60	**60**	32.95	89	**78**	**1609.21**	85	76	1338.02
WASP-STRAT2	60	**60**	31.80	89	**78**	1620.13	85	**78**	**1066.18**

the number of solved instances, and the PAR10. We recall that the PAR10 is the average solving time where unsolved instances are counted as 10 · timeout. PAR10 is a metric commonly used in machine learning and SAT communities, as it allows to consider both coverage and solved time. As a first observation, we mention that the call to the deep learning model requires on average less than one second, thus it has no negative impact on the performance of the domain-specific heuristics. Then, we observe that both WASP-STRAT1 and WASP-STRAT2 are faster than WASP-DEFAULT on coherent instances, solving 1 and 2 more instances, respectively. Additionally, WASP-STRAT2 has a PAR10 equals to 82.94 and it is approximately 21 times lower than the one of WASP-DEFAULT. The same result cannot be obtained for incoherent instances, where WASP-DEFAULT solves 4 and 5 instances more than WASP-STRAT1 and WASP-STRAT2, and also with a much lower PAR10. This result is expected since only coherent instances were used during the training and also since the heuristic is oriented towards finding a stable model. As an additional experiment, we generated, starting from the set of known incoherent instances, another set of coherent instances by randomly removing a certain number of links from the input instance. Table 3 reports the results of such an experiment, where we classified instances into three sets according to the number of nodes, i.e., 130 nodes, 135 nodes, and 140 nodes.

Interestingly, domain-specific heuristics are not effective on instances with 130 nodes, which are solved quite fast by the default version of WASP. However, on instances with 135 and 140 nodes the domain-specific WASP-STRAT2 outperforms WASP-DEFAULT solving three more instances overall and being faster in terms of PAR10. Finally, concerning the usage of memory, we observe that all the tested approaches never exceed memory limits.

5 Related Work

Several ways of combining domain heuristics and ASP are proposed in the literature. In [3], a technique which allows learning of domain-specific heuristics in DPLL-based solvers is presented. The basic idea is to analyze off-line the behavior of the solver on representative instances from the domain to learn and use a heuristic in later runs. A declarative approach to definition of domain specific heuristics in ASP is presented in [11]. The techniques presented in this paper might be also applied in combination with such a framework by properly setting the _ heuristic predicate. Andres et al. in [2] and Dodaro et al. in [8] proposed domain-specific heuristics for tackling hard problems. However, their approach was based on the implementation of the heuristic made by a domain expert. ML-solutions have been also adopted to predict the best solver for a given instance [6,14,19]. We are not aware of any attempt to experiment with automatic learning of domain heuristics in modern CDCL-based solvers.

In the context of SAT, our work is related to the one of Selsam and Bjørner [22] and their system NeuroCore. In particular, our deep learning model takes inspiration of their proposal. Nonetheless, in our model we do not fix the shape of the training instances to a unique value. Another important difference is that our training set contains coherent instances only, whereas the one used by NeuroCore is instead based on (minimal) unsatisfiable cores. This difference was motivated by the fact that the computation of (minimal) unsatisfiable cores is not currently supported by state-of-the-art ASP solvers. The integration of such techniques can be also beneficial in the context of domain-specific heuristics. Moreover, the deep learning model introduced by NeuroCore is periodically queried during the search to re-configure the branching heuristic. However, our preliminary experiments (not included in the paper for space reason) show that considering learned constraints deteriorate the performance of the solver, since multiple calls to the deep learning model on larger and larger programs were counterproductive. Wu in [25] pointed out the lack of efficiency of CDCL algorithm in solving formulae of even moderate sizes, e.g. 300 to 500 variables involved, and proposes to take advantage of ML techniques to train a model able to wisely assign initial values to branching variables in order to prevent possible conflicts and to find a solution in relatively short time. After the experimental phase, it was observed a consistent decrease in the number of conflicts. However, the computational time required to perform the preprocessing phase was non-negligible compared to the timing necessary to run the enhanced version of the solver taken as a benchmark. Moreover, Liang et al. in [18] proposed a ML-based approach to predict the so called *Literal Block Distance* (LBD), defined as the number of different decision levels of the variables in the clause. They choose to exploit an Adam SGD algorithm that autonomously triggers a restart if the next LBD exceeds the linear sample mean for 3.08 standard deviations (i.e. the 99.9^{th} percentile). The experiments show that the proposed approach performs coherently with state-of-the-art methods. Xu et al. in [26] proposed a ML-based strategy to evaluate 3-SAT instances on the phase transition. In particular, they trained a model on a 3-SAT dataset comprising instances with varying number of variables in the range 100–600. They initially opt for a random forest algorithm with the aim of discriminating between SAT or UNSAT instances basing on 61 cheap-to-compute features. Then, they progressively simplify their model and reduce the number of features considered still achieving reasonable performances.

6   Conclusion

In this paper, we presented a strategy based on deep learning to automatically generate domain-specific heuristics. In particular, we focus on one single benchmark, i.e. the graph coloring problem. This choice was motivated by the fact that *(i)* the encoding does not include advanced features such as aggregates, choice rules, and weak constraints; *(ii)* the problem allows to control the hardness of the instance by either reducing the number of nodes and/or the number of links. Moreover, the training set used to automatically generate the heuristics contains coherent instances only and, as expected, this lead to poor performance on incoherent ones. As future work, alternative strategies consist of exploiting minimal unsatisfiable cores, or automatically tuning parameters used by Algorithm 1.

Acknowledgments. This work is partially supported by MUR under PRIN project "exPlaInable kNowledge-aware PrOcess INTelligence" (PINPOINT), CUP H23C22000280006 and by MISE under project MAP4ID "Multipurpose Analytics Platform 4 Industrial Data", N. F/190138/01-03/X44.

References

1. Alviano, M., Dodaro, C., Leone, N., Ricca, F.: Advances in WASP. In: Calimeri, F., Ianni, G., Truszczynski, M. (eds.) LPNMR 2015. LNCS (LNAI), vol. 9345, pp. 40–54. Springer, Cham (2015). https://doi.org/10.1007/978-3-319-23264-5_5
2. Andres, B., Biewer, A., Romero, J., Haubelt, C., Schaub, T.: Improving coordinated SMT-based system synthesis by utilizing domain-specific heuristics. In: Calimeri, F., Ianni, G., Truszczynski, M. (eds.) LPNMR 2015. LNCS (LNAI), vol. 9345, pp. 55–68. Springer, Cham (2015). https://doi.org/10.1007/978-3-319-23264-5_6
3. Balduccini, M.: Learning and using domain-specific heuristics in ASP solvers. AI Commun. 24(2), 147–164 (2011). https://doi.org/10.3233/AIC-2011-0493
4. Bengio, Y., LeCun, Y., Hinton, G.E.: Deep learning for AI. Commun. ACM **64**(7), 58–65 (2021). https://doi.org/10.1145/3448250

5. Brewka, G., Eiter, T., Truszczynski, M.: Answer set programming at a glance. Commun. ACM **54**(12), 92–103 (2011). https://doi.org/10.1145/2043174.2043195
6. Calimeri, F., Dodaro, C., Fuscà, D., Perri, S., Zangari, J.: Efficiently coupling the I-DLV grounder with ASP solvers. TPLP **20**(2), 205–224 (2020). https://doi.org/10.1017/S1471068418000546
7. Calimeri, F., Gebser, M., Maratea, M., Ricca, F.: Design and results of the fifth answer set programming competition. Artif. Intell. **231**, 151–181 (2016). https://doi.org/10.1016/j.artint.2015.09.008
8. Dodaro, C., Gasteiger, P., Leone, N., Musitsch, B., Ricca, F., Schekotihin, K.: Combining answer set programming and domain heuristics for solving hard industrial problems (application paper). TPLP **16**(5–6), 653–669 (2016). https://doi.org/10.1017/S1471068416000284
9. Eén, N., Sörensson, N.: An extensible SAT-solver. In: Giunchiglia, E., Tacchella, A. (eds.) SAT 2003. LNCS, vol. 2919, pp. 502–518. Springer, Heidelberg (2004). https://doi.org/10.1007/978-3-540-24605-3_37
10. Erdem, E., Gelfond, M., Leone, N.: Applications of answer set programming. AI Mag. **37**(3), 53–68 (2016). https://doi.org/10.1609/aimag.v37i3.2678
11. Gebser, M., Kaufmann, B., Romero, J., Otero, R., Schaub, T., Wanko, P.: Domain-specific heuristics in answer set programming. In: Proceedings of AAAI. AAAI Press (2013)
12. Goodfellow, I., Bengio, Y., Courville, A.: Deep Learning. MIT Press, Cambridge (2016)
13. Hawkins, D.M.: The problem of overfitting. J. Chem. Inf. Comput. Sci. **44**(1), 1–12 (2004)
14. Hoos, H.H., Lindauer, M., Schaub, T.: claspfolio 2: advances in algorithm selection for answer set programming. TPLP **14**(4–5), 569–585 (2014)
15. Hornik, K., Stinchcombe, M.B., White, H.: Multilayer feedforward networks are universal approximators. Neural Netw. **2**(5), 359–366 (1989)
16. Kaufmann, B., Leone, N., Perri, S., Schaub, T.: Grounding and solving in answer set programming. AI Mag. **37**(3), 25–32 (2016). https://doi.org/10.1609/aimag.v37i3.2672
17. Kingma, D.P., Ba, J.: Adam: a method for stochastic optimization. arXiv preprint arXiv:1412.6980 (2014)
18. Liang, J.H., Oh, C., Mathew, M., Thomas, C., Li, C., Ganesh, V.: Machine learning-based restart policy for CDCL SAT solvers. In: Beyersdorff, O., Wintersteiger, C.M. (eds.) SAT 2018. LNCS, vol. 10929, pp. 94–110. Springer, Cham (2018). https://doi.org/10.1007/978-3-319-94144-8_6
19. Maratea, M., Pulina, L., Ricca, F.: A multi-engine approach to answer-set programming. TPLP **14**(6), 841–868 (2014). https://doi.org/10.1017/S1471068413000094
20. Oneto, L.: Model Selection and Error Estimation in a Nutshell. MOST, vol. 15. Springer, Cham (2020). https://doi.org/10.1007/978-3-030-24359-3
21. Rumelhart, D., Hinton, G., Williams, R.: Learning representations by back-propagating errors. Nature **323**(6088), 533–536 (1986)
22. Selsam, D., Bjørner, N.: Guiding high-performance SAT solvers with Unsat-core predictions. In: Janota, M., Lynce, I. (eds.) SAT 2019. LNCS, vol. 11628, pp. 336–353. Springer, Cham (2019). https://doi.org/10.1007/978-3-030-24258-9_24
23. Shalev-Shwartz, S., Ben-David, S.: Understanding Machine Learning: From Theory to Algorithms. Cambridge University Press, Cambridge (2014)
24. Taupe, R., Friedrich, G., Schekotihin, K., Weinzierl, A.: Solving configuration problems with ASP and declarative domain specific heuristics. In: Proceedings of CWS/ConfWS, vol. 2945, pp. 13–20. CEUR-WS.org (2021)

25. Wu, H.: Improving sat-solving with machine learning. In: Proceedings of SIGCSE, pp. 787–788. ACM (2017)
26. Xu, L., Hoos, H.H., Leyton-Brown, K.: Predicting satisfiability at the phase transition. In: Proceedings of AAAI. AAAI Press (2012)

A Qualitative Temporal Extension
of Here-and-There Logic

Thomas Eiter[1](✉) and Patrik Schneider[1,2]

[1] Institute of Logic and Computation,TU Wien, Vienna, Austria
{eiter,patrik}@kr.tuwien.ac.at
[2] Siemens AG, Munich, Germany

Abstract. Model-based Diagnosis (MBD) is an approach to diagnosis, where an
(objective) model of a system is diagnosed to find a set of *explanations* revealing
root causes for issues. Temporal behavioral models are prominent approach for
temporal MBD, where their associated temporal formulas (TBFs) by Brusoni et
al. (Artificial Intelligence, 102:39–79, 1998) can be used to relate explanations to
observations under temporal constraints based on Allen's Interval Algebra (IA).
Due to expressive limitations of the constructs, we envision an extended language
of TBFs that allows for complex formulas and nesting of formulas in temporal
constraints. To this end, we present a language that extends propositional resp. FO
logic with IA relations and provide semantics for it based on here-and-there (HT)
logic as well as on Equilibrium Logic. Furthermore, we lift a well-known tableau
calculus for propositional HT logic to the temporal setting and report about an
experimental prototype implementation. Based on these results, rich notions of
diagnostic explanations from temporal behavior models may be developed.

1 Introduction

Model-based Diagnosis (MBD) [11] is an approach to diagnosis, where an (objective)
model of a system is diagnosed to find a set of *explanations* revealing root causes for
errors. For instance in Urban Traffic Management (UTM) systems traffic flow is ana-
lyzed over longer periods to reveal root causes for traffic congestions in a road network,
e.g., frequent accidents or delays. Temporal behavioral models (TBMs) by Brusoni et al.
[5] are a prominent approach for temporal MBD, where their associated temporal formulas (TBFs) can be used to relate explanations to observations under temporal constraints
based on Allen's Interval Algebra (IA). However, TBMs are sometimes too restrictive
in expressing complex relationships between possible explanations and observations;
more details and an example are given below. Motivated by this fact, we aim at providing a language for finding possible explanations for observations, e.g., for a traffic
congestion, using temporal constraints and by extending TBMs for linking temporal
relations directly to atoms, supporting undefined time intervals, and allowing for various encodings of "explains". The extension is a step towards an abduction-based traffic
diagnosis framework that combines TBMs, a flow model for observations, e.g., as we
presented in previous work [8], and a background knowledge base (KB) that allows one
to find likely explanations.

© The Author(s), under exclusive license to Springer Nature Switzerland AG 2022
G. Gottlob et al. (Eds.): LPNMR 2022, LNAI 13416, pp. 159–176, 2022.
https://doi.org/10.1007/978-3-031-15707-3_13

Temporal Behavioral Models. According to [5], a *temporal behavioral model* (TBM) is defined as a set of *temporal behavior formulae* (TBFs) and a set of global *temporal integrity constraints*. For example, a TBF may be used to explain the causal relation between the cause *water retention* with *no fluid therapy* and the effect *high blood volume* [5]:

$$water\_ret(T_1), therapy(absent) \text{ explains } blood\_vol(high, T_2)\{T_1(before, overlaps)T_2\}.$$

Such a TBF captures the idea that statements on the left-hand-side (LHS) *explain* observation(s) on the right-hand-side (RHS) taking the *local temporal constraints* (e.g., *before*) into account, where these constraints *must* be fulfilled with respect to time intervals assigned to the variables T_1 and T_2. As Brusoni et al. noted, we may interpret *explains* in backward or forward direction. Our work aims at using TBMs for traffic diagnosis over a stream of observations to find a set of explanations that capture specific traffic patterns using Allen's Time Interval Algebra (IA). Therefore, we extend the original TBF syntax as illustrated by the following formula:

$$(a(T_1) \lor b(T_2)), c(T_3) \text{ explains } o_1(T_4), o_2(T_5) \{TC\}$$

where $TC = \{((T_1 \sqcap \sim T_3) \text{ overlaps } (T_4 \sqcup T_5)) \lor ((T_2 \sqcap T_3) \text{ overlaps } (T_4 \sqcup T_5))\}$. The atoms a and b represent the explanations for *normal congestion* and *accident-related congestion*, c represents an auxiliary atom stating whether *roadworks* occur in a time period (with $\sim T_3$ denoting it is known that it is not occurring), and o_1 and o_2 are two observations of *slow traffic*. Note that we require coalescing (denoted by $\sqcap$ and $\sqcup$) for time intervals to check the temporal constraints.

The original TBF syntax appears to be not well-suited for expressing complex relationships as above. Furthermore, a reduced syntax (not involving explains nor time intervals explicitly) may be desirable. This can be achieved by the following steps: (a) combine the LHS, RHS, and constraints to one conjunction dropping explains; (b) make the temporal information assigned to atoms implicit, with the possibility of having undefined time intervals; and (c) let temporal relations refer directly to atoms, which allows for nested sub-formulas.

Example 1. We obtain the following formula applying the steps on the TBF above:

$$(a \lor b) \land c \land ((a \land \sim c) \text{ overlaps } (o_1 \lor o_2)) \lor ((b \land c) \text{ overlaps } (o_1 \lor o_2)) \land o_1 \land o_2.$$

We aim to evaluate whether a or b are explanations supported by observations in various temporal assignments under the temporal constraints, so $(a \land \sim c)$ and $(b \land c)$ must occur on time intervals that overlap with $(o_1 \lor o_2)$. The meta directive "explains" can be replaced based on the desired reasoning task; we may e.g., conjoin the LHS and RHS for checking the consistency of the new formula according to various temporal assignments, while we may state that the LHS implies the RHS for abductive reasoning.

The new language requires a suitable semantics, where theories can be characterized and an evaluation algorithm can be developed. For this, we build on the work on here-and-there logic (HT) [12] and its extension to Equilibrium Logic [17], which can be evaluated using a tableau system or an ASP solver on restricted formulas. The novel language extends HT logic with coalescing operators, undefined time intervals, and temporal relations. For the evaluation, we extend the tableau calculus for HT logic by Pearce et al. [16] and include temporal expansion rules. We then provide soundness and completeness results for the new tableau system. Besides the technical results, we developed a prototypical implementation to enable initial experimentation with the calculus. Our contributions are developed as follows:

- After stating necessary preliminaries (Sect. 2), we present our temporal extension of HT logic including a novel syntax and semantics (Sect. 3).
- We present a temporal tableau calculus and give technical details about it (Sect. 4).
- We report on a prototypical implementation and illustrate it on a case study (Sect. 5).
- We discuss related work and compare our approach to others for (qualitative) temporal reasoning and conclude with ongoing and future work (Sect. 6).

2   Preliminaries

To analyze temporal behavioral models, we introduce a novel language that is based on an extension of here-and-there (HT) logic [12,13] with a FO semantics and strong negation called FOHT [17]. The authors of [17] also showed that HT and FOHT are *equivalently* represented by the five-valued logic N_5 and the quantified five-valued logic QN_5, respectively.

FOHT is a FO language over a signature $\Sigma = \langle C, \mathcal{F}, \mathcal{P} \rangle$, where C is a (w.l.o.g. nonempty) set of constants, $\mathcal{F}$ a set of functions, and $\mathcal{P}$ a set of predicates. We denote by $Term(C, \mathcal{F})$ and $Atom(C, \mathcal{F}, \mathcal{P})$ the sets of ground terms and atoms induced by C and $\mathcal{F}$, resp. by $C, \mathcal{F}$, and $\mathcal{P}$; furthermore, $Lit(C, \mathcal{F}, \mathcal{P}) = \{a, \sim a \mid a \in Atom(C, \mathcal{F}, \mathcal{P})\}$ is the set of ground literals, where $\sim$ is *strong negation* and a and $\sim a$ are *contrary literals*; *weak negation* is denoted by $\neg$. The notions of free/bound variables and closed formulas (sentences) are as usual.

Definition 1 (cf. [17]). *A FOHT-model is a quadruple $M = \langle D_h, H, D_t, T \rangle$, where D_h and D_t are domains s.t. $C \subseteq D_h \subseteq D_t$, and $H \subseteq T \subseteq Lit(D, \mathcal{F}, \mathcal{P})$ are sets of literals such that T does not contain contrary literals and H does not contain constants from $D_t \setminus D_h$. The satisfaction relation $M, w \models \phi$ for $w \in \{h, t\}$, where $h \leq h, h \leq t$, $t \leq t$ are totally ordered worlds, and a sentence ϕ is depending on the structure of ϕ as follows ($\mathcal{T}_w = Term(D_w, \mathcal{F})$):*

- *literal L: $w = h \wedge L \in H$ or $w = t \wedge L \in T$;*
- *$\alpha \wedge \beta$: $M, w \models \alpha$ and $M, w \models \beta$;*
- *$\alpha \vee \beta$: $M, w \models \alpha$ or $M, w \models \beta$;*
- *$\alpha \rightarrow \beta$: for every $w' \geq w$: $M, w' \not\models \alpha$ or $M, w' \models \beta$;*
- *$\forall x\ \alpha(x)$: for every $w' \geq w$ and $d \in \mathcal{T}_w$: $M, w' \models \alpha(d)$;*
- *$\exists x\ \alpha(x)$: for some $d \in \mathcal{T}_w$: $M, w \models \alpha(d)$;*
- *$\neg \alpha$: no $w' \leq w$ exists such that $M, w' \models \alpha$;*

- *$\sim(\alpha \wedge \beta)$: $M, w \models \sim\alpha$ or $M, w \models \sim\beta$;*
- *$\sim(\alpha \vee \beta)$: $M, w \models \sim\alpha$ and $M, w \models \sim\beta$;*
- *$\sim(\alpha \rightarrow \beta)$: $M, w \models \alpha$ and $M, w \models \sim\beta$;*
- *$\sim\neg\alpha$: $M, w \models \alpha$;*
- *$\sim\sim\alpha$: $M, w \models \alpha$;*
- *$\sim \forall x\ \alpha(x)$: for some $d \in \mathcal{T}_w$: $M, w \models \sim\alpha(d)$;*
- *$\sim \exists x\ \alpha(x)$: for every $w' \geq w$ and $d \in \mathcal{T}_w$: $M, w' \models \sim\alpha(d)$.*

$\mathcal{M}$ is a model of a closed formula ϕ, denoted $\mathcal{M} \models \phi$, if $\mathcal{M}, h \models \phi$ and $\mathcal{M}, t \models \phi$. A closed formula ϕ is valid in FOHT if ϕ is true in all models.

FOHT under the *constant domain* assumption, i.e., $D_h = D_t$, is denoted by $FOHT_c$; we then simplify $FOHT_c$ models to triples $\mathcal{M} = \langle D, H, T \rangle$ where $D = D_h = D_t$.

In [17], equilibrium models were defined using minimal models for $FOHT_c$ similar as in HT logic. A model $\mathcal{M} = \langle D, H, T \rangle$ of a theory Π over Σ is an *equilibrium* model, if (1) $\mathcal{M}$ is *total*, i.e., $H = T$, and (2) $\mathcal{M}$ is $\preceq$-minimal among the models of Π, where $\mathcal{M}_1 \preceq \mathcal{M}_2$ holds for $\mathcal{M}_i = \langle D_i, H_i, T_i \rangle$, $i = 1, 2$, if $D_1 = D_2$, $T_1 = T_2$, and $H_1 \subseteq H_2$ (tantamount Π has no model $\langle D, H', T \rangle$ with $H' \subset H$).

Quantified Many-Valued Logic. The (quantified) many-valued logic N_5 (QN_5) allows one to characterize the Kripke-style model semantics of HT-logic using a five-valued matrix for the set $\mathcal{T}_5 = \{-2, -1, 0, 1, 2\}$ of truth values. We also will use N_3 (QN_3) with truth-values $\mathcal{T}_3 = \{-2, -0, 2\}$, when only total models are of interest.

Each k-ary connective F has an associated *interpretation* function $f_F : \mathcal{T}_5^k \to \mathcal{T}_5$ as follows:

F	$x \wedge y$	$x \vee y$	$\sim x$	$\neg x$	$x \to y$
f_F	$\min(x,y)$	$\max(x,y)$	$-1 \cdot x$	$\begin{cases} 2 & \text{if } x \leq 0 \\ -1 \cdot x & \text{otherwise} \end{cases}$	$\begin{cases} 2 & \text{if } x \leq 0 \text{ or } x \leq y \\ y & \text{otherwise} \end{cases}$

Definition 2. *A* valuation *(or* truth-value assignment*) is a function* $\sigma : Atom(\mathcal{C}, \mathcal{F}, \mathcal{P}) \to \mathcal{T}_5$ *that can be uniquely extended to a homomorphism from* Σ *to* $\mathcal{T}_5$ *via* $\sigma(F(\phi_1, ..., \phi_i)) = f_F(\sigma(\phi_1), ..., \sigma(\phi_i))$.

For N_3, interpretations and valuations are restricted to $\mathcal{T}_3$. For $S \subseteq \mathcal{T}_k$, a formula ϕ is *S-satisfiable* (resp., an *S-tautology*) in N_k, if for some (every) valuation σ over $\mathcal{T}_k$ it holds that $\sigma(\phi) \in S$. In case $S = \{2\}$, we say Φ is *satisfiable* (resp. *valid*). For instance, we give in Fig. 1 every valuation for an implication with $\sigma(x)$, resp., $\sigma(y)$ shown on the first column, resp., first row (the grey coloring of cells is discussed in Sect. 4).

	-2	0	2
-2	2	2	2
0	2	2	2
2	-2	0	2

Fig. 1. Truth table for $x \to y$

We use $\phi \equiv_k \psi$ to denote semantic equivalence in N_k, i.e., for every valuation σ we have $\sigma(\phi) = \sigma(\psi)$. In N_3, we then have that $(x \to y) \equiv_3 (\neg x \vee y)$ as $\sigma(x \to y) = \sigma(\neg x \vee y)$ holds for all possible valuations of x and y. Note that this equivalence does not hold for N_5: e.g., for $\sigma(x) = 1$ and $\sigma(y) = -2$ we have $\sigma(x \to y) = -2$ while $\sigma(\neg x \vee y) = -1$.

Proposition 1. *The following equivalences hold for all formulas* α, β, γ *in* N_k, $k = 3, 5$:

(i) $\alpha \wedge \beta \equiv_k \beta \wedge \alpha$ *and* $\alpha \vee \beta \equiv_k \beta \vee \alpha$; *(vi)* $\sim(\alpha \vee \beta) \equiv_k (\sim\alpha \wedge \sim\beta)$ *and*

(ii) $(\alpha \wedge \beta) \wedge \gamma \equiv_k \alpha \wedge (\beta \wedge \gamma)$ $\sim(\alpha \wedge \beta) \equiv_k (\sim\alpha \vee \sim\beta)$;

(iii) $\alpha \vee (\beta \wedge \gamma) \equiv_k (\alpha \vee \beta) \wedge (\alpha \vee \gamma)$; *(vii)* $\neg(\alpha \vee \beta) \equiv_3 (\neg\alpha \wedge \neg\beta)$ *and*

(iv) $\alpha \wedge (\beta \vee \gamma) \equiv_k (\alpha \wedge \beta) \vee (\alpha \wedge \gamma)$; $\neg(\alpha \wedge \beta) \equiv_3 (\neg\alpha \vee \neg\beta)$;

(v) $\neg\neg\neg\alpha \equiv_k \neg\alpha$, *and* $\sim\sim\sim\alpha \equiv_k \sim\alpha$; *(viii)* $\alpha \to \beta \equiv_3 \neg\alpha \vee \beta$.

In [17], QN_5 models are pairs $\langle D, \sigma \rangle$, where $D \supseteq C$ is the domain and σ a valuation as above, which is extended to closed formulas by $\sigma(\forall x\ \phi(x)) = min\{\sigma(\phi(t));\ t \in \mathcal{T}\}$, and $\sigma(\exists x\ \phi(x)) = max\{\sigma(\phi(t));\ t \in \mathcal{T}\}$, where $\mathcal{T} = Term(D, \mathcal{F})$. If $D_h \neq D_t$, the many-valued semantics does not always coincide with the FOHT-semantics as quantifiers are interpreted as supremum and infimum. However, under restriction to constant domains, $FOHT_c$-models and QN_5-models tightly correspond.

Proposition 2. *(Theorem 1, [17]). A bijection f between $FOHT_c$-models $\mathcal{M}$ and QN_5-models exists s.t. for each formula ϕ, $\mathcal{M} \models \phi$ iff $f(\mathcal{M})(\phi) = 2$; hence, ϕ is is valid in $FOHT_c$ iff it is valid in QN_5.*

Propositional N_5-models (given by σ) can be converted from/to HT-models with the following table for truth-value assignments $\sigma(p)$, where $p \in Atom(\mathcal{C}, \mathcal{F}, \mathcal{P})$ and $H \subseteq T$ are as in Definition 1.

	$\sim p \in H$	$\sim p \in T \wedge \sim p \notin H$	$p \notin T \wedge \sim p \notin T$	$p \in T \wedge p \notin H$	$p \in H$
$\sigma(p)$	-2	-1	0	1	2

Furthermore, [17] showed how $\preceq$-ordering of HT-models can be transferred to N_5's many-valued semantics. Given a theory Π over Σ in N_5, the ordering $\sigma_1 \preceq \sigma_2$ of N_5-models σ_1, σ_2 holds, if for every atom $p \in Atom(\mathcal{C}, \mathcal{F}, \mathcal{P})$ the following conditions (1)–(3) hold:

$$(1)\ \sigma_1(p) = 0 \Leftrightarrow \sigma_2(p) = 0;\ (2)\ \sigma_1(p) < 1 \vee \sigma_1(p) \leq \sigma_2(p);\ \text{and}$$
$$(3)\ \sigma_1(p) > -1 \vee \sigma_1(p) \geq \sigma_2(p).$$

The equilibrium models of ϕ amount then to the $\preceq$-minimal N_5-models σ of ϕ where no atom is assigned $\{-1, 1\}$ (called *total*); intuitively, no model with less assignments in $\{-2, 2\}$ is possible.

Example 2. Consider the formula $\phi : \neg x \to y$ and the following HT-models $i_1 - i_5$ ($H \subseteq T$):

$i_1 : (\emptyset, \{x\})$, $i_2 : (\{x\}, \{x\})$, $i_3 : (\{x\}, \{x, y\})$, $i_4 : (\{y\}, \{y\})$, *and* $i_5 : (\{x, y\}, \{x, y\})$.

The corresponding N_5 models are $\sigma_1 = \{x \mapsto 1, y \mapsto 0\}$; $\sigma_2 = \{x \mapsto 2, y \mapsto 0\}$; $\sigma_3 = \{x \mapsto 2, y \mapsto 1\}$; $\sigma_4 = \{x \mapsto 0, y \mapsto 2\}$; $\sigma_5 = \{x \mapsto 2, y \mapsto 2\}$. The only equilibrium model of ϕ among them is i_4: indeed, i_1 and i_3 are not total models; i_2 and i_5 are not minimal as $i_1 \preceq i_2$ and $i_3 \preceq i_5$.

Table 1. IA relations with inverses and Allen's naming in brackets

R	Definition with start/end points	R^-	Inverse definition
$x(p)y$	$before(x,y){=}((x,y):\underline{x}<\overline{x}<\underline{y}<\overline{y})$	$x(P)y$	$after(x,y)=before(y,x)$
$x(m)y$	$meets(x,y){=}((x,y):\underline{x}<\overline{x}=\underline{y}<\overline{y})$	$x(M)y$	$metBy(x,y)=meets(y,x)$
$x(o)y$	$overlaps(x,y){=}((x,y):\underline{x}<\underline{y}<\overline{x}<\overline{y})$	$x(O)y$	$overlappedBy(x,y)=overlaps(y,x)$
$x(s)y$	$starts(x,y){=}((x,y):\underline{x}=\underline{y}<\overline{x}<\overline{y})$	$x(S)y$	$startedBy(x,y)=starts(y,x)$
$x(f)y$	$finishes(x,y){=}((x,y):\underline{y}<\underline{x}<\overline{x}=\overline{y})$	$x(F)y$	$finishedBy(x,y)=finishes(y,x)$
$x(d)y$	$during(x,y){=}((x,y):\underline{y}<\underline{x}<\overline{x}<\overline{y})$	$x(D)y$	$contains(x,y)=during(y,x)$
$x(e)y$	$equal(x,y){=}((x,y):\underline{y}=\underline{x}<\overline{x}=\overline{y})$		

Allen's Interval Algebra. For temporal constraints, we will focus on Allen's Time Interval Algebra (IA) [1] and calculus. IA is based on time intervals and the binary relations defined between them. The domain of IA relations is the set of intervals over the linear order of $\mathbb{T}$ defined as $[p_i] = [\underline{p_i}, \overline{p_i}]$ with $\underline{p_i} < \overline{p_i}$. The 13 *basic* relations are defined according to their start/end points [1] as shown in Table 1. We denote with $IA_\nu(x,y)$ that a specific relation ν holds between the two intervals. The 13 basic relations give rise to 2^{13} *general* relations. Note that several base relations can hold between two events represented by intervals that can be open.

3   Qualitative Temporal Here-and-There Logic

We now extend the language with (binary) temporal relations, which allow one to state formulas like $(a \wedge \sim c)$ *overlaps* $(o_1 \vee o_2)$ in the introductory example.

For the evaluation, we extend Σ to $\Sigma^t = \langle \mathcal{C}, \mathcal{F}, \mathcal{P}, \mathcal{A} \rangle$, where $\mathcal{A} \subseteq \mathcal{L} \times (\mathbb{Z} \times \mathbb{Z})$ is a relation that associates with each literal in $\mathcal{L} = Lit(\mathcal{C}, \mathcal{F}, \mathcal{P})$ at most one time interval from $(\mathbb{Z} \times \mathbb{Z})$, where for contrary literals g and $\sim g$ the associated intervals $[x]$ and $[y]$ must be disjoint, i.e., $[x]$ and $[y]$ have no common point in time.

Formally, $\mathcal{A}$ induces a function $\tau_\mathcal{A} : Lit(\mathcal{C}, \mathcal{F}, \mathcal{P}) \to (\mathbb{Z} \times \mathbb{Z}) \cup \{\mathbf{u}\}$ called *temporal assignment*, where $\mathbf{u}$ is the *undefined time instance*, and for each $g \in Lit(\mathcal{C}, \mathcal{F}, \mathcal{P})$:

$$\tau_\mathcal{A}(g) = \begin{cases} \mathbf{u} & \text{if } (g, (t_1, t_2)) \notin \mathcal{A}, \\ (t_1, t_2) : (g, (t_1, t_2)) \in \mathcal{A} & \text{otherwise.} \end{cases}$$

In slight abuse of terminology, we will call $\mathcal{A}$ also temporal assignment. Note that the assignment to contrary literals does not cover the whole timeline; intuitively, $\tau(g)$ expresses that for this interval the truth value of g is certain. The value $\mathbf{u}$ stands for time information that is non-evaluable, due to missing observations (at evaluation time), or due to intervals that cannot be coalesced (as seen later).

Example 3. Consider a model $\mathcal{M}_2 = \langle D, (H, \mathcal{A}_1), (T, \mathcal{A}_1) \rangle$ with $D = \{x, y, z\}$ and the formula $\phi : (p(x) \vee p(y)) \wedge ((p(x) \; before \; p(z)) \vee (p(y) \; before \; p(z)))$. A possible temporal assignment over which ϕ should be evaluated is $\mathcal{A}_1 = \{(p(x), [1,2]), p(y), [2,3]), (p(z), [4,5])\}$.

To evaluate a formula a *before* b, say, where a and b are atoms, we can readily use τ above to assess the temporal relationship of a and b. However, for complex formulas $\alpha \nu \beta$, where α and β are non-atomic, as in case of $(a \wedge \mathord{\sim} c)$ *overlaps* $o_1 \vee o_2$, an evaluation on the basis of τ is non-obvious in general. We thus restrict formulas by disallowing nested temporal relations and some connectives.

Definition 3. *A flat temporal formula (FTF) is of the form $\alpha \nu \beta$, where ν is a temporal relation and α and β are closed formulas without temporal relations, implication $\rightarrow$ and weak negation $\neg$.*

In the rest of this paper, we then consider formulas in the extended language in which each occurring subformula $\alpha \nu \beta$ is an FTF.

Coalescing. For the evaluation of formulas α and β nested in FTFs, we introduce two *coalescing* operators, where we distinguish between coalescing intervals associated with a conjunction resp. disjunction.

Definition 4. *The coalescing operators $coal_\wedge(x,y)$ and $coal_\vee(x,y)$ for the intervals $x = \tau(\alpha)$ and $y = \tau(\beta)$ associated with the literals α and β in $\alpha \wedge \beta$ resp. $\alpha \vee \beta$, are as in the following table:*[1]

x,y satisfy	$x(p)y$	$x(m)y$	$x(o)y$	$x(s)y$	$x(f)y$	$x(d)y$	$x(e)y$	$x = \mathbf{u}$ or $y = \mathbf{u}$
$coal_\wedge(x,y)$	$\mathbf{u}$	$[\overline{x},\overline{x}]$	$[y,\overline{x}]$	$[x,\overline{x}]$	$[x,\overline{x}]$	$[x,\overline{x}]$	$[x,\overline{x}]$	$\mathbf{u}$
$coal_\vee(x,y)$	$\mathbf{u}$	$[x,\overline{y}]$	$[x,\overline{y}]$	$[y,\overline{y}]$	$[y,y]$	$[y,\overline{y}]$	$[x,\overline{x}]$	$\mathbf{u}$

In Example 3, we have for instance that $coal_\vee(\tau_{\mathcal{A}_1}(p(x)), \tau_{\mathcal{A}_1}(p(y))) = [1,3]$.

Temporal assignments can then be generalized to formulas α and β inside FTFs by a *(nested)* temporal assignment $\phi \mapsto \tau_{\mathcal{A}}^*(\phi)$ where

$$
\tau_{\mathcal{A}}^*(\phi) = \begin{cases}
\tau_{\mathcal{A}}(\phi) & \text{if } \phi \in Lit(\mathcal{C}, \mathcal{F}, \mathcal{P}), \\
coal_\circ(\tau_{\mathcal{A}}^*(\phi_1), \tau_{\mathcal{A}}^*(\phi_2))) & \text{if } \phi : \phi_1 \circ \phi_2, \text{ for } \circ \in \{\wedge, \vee\}, \\
\tau_{\mathcal{A}}^*(\phi_1) & \text{if } \phi = \mathord{\sim}\mathord{\sim}\phi_1, \\
\tau_{\mathcal{A}}^*(\mathord{\sim}\phi_1 \wedge \mathord{\sim}\phi_2) & \text{if } \phi = \mathord{\sim}(\phi_1 \vee \phi_2), \\
\tau_{\mathcal{A}}^*(\mathord{\sim}\phi_1 \vee \mathord{\sim}\phi_2) & \text{if } \phi = \mathord{\sim}(\phi_1 \wedge \phi_2).
\end{cases}
$$

By convention, we regard for $\tau_{\mathcal{A}}^*$ conjunctions $\alpha \wedge \beta \wedge \gamma$ as $\alpha \wedge (\beta \wedge \gamma)$, and similar for disjunctions.

Next, we introduce FOHT_c^t-models over the extended signature Σ^t. They extend FOHT_c-models to tuples $\mathcal{M}^t = \langle D, (H, \mathcal{A}_h), (T, \mathcal{A}_t) \rangle$, where D, H, and T are as before, and $\mathcal{A}_h \subseteq \mathcal{A}_t$, are assignments.

Definition 5. *The satisfaction relations $\models$ for $w \in \{h, t\}$, where h, t are defined as before, is extended based on Definition 1 with temporal relations, denoted as ν (e.g., $\nu := before$):*

- $\mathcal{M}^t, w \models (\alpha \nu \beta)$ *if* $\mathcal{M}^t, w \models \alpha$ *and* $\mathcal{M}^t, w \models \beta$, $\tau_w^*(\alpha) \neq \mathbf{u}$, $\tau_w^*(\beta) \neq \mathbf{u}$, *and* $IA_\nu(\tau_w^*(\alpha), \tau_w^*(\beta))$ *holds;*

---

[1] The entries for the inverse relations $x(P)y$, $x(M)y$, $x(O)y$, $x(S)y$, $x(F)y$, $x(D)y$ are omitted.

$-\ \mathcal{M}^t, w \models \sim (\alpha\ \nu\ \beta)$ if $\mathcal{M}^t, w \models \alpha$ and $\mathcal{M}^t, w \models \beta$, $\tau_w^*(\alpha) \neq \mathbf{u}$, $\tau_w^*(\beta) \neq \mathbf{u}$, and $IA_\nu(\tau_w^*(\alpha), \tau_w^*(\beta))$ does not hold;

Note that $\mathcal{M}^t, w \not\models \alpha\ \nu\ \beta$ iff either (i) $\mathcal{M}^t, w \not\models \alpha$, (ii) $\mathcal{M}^t, w \not\models \beta$, (iii) $\tau_w^*(\alpha) = \mathbf{u}$, or (iv) $\tau_w^*(\beta) = \mathbf{u}$.

As previously, we call $\mathcal{M}^t$ a model of a closed formula ϕ, denoted as $\mathcal{M}^t \models \phi$ if $\mathcal{M}^t, h \models \phi$ and $\mathcal{M}^t, t \models \phi$; validity is defined accordingly.

To lift the notion of equilibrium models, we need to adjust the minimality property of FOHT$_c$ by taking temporal assignments into account.

Definition 6. *A model $\mathcal{M}^t = \langle D, (H, \mathcal{A}_h), (T, \mathcal{A}_t) \rangle$ of a theory Π over Σ^t is an equilibrium model if*

1. *M is total, i.e., $H = T$ and $\mathcal{A}_h = \mathcal{A}_t$, and*
2. *M is $\preceq'$-minimal among the models of Π, where $\mathcal{M}_1^t \preceq' \mathcal{M}_2^t$ holds, for $\mathcal{M}_i^t = \langle D, (H_i, \mathcal{A}_h^i), (T_i, \mathcal{A}_t^i) \rangle$, $i = 1, 2$, if (i) $T_1 = T_2$, (ii) $\mathcal{A}_h^1 = \mathcal{A}_h^2, \mathcal{A}_t^1 = \mathcal{A}_t^2$ and (iii) $H_1 \subseteq H_2$.*

That is, temporal assignments are frozen for model comparison. However, alternatives may be considered that view the relation between $\mathcal{A}^1$ and $\mathcal{A}^2$ differently, which we leave for further study.

In the (quantified) many-valued logics N_k resp. QN_k, truth value assignments are extended to temporal formulas, taking temporal assignments into account as follows.

Definition 7. *An extended QN_k, model is a triple $\langle D, \sigma, \tau_\mathcal{A} \rangle$, where D, σ and $\tau_\mathcal{A}$ are as before, such that σ maps non-temporal formulas ϕ to $\mathcal{T}_k$ as before, and temporal formulas $\alpha\ \nu\ \beta$ to $\mathcal{T}_k$ using $\tau_\mathcal{A}^*$, with ν as a temporal relation we have*

$$\sigma(\alpha\ \nu\ \beta) = \frac{1}{2} \cdot eval_\nu(\tau_\mathcal{A}^*(\alpha), \tau_\mathcal{A}^*(\beta)) \cdot \min(\sigma(\alpha), \sigma(\beta))$$

where (i) $eval_\nu(x, y) = 2$ if $x, y \neq \mathbf{u}$ and $IA_\nu(x, y)$ holds, (ii) $eval_\nu(x, y) = -2$ if $x, y \neq \mathbf{u}$ and $IA_\nu(x, y)$ does not hold, and (iii) $eval_\nu(x, y) = 0$ if $x = \mathbf{u}$ or $y = \mathbf{u}$.

Note that the strong negation of a temporal formula evaluates to $\sigma(\sim (\alpha\ \nu\ \beta)) = -\sigma(\alpha\ \nu\ \beta)$.

Example 3 (cont.) For the formula ϕ, we look at the following five interpretations: $i_1 : (\emptyset, \{(p(x), [1, 2])\}), i_2 : (\{(p(x), [1, 2])\}, \{(p(x), [1, 2])\}), i_3 : (\{(p(x), [1, 2]), (p(z), [4, 5])\}, \{(p(x), [1, 2]), (p(z), [4, 5])\}), i_4 : (\{(p(x), [1, 2]), (p(y), [2, 3]), (p(z), [4, 5])\}, \{(p(x), [1, 2]), (p(y), [2, 3]), (p(z), [4, 5])\})$, and $i_5 : (\{(p(y), [2, 3]), p(z), [4, 5])\}, \{(p(y), [2, 3]), (p(z), [4, 5])\})$. Only i_3 and i_5 are equilibrium models, since i_1 is not a total model, i_2 is not a model, and i_4 is not minimal since $i_3 \preceq i_4$ as well as $i_5 \preceq i_4$. If $\mathcal{A}_2 := \mathcal{A}_1 \setminus \{(p(y), [2, 3])\}$, the only equilibrium model is i_3, since $\tau_{\mathcal{A}_2}(p(y)) = \mathbf{u}$.

4 Temporal Tableau Calculus

As described in [16], the validity of a set of N_3 formulas (similarly for N_5) can be checked by a labeled tableau system, where possible truth-values are assigned as *labels* (also called signs) in tableau nodes. Then *total models* can be generated by applying the tableau rules that work with labels over the set $T_3 = \{-2, 0, 2\}$ of truth values. We first present the (labeled) non-temporal tableau system in [16], on which we then build our temporal tableau system.

Tableau system for total models. A tableau system applies expansion rules (as given in Defn. 8) on an initial tableau $\Pi = \{\phi_1, ..., \phi_n\}$ of arbitrary N_3 formulas, the *initial tableau* is defined as shown on the right:

$$\{2\} : \phi_1$$
$$...$$
$$\{2\} : \phi_n$$

Definition 8. *The tableau expansion rules capture the connectives of* N_3 *in the standard way; we show them for all connectives, where the label S is from* $S := \{\{2\}, \{0, 2\}, \{-2, 0\}, \{-2\}\}$, S^+ *from* $S^+ := \{\{2, 0\}, \{2\}\}$ *and* S^- *from* $S^- := \{\{-2, 0\}, \{-2\}\}$:

$$\frac{S^+ : \phi \wedge \psi}{\begin{array}{c} S^+ : \phi \\ S^+ : \psi \end{array}} \qquad \frac{S^- : \phi \wedge \psi}{S^- : \phi \mid S^- : \psi} \qquad \frac{S^+ : \phi \vee \psi}{S^+ : \phi \mid S^+ : \psi} \qquad \frac{S^- : \phi \vee \psi}{\begin{array}{c} S^- : \phi \\ S^- : \psi \end{array}}$$

$$\frac{S^+ : \phi \rightarrow \psi}{\{-2, 0\} : \phi \mid S^+ : \psi} \qquad \frac{S^- : \phi \rightarrow \psi}{\begin{array}{c} \{2\} : \phi \\ S^- : \psi \end{array}} \qquad \frac{S^+ : \neg \phi}{\{-2, 0\} : \phi} \qquad \frac{S^- : \neg \phi}{\{2\} : \phi} \qquad \frac{S : \sim \phi}{(-1) \cdot S : \phi}$$

where $(-1) \cdot S = \{(-1) \cdot x \mid x \in S\}$. Only the labels in S are relevant for the tableau expansion, e.g., $\{0\}$ does not occur. The expansion rules for a connective are computed based on the coverage in its truth table [7]. For instance, the implication connective was computed based on Fig. 1 with one rule for S^- covering the non-blank cells, and another rule for S^+ as disjunction covering the blank cells.

Definition 9. *A tableau* T *is generated by the tableau system for* $\Pi = \{\phi_1, ..., \phi_n\}$ *by applying the above tableau expansion rules on formulas S* : ϕ, *where* $S \in S$, *expanding it to one or more branches. After use, formulas are* marked *for each branch, so are applicable only once per branch. A branch in* T *is*

- closed, *if for a formula* ϕ *in it, there are labels* $S_1 : \phi$, $S_2 : \phi$ *with* $S_1 \cap S_2 = \emptyset$;
- finished, *if all its formulas are marked, and is* open *if it is finished and not closed.*

T *is* closed, *if every branch is closed, it is* open *if at least one branch is open, and it is* terminated *if every branch is either closed or open.*

Based on the above definition, the total models of a conjunction $\phi_1 \wedge \cdots \wedge \phi_n$ of N_3 formulas, represented as a set $\Phi = \{\phi_1, ..., \phi_n\}$, are generated by the tableau system from the open branches of a tableau T for Φ, where for an atom p_i a truth assignment $\sigma(p_i) \in S_i$ is taken from the signed literals $\Sigma = \{S_1 : p_1, ..., S_n : p_n\}$ of an open branch in T (Theorem 3 in [16]); notably, if p_i does not occur in Σ, any truth value can be assigned to it.

Example 4. For $\Phi = \{\sim q, \neg p \rightarrow q, \neg r \rightarrow p\}$ [16], the generated tableau tree is given in Fig. 2a. For the two open branches, we can derive three models: $i_1 : (\{p, \sim q, r\}, \{p, \sim q, r\})$, $i_2 : (\{p, \sim q\}, \{p, \sim q\})$, and $i_3 : (\{p, \sim q, \sim r\}, \{p, \sim q, \sim r\})$; only i_2 is minimal, as $i_2 \preceq i_1$ as well as $i_2 \preceq i_3$.

Validity of a formula ϕ in N_3 can be established via a tableau proof, which is any closed tableau $\mathfrak{T}$ for $\neg\phi$. We write $\vdash_{N_3} \phi$ in this case.

Definition 10. *A branch θ in $\mathfrak{T}$ is* satisfiable, *if for every signed formula $S_i : \phi_i$ on θ, there is a valuation such that $\sigma(\phi_i) \in S_1 \cap \cdots \cap S_n$ where $S_1 : \phi_i$ to $S_n : \phi_i$ are on branch θ. A tableau $\mathfrak{T}$ is satisfiable if at least one branch of $\mathfrak{T}$ is satisfiable.*

We recall from [9] that soundness, resp., completeness, of a tableau system is, if a theory Π has a tableau proof, then Π is a tautology, i.e., $\vdash_{N_3} \Pi$ implies $\models_{N_3} \Pi$, resp., if Π is a tautology, then Π has a tableau proof, i.e., $\models_{N_3} \Pi$ implies $\vdash_{N_3} \Pi$. Both were merely sketched in Theorem 2 of [16]. However, Fitting's method [9] can be extended to show soundness by establishing that satisfiability is a tableau system's loop invariant. For the completeness proof, we follow the generic approach by Hähnle [10] and use its machinery. Due to space limitations, we only show the proofs for the temporal tableau system since the non-temporal system is its special case.

Temporal Tableau Extension. A temporal tableau system is an extension of the non-temporal tableau of the previous section and introduces the process of *signing up* N_3 formulas with temporal labels. Besides the existing labels of tableau nodes, we also sign-up formulas in the tableau according to given temporal assignments $\mathcal{A}$, where the functions τ and τ^* are defined as before.

Definition 11. *Given a set $\mathcal{A}$ of pairs $(p, [x])$ inducing a temporal assignment τ and a formula ϕ, we let $t_\mathcal{A}(\phi) = \{(p, [x]) \in \mathcal{A} \mid p = a \text{ or } p = \sim a, a \in atm(\phi)\}$ denote the local temporal assignment for ϕ w.r.t. $\mathcal{A}$, where $atm(\phi)$ denotes the set of atoms occurring in ϕ.*

Temporal tableau system for total models. A temporal tableau system applies expansion rules on an initial tableau $\Pi = \{\phi_1, ..., \phi_n\}$ of $(\Pi, \mathcal{A})$ with the temporal assignment $\mathcal{A}$; the *initial tableau*, shown to the right, includes labels with temporal assignments denoted as $S : (\phi_i)_{t_\mathcal{A}(\phi_i)}$.

$$\{2\} : (\phi_1)_{t_\mathcal{A}(\phi_1)}$$
$$\cdots$$
$$\{2\} : (\phi_n)_{t_\mathcal{A}(\phi_n)}$$

Definition 12. *The tableau expansion rules from above are extended with temporal assignments; we show some exemplary rules; the other rules can be extended similarly:*

$$\frac{S^+ : (\phi \wedge \psi)_{\mathcal{A}'}}{S^+ : (\phi)_{t_{\mathcal{A}'}(\phi)} \\ S^+ : (\psi)_{t_{\mathcal{A}'}(\psi)}} \qquad \frac{S^+ : (\phi \vee \psi)_{\mathcal{A}'}}{S^+ : (\phi)_{t_{\mathcal{A}'}(\phi)} \mid S^+ : (\psi)_{t_{\mathcal{A}'}(\psi)}} \qquad \frac{S : (\sim\phi)_{\mathcal{A}'}}{(-1) \cdot S : (\phi)_{t_{\mathcal{A}'}(\phi)}}$$

Note that the assignments $t_{\mathcal{A}'}(\phi)$ and $t_{\mathcal{A}'}(\psi)$ are easily calculated from $\mathcal{A}'$ and ϕ resp. ψ; in any tableau extending the initial tableau, they amount to $t_\mathcal{A}(\phi)$ resp. $t_\mathcal{A}(\psi)$ for the given assignment $\mathcal{A}$. The reason for the use of (local) assignments in each branch relates (besides it is purely syntactical nature) to future work, where nested temporal formulas and multiple intervals per literal could be allowed.

Furthermore, there are additional expansion rules for temporal formulas:

$$\frac{\{2\},\{-2\}:(\phi \vee \psi)_{\mathcal{A}'}}{\begin{array}{c}\{2\}:(\phi)_{\tau^*_{\mathcal{A}'}(\phi)}\\ \{-2\}:(\phi)_{\tau^*_{\mathcal{A}'}(\phi)}\end{array}} \ \text{if } E = 0 \qquad \frac{\{0,2\},\{0,-2\}:(\phi \vee \psi)_{\mathcal{A}'}}{\{0,2\}:(\phi)_{\tau^*_{\mathcal{A}'}(\phi)}\mid\{0,-2\}:(\phi)_{\tau^*_{\mathcal{A}'}(\phi)}} \ \text{if } E = 0$$

$$\frac{S:(\phi \vee \psi)_{\mathcal{A}'}}{\begin{array}{c}S^+:(\phi)_{\tau^*_{\mathcal{A}'}(\phi)}\\ S^+:(\psi)_{\tau^*_{\mathcal{A}'}(\psi)}\end{array}} \ \tfrac{1}{2}\cdot E\cdot S = S^+ \qquad \frac{S:(\phi \vee \psi)_{\mathcal{A}'}}{S^-:(\phi)_{\tau^*_{\mathcal{A}'}(\phi)}\mid S^-:(\psi)_{\tau^*_{\mathcal{A}'}(\psi)}} \ \tfrac{1}{2}\cdot E\cdot S = S^-$$

where $E := eval_\nu(\tau^*_{\mathcal{A}'}(\phi), \tau^*_{\mathcal{A}'}(\psi))$ is as in Definition 7. Since the temporal formula must evaluate to 0 if $E = 0$, the upper left rules generate a closed branch and the upper right rules a branch that cannot be closed. The lower left rules work only for $S^+ = \{0,2\}$ and $S^+ = \{2\}$: $E \neq 0$ must hold. If $E = 2$, the input S must be $\{0,2\}$ resp. $\{2\}$ and the case amounts to conjunction; if $E = -2$, the input must be $\{0,-2\}$ resp. $\{-2\}$ and the case amounts to conjunction of the strongly negated formulas $\phi_{t_{\mathcal{A}'}(\phi)}$ and $\psi_{t_{\mathcal{A}'}(\psi)}$. The lower right rule similarly requires $E \neq 0$. It covers for $E = 2$ and $S = \{0,-2\},\{-2\}$ the conjunction of the sub-formulas, and for $E = 2$ and $S = \{0,2\}, S = \{2\}$ the conjunction of the strongly negated sub-formulas. This reflects the truth value assignment described in Definition 7.

A tableau $\mathfrak{T}^t$ is generated from the tableau system on $(\Pi, \mathcal{A})$ by applying the above expansion rules on formulas $S : \phi_{\mathcal{A}'}$ to expand it to one or more branches. The formulas are *marked* for each branch after being used. The notions of *closed*, *finished*, and *open* branch in $\mathfrak{T}^t$ can be carried over, and similarly whether $\mathfrak{T}^t$ is closed or open.

Definition 13. *Given a tableau system $(\Pi, \mathcal{A})$, a temporal tableau proof is a closed tableau $\mathfrak{T}^t$ for $\{\neg\Pi\}$ and $\mathcal{A}$; Π is a theorem in this case.*

Next, we show soundness for the temporal tableau system.

Definition 14. *Let $\Phi = \{(\phi_i)_{t_{\mathcal{A}}(\phi_i)} \mid i = 1,\ldots,n\}$ be temporal assigned formulas for $\mathcal{A}$. Then, $(\Phi, \mathcal{A})$ is satisfiable for T_3, if for some valuation σ (with τ^* embedded), $\sigma((\phi_i)_{t_{\mathcal{A}}(\phi_i)}) = 2$ for all $i = 1,\ldots,n$. A branch θ in a temporal tableau $\mathfrak{T}^t$ is satisfiable, if for some valuation σ every formula $S : (\phi)_{t_{\mathcal{A}}(\phi)}$ on θ fulfills $\sigma((\phi)_{t_{\mathcal{A}}(\phi)}) \in S$. A temporal tableau $\mathfrak{T}^t$ is satisfiable under $\mathcal{A}$, if some branch of $\mathfrak{T}^t$ is satisfiable.*

Proposition 3. *Any application of the tableau expansion rules defined in Definition 12 to a satisfiable tableau yields another satisfiable tableau.*

Proof. Assume a tableau $\mathfrak{T}^t$ that is satisfiable, and a tableau expansion rule is applied to $\mathfrak{T}^t$ to a signed formula $S_i : \phi_{\mathcal{A}'}$ resulting in the tableau $\mathfrak{T}^{t'}$; we show that $\mathfrak{T}^{t'}$ is also satisfiable. We distinguish several cases as follows, where we choose some satisfiable branch θ' in $\mathfrak{T}^t$ (which must exist):

Case 1 $\theta' \neq \theta$: The rule was applied to θ, hence θ' and $\mathfrak{T}^{t'}$ are still satisfiable.

Case 2 $\theta' = \theta$. We distinguish between sub-cases depending on the tableau expansion rule type:

Case 2a $S_i : (\phi_1 \wedge \phi_2)_{\mathcal{A}'}$: As $(\phi_1 \wedge \phi_2)_{\mathcal{A}'}$ is on the branch already, it is satisfied by some valuation σ, and w.l.o.g. $\sigma(\phi_{\mathcal{A}'}) = \sigma((\phi_1 \wedge \phi_2)_{\mathcal{A}'}) \in S_i$. If $S_i = \{0,-2\},\{-2\}$, then $\sigma(\phi_{\mathcal{A}'}) \leq 0$ and by the expansion rule $S_i : \phi_{\mathcal{A}'}$ may be put on θ', and so θ' remains satisfiable. Otherwise, if $S_i = \{0,2\}, \{2\}$, both $S_i : (\phi_1)_{t_{\mathcal{A}'}(\phi_1)}$ and $S_i : (\phi_2)_{t_{\mathcal{A}'}(\phi_2)}$ are on the branch θ', and as $\sigma((\phi_1)_{t_{\mathcal{A}'}(\phi_1)}) \leq \sigma((\phi_2)_{t_{\mathcal{A}'}(\phi_2)})$ holds $\sigma((\phi_2)_{t_{\mathcal{A}'}(\phi_2)}) \in S_i$ hold as well. Thus, θ' is satisfiable and $\mathfrak{T}^{t'}$ is satisfiable.

Case 2b $S_i : (\phi_1 \vee \phi_2)_{\mathcal{A}'}$: The argument is similar to the one on Case 2a, respecting $\max(x,y)$ for $\vee$ instead of $\min(x,y)$ for $\wedge$.

Case 2c $S_i : (\sim \phi_i)_{\mathcal{A}'}$: Here, θ was sequentially extended with $(-1) \cdot S_i : (\phi_i)_{t_{\mathcal{A}'}(\phi_i)}$ resulting in $\mathfrak{T}^{t'}$. Satisfiability is preserved since $\sigma((\phi_i)_{t_{\mathcal{A}'}(\phi_i)}) \in (-1) \cdot S_i$ iff $\sigma((\sim \phi_i)_{\mathcal{A}'}) \in S_i$ by Definition 2.

Case 2d $S_i : \neg(\phi_i)_{\mathcal{A}'}$: Based on Definition 2, we have two subcases, for $\sigma(\neg(\phi_i)_{\mathcal{A}'}) \in S_i$: where (i) $\sigma(\neg(\phi_i)_{\mathcal{A}'}) = 2$ or (ii) $\sigma(\neg(\phi_i)_{\mathcal{A}'}) = -2$. By the expansion rules of Definition 8, in case (i) θ was sequentially extended with $\{-2, 0\} : (\phi_i)_{\mathcal{A}'}$, and in case (ii) with $\{2\} : (\phi_i)_{\mathcal{A}'}$. As with Case 2c, satisfiability is preserved as $\sigma(\neg(\phi_i)_{\mathcal{A}'}) = 2$ implies $\sigma((\phi_i)_{\mathcal{A}'}) \in \{-2, 0\}$ respectively $\sigma(\neg(\phi_i)_{\mathcal{A}'}) = -2$ implies $\sigma((\phi_i)_{\mathcal{A}'}) \in \{2\}$.

Case 2e $S_i : (\phi_1 \rightarrow \phi_2,)_{\mathcal{A}'}$: Let $x := \sigma((\phi_1 \rightarrow \phi_2)_{\mathcal{A}'})$. For $S_i = \{2\}$ or $S_i = \{-2\}$, the expansion rules of Definition 8 clearly preserve satisfiability via Definition 2. For $S_i = \{0,2\}$, in case $x = 2$ satisfiability is preserved by the branch $\{-2,0\} : (\phi_1)_{t_{\mathcal{A}'}(\phi_1)}$ if $\sigma((\phi_1)_{t_{\mathcal{A}'}(\phi_1)}) = -2$ or $\sigma((\phi_1)_{t_{\mathcal{A}'}(\phi_1)}) = 0$, and by the branch $\{0,2\} : (\phi_2)_{t_{\mathcal{A}'}(\phi_2)}$ if $\sigma((\phi_2)_{t_{\mathcal{A}'}(\phi_2)}) = 2$; likewise, if $x = 0$ satisfiability is preserved by the branch $\{0,2\} : (\phi_2)_{t_{\mathcal{A}'}(\phi_2)}$ as $\sigma((\phi_2)_{t_{\mathcal{A}'}(\phi_2)}) = 0$. Finally, for $S_i = \{-2,0\}$, in case $x = -2$ (resp., $x = 0$) by Definition 2 $\sigma((\phi_1)_{t_{\mathcal{A}'}(\phi_1)}) = 2$ and $\sigma((\phi_2)_{t_{\mathcal{A}'}(\phi_2)}) = -2$ (resp., $\sigma((\phi_2)_{t_{\mathcal{A}'}(\phi_2)}) = 0$), which are in the respective labels $\{2\}$ and $\{-2,0\}$. Thus, satisfiability of $\mathfrak{T}^{t'}$ is preserved.

Case 2f $S_i : (\phi \nu \psi)_{\mathcal{A}'}$: We distinguish three cases according to $E := eval_\nu(\tau^*_{\mathcal{A}'}(\phi), \tau^*_{\mathcal{A}'}(\psi))$:

(i) $E = 0$. We have $\sigma((\phi \nu \psi)_{\mathcal{A}'}) = \frac{1}{2} \cdot \min(\sigma(\phi), \sigma(\psi)) = 0$; as θ is satisfiable, the rule for $E = 0$ cannot be applied.

(ii) $E = 2$. As θ is satisfiable, $\min(\sigma(\phi), \sigma(\psi)) \in S$. Now if the rule for $\frac{1}{2}E \cdot S = S^+$ is applied, we have $S = S^+ = \{0,2\}$ or $S = S^+ = \{2\}$; hence $\sigma(\phi) \in S^+$ and $\sigma(\psi) \in S^+$ follows, and thus θ' is satisfiable. If the rule for $\frac{1}{2}E \cdot S = S^-$ is applied, we have $S = S^- = \{0, -2\}$ or $S = S^- = \{-2\}$; thus, either $\sigma(\phi) \in S^-$ or $\sigma(\psi) \in S^-$ must hold. Hence, extending θ with $S^- : (\phi)_{\tau^*_{\mathcal{A}'}(\phi)}$ resp. $S^- : (\psi)_{\tau^*_{\mathcal{A}'}(\psi)}$ yields a satisfiable branch θ' and $\mathfrak{T}^{t'}$ is satisfiable.

(iii) $E = -2$. The argument is analogous to the one for the case $E = 2$. □

Case 2f takes nested FTFs into account, hence θ' is only expanded by non-temporal rules applied to $S_i : (\phi)_{\tau^*_{\mathcal{A}'}(\phi)}$ and $S_i : (\psi)_{\tau^*_{\mathcal{A}'}(\psi)}$ with the local temporal assignments τ^* carried over. They do not affect satisfiability in derived branches of θ', but are needed to evaluate minimal models and future work, where also nested temporal formulas are allowed.

Proposition 4. *If there is a closed tableau for* $(\Pi, \mathcal{A})$, *then* $(\Pi, \mathcal{A})$ *is not satisfiable.*

Proof. Assume towards a contradiction that we have a closed tableau while $(\Pi, \mathcal{A})$ is satisfiable. We construct a tableau $\mathfrak{T}^t$ from $(\Pi, \mathcal{A})$ with the initial branch θ that is constructed from $(\Pi, \mathcal{A})$ and is satisfiable. Then according to Proposition 3, either θ or one of the successor branches of θ will not be closed, hence we obtain a contradiction to the assumption. $\square$

Theorem 1. *(Soundness) If* $(\Pi, \mathcal{A})$ *has a tableau proof, then* $(\Pi, \mathcal{A})$ *is a tautology.*

Proof. As a consequence of Proposition 4, if there is a closed tableau for the set $\{\neg\Pi\}$ of negated temporal N_3 formulas and $\mathcal{A}$, then $\{\neg\Pi\}$ is not a satisfiable set. It follows that $(\Pi, \mathcal{A})$ is a tautology. $\square$

Completeness is shown based on propositional *Hintikka sets* for the many-valued setting, enriched with further (local) temporal assignments. We follow the generic app-roach in [10] and use its machinery.

A *many-valued sets-as-signs (mvs) Hintikka set* is a set Φ of signed formulas such that

(H1) Φ is open, i.e., there are no signed formulas $S_1 : \phi, \ldots, S_n : \phi$ in Φ such that $\bigcap_{i=1}^{n} S_i = \emptyset$, nor any formulas $S : \gamma(\phi_1, \ldots, \phi_m)$ such that $S \cap rg(\gamma) = \emptyset$, where $rg(\gamma)$ are the possible truth values for the connective γ, and

(H2) if $\phi - S : \gamma(\phi_1, \ldots, \phi_m)$ is in Φ and $\psi = \bigvee_{i=1}^{l} C_i$ is some sets-as-signs DNF representation of ϕ, then for some $C_i = \bigwedge_{j=1}^{n_i} S_{i,j} : \psi_{i,j}$, it holds that $\{S_{i,1} : \psi_{i,1}, \ldots, S_{i,n_i} : \psi_{i,n_i}\} \subseteq \Phi$.

Here γ is a connective and a *sets-as-signs DNF representation* of ϕ is a satisfiability preserving formula ψ of the given form where each $S_{i,j}$ is from $S \cup \{\{0\}\}$ and each $\psi_{i,j}$ is from $\phi_1, \ldots, \phi_m$. Then

Proposition 5 (cf. [10]). *Every mvs-Hintikka set* Φ *has a model, i.e. a truth assignment* σ *such that* $\sigma(\phi) \in S$ *for each* $S : \phi \in \Phi$.

Notably, from DNF representations corresponding tableau rules can be readily obtained.

Definition 15 (Defn. 33 in [10]). *Let* $\phi = S : \gamma(\phi_1, \ldots, \phi_m)$, $m \geq 1$, *be a signed formula. Given a sets-as-signs DNF representation* $\bigvee_{i=1}^{l} C_i$ *of* ϕ *where* $C_i = \bigwedge_{j=1}^{n_i} S_{i,j} : \phi_{i,j}$, *the corresponding sets-as-signs tableau expansion rule for* ϕ *is, where* $\bigwedge_{\psi \in F} \psi = C_i$:

$$\frac{S : \gamma(\phi_1, \ldots, \phi_m)}{F_1 \mid \cdots \mid F_l}.$$

From Proposition 5, we can then conclude that an open branch θ in a tableau $\mathfrak{T}$ for a formula $\neg\Pi$ on which all possible rules have been applied, is an mvs-Hintikka set and thus has a model; hence, $\neg\Pi$ is satisfiable. It follows that if Π is valid then a tableau proof for Π exists.

We extend mvs-Hintikka sets and sets-as-signs DNFs to the temporal setting for formulas $S : \phi_{\mathcal{A}'}$ where $S : \phi$ is a signed temporal formula labeled with a temporal assignment $\mathcal{A}'$ as in the extension of the tableau rules. As for temporal operators, we observe:

Lemma 1. *Every FTF formula $\phi = (\phi \, \nu \, \psi)$ can be viewed as a formula $\gamma_E(\phi_1, \phi_2)$ where $E := eval_\nu(\tau_\mathcal{A}^*(\phi_1), \tau_\mathcal{A}^*(\phi_2))$, i.e. as a connective γ_E depending on the operator ν and the assignment $\mathcal{A}$.*

In (H1), the notion of open set is extended by labeling each $S_i \, : \, \phi_i$ resp. $S \, :$ $\gamma(\phi_1, \ldots, \phi_m)$ with an assignment $\mathcal{A}'$; in (H2), the notion of sets-as-sign DNF representation is extended by requiring that satisfiability of $\phi = S : \gamma(\phi_1, \ldots, \gamma_m)_{\mathcal{A}'}$ is preserved by $\psi = \bigvee_{i=1}^{l} C_i$, with $C_i = \bigwedge_{j=1}^{n_i} S_{i,j} : \psi_{i,j \, \mathcal{A}'_{i,j}}$, where each formula $\alpha_{\mathcal{A}'}$ is evaluated using the assignment $\mathcal{A}'$. Proposition 5 then generalizes to the resulting temporal mvs-Hintikka sets.

For our concerns, we note that the tableau rules above ensure for the formulas on a temporal tableau Condition (H2).

Example 5. This example shows the theories $\Phi_1 = \{\{2\}:(a \vee b)_{\mathcal{A}_1}, \{2\}:(a \text{ before } c)_{\mathcal{A}_2}, \{2\}:(c)_{\mathcal{A}_3}\}$, and $\Phi_2 = \{\{2\}:(a \wedge b)_{\mathcal{A}_1}, \{2\}:(b \text{ before } c)_{\mathcal{A}_4}, \{2\}:(c)_{\mathcal{A}_3}\}$, where the temporal assignments are not given but we assume that $eval_{(p)}(\tau_{\mathcal{A}_2}^*(a), \tau_{\mathcal{A}_2}^*(c)) = 2$ and $eval_{(p)}(\tau_{\mathcal{A}_4}^*(b), \tau_{\mathcal{A}_4}^*(c)) = -2$. Then Φ_1 can be represented by a mvs-Hintikka set since Condition (H2) is fulfilled as it can be converted from CNF to sets-as-sign DNF; (H1) is fulfilled since for all formulas, the signs do overlap. Φ_2 is not representable by a mvs-Hintikka set since (H1) is violated by $\{-2\}:b$ or $\{-2\}:c$ that are derived from $\{2\}:(b \text{ before } c)$.

Lemma 2. *Every temporal tableau expansion rule of Definition 12 corresponds to a temporal set-as-signs DNF representation for $S : \gamma(\phi_1, \ldots, \phi_n)_{\mathcal{A}'}$.*

Proof. By inspecting the expansion rules of Definition 12, we can see that they are already in the form of Definition 15. The sets-as-signs representation were computed directly from the coverage of the truth tables (as illustrated by Fig. 1), which is according to [10] an eligible method.

Thus, the formulas on an open branch in a temporal tableau $\mathfrak{T}$ for $(\Pi, \mathcal{A})$ form a temporal mvs-Hintikka set and are satisfiable if each formula $S : \phi_{\mathcal{A}'}$ is evaluated with assignment $\mathcal{A}'$. However, each such $\mathcal{A}'$ is by construction the restriction of $\mathcal{A}$ to the literals relevant for ϕ, i.e. $\mathcal{A}' = t_{\mathcal{A}}(\phi)$, and thus $\sigma_{\mathcal{A}'}(\phi) = \sigma_{t_{\mathcal{A}}(\phi)}(\phi) = \sigma_{\mathcal{A}}(\phi)$ holds for every truth assignment σ. Consequently,

Proposition 6. *Every open branch θ in a temporal tableau $\mathfrak{T}$ for $(\Pi, \mathcal{A})$ on which all possible rules have been applied, has a model and hence $\neg \Pi$ is satisfiable under $\mathcal{A}$.*

We then readily obtain the claimed completeness result for the temporal tableau calculus.

Theorem 2. *(Completeness) If a temporal N_3 formula Π is a tautology with the temporal assignment $\mathcal{A}$, then $(\Pi, \mathcal{A})$ has a temporal tableau proof.*

Proof. Towards a contradiction, suppose that $(\Pi, \mathcal{A})$ has no temporal tableau proof. Hence no closed temporal tableau for $\{\neg \Pi\}$ and $\mathcal{A}$ exists, which implies that some temporal tableau $\mathfrak{T}$ for $\{\neg \Pi\}$ and $\mathcal{A}$ with an open branch θ exists on which all possible rules have been applied. By Proposition 6 $\neg \Pi$ is satisfied by some truth value assignment σ, i.e., $\sigma(\neg \Pi) = 2$; hence $\sigma(\Pi) \neq 2$, which means Π is not a tautology, which is a contradiction. $\square$

5   Prototypical Implementation

As for the implementation of a tableau prover, it may be convenient to restrict the input formulas to a specific form. Well-known such forms are CNF, DNF, as well as negation normal form (NNF). For our concerns, we may consider a temporal version of CNF.

Definition 16. *A temporal conjunctive normal form (CNF) in* N_3, *is a conjunction* $\bigwedge_{i=1}^{n} C_i$ *of clauses* $C_i = L_{i_1} \vee \dots \vee L_{i_m}$, *where each* L_{i_j} *is of the form* α, $\sim \alpha$, $\neg \alpha$, $\neg\neg\alpha$, *or* $\neg \sim \alpha$, *where* α *is either an atom or an FTF formula. Temporal disjunctive normal form (DNF) in* N_3 *is defined dually as usual.*

By means of equivalence preserving rewritings, every temporal formula in N_3 that we consider can be rewritten to temporal CNF (and similarly, to temporal DNF); indeed, Proposition 1 generalizes to the case where α, β, and γ can be FTFs. In addition, any FTF $\alpha \nu \beta$ can be due to the definition of $\tau_{\mathcal{A}}^{*}(\alpha \nu \beta)$ be rewritten into NNF (i.e. α and β become NNF) by applying Proposition 1. We remark that a temporal CNF is infeasible for N_5 as there is no equivalence preserving rewriting for implications.

Implementation. We have implemented an initial temporal tableau solver in Python 3.7, which currently evaluates N_3-theories in temporal CNF. The solver is intended for prototyping and no optimization techniques of modern tableau solvers are implemented. It also includes a model generator, and outputs all models extracted from the open branches in a tableau. The implementation is available on https://github.com/patrik999/EL-TempTableau, and is used to evaluate the cased study.

Case Study. We recall the slightly modified theory Π of Example 1 and the assignment $\mathcal{A}$:

$$\Pi = \{\neg a \vee b, \sim c, ((a \wedge \sim c)\,(o)\,(o_1 \vee o_2)) \vee ((b \wedge c)\,(o)\,(o_1 \vee o_2)), o_1, o_2\},$$
$$\mathcal{A} = \{(a, [1, 4]), (b, \boldsymbol{u}), (c, [1, 2](\sim c, [3, 5]), (o_1, [1, 3]), (o_2, [3, 5])\}.$$

The tableau tree for Π is shown in Fig. 2b, where o is short for (o) and the temporal assignments are for instance (all others are derivable accordingly): $\mathcal{A}_1 = \{(a, [1, 4]), (b, \mathrm{u})\}$, $\mathcal{A}_{3,1,1} = \{(a, [3, 4]), (\sim c, [3, 4])\}$, and $\mathcal{A}_{3,1,2} = \{(o_1, [1, 5]), (o_2, [1, 5])\}$. For the two open branches, we can derive two models, where the temporal assignments can be seen in $\mathcal{A}_{3,1,1}$ and $\mathcal{A}_{3,1,2}$. Two branches were closed since the a temporal formula was evaluated over (b, u), thus the expansion rule for $E = 0$ was applied. The leftmost branch was closed due to $\{-2\}{:}a$ and $\{2\}{:}a$ being on the same branch.

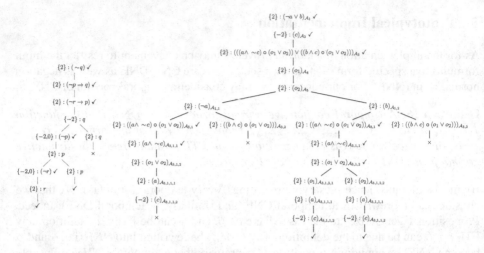

Fig. 2. Tableau tree for (a) Example 4 on the left and (b) the case study on the right

6 Related Work and Conclusion

This work is inspired by Temporal Behavioral Models [5] and builds mainly on here-and-there (HT) logic [13] and Equilibrium Logic [17], with a tableau system for reasoning [16]. The syntax/semantics presented in [17] is extended with temporal assignments/relations, which then affect the extension of the tableau system of [16]. In a broader perspective, the work is related to tableau calculi for many-valued logics [7] and to nested expressions in logic programs [15], but neither of them considers the temporal setting. Qualitative temporal reasoning was introduced to ASP by Brenton et al. [4] and Janhunen and Sioutis [14], where the former encoded temporal relations in ASP directly while the latter presented a hybrid-approach based on an extension of ASP with difference logic. Both focused on a particular encoding in ASP but did not provide a novel semantics nor a respective tableau system. With Metric Temporal ASP [6] and DatalogMTL under stable models semantics [18], Cabalar et al. and Walega et al. respectively, extended HT and Equilibrium logic, defining metric linear time connectives such as *always* or *until* over finite respectively infinite traces. Our approach is different from them regarding (a) the language, which is in [18] and [6] restricted to rules, (b) the (qualitative) temporal relations of Allen's Time Interval Algebra, and (c) the temporal annotation instead of trace-based valuation of time. Arias et al. [2] focused on goal-oriented top-down execution of Constraint ASP, which differs from our aim of model generation; in principle, one could encode intervals by fluents in this framework.

This work provides the initial step towards a framework for an abduction-based traffic diagnosis framework. Temporal behavior formulas (TBFs) [5] can be used in it to define relations between explanations and observations that take temporal constraints into account, where the constraints are based on Allen's IA [1]. Since TBFs offer limited expressive means, we have introduced a novel language that allows for nesting of temporal formulas, where associated time intervals are coalesced, and temporal assignments can express undefined time instances. We provided for this language a semantics based on an extension of HT logic and Equilibrium logic [17]. For reasoning, we have extended the three-valued propositional tableau calculus for HT logic in [16] with temporal expansion rules and provided soundness and completeness results. Furthermore, we have implemented a proof-of-concept prototype and demonstrated it on a case study.

Outlook. The work on the new language and the temporal tableau system can be extended in several directions. One direction is to equip the tableau system with minimality checking of models in order to support Equilibrium logic semantics. Pearce et al. [16] considered for this the use of sub-tableaux. However, we believe that an approach to minimality checking akin to the modular one in [3], which uses a super-dependency graph derived from an atom-clause dependency graph, could be more attractive. In connection with this, alternative notions of minimal models may be considered that allow for differences in temporal assignments. Regarding syntactic extensions of the language, richer nesting in temporal formulas may be investigated, e.g., restricted or arbitrary use of weak negation or temporal formulas. This however would require redefining (undefined) time instances and coalescing. Another direction is refined temporal semantics, where undefinedness may be avoided in some cases (e.g., (α *before* α) should always evaluate to false), or where literals are assigned with sets of intervals rather than a single interval. The current tableau system was designed for N_3, but it can be extended to N_5, moreover in combination with quantifiers. Finally, we aim to advance the proof-of-concept implementation of the prototype, using optimization techniques of tableau reasoners, and to evaluate an improved reasoner on benchmarks for temporal reasoning, e.g., on traffic flows [8].

Acknowledgements. This work was supported by the Humane AI Net project (ICT-48–2020-RIA/952026).

References

1. Allen, J.F.: Maintaining knowledge about temporal intervals. Commun. ACM **26**(11), 832–843 (1983)
2. Arias, J., Chen, Z., Carro, M., Gupta, G.: Modeling and reasoning in event calculus using goal-directed constraint answer set programming. Theor. Pract. Logic Program. **22**(1), 51–80 (2022)
3. Ben-Eliyahu-Zohary, R., Angiulli, F., Fassetti, F., Palopoli, L.: Decomposing minimal models. In: Proceedings of the Workshop on Knowledge-based Techniques for Problem Solving and Reasoning, IJCAI 2016. CEUR Workshop Proceedings, vol. 1648. CEUR-WS.org (2016)
4. Brenton, C., Faber, W., Batsakis, S.: Answer set programming for qualitative spatio-temporal reasoning: Methods and Experiments. In: ICLP 2016. vol. 52, pp. 4:1–4:15. Dagstuhl, Germany (2016)
5. Brusoni, V., Console, L., Terenziani, P., Dupré, D.T.: A spectrum of definitions for temporal model-based diagnosis. Artif. Intell. **102**(1), 39–79 (1998)
6. Cabalar, P., Diéguez, M., Schaub, T., Schuhmann, A.: Towards metric temporal answer set programming. Theor. Pract. Log. Program. **20**(5), 783–798 (2020)
7. D'Agostino, M., Gabbay, D.M., Hähnle, R., Posegga, J. (eds.): Handbook of Tableau Methods. Springer (1999)
8. Eiter, T., Falkner, A., Schneider, P., Schüller, P.: Asp-based signal plan adjustments for traffic flow optimization. In: PAIS 2020 at ECAI 2020, vol. 325, pp. 3026–3033. IOS Press (2020)

9. Fitting, M.: First-Order Logic and Automated Theorem Proving, 2nd edn. Springer, Heidelberg (1996)

10. Hähnle, R.: Tableaux for many-valued logics. In: D'Agostino et al. [7], pp. 529–580 (1999)

11. Hamscher, W., Console, L., de Kleer, J. (eds.): Readings in Model-Based Diagnosis. Morgan Kaufmann Publishers Inc., San Francisco, CA, USA (1992)

12. Heyting, A.: Die Formalen Rregeln der Iintuitionistischen Logik, pp. 42–56. Sitzungsberichte der Preussischen Akademie der Wissenschaften, Physikalisch-mathematische Klasse pp (1930)

13. Heyting, A.: On weakened quantification. J. Symb. Log. **11**(4), 119–121 (1946)

14. Janhunen, T., Sioutis, M.: Allen's interval algebra makes the difference. In: Hofstedt, P., Abreu, S., John, U., Kuchen, H., Seipel, D. (eds.) INAP/WLP/WFLP -2019. LNCS (LNAI), vol. 12057, pp. 89–98. Springer, Cham (2020). https://doi.org/10.1007/978-3-030-46714-2_6

15. Lifschitz, V., Tang, L.R., Turner, H.: Nested expressions in logic programs. Ann. Math. Artif. Intell. **25**(3–4), 369–389 (1999)

16. Pearce, D., de Guzmán, I.P., Valverde, A.: A tableau calculus for equilibrium entailment. In: Dyckhoff, R. (ed.) Automated Reasoning with Analytic Tableaux and Related Methods, pp. 352–367. Springer, Heidelberg (2000)

17. Pearce, D., Valverde, A.: Towards a first order equilibrium logic for nonmonotonic reasoning. In: Alferes, J.J., Leite, J. (eds.) JELIA 2004. LNCS (LNAI), vol. 3229, pp. 147–160. Springer, Heidelberg (2004). https://doi.org/10.1007/978-3-540-30227-8_15

18. Walega, P.A., Cucala, D.J.T., Kostylev, E.V., Grau, B.C.: DatalogMTL with negation under stable models semantics. In: Bienvenu, M., Lakemeyer, G., Erdem, E. (eds.) Proceedings of the KR 2021, pp. 609–618 (2021)

Representing Abstract Dialectical Frameworks with Binary Decision Diagrams

Stefan Ellmauthaler[1] , Sarah Alice Gaggl[2] , Dominik Rusovac[2] ,
and Johannes P. Wallner[3](✉)

[1] Knowledge-Based Systems Group, cfaed, TU Dresden, Germany
[2] Logic Programming and Argumentation Group, TU Dresden, Germany
{stefan.ellmauthaler,sarah.gaggl,dominik.rusovac}@tu-dresden.de
[3] Institute of Software Technology, TU Graz, Austria
wallner@ist.tugraz.at

Abstract. Abstract dialectical frameworks (ADFs) are a well-studied generalisation of the prominent argumentation frameworks due to Phan Minh Dung. In this paper we propose to use reduced ordered binary decision diagrams (ROBDDs) as a suitable representation of the acceptance conditions of arguments within ADFs. We first show that computational complexity of reasoning on ADFs represented by ROBDDs is milder than in the general case, with a drop of one level in the polynomial hierarchy. Furthermore, we present a framework to systematically define heuristics for search space exploitation, based on easily retrievable properties of ROBDDs and the recently proposed approach of weighted faceted navigation for answer set programming. Finally, we present preliminary experiments of an implementation of our approach showing promise both when compared to state-of-the-art solvers and when developing heuristics for reasoning.

Keywords: Abstract dialectical frameworks · Binary decision diagrams

1 Introduction

Computational argumentation is an active research topic within the broader field of Artificial Intelligence, which provides dialectical reasons in favour of or against disputed claims [3]. Deeply rooted in non-monotonic reasoning and logic programming, formal frameworks for argumentation provide the basis for heterogeneous application avenues, such as in legal or medical reasoning [2]. Within the field, formalisms in so-called abstract argumentation have proven to be useful for

This work is partly supported by the BMBF, Grant 01IS20056_NAVAS, by the Center for Scalable Data Analytics and Artificial Intelligence (ScaDS.AI), and by the DFG through the Collaborative Research Center, Grant TRR 248 project ID 38 9792660.

G. Gottlob et al. (Eds.): LPNMR 2022, LNAI 13416, pp. 177–189, 2022.
https://doi.org/10.1007/978-3-031-15707-3_14

argumentative reasoning. Here arguments are represented as abstract entities, and only the inter-argument relations decide argumentative acceptance, which is formalized via argumentation semantics. Several semantics exist, ranging from a more skeptical to a more inclusive stance towards acceptance of arguments.

Based on the prominent approach by Dung [12], a core formal approach to abstract argumentation are abstract dialectical frameworks [7], or ADFs for short, which also represent arguments as abstract entities, and allow for flexible relations between arguments, modelled as Boolean functions. Recently, ADFs were shown to be applicable in the legal field [1], in online dialog systems [20], and also for text exploration [9].

However, ADFs face the barrier of high complexity of reasoning [16,24], reaching up to the third level of the polynomial hierarchy. To address this obstacle, several approaches were proposed and studied: considering various fragments of the ADF language [18], quantified Boolean formulas [11], and utilizing advanced techniques in answer set programming [6,23].

A method for addressing high complexity, nevertheless, was not considered so far in depth for (abstract) argumentation: knowledge compilation [10]. A key principle behind knowledge compilation is that tasks of high complexity are translated to formal languages where reasoning has milder complexity, while at the same time taking possible translation performance issues into account. Applying techniques of knowledge compilation to abstract argumentation appears natural: abstract argumentation formalisms themselves can be seen as "argument compilations" of knowledge bases, e.g., ADFs can be instantiated from knowledge bases [22].

In this paper we take up the opportunity to fill this gap in the research landscape and propose to model a lingering source of complexity of ADFs, namely that of representing acceptance conditions per argument, via the prominent language of binary decision diagrams (BDDs) [8], with the following main contributions.

- We first formally introduce ADFs whose acceptance conditions are represented via BDDs.
- We show that complexity of reasoning for ADFs represented via reduced and ordered BDDs enjoys the same complexity (drop) as bipolar ADFs [24] or argumentation frameworks [13], after the compilation procedure.
- The representation via BDDs opens up a different opportunity: poly-time decidability of several tasks on BDDs allows to extract various kinds of information from the ADF. We use a recently proposed framework [15] that allows for exploring search spaces to arrive at a framework for developing heuristics for reasoning in ADFs.
- We present preliminary experiments showing promise of our approach in two directions: while at current we do not outperform the state-of-the-art ADF solver k++ADF [18], our results suggest that (i) computing the grounded semantics is as good via our approach than for k++ADF (including compilation times) and (ii) heuristics based on our framework show promise of performance increase.

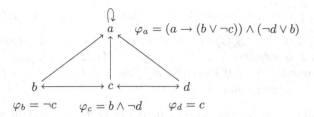

Fig. 1. Components of example ADF D_1, where the node labels represent statements and the attached formulae represent the respective acceptance condition.

2 Background

Abstract Dialectical Framework. We recall basics of Abstract Dialectical Frameworks (ADFs) and refer the interested reader to the recent Handbook of Formal Argumentation [3,7] for more details.

Definition 1. *An ADF is a triple $D := (S, L, C)$ where S is a fixed finite set of statements; $L \subseteq S \times S$ is a set of links; and $C := \{\varphi_s\}_{s \in S}$ consists of acceptance conditions for statements, which correspond to propositional formulas $\varphi ::= s \in S \mid \bot \mid \top \mid \neg\varphi \mid (\varphi \wedge \varphi) \mid (\varphi \vee \varphi) \mid (\varphi \to \varphi)$ over the parents $P(s) := \{s' \subset S \mid (s', s) \in L\}$ of statement s.*

Since links can be determined by acceptance conditions, throughout this paper we will mostly omit links and simply define ADFs as a tuple consisting of statements and their respective acceptance conditions.

Example 1. Let $D_1 = (\{a, b, c, d\}, \{(a \to (b \vee \neg c)) \wedge (\neg d \vee b), \neg c, b \wedge \neg d, c\})$. Figure 1 illustrates the components of D_1.

The semantics of ADFs are based on three-valued interpretations. An interpretation is a function $I : S \to \{\mathbf{t}, \mathbf{f}, \mathbf{u}\}$ that maps each statement to either $\mathbf{t}$ (true), $\mathbf{f}$ (false) or $\mathbf{u}$ (undefined). An interpretation I is *two-valued*, denoted by I_2, if $I(s) \in \{\mathbf{t}, \mathbf{f}\}$ for each $s \in S$. We define an *information ordering* $\leq_i$ such that $\leq_i$ is the reflexive transitive closure of $<_i$ and $\mathbf{u} <_i v$ for $v \in \{\mathbf{t}, \mathbf{f}\}$. This ordering is extended to interpretations by $I' \leq_i I$ iff $I'(s) \leq_i I(s)$ for each $s \in S$, and $I' <_i I$ if $I' \leq_i I$ and for some $s \in S$ we have $I'(s) <_i I(s)$. By $\varphi[I] := \varphi[s/\top : I(s) = \mathbf{t}][s/\bot : I(s) = \mathbf{f}]$ we define the *partial evaluation* of φ with respect to I.

Definition 2. *Let $D = (S, C)$ be an ADF and I be a three-valued interpretation over S. The characteristic operator $\Gamma_D(I) = I'$ is defined by the revisited interpretation I' of I, such that*

$$I'(s) = \begin{cases} \mathbf{t} & \text{if } \models \varphi_s[I]; \\ \mathbf{f} & \text{if } \varphi_s[I] \models \bot; \\ \mathbf{u} & \text{otherwise.} \end{cases}$$

We are now in position to define Dung's standard semantics for ADFs.

Definition 3. *Let $D = (S, C)$ be an ADF, and I a three-valued interpretation. Interpretation I is admissible in D if $I \leq_i \Gamma_D(I)$; I is complete in D if $I = \Gamma_D(I)$; I is grounded in D if I is the least fixed-point of Γ_D; and I is preferred in D if I is $\leq_i$-maximal admissible in D.*

A complete interpretation I is called a model of D if I is two-valued.

Definition 4. *Let $D = (S, C)$ be an ADF and I_2 be a two-valued interpretation. Define the reduced ADF $D^{I_2} := (S^{I_2}, C^{I_2})$ where $S^{I_2} := \{s \in S \mid I_2(s) = \mathbf{t}\}$ and $C^{I_2} := \{\varphi_s[s'/\bot : I_2(s') = \mathbf{f}] \mid s \in S^{I_2}, s' \in S\}$. If I_2 is a model of D and for the grounded interpretation G of D^{I_2} it holds that $I_2(s) = \mathbf{t}$ implies $G(s) = \mathbf{t}$, then I_2 is a* stable model *of D.*

Main reasoning tasks on ADFs under a semantics σ include credulous reasoning, i.e., asking whether there is a σ interpretation assigning a queried statement to true, and skeptical reasoning, i.e., is it the case that all σ interpretations assign a queried statement to true. Verification refers to the task of deciding whether a given interpretation is a σ interpretation.

Example 2 (cont'd). The grounded interpretation of D_1 is $\{a \mapsto \mathbf{u}, b \mapsto \mathbf{u}, c \mapsto \mathbf{u}, d \mapsto \mathbf{u}\}$. This interpretation is also complete in D_1. D_1 has no stable models.

Reduced Ordered Binary Decision Diagram. A (reduced ordered) binary decision diagram [8] is an efficient representation of a Boolean function. We follow the convention of referring to reduced ordered binary decision diagrams as BDDs.

Definition 5. *A binary decision diagram $\mathcal{B}$ over variables X is a rooted directed acyclic graph with two external nodes labeled with 0 or 1 and internal nodes u with two outgoing edges given by $low(u)$ and $high(u)$. Each internal node u is associated with a variable $x \in X$, denoted by $var(u) = x$. It is ordered, if on all paths the variables respect a linear order $x_1 < x_2 < \cdots < x_n$ and it is reduced if it satisfies the following two conditions:*

(a) if $var(u) = var(v)$, $low(u) = low(v)$ and $high(u) = high(v)$, then $u = v$, for each pair of internal nodes u, v; and

(b) $low(u) \neq high(u)$ for each internal node u.

Paths from the root to 1 correspond to partial assignments on X (true for high and false for low), and their completions (assigning remaining variables in X) to models of $\mathcal{B}$. We use $\mathcal{B}_\varphi$, for a formula φ, to denote a binary decision diagram for φ over the variables of φ s.t. the models of φ coincide with the models of $\mathcal{B}_\varphi$. Define restriction $\mathcal{B}_\varphi[x_1/v_1, \ldots, x_n/v_n]$ of $\mathcal{B}_\varphi$ s.t. each x_i is set to $v_i \in \{0, 1\}$ by

1. redirecting incoming edges of each node u with $var(u) = x_i$ to $low(u)$, if $v_i = 0$, and to $high(u)$, if $v_i = 1$; and

2. removing u.

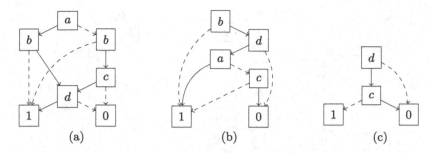

Fig. 2. BDDs of the acceptance condition φ_a with respect to D_1: (a) with ordering $a < b < c < d$; (b) with ordering $b < d < a < c$; and (c) which corresponds to (b) restricted such that a is set to 1 and b is set to 0. Solid lines denote low and dashed lines denote high.

By $vars(\mathcal{B}_\varphi) = \{var(u_0), \ldots, var(u_m)\}$ we denote the variables of internal nodes of $\mathcal{B}_\varphi$ and by $\#\mathcal{B}_\varphi := 2 \cdot m$ we denote the size of $\mathcal{B}_\varphi$, which corresponds to the number of edges for m internal nodes.

It is well-known [17] that reduced ordered binary decision diagrams admit each of the following operations in time polynomial in the size of the BDD: consistency check, validity check, clausal entailment check, implicant check, equivalence check, sentential entailment check, model counting and model enumeration.

However, note that the ordering matters when it comes to the size of a BDD. Figure 2 illustrates that the lexicographic ordering leads to a BDD (a) with 10 edges including two nodes labeled with b, whereas $b < d < a < c$ leads to a BDD (b) of size 8, including exactly one node for each variable. In fact, finding an optimal variable ordering for ordered binary decision diagrams is an NP-hard problem [5]. Even approximating it, is hard [21].

3   Representing ADFs as BDDs

An ADF is defined by acceptance conditions (propositional formulas) over statements (propositions). Utilizing BDDs directly leads to the following definition. See Fig. 3 for a BDD representation of our running example ADF.

Definition 6. *The BDD representation $\mathcal{B}(D) = (\mathcal{B}_{\varphi_{s_1}}, \ldots, \mathcal{B}_{\varphi_{s_n}})$ of an ADF $D = (S, C)$ is a tuple consisting of one BDD for each acceptance condition φ_{s_i} of $s_i \in S$ where $i = 1 \ldots n$.*

We show that complexity of reasoning on ADFs represented by BDDs coincides with complexity results of *argumentation frameworks* (AFs) [12,13]. Based on polytime procedures reducing and restricting BDDs [8], we can show a polytime result for computing the result of the characteristic operator.

Theorem 1. *Given the BDD representation $\mathcal{B}(D)$ of an ADF D, the result of applying Γ_D to any three-valued interpretation I can be computed in polynomial time.*

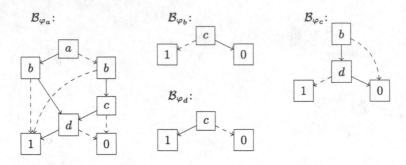

Fig. 3. The BDD representation of D_1 using lexicographic ordering.

Further, by previous results [24, Theorem 3.18], we obtain several upper bounds directly for ADFs represented by BDDs.

Theorem 2. *Given an ADF D represented by $\mathcal{B}(D)$, it holds that*

- *verification under admissibility and complete semantics is in P,*
- *credulous reasoning under admissibility, complete, and preferred semantics is in NP;*
- *verification under preferred semantics is in coNP;*
- *and skeptical reasoning under preferred semantics is in Π_2^P.*

Stable and grounded semantics are not covered by the corresponding theorem [24], nevertheless complexity exhibits a drop, as well. We first deal with grounded semantics, as an ingredient for stable semantics.

Theorem 3. *Given an ADF D represented by $\mathcal{B}(D)$, there is a polynomial algorithm that computes the grounded interpretation of D.*

Based on this result, it follows that verifying whether a model of an ADF represented by BDDs is stable is in P, and credulous and skeptical reasoning lies on the first level of the polynomial hierarchy, since all checks regarding the reduct are then polytime. For both credulous and skeptical reasoning, the membership results hold via a direct non-deterministic guess of an interpretation.

Corollary 1. *Verifying whether a three-valued interpretation is a model or is stable in an ADF represented by BDDs is in P. Moreover, credulous reasoning is in NP and skeptical reasoning in coNP.*

Regarding hardness, one can directly utilize hardness results for AFs (see [13] for an overview), since one can translate a given AF directly (in polytime) to an ADF under the BDD representation. Thus, credulous reasoning under admissible, complete, stable, and preferred semantics is NP-complete, verification of preferred interpretations is coNP-complete, and skeptical reasoning under stable is coNP-complete and Π_2^P-complete for preferred semantics.

4   Search Space Exploitation: Profiting from BDDs

Fichte et al. [15] define a navigation framework for answer set programming (ASP) [19], called *weighted faceted navigation*, that allows for quantifying the effect of navigation steps in a search space. So far it has been used to *explore* solution spaces, we utilize it to *exploit* information provided by a search space.

The idea is to navigate the search space (the set of interpretations) via heuristics that weight decisions (assigning truth values to statements). A decision, called here *facet*, is either inclusive (assigning true, denoted by $+s$) or exclusive (assigning false, denoted by $-s$). We use symbols $+$ and $-$ to distinguish true and false. A route is then an iteratively extended sequence of such facets (with the possibility of backtracking). That is, a route can be seen as a partial (two-valued) assignment on the statements, together with a partial evaluation of each acceptance condition under this partial assignment (like $\varphi[I]$ for a partial I). Weight functions then indicate heuristic goals, by assigning weights to facets, given a current route (current partial assignment). To make use of strengths of BDDs, we can include weights that are hard to compute on general formulas, but tractable on BDDs (such as number of models). We formalize these ingredients next into a generic framework for designing heuristics on ADFs represented by BDDs. We first define facets formally. The intuition behind a statement s being a facet is that it is contained in the variables of at least one BDD.

Definition 7 *We define facets of* $D = (S, C)$ *by* $\mathcal{F}(D) = \mathcal{F}(D)^+ \cup \mathcal{F}(D)^-$ *where* $\mathcal{F}(D)^+ = \{+s \mid s \in \bigcup_{B \in \mathcal{B}(D)} vars(B)\}$ *denotes inclusive facets and* $\mathcal{F}(D)^- = \{-s \mid s \in \bigcup_{B \in \mathcal{B}(D)} vars(B)\}$ *denotes exclusive facets.*

In ADFs with acceptance conditions represented via Boolean formulas, statements inside acceptance conditions might have no effect. For instance for $\phi_a = (b \vee \neg b) \wedge c$ it follows that the status of b is irrelevant for acceptance of a (formally in ADFs such links are called redundant). Reduced BDDs directly take care of such forms of redundancy, which leads to a simple observation: utilizing BDDs (for faceted navigation) reduces statements to consider. Formally, a navigation step towards facet $f \in \{+s, -s\} \subseteq \mathcal{F}(D)$ over an ADF D means that we modify $\mathcal{B}(D)$ with respect to f, denoted by $\mathcal{B}(D)[f]$, by applying a restriction to each BDD of the BDD representation $\mathcal{B}(D)$ of D s.t.

$$\mathcal{B}(D)[f] := \begin{cases} (\mathcal{B}_{\varphi_{s_1}}[s/1], \ldots, \mathcal{B}_{\varphi_{s_n}}[s/1]), & \text{if } f = +s; \\ (\mathcal{B}_{\varphi_{s_1}}[s/0], \ldots, \mathcal{B}_{\varphi_{s_n}}[s/0]), & \text{if } f = \text{-}s. \end{cases}$$

We define a *route* $\delta := \langle f_1, \ldots, f_n \rangle$ as a finite sequence of facets $f_i \in \mathcal{F}(D)$ denoting n arbitrary navigation steps over D. We assume that such a route does not contain complementary facets. By Δ_D we denote all possible routes over D. We define $\mathcal{B}(D)^\delta = \mathcal{B}(D)[f_1] \ldots [f_n]$, which means that $\mathcal{B}(D)$ is first restricted by f_1, then $\mathcal{B}(D)[f_1]$ is restricted by f_2 and so on. For simplicity, we write D^δ to denote the restriction $\mathcal{B}(D)^\delta$.

Example 3 (cont'd). Suppose we activate $+c \in \mathcal{F}(D_1)$, then $\mathcal{F}(D_1^{\langle +c \rangle}) = \mathcal{F}(D_1) \backslash \{+c, -c\}$. Proceeding by activating $-b \in \mathcal{F}(D_1^{\langle +c \rangle})$, we obtain $\mathcal{F}(D_1^{\langle +c, -b \rangle}) = \emptyset$.

That is, we "choose" to assign c true and b false, and iteratively shrink the remaining search space (available facets).

To make decisions during search, we need to make sense of the search space. The *weight* of a facet f is a parameter that quantifies what kind of effect activating f has on the search space.

Definition 8. *Let $D = (S, C)$, $\delta \in \Delta_D$ and $f \in \mathcal{F}(D^\delta)$. The weight of f is a function $\omega : \mathcal{F}(D^\delta) \times \Delta_D \to \mathbb{N}$.*

That is, $\omega(f, \delta)$ gives a weight of a facet (a potential next decision) with respect to a current route δ. In the following, we introduce several weights.

Definition 9. *Let $D = (S, C)$, $\delta \in \Delta_D$, $f \in \mathcal{F}(D^\delta)$ correspond to $s \in S$ and $\mathcal{B}_{\varphi_s} \in \mathcal{B}(D)^\delta$. We define the following weights*

- *$\omega_M(f, \delta) := |M(\varphi_s)|$ if $f = +s$, otherwise $\omega_M(f, \delta) := n - |M(\varphi_s)|$ where $M(\varphi_s)$ denotes models of φ_s and $n := 2^{|vars(\mathcal{B}_{\varphi_s})|}$* (model-counting weight)
- *$\omega_{AI}(f, \delta) := |\{\mathcal{B} \in \mathcal{B}(D^\delta) \mid s \in vars(\mathcal{B})\}|$* (active impact weight)
- *$\omega_{PI}(f, \delta) := |vars(\mathcal{B}_{\varphi_s})|$* (passive impact weight)
- *$\omega_P(f, \delta)$ is the number of paths leading to 1 (resp. 0) in $\mathcal{B}_{\varphi_s}$, if $f = +s$ (resp. $f = -s$)* (path-counting weight)
- *$\omega_{MD}(f, \delta)$ is the length of the largest simple path in $\mathcal{B}_{\varphi_s}$* (max-depth weight)

Each of the introduced weights refers to a value that can be computed in polynomial time using the BDD representation. Every weight tries to approximate information about the search space of each BDD in the ADF. The most obvious one is the model-counting weight, which counts how many models exist and is completely based on semantics notions. A bit more exact is the path-counting weight, by considering the semantics notions as well as the representation in BDD structures. The max-depth is a bit more exotic, as it computes the maximum length of the given BDD. Intuitively, this is a measurement on the maximum number of variables needed to decide the truth value of the BDD, and allows one to approximate how many additional values are required to be decided in order to ensure that the BDD represents a truth constant. Passive impact weight follows the same idea, but only allows one to see how many variables will have an impact on the BDD over all possible paths in the BDD. The active impact weight has the same idea as max-depth and the passive impact weight, but operates on a more global estimation by computing how many other BDDs might be impacted by the chosen facet.

Navigation-based heuristics, as introduced next, use weights for computing semantics. In a preliminary analysis we focus on enumerating stable interpretations. As computing stable models relies on finding two-valued models, here the objective is to use weights in order to find facets (make decisions) that ease the search for two-valued models using the characteristic operator Γ_D.

Similar to the notion of navigation modes in previous works [15], we are interested in minimal and maximal weighted facets of an ADF D^δ with respect to weight ω as defined by $min_\omega^\delta(\mathcal{F}(D^\delta)) := \{f \in \mathcal{F}(D^\delta) \mid \forall f' \in \mathcal{F}(D^\delta) : \omega(f, \delta) \leq \omega(f', \delta)\}$ and $max_\omega^\delta(\mathcal{F}(D^\delta)) := \{f \in \mathcal{F}(D^\delta) \mid \forall f' \in \mathcal{F}(D^\delta) : \omega(f, \delta) \geq \omega(f', \delta)\}$.

Table 1. Facet weights of D_1 on the empty route $\langle\rangle$.

	$+a$	$+b$	$+c$	$+d$	$-a$	$-b$	$-c$	$-d$
ω_M	11	1	1	1	5	1	3	1
ω_{AI}	1	2	3	2	1	2	3	2
ω_{PI}	4	1	2	1	4	1	2	1
ω_P	4	1	1	1	3	1	2	1
ω_{MD}	4	1	1	2	4	1	1	2

That is, we rank facets according to maximum (minimum) weight (given the current route). A navigation-based heuristic h suggests a set of facets to activate on the current route, by recursively determining minimal or maximal weighted facets in a given order with respect to specified weights. For a given ADF, a heuristic is determined by a current route and a list of weighting functions, to flexibly allow that decision shall be reached according to prioritized weight functions. For instance, $\Omega = \langle max^\delta_{\omega_M}, min^\delta_{\omega_{PI}} \rangle$ specifies that facets shall be ordered by considering maximally ω_M (highest priority) and, in case of equal ranking, consider minimizing ω_{PI} (second-level priority).

Definition 10. *Let $D = (S, C)$ be an ADF. A ranking $\Omega = \langle m_1, \ldots, m_n \rangle$ is a sequence with $m_i \in \{min^\delta_{\omega_0}, \ldots, min^\delta_{\omega_k}, max^\delta_{\omega_{k+1}}, \ldots, max^\delta_{\omega_\ell}\}$ and weights ω_j for $j = 0 \ldots \ell$. A navigation-based heuristic is a function*

$$h(\Omega, \mathcal{T}(D^\delta)) := m_n(m_{n-1}(\cdots (m_2(m_1(D^\delta)))\cdots)).$$

A heuristic is essentially defined by Ω, which specifies preferences of minimal or maximal weighted facets. Aiming at enumerating stable models, we conducted experiments using two heuristics h_0 and h_1, which should add intelligence to the search for two-valued models using BDDs as described by Algorithm 1. Heuristics h_0, h_1 are defined by $\Omega_0 = \langle max^\delta_{\omega_{PI}}, min^\delta_{\omega_{AI}}, min^\delta_{\omega_P} \rangle$ and $\Omega_1 = \langle min^\delta_{\omega_P}, max^\delta_{\omega_{PI}} \rangle$, respectively. The intuition behind Ω_0 is to find those statements, which have the highest impact on the BDDs, with a small amount of own variables and view choices in reaching a specific truth value. Ω_1 represents the approach to reduce the possible choices in one BDD to reach a specific truth value and maximises the impact on other BDDs afterwards. If the heuristic does not find a unique best option, we follow the BDD ordering.

Example 4 (cont'd). Applying rankings Ω_0 and Ω_1 on the data illustrated in Table 1, we see that heuristic h_0 suggests facet $\{-a\}$, since $max^\delta_{\omega_{PI}}(\mathcal{F}(D_1)) = \{+a, -a\}$, $min^\delta_{\omega_{AI}}(\{+a, -a\}) = \{+a, -a\}$ and finally $min^\delta_{\omega_P}(\{+a, -a\}) = \{-a\}$ for D_1 on the empty route. However, heuristic h_1 suggests to activate facet $+c$, since h_1 first considers $min^\delta_{\omega_P}(\mathcal{F}(D_1)) = \{+b, -b, +c, +d, -d\}$ and afterwards $max^\delta_{\omega_{PI}}(\{+b, -b, +c, +d, -d\}) = \{+c\}$.

The recursive Algorithm 1 uses a specified heuristic (such as Ω_0 and Ω_1), an ADF in BDD representation and an empty set of nogoods. If one of the nogoods

Algorithm 1. Recursively Enumerating Two-valued Models

Procedure: models

In: BDD representation $\mathcal{B}(D^\delta)$; set of nogoods $F \subseteq \mathcal{F}(D)$; heuristic Ω

Out: two-valued models of D;

1: set the set of two-valued models $M := \emptyset$;
2: **if** $f' = +s$ (resp. $f' = -s$) implies $\not\models \varphi_s$ (resp. $\varphi_s \not\models \bot$) for each $f' \in F$
3:     **if** $\mathcal{F}(D^\delta) \neq \emptyset$ **then** choose a facet $f \in h(\Omega, \mathcal{F}(D^\delta))$ and activate f on δ
4:         traverse routes $\delta' \in \Delta(D^\delta)$
5:             set $\mathcal{B}'$ to the BDD that corresponds to s in $\mathcal{B}(D^{\delta'})$
6:             update $\mathcal{B}(D^{\delta'})$ to obtain $\mathcal{B}''(D^{\delta'})$ where
7:                 B' is set to $\top$, **if** $f = +s$, **otherwise** B' is set to $\bot$
8:             set $M := M \cup$ models$(\mathcal{B}''(D^{\delta'}), F, \Omega)$;
9:         add the inverse facet $\overline{f}$ of f to nogoods F and activate $\overline{f}$ on δ
10:        set $M := M \cup$ models$(\mathcal{B}(D^\delta), F, \Omega)$;
11:    **else return** $\{\{s \in S \mid C \in D^\delta, C = \top, S \in D\}\}$
12: **return** M

---

is violated by the current state of the BDDs, we cannot find a two valued model with the given nogoods (Line 2 and 12). Otherwise we choose and activate a facet, based on the given heuristic. In Line 4 we now identify all interpretations of the BDD, which correspond to the activated facet value. The following four lines then propagate the truth values of one of these interpretations to all other BDDs and reduce the facet corresponding BDD to be only $\top$ (resp. $\bot$) and go one step down in the recursion by using this new BDD representation as the updated input. After the propagation of each of the corresponding interpretations, we can now deduce by tertium non datur that the truth value of the chosen facet needs to be its inverse. Therefore we now assume the inverse and add the chosen facet as a nogood. This will allow to go down the recursion depth on Line 10 with the updated nogoods. Finally in Line 11 we see that no further facet can be chosen, therefore all BDDs are either $\top$ or $\bot$ and we have found a two-valued model. Afterwards a simple stability check for the two valued models can be done.

5 Preliminary Experiments

We have implemented the presented ideas as a tool, called adf-bdd. It stands for "**A**bstract **D**ialectical **F**rameworks solved by **B**inary **D**ecision **D**iagrams, developed in **D**res**d**en". The tool allows one to compute the grounded, complete, and stable models of a given ADF. We support the currently prevalent input format for ADFs [14]. Due to this choice of compatibility we need to note that all presented tests have transformed the given acceptance conditions into ROBDDs. In a nutshell, the system allows the use of two different BDD libraries, a state of the art competitive library by the Biodivine tool [4] and our own implementation. Our own implementation can compute all of the previously introduced weights and has more efficient computations of backtracking, as well as a data structure which allows to exploit the common signature of all acceptance

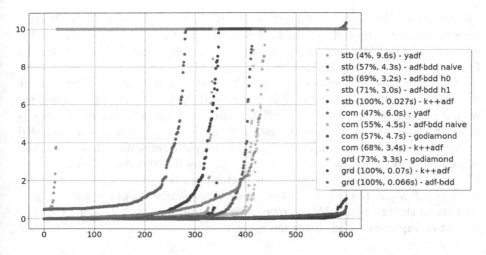

Fig. 4. Experiments on the mean run-times (seconds) of various solvers.

conditions and similar properties of BDDs and ADFs. Biodivine is more efficient in the instantiation, so we provide a combined approach too.

For the implementation we have a deterministic and straight forward approach for the grounded semantics, which computes the least fixed point of the
Γ_D operator. The complete semantics are handled by a naive approach, where all
possible three valued interpretations are constructed in a lazily evaluated list and
are checked by applying relational operations on the corresponding ROBDDs.
Stable semantics have been implemented in a similar naive way as well as with
the proposed Algorithm 1 and the two discussed heuristics. Note that we do not
exploit different variable orders so far and that we use the occurrence order of
statements from the input file as the only used variable order.

We have chosen to compare our approach[1] with the currently fastest solver
K++ADF [18] (version 2021-03-31), GODIAMOND [23] (version goDiamond 2017-
06-26), and YADF [6] (version 0.1.1). The latter two tools are using answer set solving (ASP) to solve the computational problems. The test machine specifications
are as follows: An Intel Xeon E5-2637v4 Quadcore 64bit Processor with 3.7 GHz
frequency, 384 GB working memory, running a Debian 9.13 Linux, with exclusive computation time for the tests. Note that none of the tools used an excessive
amount of the provided memory and has been capped by CPU-performance. Due
to the very different running times of the tools, we have chosen to use hyperfine
as a benchmarking tool harness. The tool decided how many runs shall be done to
reduce the load bias and provided mean performance times over up to 900 runs per
test-feature. Therefore all times are the mean run-times of all runs per instance for
each tool. In addition we imposed a ten second time-out limit for all the computations. We have seen in preliminary tests that the behaviour on the timeout-count
does not derivate noticeable with a twenty seconds time limit. As the test cases,

---

[1] https://github.com/ellmau/adf-obdd/releases/tag/v0.2.4-beta.1 v0.2.4-beta.1.

we have chosen the already multiple times used benchmarking set of 600 instances, already used by YADF and K++ADF. Due to text limitations we need to keep this analysis short, full evaluations and references of the data and the datasets can be found at https://doi.org/10.5281/zenodo.6498235.

We summarize our results in Fig. 4. Note that a missing tool indicates it does not support that semantics. For the grounded semantics our tool competes with K++ADF, suggesting that the BDD representation does not present a significant barrier for the considered instances (BDD compilation time is included in running times). The computation of the complete semantics shows that the naive approach is already as good as the ASP based GODIAMOND. For the stable models we see that our approach is better than the ASP based YADF, while there is still a gap towards K++ADF. Regarding heuristics, our results suggest that use of the two heuristics improved overall performance, suggesting that the heuristics improved search space navigation.

6   Conclusions

In this work we proposed to utilize knowledge compilation in the form of BDDs for the abstract argumentation formalism of ADFs. After showing milder complexity after the compilation process, we proceeded to present a generic framework for devising heuristics using the recently proposed framework of faceted navigation, which makes use of features (weights) that are computationally hard to obtain on Boolean formulas, but direct to retrieve from BDDs. Our preliminary experiments suggest that heuristics arising from the framework can indeed be helpful in the search space navigation, but cannot compete with the current state-of-the-art SAT-based approach of K++ADF. This latter solver is based on a candidate generation and subsequent verification procedure. Combining heuristics for search space navigation using BDDs and the SAT-based approach appear intriguing: potentially one could combine interesting heuristics on argumentation problems together with advanced SAT techniques.

References

1. Al-Abdulkarim, L., Atkinson, K., Bench-Capon, T.J.M.: A methodology for designing systems to reason with legal cases using abstract dialectical frameworks. Artif. Intell. Law **24**(1), 1–49 (2016)
2. Atkinson, K., et al.: Towards artificial argumentation. AI Mag. **38**(3), 25–36 (2017)
3. Baroni, P., Gabbay, D., Giacomin, M., van der Torre, L. (eds.) Handbook of Formal Argumentation. College Publications (2018)
4. Beneš, N., Brim, L., Kadlecaj, J., Pastva, S., Šafránek, D.: AEON: attractor bifurcation analysis of parametrised Boolean networks. In: Lahiri, S.K., Wang, C. (eds.) CAV 2020. LNCS, vol. 12224, pp. 569–581. Springer, Cham (2020). https://doi.org/10.1007/978-3-030-53288-8_28
5. Bollig, B., Wegener, I.: Improving the variable ordering of OBDDs is NP-complete. IEEE Trans. Comput. **45**(9), 993–1002 (1996)

6. Brewka, G., Diller, M., Heissenberger, G., Linsbichler, T., Woltran, S.: Solving advanced argumentation problems with answer set programming. Theory Pract. Log. Program. **20**(3), 391–431 (2020)
7. Brewka, G., Ellmauthaler, S., Strass, H., Wallner, J.P., Woltran., S.: Abstract dialectical frameworks. In Baroni, P., Gabbay, D., Giacomin, M., van der Torre, L. (eds.) Handbook of Formal Argumentation, pp. 237–285. College Publications (2018)
8. Bryant, R.E.: Graph-based algorithms for Boolean function manipulation. IEEE Trans. Comput. **100**(8), 677–691 (1986)
9. Cabrio, E., Villata, S.: Abstract dialectical frameworks for text exploration. In: Proceedings of ICAART, pp. 85–95. SciTePress (2016)
10. Darwiche, A., Marquis, P.: A knowledge compilation map. J. Artif. Intell. Res. **17**, 229–264 (2002)
11. Diller, M., Wallner, J.P., Woltran, S.: Reasoning in abstract dialectical frameworks using quantified Boolean formulas. Argument Comput. **6**(2), 149–177 (2015)
12. Dung, P.M.: On the acceptability of arguments and its fundamental role in non-monotonic reasoning, logic programming and n-person games. Artif. Intell. **77**(2), 321–358 (1995)
13. Dvořák, W., Dunne, P.E.: Computational problems in formal argumentation and their complexity. In: Baroni, P., Gabbay, D., Giacomin, M., van der Torre, L. (eds.) Handbook of Formal Argumentation, pp. 631–688. College Publications (2018)
14. Ellmauthaler, S., Wallner, J.P.: Evaluating Abstract Dialectical Frameworks with ASP. In: Proceedings of COMMA, vol. 245, pp. 505–506. IOS Press (2012)
15. Fichte, J.K., Gaggl, S.A., Rusovac, D.: Rushing and strolling among answer sets - navigation made easy. In: Proceedings of AAAI (2022)
16. Gaggl, S.A., Rudolph, S., Straß, H.: On the decomposition of abstract dialectical frameworks and the complexity of naive-based semantics. J. Artif. Intell. Res. **70**, 1–64 (2021)
17. Lai, Y., Liu, D., Wang, S.: Reduced ordered binary decision diagram with implied literals: a new knowledge compilation approach. Knowl. Inf. Syst. **35**(3), 665–712 (2013)
18. Linsbichler, T., Maratea, M., Niskanen, A., Wallner, J.P., Woltran, S.: Advanced algorithms for abstract dialectical frameworks based on complexity analysis of subclasses and SAT solving. Artif. Intell. **307**, 103697 (2022)
19. Marek, V.W., Truszczyński, M.: Stable models and an alternative logic programming paradigm. In: The Logic Programming Paradigm: A 25-Year Perspective. Artificial Intelligence, pp. 375–398 (1999)
20. Neugebauer, D.: Generating defeasible knowledge bases from real-world argumentations using D-BAS. In: Proceedings of AI ˆ3@AI*IA. Volume 2012 of CEUR Workshop Proceedings, pp. 105–110. CEUR-WS.org (2017)
21. Sieling, D.: On the existence of polynomial time approximation schemes for OBDD minimization. In: Morvan, M., Meinel, C., Krob, D. (eds.) STACS 1998. LNCS, vol. 1373, pp. 205–215. Springer, Heidelberg (1998). https://doi.org/10.1007/BFb0028562
22. Strass, H.: Instantiating rule-based defeasible theories in abstract dialectical frameworks and beyond. J. Log. Comput. **28**(3), 605–627 (2018)
23. Strass, H., Ellmauthaler, S.: goDIAMOND 0.6.6 - ICCMA 2017 system description. In: 2nd ICCMA (2017)
24. Strass, H., Wallner, J.P.: Analyzing the computational complexity of abstract dialectical frameworks via approximation fixpoint theory. Artif. Intell. **226**, 34–74 (2015)

Arguing Correctness of ASP Programs with Aggregates

Jorge Fandinno[ID], Zachary Hansen[✉][ID], and Yuliya Lierler[ID]

University of Nebraska Omaha, Omaha, NE 68182, USA
{jfandinno,zachhansen,ylierler}@unomaha.edu

Abstract. This paper studies the problem of arguing program correctness for logic programs with aggregates in the context of Answer Set Programming. Cabalar, Fandinno, and Lierler (2020) championed a modular methodology for arguing program correctness. We show how a recently proposed many-sorted semantics for logic programs with aggregates allows us to apply their methodology to this type of program. This is illustrated using well-known encodings for the Graph Coloring and Traveling Salesman problems. In particular, we showcase how this modular approach allows us to reuse the proof of correctness of a Hamiltonian Cycle encoding studied in a previous publication when considering the Traveling Salesman program.

Keywords: ASP · Program Verification · Aggregate Semantics · Modular Proofs of Correctness

1 Introduction

Answer Set Programming (ASP) [12,13] is a well-established Knowledge Representation paradigm for solving (knowledge-intensive) search/optimization problems. Based on logic programming under the *answer set semantics* [11], the ASP methodology relies on devising a logic program so that its answer sets are in one-to-one correspondence to the solutions of the target problem. The fact that this approach is fully declarative positions it as a firm candidate for producing trustworthy Artificial Intelligence (AI) systems, which require, among other qualities, the assessment that those systems produce correct judgments. Given the declarative nature of ASP, it also seems natural to consider an ASP program as a formal specification on its expected solutions [2,6]. This formal specification is usually the first program that an ASP practitioner writes and later refines to achieve higher solving efficiency [1,10]. The equivalence between the formal specification and the refined program can be manually and, in many cases, even automatically checked using existing tools [2,6,14]. Unfortunately, all these approaches deal exclusively with programs without aggregates, which are expressive constructs commonly used in practice.

J. Fandinno, Z. Hansen and Y. Lierler—Contributed equally.

G. Gottlob et al. (Eds.): LPNMR 2022, LNAI 13416, pp. 190–202, 2022.
https://doi.org/10.1007/978-3-031-15707-3_15

In this paper, we extend the *verification methodology for logic programs* (or, VLP methodology) developed in [2] to programs that contain non-recursive aggregates. This methodology is reviewed in Sect. 3. Consider the Graph Coloring (GC) problem encoded in Listing 1.1 using a choice rule with cardinality bounds. Here aggregates provide a succinct and convenient way to model the problem. Arguing correctness of this encoding was out of the scope of [2] as a choice rule with cardinality bounds (exemplified by the rule in line 1 of Listing 1.1) is an abbreviation for a pair of rules that includes an integrity constraint with a `count` aggregate [3]. We show how a recent extension of the SM operator to programs with aggregates [4] allows us to apply this methodology to programs of this kind. In addition to the GC problem, we also illustrate this

Listing 1.1. Encoding of the graph coloring problem using the ASP language.

```
1   { assign(V,C) : color(C) } = 1 :- vertex(V).
2   :- edge(V1,V2), assign(V1,C), assign(V2,C).
```

VLP methodology on the Traveling Salesman (TS) problem. These two problems are widely-studied and well understood in the ASP community, and they allow us to highlight two different use cases of aggregates. Additionally, the application of the VLP methodology to the TS problem illustrates the benefits of the "modular approach" it advocates. In particular, we are able to reuse a proof of correctness devised for another program—an encoding of the Hamiltonian Cycle problem studied in [2] that forms a subprogram of the TS encoding—as part of the argument of correctness for the TS encoding.

2   Review: Logic Programs via the Many-Sorted Approach

We start by reviewing elements of the syntax and semantics of a logic program with aggregates using the SM operator recently developed in [4]. In this approach, a logic program is considered to be an abbreviation for a many-sorted first-order sentence. The semantics of this sentence are characterized by the "agg" models of the second-order sentence obtained from the application of the SM operator to this first-order sentence. We assume familiarity with basic terminology of logic programs and the SM operator. For the sake of brevity, we focus only on the concepts necessary to understand the contributions of this paper. We refer the reader to [4] for details.

2.1   Syntax of Logic Programs with Aggregates

We consider (non-disjunctive) *rules* of the form $Head \leftarrow B_1, \ldots, B_n$ where $Head$ is an atom or the symbol $\perp$, and each B is a literal. We typically omit the $\perp$ symbol and instead write a constraint as a rule with an empty head. A *literal* is either a symbolic literal or an aggregate literal. A *symbolic literal* is either an atom or a *comparison* possibly preceded by one or two occurrences of *not*.

Listing 1.2. Encoding of a Hamiltonian Cycle problem.

```
1  vertex(X) :- edge(X,Y).
2  vertex(X) :- edge(Y,X).
3  { in(X,Y) } :- edge(X,Y).
4  ra(Y) :- in(a,Y).
5  ra(Y) :- in(X,Y), ra(X).
6  :- not ra(X), vertex(X).
7  :- in(X,Y), in(X,Z), Y != Z.
8  :- in(X,Y), in(Z,Y), X != Z.
```

Similarly, an *aggregate literal* is an aggregate atom possibly preceded by one or two occurrences of *not*. We assume familiarly with the definitions of program terms, atoms and comparisons and we focus here on describing the syntax of aggregate atoms.

An *aggregate element* is an expression of the form $t_1, \ldots, t_k$: $l_1, \ldots, l_m$, where each t_i $(1 \leq i \leq k)$ is a program term and each l_i $(1 \leq i \leq m)$ is a symbolic literal. An *aggregate atom* has the form #op$\{E\} \prec u$, where op is an operation name, E is an aggregate element, $\prec$ is a comparison symbol, and u is a program term, called the *guard*. We consider operation names count and sum. For example, the following two expressions are two aggregate atoms

$$\#\mathtt{count}\{ \; V,C \; : \; \mathtt{assign(V,C), \; color(C)} \; \} \; = \; 1 \qquad (1)$$

$$\#\mathtt{sum}\{ \; K,X,Y \; : \; \mathtt{in(X,Y), \; cost(K,X,Y)} \; \} \; > \; J \qquad (2)$$

that will be used in our examples throughout the paper.

A *choice rule* is an expression of the form

$$\{A_0 : A_1, \ldots, A_k\} \prec u \; \text{:-} \; B_1, \ldots, B_n. \qquad (3)$$

where each A_i is an atom, each B_i is a literal, $\prec$ is a comparison symbol and u is a numeral; it is understood as an abbreviation for the following pair of rules

$$A_0 \; \text{:-} \; A_1, \ldots A_k, B_1, \ldots, B_n, \; not \; not \; A_0. \qquad (4)$$

$$\text{:-} \; B_1, \ldots, B_n, \; not \; \#\mathtt{count}\{t : A_0, A_1, \ldots, A_k\} \prec u. \qquad (5)$$

where **t** is a list of program terms such that A_0 is of the form $p(\mathbf{t})$ for some symbolic constant p. As usual, we allow that "$\prec u$" or "$: A_1, \ldots A_k,$" (or both of them) are omitted from choice rules. If "$\prec u$" is omitted, then (5) is omitted; and if "$: A_1, \ldots A_k$" is omitted, then $A_1, \ldots A_k$ is omitted from (4–5).

For instance, rule 3 in Listing 1.2—capturing the Hamiltonian Cycle encoding used later in the paper as part of the TS encoding—is a choice rule where both elements are omitted and, thus, it is an abbreviation for the rule

$$\mathtt{in(X,Y)} \; \text{:-} \; \mathtt{edge(X,Y), \; not \; not \; in(X,Y).} \qquad (6)$$

As another example, rule 1 in Listing 1.1 is a choice rule where both of these elements are present, and it is understood as an abbreviation for rules

$$\mathtt{assign(V,C)} \; \text{:-} \; \mathtt{vertex(V), \; color(C), \; not \; not \; assign(V,C).} \qquad (7)$$

$$\text{:-} \; \mathtt{vertex(V), \; not \; \#count\{ \; V,C \; : \; assign(V,C), \; color(C) \; \} \; = \; 1.} \qquad (8)$$

A *program* is a finite set of rules.

2.2   From Rules to Many-Sorted First-Order Formulas

A logic program is understood as many-sorted first-order sentences over a signature σ_Π of *two sorts*, one for *program terms* and one for *sets of tuples of program terms*. We name these sorts *program* and *set*, respectively. To define the class of function symbols of the sort set we introduce the concepts of *global variables* and *set symbols*. A variable is said to be *global* in a rule if (i) it occurs in any non-aggregate literal, or (ii) it occurs in a guard of any aggregate literal. A variable that is not global is called *local*. For instance, in rule (8), variable V is global and variable C is local. In primitive rules, all variables are trivially global. A *set symbol* is a pair $E/\mathbf{X}$, where E is an aggregate element and $\mathbf{X}$ is a list of variables occurring in E. We say that $E/\mathbf{X}$ occurs in rule R if this rule contains an aggregate literal with the aggregate element E and $\mathbf{X}$ is the list of all variables in E that are global in R. For instance,

$$V, C : assign(V, C), color(C)/V \tag{9}$$

is the only set symbol occurring in rule (8). We say that $E/\mathbf{X}$ occurs in a program if $E/\mathbf{X}$ occurs in some rule of the program. For the sake of readability we associate each set symbol $E/\mathbf{X}$ with a different name $|E/\mathbf{X}|$.

As stated earlier, for a program Π, we consider a signature σ_Π over *two sorts* that contains: (i) all ground terms as object constants of the program sort; (ii) all predicate symbols occurring in Π as predicate constants with all arguments of sort program; (iii) the comparison symbols other than equality and inequality as binary predicate constants whose arguments are of the program sort; (iv) unary function constants *count* and *sum* of sort program whose unique argument is of sort set; and (v) for each set symbol $E/\mathbf{X}$ occurring in Π, a function constant $set_{|E/\mathbf{X}|}$ of the sort set. This function symbol takes as many arguments of the program sort as there are variables in $\mathbf{X}$. If $\mathbf{X}$ is an empty list, then $set_{|E/\mathbf{X}|}$ is an object constant.

We refer to [4] for the precise definition of the translation τ^* that converts a program into a finite set of first-order sentences. For the purposes of this paper it is only necessary to know the result of applying such a translation to the logic programs encoding the GC problem and the TS problem. For instance, consider rule (8). Translation τ^* applied to this rule produces the first-order sentence:

$$\forall V(vertex(V) \land \neg count(set_{asg}(V)) = 1 \rightarrow \bot), \tag{10}$$

where asg is the name for set symbol (9). The translation of the program in Listing 1.1 is completed by the following two sentences:

$$\forall V C (vertex(V) \land color(C) \land \neg\neg assign(V, C) \rightarrow assign(V, C)) \tag{11}$$

$$\forall V1\ V2\ C (edge(V1, V2) \land assign(V1, C) \land assign(V2, C) \rightarrow \bot) \tag{12}$$

Sentence (11) corresponds to rule (7). Sentences (10) and (11) together are the translation of rule 1 in Listing 1.1. Formula (12) is the the result of applying translation τ^* to rule 2 in Listing 1.1. We describe the translation of the TS encoding in Sect. 3.2. From now on, we assume that, unless otherwise made explicit, formulas with free variables stand for their universal closures.

2.3   Semantics via the SM Operator

The SM operator transforms first-order sentences into second-order sentences with equality. Ferraris, Lee and Lifschitz show that programs without aggregates can be considered as abbreviations for first-order sentences to which this operator is applied [7, Sect. 2.1]. When a set of such sentences Π is transformed by the SM operator into a second-order theory $\mathrm{SM}_{\mathbf{p}}[\Pi]$, the satisfying Herbrand interpretations of $\mathrm{SM}_{\mathbf{p}}[\Pi]$ where $\mathbf{p}$ is the list of all predicates occurring in the program are exactly the stable models of Π as defined by Gelfond and Lifschitz (1988). Fandinno, Hansen, and Lierler (2022) extend this approach to programs with aggregates by relying on a many-sorted generalization of the SM operator. We refer to [4] for the precise definition of the SM operator. For this paper it is enough to understand two properties of this operator, namely, the Splitting and Completion Theorems.

Splitting and Modules. The Splitting Theorem in [8] forms one of the foundations of the VLP methodology championed here. This theorem was recently generalised to the two-sorted case [6]; and a look to the proof shows that its generalization to the many-sorted case is straightforward. Let us recall some necessary notation for this result. An occurrence of a predicate symbol in a formula is called *negated* if it belongs to a subformula of the form $F \to \bot$ (often abbreviated as $\neg F$) and *nonnegated* otherwise. An occurrence of an expression in a formula is called *positive* if the number of implications containing that occurrence in the antecedent is even. It is called *strictly positive* if that number is 0. A *rule* of a first-order formula F is a strictly positive occurrence of an implication in F. The *dependency graph* of a formula is a directed graph that: (i) has all intensional predicate symbols as vertices; and (ii) has an edge from p to q if, for some rule $G \to H$ of F, formula G has a positive nonnegated occurrence of q and H has a strictly positive occurrence of p.

Theorem 1 *(Splitting Theorem).* *Let F and G be many-sorted first-order sentences and let $\mathbf{p}$ and $\mathbf{q}$ be two disjoint tuples of distinct predicate symbols such that (i) each strongly connected component of the dependency graph of $F \wedge G$ is a subset either of $\mathbf{p}$ or $\mathbf{q}$; (ii) F does not have strictly positive occurrences of symbols from $\mathbf{q}$; and (iii) G does not have strictly positive occurrences of symbols from $\mathbf{p}$. Then, $\mathrm{SM}_{\mathbf{pq}}[F \wedge G]$ is equivalent to $\mathrm{SM}_{\mathbf{p}}[F] \wedge \mathrm{SM}_{\mathbf{q}}[G]$.*

In the sequel, we often refer to expression $\mathrm{SM}_{\mathbf{p}}[F]$ as a module, whereas list $\mathbf{p}$ of predicate symbols is called *intensional*. The Splitting Theorem tells us how we can, at times, view a module in terms of other modules. When the list of predicate symbols $\mathbf{p}$ is empty, $\mathrm{SM}_{\mathbf{p}}[F]$ is identical to F. Thus, we may refer to any first-order sentence F as a module.

Completion. The theorem on completion presented here forms an important result that allows us, at times, to replace second-order formula (capturing a module) by an equivalent first-order formula. This is important when we construct formal arguments about models of these formulas as the later is easier to understand. Let **p** be a list of intensional predicate constants. A rule $G \rightarrow H$ is called *non-disjunctive* if H is an atomic formula or does not contain intensional symbols (i.e., elements of **p**). We say that $G \rightarrow H$ is a *constraint* with respect to **p** if H does not contain members of **p**. About a nondisjunctive rule $G \rightarrow H$ we say that it *defines* an intensional symbol p if H is an atomic formula that begins with p. In the following we assume that F is a conjunction of the universal closures of nondisjunctive rules and constraints with respect to **p**. If the argument sorts of an intensional symbol p are $s_1, \ldots, s_n$, and the rules defining p in F are

$$G_i \rightarrow p(\mathbf{t}_i) \qquad i = 1, \ldots, k,$$

then the *completed definition* of p in F is the sentence

$$\forall \mathbf{V} \left(p(\mathbf{V}) \leftrightarrow \bigvee_{i=1}^{k} \exists \mathbf{U}_i \left(G_i \wedge \mathbf{V} = \mathbf{t}_i \right) \right), \tag{13}$$

where **V** is an n-tuple of fresh variables of sorts $s_1, \ldots, s_n$, and $\mathbf{U}_i$ is the list of all variables that are free in $G_i \rightarrow p(\mathbf{t}_i)$. The expression $\mathbf{V} = \mathbf{t}_i$ here stands for the conjunction of n equalities between the corresponding members of the tuples **V** and $\mathbf{t}_i$. The *completion* $\mathrm{COMP}_\mathbf{p}[F]$ of F is the conjunction of all completed definitions of all members of **p** in F and all constraints of F. The following result immediately follows from the Main Lemma in [5]:

Theorem 2. *If the dependency graph of F is acyclic, then* $\mathrm{SM}_\mathbf{p}[F]$ *and* $\mathrm{COMP}_\mathbf{p}[F]$ *are equivalent.*

Agg-interpretations. The semantics of aggregates are defined with respect to a particular class of interpretations that we call *agg-interpretations*. Consider the following additional notation. For a tuple **X** of distinct variables, a tuple **x** of ground terms of the same length as **X**, and an expression α that contains variables from **X**, $\alpha_\mathbf{x}^\mathbf{X}$ denotes the expression obtained from α by substituting **x** for **X**. An *agg-interpretation* I is a many-sorted interpretation that satisfies the following *conditions*:

1. the domain of the program sort, denoted $|I|^{s_{prg}}$, is the set containing all ground terms of the program sort (or ground program terms, for short);
2. I interprets each ground program term as itself;
3. I interprets predicate symbols $>, \geq, <, \leq$ according to the total order chosen in [4] (this is the natural interpretation when applied to numerals, but it also apply to symbolic constants);
4. the domain of the set sort, denoted $|I|^{s_{set}}$, is the set of all sets of non-empty tuples that can be formed with elements from $|I|^{s_{prg}}$;
5. if $E/\mathbf{X}$ is a set symbol, where E is an aggregate element, **Y** is the list of all variables occurring in E that are not in **X**, and **x** and **y** are lists of ground program terms of the same length as **X** and **Y** respectively, then $set_{|E/\mathbf{X}|}(\mathbf{x})^I$ is the set of all tuples of the form $\langle (t_1)_\mathbf{xy}^\mathbf{XY}, \ldots, (t_k)_\mathbf{xy}^\mathbf{XY} \rangle$ such that I satisfies $(l_1)_\mathbf{xy}^\mathbf{XY} \wedge \cdots \wedge (l_m)_\mathbf{xy}^\mathbf{XY}$;

6. for $d \in |I|^{s_{set}}$, $count(d)^I$ is the numeral corresponding to the cardinality of d, if d is finite; and sup otherwise.

7. for $d \in |I|^{s_{set}}$, $sum(d)^I$ is the numeral corresponding to the sum of the weights of all tuples in d, if d contains finitely many tuples with non-zero weights; and 0 otherwise.(The sum of a set of integers is not always defined. We could choose a special symbol to denote this case, we chose to use 0 following the description of abstract GRINGO [9].) If d is empty, then $sum(d)^I = 0$.

An agg-interpretation satisfies the standard name assumption for object constants of the program sort, but not for function constants of the set sort.

We say that an agg-interpretation I is a *p-stable model* of program Π if it satisfies $SM_p[\tau^* \Pi]$, where p is a list of predicate symbols occurring in Π (note that this excludes predicate constants for comparisons $>, \geq, <, \leq$). An agg-interpretation I is a *stable model* of program Π if it is a p-stable model, where p is the list of *all* predicate symbols occurring in Π. The stable models of a program defined in this way correspond to the answer sets of the abstract GRINGO language [9] when the aggregates have no positive recursion [4] and with the answer sets of ASP-Core-2 [3].

3   Proving the Correctness of Logic Programs

Cabalar, Fandinno and Lierler (2020) developed a methodology for arguing the correctness of answer set programs, partially reproduced below:

Step I: Decompose the informal description of the problem into independent (natural language) statements[1].

Step II: Fix the public predicates used to represent the problem and its solutions.

Step III: Formalize the specification of the statements as a non-ground modular program, possibly introducing auxiliary predicates.

Step IV: Construct an argument (a "metaproof" in natural language) for the correspondence between the constructed program and the informal description of the problem.

An optional fifth step is to construct a formal proof from the constructed program (treated as a specification) to an alternative encoding. Here we consider proving the adherence of the constructed program to the natural language specification. We now put this methodology in practice for the case of the encodings of two problems: Graph Coloring and Traveling Salesman. The considered encodings contain aggregates. The extension of the SM operator applicable to programs with aggregates makes the use of this methodology possible in our context.

---

[1] In fact, this is also the first step that students are taught in the introduction to modeling in the ASP course taught at the University of Potsdam: https://teaching. potassco.org/.

3.1   The Graph Coloring Problem

Step I applied to the GC problem consists in identifying statements

C1 find an assignment from nodes to colors such that
C2 connected nodes do not have the same color.

Formally, an instance of the GC problem is a triple $\langle V, E, C \rangle$, where

- $\langle V, E \rangle$ is a graph with vertices V and edges $E \subseteq V \times V$, and
- C is a set of labels named *colors*.

A solution to the GC problem is

CF1 a function $asg : V \longrightarrow C$ such that
CF2 every edge $(a, b) \in E$ satisfies condition $asg(a) \neq asg(b)$.

Step II consists of choosing the public predicates to represent the problem, in this example: *vertex*/1, *edge*/2, *color*/1, and *assign*/2. **Step III** consists in formalizing the statements from **Step I** as a non-ground modular program Π. The GC problem is a great illustratory example due to the simplicity of its ASP encoding and the fact that each natural language statement is encoded as exactly one rule. In other words, in this example, each rule constitutes its own module. Rule 1 in Listing 1.1 corresponds to the module

$$\mathrm{SM}_{assign}[(10) \wedge (11)] \tag{14}$$

while rule 2 corresponds to the first-order sentence/module (12). Module (14) formalizes statement **CF1**, that is, it ensures that predicate *assign*/2 encodes a function from vertices to colors. Module (12) formalizes statement **CF2**: it ensures that the function encoded by predicate *assign*/2 satisfies the condition of the statement. By the Splitting Theorem, the conjunction of two modules—(12) and (14)—has the same *assign*-stable models as the *assign*-stable models of the conjunction (10) $\wedge$ (11) $\wedge$ (12); recall that this conjunction corresponds to τ^* applied to the GC encoding in Listing 1.1.

We now turn our attention to **Step IV**. To formalise claim **CF1** about module (14), we prove a general result about modules of a similar form. We say that relation **r** *encodes* function $f : A \longrightarrow B$ when $\mathbf{r} = \{(a, f(a)) \mid a \in A\}$. Given sets A and B, we can construct a program whose stable models encode all functions from A to B as follows. (By d^* we denote the name of domain element d, that is, an object constant whose interpretation is d.) Let $G(X)$ and $H(Y)$ be two first-order formulas such that $G(d^*)$ is satisfiable iff d belongs to A and $H(d^*)$ is satisfiable iff d belongs to B. Then, $Fun_{A,B}$ is the conjunction of formulas

$$\forall X \big(G(X) \wedge \neg count(set_{fe}(X)) = 1 \rightarrow \bot \big) \tag{15}$$

$$\forall XY \big(G(X) \wedge H(Y) \wedge \neg\neg f(X, Y) \rightarrow f(X, Y) \big) \tag{16}$$

where *fe* is the name of the set symbol $X, Y : f(X, Y), H(Y)/X$.

Proposition 1. *For an agg-interpretation I and first-order formulas $G(X)$ and $H(Y)$ containing no positive nonnegated occurrences of $f/2$, take*

$$A = \{d \mid d \in |I|^{s_{prg}} \text{ and } I \models G(d^*)\} \text{ and } B = \{d \mid d \in |I|^{s_{prg}} \text{ and } I \models H(d^*)\}.$$

Then, condition $I \models \mathrm{SM}_f[Fun_{A,B}]$ holds iff $(f/2)^I$ encodes a function from A to B.

Proof. If A is empty, then $(f/2)^I$ encodes the empty function. Hence, in the rest of the proof, we assume that A is non-empty. By the Splitting Theorem $\mathrm{SM}_f[(15) \wedge (16)]$ is equivalent to $\mathrm{SM}_f[(16)] \wedge (15)$. By the Completion Theorem, sentence $\mathrm{SM}_f[(16)]$ is equivalent to the first-order sentence

$$\forall XY\Big(f(X,Y) \leftrightarrow G(X) \wedge H(Y) \wedge \neg\neg f(X,Y))\Big). \tag{17}$$

In turn, this sentence is equivalent in first-order logic to

$$\forall XY\big(f(X,Y) \to G(X) \wedge H(Y)\big). \tag{18}$$

Let F denote the conjunction of (15) and (18), which is equivalent to $\mathrm{SM}_f[Fun_{A,B}]$. *Left-to-right.* Assume that $I \models F$. Pick any $a \in A$. Then, $I \models G(a^*)$ and, since $I \models (15)$, it follows that $I \models (count(set_{fe}(a^*)) = 1)$. Hence, $set_{fe}(a^*)^I = \{\langle a, b_a\rangle\}$ for some $b_a \in |I|^{s_{prg}}$ such that $I \models f(a^*, b_a^*) \wedge H(b_a^*)$. Let $\hat{f}$ be the function such that $\hat{f}(a) = b_a$; $\hat{f}$ is a function from A to B encoded by $(f/2)^I$. *Right-to-left.* Let $\hat{f}$ be a function from A to B such that $(f/2)^I = \{(a, \hat{f}(a)) \mid a \in A\}$; in other words $(f/2)^I$ encodes $\hat{f}$. Let us show that $I \models F$. First, for any term $a \in |I|^{s_{prg}}$ such that $I \models G(a^*)$, it follows that $a \in A$ and, thus, $set_{fe}(a^*)^I = \{\langle a, \hat{f}(a)\rangle\}$. This implies that $I \models (15)$. Second, for any $a \in |I|^{s_{prg}}$ and $b \in |I|^{s_{prg}}$ such that $I \models f(a^*, b^*)$ it follows by construction that $a \in A$ and $b = \hat{f}(a)$ and $b \in B$. Hence, $I \models G(a^*) \wedge H(b^*)$ and, thus, $I \models (18)$.

Claim **CF2** about module (12) is argued within the proof of the following theorem that can also be seen as a proof of correctness for the GC encoding presented in Listing 1.1.

Theorem 3. *Let I be an agg-interpretation such that $\langle vertex^I, edge^I, color^I\rangle$ forms an instance of the Graph Coloring problem. Then, $I \models (12) \wedge (14)$ iff $(assign/2)^I$ encodes a function that forms a solution to the considered instance.*

Proof. From Proposition 1, we get that $I \models (14)$ iff $(assign/2)^I$ encodes a function $asg : vertex^I \longrightarrow color^I$ such that $(assign/2)^I = \{(a, asg(a)) \mid a \in vertex^I\}$. Sentence (12) is equivalent to

$$\forall V1\, V2\, C1\, C2\big(edge(V1,V2) \wedge assign(V1,C1) \wedge assign(V2,C2) \to C1 \neq C2\big).$$

This sentence is satisfied by I iff every edge $(a,b) \in edge^I$ satisfies $asg(a) \neq asg(b)$.

The use of the SM operator allows us to argue the correctness of an encoding in isolation from the way its instances are obtained. In Theorem 3, we only implicitly refer to a specific instance of the GC problem by considering an interpretation I such that $\langle vertex^I, edge^I, color^I \rangle$ forms this instance. In practice, to compute a solution for a considered GC instance one has to extend the program corresponding to the GC problem with an encoding of the instance. Such an instance can be represented by a set of facts utilizing predicates chosen for the representation. For example, facts

$$vertex(a).\ vertex(b).\ edge(a,b).\ color(g).\ color(b).\ color(r).$$

encode an instance $\langle \{a, b\}, \{(a, b)\}, \{g, b, r\} \rangle$ of the GC problem. Answer sets of the program in Listing 1.1 extended with these facts will encode the solutions to the specified instance. However, the general approach followed in Theorem 3 actually allows those facts to be generated by a, perhaps very complex, logic program, as long as it does not use the predicate symbols used in the GC encoding other than the ones used to describe the problem instance. We take the same approach of implicit reference to an instance when arguing the correctness of the TS problem.

3.2 The Traveling Salesman Problem

Let us look into the following variant of the Traveling Salesman problem:

We are given a directed graph with nodes as cities and edges as roads. We assume the presence of a city named "a". Each road directly connects a pair of cities, and costs a salesman some time to traverse (time is expressed as an integer value). The salesman may pass each city exactly once. Find: *a route* traversing *all the cities under* a certain *maximum cost* of total time starting and finishing at city a.

Formally, an instance of the TS problem is a quadruple $\langle V, E, cst, m \rangle$, where

- $\langle V, E \rangle$ is a graph assuming one vertex in V named a,
- cst is a function from edges E to integers, and
- m is some integer.

A solution to this instance is a subset of edges $P \subseteq E$ such that

T1 P forms a Hamiltonian cycle of graph $\langle V, E \rangle$ and
T2 the following inequality holds

$$\sum_{e \in P} cst(e) \leq m. \tag{19}$$

This constitutes the application of **Step I** to the TS problem. **Step II** consists in choosing the public predicates to represent the problem: $vertex/1$, $edge/2$, $cost/3$, $maxCost/1$, and $in/2$. We say that an agg-interpretation I *encodes* instance $\langle V, E, cst, m \rangle$ if it satisfies the following conditions:

- $(vertex/1)^I = V$ and $(edge/2)^I = E$;
- $(cost/3)^I = \{(c, v_1, v_2) \mid (v_1, v_2) \in E$ and $cst((v_1, v_2)) = c\}$;
- $(maxCost/1)^I = \{m\}$;

Predicate symbol $in/2$ is meant to capture a solution to the TS problem, i.e., an agg-interpretation I encoding an instance of the TS problem also *encodes* a solution P whenever $(in/2)^I = P$. Using the mentioned predicate symbols, we can capture the TS problem by adding the following rule to the encoding of the Hamiltonian Cycle problem in Listing 1.2:

```
:- #sum{ K,X,Y : in(X,Y), cost(K,X,Y) } > J, maxCost(J).          (20)
```

Translation τ^* applied to the rules in Listing 1.2 and rule (20) results in the sentences (recall that we identify formulas below with their universal closures):

$$edge(X, Y) \rightarrow vertex(X) \tag{21}$$
$$edge(Y, X) \rightarrow vertex(X) \tag{22}$$
$$\neg\neg in(X, Y) \wedge edge(X, Y) \rightarrow in(X, Y) \tag{23}$$
$$in(a, Y) \rightarrow ra(Y) \tag{24}$$
$$in(X, Y) \wedge ra(X) \rightarrow ra(Y) \tag{25}$$
$$\neg ra(X) \wedge vertex(X) \rightarrow \bot \tag{26}$$
$$in(X, Y) \wedge in(X, Z) \wedge Y \neq Z \rightarrow \bot \tag{27}$$
$$in(X, Y) \wedge in(Z, Y) \wedge X \neq Z \rightarrow \bot \tag{28}$$
$$maxCost(J) \wedge sum(set_{tp}) > J \rightarrow \bot, \tag{29}$$

where tp is the name of the set symbol

$$K, X, Y : in(X, Y), cost(K, X, Y).$$

Note that this set symbol has no global variables in rule (20). By HC we denote the conjunction of sentences (21–28). By **hc** we denote the tuple containing all predicate symbols in HC except $edge/2$ and $vertex/1$. By the Splitting Theorem, $SM_{\mathbf{hc}}[HC \wedge (29)]$ is equivalent to $SM_{\mathbf{hc}}[HC] \wedge (29)$ so that $SM_{\mathbf{hc}}[HC]$ and (29) form modules. The former module, corresponding to a program in Listing 1.2, formalizes statement **T1**; the latter module formalizes statement **T2**. Thus, we have completed **Step III**.

We turn our attention to **Step IV**. Propositions 5 and 8 in [2] prove that module $SM_{\mathbf{hc}}[HC]$ correctly encodes the Hamiltonian Cycle problem. The proof of that claim used the one-sorted version of the SM operator. It is easy to see that for formulas that include only predicates of one sort, such as HC, there is an immediate correspondence between the one-sorted and the many-sorted models of the formula. Hence, the following is an immediate consequence of Propositions 5 and 8 mentioned above.

Proposition 2. *Let I be an agg-interpretation s.t. $G = \langle vertex^I, edge^I \rangle$ is a graph with $a \in vertex^I$. Then, $I \models SM_{\mathbf{hc}}[HC]$ iff $(in/2)^I$ forms a Hamiltonian cycle of G.*

All that remains is to prove the following result about sentence (29).

Lemma 1. *Let I be an agg-interpretation that encodes an instance $\langle V, E, cst, m \rangle$ of the Traveling Salesman problem such that $in^I \subseteq edge^I$. Then, $I \models$ (29) iff inequality (19) holds, where $P = (in/2)^I$.*

Proof. Since I is an agg-interpretation that encodes $\langle V, E, cst, m \rangle$ and satisfies $in^I \subseteq edge^I$, it follows that

$$set^I_{tp} = \{\langle c, a, b \rangle \mid \langle a, b \rangle \in in^I \text{ and } \langle c, a, b \rangle \in cost^I\}$$
$$= \{\langle c, a, b \rangle \mid \langle a, b \rangle \in in^I \text{ and } \langle a, b \rangle \in edge^I \text{ and } cst(\langle a, b \rangle) = c\}$$
$$= \{\langle c, a, b \rangle \mid \langle a, b \rangle \in in^I \text{ and } cst(\langle a, b \rangle) = c\}$$

Therefore, $sum(set_{tp})^I = \sum_{e \in P} cst(e)$. Finally, since I encodes $\langle V, E, cst, m \rangle$, it follows that $maxCost^I = \{m\}$ and, thus, $I \models$ (29) iff (19) holds.

The following auxiliary lemma follows from the Splitting and Completion Theorems and is due to the presence of sentence (23) in HC. It allows us to complete the argument for the TS problem.

Lemma 2. $SM_{\mathbf{hc}}[HC] \models \forall XY (in(X, Y) \rightarrow edge(X, Y))$.

Theorem 4. *Let I be an agg-interpretation encoding an instance $\langle V, E, cst, m \rangle$ of the Traveling Salesman problem. Then, $I \models SM_{\mathbf{hc}}[HC \wedge (29)]$ iff I encodes a solution to the considered instance of the problem.*

Proof. By the Splitting Theorem, $I \models SM_{\mathbf{hc}}[HC \wedge (29)]$ iff $I \models SM_{\mathbf{hc}}[HC] \wedge (29)$. Then, from Proposition 2, it follows that the latter holds iff $(in/2)^I$ forms a Hamiltonian cycle of $G = \langle vertex^I, edge^I \rangle$ and $I \models$ (29). Finally, by Lemma 2, we get that $I \models SM_{\mathbf{hc}}[HC]$ implies $I \models \forall XY (in(X, Y) \rightarrow edge(X, Y))$ and, thus, that $in^I \subseteq edge^I$. Therefore, the result follows from Lemma 1.

Theorem 4 can be seen as a proof of correctness for the TS encoding consisting of rules in Listing 1.2 and rule (20).

4   Conclusions and Future Work

We have shown how the semantics for programs with aggregates based on a many-sorted extension of the SM operator [4] can be used for arguing correctness of logic programs of this kind. For this we followed a modular methodology [2] and showed how it allows us to reuse the proof of correctness of other programs when they form sub-modules in the encoding of a new problem. One of the limitations of our approach is that it is only applicable to programs where aggregates do not have positive recursion. This limitation is inherited from the semantics for programs with aggregates in which it is based. Although aggregates with positive recursion are rare in practical applications, future work should be directed towards removing this limitation. It will be also interesting to consider programs with weak constraints.

The work by Yuliya Lierler was partially supported by NSF grant 1707371.

References

1. Buddenhagen, M., Lierler, Y.: Performance tuning in answer set programming. In: Calimeri, F., Ianni, G., Truszczynski, M. (eds.) LPNMR 2015. LNCS (LNAI), vol. 9345, pp. 186–198. Springer, Cham (2015). https://doi.org/10.1007/978-3-319-23264-5_17
2. Cabalar, P., Fandinno, J., Lierler, Y.: Modular answer set programming as a formal specification language. Theor. Pract. Logic Program. **20**(5), 767–782 (2020)
3. Calimeri, F., et al.: ASP-Core-2: input language format (2012). https://www.mat.unical.it/aspcomp2013/ASPStandardization
4. Fandinno, J., Hansen, Z., Lierler, Y.: Axiomatization of aggregates in answer set programming. In: Proceedings of the 36th National Conference on Artificial Intelligence, AAAI 2022. AAAI Press (2022)
5. Fandinno, J., Lifschitz, V.: Verification of locally tight programs (2022). http://www.cs.utexas.edu/users/ai-labpub-view.php?PubID=127938
6. Fandinno, J., Lifschitz, V., Lühne, P., Schaub, T.: Verifying tight logic programs with anthem and vampire. Theor. Pract. Logic Program. **20**(5), 735–750 (2020)
7. Ferraris, P., Lee, J., Lifschitz, V.: Stable models and circumscription. Artif. Intell. **175**(1), 236–263 (2011)
8. Ferraris, P., Lee, J., Lifschitz, V., Palla, R.: Symmetric splitting in the general theory of stable models. In: Boutilier, C. (ed.) Proceedings of the 21st International Joint Conference on Artificial Intelligence, IJCAI 2009, pp. 797–803. AAAI/MIT Press (2009)
9. Gebser, M., Harrison, A., Kaminski, R., Lifschitz, V., Schaub, T.: Abstract Gringo. Theor. Pract. Logic Program. **15**(4–5), 449–463 (2015). https://doi.org/10.1017/S1471068415000150
10. Gebser, M., Kaminski, R., Kaufmann, B., Schaub, T.: Challenges in answer set solving. In: Balduccini, M., Son, T.C. (eds.) Logic Programming, Knowledge Representation, and Nonmonotonic Reasoning. LNCS (LNAI), vol. 6565, pp. 74–90. Springer, Heidelberg (2011). https://doi.org/10.1007/978-3-642-20832-4_6
11. Gelfond, M., Lifschitz, V.: The stable model semantics for logic programming. In: Kowalski, R., Bowen, K. (eds.) Proceedings of the 5th International Conference and Symposium of Logic Programming, ICLP 1988, pp. 1070–1080. MIT Press (1988). https://doi.org/10.1201/b10397-6
12. Marek, V.W., Truszczyński, M.: Stable models and an alternative logic programming paradigm. In: Apt, K.R., Marek, V.W., Truszczynski, M., Warren, D.S. (eds.) The Logic Programming Paradigm, pp. 375–398. Springer, Heidelberg (1999). https://doi.org/10.1007/978-3-642-60085-2_17
13. Niemelä, I.: Logic programs with stable model semantics as a constraint programming paradigm. Ann. Math. Artif. Intell. **25**(3–4), 241–273 (1999)
14. Oetsch, J., Seidl, M., Tompits, H., Woltran, S.: Beyond uniform equivalence between answer-set programs. ACM Trans. Comput. Log. **22**(1), 2:1-2:46 (2021)

Efficient Computation of Answer Sets via SAT Modulo Acyclicity and Vertex Elimination

Masood Feyzbakhsh Rankooh[(✉)] and Tomi Janhunen[iD]

Tampere University, Tampere, Finland
{masood.feyzbakhshrankooh,tomi.janhunen}@tuni.fi

Abstract. Answer set programming (ASP) is a declarative programming paradigm where the solutions of a search problem are captured by the answer sets of a logic program describing its solutions. Besides native algorithms implemented as answer-set solvers, the computation of answer sets can be realized (i) by translating the logic program into propositional logic or its extensions and (ii) by finding satisfying assignments with appropriate solvers. In this work, we recall the graph-based extension of propositional logic, viz. SAT modulo graphs, and the case of acyclicity constraint which keeps a digraph associated with each truth assignment acyclic. This particular extension lends itself very well for answer set computation, e.g., using extended SAT solvers, such as GRAPHSAT, as back-end solvers. The goal of this work, however, is to translate away the acyclicity extension altogether using a vertex elimination technique, giving rise to a translation from ASP into propositional clauses only. We use non-tight benchmarks and a state-of-the-art SAT solver, KISSAT, to illustrate that performance obtained in this way can be competitive against GRAPHSAT and native ASP solvers such as CLASP and WASP.

1 Introduction

Answer set programming (ASP) is a paradigm for declarative programming where the solutions of a search problem are described in terms of rules (see, e.g., [6,15] for overviews). A central idea behind the paradigm is that the solutions of the problem are captured by the *answer sets* [16] of the *logic program* formed by the rules. Then, solutions can be sought using dedicated search engines, known as *answer-set solvers*, for the computation of answer sets. The performance of answer-set solvers has been evaluated in a series of ASP competitions, see [12] for the results of the seventh competition. The latest competitions have been dominated by native answer-set solvers CLASP [11] and WASP [1], making them as natural targets for comparison when improving answer set computation.

Besides native native answer-set solvers, the computation of answer sets can be realized via translations into propositional (Boolean) logic such that Boolean satisfiability (SAT) checkers, also known as SAT solvers, can be used to find satisfying assignments corresponding to answer sets. Such a strategy for answer

The original version of this chapter was revised: this chapter was previously published non-open access. The correction to this chapter is available at
https://doi.org/10.1007/978-3-031-15707-3_40

G. Gottlob et al. (Eds.): LPNMR 2022, LNAI 13416, pp. 203–216, 2022.
https://doi.org/10.1007/978-3-031-15707-3_16

set computation is more generally known as *translation-based* ASP [14] that was originally proposed to combine the knowledge representation capabilities of ASP with the efficiency of existing solver technology. There is some variety of translations from ASP to pure SAT, including worst-case exponential [18], quadratic [17], and sub-quadratic [13] ones. Yet more compact (linear) translations are enabled if one considers extensions of propositional logic such as *difference logic* (DL) [20] and *SAT modulo graphs* [9]. The latter is particularly relevant for the purposes of this work in the case of *acyclicity constraint* which keeps a digraph associated with each truth assignment acyclic. This primitive is well-suited for expressing the essentials of answer sets [8] as well as for their computation, e.g., using extended SAT solvers, such as GRAPHSAT [10], as back-ends. As reflected by ASP competition results, the level of performance obtained via translations can be sometimes comparable to that of native solvers, but no translation-based approach has really been able to challenge native ASP solvers so far. At best, non-native back-end solvers scale similarly, but the performance is degraded by slower propagation due to blow-ups and primitives used in translation.

In this work, however, we take advantage of a recently introduced method that translates away the acyclicity constraints altogether using a vertex elimination technique [21]. Our translation is therefore from ASP into pure SAT. While GRAPHSAT relies on a specialized algorithm for satisfying the acyclicity constraint, our method offers an easy way to use any state-of-the-art SAT solver as the back-end solver without additional implementation effort.

Our translation of ASP into pure SAT is produced through four stages, which respectively are normalization, instrumentation with acyclicity constraint, program completion, and translating the acyclicity constraint to propositional clauses using vertex elimination. We theoretically show how the correctness of our method can be derived from the correctness of the mentioned stages. As for the empirical analysis, by considering non-tight decision problem sets of previous ASP competitions, we show that our new translation-based method, when accompanied by a state-of-the-art SAT solver, KISSAT [2], outperforms previous translation-based methods, and is also quite competitive against state-of-the-art native ASP solvers such as CLASP and WASP. To the best of our knowledge and referring to ASP Competition results, this is the first time when a translation-based approach to answer-set solving has actualized its intended potential.

The rest of this article is organized as follows. In Sect. 2, we recall basic concepts and definitions of ASP and identify the class of *weight constraint programs* (WCPs) that is central for this study. Then, in Sect. 3, we discuss the three basic steps required to transform a WCP P into a set of clauses amended by a dynamically varying digraph that is enforced to be acyclic. In Sect. 4, we recall how vertex elimination can be used to check whether a given digraph is acyclic. Then, we describe how SAT modulo acyclicity can be translated back to pure SAT using vertex elimination in Sect. 5. In Sect. 6, we combine the techniques presented so far and present a novel translation of WCPs into pure SAT, improving the efficiency of computing answer sets with SAT solvers. To this end, we present practical evidence in Sect. 7 based on an experimental evaluation of the resulting method for answer set computation. The analysis is based on six non-tight benchmark problems. Finally, we conclude the paper in Sect. 8.

2   Preliminaries

In the sequel, *weight constraint programs* (WCPs) consist of *rules* of the forms:

$$a \leftarrow b_1, \ldots, b_n, \text{not } c_1, \ldots, \text{not } c_m. \tag{1}$$

$$\{a\} \leftarrow b_1, \ldots, b_n, \text{not } c_1, \ldots, \text{not } c_m. \tag{2}$$

$$a \leftarrow k \leq [b_1 = w_1, \ldots, b_n = w_n, \text{not } c_1 = w_{n+1}, \ldots, \text{not } c_m = w_{n+m}]. \tag{3}$$

The symbols a, $b_1, \ldots, b_n$ with $n \geq 0$, and $c_1, \ldots, c_m$ with $m \geq 0$ occurring in the rules are (propositional) *atoms* and "not" denotes *negation by default*. The *bound* k and the *weights* $w_1, \ldots, w_{n+m}$ in (3) are non-negative integers. Rules of the forms (1)–(3) are known as *normal, choice,* and *weight rules*, respectively [23]. Intuitively, each rule r gives a reason to derive its *head* head$(r) = a$ if the conditions in its *body* body(r) are met, i.e., atoms involved can be either derived or not by other rules. For a choice rule r of form (2), the derivation of head(r) is optional and, for a weight rule r of form (3), the sum of weights associated with *satisfied* body conditions must reach k. We write body$^+(r)$ and body$^-(r)$ for the sets of atoms $b_1, \ldots, b_n$ (resp. $c_1, \ldots, c_m$) occurring positively (resp. negatively) in body(r). A *normal* logic program (NLP) consists of normal rules only whereas the rules of a *positive* logic program satisfy $m = 0$, i.e., are negation free. Given a WCP P, the *definition* of an atom a in P is def$_P(a) = \{r \in P \mid$ head$(r) = a\}$.

The *signature* of a WCP P is the set of atoms At$(P) = \bigcup_{r \in P}(\{\text{head}(r)\} \cup$ body$^+(r) \cup$ body$^-(r))$ that occur in P. The *positive dependency graph* of P is DG$^+(P)\langle$At$(P), \succeq\rangle$ where $a \succeq b$ holds for $a, b \in$ At(P) if head$(r) = a$ and $b \in$ body$^+(r)$ for some rule $r \in P$. A *strongly connected component* (SCC) of DG$^+(P)$ is a maximal subset $S \subseteq$ At(P) such that all distinct atoms $a, b \in S$ depend (transitively) on each other via a directed path in DG$^+(P)$.

An *interpretation* $I \subseteq$ At(P) determines which atoms $a \in$ At(P) are *true* $(a \in I)$ and which are *false* $(a \notin I)$. Then I satisfies a rule $r \in P$ of forms (1) and (3), denoted $I \models r$, if the satisfaction of the body, denoted $I \models$ body(r), implies that head$(r) \in I$, i.e., $I \models$ head(r). For a choice rule r of form (2), $I \models r$ unconditionally. Moreover, the interpretation I is a (classical) *model* of P if $I \models r$ holds for every $r \in P$. Each positive program P has a unique *least model* LM(P) obtained as the intersection $\bigcap\{I \subseteq$ At$(P) \mid I \models P\}$.

Given an interpretation I, the *reduct* r^I of r with respect to I is obtained by partially evaluating the negative conditions of r. For a normal rule (1), $r^I = \emptyset$ if $c_i \in I$ for some $1 \leq i \leq m$ and $r^I = \{a \leftarrow b_1, \ldots, b_n\}$ otherwise. For a choice rule (2), the latter case additionally requires that $a \in I$. For a weight rule (3), $r^I = \{a \leftarrow l \leq [b_1 = w_1, \ldots, b_n = w_n]\}$ where the revised bound l is obtained from k by deducing w_{n+i} for each $1 \leq i \leq m$ such that $c_i \notin I$. Finally, for an entire WCP P, the reduct $P^I = \bigcup\{r^I \mid r \in P\}$ and I is a *stable model* of P iff $I = $ LM(P^I). For the purposes of this work, it is also useful to distinguish the *supporting rules* of P with respect to I, i.e., SR$_P(I) = \{r \in P \mid$ head$(r) \in I, I \models$ body$(r)\}$. Then, a model $I \models P$ is *supported* (by P) when $I = \{$head$(r) \mid r \in$ SR$_P(I)\}$. Each stable model of P is supported by P, but supported models are not necessarily stable, such as $I = \{a\}$ for $P = \{a \leftarrow a.\}$.

Example 1. Consider a WCP P consisting of the following three rules:

$$a \leftarrow b, c. \qquad \{b\}. \qquad c \leftarrow 3 \leq [a = 1, b = 2, \text{not } b = 3].$$

The signature $\mathrm{At}(P) = \{a, b, c\}$ and $\mathrm{DG}^+(P)$ has SCCs $S_1 = \{a, c\}$ and $S_2 = \{b\}$. There are two stable models $M_1 = \{b\}$ and $M_2 = \{c\}$ justified by reducts $P^{M_1} = \{a \leftarrow b, c. \ b. \ c \leftarrow 3 \leq [a = 1, b = 2].\}$ and $P^{M_2} = \{a \leftarrow b, c. \ c \leftarrow 0 \leq [a = 1, b = 2]\}$. But the model $M_2 = \{a, b, c\}$ is only supported, not stable.   ∎

3   Translating ASP into SAT Modulo Graphs/Acyclicity

In this section, we recall the translation of logic programs under answer set semantics into SAT modulo Graphs. The original translation [8] was formulated directly from normal programs into SAT modulo acyclicity. This approach presumes that WCPs are first *normalized* in the sense of [3], i.e., rewritten in terms of normal rules only. An improved translation [4] instruments a WCP with extra rules that make the acyclicity constraint explicit in the program. The resulting logic program encodes the minimality of answer sets in two parallel ways if the program is interpreted under the *ASP modulo acyclicity* semantics [4]. Since instrumentation covers WCPs in general, it is possible to postpone normalization after this phase, which can be deemed beneficial for the size of the resulting NLP because normalization tends to enlarge SCCs in logic programs. The final step of the translation is based on Clark's *completion* [7] but to keep the resulting blow-up linear, new atoms in the sense of Tseitin [24] are required. Moreover, the interpretation of atoms involved in the acyclicity constraint must be kept intact. In what follows, we review the essentials of normalization (Sect. 3.1), instrumentation (Sect. 3.2), and program completion (Sect. 3.3).

3.1   Normalization

The extended rule types [23] can be rewritten using normal rules only [3], but for the sake of compactness new atoms are necessary. For instance a choice rule r in (2), can be expressed using a new atom $\bar{a}$ for the head along with normal rules $a \leftarrow \text{not } \bar{a}, \text{body}(r)$ and $\bar{a} \leftarrow \text{not } a$. The normalization schemes for weight rules (3) are far more complex. For instance, the normalization of $a \leftarrow k \leq [b_1 = 1, \ldots, b_n = 1]$ would require $\binom{n}{k}$ positive normal rules without new atoms. Fortunately, there are (low-degree) polynomial designs based on, e.g., binary decision diagrams, sorting networks, and mixed radix number systems [3]. Given a WCP P, we write $\mathrm{Tr}_{\mathrm{NORM}}(P)$ for the result of normalizing P using some (fixed) normalization schemes for choice (2) and weight (3) rules.

Proposition 1 ([3,5]). *Let P be a WCP.*

1. *If an interpretation $M \subseteq \mathrm{At}(P)$ is a stable model of P, then there is a stable model N of the normalization $\mathrm{Tr}_{\mathrm{NORM}}(P)$ such that $M = N \cap \mathrm{At}(P)$.*
2. *If $N \subseteq \mathrm{At}(P)$ is a stable model of the normalization $\mathrm{Tr}_{\mathrm{NORM}}(P)$, then $M = N \cap \mathrm{At}(P)$ is a stable model of P.*

Most normalization schemes [3,5] are faithful in even a stronger (bijective) sense, i.e., the program P and its normalization $\mathrm{Tr}_{\mathrm{NORM}}(P)$ are *visibly equivalent* [13]: their answer sets are in one-to-one correspondence and coincide up to $\mathrm{At}(P)$.

Example 2. Recalling WCP P from Example 1, one potential normalization is:

$$a \leftarrow b, c. \qquad b \leftarrow \mathbf{not}\ \bar{b}. \qquad \bar{b} \leftarrow \mathbf{not}\ b. \qquad c \leftarrow a, b. \qquad c \leftarrow \mathbf{not}\ b.$$

Its stable models $N_1 = \{b\}$ and $N_2 = \{\bar{b}, c\}$ correspond to the earlier ones. ∎

3.2 Instrumentation with Acyclicity Constraint

Our next target is to recall the *acyclicity translation* $\mathrm{Tr}_{\mathrm{ACYC}}(P)$ of a WCP P [4] that deploys special *dependency atoms* $\mathrm{dep}(a, b)$ to express the activation of the respective edge $\langle a, b \rangle \in \mathrm{DG}^+(P)$ in the acyclicity constraint. This transformation is feasible on an atom-by-atom basis and required only for atoms $a \in \mathrm{At}(P)$ involved in non-trivial SCCs S of P with $|S| > 1$. Given such an S and an atom $a \in S$, the idea is to *instrument* P with additional rules that capture *well-support* for a (cf. [4]). For each edge $\langle a, b \rangle \in \mathrm{DG}^+(P)$ specific to S, the potential dependency of a on b is expressed using a choice rule $\{\mathrm{dep}(a, b)\} \leftarrow b$. Besides this, special atoms $\mathrm{ws}(r_1), \ldots, \mathrm{ws}(r_k)$ for the defining rules $\{r_1, \ldots, r_k\} = \mathrm{def}_P(a)$ enforce the well support for a in terms of a constraint $f \leftarrow a, \mathbf{not}\ \mathrm{ws}(r_1), \ldots, \mathbf{not}\ \mathrm{ws}(r_k), \mathbf{not}\ f$ where f is new. Given the SCC S of a in P, we assume that each $\mathrm{body}^+(r)$ in (1)–(3) is ordered so that for some $0 \leq l \leq n$, $b_1 \in S, \ldots, b_l \in S$ while $b_{l+1} \notin S, \ldots, b_n \notin S$. Then, if a *defining* rule $r \in \mathrm{def}_P(a)$ is of the form (1) or (2), the rule (4) below captures well-support mediated by r, but if it is of the form (3), then the rule is (5).

$$\mathrm{ws}(r) \leftarrow \mathrm{dep}(a, b_1), \ldots, \mathrm{dep}(a, b_l), b_{l+1}, \ldots, b_n, \mathbf{not}\ c_1, \ldots, \mathbf{not}\ c_m. \qquad (4)$$

$$\mathrm{ws}(r) \leftarrow k \leq [\mathrm{dep}(a, b_1) = w_1, \ldots, \mathrm{dep}(a, b_l) = w_l, b_{l+1} = w_{l+1}, \ldots, b_n = w_n,$$
$$\mathbf{not}\ c_1 = w_{n+1}, \ldots, \mathbf{not}\ c_m = w_{n+m}]. \qquad (5)$$

For the program $\mathrm{Tr}_{\mathrm{ACYC}}(P)$ obtained in this way, the distinction between stable and supported models disappears if we insist on *acyclic models* I for which the digraph induced by the set of arcs $\{\langle a, b \rangle \mid \mathrm{dep}(a, b) \in I\}$ is acyclic.

Proposition 2 ([4, Theorem 3.11]). *Let P be a WCP.*

1. *If M is a stable model of P, then $\mathrm{Tr}_{\mathrm{ACYC}}(P)$ has an acyclic supported model N such that $M = N \cap \mathrm{At}(P)$.*
2. *If N is an acyclic supported model of $\mathrm{Tr}_{\mathrm{ACYC}}(P)$, then $M = N \cap \mathrm{At}(P)$ is a stable model of P and well-supported by $R = \{r \in P \mid \mathrm{ws}(r) \in N, \mathrm{head}(r) \in N\}$.*

Example 3. Normalization in Example 2 preserves SCCs as is, in particular, the SCC $S = \{a, c\}$. Let r_1 be the defining rule for a, and r_2 and r_3 the ones for c.

Adding

$$\{\mathtt{dep}(a,c)\} \leftarrow c. \qquad\qquad \{\mathtt{dep}(c,a)\} \leftarrow a.$$
$$\mathtt{ws}(r_1) \leftarrow \mathtt{dep}(a,c), b. \qquad \mathtt{ws}(r_2) \leftarrow \mathtt{dep}(c,a), b. \qquad \mathtt{ws}(r_3) \leftarrow \mathrm{not}\ b.$$
$$f \leftarrow a, \mathrm{not}\ \mathtt{ws}(r_1), \mathrm{not}\ f. \qquad f \leftarrow c, \mathrm{not}\ \mathtt{ws}(r_2), \mathrm{not}\ \mathtt{ws}(r_3), \mathrm{not}\ f.$$

ensure that acyclic supported models are stable. In particular, note that $N = \{a, b, c, \mathtt{dep}(a, c), \mathtt{dep}(c, a), \mathtt{ws}(r_1), \mathtt{ws}(r_2)\}$ is supported, but not acyclic.   ∎

3.3   Program Completion Modulo Acyclicity

The final phase of translating logic programs into SAT modulo acyclicity presumes an NLP P as input, potentially involving dependency atoms $\mathtt{dep}(a,b)$ where a and b are ordinary (non-dependency) atoms in P, see Sect. 3.2. Given a normal rule $r \in P$ of the form (1), we introduce a new atom $\mathtt{bt}(r)$ denoting the satisfaction of $\mathrm{body}(r)$, thus following the idea of Tseitin-transformation [24]. The equivalence (6) below gives a name $\mathtt{bt}(r)$ for $\mathrm{body}(r)$ and then the definition $\mathrm{def}_P(a)$ of an ordinary atom a can be written as the equivalence (7).

$$\mathtt{bt}(r) \leftrightarrow \bigwedge_{b\,\in\,\mathrm{body}^+(r)} b \;\wedge\; \bigwedge_{c\,\in\,\mathrm{body}^-(r)} \neg c \tag{6}$$

$$a \leftrightarrow \bigvee_{r\,\in\,\mathrm{def}_P(a)} \mathtt{bt}(r) \tag{7}$$

Choice rules $\{\mathtt{dep}(a, b)\} \leftarrow b$ introduced by $\mathrm{Tr}_{\mathrm{ACYC}}$ are completed as $\mathtt{dep}(a, b) \leftrightarrow b \wedge \mathtt{dep}(a, b)$. What remains is the clausification of these formulas, (6) for every $r \in P$, and (7) for each ordinary atom $a \in \mathrm{At}(P)$. Omitting details, we denote the resulting set by $\mathrm{Tr}_{\mathrm{COMP}}(P)$. The correctness of $\mathrm{Tr}_{\mathrm{COMP}}$ builds on the following.

Proposition 3 ([4,8]). *Let P be an NLP subject to acyclicity constraint.*

1. *If an interpretation $I \subseteq \mathrm{At}(P)$ is an acyclic supported model of P, then $I \cup \{\mathtt{bt}(r) \mid r \in P, I \models \mathrm{body}(r)\}$ is an acyclic model of $\mathrm{Tr}_{\mathrm{COMP}}(P)$.*
2. *If an interpretation $I \subseteq \mathrm{At}(\mathrm{Tr}_{\mathrm{COMP}}(P))$ is an acyclic model of $\mathrm{Tr}_{\mathrm{COMP}}(P)$, then $I \cap \mathrm{At}(P)$ is an acyclic supported model of P.*

Example 4. The rules introduced by normalization (Example 2) and by instrumentation for well-support (Example 3) effectively yield the following clauses:

$$
\begin{array}{llll}
a \vee \neg b \vee \neg c, & \neg a \vee b, & \neg a \vee c, & b \vee \bar{b}, \qquad\qquad \neg b \vee \neg \bar{b}, \\
c \vee \neg a, & c \vee b, & \neg c \vee a \vee \neg b, & \neg\mathtt{dep}(a, c) \vee c, \quad \neg\mathtt{dep}(c, a) \vee a, \\
& & \neg\mathtt{ws}(r_1) \vee \mathtt{dep}(a, c), & \neg\mathtt{ws}(r_1) \vee b, \quad \mathtt{ws}(r_1) \vee \neg b \vee \neg\mathtt{dep}(a, c), \\
& & \neg\mathtt{ws}(r_2) \vee \mathtt{dep}(c, a), & \neg\mathtt{ws}(r_2) \vee b, \quad \mathtt{ws}(r_2) \vee \neg b \vee \neg\mathtt{dep}(c, a), \\
& & & \neg\mathtt{ws}(r_3) \vee b, \quad \mathtt{ws}(r_3) \vee \neg b, \\
& & & \mathtt{ws}(r_1) \vee \neg a, \quad \mathtt{ws}(r_2) \vee \mathtt{ws}(r_3) \vee \neg c.
\end{array}
$$

Then, the stable models of the original WCP P are captured by *acyclic* models $I_1 = \{b\}$ and $I_2 = \{c, \bar{b}, \mathtt{ws}(r_3)\}$ while N from Example 3 is a model with a cycle.   ∎

4 Vertex Elimination

Vertex elimination for digraphs was originally introduced by Rose and Tarjan [22]. Quite recently, it was successfully used to prevent cycles in digraphs associated with propositional formulas [21]. We now recall these methods.

Given a digraph $G = \langle V, E \rangle$, an ordering of V is a bijection $\alpha : \{1, \ldots, n\} \rightarrow V$. For a vertex v, the *fill-in* of v, denoted by $F(v)$, is the set of edges from the in-neighbors of v to the out-neighbors of v, formally defined by

$$F(v) = \{\langle x, y \rangle | \langle x, v \rangle \in E, \langle v, y \rangle \in E, x \neq y\}. \tag{8}$$

The *v-elimination* graph of G is produced by removing v from G, and adding the fill-in of v to the resulting graph. Formally, $G(v) = (V - \{v\}, E(v) \cup F(v)$, where $E(v) = \{\langle x, y \rangle | \langle x, y \rangle \in E, x \neq v, y \neq v\}$.

Given a digraph G and an ordering α of its vertices, the *elimination process* of G according to α is the sequence $G = G_0, G_1, \ldots, G_{n-1}$, where G_i is the $\alpha(i)$-elimination graph of G_{i-1} for $i = 1, \ldots, n - 1$.

The fill-in of the digraph G according to α, denoted by $F_\alpha(G)$, is the set of all edges added to G in the elimination process. Formally, $F_\alpha(G)$ is defined by (9), where $F_{i-1}(\alpha(i))$ is the fill-in of $\alpha(i)$ in G_{i-1}.

$$F_\alpha(G) = \bigcup_{i=1}^{|V|-1} F_{i-1}(\alpha(i)) \tag{9}$$

The vertex elimination graph of G according to α, denoted by G_α^*, is the union of all graphs produced in the elimination process of G according to α:

$$G_\alpha^* = \langle V, E \cup F_\alpha(G) \rangle. \tag{10}$$

For any digraph G, the number of arcs of the vertex elimination graph depends on the ordering function α. It has been shown that the problem of finding the optimal ordering function, the one resulting in the smallest number of arcs in the vertex elimination graph, is NP-complete [22]. Nevertheless, there are effective heuristics for finding empirically usable orderings. Examples are the *minimum fill-in* and *minimum degree* that accordingly choose a vertex for removal at each step during the elimination process.

One important property of vertex elimination graphs is that if the original graph G has a directed cycle, no matter what the ordering α is, the vertex elimination graph G_α^* will have a cycle of length 2. Example 5 shows how cycles go through contraction during the vertex elimination process.

Example 5. Let G be the cycle depicted in Fig. 1a. Figure 1a to 1g show the vertex elimination process of G according to α, where $\alpha(1)$ to $\alpha(8)$ are 2, 4, 6, 8, 1, 5, 3, and 7, respectively. Figure 1h depicts the vertex elimination graph according to α. As it can be seen in Fig. 1, after elimination of each node, the size of the remaining cycle decreases by one node. Therefore, the produced vertex elimination graph must have a cycle of length 2.

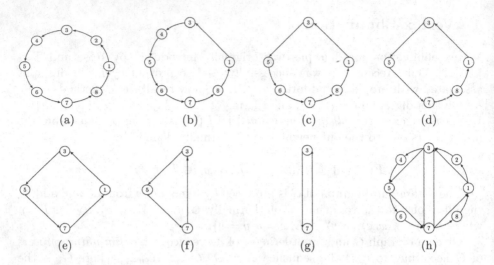

Fig. 1. The vertex elimination process of an eight-node cycle

5 Translating SAT Modulo Acyclicity into Pure SAT

Let ϕ be a propositional formula associated with graph $G = \langle V, E \rangle$, such that arc $\langle v_i, v_j \rangle \in E$ is represented by the atom $e_{i,j} \in At(\phi)$. An interpretation I is an acyclic model of formula ϕ iff $I \models \phi$ in the classical sense and the digraph $G_I = (V, \{\langle v_i, v_j \rangle | e_{i,j} \in I\})$ is acyclic. We are interested in producing a propositional formula ϕ', such that ϕ' is satisfiable in the classical sense if and only if there is an acyclic model for ϕ.

Vertex elimination has recently been used for translating SAT modulo acyclicity into pure SAT [21]. This is achieved by adding atoms and clauses to ϕ that dynamically simulate the vertex elimination process of G_I for a classical model I of ϕ. Considering the cycle contraction property of vertex elimination graphs mentioned above, the acyclicity of G_I can then be ensured by prohibiting cycles of length 2 in the vertex elimination graph of G_I.

Let α be an arbitrary ordering of V. Without loss of generality, we assume that members of V are indexed such that for $i = 1, \ldots, n$, $\alpha(i) = v_i$. For the sake of simplicity, we denote the vertex elimination graphs of G and G_I according to α, simply by $G^* = \langle V, E^* \rangle$ and $G_I^* = \langle V, E_I^* \rangle$, respectively. To simulate the vertex elimination process of G_I, we need atoms $e'_{i,j}$ to represent the arcs of G_I^*. We know that every arc of G_I is also an arc of G_I^*. In other words, $e_{i,j}$ implies $e'_{i,j}$. Hence, we add to the original formula

$$\bigwedge_{\langle v_i, v_j \rangle \,\in\, E} e_{i,j} \rightarrow e'_{i,j}. \tag{11}$$

Let $G = G_0, G_1, \ldots, G_{n-1}$ be the vertex elimination process of G, and $G_I = G'_0, G'_1, \ldots, G'_{n-1}$ be the vertex elimination process of G_I. Since G_I is a subgraph of G, G'_i must be a subgraph of G_i for $i = 1, \ldots, n - 1$. Therefore, the fill-in of

v_i in G'_{i-1} is also a subset of the fill-in of v_i in G_{i-1}. Since the fill-in of v_i in G_{i-1} can be computed statically, we can use it to reduce the number of formulas and atoms needed for dynamic computation of the fill-in of v_i in G'_{i-1}. Based on this, we add formula (12) to ensure that for $i = 1, \ldots, n-1$, the fill-in of v_i in G'_{i-1} is included in G^*_I. In (12), $F_{i-1}(v_i)$ denotes the fill-in of v_i in G_{i-1}.

$$\bigwedge_{v_i \in V, \langle v_j, v_k \rangle \in F_{i-1}(v_i)} (e'_{j,i} \wedge e'_{i,k}) \to e'_{j,k} \tag{12}$$

Finally, we guarantee the acyclicity of G_I by prohibiting cycles of length 2 in the vertex elimination graph of G_I, using formula (13).

$$\bigwedge_{\langle v_i, v_j \rangle \in E^*, \langle v_j, v_i \rangle \in E^*, i<j} e'_{i,j} \to \neg e'_{j,i} \tag{13}$$

Consider ϕ' to be the conjunction of ϕ and formulas (11) to (13). Theorem 1 and Theorem 2 of [21] show that for any given ordering α of V, ϕ' is satisfiable in classical sense iff there is an acyclic model for ϕ. Nevertheless, by straightforward consideration, one can reach to a stronger theoretical result as follows.

Proposition 4. *Let ϕ be a propositional formula subject to acyclicity constraint, associated with graph $G = \langle V, E \rangle$, and α be any ordering of V.*

1. *If an interpretation $I \subseteq \mathrm{At}(\phi)$ is an acyclic model of ϕ, then the interpretation $J = I \cup \{e'_{i,j} \mid \langle v_i, v_j \rangle \in E^*_I\}$ is a classical model of ϕ'.*
2. *If an interpretation $J \subseteq \mathrm{At}(\phi')$ is a classical model of ϕ', then the interpretation $I = J \cap \mathrm{At}(\phi)$ is an acyclic model of ϕ.*

6 Translating ASP into Pure SAT

Considering a WCP P, let ϕ denote the conjunction of all clauses produced by the translation $\mathrm{Tr_{COMP}}(\mathrm{Tr_{ACYC}}(\mathrm{Tr_{NORM}}(P)))$. By construction, ϕ is a propositional formula with acyclicity constraint imposed on a graph $G = \langle V, E \rangle$, where V is the set of ordinary (non-dependency) atoms in $\mathrm{Tr_{NORM}}(P)$, and E is the set of pairs $\langle a, b \rangle$ such that $\mathrm{dep}(a, b)$ is an atom in $\mathrm{Tr_{ACYC}}(\mathrm{Tr_{NORM}}(P))$. Let $G = G_0, G_1, \ldots, G_{n-1}, F_{i-1}(v_i)$, and $G^* = \langle V, E^* \rangle$ be defined as in Sect. 5 and $\mathrm{Tr_{SAT}}(P)$ the set of clauses in ϕ extended by clauses derived from formulas (11)–(13). Theorem 1 is a direct consequence of Propositions 1–4.

Theorem 1. *Let P be a WCP.*

1. *If an interpretation $M \subseteq \mathrm{At}(P)$ is a stable model of P, then there is a classical model N of $\mathrm{Tr_{SAT}}(P)$ such that $M = N \cap \mathrm{At}(P)$.*
2. *If an interpretation $N \subseteq \mathrm{At}(\mathrm{Tr_{SAT}}(P))$ is a classical model of $\mathrm{Tr_{SAT}}(P)$, then $M = N \cap \mathrm{At}(P)$ is a stable model of P.*

Theorem 1 does not provide a bijection between the set of classical models of $\mathrm{Tr_{SAT}}(P)$ and the set of stable modes of P but admits the following result.

Table 1. Comparison of coverage of competing methods

Problem Set	Problems	Solved				
		SAT	CLASP	WASP	GRAPHSAT	BIN
CombinedConfiguration	99	**66**	65	19	26	33
Hamiltonian	300	282	199	276	**300**	194
KnightTourWithHoles	300	**44**	40	37	31	26
Labyrinth	246	205	**209**	191	109	156
MazeGeneration	50	**50**	**50**	**50**	**50**	22
RandomNonTight	14	**14**	**14**	12	**14**	**14**
Total	1219	**661**	577	585	530	445

Corollary 1. *Let P be a WCP. The set of projections of classical models of* $\mathrm{Tr}_{\mathrm{SAT}}(P)$ *to* $\mathrm{At}(P)$ *is equal to the set of stable models of P.*

Example 6. Consider the clauses of Example 4. After our vertex elimination based translation, clauses $\neg\mathbf{dep}(a,c) \vee \mathbf{dep}'(a,c)$ and $\neg\mathbf{dep}(c,a) \vee \mathbf{dep}'(c,a)$ are produced according to formula (11), and $\mathbf{dep}'(a,c) \vee \neg\mathbf{dep}'(c,a)$ is produced by formula (13), rendering $\mathrm{Tr}_{\mathrm{SAT}}(P)$ not satisfiable by any superset of N from Example 3.   ∎

7   Experimental Evaluation

We have implemented our vertex elimination based translation of SAT modulo acyclicity into pure SAT as GRAPH2SAT 1.0 within the ASPTOOLS[1] collection [14]. To translate ASP to SAT modulo acyclicity, we use LP2ACYC 1.30, LP2NORMAL2 1.14, LP2SAT 1.26, all provided by the ASPTOOLS collection. All experiments are run on a cluster of Linux machines with Intel Xeon 2.40 GHz CPUs, using a timeout of 600 s per problem, and, a memory limit of 16 GB. For determining the vertex elimination order, we implemented the *minimum degree* heuristic. As the SAT solver, we use KISSAT 1.0.3 [2].

As regards competing methods, we compare against state-of-the-art native ASP solvers CLASP 3.3.5 and WASP 2.0, the translation-based method using SAT modulo acyclicity formulas fed to GRAPHSAT as the solver, as well as the previously introduced binary counter encoding of acyclicity constraint into pure SAT [13] accompanied by KISSAT as the solver, henceforth denoted by BIN. As the benchmark set, we use all problem sets of previous ASP competitions whose complexity is not beyond NP and are in the non-tight decision category.

---

[1] https://github.com/asptools.

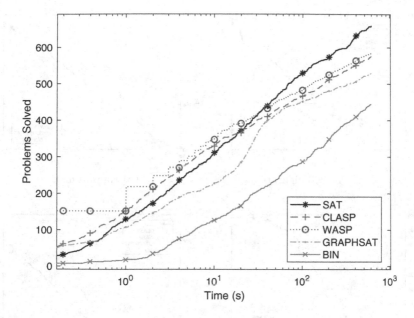

Fig. 2. Cumulative numbers of problems solved by the competing methods

The problem sets with such properties are: CombinedConfiguration, KnightTour-WithHoles, Labyrinth, MazeGeneration, and RandomNonTight. We also use the Hamiltonian cycle encoding presented in [19]. This problem set includes 30 randomly generated *planar graphs* with 60, 70, . . . , 150 nodes, summing up to 300 instances. In total, 1219 problem instances are used in our experiments. Here, we report the solving times of the competing methods. The time spent by our method on translation is negligible compared to the solving time. We checked that taking the translation time into account would not render any of the currently solved instances unsolvable within the time limit of 600 s.

The number of problems solved by the mentioned methods on our benchmark suite is stated in Table 1. In total, our method solves 84, 76, 131, and 221 problems more than CLASP, WASP, GRAPHSAT, and BIN, respectively. Figure 2 shows the cumulative number of problems solved by the competing methods. As it can be observed, when given more than 30 s, our method solves more problems than any other competing solver. Also, Fig. 3, which depicts the cumulative number of problems solved by the competing methods in each problem set, shows that our method is among the top two solvers in every problem set.

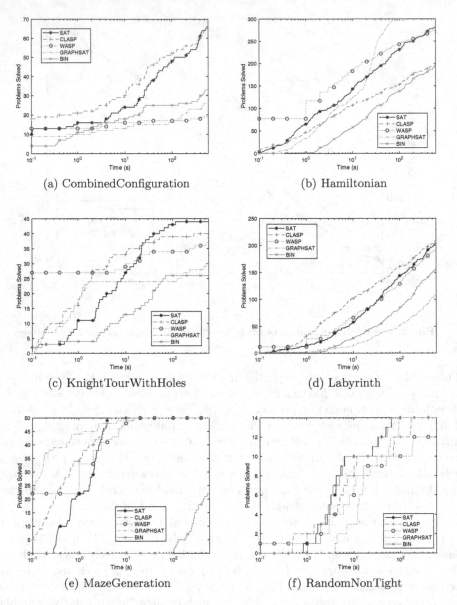

(a) CombinedConfiguration

(b) Hamiltonian

(c) KnightTourWithHoles

(d) Labyrinth

(e) MazeGeneration

(f) RandomNonTight

Fig. 3. Cumulative numbers of problems solved by the competing methods in each problem set

8   Discussion and Conclusion

In this work, we take into reconsideration the translation of ASP into SAT modulo graphs and, more specifically, SAT modulo acyclicity [8,9]. This transformation along its refactored version [4] enable the computation of answer sets using appropriately extended SAT solvers such as GRAPHSAT. The recent app-roach of [21] makes the graph extension involved in SAT modulo acyclicity obso-lete using yet another transformation based on vertex elimination. The central goal of this work is to check the effect on performance if the composition of these translations is deployed and a state-of-the-art SAT solver [2] is used as the back-end solver. The results obtained for six non-tight benchmarks are very promising as the approach presented in this work turns out to be competitive against GRAPHSAT and the native ASP solvers CLASP and WASP. This can be interpreted as a realization of the long-term objective of translation-based ASP, i.e., taking advantage of the development of solver technology. An immediate conclusion is that the designs of native ASP solvers should be revised to reflect recent developments in SAT solvers. Otherwise, the performance gap is to grow.

Acknowledgments. Financial support from the Academy of Finland (Project XAILOG, #345633) is gratefully acknowledged.

References

1. Alviano, M., Dodaro, C., Leone, N., Ricca, F.: Advances in WASP. In: Calimeri, F., Ianni, G., Truszczynski, M. (eds.) LPNMR 2015. LNCS (LNAI), vol. 9345, pp. 40–54. Springer, Cham (2015). https://doi.org/10.1007/978-3-319-23264-5_5
2. Biere, A., Fazekas, K., Fleury, M., Heisinger, M.: CaDiCal, Kissat, Paracooba, Plin-geling and Treengeling entering the SAT Competition 2020. In: SAT Competition 2020, pp. 50–54 (2020)
3. Bomanson, J., Gebser, M., Janhunen, T.: Improving the normalization of weight rules in answer set programs. In: Fermé, E., Leite, J. (eds.) JELIA 2014. LNCS (LNAI), vol. 8761, pp. 166–180. Springer, Cham (2014). https://doi.org/10.1007/978-3-319-11558-0_12
4. Bomanson, J., Gebser, M., Janhunen, T., Kaufmann, B., Schaub, T.: Answer set programming modulo acyclicity. Fundam. Informaticae **147**(1), 63–91 (2016)
5. Bomanson, J., Janhunen, T., Niemelä, I.: Applying visible strong equivalence in answer-set program transformations. ACM Trans. Comput. Log. **21**(4), 33:1-33:41 (2020)
6. Brewka, G., Eiter, T., Truszczynski, M.: Answer set programming at a glance. Commun. ACM **54**(12), 92–103 (2011)
7. Clark, K.: Negation as failure. In: Gallaire, H., Minker, J. (eds.) Logic and Data Bases, pp. 293–322. Plenum Press (1978)
8. Gebser, M., Janhunen, T., Rintanen, J.: SAT modulo graphs: acyclicity. In: Fermé, E., Leite, J. (eds.) JELIA 2014. LNCS (LNAI), vol. 8761, pp. 137–151. Springer, Cham (2014). https://doi.org/10.1007/978-3-319-11558-0_10
9. Gebser, M., Janhunen, T., Rintanen, J.: SAT modulo graphs: acyclicity. In: Fermé, E., Leite, J. (eds.) JELIA 2014. LNCS (LNAI), vol. 8761, pp. 137–151. Springer, Cham (2014). https://doi.org/10.1007/978-3-319-11558-0_10
10. Gebser, M., Janhunen, T., Rintanen, J.: Declarative encodings of acyclicity prop-erties. J. Log. Comput. **30**(4), 923–952 (2020)
11. Gebser, M., Kaminski, R., Kaufmann, B., Romero, J., Schaub, T.: Progress in *clasp* Series 3. In: Calimeri, F., Ianni, G., Truszczynski, M. (eds.) LPNMR 2015. LNCS (LNAI), vol. 9345, pp. 368–383. Springer, Cham (2015). https://doi.org/10.1007/978-3-319-23264-5_31

12. Gebser, M., Maratea, M., Ricca, F.: The seventh answer set programming competition: design and results. Theory Pract. Log. Program. **20**(2), 176–204 (2020)
13. Janhunen, T.: Some (in)translatability results for normal logic programs and propositional theories. J. Appl. Non Class. Logics **16**(1–2), 35–86 (2006)
14. Janhunen, T.: Cross-translating answer set programs using the ASPTOOLS collection. Künstliche Intell. **32**(2–3), 183–184 (2018)
15. Janhunen, T., Niemelä, I.: The answer set programming paradigm. AI Mag. **37**(3), 13–24 (2016)
16. Lifschitz, V.: What is answer set programming? In: AAAI 2008, pp. 1594–1597 (2008)
17. Lin, F., Zhao, J.: On tight logic programs and yet another translation from normal logic programs to propositional logic. In: IJCAI 2003, pp. 853–858 (2003)
18. Lin, F., Zhao, Y.: ASSAT: computing answer sets of a logic program by SAT solvers. In: AAAI 2002, pp. 112–118 (2002)
19. Niemelä, I.: Logic programs with stable model semantics as a constraint programming paradigm. Ann. Math. Artif. Intell. **25**(3–4), 241–273 (1999)
20. Nieuwenhuis, R., Oliveras, A.: DPLL(T) with exhaustive theory propagation and its application to difference logic. In: Etessami, K., Rajamani, S.K. (eds.) CAV 2005. LNCS, vol. 3576, pp. 321–334. Springer, Heidelberg (2005). https://doi.org/10.1007/11513988_33
21. Rankooh, M.F., Rintanen, J.: Propositional encodings of acyclicity and reachability by using vertex elimination. In: AAAI 2022 (2022, to appear)
22. Rose, D.J., Tarjan, R.E.: Algorithmic aspects of vertex elimination. In: Proceedings of the 7th Annual ACM Symposium on Theory of Computing, pp. 245–254 (1975)
23. Simons, P., Niemelä, I., Soininen, T.: Extending and implementing the stable model semantics. Artif. Intell. **138**(1–2), 181–234 (2002)
24. Tseitin, G.: On the complexity of derivation in the propositional calculus. Zapiski Nauchnykh Seminarov LOMI **8**, 234–259 (1968)

IASCAR: Incremental Answer Set Counting by Anytime Refinement

Johannes Klaus Fichte[1], Sarah Alice Gaggl[2], Markus Hecher[1],
and Dominik Rusovac[2(✉)]

[1] Institute of Logic and Computation, TU Wien, Vienna, Austria
{johannes.fichte,markus.hecher}@tuwien.ac.at
[2] Logic Programming and Argumentation Group, TU Dresden, Dresden, Germany
{sarah.gaggl,dominik.rusovac}@tu-dresden.de

Abstract. Answer set programming (ASP) is a popular declarative programming paradigm with various applications. Programs can easily have so many answer sets that they cannot be enumerated in practice, but counting still allows to quantify solution spaces. If one counts under assumptions on literals, one obtains a tool to comprehend parts of the solution space, so called *answer set navigation*. But navigating through parts of the solution space requires counting many times, which is expensive in theory. There, *knowledge compilation* compiles instances into representations on which counting works in polynomial time. However, these techniques exist only for CNF formulas and compiling ASP programs into CNF formulas can introduce an exponential overhead. In this paper, we introduce a technique to iteratively count answer sets under assumptions on knowledge compilations of CNFs that encode supported models. Our anytime technique uses the principle of inclusion-exclusion to systematically improve bounds by over- and undercounting. In a preliminary empirical analysis we demonstrate promising results. After compiling the input (offline phase) our approach quickly (re)counts.

Keywords: ASP · Answer set counting · Knowledge compilation

1 Introduction

Answer set programming (ASP) [11] is a widely used declarative problem modeling and solving paradigm with many applications in knowledge representation, artificial intelligence, planning, and many more. It is widely used to solve difficult search problems while allowing compact modeling [7]. In ASP, a problem is represented as a set of rules, called *logic program*, over atoms. Models of a program under the stable semantics form its solutions, so-called *answer sets*. Beyond the search for one solution or an optimal solution, an increasingly popular question is counting answer sets, which provides extensive applications for quantitative reasoning. For example, counting is crucial for probabilistic logic programming, c.f., [6,13] or encoding Bayesian networks and their inference [12]. Interestingly, counting also facilitates more fine-grained reasoning modes between brave

G. Gottlob et al. (Eds.): LPNMR 2022, LNAI 13416, pp. 217–230, 2022.
https://doi.org/10.1007/978-3-031-15707-3_17

218   J. K. Fichte et al.

and cautious reasoning. To this end, one examines the ratio of an atom occurring in answer sets over all answer sets, which yields a notion of *plausibility* of an atom. When considering sets of literals, which represent assumptions, one obtains a detailed tool to *comprehend search spaces* that contain a large number of answer sets [5]. However, already for ground normal programs, answer set counting is #·P-complete, making it harder than decision problems. Recall that brave reasoning is just NP-complete, but by Toda's Theorem we know that $PH \subseteq P^{\#\cdot P}$ where $\bigcup_{k \in \mathbb{N}} \Delta_k^P = PH$ and $NP \subseteq \Delta_2^P = P^{NP}$. Approximate counting is in fact easier, i.e., approx-#·P $\subseteq BPP^{NP} \subseteq \Sigma_3^P$, and approximate answer set counters have very recently been suggested [8]. Still, when navigating large search spaces, we need to count answer sets many times rendering such tools conceptually ineffective. There, knowledge compilation comes in handy [3].

In *knowledge compilation*, computation is split in two phases. Formulas are compiled in a potentially very expensive step into a representation in an *offline phase* and reasoning is carried out in polynomial time on such representations in an *online phase*. Such a conceptual framework would be perfectly suited when answer sets are counted many times, providing us with quick re-counting. While we can translate programs into propositional formulas and directly apply techniques from propositional formulas, it is widely known that one can easily run into an exponential blowup [10] or introduce level mappings that are oftentimes large grids and hence expensive for counters. In practice, solvers that find one answer set or optimal answer sets can avoid a blowup by computing supported models, which can be encoded into propositional formulas with limited overhead, and implementing propagators on top [7].

In this paper, we explore a counterpart of a propagator-style approach for counting answer sets. We encode finding supported models as a propositional formula and use a knowledge compiler to obtain, in an offline phase, a representation, which allows us to construct a counting graph that in turn can be used to efficiently compute the number of supported models. The resulting counting graph can be quite large, but can be evaluated in parallel. Counting supported models provides us only with an upper bound on the number of answer sets. We suggest a combinatorial technique to systematically improve bounds by over- and undercounting while incorporating the external support, whose absence can be seen as cause of overcounting in the first place. Our technique can be used to approximate the counts, but also provides the exact count on the number of answer sets when taking the entire external support into account.

Contributions. Our main contributions are as follows.

1. We consider knowledge compilation from an ASP perspective. We recap features such as counting under assumptions, known as conditioning, that make knowledge compilations (sd-DNNFs) quite suitable for navigating search spaces. We suggest a domain-specific technique to compress counting graphs that were constructed for supported models using Clark's completion.
2. We establish a novel combinatorial algorithm that takes an sd-DNNF of a completion formula and allows for systematically improving bounds by over-

and undercounting. The technique identifies not supported atoms and compensates overcounting on the sd-DNNF.
3. We apply our approach to instances tailored to navigate incomprehensible answer set search spaces. While the problem is challenging in general, we demonstrate feasibility and promising results on quickly (re-)counting. We can quickly (re-)count after every search space navigation step.

Related Works. Previous work [1] considered knowledge compilation for logic programs. There an eager incremental approximation technique incrementally computes the result whereas our approach can be seen as an incremental lazy approach on the counting graph. Moreover, the technique by Bogarts and Broeck focuses on well-founded models and stratified negation, which does not work for normal programs in general without translating ASP programs into CNFs directly. Note that common reasoning problems on answer set programs without negation can be solved in polynomial time. Model counting can significantly benefit from preprocessing techniques, which eliminate variables. Widely used propositional knowledge compilers are c2d [2] and d4 [9].

2   Preliminaries

We assume familiarity with propositional satisfiability, graph theory, propositional ASP [7]. Recall that a *cycle* C on a (di)graph G is a (directed) walk of G where the first and the last vertex coincide. For cycle C, we let V_C be its vertices and $cycles(G) := \{V_C \mid C \text{ is a cycle of } G\}$. We consider propositional *variables* and mean by formula a propositional formula. By $\top$ and $\bot$ we refer to the variables that are always evaluated to 1 or 0 (constants). A literal is an atom a or its negation $\neg a$, we assume $\neg\neg a = a$, and $vars(\varphi)$ denotes the set of variables that occur in formula φ. The set of models of a formula φ is given by $\mathcal{M}(\varphi)$.

Answer Set Programming (ASP). In the context of ASP, we usually say atom instead of variable. A *(logic) program* Π is a finite set of *rules* r of the form $a_0 \leftarrow a_1, \ldots, a_m, \neg a_{m+1}, \ldots, \neg a_n$ where $0 \leq m \leq n$ and $a_0, \ldots, a_n$ are atoms and usually omit $\top$ and $\bot$. For a rule r, we define $H(r) := \{a_0\}$ called *head* of r. The *body* consists of $B^+(r) := \{a_1, \ldots, a_m\}$ and $B^-(r) := \{a_{m+1}, \ldots, a_n\}$. The set $at(r)$ of atoms of r consists of $H(r) \cup B^+(r) \cup B^-(r)$. Let Π be a program. Then, we let the set $at(\Pi) := \bigcup_{r \in \Pi} at(r)$ of Π contain its atoms. Its *positive dependency digraph* $DP(\Pi) = (V, E)$ is defined by $V := at(\Pi)$ and $E := \{(a_1, a_0) \mid a_1 \in B^+(r), a_0 \in H(r), r \in \Pi\}$. The *cycles of* Π are given by $cycles(\Pi) := cycles(DP(\Pi))$. Π is *tight*, if $DP(\Pi)$ is acyclic. An *interpretation* of Π is a set $I \subseteq at(\Pi)$ of atoms. I *satisfies* a rule $r \in \Pi$ if $H(r) \cap I \neq \emptyset$ whenever $B^+(r) \subseteq I$ and $B^-(r) \cap I = \emptyset$. I satisfies Π, if I satisfies each rule $r \in \Pi$. The *GL-reduct* Π^I is defined by $\Pi^I := \{H(r) \leftarrow B^+(r) \mid I \cap B^-(r) = \emptyset, r \in \Pi\}$. I is an *answer set*, sometimes also called stable model, if I satisfies Π^I and I is subset-minimal. The *completion* of Π is the formula $comp(\Pi) := \{a \leftrightarrow \bigvee_{r \in \Pi, H(r)=a} BF(r) \vee \bot \mid a \in at(\Pi)\}$ where $BF(r) := \bigwedge_{b \in B^+(r)} b \wedge \bigwedge_{c \in B^-(r)} \neg c \wedge \top$. An interpretation I is a *supported model*

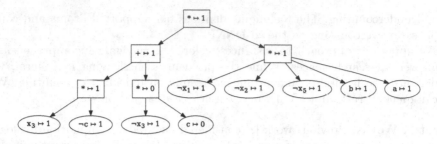

Fig. 1. Counting graph $\mathcal{G}(\varphi \wedge \neg c)$ labeled with literals, operations and val.

of Π, if it is a model of the formula comp(Π). Let $\mathcal{S}(\Pi)$ be the set of all supported models of Π. It holds that $\mathcal{AS}(\Pi) \subseteq \mathcal{S}(\Pi)$, but not vice-versa. If Π is tight, then $\mathcal{AS}(\Pi) = \mathcal{S}(\Pi)$. In practice, we use the completion in CNF, thereby introducing auxiliary variables and still preserving the number of supported models.

Example 1. Let $\Pi_1 = \{a \leftarrow b; b \leftarrow; c \leftarrow c\}$. We see that $DP(\Pi_1)$ is cyclic due to rule $c \leftarrow c$. Thus, Π_1 is not tight and its respective answer sets $\mathcal{AS}(\Pi_1) = \{\{a, b\}\}$ and supported models $\mathcal{S}(\Pi_1) = \{\{a, b\}, \{a, b, c\}\}$ differ.

Assumptions. We define $\neg L := \{\neg a \mid a \in L\}$ for a set L of literals. Let Π be a program and $\mathcal{L}(\Pi) := at(\Pi) \cup \neg at(\Pi)$ be its literals. An *assumption* is a literal $\ell \in \mathcal{L}(\Pi)$ interpreted as rule $ic(\ell) := \{\bot \leftarrow \neg \ell\}$. For set L of assumptions of Π, we say that L is *consistent*, if there is no atom $a \in L$ for which $\neg a \in L$. Throughout this paper, by L we refer to consistent assumptions. Furthermore, we define $ic(L) := \bigcup_{\ell \in L} ic(\ell)$ and let $\Pi^L := \Pi \cup ic(L)$.

Example 2 (cont'd). Since $\mathcal{AS}(\Pi_1) = \{\{a, b\}\}$, we see that if $L \subseteq \{a, b, \neg c\}$, we obtain $\mathcal{AS}(\Pi_1) = \mathcal{AS}(\Pi_1^L)$, and otherwise $\mathcal{AS}(\Pi_1^L) = \emptyset$.

3   Counting Supported Models

In our applications mentioned in the introduction, we are interested in counting multiple times under assumptions. Therefore, we extend known techniques from knowledge compilation [3]. The general outline for a given program Π is as follows: (i) we construct the formula comp(Π) that can (ii) be compiled in a computationally expensive step into a formula $\Phi_{comp(\Pi)}$ in a normal form, so-called sd-DNNF by existing knowledge compilers. Then, (iii) on the sd-DNNF $\Phi_{comp(\Pi)}$ counting can be done in polynomial time in the size of $\Phi_{comp(\Pi)}$. We can even count under a set L of propositional assumptions by a technique used as conditioning. However, this approach yields only the number of supported models under assumptions and we overcount compared to the number of answer sets. To this end, in Sect. 4, (iv) we present a technique to incrementally reduce the overcount. First, we recall how knowledge compilation can be used to count formulas under assumptions by assuming that a formula is in sd-DNNF and constructing a counting graph.

Knowledge Compilation [3] and Counting on Formulas in sd-DNNF. Let φ be a formula. φ is in *NNF (negation normal form)* if negations ($\neg$) occur only directly in front of variables and the only other operators are conjunction ($\wedge$) and disjunction ($\vee$). NNFs can be represented in terms of *rooted directed acyclic graphs* (DAGs) where each leaf node is labeled with a literal, and each internal node is labeled with either a conjunction ($\wedge$-*node*) or a disjunction ($\vee$-*node*). We use an NNF and its DAG interchangeably. The *size of an NNF* φ, denoted by $|\varphi|$, is given by the number of edges in its DAG. Formula φ is in *DNNF*, if it is in NNF and it satisfies the *decomposability* property, that is, for any distinct subformulas ψ_i, ψ_j in a conjunction $\psi = \psi_1 \wedge \cdots \wedge \psi_n$ with $i \neq j$, we have vars$(\psi_i) \cap$ vars$(\psi_j) = \emptyset$. φ is in *d-DNNF*, if it is in DNNF and it satisfies the *decision* property, that is, disjunctions are of the form $\psi = (x \wedge \psi_1) \vee (\neg x \wedge \psi_2)$. Note that x does not occur in ψ_1 and ψ_2 because of decomposability. ψ_1 and ψ_2 may be conjunctions. φ is in *sd-DNNF*, if all disjunctions in ψ are smooth, meaning for $\psi = \psi_1 \vee \psi_2$ we have vars$(\psi_1) =$ vars(ψ_2). Determinism and smoothness permit traversal operations on sd-DNNFs to count models of φ in linear time in $|\varphi|$. The traversal takes place on the so called counting graph of an sd-DNNF. The *counting graph* $\mathcal{G}(\varphi)$ is the DAG of φ where each node N is additionally labeled by val$(N) := 1$, if N consists of a literal, labeled by val$(N) := \Sigma_i$ val(N_i), if N is an $\vee$-node with children N_i; labeled by val$(N) := \Pi_i$ val(N_i), if N is an $\wedge$-node. By val$(\mathcal{G}(\varphi))$ we refer to val(N) for the root N of $\mathcal{G}(\varphi)$. Function val can be constructed by traversing $\mathcal{G}(\varphi)$ in post-order in polynomial time. It is well-known that val$(\mathcal{G}(\varphi))$ equals the model count of φ. For a set L of literals, counting of $\varphi^L := \varphi \wedge \bigwedge_{\ell \in L} \ell$ can be carried out by *conditioning* of φ on L [2]. Therefore, the function val on the counting graph is modified by setting val$(N) = 0$, if N consists of ℓ and $\neg \ell \in L$. This corresponds to replacing each literal ℓ of the NNF φ by constant $\bot$ or $\top$, respectively. From now on, we denote by Φ_{Π^L} an equivalent sd-DNNF of comp(Π^L) and its counting graph by $\mathcal{G}_{\Pi^L}$. Note that $\Pi^L = \Pi$ for $L = \emptyset$. The conditioning of $\mathcal{G}_\Pi$ on L is denoted by $(\mathcal{G}_\Pi)^L$.

Example 3. Consider sd-DNNF $\varphi_1 = ((x_3 \wedge \neg c) \vee (\neg x_3 \wedge c)) \wedge (\neg x_1 \wedge \neg x_2 \wedge \neg x_5 \wedge a \wedge b)$. We observe in Fig. 1 that its DAG has 14 nodes, 7 variables and 13 edges, so that $|\varphi_1| = 13$. By conditioning, each variable in L will be removed from $\mathcal{G}(\varphi_1)$ and $\varphi_1 \wedge \neg c = ((x_3 \wedge \neg \bot) \vee (\neg x_3 \wedge \bot)) \wedge (\neg x_1 \wedge \neg x_2 \wedge \neg x_5 \wedge a \wedge b)$. From Fig. 1, we observe that the model count val$(\mathcal{G}(\varphi \wedge \neg c))$ of $\varphi \wedge \neg c$ is 1.

Counting Supported Models. Using the techniques as described above, we can compile the formula comp(Π) into an sd-DNNF $\Phi_{\text{comp}(\Pi)}$ and count the number $|\mathcal{S}(\Pi)|$ of supported models. We illustrate this in the following example.

Example 4. Consider Π_1 from Example 1. When constructing comp(Π_1) in CNF, we obtain 10 clauses with 4 new auxiliary variables x_1, x_2, x_3, x_5. We can compile it into an sd-DNNF Φ_{Π_1} which is logically equivalent to comp(Π_1). For illustration purposes, we chose φ_1 from Example 3 such that Φ_{Π_1} is equivalent to φ_1. Hence, we can obtain the number $|\mathcal{S}(\Pi_1)|$ of supported models from val$(\mathcal{G}_{\Pi_1})$.

3.1 Counting Supported Models Under Assumptions

Since assumptions of formulas and programs slightly differ, it is not immediately clear that we can use conditioning to obtain the number of supported models of a program under given assumptions. However, supported models of Π under assumptions L coincide with models of Φ_{Π^L}.

Observation 1. $\mathcal{M}(\Phi_{\Pi^L}) = \mathcal{S}(\Pi^L)$ *for program Π and assumptions L.*

For any program Π the conditioning $(\Phi_\Pi)^L$ on assumptions L allows us to identify supported models of a program Π^L.

Lemma 1 ($\star^1$). $\mathcal{M}((\Phi_\Pi)^L) = \mathcal{S}(\Pi^L)$ *for program Π and assumptions L.*

Immediately, we obtain that we can count the number of supported models by first compiling the completion into an sd-DNNF and then applying conditioning. For tight programs, this already yields the number of answer sets.

Corollary 1. $\mathrm{val}((\mathcal{G}_\Pi)^L) = |\mathcal{M}((\Phi_\Pi)^L)| = |\mathcal{S}(\Pi^L)|$ *for program Π and assumptions L. If Π is tight, also $\mathrm{val}((\mathcal{G}_\Pi)^L) = |\mathcal{AS}(\Pi^L)|$ holds. Furthermore, counting can be done in time linear in $|\Phi_\Pi|$.*

Example 5 (cont'd). Π_1 has two supported models $\{a, b\}$ and $\{a, b, c\}$. Without setting $\mathrm{val}(c)$ to 0 in Fig. 1, we would obtain 2, which corresponds to these two models. By assumption $\neg c$, we set $\mathrm{val}(c)$ to 0, which results in total count of 1 as the $\wedge$-node (+) gives only one count in the subgraph.

3.2 Compressing Counting Graphs

When computing the counting graph of the completion of a program Π, in practice, we usually construct a CNF of the completion by the well-known Tseitin transformation. It is well-known that there is a one-to-one correspondence, however, auxiliary variables are introduced. For counting, the one-to-one correspondence immediately allows to establish a bijection between the models of the CNF and the supported models making it practicable on CNFs.

However, from Corollary 1, we know that the runtime counting models on $(\mathcal{G}_\Pi)^L$ depends on the size of Φ_Π. In consequence, introducing auxiliary variables affects the runtime of our approach. To this end, we introduce a compressing technique in Algorithm 1 that takes a counting graph $\mathcal{G}_\Pi$ and produces a *compressed counting graph* (CCG) $\tau(\mathcal{G}_\Pi)$, thereby removing auxiliary variables that have been introduced by the Tseitin transformation, which we describe by Algorithm 1. Algorithm 1 takes as input an sd-DNNF Φ_Π, and literals $\mathcal{L}(\Pi)$; and returns the compressed counting graph $\tau(\mathcal{G}_\Pi)$. In Line 2, we check whether the literal node consists of an auxiliary variable, and if so, it will be ignored. The case distinction in Lines 5–7 distinguishes how many not ignored children a non-literal node still has. Remember that each non-literal node is either an $\wedge$-node or an $\vee$-node. In Line 5, the node can be removed, as it has no child.

Algorithm 1. Counting Graph Compression

In: Program Π, sd-DNNF Φ_Π; **Out**: $\tau(\mathcal{G}_\Pi)$

1: initialize array t and traverse nodes $N \in \Phi_\Pi$ bottom-up such that
2:   **if** N contains a literal $\ell \in \mathcal{L}(\Pi)$ **then** label N with val(N)
3:   **else if** N contains a literal $\ell \notin \mathcal{L}(\Pi)$ **then** mark N as `ignored`
4:   **else** check the number of children of N that are not marked as `ignored`
5:     **if** N has no remaining children **then** mark N as `ignored`
6:     **else if** N has one remaining child C **then** $N \leftarrow C$ and mark N as `ignored`
7:     **else** $v \leftarrow$ val(N) w.r.t. t and remaining children of N and label N with v
8:     add N to t
9: remove all nodes marked with `ignored` from t
10: **return** t

In Line 6, the node needs to be absorbed, as it has only one child meaning that the node ultimately becomes its child. In all other cases (Line 7), the node needs to be evaluated on the CCG t such that the ignored nodes are treated as neutral element of the respective sum or product. Ignored nodes are then removed from t. It remains to show that compressing $\mathcal{G}_\Pi$ leaves val unchanged.

Lemma 2 ($\star$). *Let Π be a program, Φ_Π an sd-DNNF of* comp(Π) *after a transformation that preserves the number of models, but introduces auxiliary variables, and $\mathcal{G}_\Pi$ its counting graph. Then,* val($\tau(\mathcal{G}_\Pi)$) $=$ val($\mathcal{G}_\Pi$) *and $\tau(\mathcal{G}_\Pi)$ can be constructed in time $\mathcal{O}(2 \cdot |\Phi_\Pi|)$.*

Corollary 2. *If Π is tight, then* val($\tau(\mathcal{G}_\Pi)$) $= |\mathcal{AS}(\Pi)|$.

4   Incremental Counting by Inclusion-Exclusion

In the previous section, we illustrated how counting on tight programs works and introduced a technique to speed-up practical counting. To count answer sets of a non-tight program, we need to distinguish supported models from answer sets on $\tau(\mathcal{G}_\Pi)$, which can become quite tedious. Therefore, we use the positive dependency graph $DP(\Pi)$ of Π. A set $X \subseteq at(\Pi)$ of atoms is an answer set, whenever it can be derived from Π in a finite number of steps. In particular, the mismatch between answer sets and supported models is caused by cyclic atoms $C \in cycles(\Pi)$ in $DP(\Pi)$ that are not supported by atoms from outside the cycle. We call those supporting atoms of C the *external support* of C.

Definition 1. *Let Π be a program and $r \in \Pi$. An atom $a \in B^+(r)$ is an external support[2] of $C \in cycles(\Pi)$, whenever $H(r) \subseteq C$ and $a \notin C$. By $ES(C)$ we denote the set of all external supports of C.*

Next, we illustrate the effect of external supports on the answer sets derivation.

---

[2] Note that external supports are sets of literals. However, we can simulate such a set by introducing an auxiliary atom; hence one atom, as in this definition, is sufficient [7].

Example 6. Let $\Pi_2 = \{a \leftarrow b; b \leftarrow a; a \leftarrow c; c \leftarrow \neg d; d \leftarrow \neg c\}$. We obtain a cycle $C = \{a, b\}$ due to rules $a \leftarrow b$ and $b \leftarrow a$ with external support $ES(C) = \{c\}$ due to rule $a \leftarrow c$. However, due to rules $c \leftarrow \neg d$ and $d \leftarrow \neg c$, we see that whenever d is true, c is false, so that d deactivates the support of C, which means that $\{a, b, d\}$ cannot be derived from Π_2 in a finite number of steps. Accordingly, we have $\mathcal{S}(\Pi_2) = \{\{a, b, c\}, \{a, b, d\}, \{d\}\}$, but $\mathcal{AS}(\Pi_2) = \{\{a, b, c\}, \{d\}\}$.

Example 7. Let $a \leftarrow b$, $b \leftarrow a$, and $b \leftarrow c, \neg d$ be rules. Then the external support of cyclic atoms $\{a, b\}$ is $\{c, \neg d\}$. If instead of $b \leftarrow c, \neg d$ we use two alternative rules $b_r \leftarrow c, \neg d$ and $b \leftarrow b_r$, we have $ES(\{a, b\}) = \{b_r\}$, see Footnote (see Footnote 2).

To approach the answer set count of a non-tight program under assumptions, we employ the well-known *inclusion-exclusion principle*, which is a counting technique to determine the number of elements in a finite union of finite sets $X_1, \ldots, X_n$. Therefore, first the cardinalities of the singletons are summed up. Then, to compensate for potential overcounting, the cardinalities of all intersections of two sets are subtracted. Next, the number of elements that appear in at least three sets are added back, i.e., the cardinality of the intersection of all three sets – to compensate for potential undercounting – and so on. As an example, for three sets X_1, X_2, X_3 the procedure can be expressed as $|X_1 \cup X_2 \cup X_3| = |X_1| + |X_2| + |X_3| - |X_1 \cap X_2| - |X_1 \cap X_2| - |X_2 \cap X_3| + |X_1 \cap X_2 \cap X_3|$. This principle can be used to count answer sets via supported model counting.

We define the *unsupported constraint* $\lambda(C)$ for a set $C = \{c_0, \ldots, c_n\} \in cycles(\Pi)$ of cyclic atoms and its resp. external supports $ES(C) = \{s_0, \ldots, s_m\}$ by $\lambda(C) := \bot \leftarrow c_0, \ldots, c_n, \neg s_0, \ldots, \neg s_m$. The unsupported constraints as defined here contain the whole set C, which is slightly weaker than constraints (nogoods) defined in related work [7], but sufficient for characterizing answer sets.

Lemma 3 ($\star$). *For any given program Π where $C_i \in cycles(\Pi)$ and $1 \leq i \leq n$, we have that $\mathcal{AS}(\Pi) = \mathcal{S}(\Pi \cup \{\lambda(C_1), \ldots, \lambda(C_n)\})$.*

Before we discuss our approach on incremental answer set counting, we need some further notation. From now on, by $\Lambda_d(\Pi) := \{\{\lambda(C_1), \ldots, \lambda(C_d)\} \mid \{C_1, \ldots, C_d\} \subseteq cycles(\Pi)\}$ we denote the set of all combinations of unsupported constraints of cycles that occur in any subset of $cycles(\Pi)$ with cardinality $0 \leq d \leq n$, where $n := |cycles(\Pi)|$. Now, we define the approach of $|\mathcal{AS}(\Pi^L)|$ by a_d^L, using the combinatorial principle of inclusion-exclusion as follows:

$$a_d^L := \sum_{i=0}^{d} (-1)^i \sum_{\Gamma \in \Lambda_i(\Pi)} |\mathcal{S}(\Pi^L \cup \Gamma)| = |\mathcal{S}(\Pi^L)| - \sum_{\Gamma \in \Lambda_1(\Pi)} |\mathcal{S}(\Pi^L \cup \Gamma)|$$

$$+ \sum_{\Gamma \in \Lambda_2(\Pi)} |\mathcal{S}(\Pi^L \cup \Gamma)| - \cdots + (-1)^d \sum_{\Gamma \in \Lambda_d(\Pi)} |\mathcal{S}(\Pi^L \cup \Gamma)|$$

By subtracting $|\mathcal{S}(\Pi^L \cup \Gamma)|$ for each $\Gamma \in \Lambda_1(\Pi)$ we subtract the number of supported models that are *not answer sets* under assumptions L with respect to each cycle $C \in cycles(\Pi)$. However, we need to take into account the interaction of cycles and their respective external supports under assumptions L. Thus we enter the first alternation step, where we proceed by adding back $|\mathcal{S}(\Pi^L \cup \Gamma)|$

Algorithm 2. Incremental Counting by Anytime Refinement

In: program Π; assumptions L; compressed counting graph $\tau(\mathcal{G}_\Pi)$; alternation depth d; **Out:** a_d^L

1: count $\leftarrow$ val$(\tau(\mathcal{G}_\Pi)^L)$ and $c \leftarrow 0$
2: **if** d is odd **then** $d \leftarrow d + 1$
3: **for** every $1 \leq i \leq d$
4:      **if** $c =$ count **then** break **else** $c \leftarrow$ count
5:      **for** every $1 \leq j \leq i$
6:          $c' \leftarrow$ val$(\tau(\mathcal{G}_\Pi)^{L \cup L'})$ where L' is the set of literals appearing in $\Gamma_j \in \Lambda_i(\Pi)$
7:          count $\leftarrow$ count $- c'$ **if** i is odd **otherwise** count $\leftarrow$ count $+ c'$
8: **return** count

---

for each $\Gamma \in \Lambda_2(\Pi)$, which means that we add back the number of supported models that were mistakenly subtracted from $|\mathcal{S}(\Pi^L)|$ in the previous step, and so on, until we went through all Λ_i where $0 \leq i \leq d$. Note that therefore in total we have d alternations. In general, we show that $a_n^L = |\mathcal{AS}(\Pi^L)|$ as follows.

Theorem 1 ($\star$). *Let Π be a program, cycles$(\Pi) = \{C_1, \ldots, C_n\}$, and further $U := \{\lambda(C_1), \ldots, \lambda(C_n)\}$ be the set of all unsupported constraints of Π. Then, $|\mathcal{S}(\Pi^L \cup U)| = \sum_{i=0}^{n}(-1)^i \sum_{\Gamma \in \Lambda_i(\Pi)} |\mathcal{S}(\Pi^L \cup \Gamma)|$ for assumptions L.*

Finally, one can count answer sets correctly.

Corollary 3 ($\star$). *Let $n = |cycles(\Pi)|$. Then, $a_n^L = |\mathcal{AS}(\Pi^L)|$ for program Π and assumptions L.*

In fact, we can characterize a_n^L with respect to alternation depths. If there is no change from one alternation to another, the point is reached where the number of answer sets is obtained, as the following lemma states.

Lemma 4 ($\star$). *Let Π be a program and L be assumptions. If $a_i^L = a_{i+1}^L$ for some integer $i \geq 0$, then $a_i^L = |\mathcal{AS}(\Pi^L)|$.*

Using our approach on computing a_n^L, we end up with 2^n (supported model) counting operations where $n := |cycles(\Pi)|$ on the respective compressed counting graph $\tau(\mathcal{G}_\Pi)$, which, since counting is linear in $k := |\tau(\mathcal{G}(\Pi))|$, gives us that approaching the answer set count under assumptions is by $2^n \cdot k$ exponential in time. However, we can restrict the alternation depth to d such that $0 \leq d < n$ in order to stop after $\Lambda_d(\Pi)$. Then we need to count n times for each cycle and its respective unsupported constraints and another $\binom{n}{i}$ times for $1 < i \leq d$, that is, for each number of subsets of cycles and their respective unsupported constraints with cardinality i. These considerations yield the following result.

Theorem 2. *Let Π be a program, L be assumptions, and $0 \leq d \leq n$ with $n := |cycles(\Pi)|$. We can compute a_d^L in time $\mathcal{O}(m \cdot |\tau(\mathcal{G}(\Pi))|)$ where $m = \sum_{i \leq d} \binom{n}{i}$.*

Note that if we choose an even d, we will stop on adding back, potentially overcounting, and otherwise we will stop on subtracting, potentially undercounting. Algorithm 2 ensures that we end on an add-operation to avoid undercounting in Line 2. Furthermore, it uses Lemma 4 as a termination criterion in Line 4.

Table 1. Runtimes of compiling input program to an NNF when directly counting answer sets (sat), counting supported models (comp), compressing counting graphs (T) and approaching the answer set count (A) under assumptions with specified alternation depth (d) of several instances with varying numbers of simple cycles (#SC) and supported models ($\#\mathcal{S}$), sd-DNNF sizes (NNF size) and CCG sizes (CCG size). Depths marked with * indicates restricting alternation depths. IASCAR# corresponds to the approximation of the number of answer sets.

Instance	sat[s]	comp[s]	NNF size	T[s]	CCG size	$\#\mathcal{S}$	#SC	d	IASCAR#	A[s]
8_queens	5.2	4.5	48,791	0.0	3,490	$9.200 \cdot 10^1$	0	0	$0.000 \cdot 10^0$	0.0
10_queens	9.7	6.9	532,645	0.0	31,172	$7.240 \cdot 10^2$	0	0	$1.200 \cdot 10^1$	0.0
12_queens	**95.6**	**46.0**	**12,529,332**	**0.7**	**649,354**	$1.420 \cdot 10^4$	0	0	$7.500 \cdot 10^1$	0.1
3x3_grid	5.7	4.5	788,711	0.1	210,893	$3.629 \cdot 10^5$	0	0	$7.200 \cdot 10^2$	0.0
AF_stable	3.0	2.9	11,141	0.0	3,284	$7.696 \cdot 10^3$	0	0	$3.080 \cdot 10^3$	0.0
3_coloring	8.5	7.2	6,677	0.0	2,839	$1.026 \cdot 10^{17}$	0	0	$3.028 \cdot 10^{16}$	0.0
arb_2_coloring	0.4	0.4	1,061	0.0	446	$5.193 \cdot 10^{33}$	0	0	$6.490 \cdot 10^{32}$	0.0
simple	1.3	0.1	90	0.0	59	$1.400 \cdot 10^1$	3	3	$0.000 \cdot 10^0$	0.0
nrp_accenture	6.0	0.3	119	0.0	84	$6.000 \cdot 10^0$	5	5	$0.000 \cdot 10^0$	0.0
nrp_autorit	6.6	0.4	166	0.0	123	$1.600 \cdot 10^1$	5	5	$4.000 \cdot 10^1$	0.0
nrp_california	**12.8**	**0.5**	**201**	**0.0**	**133**	$8.000 \cdot 10^0$	**15**	**15**	$0.000 \cdot 10^0$	**0.5**
nrp_hanoi	**280.2**	**4.1**	**4,119**	**0.0**	**3,128**	$1.017 \cdot 10^{14}$	**77**	***2**	$3.197 \cdot 10^{12}$	**0.3**
nrp_berkshire	**311.3**	**2.7**	**10,626**	**0.0**	**7,914**	$1.162 \cdot 10^{13}$	**206**	***2**	$0.000 \cdot 10^0$	**5.0**
nrp_benton	20.4	0.7	642	0.0	446	$5.200 \cdot 10^1$	38	*2	$0.000 \cdot 10^0$	0.0
nrp_bart	105.1	2.1	1,645	0.0	1,223	$2.295 \cdot 10^7$	46	*2	$5.767 \cdot 10^6$	0.1
nrp_aircoach	253.8	3.2	8,874	0.0	6,667	$8.563 \cdot 10^{11}$	130	*2	$0.000 \cdot 10^0$	1.6
nrp_a1210993	64.7	1.6	1,280	0.0	954	$3.642 \cdot 10^5$	29	*2	$0.000 \cdot 10^0$	0.0
nrp_kyoto	0.0	0.0	57	0.0	38	$2.000 \cdot 10^0$	2	2	$0.000 \cdot 10^0$	0.0

Example 8. Let $\Pi_3 = \Pi_2 \cup \{b \leftarrow g; f \leftarrow g; e \leftarrow f; f \leftarrow e\}$, which has 2 cycles $C_0 = \{a, b\}$ and $C_1 = \{e, f\}$. Their corresponding external supports are $ES(C_0) = \{c, g\}$ and $ES(C_1) = \{g\}$. Program Π_3 has 6 supported models $\{\{d\}, \{d, e, f\}, \{a, b, d\}, \{a, b, c\}, \{a, b, c, e, f\}, \{a, b, d, e, f\}\}$ of which $\{d\}$ and $\{a, b, c\}$ are answer sets. Suppose we want to determine $a_1^{\{d\}}$, then: $a_1^{\{d\}} = |\mathcal{S}(\Pi^{\{d\}})| - |\mathcal{S}(\Pi^{\{d\}} \cup \{\bot \leftarrow a, b, \neg c, \neg g\})| - |\mathcal{S}(\Pi^{\{d\}} \cup \{\bot \leftarrow e, f, \neg g\})| = 4 - 2 - 2 = 0$. We see that restricting the alternation depth to 1, leads to undercounting. However, not restricting the depth leads to the exact count as: $a_2^{\{d\}} = a_1^{\{d\}} + |\mathcal{S}(\Pi^{\{d\}} \cup \{\bot \leftarrow a, b, \neg c, \neg g; \bot \leftarrow e, f, \neg g\})| = 0 + 1 = 1 = |\mathcal{AS}(\Pi_3^{\{d\}})|$.

5 Preliminary Empirical Evaluation

To demonstrate the capability of our approach, we implemented a prototypical system, called IASCAR. The system binary is publicly available for download[3]. Our system counts on CCGs constructed from sd-DNNFs. Therefore, we implement Algorithms 1 and 2, which first construct a CCG and then count based on

---

[3] See https://tinyurl.com/iascar-b for a Linux binary, instances, and raw data.
gringo cuts off trivial supported models when grounding, not affecting us here.

the inclusion-exclusion technique. However, for simplicity in our experiments we use IASCAR only on simple cycles, i.e., only first and last vertex repeat. While in theory, as stated in Corollary 3, we need to take all cycles into account to obtain an exact result, our use of IASCAR *approximates by overcounting*.

In order to obtain the CCGs, we use a chain that consists of (a) constructing a positive dependency graph from ground input program and encoding simple cycles as unsupported constraints for later use separately; (b) converting extended rules of the ground input program (gringo) into normal rules (lp2normal); (c) constructing as CNF the completion of the resulting program (lp2sat); and (d) compiling CNF into an (sd-D)NNF (c2d). Alternatively, when converting programs into CNF instances for directly counting the number of answer sets, we insert a Step (b1) after (b) which adds loop formulas (lp2atomic) and obtain the count after Step (d) without using IASCAR.

We design a small experiment to study the questions: (1) are modern knowledge compilers capable of outputting sd-DNNFs that allow for counting supported models or can we even output sd-DNNFs that allow for counting answer sets; (2) do we benefit from counting on sd-DNNFs when counting many times for counting under assumptions; (3) how much do we benefit from our approach to systematically reduce overcounting.

We take instances that encode a prototypical ASP domain with reachability (nrp_*) and use of transitive closure [4] containing cycles. This problem distinguishes from simple SAT for which we could use knowledge compilers without encoding a program into CNF by using level mappings or loop formulas. Therefore, we take as instances real-world graphs of public transport networks from all over the world, which were used in the PACE'16 and '17 challenges. In addition, we chose the well-known n-queens problem for $n \in \{8, 10, 12\}$; a sudoku sub-grid (3x3_grid) that has to be filled uniquely with numbers from 1 to 9; an encoding for stable extensions of an argumentation framework instance (AF_stable) [5]; the 3-coloring problem on a graph (3_coloring); an encoding that ensures arbitrary 2-coloring for the same graph (arb_2_coloring). These instances admit no simple cycles. In general, the instances result in varying NNF sizes, CCG sizes, and number of simple cycles, answer sets and supported models. Prototypical problems benefiting from counting many times are probabilistic settings or navigation problems. These domains are quite unexplored due to absence of ASP systems, and to the best of our knowledge, there are no standard benchmark sets for counting under assumptions. For counting under assumptions, we selected a small number of atoms (3) in the program to keep it consistent and having a sufficiently high number of solutions. We selected uniform at random.

We ran the experiments on an 8-core intel I7-10510U CPU 1.8 GHz with 16 GB of RAM on Manjaro Linux 21.1.1 (Kernel 5.10.59-1-MANJARO). We follow standard guidelines for empirical evaluations; runtime is measured by perf.

Before we state the results, we formulate expectations from the design of experiment and our theoretical understanding. (E1): We anticipate limitations of counting answer sets when compiling plain level encodings/loop formulas, as generating sd-DNNF takes long. (E2.1): Compressing the counting graph can significantly reduce its size and works fast. (E2.2): The runtime of IASCAR depends on the number of cycles and size of the CCG due to the structural parameter of the underlying algorithm. (E2.3): Counting works fast on instances with few cycles. Otherwise, depth restriction makes our approach utilizable. (E3): There are instances on which simple cycles are insufficient for counting answer sets.

We summarize our results in Table 1. (O1): From column sat[s], we can see that constructing an sd-DNNF of a CNF, which encodes answer sets of an input program, and subsequent counting varies notably. For example, on smaller instances such as 8_queens, 3x3_grid, or arb_2_coloring, we can compile and count answer sets in reasonable time. Whereas on instances such as nrp_california, nrp_hanoi, or nrp_berkshire we observe a high runtime; in particular, there we see that sd-DNNFs can become quite large. By correlating this observation with column #S, we can see that instances, which can be solved fast, have no simple cycles. This matches with our expectation E1 and the knowledge on how CNFs are generated from a program as cycles are a primary source of hardness in ASP. Unsurprisingly, compiling CNFs without level encodings/loop formulas, as stated in column comp[s], works much faster. This is particularly visible for instances nrp_california, nrp_hanoi, nrp_berkshire, nrp_bart, nrp_aircoach, or nrp_a1210993. (O2): From column T[s], we can see that compressing the counting graph can significantly reduce its size. On many instances, we see a reduction by one order, for example, 10_queens by factor 17.1, 12_queens by 19.3, 3x3_grid by 3.7, or AF_stable by 3.4. This confirms Expectation (E2.1). However, compressing instances with a large number of cycles, such as nrp_berkshire, is less effective than on those with a small number of cycles, such as nrp_kyoto and 12_queens. (O3): From columns #SC, depth, and A[s], we can see that the runtime depends on both parameters. A medium number of simple cycles and depth effects the runtime; similar to high number of simple cycles and small depth. Still, with a high number of simple cycles and a small depth, we can obtain the count under assumption sufficiently fast. This partially confirms our Expectation (E2.2). Interestingly, the size of the CCG itself has a much less impact than anticipated, see instance 12_queens. (O4): The runtime, as stated in column A[s], indicates that we can still obtain a reasonable count for instances, which ran with restricted depth, marked by *; see for example nrp_hanoi, nrp_aircoach, or nrp_berkshire. Restricting depth d to 2 led to overcounting for instance nrp_hanoi. (O5): Finally, there is one instance, namely, nrp_autorit, for which we overcounted by 3 when restricting to simple cycles, which confirms Expectation (E3). However, on all other instances, we obtained the exact number of answer sets.

The evaluation indicates that our approach clearly pays off on instances containing reasonably many cycles. In particular, we see promising results when counting under assumptions, clearly benefiting from knowledge compilation.

6   Conclusion and Future Work

We establish a novel technique for counting answer sets under assumptions combining ideas from knowledge compilation and combinatorial solving. Knowledge compilation and known transformations of ASP programs into CNF formulas already provide us with a basic toolbox for counting answer sets. However, compilations suffer from an overhead when constructing CNFs. One can view our approach similar to propagation-based solving when searching for one solution. We construct compilations that allow reasoning for supported models and apply a combinatorial principle to count answer sets. Our approach gradually reduces overcounting that we obtain when simply considering supported models. Further, we introduce domain specific simplification techniques on counting graphs.

We expect our technique to be useful for navigating answer sets or answering probabilistic questions on ASP programs, requiring counting under assumptions. For future work, we plan to investigate techniques to reduce the size of compilations for supported models, which can in fact already be a bottleneck due to the added clauses modeling the support of an atom. There, domain specific preprocessing or an alternative compilation could be promising. A large scale in-depth analysis of benefits of various counting techniques, such as enumeration on instances with few expected answer sets, approximations if one needs to count only once, or knowledge compilations could be fruitful for users. From the theoretical side, questions on effectiveness of knowledge compilations in ASP might be interesting similar to considerations for formulas [3].

Acknowledgements. Research was funded by the DFG through the Collaborative Research Center, Grant TRR 248 project ID 389792660, the BMBF, Grant 01IS20056_NAVAS, the Vienna Science and Technology Fund (WWTF) grant ICT19-065, and the Austrian Science Fund (FWF) grants P32830 and Y698.

References

1. Bogaerts, B., den Broeck, G.V.: Knowledge compilation of logic programs using approximation fixpoint theory. TPLP **15**(4–5), 464–480 (2015)
2. Darwiche, A.: Compiling knowledge into decomposable negation normal form. In: IJCAI 1999, pp. 284–289. Morgan Kaufmann (1999)
3. Darwiche, A., Marquis, P.: A knowledge compilation map. J. Artif. Intell. Res. **17**, 229–264 (2002)
4. Eiter, T., Hecher, M., Kiesel, R.: Treewidth-aware cycle breaking for algebraic answer set counting. In: KR 2021, vol. 18, pp. 269–279 (2021)
5. Fichte, J.K., Gaggl, S.A., Rusovac, D.: Rushing and strolling among answer sets - navigation made easy. In: AAAI 2022 (2022)
6. Fierens, D., et al.: Inference and learning in probabilistic logic programs using weighted Boolean formulas. TPLP **15**(3), 358–401 (2015)
7. Gebser, M., Kaufmann, B., Schaub, T.: Conflict-driven answer set solving: From theory to practice. Artif. Intell. **187–188**, 52–89 (2012)
8. Kabir, M., Everardo, F., Shukla, A., Fichte, J.K., Hecher, M., Meel, K.: ApproxASP - a scalable approximate answer set counter. In: AAAI 2022 (2022, in Press)

9. Lagniez, J.M., Marquis, P.: An improved decision-DDNF compiler. In: IJCAI 2017, pp. 667–673. The AAAI Press (2017)

10. Lifschitz, V., Razborov, A.: Why are there so many loop formulas? ACM Trans. Comput. Log. **7**(2), 261–268 (2006)

11. Marek, V.W., Truszczyński, M.: Stable models and an alternative logic programming paradigm. In: Apt, K.R., Marek, V.W., Truszczynski, M., Warren, D.S. (eds.) The Logic Programming Paradigm, pp. 375–398. Springer, Heidelberg (1999). https://doi.org/10.1007/978-3-642-60085-2_17

12. Sang, T., Beame, P., Kautz, H.: Performing Bayesian inference by weighted model counting. In: AAAI 2005. The AAAI Press (2005)

13. Wang, Y., Lee, J.: Handling uncertainty in answer set programming. In: AAAI 2015, pp. 4218–4219. The AAAI Press (2015)

Reasoning About Actions with $\mathcal{EL}$ Ontologies and Temporal Answer Sets for DLTL

Laura Giordano[1], Alberto Martelli[2], and Daniele Theseider Dupré[1(✉)]

[1] DISIT, Università del Piemonte Orientale, Alessandria, Italy
{laura.giordano,dtd}@uniupo.it
[2] Dipartimento di Informatica, Università di Torino, Torino, Italy
mrt@di.unito.it

Abstract. We propose an approach for reasoning about actions with domain descriptions including an $\mathcal{EL}^{\perp}$ ontology in a temporal action theory. The action theory is based on a Dynamic Linear Time Temporal Logic, whose extensions are defined through temporal answer sets. The work provides conditions under which action consistency can be guaranteed with respect to an $\mathcal{EL}^{\perp}$ ontology, by polynomially encoding an $\mathcal{EL}^{\perp}$ knowledge base into a domain description of the temporal action theory.

1 Introduction

The integration of description logics and action formalisms has gained a lot of interest in the past years [2,5,6,13]. In this paper we explore the combination of a temporal action logic [22] and $\mathcal{EL}^{\perp}$ ontologies [3], with the aim of allowing reasoning about action execution in the presence of the constraints given by an $\mathcal{EL}^{\perp}$ knowledge base.

As usual in many formalisms integrating Description Logics (DLs) and action languages [2,6,7,13], we regard inclusions in the KB as state constraints of the action theory, which we expect to be satisfied in all states resulting after action execution. In the literature of reasoning about actions it is well known that causal laws and their interplay with domain constraints are crucial for solving the ramification problem [14,20,25,31,33,34]. When domain knowledge is expressed in a description logic, the issue has been considered, e.g., in [5] where causal laws are used to ensure the consistency with the TBox (the set of terminological axioms) of the resulting state, after action execution. For instance, given a TBox containing $\exists Teaches.Course \sqsubseteq Teacher$, and an ABox (i.e., a set of assertions on individuals) containing the assertion $Course(math)$, an action which adds the assertion $Teaches(john, math)$, without also adding $Teacher(john)$, will not give rise to a consistent next state with respect to the knowledge base. The addition of the causal law **caused** $Teacher(john)$ **if** $Teaches(john, math) \wedge Course(math)$ would force, for instance, the above TBox inclusion to be satisfied in the resulting state.

The approach by Baader et al. [5] uses causal relationships to deal with the ramification problem in an action formalism based on description logics; it exploits a semantics in the style of Winslett's [35] and McCain and Turner's [33] fixpoint semantics. In this paper, we aim at extending this approach to reason about actions with an $\mathcal{EL}^\perp$ ontology with *temporal answer sets*, building on previous work [22,23] defining a temporal logic programming language for reasoning about *complex actions* and *infinite computations*. This language, besides the usual LTL operators, allows for general Dynamic Linear Time Temporal Logic (DLTL) formulas [28] to be included in domain descriptions to constrain the space of possible extensions. In [22], *temporal answer sets* for domain descriptions are proposed as a generalization of *answer sets* [18], and a translation to ASP is provided; a *bounded model checking (BMC) technique* is used for the verification of DLTL constraints, extending the approach developed by Helianko and Niemela [27] for bounded LTL model checking with Stable Models. An alternative ASP translation is investigated in [23], with a BMC approach exploiting the Büchi automaton construction to achieve completeness. Our temporal action logic has been shown to be related to extensions of the $\mathcal{A}$ language [8,10,15,19,25]. Its LTL fragment also relates to the recent temporal extension of Clingo, *telingo* [11], dealing with finite computations, and with the LTL fragment of Temporal Equilibrium Logic (TEL), as the restriction of TEL to the rule based case leads to a linear-time temporal ASP [16].

The paper studies *extended temporal action theories*, combining the temporal action logic mentioned above with an $\mathcal{EL}^\perp$ ontology. It is shown that, for $\mathcal{EL}^\perp$ knowledge bases in normal form, the consistency of the action theory extensions with the ontology can be assured by adding to the action theory a set of causal laws and state constraints, by exploiting the fragment for $\mathcal{EL}^\perp$ of the materialization calculus by Krötzsch [29]. Sufficient conditions on the action theory can be defined to repair the states resulting from action execution and guarantee consistency with TBox. To this purpose, for each inclusion axiom in TBox, a suitable set of causal laws can be added to the action theory. Our approach provides a polynomial encoding of an action theory, extended with an $\mathcal{EL}^\perp$ ontology, into the language of the (DLTL) temporal action logic studied in [22]. The proof methods for this temporal action logic, based on bounded model checking in ASP, can then be exploited for reasoning about actions in the extended action theory.

A preliminary version of the work was presented in the ICLP 2021 workshops [1].

2   The Description Logic $\mathcal{EL}^\perp$

We consider a fragment of the logic $\mathcal{EL}^{++}$ [3] that, for simplicity of presentation, does not include role inclusions and concrete domains. The fragment, let us call it $\mathcal{EL}^\perp$, includes the concept $\perp$ (the inconsistent concept) as well as nominals $\{a\}$.

We let N_C be a set of concept names, N_R a set of role names and N_I a set of individual names. Concepts in $\mathcal{EL}^\perp$ are defined inductively as $C := A \mid \top \mid \perp \mid C \sqcap C \mid \exists r.C \mid \{a\}$, where $a \in N_I$, $A \in N_C$ and $r \in N_R$; $\{a\}$ is the concept only containing a. Complement, disjunction and universal restriction are not allowed.

A knowledge base K is a pair $(\mathcal{T}, \mathcal{A})$, where $\mathcal{T}$ is a TBox containing a finite set of concept inclusions $C_1 \sqsubseteq C_2$ and $\mathcal{A}$ is an ABox containing assertions of the form $C(a)$ and $r(a, b)$, where C, C_1, C_2 concepts, $r \in N_R$ and $a, b \in N_I$.

We will assume that the TBox is in normal form [4]. Let BC_K be the smallest set of concepts containing $\top$, all the concept names occurring in K and all nominals $\{a\}$, for any individual name a occurring in K. An inclusion is in *normal form* if it has one of the following forms: $C_1 \sqsubseteq D$, $C_1 \sqcap C_2 \sqsubseteq D$, $C_1 \sqsubseteq \exists r.C_2$, $\exists r.C_2 \sqsubseteq D$, where $C_1, C_2 \in BC_K$, and $D \in BC_K \cup \{\bot\}$. In [4] it is shown that any TBox can be normalized in linear time, by introducing new concept and role names.

In the following we will denote with $N_{C,K}$, $N_{R,K}$ and $N_{I,K}$ the (finite) sets of concept names, role names and individual names occurring in K.

Definition 1 (Interpretations and models). *An interpretation in $\mathcal{EL}^{\bot}$ is any structure $(\Delta^I, \cdot^I)$ where: Δ^I is a domain; $\cdot^I$ is an interpretation function that maps each concept name A to set $A^I \subseteq \Delta^I$, each role name r to a binary relation $r^I \subseteq \Delta^I \times \Delta^I$, and each individual name a to an element $a^I \in \Delta^I$. Furthermore: $\top^I = \Delta^I$, $\bot^I = \emptyset$; $\{a\}^I = \{a^I\}$; $(C \sqcap D)^I = C^I \cap D^I$; $(\exists r.C)^I = \{x \in \Delta \mid \exists y \in C^I : (x, y) \in r^I\}$. An interpretation $(\Delta^I, \cdot^I)$ satisfies an inclusion $C \sqsubseteq D$ if $C^I \subseteq D^I$; it satisfies an assertion $C(a)$ if $a^I \in C^I$; it satisfies an assertion $r(a, b)$ if $(a^I, b^I) \in r^I$.*

Given a knowledge base $K = (\mathcal{T}, \mathcal{A})$, an interpretation $(\Delta^I, \cdot^I)$ is a model of $\mathcal{T}$ if $(\Delta^I, \cdot^I)$ satisfies all inclusions in $\mathcal{T}$; $(\Delta^I, \cdot^I)$ is a model of K if $(\Delta^I, \cdot^I)$ satisfies all inclusions in $\mathcal{T}$ and all assertions in $\mathcal{A}$. $\mathcal{A}$ is consistent with $\mathcal{T}$ if there is a model of $\mathcal{T}$ satisfying all the assertions in $\mathcal{A}$.

3 Temporal Action Theories in DLTL and Temporal Answer Sets

In this paper we refer to the notion of the temporal action theory in [21], a rule based fragment of which has been studied in [22,23]; it exploits the dynamic extension of LTL called Dynamic Linear Time Temporal Logic (DLTL) [28]. In DLTL the next state modality is indexed by actions and the until operator $\mathcal{U}^{\pi}$ is indexed by a program π which, as in PDL, can be any regular expression (*complex action*) built from atomic actions in a finite non-empty set Σ, using sequence (;), nondeterministic choice (+) and finite iteration (*). The derived modalities $\langle\pi\rangle$ and $[\pi]$ can be defined as: $\langle\pi\rangle\alpha \equiv \top\mathcal{U}^{\pi}\alpha$ and $[\pi]\alpha \equiv \neg\langle\pi\rangle\neg\alpha$. Similarly, $\bigcirc$ (next), $\Diamond$ and $\Box$ operators of LTL can be defined.

A *domain description* Π is a set of laws describing the effects of actions and their executability preconditions. Atomic propositions describing the state of the domain are called *fluents*. Actions may have direct effects, described by action laws, and indirect effects, described by causal laws capturing the causal dependencies among fluents.

Let $\mathcal{L}$ be a first order language which includes a finite number of constants and variables, but no function symbol. Let $\mathcal{P}$ be the set of predicate symbols, Var the set of variables and $Cons$ the set of constant symbols. We call *fluents* atomic literals of the form $p(t_1, \ldots, t_n)$, where, for each i, $t_i \in Var \cup Cons$. A *simple fluent literal* (or *s-literal*) l is an atomic literals $p(t_1, \ldots, t_n)$ or its negation $\neg p(t_1, \ldots, t_n)$. We denote by Lit_S the set of all simple fluent literals. Lit_T is the set of *temporal fluent literals*: if $l \in Lit_S$, then $[a]l, \bigcirc l \in Lit_T$, where a is an action name (an atomic proposition, possibly containing variables), and $[a]$ and $\bigcirc$ are the temporal operators introduced in the previous paragraph. Let $Lit = Lit_S \cup Lit_T \cup \{\bot, \top\}$, where $\bot$ represents the inconsistency and $\top$ truth. A (simple or temporal) fluent literal l, and its negation *not* l (representing the default negation of l) are called *extended fluent literals*.

The laws are formulated as rules of a temporally extended logic programming language. Rules have the form $\Box(l_0 \leftarrow l_1, \ldots, l_m, not\ l_{m+1}, \ldots, not\ l_n)$, where the l_i's are either simple or temporal fluent literals, with the following restrictions: (i) If l_0 is a simple literal, then the body cannot contain temporal literals; (ii) If $l_0 = [a]l$, then the temporal literals in the body must have the form $[a]l'$; (iii) If $l_0 = \bigcirc l$, then the temporal literals in the body must have the form $\bigcirc l'$. As usual in ASP, the rules with variables will be used as a shorthand for the set of their ground instances.

In the following we use of a notion of *state*: a set of ground fluent literals. A state is said to be *consistent* if it is not the case that both f and $\neg f$ belong to the state, or that $\bot$ belongs to the state. A state is said to be *complete* if, for each fluent f, either f or $\neg f$ belong to the state. The execution of an action in a state may possibly change the values of fluents in the state through its direct and indirect effects, thus giving rise to a new state. While the law above can be applied in all states, a law

$$l_0 \leftarrow l_1, \ldots, l_m, not\ l_{m+1}, \ldots, not\ l_n$$

which is not prefixed by $\Box$, only applies to the initial state.

The following action laws describe the deterministic effects of actions $assign(y, x)$, of assigning a course to a teacher, and $retire(x)$, of retiring from work (rules with variables stand for all their propositional groundings, as usual in ASP):

$$\Box([assign(y,x)]teaches(x,y) \leftarrow course(y)) \qquad\qquad \Box[retire(x)]\neg teacher(x)$$

The following precondition law: $\Box([assign(y,x)]\bot \leftarrow not\ likes(x,y))$ specifies that y cannot be assigned to x, if x does not like y.

The following program $\pi(x,y)$ repeatedly tries to convince that course y is a good choice for x, until either x likes y and y is assigned to x, or the assignment is rejected:

$$(\neg likes(x,y)?; convince(x,y))^*; (likes(x,y)?; assign(x,y)+reject(x,y)?)$$

where $(likes(x,y)?$ and $(\neg likes(x,y)?$ are test actions (only executable if the corresponding fluent holds, see [22]). The constraint $\Diamond\langle\pi(a,c)\rangle\top$ can, e.g., be included in the set of temporal constraints $\mathcal{C}$, meaning that all runs must eventually include an execution of $\pi(a,c)$. Nondeterministic actions can be represented using default negation, e.g., $\Box([flip]head \leftarrow not\ [flip]\neg tail)$ and $\Box([flip]\neg tail \leftarrow not\ [flip]head)$. *Static* and *dynamic causal laws* (see below), similar to the ones in the action languages $\mathcal{K}$ [15] and $\mathcal{C}^+$ [25], can represent different kinds of causal dependencies among fluents.

The semantics of a domain description has been defined based on *temporal answer sets* [22,23], extending the notion of *answer set* [17] to the linear structure of temporal models. In the following, we consider the ground instantiations of the domain description Π, and we denote by Σ the set of ground instances of the action names in Π.

A temporal interpretation is defined as a pair (σ, S), where $\sigma \in \Sigma^\omega$ is a sequence of actions and S is a consistent set of ground literals of the form $[a_1; \ldots; a_k]l$, where $a_1 \ldots a_k$ is a prefix of σ and l is a ground simple fluent literal, meaning that l holds in the state obtained by executing $a_1 \ldots a_k$. S is *consistent* iff it is not the case that both $[a_1; \ldots; a_k]l \in S$ and $[a_1; \ldots; a_k]\neg l \in S$, for some l, or $[a_1; \ldots; a_k]\bot \in S$. A temporal interpretation (σ, S) is said to be *total* if either $[a_1; \ldots; a_k]p \in S$ or $[a_1; \ldots; a_k]\neg p \in S$, for each $a_1 \ldots a_k$ prefix of σ and for each fluent name p.

We define the *satisfiability of a simple, temporal or extended literal t in a partial temporal interpretation* (σ, S) after $a_1 \ldots a_k$, (written $(\sigma, S), a_1 \ldots a_k \models t$) as:

$(\sigma, S), a_1 \ldots a_k \models \top, \qquad (\sigma, S), a_1 \ldots a_k \not\models \bot$

$(\sigma, S), a_1 \ldots a_k \models l$ *iff* $[a_1; \ldots; a_k]l \in S$, for l s-literal

$(\sigma, S), a_1 \ldots a_k \models [a]l$ *iff* $[a_1; \ldots; a_k; a]l \in S$ or $a_1 \ldots a_k, a$ is not a prefix of σ

$(\sigma, S), a_1 \ldots a_k \models \bigcirc l$ *iff* $[a_1; \ldots; a_k; b]l \in S$, where $a_1 \ldots a_k b$ is a prefix of σ

$(\sigma, S), a_1 \ldots a_k \models$ *not* l *iff* $(\sigma, S), a_1 \ldots a_k \not\models l$

The satisfiability of rule bodies in a temporal interpretation (σ, S) is defined as usual. A rule $\Box(H \leftarrow Body)$ is satisfied in (σ, S) if, for all action sequences $a_1 \ldots a_k$ (including the empty one ε), $(\sigma, S), a_1 \ldots a_k \models Body$ implies $(\sigma, S), a_1 \ldots a_k \models H$. A rule $H \leftarrow Body$ is satisfied in (σ, S) if, $(\sigma, S), \varepsilon \models Body$ implies $(\sigma, S), \varepsilon \models H$.

Let Π be a set of rules not containing default negation, and let $\sigma \in \Sigma^\omega$.

Definition 2. *A temporal interpretation* (σ, S) *is a temporal answer set of* Π *if* S *is minimal (with respect to set inclusion) among the* S' *such that* (σ, S') *is a partial interpretation satisfying the rules in* Π.

To define answer sets of a program Π containing negation, the *reduct*, $\Pi^{(\sigma, S)}$, *of* Π *relative to a temporal interpretation* (σ, S) is defined, extending Gelfond and Lifschitz' transform [18], to compute a different reduct of Π for each prefix $a_1, \ldots, a_h$ of σ.

Definition 3. *The reduct,* $\Pi^{(\sigma, S)}_{a_1, \ldots, a_h}$, *of* Π *relative to* (σ, S) *and to the prefix* $a_1, \ldots, a_h$ *of* σ , *is the set of all the rules* $[a_1; \ldots; a_h](H \leftarrow l_1, \ldots, l_m)$ *such that* $\Box(H \leftarrow l_1, \ldots, l_m,$ *not* $l_{m+1}, \ldots,$ *not* $l_n)$ *is in* Π *and* $(\sigma, S), a_1, \ldots, a_h \not\models l_i$, *for all* $i = m + 1, \ldots, n$ *(and similarly for prefix* ε). *The reduct* $\Pi^{(\sigma, S)}$ *of* Π *relative to* (σ, S) *is the union of all reducts* $\Pi^{(\sigma, S)}_{a_1, \ldots, a_h}$ *for all prefixes* $a_1, \ldots, a_h$ *of* σ.

In definition above, we say that rule $[a_1; \ldots; a_h](H \leftarrow Body)$ is satisfied in a temporal interpretation (σ, S) if $(\sigma, S), a_1 \ldots a_k \models Body$ implies $(\sigma, S), a_1 \ldots a_k \models H$.

Definition 4 ([22]). *A temporal interpretation* (σ, S) *is an answer set of* Π *if* (σ, S) *is an answer set of the reduct* $\Pi^{(\sigma, S)}$.

Observe that a partial interpretation (σ, S) provides, for each prefix $a_1 \ldots a_k$, a partial evaluation of fluents in the state corresponding to that prefix. The state obtained by the execution of the actions $a_1 \ldots a_k$ can be defined as: $w^{(\sigma, S)}_{a_1 \ldots a_k} = \{l : [a_1; \ldots; a_k]l \in S\}$.

Although the answer sets of a domain description Π are partial interpretations, in some cases, e.g., when the initial state is complete and all fluents are inertial, it is possible to guarantee that the temporal answer sets of Π are total. The case of total temporal answer sets is of special interest as a total temporal answer set (σ, S) can be regarded as a temporal model (σ, V_S), where, for each finite prefix $a_1 \ldots a_k$ of σ, $V_S(a_1, \ldots, a_k) = \{p : [a_1, \ldots, a_k]p \in S\}$. In the following, we restrict our consideration to domain descriptions Π whose answer sets are total (called *well-defined* in [22]). We say that a total answer set S over σ satisfies a DLTL formula α if $M_S, \varepsilon \models \alpha$.

We can now introduce the notion of *extension of a well-defined domain description* $D = (\Pi, \mathcal{C})$ over Σ in two steps: first, we find the temporal answer sets of Π; second, we filter out all the temporal answer sets which do not satisfy the constraints in $\mathcal{C}$.

Definition 5 ([22]). *An extension of a well-defined domain description* $D = (\Pi, \mathcal{C})$ *over* Σ *is a (total) answer set* (σ, S) *of* Π *which satisfies the constraints in* $\mathcal{C}$.

4   Combining Temporal Action Theories with $\mathcal{EL}^\perp$ Ontologies

In this section we define a notion of *extended temporal action theory*, consisting of a temporal action theory plus an $\mathcal{EL}^\perp$ knowledge base. Our approach, following most of the proposals for reasoning about actions in DLs [2,5–7,13], is to regard TBox as a set of state constraints, i.e. conditions that must be satisfied in all states and extensions of the action theory, and ABox as a set of constraints on all possible initial states.

We regard DL assertions as fluents that may occur in our action laws as well as in the states of the action theory. Given a (normalized) $\mathcal{EL}^\perp$ knowledge base $K = (\mathcal{T}, \mathcal{A})$, we require that: (a) for each (possibly complex) concept C occurring in K there is a unary predicate $C \in \mathcal{P}$; (b) for each role name $r \in N_{R,K}$ there is a binary predicate $r \in \mathcal{P}$; (c) the set $Cons$ includes all the individual names occurring in K, i.e. $N_{I,K} \subseteq Cons$.

Observe that if a concept such as $\exists r.C$ occurs in K, there exists a predicate name $\exists r.C \in \mathcal{P}$ and, for each $a \in N_{I,KB}$, the fluent literals $(\exists r.C)(a)$ and $\neg(\exists r.C)(a)$ belong to the set Lit. We will still call such literals assertions. Although classical negation is not allowed in $\mathcal{EL}^\perp$, we use *explicit negation* [17] to allow negative literals of the form $\neg C(a)$ in the action language (to allow for deleting an assertion from a state).

A simple literal in Lit is said to be a *simple assertion* if it has the form $B(a)$ or $r(a,b)$ or $\neg B(a)$ or $\neg r(a,b)$, where $B \in BC_K$ is a base concept in K, $r \in N_{R,K}$ and $a,b \in N_{I,K}$. Observe that $\{a\}(c)$ and $\neg\{a\}(c)$ are simple assertions, while $(\exists r.C)(a)$ and $\neg(\exists r.C)(a)$ are non-simple assertions.

In order to deal with existential restrictions, in addition to the individual names $N_{I,KB}$ occurring in the KB we introduce a finite set Aux of auxiliary individual names, as proposed in [29] to encode $\mathcal{EL}^\perp$ inference in Datalog, where Aux contains a new individual name $aux^{A \sqsubseteq \exists r.B}$, for each inclusion $A \sqsubseteq \exists r.B$ occurring in the KB. We further require that $Aux \subseteq Cons$.

Definition 6 (Extended action theory). *An* extended action theory *is a tuple* $(K, \Pi, \mathcal{C})$, *where:* $K = (\mathcal{T}, \mathcal{A})$ *is an* $\mathcal{EL}^\perp$ *knowledge base;* Π *is a set of laws: action, causal, executability and initial state laws (see below);* $\mathcal{C}$ *is a set of DLTL formulae (constraints).*

Besides *action laws* $\square([a]l \leftarrow l_1,\ldots,l_m, not\ l_{m+1},\ldots, not\ l_n)$ which describe the immediate effects of actions, including nondeterministic ones, Π allows for two kinds of *causal laws: Static causal laws* $\square(l_0 \leftarrow l_1,\ldots,l_m, not\ l_{m+1},\ldots, not\ l_n)$, where the l_i's are simple fluent literals, whose meaning is: if $l_1,\ldots,l_m$ hold in a state and $l_{m+1},\ldots,l_n$ do not hold in that state, than l_0 is caused to hold in that state. *Dynamic causal laws* $\square(\bigcirc l_0 \leftarrow t_1,\ldots,t_m, not\ t_{m+1},\ldots, not\ t_n)$, where l_0 is a simple fluent literal and the t_i's are simple fluent literals or temporal fluent literals of the form $\bigcirc l_i$, e.g., $\bigcirc Teacher(x) \leftarrow \bigcirc Teaches(x,y) \wedge Course(y)$. Differently from [5,6], direct and indirect effects of actions are not required to be simple DL assertions.

Precondition laws describe the executability conditions of actions. They have the form: $\square([a]\perp \leftarrow l_1,\ldots,l_m, not\ l_{m+1},\ldots, not\ l_n)$ where $a \in \Sigma$ and the l_i's are simple fluent literals.

Initial state laws are needed to introduce conditions that have to hold in the initial state. They have the form: $l_0 \leftarrow l_1,\ldots,l_m, not\ l_{m+1},\ldots, not\ l_n$ where the l_i's are simple fluent literals. As a special case, the initial state can be defined as a set of simple fluent literals (and simple assertions).

State constraints, that apply to the initial state or to all states, can be obtained when $\perp$ occurs in place of l_0 in the head of initial state laws or static causal laws.

Following Lifschitz [30] we call *frame fluents* the fluents to which the law of inertia applies. Persistency of frame fluents from a state to the next one can be captured by introducing in Π a set of causal laws, said *persistency laws* for all frame fluents f:

$$\Box(\bigcirc f \leftarrow f,\ not \bigcirc \neg f) \qquad \Box(\bigcirc \neg f \leftarrow \neg f,\ not \bigcirc f)$$

meaning that, if f holds in a state, then f will hold in the next state, unless its negation $\neg f$ is caused to hold (and similarly for $\neg f$). Persistency of a fluent is blocked by the execution of an action which causes the value of the fluent to change. The persistency laws above play the role of *inertia rules* in $\mathcal{C}$ [26], $\mathcal{C}+$ [25] and $\mathcal{K}$ [15].

If f is *non-frame* with respect to an action a, f is not expected to persist and may change its value when an action α is executed, either non-deterministically, by laws

$$\Box(\bigcirc f \leftarrow not \bigcirc \neg f) \qquad \Box(\bigcirc \neg f \leftarrow not \bigcirc f)$$

(*non-frame laws*), or by taking some default value (see [22] for examples).

In the following we assume that persistency laws and non-frame laws can be applied to simple assertions but not to non-simple ones (such as $(\exists r.B)(x)$), whose value in a state (as we will see) is determined from the value of simple assertions. For simple assertions $A(c)$ in a domain description, one has to choose whether the concept A is frame or non-frame (so that either persistency laws or non-frame laws can be introduced). We assume that nominals are frame fluents, that is, $(\neg)\{a\}(b)$ persists from a state to the next one unless cancelled by the direct or indirect effects of an action.

ABox assertions may incompletely specify the initial state. As we want to reason about states corresponding to $\mathcal{EL}^{\perp}$ interpretations, we assume that the laws: $f \leftarrow not \neg f$ and $\neg f \leftarrow not f$ for *completing the initial state* are introduced in Π for all simple literals f (including assertions with nominals). As shown in [22], the assumption of complete initial states, together with suitable conditions on the laws in Π, gives rise to semantic interpretations (extensions) of the domain description in which all states are complete. In particular, for simple assertions it is sufficient to assume that either persistency laws or non-frame laws are introduced, as for all simple fluents. Under such condition, starting from an initial state, complete for simple fluents, all the reachable states are also complete for simple fluents, that is, the domain description is well-defined.

The third component $\mathcal{C}$ of a domain description $(K, \Pi, \mathcal{C})$ is the set of *temporal constraints* in DLTL, which allow general temporal conditions to be imposed on the executions of the domain description, restricting the space of the possible executions (or *extensions*), as shown in Sect. 3. The next section generalizes the notion of extension to domain descriptions $(K, \Pi, \mathcal{C})$ including an $\mathcal{EL}^{\perp}$ ontology K.

5   Ontology Axioms as State Constraints

Given an action theory $(K, \Pi, \mathcal{C})$, where $K = (\mathcal{T}, \mathcal{A})$, we define an extension of $(K, \Pi, \mathcal{C})$ as an extension (σ, S) of the action theory $(\Pi, \mathcal{C})$ satisfying all axioms of the ontology K. Informally, each state w in the extension is required to correspond to an $\mathcal{EL}^{\perp}$ interpretation and to satisfy all inclusion axioms in TBox $\mathcal{T}$. Additionally, the initial state must satisfy all assertions in the ABox $\mathcal{A}$.

To define the extensions of an action theory $(K, \Pi, \mathcal{C})$, we restrict to well-defined domain descriptions $(K, \Pi, \mathcal{C})$, so that all states in an extension are complete for simple fluents (and for simple assertions). We prove that such states represent $\mathcal{EL}^{\perp}$ interpretations on the language of K, provided an additional set of laws $\Pi_{\mathcal{L}(K)}$ is included in the action theory. Next, we further add to Π a set $\Pi_{\mathcal{T}}$ of constraints, to guarantee that each state satisfies the inclusion axioms in $\mathcal{T}$, and a set of laws $\Pi_{\mathcal{A}}$, to guarantee that all assertions in $\mathcal{A}$ are satisfied in the initial state.

Overall, this provides a transformation of the action theory $(K, \Pi, \mathcal{C})$ into a new DLTL action theory $(\Pi \cup \Pi_K, \mathcal{C})$, by eliminating the ontology while introducing the set of static causal laws and constraints $\Pi_K = \Pi_{\mathcal{L}(K)} \cup \Pi_{\mathcal{T}} \cup \Pi_{\mathcal{A}}$, intended to exclude those extensions which do not satisfy the axioms in K.

The set of domain constraints and causal laws in $\Pi_{\mathcal{L}(K)}$ is intended to guarantee that any state w of an extension respects the semantics of DL concepts occurring in K. The definition of $\Pi_{\mathcal{L}(K)}$ is based on a fragment of the materialization calculus for $\mathcal{EL}^{\perp}$ [29], which provides a Datalog encoding of an $\mathcal{EL}^{\perp}$ ontology. Here, the idea is that of regarding an assertion $C(a)$ in a state w as the evidence that $a^I \in C^I$ in the corresponding interpretation. Let $\Pi_{\mathcal{L}(K)}$ be the following set of causal laws:

(1) $\Box(\perp \leftarrow \perp(x))$ (2) $\Box(\top(x) \leftarrow)$ (3) $\Box(\{a\}(a) \leftarrow)$

(4) $\Box(exists\_r\_B(x) \leftarrow r(x,y) \wedge B(y))$

(5) $\Box((\exists r.B)(x) \leftarrow exists\_r\_B(x))$ (6) $\Box(\neg(\exists r.B)(x) \leftarrow not\ exists\_r\_B(x))$

(7) $\Box(\perp \leftarrow \{a\}(x) \wedge B(x) \wedge not\ B(a))$, for $x \neq a$

(8) $\Box(\perp \leftarrow \{a\}(x) \wedge B(a) \wedge not\ B(x))$, for $x \neq a$

(9) $\Box(\perp \leftarrow \{a\}(x) \wedge r(z,x) \wedge not\ r(z,a))$, for $x \neq a$

for all $x, y \in \Delta$, $a \in N_{I,K}$, $B \in BC_K$ (the base concepts occurring in K) and $r \in N_{R,K}$ (the roles occurring in K). Observe that the first constraint has the effect that a state S, in which the concept $\perp$ has an instance, is made inconsistent. Law (4) makes $exists\_r\_B(x)$ hold in any state in which there is a domain element y such that $r(x,y)$ and $B(y)$ hold (where $exists\_r\_B$ is an additional auxiliary predicate for $B \in BC_K$ and $r \in N_{R,K}$). Laws (5) and (6) guarantee that, for all $x \in \Delta$, either $(\exists r.B)(x)$ or $\neg(\exists r.B)(x)$ is contained in the state. State constraints (7–9) are needed for the treatment of nominals and are related to rules (27–29) of the materialization calculus [29].

Let (σ, S) be an extension of the action theory $(\Pi \cup \Pi_{\mathcal{L}(K)}, \mathcal{C})$. It can be proven that any state w of (σ, S) represents an $\mathcal{EL}^{\perp}$ interpretation. Given a state w, let w^+ be the set of $\mathcal{EL}^{\perp}$ assertions $C(a)$ $(r(a,b))$, such that $C(a) \in w$ (resp., $r(a,b) \in w$). Let w^- be the set of $\mathcal{EL}^{\perp}$ assertions $C(a)$ $(r(a,b))$, such that $\neg C(a) \in w$ (resp., $\neg r(a,b) \in w$).

Proposition 1. *Let* (σ, S) *be an extension of action theory* $(\Pi \cup \Pi_{\mathcal{L}(K)}, \mathcal{C})$ *and* w *be a state of* (σ, S). *Then there is an interpretation* $(\Delta^I, \cdot^I)$ *that satisfies all the assertions in* w^+ *and falsifies all assertions in* w^- *(and we say that* $(\Delta^I, \cdot^I)$ *agrees with state* w*).*

As mentioned, we are interested in the states satisfying the TBox $\mathcal{T}$ of K. Provided Π is well-defined, for each extension (σ, S) of the action theory $(\Pi \cup \Pi_{\mathcal{L}(K)}, \mathcal{C})$, any state w is consistent and complete for all simple literals (and hence, by (5) and (6), for all assertions). We say that w *satisfies the TBox* $\mathcal{T}$ if for all interpretations $(\Delta^I, \cdot^I)$ such that $(\Delta^I, \cdot^I)$ agrees with state w, $(\Delta^I, \cdot^I)$ is a model of $\mathcal{T}$.

The requirement that each w should satisfy $\mathcal{T}$ can be incorporated in the action theory through a set of constraints $\Pi_{\mathcal{T}}$, exploiting the fact that $\mathcal{T}$ is in normal form. $\Pi_{\mathcal{T}}$ contains the following state constraints:

$\quad \Box(\bot \leftarrow A(x) \land not\ D(x))$, for each $A \sqsubseteq D$ in $\mathcal{T}$;
$\quad \Box(\bot \leftarrow A(x) \land B(x) \land not\ D(x))$, for each $A \sqcap B \sqsubseteq D$ in $\mathcal{T}$;
$\quad \Box(\bot \leftarrow A(x) \land not\ (\exists r.B)(x))$, for each $A \sqsubseteq \exists r.B$ in $\mathcal{T}$;
$\quad \Box(\bot \leftarrow (\exists r.B)(x) \land not\ D(x))$, for each $\exists r.B \sqsubseteq D$ in $\mathcal{T}$;

where $A, B \in BC_K$, $D \in BC_K \cup \{\bot\}$ and $x \in N_{I,K} \cup Aux$. For $D = \bot$, the condition $not\ D(x)$ is omitted. The following proposition can be proved for a well-defined Π.

Proposition 2. *Let* (σ, S) *be an extension of the action theory* $(\Pi \cup \Pi_{\mathcal{L}(K)}, \mathcal{C})$. *A state* w *of* (σ, S) *satisfies* $\mathcal{T}$ *iff* w *satisfies all constraints in* $\Pi_{\mathcal{T}}$.

We can then add the constraints in $\Pi_{\mathcal{T}}$ to an action theory $(\Pi \cup \Pi_{\mathcal{L}(K)}, \mathcal{C})$ to single out the extensions (σ, S) whose states all satisfy the TBox $\mathcal{T}$. In a similar way, we can restrict to answer sets (σ, S) whose initial state $w_{\varepsilon}^{(\sigma,S)}$ satisfies all assertions in $\mathcal{A}$, by defining a set of initial state constraints as:

$$\Pi_{\mathcal{A}} = \{\bot \leftarrow not\ A(c)) \mid A(c) \in \mathcal{A}\} \cup \{\bot \leftarrow not\ r(c,d)) \mid r(c,d) \in \mathcal{A}\}$$

We define the *extensions of the extended action theory* $(K, \Pi, \mathcal{C})$ as the extensions of the action theory $(\Pi \cup \Pi_K, \mathcal{C})$, where $\Pi_K = \Pi_{\mathcal{L}(K)} \cup \Pi_{\mathcal{T}} \cup \Pi_{\mathcal{A}}$.

6   Causal Laws for Repairing Inconsistencies: Sufficient Conditions

Introducing state constraints corresponding to Tbox inclusions is not enough to take them into account across state changes. Consider the example in the introduction.

Example 1. Let $K = (\mathcal{T}, \mathcal{A})$ be a knowledge base such that $\mathcal{T} = \{\exists Teaches.Course \sqsubseteq Teacher\}$ and $\mathcal{A} = \{Person(john), Course(cs1)\}$. We assume that all simple assertions, i.e., $Person(x)$, $Teacher(x)$, $Course(x)$, $Teaches(x, y)$, are frame for all $x, y \in N_{I,K} \cup Aux$. Let us consider a state w_0 where John does not teach any course and is not a teacher. If an action $Assign(cs1, john)$ were executed in w_0, given a Π containing the action law $[Assign(cs1, john)] Teaches(john, cs1)$, the resulting state would contain $Teaches(john,cs1)$ and $(\exists Teaches.Course)(john)$, but would not contain $Teacher(john)$, thus violating the state constraint $\Box(\bot \leftarrow (\exists Teaches.Course)(x) \land not\ Teacher(x))$, in $\Pi_{\mathcal{T}}$. In this case, there is no extension of the action theory in which action $Assign(cs1, john)$ can be executed in the initial state.

As observed in [5], when this happens, the action specification can be regarded as being underspecified, as it is not able to capture the dependencies among fluents which occur in the TBox. To guarantee that TBox is satisfied in the new state, causal laws are needed which allow the state to be *repaired*. In the specific case, adding the causal law $\Box(Teacher(x) \leftarrow Teaches(x, y) \land Course(y))$ to Π would suffice to cause $Teacher(x)$ in the resulting state, as an indirect effect of action $Assign(cs1, john)$.

Can we identify the conditions needed to guarantee that an action theory is able to repair the state, after executing an action, so to satisfy all inclusions of a (normalized) $\mathcal{EL}^\perp$ TBox, when possible? Let us continue Example 1.

Example 2. Consider the case when action *retire(john)* is executed in a state w_1 where *Person(john)*, *Course(cs1)*, *Teaches(john,cs1)* and *Teacher(john)* hold. Suppose that the action law: $[retire(john)]\neg Teacher(john)$ is in Π. Then, $\neg Teacher(john)$ will belong to the new state w_2, but w_2 would still contain *Course(cs1)*, *Teaches(john,cs1)*, persisting from the previous state (as *Course* and *Teaches* are frame fluents). Hence, w_2 would violate the TBox $\mathcal{T}$. The causal law $\Box(\neg Teaches(x,y) \leftarrow \neg Teacher(x) \land Course(y))$ would repair the inconsistency: when John retires he stops teaching all the courses he was teaching before. In particular, he stops teaching $cs1$. On the contrary, $\Box(\neg Course(y) \leftarrow \neg Teacher(x) \land Teaches(x,y))$ is presumably unintended.

As we can see, the causal laws needed to restore consistency when an action is executed can be obtained from the inclusions in the TBox also considering some of their contrapositives, even though not all them are always intended. The choice of the causal rules to include should not be done automatically. For $\mathcal{EL}^\perp$ knowledge bases in normal form, the set of constraints in Π_T can be replaced by a set of repair rules, i.e., a set of causal laws which can be used to recover a consistent state, whenever possible. In the following we identify the set of repair rules for each axiom in normal form and sufficient conditions to guarantee that Tbox $\mathcal{T}$ is satisfied.

The case of a (normalized) inclusion $A \sqsubseteq B$, with $A, B \in N_C$, is relatively simple; the execution of an action α with effect $A(c)$ (but not $B(c)$), in a state in which none of $A(c)$ and $B(c)$ holds, would lead to a state which violates the constraints in the KB. Similarly for an action β with effect $\neg B(c)$. Deleting $B(c)$ should cause $A(c)$ to be deleted as well, if we want the inclusion $A \sqsubseteq B$ to be satisfied. Hence, to guarantee that the TBox is satisfied in the new state, for each inclusion $A \sqsubseteq B$, two causal laws are needed: $\Box(B(x) \leftarrow A(x))$ and $\Box(\neg A(x) \leftarrow \neg B(x))$.

For an axiom $A \sqcap B \sqsubseteq \perp$, consider the concrete case *pending* $\sqcap$ *approved* $\sqsubseteq \perp$, representing mutually exclusive states of a claim in a process of dealing with an insurance claim, we expect the following causal laws to be included:

$$\Box(\neg pending(x) \leftarrow approved(x)) \qquad \Box(\neg approved(x) \leftarrow pending(x))$$

even though the second one is only useful if a claim can become pending again after having become (temporarily) approved. For the general case, let us define, for each possible axiom in normal form, a set of causal laws or *repair laws* as follows:

1- For $A \sqsubseteq B$ in $\mathcal{T}$: $\Box(B(x) \leftarrow A(x))$ and $\Box(\neg A(x) \leftarrow \neg B(x))$;
2- For $A \sqcap B \sqsubseteq D$ in $\mathcal{T}$: $\Box(D(x) \leftarrow A(x) \land B(x))$, $\Box(\neg A(x) \leftarrow \neg D(x) \land B(x))$ and $\Box(\neg B(x) \leftarrow \neg D(x) \land A(x))$;
3- For $A \sqsubseteq \exists r.B$ in $\mathcal{T}$: $\Box(r(x, aux^{A \sqsubseteq \exists r.B}) \leftarrow A(x))$, $\Box(B(aux^{A \sqsubseteq \exists r.B}) \leftarrow A(x))$ and $\Box(\neg A(x) \leftarrow \neg(\exists r.B)(x))$;
4- For $\exists r.B \sqsubseteq A$ in $\mathcal{T}$: $\Box(A(x) \leftarrow (\exists r.B)(x))$, $\Box(\neg r(x,y) \leftarrow \neg A(x) \land B(y))$ and $\Box(\neg B(y) \leftarrow \neg A(x) \land r(x,y))$.

Let $\Pi_{C(\mathcal{T})}$ be a set of causal laws containing at least: one law for each axiom of type 1, 2 and 4, and the first two rules or the third one for each axiom of type 3.

Proposition 3. *Given a well-defined action theory* $(\Pi, \mathcal{C})$ *and a TBox* $\mathcal{T}$*, any state* w *of an extension* (σ, S) *of* $(\Pi \cup \Pi_{\mathcal{L}(K)} \cup \Pi_{C(\mathcal{T})} \cup \Pi_A, \mathcal{C})$ *satisfies* $\mathcal{T}$*.*

Observe that, for the case for $A \sqsubseteq \exists r.B$, from $r(x, aux^{A \sqsubseteq \exists r.B})$ and $B(aux^{A \sqsubseteq \exists r.B})$ $(\exists r.B)(x)$ is caused by laws (4–5) in $\Pi_{\mathcal{L}(K)}$. While the causal laws in $\Pi_{C(\mathcal{T})}$ are sufficient to guarantee the consistency of a resulting state with TBox $\mathcal{T}$, one cannot exclude that an action has effects inconsistent with TBox (e.g., an action with direct effects $A(c)$ and $\neg B(c)$, conflicting with an axiom $A \sqsubseteq B$ in $\mathcal{T}$). In such a case, the action would not be executable. The more are the repair causal laws considered, the more is the repair ability and the more are the extensions of the domain description.

Notice that the above encoding of an $\mathcal{EL}^{\perp}$ TBox into a set of temporal action laws requires a polynomial number of laws to be added to the action theory (in the size of K). Based on this mapping, the proof methods for our temporal action logic, which are based on the ASP encodings of bounded model checking [22,23], can be exploited (with the same PSPACE complexity) for reasoning about actions in an action theory extended with an $\mathcal{EL}^{\perp}$ knowledge base.

7 Conclusions and Related Work

In this paper we have proposed an approach for reasoning about actions by combining a temporal action logic [22], whose semantics is based on a notion of temporal answer set, and an $\mathcal{EL}^{\perp}$ ontology. It is shown that, for $\mathcal{EL}^{\perp}$ knowledge bases in normal form, the consistency of the action theory extensions with respect to an ontology can be verified by adding to the action theory a set of causal laws and state constraints, by exploiting a fragment of the materialization calculus by Krötzsch [29]. Starting from the idea by Baader et al. [5] that causal rules can be used to ensure the consistency of states with the TBox, we have defined sufficient conditions on the action theory to repair the states resulting from action execution and guarantee consistency with TBox. Our approach provides a polynomial encoding of an action theory extended with an $\mathcal{EL}^{\perp}$ knowledge base in normal form, into the language of the (DLTL based) temporal action logic studied in [22]. The proof methods for this temporal action logic, based on ASP encodings of bounded model checking [22,23], can then be exploited for reasoning about actions in an extended action theory. It would be interesting, for action domains with finite executions, to investigate whether the action theories in [22] can be encoded in *telingo* [11], so to exploit the optimized implementation of *telingo*.

Many of the proposals in the literature for combining DLs with action theories focus on expressive DLs. In their seminal work [6], Baader et al. study the integration of action formalisms with expressive DLs, from $\mathcal{ALC}$ to $\mathcal{ALCOIQ}$, under Winslett's *possible models approach* (PMA) [35], based on the assumption that TBox is acyclic and on the distinction between defined and primitive concepts, where only primitive concepts are allowed in action effects. They determine the complexity of the executability and projection problems and show that they get decidable fragments of the situation calculus. Our semantics departs from PMA as causal laws are considered. As [5,32] we do not require a restriction to acyclic TBoxes and primitive concepts in postconditions.

The requirement of acyclic TBoxes is lifted in the work by Liu et al. [32], where an approach to the ramification problem is proposed which does not use causal relationships, but exploits *occlusion* to provide a specification of the predicates that can change through the execution of actions. The idea is to leave to the designer of an action domain the control of the ramification of the actions.

Similar considerations are at the basis of the approach by Baader et al. [5] that, instead, exploits causal relationships for modeling ramifications in an action language for $\mathcal{ALCO}$, and defines its semantics in the style of McCain and Turner fixpoint semantics [33]. Temporal projection is proven decidable and EXPTIME-complete. In this paper, following [5], we exploit causal laws for modeling ramifications in the context of a temporal action language for $\mathcal{EL}^\perp$. We allow for non-deterministic effects of actions (not allowed in [5]) and for the distinction between frame and non-frame fluents [30], which is strongly related to occlusion used in [32]. We have also provided sufficient conditions for an action specification to be consistent with a normalized $\mathcal{EL}^\perp$ ontology.

Ahmetai et al. [2] study the evolution of Graph Structured Data as a result of updates expressed in an action language. They provide decidability and complexity results for expressive DLs such as $\mathcal{ALCHOIQbr}$ (under finite satisfiability) as well as for variants of DL-*lite*. Complex actions including action sequence and conditional actions are considered. Complex actions are considered as well in [13], where an action formalism is introduced for a family DLs, from $\mathcal{ALCO}$ to $\mathcal{ALCHOIQ}$, exploiting PDL program constructors to define complex actions. As in [6], the TBox is assumed to be acyclic.

In [9] Description Logic and Action Bases are introduced, where an initial Abox evolves over time due to actions which have conditional effects. In [12] the approach is extended to allow for different notions of *repair* of the resulting state, such as a maximal subset consistent with the Tbox, or the intersection of all such subsets. In this paper, we rely on causal laws for repairing states; selecting the appropriate causal laws means acquiring more knowledge, and allows for a finer control on the resulting state.

Our semantics for actions, as many of the proposals in the literature, requires that a state provides a complete description of the world and is intended to represent an interpretation of the $\mathcal{EL}^\perp$ knowledge base. An alternative approach has been adopted in [9], where a state can provide an incomplete specification of the world. In our approach, an incomplete state could be represented as an epistemic state, to distinguish what is known to be true (or to be false) and what is unknown. An epistemic extension of our action logic, based on temporal answer sets, has been developed in [23], and it can potentially be exploited for reasoning about actions with incomplete states also in presence of ontological knowledge. We leave the study of this case for future work, as well as the investigation of ASP approaches for combining temporal reasoning with weighted conditional knowledge bases for lightweight DLs [24].

Acknowledgements. The work in this paper was partly supported by INDAM-GNCS.

References

1. Proceedings of ICLP 2021 Workshops, Porto, Portugal (virtual). CEUR Workshop Proceedings, vol. 2970. CEUR-WS.org (2021). http://ceur-ws.org/Vol-2970

2. Ahmetaj, S., Calvanese, D., Ortiz, M., Simkus, M.: Managing change in graph-structured data using description logics. In: Proceedings of the AAAI 2014, pp. 966–973 (2014)
3. Baader, F., Brandt, S., Lutz, C.: Pushing the $\mathcal{EL}$ envelope. In: Kaelbling, L., Saffiotti, A. (eds.) Proceedings of the IJCAI 2005, Edinburgh, Scotland, UK, pp. 364–369, August 2005
4. Baader, F., Brandt, S., Lutz, C.: Pushing the $\mathcal{EL}$ envelope. In: LTCS-Report LTCS-05-01. Institute for Theoretical Computer Science, TU Dresden (2005)
5. Baader, F., Lippmann, M., Liu, H.: Using causal relationships to deal with the ramification problem in action formalisms based on description logics. In: LPAR-17, pp. 82–96 (2010)
6. Baader, F., Lutz, C., Milicic, M., Sattler, U., Wolter, F.: Integrating description logics and action formalisms: first results. In: Proceedings of the AAAI 2005, pp. 572–577 (2005)
7. Baader, F., Liu, H., ul Mehdi, A.: Verifying properties of infinite sequences of description logic actions. In: ECAI, pp. 53–58 (2010)
8. Babb, J., Lee, J.: Cplus 2ASP: computing action language $\mathcal{C}$+ in answer set programming. In: Cabalar, P., Son, T.C. (eds.) LPNMR 2013. LNCS (LNAI), vol. 8148, pp. 122–134. Springer, Heidelberg (2013). https://doi.org/10.1007/978-3-642-40564-8_13
9. Bagheri Hariri, B., Calvanese, D., Montali, M., De Giacomo, G., De Masellis, R., Felli, P.: Description logic knowledge and action bases. J. Artif. Intell. Res. **46**, 651–686 (2013)
10. Baral, C., Gelfond, M.: Reasoning agents in dynamic domains. In: Minker, J. (ed.) Logic-Based Artificial Intelligence, pp. 257–279. Springer, Boston, MA (2000). https://doi.org/10.1007/978-1-4615-1567-8_12
11. Cabalar, P., Kaminski, R., Morkisch, P., Schaub, T.: telingo = ASP + Time. In: Balduccini, M., Lierler, Y., Woltran, S. (eds.) Logic Programming and Nonmonotonic Reasoning: Proceedings of the 15th International Conference, LPNMR 2019, Philadelphia, PA, USA, 3–7 June 2019, pp. 256–269. Springer, Cham (2019). https://doi.org/10.1007/978-3-030-20528-7_19
12. Calvanese, D., Kharlamov, E., Montali, M., Santoso, A., Zheleznyakov, D.: Verification of inconsistency-aware knowledge and action bases. In: Proceedings of the IJCAI 2013 (2013)
13. Chang, L., Shi, Z., Gu, T., Zhao, L.: A family of dynamic description logics for representing and reasoning about actions. J. Autom. Reason. **49**(1), 1–52 (2012)
14. Denecker, M., Theseider Dupré, D., Van Belleghem, K.: An inductive definitions approach to ramifications. Electron. Trans. Artif. Intell. **2**, 25–97 (1998)
15. Eiter, T., Faber, W., Leone, N., Pfeifer, G., Polleres, A.: A logic programming approach to knowledge-state planning: semantics and complexity. ACM TOCL **5**(2), 206–263 (2004)
16. Aguado, F., et al.: Linear-time temporal answer set programming. TPLP, 1–55 (2021). https://www.cambridge.org/core/journals/theory-and-practice-of-logic-programming/article/lineartime-temporal-answer-set-programming/AB07F1F913DC0068B22E2A929276EDD2
17. Gelfond, M.: Answer sets, Chap. 7. In: Handbook of Knowledge Representation. Elsevier (2007)
18. Gelfond, M., Lifschitz, V.: The stable model semantics for logic programming. In: Proceedings of the 5th International Conference and Symposium on Logic Programming, pp. 1070–1080 (1988)
19. Gelfond, M., Lifschitz, V.: Action languages. Electron. Trans. Artif. Intell. **2**, 193–210 (1998)
20. Giordano, L., Martelli, A., Schwind, C.: Ramification and causality in a modal action logic. J. Log. Comput. **10**(5), 625–662 (2000)
21. Giordano, L., Martelli, A., Schwind, C.: Reasoning about actions in dynamic linear time temporal logic. Logic J. IGPL **9**(2), 289–303 (2001)
22. Giordano, L., Martelli, A., Theseider Dupré, D.: Reasoning about actions with temporal answer sets. Theor. Pract. Logic Program. **13**, 201–225 (2013)
23. Giordano, L., Martelli, A., Theseider Dupré, D.: Achieving completeness in the verification of action theories by bounded model checking in ASP. J. Log. Comp. **25**(6), 1307–30 (2015)

24. Giordano, L., Theseider Dupré, D.: An ASP approach for reasoning on neural networks under a finitely many-valued semantics for weighted conditional knowledge bases (2022). To appear in TPLP, https://arxiv.org/abs/2202.01123

25. Giunchiglia, E., Lee, J., Lifschitz, V., McCain, N., Turner, H.: Nonmonotonic causal theories. Artif. Intell. **153**(1–2), 49–104 (2004)

26. Giunchiglia, E., Lifschitz, V.: An action language based on causal explanation: preliminary report. In: Proceedings of the AAAI/IAAI 1998, pp. 623–630 (1998)

27. Heljanko, K., Niemelä, I.: Bounded LTL model checking with stable models. Theor. Pract. Logic Program. **3**(4–5), 519–550 (2003)

28. Henriksen, J., Thiagarajan, P.: Dynamic linear time temporal logic. Ann. Pure Appl. Logic **96**(1–3), 187–207 (1999)

29. Krötzsch, M.: Efficient inferencing for OWL EL. In: Janhunen, T., Niemelä, I. (eds.) JELIA 2010. LNCS (LNAI), vol. 6341, pp. 234–246. Springer, Heidelberg (2010). https://doi.org/10.1007/978-3-642-15675-5_21

30. Lifschitz, V.: Frames in the space of situations. Artif. Intell. **46**, 365–376 (1990)

31. Lin, F.: Embracing causality in specifying the indirect effects of actions. In: IJCAI 1995, Montréal Québec, Canada, 20–25 August 1995, vol. 2, pp. 1985–1993 (1995)

32. Liu, H., Lutz, C., Miličić, M., Wolter, F.: Reasoning about actions using description logics with general TBoxes. In: Fisher, M., van der Hoek, W., Konev, B., Lisitsa, A. (eds.) JELIA 2006. LNCS (LNAI), vol. 4160, pp. 266–279. Springer, Heidelberg (2006). https://doi.org/10.1007/11853886_23

33. McCain, N., Turner, H.: A causal theory of ramifications and qualifications. In: Proceedings of the IJCAI 1995, pp. 1978–1984 (1995)

34. Thielscher, M.: Ramification and causality. Artif. Intell. **89**(1–2), 317–364 (1997)

35. Winslett, M.: Reasoning about action using a possible models approach. In: Proceedings of the AAAI, St. Paul, MN, 21–26 August, pp. 89–93 (1988)

Inference to the Stable Explanations

Guido Governatori[1]([✉]), Francesco Olivieri[2], Antonino Rotolo[3],
and Matteo Cristani[4]

[1] Cooroibah, QLD 4565, Australia
guido@governatori.net
[2] School of ICT, Institute for Integrated and Intelligent Systems,
Griffith University, Nathan, QLD 4111, Australia
f.oliveri@griffith.edu.au
[3] ALMA AI, University of Bologna, Bologna, Italy
antonino.rotolo@unibo.it
[4] University of Verona, 37134 Verona, Italy
matteo.cristani@univr.it

Abstract. The process of explaining a piece of evidence by constructing a set of assumptions that are a good explanation for that evidence
is ubiquitous in real-life (e.g. in legal systems). In this paper, we introduce, discuss, and formalise the notion of *stable explanations* in a non-
monotonic setting. We show how, while applying it to the process of (1)
computing a set of literals able to (2) derive a conclusion (3) from a set
of defeasible rules, we obtain a restricted version of the notion of abduction. This is both interesting and useful: when an explanation for a given
conclusion is stable, it can, in fact, be used to infer the same conclusion
independently of other pieces of evidence that are found afterwards.

1 Introduction

Abduction is the inference process of finding a set of assumptions able to derive
a given conclusion, possibly under a given set of restrictions on how the assumptions or the rules used to derive the desired conclusions can be selected. When
this reasoning is performed in a non-monotonic setting, where the classical
derivation rules such as Modus Ponens, or Ex Falso Sequitur Quodlibet, are
substituted by rules specified within the theory itself, we encounter novel issues.

The abduction literature is vast, encompassing philosophy, logic, and computing science. When looking at the general picture, we may imagine that we should
be processing a logical theory where we have a piece of evidence, something the
theory actually proves. We aim at devising a set of assumptions actually able to
derive those conclusions through that theory. We are looking for the best explanation of a conclusion that has been reached. Hartman mastered this concept in
its foundational work on abduction [17].

Clearly, when we look at the mentioned vast literature, we come across several papers that analyse the powerful concept of abduction in a classical way,
including some from the perspective of non-monotonic systems [3,8,11].

© The Author(s), under exclusive license to Springer Nature Switzerland AG 2022
G. Gottlob et al. (Eds.): LPNMR 2022, LNAI 13416, pp. 245–258, 2022.
https://doi.org/10.1007/978-3-031-15707-3_19

There is, however, a neatly different notion that has not yet been studied: the *stability* of an explanation. Non-monotonic systems have indeed a substantially different behaviour than classical theories. In a classical theory, the operation of adding a new axiom to the theory itself (since this means that new constraints are added for the models of the theory) causes, simultaneously (i) the expansion of the set of conclusions that can be obtained from the theory itself, and (ii) a contraction of the set of models the theory is interpreted with. This does not happen with non-monotonic theories that could both expand and contract conclusions and models as an effect of changing the theory (by either adding or removing an axiom/rule).

The notion we introduce in this paper is as simple as this: an explanation for a given conclusion is stable when adding new elements to that explanation does not affect its power to explain the observed conclusion. This property can be observed in both monotonic and non-monotonic systems. (The most general case is, however, the here-studied non-monotonic one.)

In non-monotonic settings, and in particular, in Defeasible Logic (henceforth DL), we have three types of elements: (1) facts (2) rules, and (3) superiority relations. Facts describe those indisputable things that are true beyond any doubts. Rules are instead ways to obtain conclusions that are considered plausible (or typical), whereas the superiority relation is thought as a means to establish whether one rule for a conclusion might prevail against another rule for the opposite conclusion. In fact, the formalism sceptically concludes only those literals that are either factual or are concluded by a sequence of derivation steps involving rules that are never beaten by rules for the opposite conclusion.

Let us introduce an actual example of an abductive process based upon the determination of a candidate set of literals, whose assumption would be sufficient to prove a given conclusion.

Let us consider a (simplified) fragment of the Australian National Consumer Credit Protection Act 2009, in particular, Section 29 forbidding engaging in credit activities without a credit license. Furthermore, Section 29 (Subsection 3) permits such activities for a person acting on behalf of another person (the principal), when the person is an employee or the director of the principal, and the principal holds a credit license. Moreover, Section 80 specifies conditions under which a person could be banned for credit activities. Thus, for example, a person is banned if they became insolvent or was convicted of fraud. The conditions can be represented by the following rules:

$$s29.1:\ person \Rightarrow \neg creditActivity$$
$$s29.1e:\ person, creditLicense \Rightarrow creditActivity$$
$$s29.3a:\ actsOnBehalfPrincipal, principalCreditLicense \Rightarrow creditActivity$$
$$s80:\ banned \Rightarrow \neg creditActivity$$
$$s80.1b:\ insolvent \Rightarrow banned$$
$$s80.1c:\ convictedFraud \Rightarrow banned$$

where the superiority relation contains the following instances $s29.1e > s29.1$, $29.3a > s29.1$ and $s80 > s29.3a$.

Suppose that person A wants to engage in a credit activity. What are the conditions that person A has to satisfy to legally engage in a credit activity? According to rule $s29.1e$ if person A holds a credit license, then they can legally engage in a credit activity, and we do not have to look for other conditions. In case A does not have a credit activity, they can still legally engage if A acts on behalf of the principal and the principal has a credit license. Those two conditions, in absence of additional information, would allow us to say that A is legally permitted to engage in credit activities. However, if the further information that A was insolvent is provided, then we conclude that A was banned, and then rule $s80$ becomes applicable preventing us to conclude that A is entitled to engage in credit activities. Thus, in the first case, after we have established that A holds a credit license, we do not have to investigate other conditions. On the contrary, in the second case, being able to determine that A acts on behalf of a principal that holds a credit license is not enough. We have to see if A was banned. This, in turn, requires us to check if A was either insolvent or convicted of fraud. To sum up the set of facts $\{person, creditLicence\}$ is *stable* for the conclusion *creditActivity*, in the sense that it is resilient to the addition of other facts; on the other hand, $\{person, actsOnBehalfPrincipal, principalCreditLicense\}$ is not stable for *creditActivity* since the addition of *insolvent* prevents the derivation of such conclusion.

By the example above, we can conclude that stable explanations are more naturally considered because they are insensitive to the change in knowledge of the facts. In other terms, stable explanations are, to some extent, *monotonic*. In this paper, we concentrate on those abductive processes that only involve the *expansion* of the set of facts (to determine stability), and do not involve contraction of facts, revision of facts, or manipulation of rules.

Before going into the details of this study, let us make some observations regarding the complexity of the revision processes mentioned before. So far, in the current literature on these processes, only negative results have been obtained. In fact, both rules and preference revision processes are problems that are NP-hard, and, as we shall see in the remainder of this study, the same happens in the case of fact revision. There is, however, an important difference. In order to achieve the desired result of abductive reasoning, we shall be forced to employ the discussed notion of stability.

When a theory is revised in a way that *only* involves stable literals, the process of revision is simpler than it is when unstable literals are involved. This is a strong suggestion in the direction of finding out a subset of instances of the abduction of facts that could be treated polynomially. This is however compensated by the unfortunate condition that testing the stability of a literal is a coNP-complete problem, thus making imaginable a process of preliminary analysis (typically expensive in computational terms) followed by an overhead of tests that works on stable literals and is performed in a better computational fashion.

The interest in these notions is also general. With this investigation we have provided a third and potentially final chapter of the analysis of revision processes as discussed in the literature on Defeasible Logic.

The rest of the paper is organised as follows. Section 2 provides an introduction to the logical framework of defeasible logic. Section 3 introduces the formal definitions of when a case is stable as well as some related notions. Section 4 studies the asymptotic computational analysis of the problems. Section 5 establishes the relationships between the problem of determining whether a case is stable to the notion of theory change (or belief revision in Defeasible Logic parlance). Section 6 discusses some related relevant works and Sect. 7 takes some conclusions and sketches how this research can be taken further.

2   The Logical Framework of Defeasible Logic

The logical apparatus we shall utilise for our investigation is the Standard Defeasible Logic (SDL) [1]. We start by defining the language.

Let PROP be the set of propositional atoms, then the set of literals Lit = PROP $\cup$ $\{\neg p \mid p \in$ PROP$\}$. The *complementary* of a literal p is denoted by $\sim p$: if p is a positive literal q then $\sim p$ is $\neg q$, if p is a negative literal $\neg q$ then $\sim p$ is q. Literals are denoted by lower-case Roman letters. Let Lab be a set of labels to represent names of rules, which will be denoted as lower-case Greek letters.

A defeasible theory D is a tuple $(F, R, >)$, where F is the set of facts (indisputable statements), R is the rule set, and $>$ is a binary relation over R.

R is partitioned into three distinct sets of rules, with different meanings to draw different "types of conclusions". *Strict rules* are rules in the classical sense: whenever the premises are the case, so is the conclusion. We then have *defeasible rules* which represent the non-monotonic part (along which defeaters) of the logic: if the premises are the case, then typically the conclusion holds as well unless we have contrary evidence that opposes and prevents us from drawing such a conclusion. Lastly, we have *defeaters*, which are special rules whose purpose is to prevent contrary evidence from being the case. It follows that in DL, through defeasible rules and defeaters, we can represent in a natural way exceptions (and exceptions to exceptions, and so forth).

We finally have the superiority relation $>$, a binary relation among couples of rules that is the mechanism to solve conflicts. Given the two rules α and β, we have $(\alpha, \beta) \in >$ (or simply $\alpha > \beta$), in the scenario where both rules may fire (can be activated), α's conclusion will be preferred to β's.

A rule $\alpha \in R$ has the form $\alpha\colon A(\alpha) \leadsto C(\alpha)$, where: (i) $\alpha \in$ Lab is the unique name of the rule (ii) $A(\alpha) \subseteq$ Lit is α's (set of) antecedents (iii) $C(\alpha) = l \in$ Lit is its conclusion, and (iv) $\leadsto \in \{\rightarrow, \Rightarrow, \leadsto\}$ defines the type of rule, where: $\rightarrow$ is for strict rules, $\Rightarrow$ is for defeasible rules, and $\leadsto$ is for defeaters.

Some standard abbreviations. R_s denotes the set of strict rules in R, and the set of strict and defeasible rules by Rs; $R[l]$ denotes the set of all rules whose conclusion is l.

A *conclusion* of D is a *tagged literal* with one of the following forms:

$\pm\Delta l$ means that l is *definitely proved* (resp. *strictly refuted/non provable*) in D, i.e., there is a definite proof for l in D (resp. a definite proof does not exist).

$\pm\partial l$ means that l is *defeasibly proved* (resp. *defeasibly refuted*) in D, i.e., there is a defeasible proof for l in D (resp. a definite proof does not exist).

The definition of proof is also the standard in DL. Given a defeasible theory D, a proof P of length n in D is a finite sequence $P(1), P(2), \dots, P(n)$ of tagged formulas of the type $+\Delta l, -\Delta l, +\partial l, -\partial l$, where the proof conditions defined in the rest of this section hold. $P(1..n)$ denotes the first n steps of P.

All proof tags for literals are standard in DL [1]. We present only the positive ones as the negative proof tags can be straightforwardly obtained by applying the *strong negation principle* to the positive counterparts. The strong negation principle applies the function that simplifies a formula by moving all negations to an innermost position in the resulting formula, replaces the positive tags with the respective negative tags, and the other way around see [16].

Positive proof tags ensure that there are effective decidable procedures to build proofs; the strong negation principle guarantees that the negative conditions provide a constructive and exhaustive method to verify that a derivation of the given conclusion is not possible.

The definition of $+\Delta$ describes forward-chaining of strict rules.

Definition 1 $(+\Delta)$.
$+\Delta l$: If $P(n+1) = +\Delta l$ then either

> (1) $l \in F$, or
> (2) $\exists \alpha \in R_s[l].\forall a \in A(\alpha). +\Delta a \in P(1..n).$

A literal is strictly proved if it is a(n initial) fact of the theory or a strict rule exists.

Defeasible derivations are based on the notions of a rule being applicable or discarded. A rule is *applicable* at a given derivation step when every antecedent has been proved at any previous derivation step. Symmetrically, a rule is *discarded* when at least one antecedent has been previously refuted.

Definition 2 (Applicable & Discarded).
Given a defeasible theory D, a literal l, and a proof $P(n)$, we say that

- $\alpha \in R[l]$ *is applicable at* $P(n+1)$ *iff* $\forall a \in A(\alpha). +\partial a \in P(1..n).$
- $\alpha \in R[l]$ *is discarded at* $P(n+1)$ *iff* $\exists a \in A(\alpha). -\partial a \in P(1..n).$

Note that a strict rule can be used to derive defeasible conclusions when it is applicable and at least one of its premises is defeasibly but not strictly proved.

Definition 3 $(+\partial)$.
$+\partial l$: If $P(n+1) = +\partial l$ then either

(1) $+\Delta l \in P(1..n)$, or
(2.1) $-\Delta\sim l \in P(1..n)$, and
(2.2) $\exists \alpha \in R[l]$ applicable s.t.
(2.3) $\forall \beta \in R[\sim l]$ either
(2.3.1) β discarded, or
(2.3.2) $\exists \zeta \in R[l]$ applicable s.t. $\zeta > \beta$.

A literal is defeasibly proved if (1) it has already proved as a strict conclusion, or (2.1) the opposite is not and (2.2) there exists an applicable, defeasible or strict, rule such that any counter-attack is either (2.3.1) discarded or (2.3.2) defeated by an applicable, stronger rule supporting l. Note that, whereas β and ζ may be defeaters, α *may not*, as we need a strict or defeasible, applicable rule to draw a conclusion.

The last notions introduced in this section are those of extension of a defeasible theory. Informally, an extension is everything that is derived and disproved.

Definition 4 (Theory Extension). *Given a defeasible theory D, we define the set of positive and negative conclusions of D as its extension:*

$$E(D) = (+\Delta, -\Delta, +\partial, -\partial),$$

where $\pm\# = \{l | l$ appears in D and $D \vdash \pm\#l\}$, $\# \in \{\Delta, \partial\}$.

Example 1. Assume theory $D = (F = \{a, b\}, R, \{(\zeta, \gamma)\})$, with

$$R = \{ \ \alpha: a \Rightarrow z \qquad \beta: b \rightarrow c \qquad \gamma: c \Rightarrow \sim l \qquad \zeta: z \rightarrow l \ \}.$$

As a and b are facts, by Condition 1 of $+\Delta$, we have $D \vdash +\Delta a, +\Delta b$, which by Condition 2 of $+\Delta$ concludes $D \vdash +\Delta c$. Given that there are no rules that support $\sim z$ and α is applicable, Conditions (2.2) and (2.3.1) of $+\partial$ are satisfied and we conclude $D \vdash +\partial z$. Both γ and ζ are applicable (ζ is indeed a strict rule, but as its only consequence z is here defeasibly but not strictly proved it can be used to support the defeasible derivability of l): given that $\zeta > \gamma$, we have $D \vdash +\partial l$ and $D \vdash -\partial\sim l$. The resulting extension is thus $E(D) =$

$$(+\Delta = \{a, b, c\}, \quad -\Delta = \{\sim a, \sim b, \sim c, l, \sim l, z, \sim z\},$$

$$+\partial = \{a, b, c, l, z\}, \quad -\partial = \{\sim a, \sim b, \sim c, \sim l, \sim z\} \ ).$$

Theorem 1. *[19] Given a defeasible theory D, its extension $E(D)$ can be computed in time polynomial to the size of the theory. (The size of the theory is given by the number of occurrences of literals, rules, and instances of the superiority relation in it).*

3   Computational Problem and Methodology

As outlined in the previous sections, the output theory, as well as the whole operations, must satisfy certain properties. First, we shall impose that only literals that do not appear as a consequence of any rule can be facts of the output theory, as in Definition 5 below.

Definition 5 (Admissible factual literals).   *Given (an initial) theory $D_{init} = (\emptyset, R, >)$, we define the set of* admissible factual literals *(shortly* factual literals*) as*

$$\{p, \neg p \mid R[p] \cup R[\neg p] = \emptyset\}.$$

It follows that the set of factual literals is the set of literals for which there are no rules and, consequently, such literals can only be derived if they are facts.

A set of literals is *consistent* if it does not contain any pair of literals $(p, \neg p)$.

Example 2. Assume D_{init} is $(\emptyset, R, \emptyset)$, with

$$R = \{\alpha \colon a \Rightarrow z \qquad \zeta \colon z \Rightarrow l \qquad \beta \colon b \Rightarrow \sim l \qquad \gamma \colon g \Rightarrow l\}.$$

Here, a, b, and g are (admissible) factual literals, whilst z, l, and $\sim l$ are not.

Secondly, the output theory must be stable, i.e., consistently adding facts does not change the provability of the target literal. In order to formalise a theory being stable, we firstly define which characteristics the output theory must satisfy, and we name such "valid" output theories *cases*.

Definition 6 (Case). *Given the initial theory $D_{init} = (\emptyset, R, >)$ and the target literal l, we say that a theory $D = (F, R, >)$ is a* case for l of D_{init} *iff*

1. *F is consistent,*
2. *for all $f \in F$, f is a factual literal, and*
3. *$D \vdash +\partial l$.*

When l or D_{init} are clear from the context, we shortly say that D is a *case*. Moreover, whenever clear from the context, we use the term case for both the theory and the set of facts in it. Referring to Example 2, theory $D = (F = \{a\}, R, \emptyset)$ is a case for l of D_{init}.

Definition 7 (Stable Case). *Given the initial theory $D_{init} = (\emptyset, R, >)$ and the target l, we say that a theory $D = (F, R, >)$ is a* stable case for l of D_{init} *iff (1) D is a case for l (of D_{init}), and (2) for all $D' = (F', R, >)$ s.t. if $F \subsetneq F'$ and F' is consistent, then $D' \vdash +\partial l$.*

The case theory $D = (F = \{a\}, R, \emptyset)$ is not stable as $D' = (F' = \{a, b\}, R, \emptyset)$ defeasibly rejects l. On the contrary, theories with set of facts $\{a, \sim b\}$, $\{c, \sim b\}$, or $\{a, \sim b, c\}$ are stable cases for l as motivated in Sect. 1, even if $\sim b$ does not appear in any rule antecedent/consequent, we may impose $\sim b \in F$, provided that the letter from which the literal is obtained appears in a rule either as an antecedent or as a consequent.

In the current investigation, we will not concern ourselves with finding *minimal* stable cases and leave such an investigation for future works.

Symmetric to the concept of case, we now introduce the notion of *refutation case*, which is the base to consequently define the notion of *stable refutation case*.

Definition 8 (Refutation case). *Given the initial theory $D_{init} = (\emptyset, R, >)$ and the target literal l, we say that a theory $D = (F, R, >)$ is a refutation case for l of D_{init} iff*

1. F is consistent,
2. for all $f \in F$, f is a factual literal, and
3. $D \vdash -\partial l$.

Definition 9 (Stable Refutation Case). *Given the initial theory $D_{init} = (\emptyset, R, >)$ and the target literal l, we say that a theory $D = (F, R, >)$ is a stable refutation case for l of D_{init} iff (1) D is a refutation case for l (of D_{init}), and (2) for all $D' = (F', R, >)$ s.t. if $F \subsetneq F'$ and F' is consistent, then $D' \vdash -\partial l$.*

The last notion introduced is that of *unstable case*, namely the situation when a case is not resilient to the addition of facts to the theory.

Definition 10 (Unstable Case). *Given the initial theory $D_{init} = (\emptyset, R, >)$ and the target l, we say that a theory $D = (F, R, >)$ is an iff (1) D is a case for l (of D_{init}), and (2) there exists $D' = (F', R, >)$ s.t. if $F \subsetneq F'$ and F' is consistent, then $D' \vdash +\partial \sim l$.*

Note that, naturally, D is "just" a case for l, and not a stable (refutation) case.

4   Complexity Results

We shall prove the complexity results of the three problems of determining whether: a case is stable, a refutation case is stable, or a case is unstable.

Theorem 2. *Given a Defeasible Theory and a case, the problem of determining if the case is stable is co-NP-complete.*

Proof. To prove that the problem is co-NP-complete, we show that its complement is NP-complete. Namely, given the theory and the case, to show that the case is not stable. Hence, we have to show that a superset of the case that does not prove the target literal exists. As usual, the proof consists of two parts. Given an oracle that guesses a theory where the set of facts is a superset of the case, we can check polynomially whether this theory proves the target literal or not (Theorem 1). For the second part, we provide a polynomial encoding of 3-SAT, and we demonstrate that if the theory encoding the 3-SAT instance is not stable, then the 3-SAT instance is satisfiable. A 3-SAT instance is given by

$$\bigwedge_{i=1}^{n} d_i$$

where $d_i = c_i^1 \vee c_i^2 \vee c_i^3$. Its encoding in Defeasible Logic is given by the theory $D = (\emptyset, R, \emptyset)$ where R contains, for every clause d_i, the following rules[1]:

$$r_{i,j}: c_i^j \Rightarrow d_i \qquad j \in \{1, 2, 3\}$$

plus the two rules:

$$r_{sat}: d_1, \dots, d_n \Rightarrow sat$$
$$r_{nsat}: \Rightarrow \neg sat$$

Clearly, the encoding is polynomial (actually, linear) in the size of the 3-SAT instance. We consider the case given by the empty set of facts and $\neg sat$ as the target literal. It is immediate to verify that $D \vdash +\partial \, sat$: r_{nsat} is the only applicable rule; all other rules are discarded. The set of admissible literals consists of all literals c_i^j and $\sim c_i^j$. To show that $\emptyset$ is not stable we have to find a subset of admissible literals C such that $D' = (C, R, \emptyset) \vdash -\partial \neg sat$. For a (consistent) set of admissible literals C, we build the interpretation I as follows:

$$I(c_i^j) = \begin{cases} TRUE & c_i^j \in C \\ FALSE & \text{otherwise} \end{cases}$$

We can not prove that $D' \vdash -\partial \neg sat$ iff $I \models \bigwedge_{i=1}^{n} d_i$. To prove $-\partial \neg sat$, the rule r_{sat} has to be applicable. This means we need to have $+\partial d_i$. This implies that for each d_i at least of the rules $r_{i,1}$, $r_{i,2}$ and $r_{i,3}$ is applicable too. Consequently, one of c_i^1, c_i^2, and c_i^3 is defeasible derivable. Given there are no rules for c_i^j, $+\partial c_i^j$ iff $c_i^j \in C$. Accordingly, $I(c_i^j) = TRUE$. Thus, for every clause we have an element in it that makes the clause true, thus $I(d_i) = TRUE$, for every i and so the 3-SAT instance is satisfiable. Conversely, when $I \models \bigwedge_{i=1}^{n} d_i$, $I \models d_i$ for every $1 \leq i \leq n$. Thus, for each d_i, there is a c_i^j such that $I(c_i^j) = TRUE$, and so $c_i^j \in C$. Therefore, $D' \vdash +\partial c_i^j$, from which we derive that for every i, $D' \vdash +\partial d_i$, making r_{sat} applicable, which implies $D' \vdash -\partial \neg sat$.

Theorem 3. *Given a Defeasible Theory and a refutation case, the problem of determining if the refutation case is stable is co-NP-complete.*

Proof. We can use the proof of Theorem 2, but we set the target literal to $-\partial sat$.

Theorem 4. *Given a Defeasible Theory and a case, the problem of determining if the case is unstable is NP-complete.*

Proof. We can use the same transformation of Theorem 2 and add the instance of the superiority relation $r_{sat} > r_{nsat}$.

---

[1] Notice that we use d_i as a variable for a clause in the 3-SAT instance and as a literal (representing the clause) in the corresponding defeasible logic encoding.

5 Abduction and Theory Change

In Sect. 3, we defined the issue of whether a case is stable or not, namely, the problem of determining whether adding new facts makes the target literal no longer derivable. In Sect. 4, we then investigated the complexity of such a problem. To this end, we examined the complement of the problem: whether it is possible to find a superset of the case that can change the derivability status of the target literal. It should be clear that this operation is a form of belief revision.

In the literature of DL [13,15], belief revision is more appropriately called "theory change". Three types of theory changes are identified in DL: expansion, revision, and contraction. Expansion is the process of transitioning from a theory where "something" is refuted to a theory where that something is proved. Contraction is conceptually the opposite operation, from derived to refuted. Lastly, revision is going from something being proved to the opposite being proved.

The authors of [4] provide simple (constant time) operations to change a theory via adding new rules. The problem of changing a theory by modifying the superiority relation (either by adding or removing instances of it) was proved to be computationally intractable in [12,13]. In this section, we show how to use the results of Sect. 4 to establish the computational complexity results for the problem of theory change by adding facts (different from the target literal).

Formally, given the initial theory D_{init}, the output theory D, and the target literal l, we can formally define such operations under a (DL's) proof theoretical perspective as

Expansion: from $D_{init} \vdash -\partial l$ to $D \vdash +\partial l$.
Contraction: from $D_{init} \vdash +\partial l$ to $D \vdash -\partial l$.
Revision: from $D_{init} \vdash +\partial l$ to $D \vdash +\partial \sim l$.

Using the results in Sect. 4, we can establish the following complexity results:

Theorem 5. *When the target literal is not admissible and the new set of facts does not include it or its complement, then*

1. *The problem of determining whether it is possible to expand a theory by only adding facts is equivalent to the problem of determining whether the case corresponding to the initial theory is not a stable refutation case.*
2. *The problem of determining whether it is possible to contract a theory by only adding facts is equivalent to the problem of determining whether the case corresponding to the initial theory is not a stable case.*
3. *The problem of determining whether it is possible to expand a theory by only adding facts is equivalent to the problem if determining whether the case corresponding to the initial theory is an unstable case.*

Moreover, the three problems above are NP-complete.

First of all, we recall a result of [1] where the authors show that there is a polynomial transformation of a theory into an equivalent one, where the set of facts is empty. After this step, we can immediately use Theorems 2–4 to set the complexity of the above theory change problems.

6   Related Work

The abduction process as devised by [17] is the process of understanding which explanations could be found that come from the assumption that a given conclusion has to be accepted. The literature on abduction is vast as we already observed in Sect. 1.

The non-monotonic nature of revision of beliefs has been stressed out since the beginnings. In primis, the idea of non-monotonicity has been investigated as a means to represent the way in which conclusions are derived when the derivations are not universal but only typical [1,14,20]. In a closely related but parallel approach it has been regarded as a way to represent theory change [22].

Another fruitful area of investigation for revision that involves also abduction is the argumentation theory. In particular Snaith and Reed [23] discussed the ways in which arguments can be revised, and Augusto and Simar [2] the nature of temporal arguments.

Naturally, a computational perspective on this arose rather soon in the various communities that studied these issues. The initial investigations on this topic have been reviewed by the authors of [7] and devised in terms of their complexity. However, until some years further, no study was able to focus the main point of abduction processes from a computational point of view: the nature of abduction is to make a *case* for a proven conclusion, not only to find an explanation for that conclusion that aims at a general and philosophical perspective. When Eiter and Gotlob discussed this point in [9], a somehow disruptive approach to the issue was adopted by the majority of scholars and neat progresses have been made in understanding how to treat the problem in a correct way.

Recent advances in this investigation line, relatively to the complexity of abduction have been focusing on the notion of *adaptation*, where a theory adapts to the conclusions have not a factual nature [18]. A relevant issue in abduction methods relates to minimisation, as devised in [21] lately.

Another interesting recent work is [5,6] where the concept of strong explanation has been introduced for non-monotonic reasoning. The addressed problem is precisely how to determine minimal subsets of the knowledge base entailing a certain formula. The authors show that strong explanations coincide with the standard notion for monotonic logics, but also handle the nonmonotonic case adequately. This contribution does not consider DL, but we see interesting overlaps, which we will explore in future works.

Case-based reasoning issues in abduction led to considering, in fact, not only a general process for propositional theories, but also the base for a large set of methodological issues related to non-monotonic systems such as default logic [10,11].

7   Conclusions and Future Investigations

In this paper we introduced a novel concept for abduction in non-monotonic systems: the one of stability. An explanation is stable, when adding new facts does not prevent such an explanation to work for that literal.

Stable explanations are provided for abduction processes that only *increase* the set of facts; without loss of generality, we assumed the initial set of facts to be empty. Computing stability is hence the prime problem to be solved in order to obtain a good explanation for a literal. However, determining whether an explanation exists is computationally hard. We have also proven that the revision problem of a theory with an empty set of facts is related to the stability problem, thus providing a proof that the revision problem is computationally hard as well.

There are diverse research lines that are worth to pursuing. First of all, all our results are for a single target literal. It is not possible to extend them trivially to a set of literals. In fact, though the problem is similar, it is technically not true that we can derive separately such elements of a set to conclude, somehow, that a set operation on the resulting sets of assumptions gives us an answer on it. Analogously, establishing whether a set of literals is stable does not consist in proving stability for each literal separately.

Further, it is important to understand how to introduce specific constraints on what can be changed, and what may not. In particular, what if we assume that some facts cannot be changed/eliminated. This could be important, for instance, if we have a situation like the one depicted in Sect. 1.

Rather naturally, it would also be an issue to study the behaviour of the facts contraction operator, that completes, along the facts expansion operator, the range of possible ways in which a set of facts can be abducted on a non-monotonic theory. Contraction alone could possibly be interesting, as well as paired with expansion.

Last but not least: the problems introduced here are computationally hard, and some of the ones that we can define as future work actually include these problems (expansion of sets, constrained expansion) while the contraction and revision problems cannot be trivially considered as supersets of the expansion of a single literal. Is there any way to reduce the complexity? In particular, are there any subsets of the instances of the defined problems that are polynomially tractable? If this is the case we can reduce the computational cost by detecting whether a single instance belongs to one of these classes, and then solve it polynomially.

References

1. Antoniou, G., Billington, D., Governatori, G., Maher, M.: Representation results for defeasible logic. ACM Trans. Comput. Log. **2**(2), 255–287 (2001). https://doi.org/10.1145/371316.371517
2. Augusto, J., Simari, G.: Temporal argumentative system. AI Commun. **12**(4), 237–257 (1999)
3. Batens, D.: Abduction logics: Illustrating pitfalls of defeasible methods. Logic Argumentation Reasoning **14**, 169–193 (2017). https://doi.org/10.1007/978-3-319-58507-9_8

4. Billington, D., Antoniou, G., Governatori, G., Maher, M.: Revising nonmonotonic theories: the case of defeasible logic. In: Burgard, W., Cremers, A.B., Cristaller, T. (eds.) KI 1999. LNCS (LNAI), vol. 1701, pp. 101–112. Springer, Heidelberg (1999). https://doi.org/10.1007/3-540-48238-5_8
5. Brewka, G., Thimm, M., Ulbricht, M.: Strong inconsistency. Artif. Intell. **267**, 78–117 (2019). http://dblp.uni-trier.de/db/journals/ai/ai267.html#BrewkaTU19
6. Brewka, G., Ulbricht, M.: Strong explanations for nonmonotonic reasoning. In: Lutz, C., Sattler, U., Tinelli, C., Turhan, A.-Y., Wolter, F. (eds.) Description Logic, Theory Combination, and All That. LNCS, vol. 11560, pp. 135–146. Springer, Cham (2019). https://doi.org/10.1007/978-3-030-22102-7_6
7. Bylander, T., Allemang, D., Tanner, M.C., Josephson, J.R.: The computational complexity of abduction. Artif. Intell. **49**(1), 25–60 (1991). https://doi.org/10.1016/0004-3702(91)90005-5
8. Delrieux, C.: Abductive inference in defeasible reasoning: A model for research programmes. J. Appl. Log. **2**(4), 409–437 (2004). https://doi.org/10.1016/j.jal.2004.07.003
9. Eiter, T., Gottlob, G.: The complexity of logic-based abduction. J. ACM (JACM) **42**(1), 3–42 (1995). https://doi.org/10.1145/200836.200838
10. Eiter, T., Gottlob, G., Leone, N.: Abduction from logic programs: semantics and complexity. Theoret. Comput. Sci. **189**(1–2), 129–177 (1997). https://doi.org/10.1016/s0304-3975(96)00179-x
11. Eiter, T., Gottlob, G., Leone, N.: Semantics and complexity of abduction from default theories. Artif. Intell. **90**(1–2), 177–223 (1997). https://doi.org/10.1016/s0004-3702(96)00040-9
12. Governatori, G., Olivieri, F., Cristani, M., Scannapieco, S.: Revision of defeasible preferences. Int. J. Approximate Reasoning **104**, 205–230 (2019). https://doi.org/10.1016/j.ijar.2018.10.020
13. Governatori, G., Olivieri, F., Scannapieco, S., Cristani, M.: Superiority based revision of defeasible theories. In: Dean, M., Hall, J., Rotolo, A., Tabet, S. (eds.) RuleML 2010. LNCS, vol. 6403, pp. 104–118. Springer, Heidelberg (2010). https://doi.org/10.1007/978-3-642-16289-3_10
14. Governatori, G., Maher, M.J., Billington, D., Antoniou, G.: Argumentation semantics for defeasible logics. J. Log. Comput. **14**(5), 675–702 (2004)
15. Governatori, G., Olivieri, F., Cristani, M., Scannapieco, S.: Revision of defeasible preferences. Int. J. Approx. Reason. **104**, 205–230 (2019). https://doi.org/10.1016/j.ijar.2018.10.020
16. Governatori, G., Padmanabhan, V., Rotolo, A., Sattar, A.: A defeasible logic for modelling policy-based intentions and motivational attitudes. Log. J. IGPL **17**(3), 227–265 (2009). https://doi.org/10.1093/jigpal/jzp006
17. Harman, G.H.: The inference to the best explanation. Philos. Rev. **74**(1), 88–95 (1965). https://doi.org/10.2307/2183532
18. Lycke, H.: A formal explication of the search for explanations: the adaptive logics approach to abductive reasoning. Logic J. IGPL **20**(2), 497–516 (2012). https://doi.org/10.1093/jigpal/jzq053
19. Maher, M.J.: Propositional defeasible logic has linear complexity. Theory Pract. Logic Program. **1**(6), 691–711 (2001)
20. Nute, D.: Defeasible reasoning. In: Proceedings of the Hawaii International Conference on System Science, vol. 3, pp. 470–477 (1987)
21. Pfandler, A., Pichler, R., Woltran, S.: The complexity of handling minimal solutions in logic-based abduction. J. Log. Comput. **25**(3), 805–825 (2014). https://doi.org/10.1093/logcom/exu053

258   G. Governatori et al.

22. Shoham, Y.: Chronological ignorance: Experiments in nonmonotonic temporal reasoning. Artif. Intell. **36**(3), 279–331 (1988). https://doi.org/10.1016/0004-3702(88)90085-9
23. Snaith, M., Reed, C.: Argument revision. J. Log. Comput. **27**(7), 2089–2134 (2017). https://doi.org/10.1093/logcom/exw028

Semantics for Conditional Literals via the SM Operator

Zachary Hansen and Yuliya Lierler[✉]

University of Nebraska Omaha, Omaha, NE 68182, USA
{zachhansen,ylierler}@unomaha.edu

Abstract. Conditional literals are an expressive Answer Set Programming language construct supported by the solver CLINGO. Their semantics are currently defined by a translation to infinitary propositional logic, however, we develop an alternative characterization with the SM operator which does not rely on grounding. This allows us to reason about the behavior of a broad class of CLINGO programs/encodings containing conditional literals, without referring to a particular input/instance of an encoding. We formalize the intuition that conditional literals behave as nested implications, and prove the equivalence of our semantics to those implemented by CLINGO.

Keywords: ASP · Semantics · Conditional Literals

1 Introduction

Answer Set Programming (ASP) [13,14] is a widely utilized branch of logic programming that combines an expressive modeling language with efficient grounders and solvers. It has found a number of prominent applications since its inception, such as diagnostic AI and space shuttle decision support systems [1]. For various classes of logic programs, there are multiple equivalent ways to characterize their semantics [12]. Most of the semantics for non-propositional programs (used in the practice of ASP) are defined via grounding – a process of instantiating variables for passing constants. This often makes it difficult to reason about parts of logic programs in isolation. The SM operator [7] is one of the few approaches to interpreting logic programs without reference to grounding. In this approach, a logic program is viewed as an abbreviation for a first-order sentence. The semantics of a program are defined by means of an application of the SM operator to the program, which results in a second-order formula. The Herbrand models of this formula coincide with the answer sets of the considered logic program. In this work, we extend the class of programs to which the SM operator is applicable by providing a translation to first-order formulas for constructs known as "conditional" literals. We then illustrate that the newly defined semantics via the SM operator for programs with conditional literals coincides with that by Harrison, Lifschitz, and Yang (2014). In that work, the authors

---

Z. Hansen and Y. Lierler—These authors contributed equally.

captured the meaning of programs with conditional literals via grounding/trans-formation of a logic program into infinitary propositional formulas. Importantly, the answer set system CLINGO [9] obeys their semantics.

Rules with conditional literals are common in so-called meta-programming [11], where reification of constructs is utilized to build ASP-based reasoning engines that may go beyond the ASP paradigm itself. The meta-programming technique is well illustrated in [11] by means of multiple examples, where conditional literals are widespread. For instance, Kaminski et al. (2021) use this technique in the implementation of optimization statements, reasoning about actions, reasoning about preferences, and guess-and-check programming. Here, we showcase the utility of conditional literals on the well-studied graph (k) coloring problem. This problem has a simple specification: *For an undirected graph, the k-coloring problem assigns one of k colors to each vertex such that no two vertices connected by an edge share a color.* It is an NP-complete problem to decide if a given graph admits a k-coloring for any $k \geq 3$. This problem can be elegantly encoded in a few lines of ASP code. First consider the encoding in Listing 1.1, where $color(I; J)$ and $vtx(V; W)$ abbreviate expressions $color(I); color(J)$ and $vtx(V); vtx(W)$, respectively. This is an instructional encoding by Lierler (2017, Sect. 5) modulo the changes in predicate names.

Listing 1.1. 3-coloring problem encoding.

```
1   {asg(V,I)} :- vtx(V); color(I).
2   :- not asg(V,r); not asg(V,g); not asg(V,b); vtx(V).
3   :- asg(V,I); asg(V,J); I != J; vtx(V); color(I;J).
4   :- asg(V,I); asg(W,I); vtx(V;W); color(I); edge(V,W).
```

Given an instance of a graph, the program in Listing 1.1 assigns colors from the set $\{r, g, b\}$ to its vertices. Yet, however concise and self-explanatory this solution is, it lacks elaboration tolerance. It is restricted to the color names hard-coded into the program, and it only solves the 3-coloring problem as opposed to the k-coloring problem. Conditional literals provide us with a convenient means to address this shortcoming. Consider the encoding in Listing 1.1 with line 2 replaced by

$$:- \textsf{not asg(V, I)} : \textsf{color(I)}; \textsf{vtx(V)}. \tag{1}$$

where expression $not\ asg(V, I) : color(I)$ constitutes a conditional literal. The original rule in line 2 forbade solutions that did not assign any of the three colors to a vertex. In rule (1), the conditional literal is satisfied when no colors are assigned to a given vertex. In the sequel, we refer to the program consisting of the rules in lines 1, 3, and 4 of Listing 1.1 and rule (1) as the k-coloring encoding. Note how the k-coloring encoding is agnostic to the naming and number of colors, providing us with a truly elaboration tolerant solution for the k-coloring problem.

The remainder of this paper is organized as follows. Section 2 starts by presenting the syntax of logic programs considered in this paper. These programs contain conditional literals and we call them conditional programs. Section 3 continues by defining a translation from conditional programs to first-order formulas, and uses the SM operator to provide their semantics. Section 4 describes the semantics of conditional programs using infinitary propositional logic. In Sect. 5 we connect these two characterizations of conditional programs, formally illustrating that they coincide. Thus, the SM-based semantics introduced here for conditional programs captures the behavior of CLINGO. In Sect. 6, we illustrate the utility of the SM-based semantics by arguing the correctness of the *k-coloring* program.

2 Syntax of Conditional Programs

In this section, we introduce a fragment of the input language of CLINGO with conditional literals. A *term* is a variable, or an object constant, or an expression of the form $f(\mathbf{t})$, where f is a function constant of arity k and $\mathbf{t}$ is a k-tuple of terms. When a term does not contain variables we call it *ground*. An *atomic formula* is either (i) an expression of the form $t = t'$ where t and t' are terms or (ii) an *atom* $p(t_1, \ldots, t_n)$, where p is a predicate symbol of arity n and t_i $(1 \leq i \leq n)$ is a term; if $n = 0$, we omit the parentheses and write p (p is a propositional atom). A *basic literal* is an atomic formula optionally preceded by *not*; we identify a basic literal of the form *not* $t = t'$ with the expression $t \neq t'$. A *conditional literal* is an expression of the form $H : l_1, \ldots, l_m$, where H is a basic literal or the symbol $\bot$ (denoting falsity) and $l_1, \ldots, l_m$ is a nonempty list of basic literals. We often abbreviate such an expression as $H : \mathbf{L}$.

A *(conditional logic) program* is a finite set of *rules* of the form

$$H_1 \mid \cdots \mid H_m \leftarrow B_1; \ldots; B_n. \tag{2}$$

$(m, n \geq 0)$, where each H_i, B_i is a basic or conditional literal; if $m = 0$ then we identify the *head* of the rule (left hand side of rule operator $\leftarrow$) with $\bot$. The right hand side of the rule operator $\leftarrow$ is called the *body*. We call a rule, where $m = 1$ and $n = 0$ a *fact*. We consider rules of the form $\{p(\mathbf{t})\} \leftarrow B_1; \ldots; B_n$ to be shorthand for $p(\mathbf{t}) \mid not\ p(\mathbf{t}) \leftarrow B_1; \ldots; B_n$, where p is a predicate constant of arity k and $\mathbf{t}$ is a k-tuple of terms.

Let $\sigma = (\mathcal{O}, \mathcal{F}, \mathcal{P})$ be a signature of a first-order language, where $\mathcal{O}$ is the set of object constants, $\mathcal{F}$ is the set of function constants of non-zero arity, and $\mathcal{P}$ is the set of predicate constants; by $\mathcal{G}_\sigma$ we denote the set of all ground terms that one may construct from the sets $\mathcal{O}$ and $\mathcal{F}$ of σ. For example, take $\mathcal{O} = \{a\}$ and $\mathcal{F} = \{f/1\}$ in some σ: then, $\mathcal{G}_\sigma = \{a, f(a), f(f(a)), \ldots\}$. It is customary in logic programming that a program defines its signature implicitly, yet here it is convenient to make it explicit. For a program Π, we refer to its signature as a triple $(\mathcal{O}_\Pi, \mathcal{F}_\Pi, \mathcal{P}_\Pi)$, where $\mathcal{O}_\Pi$, $\mathcal{F}_\Pi$, and $\mathcal{P}_\Pi$ contain all the object constants, function symbols of non-zero arity, and predicate constants occurring in Π, respectively. To simplify the notation, we use $\mathcal{G}_\Pi$ to denote $\mathcal{G}_{(\mathcal{O}_\Pi, \mathcal{F}_\Pi, \mathcal{P}_\Pi)}$.

3 Semantics via the SM Operator

We now propose a syntactic transformation ϕ from logic programs to first-order sentences. The majority of this translation is implicitly described in

[7, Section 2.1], where rules are viewed as an alternative notation for particular types of first-order sentences. We extend these ideas to programs with conditional literals.

First, we define some required concepts. A variable is *global* in a conditional literal $H : \mathbf{L}$ if it occurs in H but not in $\mathbf{L}$. Given a rule, all variables occurring in basic literals outside of conditional literals are considered *global*. A variable is *global in a rule* if it is global in one or more of the rule's literals. For example, in rule (1), variable V is global whereas variable I is not. Let R be a rule of the form (2) such that at least one H_i or B_i in the rule is a conditional literal $\mathcal{L}$. Let $\mathbf{v}$ be the list of variables occurring in $\mathcal{L}$. Let $\mathbf{z}$ be the list of the global variables in R. Then we call $\mathbf{x} = \mathbf{v} \setminus \mathbf{z}$ the *local* variables of $\mathcal{L}$ within R.

To transform a rule R of the form (2) into a first order sentence, we define a translation $\phi_\mathbf{z}$, where $\mathbf{z}$ is the list of global variables occurring in R:

1. $\phi_\mathbf{z}(\bot)$ is $\bot$;
2. $\phi_\mathbf{z}(A)$ is A for an atomic formula A;
3. $\phi_\mathbf{z}(not\,A)$ is $\neg\phi_\mathbf{z}A$ for an atomic formula A;
4. $\phi_\mathbf{z}(\mathbf{L})$ is $\phi_\mathbf{z}(l_1) \wedge \cdots \wedge \phi_\mathbf{z}(l_m)$ for a list $\mathbf{L}$ of basic literals;
5. for a conditional literal $H : \mathbf{L}$ occurring in the body of R with local variables $\mathbf{x}$,
   $\phi_\mathbf{z}(H : \mathbf{L})$ is $\forall\mathbf{x}\,(\phi_\mathbf{z}(\mathbf{L}) \rightarrow \phi_\mathbf{z}(H))$;
6. for a conditional literal $H : \mathbf{L}$ occurring in the head of R with local variables $\mathbf{x}$,
   $\phi_\mathbf{z}(H : \mathbf{L})$ is $\exists\mathbf{x}\big((\phi_\mathbf{z}(\mathbf{L}) \rightarrow \phi_\mathbf{z}(H)) \wedge \neg\neg\phi_\mathbf{z}(\mathbf{L})\big)$.

Recall rule (1) containing the conditional literal $not\ asg(V, I) : color(I)$. Variable V is the only global variable of that rule, whereas variable I is local within this conditional literal. Hence, ϕ_V turns this conditional literal into formula $\forall i\,(color(i) \rightarrow \neg asg(v, i))$, where in accordance with the convention of first-order logic we turn variables into lower case.

We now define the translation ϕ on rules and programs as follows:

1. for every rule R of the form (2), its translation $\phi(R)$ is the formula

$$\forall\mathbf{z}(\phi_\mathbf{z}(B_1) \wedge \cdots \wedge \phi_\mathbf{z}(B_n) \rightarrow \phi_\mathbf{z}(H_1) \vee \cdots \vee \phi_\mathbf{z}(H_m)),$$

   where $\mathbf{z}$ is the list of the global variables of R;
2. for every program Π, its translation $\phi(\Pi)$ is the first-order sentence formed by the conjunction of $\phi(R)$ for every rule R in Π.

As a result, the rules of the *k-coloring* conditional program discussed in the Introduction are identified with the following sentences by translation ϕ:

$$\forall vi\big((vtx(v) \wedge color(i)) \rightarrow asg(v, i) \vee \neg asg(v, i)\big) \tag{3}$$

$$\forall v\big((\forall i(color(i) \rightarrow \neg asg(v, i)) \wedge vtx(v)) \rightarrow \bot\big) \tag{4}$$

$$\forall vij\big((asg(v, i) \wedge asg(v, j) \wedge i \neq j \wedge vtx(v) \wedge color(i) \wedge color(j)) \rightarrow \bot\big) \tag{5}$$

$$\forall viw\big((asg(v, i) \wedge asg(w, i) \wedge vtx(v; w) \wedge color(i) \wedge edge(v, w)) \rightarrow \bot\big) \tag{6}$$

where $vtx(v; w)$ abbreviates $vtx(v) \wedge vtx(w)$. The first-order sentence corresponding to the *k-coloring* program consists of the conjunction of Formulas (3-6). We refer to this first-order sentence as KC.

We now review the operator SM following Ferraris, Lee, and Lifschitz (2011). The symbols $\perp, \wedge, \vee, \rightarrow, \forall$, and $\exists$ are viewed as primitives. The formulas $\neg F$ and $\top$ are abbreviations for $F \rightarrow \perp$ and $\perp \rightarrow \perp$, respectively. If p and q are predicate symbols of arity n then $p \leq q$ is an abbreviation for the formula $\forall \mathbf{x}(p(\mathbf{x}) \rightarrow q(\mathbf{x}))$, where $\mathbf{x}$ is a tuple of variables of length n. If $\mathbf{p}$ and $\mathbf{q}$ are tuples $p_1, \ldots, p_n$ and $q_1, \ldots, q_n$ of predicate symbols then $\mathbf{p} \leq \mathbf{q}$ is an abbreviation for the conjunction $(p_1 \leq q_1) \wedge \cdots \wedge (p_n \leq q_n)$, and $\mathbf{p} < \mathbf{q}$ is an abbreviation for $(\mathbf{p} \leq \mathbf{q}) \wedge \neg (\mathbf{q} \leq \mathbf{p})$. We apply the same notation to tuples of predicate variables in second-order logic formulas. If $\mathbf{p}$ is a tuple of predicate symbols $p_1, \ldots, p_n$ (not including equality), and F is a first-order sentence then $\mathrm{SM}_{\mathbf{p}}[F]$ (called the *stable model operator with intensional predicates* $\mathbf{p}$) denotes the second-order sentence $F \wedge \neg \exists \mathbf{u}(\mathbf{u} < \mathbf{p}) \wedge F^*(\mathbf{u})$, where $\mathbf{u}$ is a tuple of distinct predicate variables $u_1, \ldots, u_n$, and $F^*(\mathbf{u})$ is defined recursively:

- $p_i(\mathbf{t})^*$ is $u_i(\mathbf{t})$ for any tuple $\mathbf{t}$ of terms;
- F^* is F for any atomic formula F that does not contain members of $\mathbf{p}$;
- $(F \wedge G)^*$ is $F^* \wedge G^*$;
- $(F \vee G)^*$ is $F^* \vee G^*$;
- $(F \rightarrow G)^*$ is $(F^* \rightarrow G^*) \wedge (F \rightarrow G)$;
- $(\forall x F)^*$ is $\forall x F^*$;
- $(\exists x F)^*$ is $\exists x F^*$.

We define the semantics of conditional logic programs using the SM operator. We note that if $\mathbf{p}$ is the empty tuple then $\mathrm{SM}_{\mathbf{p}}[F]$ is equivalent to F. We call an interpretation a $\mathbf{p}$-*stable model* of F when it is a model of $\mathrm{SM}_{\mathbf{p}}[F]$. For a conditional logic program Π and a Herbrand interpretation I over the signature $(\mathcal{O}_\Pi, \mathcal{F}_\Pi, \mathcal{P}_\Pi)$, I is an *answer set* of Π when I is a $\mathcal{P}_\Pi$-stable model of $\phi(\Pi)$.

As is customary, the concept of an answer set is defined for Herbrand interpretations. It is common to identify Herbrand interpretations with the set of ground atoms that are evaluated to true by this interpretation. When convenient, we follow this convention. It is worth noting that dropping the word Herbrand from the definition of an answer set allows us to extend the notion of an answer set/stable model to non-Herbrand interpretations following, for example, the tradition of [7,15]. Also, the provided definitions allow us to consider $\mathbf{p}$-stable models of conditional programs, where $\mathbf{p}$ is a tuple of predicate symbols in Π to characterize interesting properties of conditional programs. We articulate the utility of $\mathbf{p}$-stable models in Sect. 6. In that section we extend the *k-coloring* program with a sample set of facts encoding an instance of the *k-coloring* problem and argue how the answer sets of the resulting program correspond to the solutions of this instance.

4   Semantics via Infinitary Propositional Logic

Programs with conditional literals were first formalized by (i) their reduction to infinitary (propositional logic) formulas [10] and (ii) utilizing the definition of a stable model for such formulas introduced by Truszczyński (2012). We refer the reader to Definition 1 in [15] for the details on what constitutes a stable model for an infinitary formula as its details are not required in understanding the content of this paper. We now review the syntax of an infinitary formula and the details of the translation of conditional programs to infinitary formulas by Harrison, Lifschitz, and Yang (2014).

Let A be a set of ground atoms. We define sets $\mathcal{F}_0, \mathcal{F}_1, \ldots$ by induction:

- $\mathcal{F}_0 = A$;
- $\mathcal{F}_{i+1}$ adds to $\mathcal{F}_i$ all expressions $\mathcal{H}^\wedge, \mathcal{H}^\vee$ for all subsets $\mathcal{H}$ of $\mathcal{F}_i$, and $F \to G$ for all $F, G \in \mathcal{F}_i$.

The set of *infinitary formulas* over A is defined as $\cup_{i=0}^\infty \mathcal{F}_i$. $\{F, G\}^\wedge$ can be written as $F \wedge G$, and $\{F, G\}^\vee$ can be written as $F \vee G$. The symbols $\bot$ and $\top$ will be understood as abbreviations for $\emptyset^\vee$ and $\emptyset^\wedge$, respectively. Expression $\neg F$ is understood as $F \to \bot$.

Harrison, Lifschitz, and Yang (2014) define the semantics of programs with conditional literals using a translation τ that transforms rules of a given program into infinitary propositional formulas. It is worth noting that they allow a broader syntactic class of rules than we consider here. For instance, rules with aggregates are allowed; these rules are outside the scope of this paper, but we refer interested readers to [4] for a review of how the SM operator can define semantics for programs with aggregates. Here, we restrict our review of τ to conditional programs. The translation τ is summarized below using the following notation: if t is a term, $\mathbf{x}$ is a tuple of variables, and $\mathbf{r}$ is a tuple of terms of the same length as $\mathbf{x}$, then $[t]_\mathbf{r}^\mathbf{x}$ (equivalently, $t_\mathbf{r}^\mathbf{x}$) is the term obtained from t by substituting $\mathbf{x}$ by $\mathbf{r}$. We use similar notation for other expressions such as literals or their lists, e.g., we may write $[l_1, \ldots, l_m]_\mathbf{r}^\mathbf{x}$ which stands for $[l_1]_\mathbf{r}^\mathbf{x}, \ldots, [l_m]_\mathbf{r}^\mathbf{x}$ and $[H : \mathbf{L}]_\mathbf{r}^\mathbf{x}$ which stands for $H_\mathbf{r}^\mathbf{x} : \mathbf{L}_\mathbf{r}^\mathbf{x}$. A conditional literal or a rule is *closed* if it contains no global variables. $|\mathbf{x}|$ denotes the number of elements in a list $\mathbf{x}$.

To transform a closed rule R into an infinitary propositional formula w.r.t. a set $\mathcal{G}$ of ground terms, translation τ is defined as follows:

1. $\tau(\bot)$ is $\bot$;
2. $\tau(A)$ is A for a ground atom A;
3. $\tau(t_1 = t_2)$ is $\top$ if t_1 is identical to t_2, and $\bot$ otherwise, for ground terms t_1, t_2;
4. τ (*not* A) is $\neg \tau A$;
5. $\tau(\mathbf{L})$ is $\tau(l_1) \wedge \cdots \wedge \tau(l_m)$ for a list $\mathbf{L}$ of basic literals;
6. for a closed conditional literal $H : \mathbf{L}$ occurring in the body of rule R, $\tau(H : \mathbf{L})$ is the conjunction of the formulas $\tau(\mathbf{L}_\mathbf{r}^\mathbf{x}) \to \tau(H_\mathbf{r}^\mathbf{x})$ where $\mathbf{x}$ is the list of variables occurring in the conditional literal, over all tuples of ground terms $\mathbf{r} \in \mathcal{G}^{|\mathbf{x}|}$ (recall that $\mathcal{G}^n$ denotes the Cartesian product $\mathcal{G} \times \cdots \times \mathcal{G}$ of length n);
7. for a closed conditional literal $H : \mathbf{L}$ occurring in the head of rule R, $\tau(H : \mathbf{L})$ is the disjunction of formulas $\left(\tau(\mathbf{L}_\mathbf{r}^\mathbf{x}) \to \tau(H_\mathbf{r}^\mathbf{x})\right) \wedge \neg\neg\tau(\mathbf{L}_\mathbf{r}^\mathbf{x})$ where $\mathbf{x}$ is the list of variables occurring in the conditional literal, over all tuples of ground terms $\mathbf{r} \in \mathcal{G}^{|\mathbf{x}|}$;
8. for a closed rule r of form (2), $\tau(r)$ is $\tau B_1 \wedge \cdots \wedge \tau B_n \to \tau H_1 \vee \cdots \vee \tau H_m$.

Now, we formalize the rule instantiation process from [10]. Let $\mathbf{z}$ denote the global variables of rule R. By $inst_{\mathcal{G}}(R)$ we denote the *instantiations* of rule R w.r.t. a set $\mathcal{G}$ of ground terms, i.e., $inst_{\mathcal{G}}(R) = \{R_{m}athbfu^{\mathbf{z}} \mid mathbfu \in \mathcal{G}^{|\mathbf{z}|}\}^{\wedge}$. Clearly, every rule $r \in inst_{\mathcal{G}}(R)$ is closed, as is each (conditional) literal occurring in r.

Let Π be a conditional program. For a rule R in Π, its translation is defined as $\tau(R) = \{\tau(r) \mid r \in inst_{\mathcal{G}_{\Pi}}(R)\}^{\wedge}$. Similarly, $\tau(\Pi) = \{\tau(R) \text{ w.r.t. } \mathcal{G}_{\Pi} \mid R \in \Pi\}^{\wedge}$. A set of ground atoms constructed over the signature of Π forms a CLINGO *answer set* of a program Π when it is a stable model of $\tau(\Pi)$ in the sense of Definition 1 by Truszczyński (2012).

5 Connecting Two Semantics of Conditional Programs

In this section our goal is to connect our proposed semantics for conditional (logic) programs via the SM operator (Sect. 3) to the semantics defined for such programs in [10] (Sect. 4). For that purpose we review some of the details of [15] that help us to construct an argument for the formal relationship between the considered semantics for conditional programs.

Truszczynski (2012) provides a definition of stable models for first-order sentences. These models may be Herbrand and non-Herbrand interpretations. He defines *the grounding of a sentence F w.r.t. interpretation I*, denoted by $gr_I(F)$, as a transformation of F into infinitary propositional formulas over a given signature [15, Section 3]. If we restrict our attention to Herbrand interpretations, we may note that: *For arbitrary Herbrand interpretations I_1 and I_2 of a first-order sentence F, $gr_{I_1}(F)$ is identical to $gr_{I_2}(F)$*. Thus, we drop the subscript I from the definition of $gr_I(F)$ when we review this concept.

Let σ be a signature and let I be a Herbrand interpretation over σ. For a ground term c in $\mathcal{G}_{\sigma}$, we use c to denote both this ground term and its respective domain element in I, i.e., $c = c^I$. Let F be a first-order sentence over σ. The *grounding of F* (w.r.t. σ), denoted by $gr(F)$, is defined recursively, mapping F into an infinitary propositional formula:

1. $gr(\bot) = \bot$;
2. $gr(A) = A$ for a ground atom A;
3. $gr(t_1 = t_2)$ is $\top$ if t_1 is identical to t_2, and $\bot$ otherwise, for ground terms t_1, t_2;
4. If $F = G \vee \ldots \vee H$, then $gr(F) = gr(G) \vee \cdots \vee gr(H)$;
5. If $F = G \wedge \ldots \wedge H$, then $gr(F) = gr(G) \wedge \cdots \wedge gr(H)$;
6. If $F = G \rightarrow H$, then $gr(F) = gr(G) \rightarrow gr(H)$;
7. If $F = \exists \mathbf{x} G(\mathbf{x})$, then $gr(F) = \{gr(G(mathbfu)) \mid mathbfu \in \mathcal{G}_{\sigma}^{|\mathbf{x}|}\}^{\vee}$;
8. If $F = \forall \mathbf{x} G(\mathbf{x})$, then $gr(F) = \{gr(G(mathbfu)) \mid mathbfu \in \mathcal{G}_{\sigma}^{|\mathbf{x}|}\}^{\wedge}$.

We now observe a key property relating gr, ϕ, and τ transformations that is essential in connecting the SM-based semantics proposed for conditional programs and the infinitary logic-based semantics reviewed in the previous section.

Theorem 1 (Syntactic Identity). *For any conditional logic program Π containing at least one object constant, $gr(\phi(\Pi))$ is identical to $\tau(\Pi)$.*

By Theorem 5 from [15], it follows that for a first-order sentence F, Herbrand interpretations of F are answer sets of F if and only if they are stable models of $gr(F)$ in the sense of Definition 1 by Truszczyński (2012). The following theorem is an immediate consequence of this formal result and the Theorem on Syntactic Identity.

Theorem 2 (Main Theorem). *For any conditional logic program Π containing at least one object constant and any Herbrand interpretation I over $(\mathcal{O}_\Pi, \mathcal{F}_\Pi, \mathcal{P}_\Pi)$, the following conditions are equivalent:*

- *I is an answer set of Π as defined in Sect. 3;*
- *I is a CLINGO answer set of Π as defined in Sect. 4.*

The remainder of this section presents auxiliary results required in constructing the proof of the Theorem on Syntactic Identity, followed by the theorem's proof. The following lemma captures basic equivalences between ϕ, function composition $gr \circ \phi$, and τ transformations.

Lemma 1. *Let $\mathbf{z}$ be a list of variables. Then, the following equivalences hold:*

1. *$\phi_{\mathbf{z}}(\bot) = \tau(\bot)$;*
2. *$gr(\phi_{\mathbf{z}}\bot) = \tau(\bot)$;*

Let A be an atom, $\mathbf{x}$ be a list that includes all variables in A, and $\mathbf{r}$ be a list of ground terms of the same length as $\mathbf{x}$. Then, the following equivalences hold:

3. *$\phi_{\mathbf{z}}(A_{\mathbf{r}}^{\mathbf{x}}) = \tau(A_{\mathbf{r}}^{\mathbf{x}})$;*
4. *$\phi_{\mathbf{z}}(not\ A_{\mathbf{r}}^{\mathbf{x}}) = \tau(not\ A_{\mathbf{r}}^{\mathbf{x}})$.*
5. *$gr(\phi_{\mathbf{z}}(A_{\mathbf{r}}^{\mathbf{x}})) = \tau(A_{\mathbf{r}}^{\mathbf{x}})$;*
6. *$gr(\phi_{\mathbf{z}}(not\ A_{\mathbf{r}}^{\mathbf{x}})) = \tau(not\ A_{\mathbf{r}}^{\mathbf{x}})$.*

Let A be an atomic formula of the form $t_1 = t_2$, $\mathbf{x}$ be a list that includes all variables in A, and $\mathbf{r}$ be a list of ground terms of the same length as $\mathbf{x}$. Then, the following equivalences hold:

7. *$gr(\phi_{\mathbf{z}}(A_{\mathbf{r}}^{\mathbf{x}})) = \tau(A_{\mathbf{r}}^{\mathbf{x}})$;*
8. *$gr(\phi_{\mathbf{z}}(not\ A_{\mathbf{r}}^{\mathbf{x}})) = \tau(not\ A_{\mathbf{r}}^{\mathbf{x}})$.*

Let $\mathbf{L}$ be a list of basic literals, $\mathbf{x}$ be a list that includes all variables in $\mathbf{L}$, and $\mathbf{r}$ be a list of ground terms of the same length as $\mathbf{x}$. The equivalence below holds:

9. *$gr(\phi_{\mathbf{z}}(\mathbf{L}_{\mathbf{r}}^{\mathbf{x}})) = \tau(\mathbf{L}_{\mathbf{r}}^{\mathbf{x}})$.*

Proof. Equivalences 1-5, 7 follow immediately from the definitions of ϕ, gr, and τ transformations (and preceding equivalences, e.g., proof of equivalence 2 takes into account equivalence 1.). The claim of equivalences 6 and 8 relies on equivalences 5 and 7, respectively, and is supported by the following chain

$$gr(\phi_{\mathbf{z}}(not\ A_{\mathbf{r}}^{\mathbf{x}})) = gr(\neg\phi_{\mathbf{z}}(A_{\mathbf{r}}^{\mathbf{x}})) = gr(\phi_{\mathbf{z}}(A_{\mathbf{r}}^{\mathbf{x}}) \to \bot) =$$
$$gr(\phi_{\mathbf{z}}(A_{\mathbf{r}}^{\mathbf{x}})) \to gr(\bot) = \tau(A_{\mathbf{r}}^{\mathbf{x}}) \to \bot = \neg\tau(A_{\mathbf{r}}^{\mathbf{x}}) = \tau(not\ A_{\mathbf{r}}^{\mathbf{x}}).$$

Equivalence 9 follows immediately from the definitions of ϕ, gr, and τ transformations and equivalences 5-8. The remaining lemmas of this section capture less trivial equivalences between $gr \circ \phi$ and τ transformations.

Lemma 2. *Let Π be a conditional logic program containing at least one object constant. Let B be a literal in the body of a rule R in Π, where $\mathbf{z}$ is the list of global variables occurring in R and $\mathbf{u}$ is a list of ground terms of the same length as $\mathbf{z}$. Then, $gr\Big(\phi_{\mathbf{z}}([B]_{\mathbf{u}}^{\mathbf{z}})\Big)$ is identical to $\tau([B]_{\mathbf{u}}^{\mathbf{z}})$ w.r.t. $\mathcal{G}_{\Pi}$.*

Proof. For the case when B is a basic literal, the claim immediately follows from Lemma 1. What remains to be shown is that it is also the case when B is a conditional literal of the form $H : \mathbf{L}$. Take $\mathbf{x}$ to denote the set of local variables in B. Per condition 5 of the definition of $\phi_{\mathbf{z}}$, $\phi_{\mathbf{z}}(H : \mathbf{L}) = \forall\mathbf{x}\,(\phi_{\mathbf{z}}(\mathbf{L}) \to \phi_{\mathbf{z}}(H))$.

$$gr(\phi_{\mathbf{z}}([H : \mathbf{L}]_{\mathbf{u}}^{\mathbf{z}})) = gr\Big(\forall\mathbf{x}\big(\phi_{\mathbf{z}}(\mathbf{L}_{\mathbf{u}}^{\mathbf{z}}(\mathbf{x})) \to \phi_{\mathbf{z}}(H_{\mathbf{u}}^{\mathbf{z}}(\mathbf{x}))\big)\Big)$$
$$= \{gr(\phi_{\mathbf{z}}(\mathbf{L}_{\mathbf{u}mathbfv}^{\mathbf{zx}}) \to \phi_{\mathbf{z}}(H_{\mathbf{u}mathbfv}^{\mathbf{zx}})) \mid mathbfv \in \mathcal{G}_{\Pi}^{|\mathbf{x}|}\}^{\wedge}$$
$$= \{gr(\phi_{\mathbf{z}}(\mathbf{L}_{\mathbf{u}mathbfv}^{\mathbf{zx}})) \to gr(\phi_{\mathbf{z}}(H_{\mathbf{u}mathbfv}^{\mathbf{zx}})) \mid mathbfv \in \mathcal{G}_{\Pi}^{|\mathbf{x}|}\}^{\wedge}$$
$$= \{\tau(\mathbf{L}_{\mathbf{u}mathbfv}^{\mathbf{zx}}) \to \tau(H_{\mathbf{u}mathbfv}^{\mathbf{zx}}) \mid mathbfv \in \mathcal{G}_{\Pi}^{|\mathbf{x}|}\}^{\wedge}$$
$$= \tau([H : \mathbf{L}]_{\mathbf{u}}^{\mathbf{z}})$$

Condition 8 of the definition of the gr transformation allows us to move from the first line to the second in the chain above. Condition 6 of that definition allows us to move from the second line to the third. Lemma 1 provides us with grounds to move from the third to the fourth line. The final step is due to condition 6 of the τ transformation definition.

Lemma 3. *Let Π be a conditional logic program containing at least one object constant. Let H be a literal in the head of a rule R in Π, where $\mathbf{z}$ is the list of global variables occurring in R and $\mathbf{u}$ is a list of ground terms of the same length as $\mathbf{z}$. Then, $gr\Big(\phi_{\mathbf{z}}([H]_{\mathbf{u}}^{\mathbf{z}})\Big)$ is identical to $\tau([H]_{\mathbf{u}}^{\mathbf{z}})$ w.r.t. $\mathcal{G}_{\Pi}$.*
The proof of Lemma 3 is similar in structure to the proof of Lemma 2.

Lemma 4. *Let Π be a conditional logic program containing at least one object constant. For any rule R in Π, $gr(\phi(R))$ is identical to $\tau(R)$ w.r.t. $\mathcal{G}_{\Pi}$.*

Proof. Let $\mathbf{z}$ be the list of the global variables of R.

$$gr\big(\phi(R)\big) = gr\Big(\forall \mathbf{z}\big(\phi_{\mathbf{z}}(B_1) \wedge \cdots \wedge \phi_{\mathbf{z}}(B_n) \to \phi_{\mathbf{z}}(H_1) \vee \cdots \vee \phi_{\mathbf{z}}(H_m)\big)\Big)$$

$$= \{gr\Big(\phi_{\mathbf{z}}([B_1]_{\mathbf{u}}^{\mathbf{z}}) \wedge \cdots \wedge \phi_{\mathbf{z}}([B_n]_{\mathbf{u}}^{\mathbf{z}}) \to \phi_{\mathbf{z}}([H_1]_{\mathbf{u}}^{\mathbf{z}}) \vee \cdots \vee \phi_{\mathbf{z}}([H_m]_{\mathbf{u}}^{\mathbf{z}})\Big)$$
$$\mid \mathbf{u} \in \mathcal{G}_{\Pi}^{|\mathbf{z}|}\}^{\wedge}$$

$$= \{gr\Big(\phi_{\mathbf{z}}([B_1]_{\mathbf{u}}^{\mathbf{z}})\Big) \wedge \cdots \wedge gr\Big(\phi_{\mathbf{z}}([B_n]_{\mathbf{u}}^{\mathbf{z}})\Big)$$
$$\to gr\Big(\phi_{\mathbf{z}}([H_1]_{\mathbf{u}}^{\mathbf{z}})\Big) \vee \cdots \vee gr\Big(\phi_{\mathbf{z}}([H_m]_{\mathbf{u}}^{\mathbf{z}})\Big) \mid \mathbf{u} \in \mathcal{G}_{\Pi}^{|\mathbf{z}|}\}^{\wedge}$$

$$= \{\tau([B_1]_{\mathbf{u}}^{\mathbf{z}}) \wedge \cdots \wedge \tau([B_n]_{\mathbf{u}}^{\mathbf{z}}) \to \tau([H_1]_{\mathbf{u}}^{\mathbf{z}}) \vee \cdots \vee \tau([H_m]_{\mathbf{u}}^{\mathbf{z}}) \mid \mathbf{u} \in \mathcal{G}_{\Pi}^{|\mathbf{z}|}\}^{\wedge}$$

$$= \{\tau(R_{\mathbf{u}}^{\mathbf{z}}) \mid \mathbf{u} \in \mathcal{G}_{\Pi}^{|\mathbf{z}|}\}^{\wedge} = \{\tau(r) \mid r \in inst_{\mathcal{G}_{\Pi}}(R)\}^{\wedge}$$

$$= \tau(R)$$

Lemmas 2 and 3 provide grounds for the fourth equality in the chain. The remainder follows from the definitions of gr, ϕ and τ transformations. The case when the head of the rule is $\perp$ follows the same lines.

The following equality follows immediately from Lemma 4 and constitutes a proof of the Theorem on Syntactic Identity:

$$gr\big(\phi(\Pi)\big) = \{gr(\phi(R)) \mid R \in \Pi\}^{\wedge} = \{\tau(R) \mid R \in \Pi\}^{\wedge} = \tau(\Pi).$$

6   Arguing Correctness of the K-Coloring Problem

In this section, we apply the *verification methodology for logic programs* proposed in [2] to the *k-coloring* encoding containing conditional literals. This methodology consists of four steps:

1. Decompose the informal description of the problem into independent (natural language) statements.
2. Fix the vocabulary/predicate constants used to represent the problem and its solutions.
3. Formalize the specification of the statements as a logic (modular) program.
4. Construct a "metaproof" in natural language for the correspondence between the constructed program and the informal description of the problem.

An instance of the k-coloring problem is a triple $\langle V, E, C \rangle$, where

- $\langle V, E \rangle$ is a graph with vertices V and edges $E \subseteq V \times V$, and
- C is a set of labels named *colors*, whose cardinality is k.

A solution to the *k-coloring* problem is

K1 a function $\widetilde{asg} : V \longrightarrow C$ such that
K2 every edge $(a, b) \in E$ satisfies condition $\widetilde{asg}(a) \neq \widetilde{asg}(b)$.

We view statements **K1** and **K2** as the formalization of Step 1. In fact, this formalization of Step 1 follows the lines by Fandinno, Hansen, and Lierler (2022), who considered another encoding of *k-coloring* problem (containing aggregates) and argued its correctness.

We fix predicate constants $vtx/1$, $edge/2$, $color/1$, $asg/2$ to represent the *k-coloring* problem and its solutions. In particular, predicate constants $vtx/1$, $edge/2$, and $color/1$ are used to encode a specific instance of the problem; whereas predicate constant $asg/2$ is used to encode the function $\widetilde{asg}$. Formally, we call a binary relation **r** *functional* when for all pairs (a_1, b_1), (a_2, b_2) in **r**, if $a_1 = a_2$, then $b_1 = b_2$. Clearly, functional relations can be used to *encode* functions in an intuitive manner, where each pair (a, b) in functional relation **r** suggests a mapping from element a to element b. In other words, $asg/2$ will encode a functional relation meant to capture mapping $\widetilde{asg}$ that forms a solution to the considered instance of the *k-coloring* problem. This constitutes Step 2.

Splitting Theorem [8] is a fundamental result that allows us to uncover the internal structure of a logic program. For example, consider the context of the *k-coloring* program. Using the ϕ-transformation, we identify this program with sentence KC that is the conjunction of formulas (3-6). By K_1 we denote the conjunction of formulas (3-5) and by K_2 we denote formula (6). The Splitting Theorem tells us that

$$\mathrm{SM}_{asg}[KC] \equiv \mathrm{SM}_{asg}[K_1] \wedge K_2. \tag{7}$$

Within this verification methodology, Step 3 can be implemented by considering $\mathrm{SM}_{asg}[K_1]$ and K_2 as two modules of a logic (modular) program that formalize statements **K1** and **K2**, respectively. We now make this claim precise by stating formal results that culminate in capturing Step 4. Intuitively, the following Lemmas 5 and 6 state that modules $\mathrm{SM}_{asg}[K_1]$ and K_2 formalize statements **K1** and **K2**, respectively.

Lemma 5. *Let I be an Herbrand interpretation such that $\langle vtx^I, edge^I, color^I \rangle$ forms an instance of the k-coloring problem. Then, $I \models \mathrm{SM}_{asg}[K_1]$ if and only if relation asg^I encodes a function from vtx^I to $color^I$.*

Lemma 6. *Let I be an Herbrand interpretation such that $\langle vtx^I, edge^I, color^I \rangle$ forms an instance of the k-coloring problem and asg^I encodes a function $\widetilde{asg}$ from vtx^I to $color^I$. Then, $I \models K_2$ if and only if every edge $(a, b) \in edge^I$ satisfies condition $\widetilde{asg}(a) \neq \widetilde{asg}(b)$.*

By equivalence (7) and the two preceding lemmas the following theorem immediately follows. This theorem can be seen as a proof of correctness for the *k-coloring* encoding.

Theorem 3. *Let I be an Herbrand interpretation such that $\langle vtx^I, edge^I, color^I \rangle$ forms an instance of the k-coloring problem. Then, $I \models \mathrm{SM}_{asg}[KC]$ if and only if $(asg/2)^I$ encodes a function that forms a solution to the considered instance.*

Due to space constraints, we omit the proofs of the formal results of this section. We refer the reader to similar arguments, namely, the proofs by Cabalar,

Fandinno, and Lierler (2020) when they argue correctness of logic program modules for the Hamiltonian Cycle problem, and the proofs by Fandinno, Hansen, and Lierler (2022) when they do the same for the Traveling Salesman problem and an alternative encoding of the *k-coloring* problem.

We note that in practical settings answer set systems accept instances of problems, typically encoded as sets of facts. For instance, the set Π_G of facts

$$\text{vtx(a). vtx(b). edge(a, b). color(g). color(b). color(r).} \tag{8}$$

corresponds to the following instance of the 3-coloring problem:

$$\langle\{a, b\}, \{(a, b)\}, \{g, b, r\}\rangle. \tag{9}$$

Consider module $\text{SM}_{vtx,edge,color}[\phi(\Pi_G)]$. It captures the considered set of facts. For a Herbrand model I of this module, the extension $\langle vtx^I, edge^I, color^I \rangle$ forms (9). This claim trivially follows from Theorem on Completion [8]. Note that the program composed of the facts in Π_G and the *k-coloring* rules has answer sets that are the Herbrand models of formula $\text{SM}_{vtx,edge,color,asg}[\phi(\Pi_G) \wedge KC]$. By the Splitting Theorem, it is equivalent to $\text{SM}_{vtx,edge,color}[\phi(\Pi_G)] \wedge \text{SM}_{asg}[KC]$. By Theorem 3 we may immediately conclude that any answer set of a program composed of the facts in Π_G and rules in the *k-coloring* program is such that the extension of predicate constant $asg/2$ encodes a solution to instance (9) of the 3-coloring problem.

The previous paragraph illustrates an important idea stemming from [3]. Given a problem P and a signature σ_P to encode it, in place of discussing the specifics of encoding of a particular instance of problem P, we may associate Herbrand interpretations over σ_P satisfying some conditions with this instance. This way we may speak of an encoding for problem P in separation from details on how an instance for this problem is encoded. The statement of the final theorem illustrates this idea. For example, the following rules `vtx(X):-edge(X,Y).` `vtx(Y):-edge(X,Y).` can be used to replace the first two facts in (8) to encode the same instance of the *k-coloring* problem. As long as we may associate this new encoding of an instance with an Herbrand interpretation capturing that instance from the perspective of the claim of Theorem 3, we can claim the correctness of the resulting ASP program composed of a newly encoded instance and the *k-coloring* encoding. This is true whenever the Splitting Theorem supports modularization of a program as illustrated.

Conclusions, Future Work, Acknowledgements

In this paper we present semantics for conditional programs that do not refer to grounding. These semantics demonstrate that conditional literals represent nested implications within rules. The benefits of this contribution are three-fold. First, it has pedagogical value. The nested implication approach provides a simple characterization of conditional literals, supplying students with an intuitive perspective on their behavior. Our work provides rigorous support for this previously informal intuition. Second, conditional literals are a step towards developing ASP rules with complex, nested bodies that are closer to classical logic languages. This makes the language more expressive. Finally, we have broadened the class of ASP programs that can be formally verified without referring to grounding. For instance, the final section of this paper illustrates the use of the proposed semantics by arguing the correctness of the k-coloring encoding. In the Introduction we mentioned how conditional literals are omnipresent in meta-programming. The users of meta-programming may now apply similar ideas in constructing proofs of correctness for their formalizations.

We also note that for so called tight conditional programs [8], our characterization provides a way to associate such programs with classical first-order logic formulas by means of the Theorem on Completion [5, Section A.3]. This fact forms a theoretical foundation for a possible extension of the software verification tool ANTHEM [6] to programs with conditional literals. This tool allows its users to formally and automatically verify the correctness of tight logic programs (without conditional literals). The k-coloring program presented in this paper is tight and the suggested extension of ANTHEM would therefore be applicable to it. Implementing the corresponding extension in ANTHEM is a direction of future work.

Acknowledgements. The work was partially supported by NSF grant 1707371. We are grateful to Jorge Fandinno, Vladimir Lifschitz, and Miroslaw Truszczynski for valuable discussions and comments on this paper.

References

1. Brewka, G., Eiter, T., Truszczyński, M.: Answer set programming at a glance. Commun. ACM **54**(12), 92–103 (2011). https://doi.org/10.1145/2043174.2043195
2. Cabalar, P., Fandinno, J., Lierler, Y.: Modular answer set programming as a formal specification language. Theory Pract. Logic Program. **20**(5), 767–782 (2020)
3. Fandinno, J., Hansen, Z., Lierler, Y.: Arguing correctness of asp programs with aggregates (2022), (Accepted to LPNMR-22)
4. Fandinno, J., Hansen, Z., Lierler, Y.: Axiomatization of aggregates in answer set programming. In: Proceedings of the Thirty-six National Conference on Artificial Intelligence (AAAI 2022). AAAI Press (2022)
5. Fandinno, J., Lifschitz, V.: Verification of locally tight programs (2022). http://www.cs.utexas.edu/users/ai-labpub-view.php?PubID=127938
6. Fandinno, J., Lifschitz, V., Lühne, P., Schaub, T.: Verifying tight logic programs with anthem and vampire. Theory Pract. Logic Program. **20**(5), 735–750 (2020)
7. Ferraris, P., Lee, J., Lifschitz, V.: Stable models and circumscription. Artif. Intell. **175**(1), 236–263 (2011)
8. Ferraris, P., Lee, J., Lifschitz, V., Palla, R.: Symmetric splitting in the general theory of stable models. In: Boutilier, C. (ed.) Proceedings of the Twenty-First International Joint Conference on Artificial Intelligence (IJCAI 2009), pp. 797–803. AAAI/MIT Press (2009)
9. Gebser, M., Kaminski, R., Kaufmann, B., Ostrowski, M., Schaub, T., Thiele, S.: A user's guide to `gringo`, `clasp`, `clingo`, and `iclingo`. http://potassco.org

10. Harrison, A., Lifschitz, V., Yang, F.: The semantics of gringo and infinitary propositional formulas. In: Baral, C., De Giacomo, G., Eiter, T. (eds.) Proceedings of the Fourteenth International Conference on Principles of Knowledge Representation and Reasoning (KR 2014). AAAI Press (2014)

11. Kaminski, R., Romero, J., Schaub, T., Wanko, P.: How to build your own ASP-based system?! Theory and Practice of Logic Programming, p. 1–63 (2021). https://doi.org/10.1017/S1471068421000508

12. Lifschitz, V.: Thirteen definitions of a stable model. In: Fields of Logic and Computation: Essays Dedicated to Yuri Gurevich on the Occasion of his 70th Birthday (2010)

13. Marek, V.W., Truszczyński, M.: Stable Models and an Alternative Logic Programming Paradigm, pp. 375–398. Springer, Heidelberg (1999). https://doi.org/10.1007/978-3-642-60085-2_17

14. Niemelä, I.: Logic programs with stable model semantics as a constraint programming paradigm. Ann. Math. Artif. Intell. **25**(3), 241–273 (1999). https://doi.org/10.1023/A:1018930122475

15. Truszczynski, Miroslaw: Connecting first-order ASP and the logic FO(ID) through reducts. In: Erdem, Esra, Lee, Joohyung, Lierler, Yuliya, Pearce, David (eds.) Correct Reasoning. LNCS, vol. 7265, pp. 543–559. Springer, Heidelberg (2012). https://doi.org/10.1007/978-3-642-30743-0_37

State Transition in Multi-agent Epistemic Domains Using Answer Set Programming

Yusuf Izmirlioglu$^{(\boxtimes)}$, Loc Pham, Tran Cao Son, and Enrico Pontelli

New Mexico State University, Las Cruces, NM, USA
{yizmir,locpham}@nmsu.edu, {tson,epontell}@cs.nmsu.edu

Abstract. In this paper we develop a state transition function for partially observable multi-agent epistemic domains and implement it using Answer Set Programming (ASP). The transition function computes the next state upon an occurrence of a single action. Thus it can be used as a module in epistemic planners. Our transition function incorporates ontic, sensing and announcement actions and allows for arbitrary nested belief formulae and general common knowledge. A novel feature of our model is that upon an action occurrence, an observing agent corrects his (possibly wrong) initial beliefs about action precondition and his observability. By examples, we show that this step is necessary for robust state transition. We establish some properties of our state transition function regarding its soundness in updating beliefs of agents consistent with their observability.

Keywords: Answer Set Programming · Multi-agent systems · Epistemic planning · State transition

1 Introduction

Many Artificial Intelligence applications involve multiple autonomous agents interacting with each other and the environment. Agents can take actions that may change the physical state of the world as well as beliefs of agents. A typical problem in a multi-agent setting is how to update agents' beliefs in a sound manner upon an action occurrence, especially when some agents initially have incorrect or incomplete beliefs about the world and other agents. Another challenge is that not all agents might be able to fully observe the effect of the action. Some agents might only observe that the action takes place but not its effects (partial observer agents) and some agents might be completely unaware of the action occurrence (oblivious agents).

In this paper, we study the abovementioned problem of robust state transition upon an action occurrence in multi-agent epistemic settings. We use possible world semantics in the form of Kripke structure [11] to represent agents' beliefs and investigate action occurrences in possible world semantics. We classify actions into three categories: An *ontic* action changes the actual state of the world by changing the value of fluent(s). A *sensing* action allows an agent to learn the value of a set of fluent variable(s). An *announcement* action conveys

G. Gottlob et al. (Eds.): LPNMR 2022, LNAI 13416, pp. 273–286, 2022.
https://doi.org/10.1007/978-3-031-15707-3_21

the value of a set of fluent variable(s) to other agents. We develop a novel state transition function for ontic, sensing, announcement actions using Answer Set Programming (ASP), a popular logic programming paradigm. Our model allows for different levels of observability, uncertainity of the initial state, arbitrarily nested belief formulae and general common knowledge. Hence our ASP program can be imported as a module into single and multi agent epistemic planners to compute the next state. Our choice of ASP is due to its capability in writing compact and understandable rules in recursive form for state transition and entailment of belief formulae.

One important feature of our state transition is that when an action occurs, full and partial observer agents correct their initial (possibly wrong) beliefs about action precondition and their observability before the effect is realized. Namely, an observing agent realizes that the precondition of the action holds and he is not ignorant of the action. This correction step is vital for robust state transition because whether the effect of the action is applicable to a world in the Kripke structure depends on satisfaction of precondition and observability conditions at that world. We provide some examples to illustrate that without correcting beliefs, state transition is not robust[1] This is indeed the problem with the existing models of state transition.

One method to compute state transition is to employ *action models*, introduced in [1,2] and later extended to *event update models* in [6,10]. Event update models involve different events and agents' accessibility relations between events depending on their observability. The next state is computed by cross product of the initial Kripke structure with the event update model. However, Example 1 shows that the standard event update model [4,6], by itself, is not capable of correcting agents' beliefs and robust state transition.

Example 1. We examine a scenario with two agents A, B in a power plant. Agent B has a voltmeter device which senses the level of the voltage. At the actual state, the voltmeter is sound and the voltage level is normal. Agent A initially believes that the voltmeter is defective and he does not know the voltage level. This state is represented as a pointed Kripke structure, as in Fig. 1(a), top. Possible worlds are represented by circles. A double circle represents the true world. Links between worlds encode the belief accessibility relations of agents. Suppose that agent B takes the *check_voltage* action which senses the voltage level. Its precondition is the device being sound, i.e., *sound* and the condition for full observability is ⊤. Hence A and B are full observers at all worlds. The event update model for *check_voltage* is given in Fig. 1(a), bottom left. The σ event corresponds to sensed value being *normal* and the τ event corresponds to ¬*normal*. The result of applying this event model to the initial state is given in Fig. 1(a) bottom right. The action model removes the accessibility relation of agent A from world s to u and v because u, v do not satisfy action precondition. In the next state, A has no accessibility relation and believes in every formula.

---

[1] Details of state transition in these examples can be found in our online appendix at https://github.com/yizmirlioglu/Epistemic.

Intuitively, when A observes the action, he should realize that the meter is sound and learn the voltage level. Therefore, the event model in [4, 6], by itself, is not capable of correcting agent's beliefs and robust state transition.

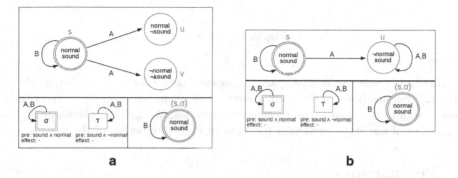

Fig. 1. (a) The first example   (b) The second example

Example 2. Consider a variation of Example 1 depicted in Fig. 1 (b). Now agent A initially knows that the meter is sound, but he has incorrect belief that the voltage level is not normal. Agent B performs the *check_voltage* action as before. Applying the event model for the *check_voltage* action to the initial Kripke structure, we obtain the next state shown in Fig. 1(b) (bottom right). Again agent A ends up having no accessibility relation. Ideally A should change his belief and knows that the voltage level is normal. Hence the next state is counter-intuitive.

[7] has constructed a model of state transition where agents correct their beliefs about action precondition. However, their transition function does not involve belief correction for observability. Their framework requires two separate operators for belief and knowledge. As the next example suggests, correcting beliefs for an agent's own observability as well as his beliefs about other agents' observability are necessary for robust state transition.

Example 3. We examine another scenario in Fig. 2(left) with two agents A, B. The knowledge and beliefs of the agents are encoded with the knowledge and the belief accessibility relations. At the actual world, the door is closed and both agents are near to the door. Initially agent A believes that both A, B are near the door, however B believes that A is near but B is far from the door (wrong initial belief). Agent A performs the *open_door* action whose precondition is *haskey_a* and effect is *open*. The condition for full observability of agent A, B is *near_a*, *near_b* respectively. The next state according to transition function of [7] is shown in Fig. 2 (right). At the next state according to [7], agent B believes that the door is open but believes that he is far from the door. This is not a realistic outcome because B wouldn't observe opening the door if he were far from the door.

The above discussion inspires us to develop a robust state transition function for multi-agent domains. Using ASP, we compute state transition which corrects agents' beliefs about action precondition, observability and effect of the action. In

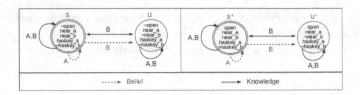

Fig. 2. Example 3

sensing/announcement actions, partial observer agents correct their beliefs about precondition and observability; full observer agents, in addition, also correct their beliefs about the sensing/announcement variables. We provide theorems about soundness of our state transition function in updating beliefs of the agents.

2 Preliminaries

Possible World Semantics: Let $\mathcal{AG}$ be a finite and non-empty set of agents and $\mathcal{F}$ be a set of fluents encoding the properties of the world. *Belief formulae* over $\langle \mathcal{AG}, \mathcal{F} \rangle$ are defined by the BNF:

$$\varphi ::= p \mid \neg\varphi \mid (\varphi \wedge \varphi) \mid (\varphi \vee \varphi) \mid \mathbf{B}_i\varphi$$

where $p \in \mathcal{F}$ is a fluent and $i \in \mathcal{AG}$. We refer to a belief formula which does not contain any occurrence of $\mathbf{B}_i$ as *a fluent formula*. In addition, for a formula γ and a non-empty set $\alpha \subseteq \mathcal{AG}$, $\mathbf{B}_\alpha\gamma$ and $\mathbf{C}_\alpha\gamma$ denote $\bigwedge_{i\in\alpha} \mathbf{B}_i\gamma$ and $\bigwedge_{k=0}^{\infty} \mathbf{B}_\alpha^k\gamma$, where $\mathbf{B}_\alpha^0\gamma=\gamma$ and $\mathbf{B}_\alpha^{k+1}\gamma=\mathbf{B}_\alpha^k\mathbf{B}_\alpha\gamma$ for $k \geq 0$, respectively. Let $\mathcal{L}_{\mathcal{AG}}$ denote the set of belief formulae over $\langle \mathcal{AG}, \mathcal{F} \rangle$.

Satisfaction of belief formulae is defined over *pointed Kripke structures* [11]. A Kripke structure M is a tuple $\langle S, \pi, \mathcal{B}_1, \ldots, \mathcal{B}_n \rangle$, where S is a set of worlds (denoted by $M[S]$), $\pi : S \mapsto 2^{\mathcal{F}}$ is a function that associates an interpretation of $\mathcal{F}$ to each element of S (denoted by $M[\pi]$), and for $i \in \mathcal{AG}$, $\mathcal{B}_i \subseteq S \times S$ is a binary relation over S (denoted by $M[i]$). For convenience, we will often draw a Kripke structure M as a directed labeled graph, whose set of labeled nodes represent S and whose set of labeled edges contains $s \xrightarrow{i} t$ iff $(s,t) \in \mathcal{B}_i$. The label of each node is its interpretation and the name of the world is written above the node. For $u \in S$ and a fluent formula φ, $M[\pi](u)$ and $M[\pi](u)(\varphi)$ denote the interpretation associated to u via π and the truth value of φ with respect to $M[\pi](u)$. For a world $u \in M[S]$, (M,u) is a *pointed Kripke structure*, also called *state* hereafter.

Given a belief formula φ and a state (M,u), $(M,u) \vDash \mathbf{B}_i\varphi$ if $(M,t) \vDash \varphi$ for every t such that $(u,t) \in \mathcal{B}_i$. $(M,u) \vDash \mathbf{C}_G\varphi$ if $(M,u) \vDash \varphi$ and $(M,t) \vDash \varphi$ for every t such that $(u,t) \in \mathbf{R}_G^*$ where $\mathbf{R}_G^*$ is the transitive closure of $\mathcal{B}_i$, $i \in G$.

For a fluent $f \in \mathcal{F}$, let $\bar{f} = \neg f$ and $\overline{\neg f} = f$; and for a set of fluent literals X, let $\overline{X} = \{\bar{\ell} \mid \ell \in X\}$. If $\chi = b_1 \wedge \ldots \wedge b_e$ and $\gamma = l_1 \wedge \ldots \wedge l_g$ are conjunctions of fluent literals, $\chi \cup \gamma$ denotes the set $\{b_1, \ldots, b_e, l_1, \ldots, l_g\}$.

Domain Description: Let $D = \langle \mathcal{AG}, \mathcal{F}, \mathcal{A} \rangle$ be a multi-agent epistemic domain. We assume that the precondition of an action is of the form $\psi = h_1 \wedge \ldots \wedge h_r \wedge \xi$ where ξ is a belief formula. In the multi-agent action language m$\mathcal{A}^*$ [4], the precondition of action a is encoded by the statement "**executable** a **if** ψ". We allow for conditional effects of an ontic action a. In m$\mathcal{A}^*$, effect of an ontic action a is described by "a **causes** β **if** μ", where μ is a fluent formula and β is a set of literals. Intuitively, if condition μ holds at a world u, the action replaces the relevant literals in the world with the ones in β. Let $Effects_a$ be the set of (μ, β) pairs. We assume that if (μ, φ) and (μ', φ') are in $Effects_a$ then $\mu \wedge \mu'$ is inconsistent. $M'[\pi](u') = \phi(a, \pi(u))$ stands for interpretation of the resultant world u' upon applying the action a on the world u. Formally, if $(M, u) \vDash \mu$ and $(\mu, \beta) \in Effects_a$, then $M'[\pi](u') = (\pi(u) \setminus \overline{\beta}) \cup \beta$. If $(M, u) \nvDash \mu$ for any $(\mu, \beta) \in Effects_a$ then $M'[\pi](u') = \pi(u)$.

m$\mathcal{A}^*$ describes the effects of sensing and announcement actions by the statements "a **determines** φ" and "a **announces** φ" respectively. In the sensing actions, $\varphi = \{\rho_1, \ldots, \rho_o\}$ is the set of fluents that the agent senses, whereas in the announcement actions, φ is the set of fluents that the agent announces.

Full and partial observability conditions are encoded in m$\mathcal{A}^*$ as "i **observes** a **if** $\delta_{i,a}$" and "i **aware_of** a **if** $\theta_{i,a}$" respectively. We assume $\delta_{i,a}$, $\theta_{i,a}$ are conjunction of literals and they are pairwise disjoint. Note that observability depends on a world and it is defined over pointed Kripke structures. In case neither $\delta_{i,a}$ nor $\theta_{i,a}$ holds at (M, u), then agent i is oblivious at (M, u).

We say that a domain D is consistent if it satisfies the above conditions for action description and observability rules. We define the initial state as $T = (M, s)$ where s is the actual world.

Answer Set Programming: Answer Set Programming (ASP) is a knowledge representation and reasoning paradigm [12,13] which provides a formal framework for declaratively solving problems. The idea of ASP is to model a problem by a set of logical formulas (called rules), so that its models (called answer sets) characterize the solutions of the problem. Our ASP formulation is based on stable model semantics [12]. ASP provides logical formulas, called rules, of the form

$$Head \leftarrow L_1, \ldots, L_k, not\ L_{k+1}, \ldots, not\ L_l \tag{1}$$

where $l \geq k \geq 0$, $Head$ is a literal (i.e., an atom A or its negation $\neg A$) or $\bot$, and each L_i is a literal. A rule is called a *constraint* if $Head$ is $\bot$, and a *fact* if $l = 0$. A set of rules is called a *program*. ASP provides special constructs to express nondeterministic choices, cardinality constraints, and aggregates. Programs using these constructs can be viewed as abbreviations for programs that consist of rules of the form (1). Further information about ASP can be found in [14].

3   State Transition Using ASP

Let $D = \langle \mathcal{AG}, \mathcal{F}, \mathcal{A} \rangle$ be a consistent multi-agent domain and (M, s) be the initial state. We study the problem of computing the next state $\Phi_D(a, (M, s))$ given the initial state (M, s) and the occurrence of action a. Our state transition function

$\Phi_D(\mathsf{a}, (M, s))$ works as follows: In ontic actions, we first correct full observer agents' beliefs about action precondition and observability, and then apply the effect of the action by modifying the relevant fluents. Namely, full observers observe the effects of the action and correct their beliefs, while oblivious agents remain in the old state.

Sensing and announcement actions do not alter the actual world, they only change beliefs of the agents. We assume that agents always announce truthfully and the listening agents always believe in the announced value of variables and update their beliefs accordingly. In sensing/announcement actions, a full observer agent i will correct his beliefs about precondition, his observability, and the sensing/announcement variables, i.e., he will correct the literals in ψ, $\delta_{i,\mathsf{a}}$ and φ. A partial observer agent i will correct his beliefs about only precondition and his observability, but not about the sensing/announcement variables. Beliefs of oblivious agents do not change. By construction, agents also correct their beliefs about belief of other agents, for all types of actions.

Below we build the ASP program $\Pi_{D,T,\mathsf{a}}$ which computes the next state $\Phi_D(\mathsf{a}, T)$ given an initial state $T = (M, s)$ and occurrence of an action a. Due to limited space, we provide only the core ASP rules that illustrate the idea behind the formulation; for the full code we refer to our online repository[2].

Input: We represent agents and agent sets by $ag(I)$, $ag\_set(G)$ atoms. $formula(F)$ atom shows the belief formulae that appear in the domain D. Actions are described by $action(A)$, $type(A, Y)$, $exec(A, F)$, $causes(A, L, F)$, $determines(A, F)$, $announces(A, F)$ atoms. $observes(I, A, F)$ and $aware(I, A, F)$ atoms state the condition for full observability and partial observability of agent I, respectively. $pre\_lit(A, F)$ denote the literals $h_1, ..., h_r$ in action precondition ψ, $full\_lit(I, A, F)$ denote the literals in $\delta_{i,\mathsf{a}}$ and $partial\_lit(I, A, F)$ denote the literals in $\theta_{i,\mathsf{a}}$. Sensing/announcement variables are identified by $varphi(A, F)$ atoms.

The worlds, accessibility relations and the valuations at the initial state T are encoded by $world(U)$, $access(I, U, V)$, $val(U, F)$ atoms, respectively, where I denotes an agent, U and V are worlds, and F is a fluent. For efficiency, we state only the positive literals in the valuation of a world. $actual(S)$ stands for the actual world S. $occ(\mathsf{a})$ atom shows the action a that occurs. The next state is represented by $world\_n(U)$, $actual\_n(Z)$, $access\_n(I, U, V)$, $val\_n(U, F)$.

State Transition: We first compute entailment of belief formulae at the initial state T. $entails(U, F)$ atom denotes that the world $U \in M[S]$ satisfies the belief formula F. Some of the rules that compute entailment of belief formula are:

$$entails(U, F) \leftarrow world(U),\ val(U, F),\ fluent(F). \tag{2}$$

$$entails(U, \neg F) \leftarrow world(U),\ not\ val(U, F),\ fluent(F). \tag{3}$$

$$entails(U, F1 \wedge F2) \leftarrow world(U),\ entails(U, F1),\ entails(U, F2),$$
$$formula(F1 \wedge F2). \tag{4}$$

$$\neg entails(U, B_I F) \leftarrow world(U),\ access(I, U, V),\ not\ entails(V, F),$$
$$formula(B_I F). \tag{5}$$

---

[2] https://github.com/yizmirlioglu/Epistemic.

$$entails(U, B_I F) \leftarrow not\ \neg entails(U, B_I F),\ world(U),\ formula(B_I F). \qquad (6)$$

Rule (5) states that the belief formula $B_I F$ is not entailed at world U if there is a world V (that agent I considers at U) and V does not satisfy F. If there is no such case, U entails $B_I F$ by the rule (6).

Then we compute observability of the agents at each world by

$$f\_obs(I, A, U) \leftarrow observes(I, A, F),\ entails(U, F),\ world(U),\ occ(A). \qquad (7)$$

$$p\_obs(I, A, U) \leftarrow aware(I, A, F),\ entails(U, F),\ world(U),\ occ(A). \qquad (8)$$

$$obliv(I, A, U) \leftarrow not\ f\_obs(I, A, U),\ not\ p\_obs(I, A, U),\ world(U),\ ag(I),\ occ(A). \qquad (9)$$

The rule below checks whether the action is executable i.e. the precondition of the action a holds at the actual world (M, s). In this case, s' is the actual world at the next state.

$$pre\_hold(S) \leftarrow actual(S),\ entails(S, F),\ exec(A, F),\ occ(A). \qquad (10)$$

$$actual\_n(S') \leftarrow actual(S),\ pre\_hold(S),\ occ(A). \qquad (11)$$

We identify the worlds in the next state M' by the rules below. If the precondition of the action holds at (M, s), then s' is a world in M'. The worlds that are reachable from s' are also worlds in M'.

$$world\_n(S') \leftarrow actual(S),\ pre\_hold(S),\ occ(A). \qquad (12)$$

$$world\_n(V) \leftarrow actual\_n(Z),\ access\_n(I, Z, V). \qquad (13)$$

$$world\_n(V) \leftarrow world\_n(U),\ access\_n(I, U, V). \qquad (14)$$

We construct the accessibility relations of full observers in the next state M' for an ontic action as below. Full observers correct their beliefs about action precondition and observability and observe the effect of the action. Suppose that $(M, U) \models \delta_{i,a}$ and $(U, V) \in M[i]$. In the next state, we keep only the accessibility relations of agent i from U to the worlds V which satisfy action precondition and observability of i. In this case we apply the effect of the action to world V, obtain $V' \in M'[S]$ and create the accessibility relation $(U', V') \in M'[i]$. However, if all the V worlds that agent i considers possible at U violate precondition and/or observability (indicated by the $ontic\_cond(i, U)$ atom), we cannot remove all the edges, thus we amend the worlds to obtain V_i and create relations from U' to V_i.

$$formula\_full(I, A, F1 \wedge F2) \leftarrow exec(A, F1),\ observes(I, A, F2),\ ag(I). \qquad (15)$$

$$\neg ontic\_cond(I, U) \leftarrow access(I, U, V),\ entails(V, F),\ formula\_full(I, A, F),$$
$$occ(A),\ type(A, ontic). \qquad (16)$$

$$access\_n(I, U', V') \leftarrow world\_n(U'),\ access(I, U, V),\ f\_obs(I, A, U),$$
$$entails(V, F),\ formula\_full(I, A, F),\ occ(A),\ type(A, ontic). \qquad (17)$$

$$access\_n(I, U', V_I) \leftarrow world\_n(U'),\ access(I, U, V),\ f\_obs(I, A, U),$$
$$not\ \neg ontic\_cond(I, U),\ occ(A),\ type(A, ontic). \qquad (18)$$

Oblivious agents remain at the old state and their beliefs do not change. We keep all accessibility relations in M so that beliefs of oblivious agents remain the same, namely $M[i] \subseteq M'[i]$ for all $i \in \mathcal{AG}$.

$$access\_n(I,U,V) \leftarrow world\_n(U),\ access(I,U,V),\ occ(A). \tag{19}$$

$$access\_n(I,U',V) \leftarrow world\_n(U'),\ access(I,U,V),\ obliv(I,A,U),$$
$$occ(A),\ type(A,ontic). \tag{20}$$

$$access\_n(I,U_J,V) \leftarrow I \neq J,\ world\_n(U_J),\ access(I,U,V),\ obliv(I,A,U),$$
$$occ(A),\ type(A,ontic). \tag{21}$$

For sensing/announcement actions, we need to check whether sensing/announcement variables are the same across two worlds $U, V \in M[S]$. $var\_diff(U,V)$ indicates that at least one variable differs across U and V.

$$var\_diff(U,V) \leftarrow access(I,U,V),\ val(U,F),\ not\ val(V,F),\ varphi(A,F),\ occ(A). \tag{22}$$

$$var\_diff(U,V) \leftarrow access(I,U,V),\ not\ val(U,F),\ val(V,F),\ varphi(A,F),\ occ(A). \tag{23}$$

Now we create accessibility relations in the next state for a sensing/announcement action. We first consider full observers. Suppose that $(M,U) \models \delta_{i,a}$ and $(U,V) \in M[i]$. In the next state agent i keeps links to those V worlds which satisfy precondition, observability of i and whose value of sensing/announcement variables are the same as U; and removes links to V worlds which do not satisfy such conditions. If all V worlds that agent i considers possible at U, violate precondition and/or observability and/or value of sensing/announcement variables (indicated by the $sa\_f\_cond(i,U)$ atom), then i will amend all these V worlds and create link to amended $V_{i,U}^f$ worlds.

$$\neg sa\_f\_cond(I,U) \leftarrow access(I,U,V),\ entails(V,F),\ formula\_full(I,A,F),$$
$$not\ var\_diff(U,V),\ occ(A),\ type(A,sa). \tag{24}$$

$$access\_n(I,U',V') \leftarrow world\_n(U'),\ access(I,U,V),\ f\_obs(I,A,U),\ entails(V,F),$$
$$formula\_full(I,A,F),\ not\ var\_diff(U,V),\ occ(A),\ type(A,sa). \tag{25}$$

$$access\_n(I,U',V_{I,U}^f) \leftarrow world\_n(U'),\ access(I,U,V),\ f\_obs(I,A,U),$$
$$not\ \neg sa\_f\_cond(I,U),\ occ(A),\ type(A,sa). \tag{26}$$

Partial observers correct for only the precondition and observability, but not for the sensing/announcement variables. Suppose that $(M,U) \models \theta_{i,a}$ and $(U,V) \in M[i]$. In the next state, agent i keeps links to those V worlds which satisfy precondition and observability of i; and remove links to V worlds which do not satisfy precondition and observability. However, if all V worlds that agent i considers possible at U violate precondition and/or observability (indicated by the $sa\_p\_cond(i,U)$ atom), then i will amend all these V worlds and create links to amended V_i^p worlds.

$$formula\_partial(I,A,F1 \wedge F2) \leftarrow exec(A,F1),\ aware(I,A,F2),\ ag(I). \tag{27}$$

$$\neg sa\_p\_cond(I,U) \leftarrow access(I,U,V),\ entails(V,F),\ formula\_partial(I,A,F),$$
$$occ(A),\ type(A,sa). \tag{28}$$

$$access\_n(I, U', V') \leftarrow world\_n(U'), access(I, U, V), p\_obs(I, A, U),$$
$$entails(V, F), formula\_partial(I, A, F), occ(A), type(A, sa). \quad (29)$$
$$access\_n(I, U', V_I^p) \leftarrow world\_n(U'), access(I, U, V), p\_obs(I, A, U),$$
$$not \, \neg sa\_p\_cond(I, U), occ(A), type(A, sa). \quad (30)$$

Accessibility relations of oblivious agents are constructed in a similar manner to the ontic actions. We also need to compute the valuation function at the next state M'. We first consider ontic actions. Note that μ, β for an ontic action may include common fluent(s) with precondition and/or observability formula. For robust state transition, the observing agent should first correct for precondition and observability, and then apply the effect of the action. Let $\lambda(U_i) = (\pi(U) \setminus (\overline{\psi \cup \delta_{i,a}})) \cup (\psi \cup \delta_{i,a})$ be an interpretation such that agent i corrects his beliefs at world $U \in M[S]$ about precondition and his observability. We compute $\lambda(U_i)$ by the rules

$$lambda(U_I, H) \leftarrow world\_n(U_I), pre\_lit(A, H), fluent(H),$$
$$occ(A), type(A, ontic). \quad (31)$$
$$lambda(U_I, H) \leftarrow world\_n(U_I), full\_lit(I, A, H), fluent(II),$$
$$occ(A), type(A, ontic). \quad (32)$$
$$lambda(U_I, H) \leftarrow world\_n(U_I), val(U, H), not \, pre\_lit(A, \neg H),$$
$$not \, full\_lit(I, A, II), fluent(H), occ(A), type(A, ontic) \quad (33)$$

Whether the interpretation $\lambda(U_i)$ satisfies a belief formula is denoted by $entails\_lambda(U_i, F)$ atom and can be computed by the ASP rules similar to (2)–(6). Valuation of U', $U_i \in M'[S]$ are computed by $M'[\pi](U') = \phi(\mathsf{a}, \pi(U))$ and $M'[\pi](U_i) = \phi(\mathsf{a}, \lambda(U_i))$ respectively. Namely, if $\pi(U)$ (resp. $\lambda(U_i)$) satisfies μ, then the literals in β are placed into the valuation of U' (resp. U_i).

$$val\_n(U', E) \leftarrow world\_n(U'), entails(U, F), causes(A, E, F), fluent(E),$$
$$occ(A), type(A, ontic). \quad (34)$$
$$val\_n(U', H) \leftarrow world\_n(U'), val(U, H), entails(U, F), not \, causes(A, \neg H, F),$$
$$fluent(H), occ(A), type(A, ontic). \quad (35)$$
$$val\_n(U_I, E) \leftarrow entails\_lambda(U_I, F), causes(A, E, F), fluent(E),$$
$$occ(A), type(A, ontic). \quad (36)$$
$$val\_n(U_I, H) \leftarrow lambda(U_I, H), entails\_lambda(U_I, F), not \, causes(A, \neg H, F),$$
$$fluent(H), occ(A), type(A, ontic). \quad (37)$$

Last, we compute the valuation of worlds at the next state for a sensing/announcement action. The valuation of the world $U' \in M'[S]$ is the same as valuation of $U \in M[S]$. Valuation of U_i^p and $V_{i,U}^f$ worlds may be different from $\pi(U)$. Recall that U_i^p is created for partial observer agent i where he corrects for action precondition and observability; and $V_{i,U}^f$ is created for full observer agent i where he corrects for precondition, observability and sensing/announcement variables (with respect to $U \in M[S]$).

$$val\_n(U_I^p, H) \leftarrow world\_n(U_I^p),\ pre\_lit(A, H),\ fluent(H),\ occ(A),\ type(A, sa). \qquad (38)$$

$$val\_n(U_I^p, H) \leftarrow world\_n(U_I^p),\ partial\_lit(I, A, H),\ fluent(H),$$
$$occ(A),\ type(A, sa). \qquad (39)$$

$$val\_n(U_I^p, H) \leftarrow world\_n(U_I^p),\ val(U, H),\ not\ pre\_lit(A, \neg H),$$
$$not\ partial\_lit(I, A, \neg H),\ fluent(H),\ occ(A),\ type(A, sa). \qquad (40)$$

$$val\_n(V_{I,U}^f, H) \leftarrow world\_n(V_{I,U}^f),\ pre\_lit(A, H),\ fluent(H),\ occ(A),\ type(A, sa). \qquad (41)$$

$$val\_n(V_{I,U}^f, H) \leftarrow world\_n(V_{I,U}^f),\ full\_lit(I, A, H),\ fluent(H),$$
$$occ(A),\ type(A, sa). \qquad (42)$$

$$val\_n(V_{I,U}^f, F) \leftarrow world\_n(V_{I,U}^f),\ varphi(A, F),\ val(U, F),\ occ(A),\ type(A, sa). \qquad (43)$$

$$val\_n(V_{I,U}^f, h) \leftarrow world\_n(V_{I,U}^f),\ val(V, H),\ not\ pre\_lit(A, \neg H),$$
$$not\ full\_lit(I, A, \neg H),\ not\ varphi(A, H),\ fluent(H),\ occ(A),\ type(A, sa). \qquad (44)$$

To compute the entailment of belief formulae at the next state, we add rules that are analogous to the rules (2)–(6) by replacing $entails(U, F)$, $world(U)$, $access(I, U, V)$, $val(U, F)$ atoms with $entails\_n(U, F)$, $world\_n(U)$, $access\_n(I, U, V)$, $val\_n(U, F)$ respectively.

4   Properties of the State Transition Function

We now provide results that our ASP formulation updates the state and beliefs of agents in a robust way. The proof of the theorems can be found in the appendix, available online[3]. Throughout the section, we assume $D = \langle \mathcal{AG}, \mathcal{F}, \mathcal{A} \rangle$ is a multi-agent epistemic domain and $T = (M, s)$ is the initial state where s is the actual world. We first ensure that the ASP program $\Pi_{D,T,\mathsf{a}}$ yields an answer set.

Theorem 1. *The ASP program* $\Pi_{D,T,\mathsf{a}}$ *has an answer set provided that D is a consistent domain.*

Theorem 2 describes how beliefs of full observer and oblivious agents change due to the occurrence of an ontic action. Full observers observe the effect of the action and update their beliefs accordingly. Beliefs of oblivious agents do not change. Moreover a full observer agent knows that another full observer agent has updated his beliefs and beliefs of oblivious agents stay the same.

Theorem 2. *Suppose that* a *is an ontic action,* $(\mu, \beta) \in Effects_\mathsf{a}$, *$Z$ is an answer set of the ASP program* $\Pi_{D,T,\mathsf{a}}$ *and* $occ(\mathsf{a})$, $pre\_hold(s) \in Z$.

1. *For $i \in \mathcal{AG}$, if $entails(s, \delta_{i,\mathsf{a}})$, $entails(s, \mathbf{B}_i\, \mu) \in Z$ then $entails\_n(s', \mathbf{B}_i\, \ell) \in Z$ for $\ell \in \beta$.*
2. *Suppose that $entails(s, \neg \delta_{i,\mathsf{a}}) \in Z$. For a belief formula η, $entails\_n(s', \mathbf{B}_i\, \eta) \in Z$ if and only if $entails(s, \mathbf{B}_i\, \eta) \in Z$.*

---

[3] https://github.com/yizmirlioglu/Epistemic.

3. *Suppose that entails$(s, \delta_{i,a})$, entails$(s, \mathbf{B}_i\,\delta_{j,a}) \in Z$ where $i \neq j$, $i, j \in \mathcal{AG}$. If entails$(s, \mathbf{B}_i\,\mathbf{B}_j\,\mu) \in Z$ then entails_n$(s', \mathbf{B}_i\,\mathbf{B}_j\,\ell) \in Z$ holds, for $\ell \in \beta$.*
4. *Suppose that entails$(s, \mathbf{B}_i\,\neg\delta_{j,a}) \in Z$ holds where $i \neq j$, $i, j \in \mathcal{AG}$. For a belief formula η, if entails$(s, \mathbf{B}_i\,\mathbf{B}_j\,\eta) \in Z$ then entails_n$(s', \mathbf{B}_i\,\mathbf{B}_j\,\eta) \in Z$.*

Theorem 3 states that full observers learn the value of the sensing/announcement variables $\ell \in \varphi$ while partial observers know that full observers know the value of sensing variables; belief of oblivious agents stays the same.

Theorem 3. *Suppose that a is a sensing/announcement action, Z is an answer set of the ASP program $\Pi_{D,T,a}$ and occ(a), pre_hold$(s) \in Z$.*

1. *For $i \in \mathcal{AG}$, $\ell \in \varphi$, if entails$(s, \delta_{i,a})$, entails$(s, \ell) \in Z$ then entails_n$(s', \mathbf{B}_i\ell) \in Z$.*
2. *For $i \in \mathcal{AG}$, $\ell \in \varphi$, if entails$(s, \delta_{i,a})$, entails$(s, \neg\ell) \in Z$ then entails_n$(s', \mathbf{B}_i\neg\ell) \in Z$.*
3. *Suppose that entails$(s, \theta_{i,a})$, entails$(s, \mathbf{B}_i\,\delta_{j,a}) \in Z$ where $i \neq j$, $i, j \in \mathcal{AG}$. Then entails_n$(s', \mathbf{B}_i\,(\mathbf{B}_j\,\ell \vee \mathbf{B}_j\,\overline{\ell})) \in Z$ for $\ell \in \varphi$.*
4. *Suppose that obliv$(i, a, s) \in Z$. For a belief formula η, entails_n$(s', \mathbf{B}_i\,\eta) \in Z$ if and only if entails$(s, \mathbf{B}_i\,\eta) \in Z$.*

5   Example Scenarios

This section demonstrates our state transition function by applying it to the example scenarios in the introduction. We consider the belief operator in the Kripke structures at Fig. 1, 2. The ASP encoding of input and output for these scenarios can be found in our online repository. For instance, the initial state and the computed next state of the first scenario are

$actual(s)$. $world(s)$. $world(u)$. $world(v)$.

$val(s, normal)$. $val(s, sound)$. $val(u, normal)$. $access(a, s, u)$. $access(a, s, v)$. $access(b, s, s)$.

$actual\_n(prime(s))$. $world\_n(prime(s))$. $world\_n(subf(u, a, s))$. $world\_n(subf(v, a, s))$.

$val\_n(prime(s), normal)$. $val\_n(prime(s), sound)$. $val\_n(subf(u, a, s), normal)$.

$val\_n(subf(u, a, s), sound)$. $val\_n(subf(v, a, s), normal)$. $val\_n(subf(v, a, s), sound)$.

$access\_n(a, prime(s), subf(u, a, s))$. $access\_n(a, prime(s), subf(v, a, s))$. $access\_n(b, prime(s), prime(s))$.

The next state of each scenario is depicted in Fig. 3 according to the ASP output. Now the next state is intuitive: In the first scenario, agent A has corrected his beliefs at world u, v and he believes that the meter is sound and the voltage level is normal. In the second scenario, the transition function was able to revert agent A's initial incorrect belief about the sensing variable *normal*. After the sensing action, A believes that the voltage level is normal as expected. In the third scenario, at the next state B knows that the door is open and he has realized that he is full observer (*near_b*). Besides agent A believes that B is full observer and A believes that B believes that B is full observer.

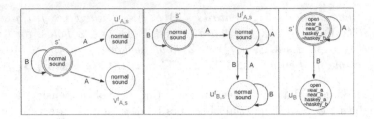

Fig. 3. Solution of example scenarios in the introduction

6   Related Literature

In dynamic epistemic logic literature, state transition in possible world semantics have been studied by [3,4,7,15]. Event update models have also been employed for state transition [1,2,6]. For multi-agent contexts, [4,16] have developed action languages that describe the domain, actions and observability of agents. [4] utilizes a simple belief correction mechanism for sensing/announcement actions where the full observer agents "directly learn the actual state of the world".

[7] proposed an alternative state transition function, where full and partial observers correct their beliefs about action precondition, but not about observability. Observability of agents is computed at the actual world and assumed to be fixed across worlds. Thus an agent corrects his beliefs even in those worlds where he is not a full or partial observer. Conditional effects are not allowed for an ontic action. The authors do not examine how an agent's beliefs about other agents change during state transition. In our model, the knowledge operator is not required and the belief operator is sufficient for belief correction. Besides, we do not assume a fixed observability across all worlds. By construction, our state transition function corrects an agent's first order beliefs and beliefs about other agents (higher order beliefs).

Our work also contributes to the field on applications of Answer Set Programming. ASP has been utilized in epistemic reasoning literature by [5,8,9,17]. [5] have used ASP to encode Kripke structures and showed that epistemic problems such as "Muddy child", "Sum and Product" can be solved in this setting. [9,17] have developed conditional epistemic planners for single agent setting. A multi-agent planner have been implemented using ASP by [8].

7   Conclusion

We have developed an ASP-based state transition function for ontic, sensing and announcement actions for partially observable multi-agent epistemic domains. One novel feature of our transition function is that agents correct their belief about precondition, observability and sensing/announcement variables upon an action occurrence. By examples, we have shown that this step is crucial for observing the effect of the action, and thus for robust state transition.

Answer Set Programming enables us to write state transition in terms of simple, understandable logical rules in recursive form. We establish some properties of our planner regarding its robustness in updating beliefs of agents consistent with their level of observability. For future work, we aim to implement a planner using this ASP formulation. Our transition function can also be used in existing conformant and conditional epistemic planning systems as a module to compute the next state.

Acknowledgment. The authors have been partially supported by NSF grants 2151254, 1914635 and 1757207. Tran Cao Son was also partially supported by NSF grant 1812628.

References

1. Baltag, A., Moss, L.: Logics for epistemic programs. Synthese (2004)
2. Baltag, A., Moss, L., Solecki, S.: The logic of public announcements, common knowledge, and private suspicions. In: 7th TARK, pp. 43–56 (1998)
3. Baral, C., Gelfond, G., Pontelli, E., Son, T.C.: An action language for reasoning about beliefs in multi-agent domains. In: Proceedings of NMR (2012)
4. Baral, C., Gelfond, G., Pontelli, E., Son, T.C.: An action language for multi-agent domains. Artif. Intell. **302**, 103601 (2022)
5. Baral, C., Gelfond, G., Son, T.C., Pontelli, E.: Using answer set programming to model multi-agent scenarios involving agents' knowledge about other's knowledge. In: Proceedings of the 9th International Conference on Autonomous Agents and Multiagent Systems, vol. 1, pp. 259–266 (2010)
6. Benthem, J.V., Eijck, J.V., Kooi, B.P.: Logics of communication and change. Inf. Comput. **204**(11), 1620–1662 (2006)
7. Buckingham, D., Kasenberg, D., Scheutz, M.: Simultaneous representation of knowledge and belief for epistemic planning with belief revision, 172–181 (2020). https://doi.org/10.24963/kr.2020/18
8. Burigana, A., Fabiano, F., Dovier, A., Pontelli, E.: Modelling multi-agent epistemic planning in asp. Theory Pract. Logic Program. **20**(5), 593–608 (2020)
9. Cabalar, P., Fandinno, J., del Cerro, L.F.: Dynamic epistemic logic with asp updates: application to conditional planning. arXiv preprint arXiv:1905.10621 (2019)
10. Ditmarsch, H.V., van der Hoek, W., Kooi, B.: Dynamic Epistemic Logic, 1st edn. Springer (2007)
11. Fagin, R., Halpern, J., Moses, Y., Vardi, M.: Reasoning About Knowledge. MIT Press (1995)
12. Gelfond, M., Lifschitz, V.: The stable model semantics for logic programming. In: Kowalski, R., Bowen, K. (eds.) Logic Programming: Proceedings of the Fifth International Conference and Symposium, pp. 1070–1080 (1988)
13. Gelfond, M., Lifschitz, V.: Classical negation in logic programs and disjunctive databases. New Gen. Comput. 365–387 (1991)
14. Lifschitz, V.: Answer Set Programming. Springer, Cham (2019). https://doi.org/10.1007/978-3-030-24658-7

15. Pontelli, E., Son, T.C., Baral, C., Gelfond, G.: Answer set programming and planning with knowledge and world-altering actions in multiple agent domains. In: Erdem, E., Lee, J., Lierler, Y., Pearce, D. (eds.) Correct Reasoning. LNCS, vol. 7265, pp. 509–526. Springer, Heidelberg (2012). https://doi.org/10.1007/978-3-642-30743-0_35
16. Rajaratnam, D., Thielscher, M.: Representing and reasoning with event models for epistemic planning. In: Proceedings of the International Conference on Principles of Knowledge Representation and Reasoning, vol. 18, pp. 519–528 (2021)
17. Tu, P.H., Son, T.C., Baral, C.: Reasoning and planning with sensing actions, incomplete information, and static causal laws using answer set programming. Theory Pract. Logic Program. **7**(4), 377–450 (2007)

Towards Provenance in Heterogeneous Knowledge Bases

Matthias Knorr$^{(\boxtimes)}$ ⓘ, Carlos Viegas Damásio ⓘ, Ricardo Gonçalves ⓘ,
and João Leite ⓘ

Departamento de Informática, NOVA LINCS, FCT NOVA,
Caparica, Portugal
{mkn,cd,rjrg,jleite}@fct.unl.pt

Abstract. A rapidly increasing amount of data, information and knowledge is becoming available on the Web, often written in different formats and languages, adhering to standardizations driven by the World Wide Web Consortium initiative. Taking advantage of all this heterogeneous knowledge requires its integration for more sophisticated reasoning services and applications. To fully leverage the potential of such systems, their inferences should be accompanied by justifications that allow a user to understand a proposed decision/recommendation, in particular for critical systems (healthcare, law, finances, etc.). However, determining such justifications has commonly only been considered for a single formalism, such as relational databases, description logic ontologies, or declarative rule languages. In this paper, we present the first approach for providing provenance for heterogeneous knowledge bases building on the general framework of multi-context systems, as an abstract, but very expressive formalism to represent knowledge bases written in different formalisms and the flow of information between them. We also show under which conditions and how provenance information in this formalism can be computed.

Keywords: Provenance · Heterogeneous knowledge bases · Multi-context systems

1 Introduction

A rapidly increasing amount of data, information and knowledge is becoming available on the Web, driven by the Semantic Web initiative led by the World Wide Web Consortium (W3C).[1] A number of language standards have been established in this initiative and to take advantage of all this available knowledge often requires their integration. This is particularly true for (but not limited to) integrations of rule languages, e.g., under answer set semantics [4] and ontology languages based on description logics [1], that are both highly expressive, but with orthogonal/complementary characteristics and modelling features (see, e.g., [12,21,23,24] and references therein).

---

[1] https://www.w3.org/.

G. Gottlob et al. (Eds.): LPNMR 2022, LNAI 13416, pp. 287–300, 2022.
https://doi.org/10.1007/978-3-031-15707-3_22

However, in the course of the integration of such heterogeneous knowledge, it becomes increasingly difficult to trace the causes for a certain inference, or find the justification for some proposed decision, in particular, if the pieces of knowledge originate from different authors. It would therefore be important to provide methods that accompany inferences/decisions with explanations/justifications in a way a user can understand to allow for the validation of reasoning results, in particular for critical systems (healthcare, law, finances, etc.).

This has been recognized in different areas of Artificial Intelligence, and for several Knowledge Representation and Reasoning formalisms, the problem of finding justifications has been considered. In particular, a lot of work has focussed on tracing the origins of derivations, commonly under the name of provenance [5], e.g., in relational databases and Datalog [18,19], Logic Programming [8], Answer Set Programming [13], Description Logics ontology languages [2,6,20], as well as in SPARQL [7] and data streams [16]. Yet, provenance for heterogeneous knowledge bases has mostly been ignored, with the exception of [10], though limited to two very restricted settings.

In this paper, we investigate provenance for heterogeneous knowledge bases, utilising multi-context systems (MCSs) [3] as our formalism of choice. MCSs allow for the integration of a large variety of logic-based formalisms, and model the flow of information between them. They cover very general approaches for integrating ontologies and rules [22], thus allowing to study provenance in a more general manner, which then paves the way towards provenance in related approaches in the literature. We focus on providing justifications of inferences (the only question that has been handled in the literature are explanations of inconsistencies when repairing inconsistent multi-context systems [11], which is inherently different). Our contributions can be summarized as follows:

- We develop the first general approach for provenance in heterogeneous knowledge bases, and in multi-context systems in particular, annotating inferences with their justifying provenance information.
- We provide means to compute this provenance information annotating models, so-called equilibria, in MCSs.
- We establish under which conditions this provenance information can indeed be computed, showing its applicability to a wide class of formalisms.

The remainder of the paper is structured as follows. We recall notions on provenance semirings in Sect. 2. Then, in Sect. 3, we introduce provenance multi-context systems as a non-trivial extension of MCSs. In Sect. 4, we show how and when model notions for such provenance MCSs can be computed and provide considerations on complexity, before we conclude in Sect. 5.

2 Provenance Semirings

In the context of databases, commutative semirings have been introduced as a means of representing provenance information [18,19], such as providing information regarding what combination of tuples in a database certain query results were obtained from. Subsequently, commutative semirings have been adopted for representing provenance information in a wide variety of different logic formalisms and it has been shown that they cover other related approaches in the literature, such as finding minimal explanations/justifications [15]. They are thus well-suited to capture provenance information in formalisms composed of knowledge bases written in different (knowledge representation) languages, and we recall the main notions here.

A *commutative semiring* is an algebraic structure $\mathcal{K} = (K, \oplus_\mathcal{K}, \otimes_\mathcal{K}, 0_\mathcal{K}, 1_\mathcal{K})$ where $\oplus_\mathcal{K}$ and $\otimes_\mathcal{K}$ are commutative and associative binary operators over a set K, called the annotation domain of $\mathcal{K}$. The operators $\oplus_\mathcal{K}$ and $\otimes_\mathcal{K}$ have neutral elements $0_\mathcal{K}$ and $1_\mathcal{K}$, respectively, where $\otimes_\mathcal{K}$ distributes over $\oplus_\mathcal{K}$, and $0_\mathcal{K}$ is an annihilating element of $\otimes_\mathcal{K}$. This allows the definition of functions (so-called $\mathcal{K}$-relations) that map tuples (in the case of databases) to annotations over K such that only finitely many tuples are annotated with a value different from $0_\mathcal{K}$.

As an example in the case of databases, we may consider a commutative semiring where each tuple in any given table is annotated with an annotation name. Then, the annotations of query results correspond to the combinations of these annotations names, i.e., those corresponding to tuples, using $\oplus_\mathcal{K}$ to represent alternatives and $\otimes_\mathcal{K}$ to represent the join of tuples.

This idea is captured in general in the provenance polynomials semiring $\mathbb{N}[X] = (\mathbb{N}[X], +, \times, 0, 1)$ where polynomials over annotation variables X are used with natural number coefficients and exponents over these variables. Other relevant semirings in the literature can be obtained from it by introducing additional properties on the operations such as idempotence on $+$ and/or $\times$, or absorption, giving rise to a hierarchy of semirings [19]. Several such semirings have been used for notions of provenance in different logic-based formalisms (e.g., [2,6], and also [15] for further references). Among these semirings, $\mathbb{N}[X]$ is the most general one and universal, in the sense that for any other commutative semiring $\mathcal{K}$, a semiring homomorphism can be defined, allowing the computations for $\mathcal{K}$ to be done in $\mathbb{N}[X]$.

Monus semirings or *m-semirings* [14] extend such commutative semirings by adding natural orders $\preceq_\mathcal{K}$, which are partial orders that order elements of the annotation domain based on the $\oplus_\mathcal{K}$ operation, namely, $k_1 \preceq_\mathcal{K} k_2$ if there exists k_3 such that $k_1 \oplus_\mathcal{K} k_3 = k_2$. The monus operation $k_1 \ominus_\mathcal{K} k_2$ then refers to the unique smallest element k_3 in such a partial order such that $k_2 \oplus_\mathcal{K} k_3 \preceq_\mathcal{K} k_1$. This allows capturing negation and has been generalized to recursive Datalog queries and logic programs under different semantics [8] using a semiring that utilizes boolean formulas over two sets of variables – positive facts and their negations. Similar ideas have been applied to handle semiring provenance for First-Order Logic [17,25], utilizing first-order formulas in negation normal form.

3   Provenance Multi-context Systems

Multi-context systems (MCSs) [3] are defined as a collection of components, so-called contexts, each of which allows one to represent knowledge in some logic-based formalism. Each such logic is associated with a set of well-formed knowledge bases in the logic (its admitted syntax), possible belief sets, indicating how models are defined in this logic (its admitted semantics), and a function assigning to each possible knowledge base a set of acceptable such belief sets. MCSs use so-called bridge rules that allow one to model the flow of information between these contexts, in the sense that they admit the incorporation of knowledge in one context based on the beliefs considered true in other contexts. The semantics of MCSs is then assigned using equilibria that take the acceptable belief sets and the interaction between contexts into account.

In this section, we introduce provenance multi-context systems that extend MCSs with the means to explain inferences obtained from the modular integration of its contexts. Here, rather than recalling first MCSs and then introduce their extension, to not unnecessarily burden the presentation with partially repetitive technical definitions, we introduce provenance multi-context systems right away clarifying in the course of this introduction how and where our notion extends the previous one.

The first important question is how provenance should be represented in such a modular framework. Given that different notions of provenance have been introduced for different logical formalisms, with varying granularity of the provided provenance information, our objective is to maintain the modular character of MCSs, and admit that possibly different notions of provenance be used in each of the contexts, and provide provenance annotations for inferences in the contexts taking into account provenance information from other contexts via bridge rules.

We start by defining the set of variables allowed to be used as annotations. To account for possibly varying algebras in different contexts with differing binary operators, we introduce a number of different annotation languages V_i, each intended to correspond to one of the contexts, that can be interleaved by means of one particular language V_*, which is meant to correspond to the integration of information in bridge rules between contexts.

Definition 1. Let $N = N_* \cup \bigcup N_i$ be a countably infinite set of names and $\Sigma = \Sigma_* \cup \bigcup \Sigma_i$ be a countably infinite set of binary operators such that, for all i, all N_i are mutually distinct, $N_* \cap N_i = \emptyset$, and $N \cap \Sigma = \emptyset$. The set of annotation variables $V = V_* \cup \bigcup V_i$ is defined inductively for all i with $1 \leq i \leq n$:

(1) $N_i \subseteq V_i$;
(2) $(v_1 \circ v_2) \in V_i$ for $v_1, v_2 \in V_i$ and $\circ \in \Sigma_i$;
(3) $(r \circ v_1 \circ \cdots \circ v_m) \in V_*$ for $r \in N_*$, for all k, $1 \leq k \leq m$, $v_k \in V_i$ for some i, $\circ \in \Sigma_*$, and $m \geq 0$;
(4) $V_* \subseteq V_i$.

Condition (1) specifies that names intended to annotate formulas are valid annotation variables within the respective sublanguage. Then, condition (2) indicates how to obtain complex annotations within each of the defined sublanguages. Condition (3) defines that annotation variables in the language V_* are composed of one name from N_* and 0 or more annotations from the other languages, which is intended to represent the composition of annotations v_k within a bridge rule (as defined in the following). Finally, condition (4) admits that annotations from V_* be used in the other annotation languages.

Note that names, which are meant to be used to identify formulas in individual contexts, are distinct, while operators may overlap in between different Σ_i, and between Σ_* and different Σ_i, to account for the possibility that different contexts may use the same provenance formalism.

Based on this, we can introduce provenance logics as a means to capture a large variety of formalisms that allow tracing the reasons for inferences, thus generalizing the logics of MCSs as described in the beginning of this section.

Definition 2. *A provenance logic L is a tuple $(\mathcal{K}, \mathbf{KB}, \mathbf{BS}, \mathbf{ACC})$ where*

(1) $\mathcal{K}$ is a commutative semiring over polynomials over some V_i with $\oplus_{\mathcal{K}}, \otimes_{\mathcal{K}} \in \Sigma_i$, and a natural order $\preceq_{\mathcal{K}}$;

(2) $\mathbf{KB}$ is the set of well-formed knowledge bases of L such that each $kb \in \mathbf{KB}$ is a set composed of formulas distinctly annotated with elements from V_i;

(3) $\mathbf{BS}$ is the set of possible annotated belief sets, i.e., functions that map beliefs from the set of possible beliefs B_L of L to V_i, such that false beliefs are mapped to $0_{\mathcal{K}}$;

(4) $\mathbf{ACC} : \mathbf{KB} \to 2^{\mathbf{BS}}$ is a function describing the semantics of L by assigning to each knowledge base a set of acceptable annotated belief sets.

In comparison to logics for MCSs [3], provenance logics include a commutative semiring $\mathcal{K}$ and formulas in knowledge bases are in addition annotated according to one of the languages V_i (see Definition 1). Also, the idea of possible belief sets from MCSs is extended in that sets of annotated beliefs are used. I.e., rather than using sets of beliefs that are meant to be true, sets of beliefs with their corresponding annotations are considered. The function $\mathbf{ACC}$ then assigns semantics to knowledge bases by associating them with acceptable annotated belief sets.

Note that some approaches in the literature assign polynomials to beliefs that are not true, e.g., to account for possible changes so that something becomes true, but here, for the sake of generality and in the spirit of MCSs, we omit this, and focus on determining the provenance of true elements.

Example 1. We present some example provenance logics.

- L_{db} – Databases with provenance under bag semantics [18]:
  - $\mathcal{K}_{db}$: $\mathbb{N}[X]$;
  - $\mathbf{KB}_{db}$: the set of annotated databases together with queries expressed in an appropriate query language, such as Datalog;
  - $\mathbf{BS}_{db}$: the set of sets of atoms with annotations;
  - $\mathbf{ACC}_{db}(kb)$: the set of tuples in kb and query results over db with their annotation according to $\mathcal{K}_{db}$;
- L_{dl} – Description Logic $\mathcal{ELH}^r$ [2]:
  - $\mathcal{K}_{dl}$: $Trio[X]$, i.e., $\mathbb{N}[X]$ with idempotent $\times$;
  - $\mathbf{KB}_{dl}$: set of well-formed annotated $\mathcal{ELH}^r$ ontologies;
  - $\mathbf{BS}_{dl}$: the set of sets of annotated atomic inferences;
  - $\mathbf{ACC}_{dl}(kb)$: the set of atomic inferences from kb with their annotation according to $\mathcal{K}_{dl}$;

- L_{lp} – Normal logic programs under answer set semantics (adapted from [8]):
  - $\mathcal{K}_{lp}$: $PosBool[X]$, i.e., $\mathbb{N}[X]$ with idempotent $+$ and $\times$ and absorption on $+$, over positive atoms;
  - $\mathbf{KB}_{lp}$: the set of annotated normal logic programs;
  - $\mathbf{BS}_{lp}$: the set of sets of atoms with annotations;
  - $\mathbf{ACC}_{lp}(kb)$: the answer sets of kb with annotations according to $\mathcal{K}_{lp}$;

Similar to MCSs, bridge rules are used to specify how knowledge is transferred between the different components, but here we also have to take provenance information into account.

Definition 3. *Given a collection of provenance logics $L = \langle L_1, \ldots, L_n \rangle$, an L_i-bridge rule over L, $1 \leq i \leq n$, is of the form:*

$$\pi@s \leftarrow (r_1 : p_1), \ldots, (r_j : p_j), \tag{1}$$
$$\mathbf{not}\,(r_{j+1} : p_{j+1}), \ldots, \mathbf{not}\,(r_m : p_m)$$

where $\pi \in N_*$ and, for $1 \leq k \leq m$, $1 \leq r_k \leq n$ and $p_k \in B_{L_{r_k}}$, and, for each $kb \in \mathbf{KB}_i$, $kb \cup \{v@s\} \in \mathbf{KB}_i$ for every $v \in V_*$. We refer with $H(\pi)$ and $B(\pi)$ to the head and the body of the bridge rule, respectively. A bridge rule is called monotonic if it does not contain elements of the form $\mathbf{not}\,(r : p)$, and non-monotonic otherwise.

Note that each of the r_k refer to one of the logics and the beliefs p_k belong to the corresponding set of possible beliefs $B_{L_{r_k}}$ of logic L_{r_k} (cf. (3) of Definition 1). Also note that π is the annotation name of the bridge rule itself, whereas v is an annotation variable associated to the bridge rule head s, intended to be incorporated into the knowledge base kb_i, such that v takes the annotations of the bridge rule elements into account (as made precise when we define the semantics).

With this in place, we can introduce provenance multi-context systems.

Definition 4. *A provenance multi-context system (pMCS) is a collection of contexts $M = \langle C_1, \ldots, C_n \rangle$ where $C_i = (L_i, kb_i, br_i)$, $L_i = (\mathcal{K}_i, \mathbf{KB}_i, \mathbf{BS}_i, \mathbf{ACC}_i)$ is a provenance logic, $kb_i \in \mathbf{KB}_i$ a knowledge base, and br_i is a set of L_i-bridge rules over $\langle L_1, \ldots, L_n \rangle$.*

We assume that the annotations used for the elements occurring in the individual kb_i are unique elements from N_i, and that each context uses a different set of annotations V_i. Also, while different forms of specifying the annotations of formulas can be found in the literature, here we use uniformly the notation introduced for bridge rules, i.e., the annotation is given in front of a formula with @ as separator.

Example 2. Consider $M = \langle C_1, C_2, C_3 \rangle$ such that:

- C_1 is a database context with L_{db}, $kb = \{d_1@p(1,1), d_2@p(1,2)\}$ with a single relation $p/2$ with two tuples, $br_1 = \emptyset$, and query q defined by $q(x,y) \leftarrow p(e,x), p(e,y)$;

- C_2 a DL context with L_{dl}, $kb_2 = \{o_1@A \sqsubseteq B\}$, and
  $br_2 = \{b_1@A(w) \leftarrow \mathbf{not}\,(3:l)\}$;
- C_3 an ASP context with L_{lp}, $kb_3 = \{r_1@l \leftarrow \mathbf{not}\,m, n\}$, and
  $br_3 = \{c_1@n \leftarrow (1:q(1,1)), c_2@m \leftarrow (2:B(w))\}$.

As C_1 has no bridge rules, we obtain $\mathbf{ACC}_{db}(kb_1) = \{S_1\}$ with $S_1(p(1,1)) = d_1$, $S_1(p(1,2)) = d_2$, $S_1(q(1,1)) = d_1^2$, $S_1(q(1,2)) = S_1(q(2,1)) = d_1 \times d_2$, and $S_1(q(2,2)) = d_2^2$. For both kb_2 and kb_3, $\mathbf{ACC}_i(kb_i) = \{S_i\}$ with S_i mapping every atomic inference/atom to 0 (as the bridge rules are not considered for the semantics of individual contexts).

We now turn to the semantics of pMCSs. We first introduce belief states that contain one possible annotated belief set for each context and serve as suitable model candidates.

Definition 5. *Let $M = \langle C_1, \ldots, C_n \rangle$ be a pMCS. A belief state of M is a collection $S = \langle S_1, \ldots, S_n \rangle$ such that each S_i is an element of $\mathbf{BS}_i$.*

We next identify specific belief states, called equilibria, that take bridge rules into account for determining acceptable belief states, similar to MCSs. We adapt this with annotations building on the algebraic approach for non-monotonic rules [8] to pass annotation information via bridge rules. The main idea is to use annotations from V_* assuming the existence of distinct negative names (using $\mathbf{not}$) in the respective N_i, one per negated p_k with $j+1 \leq k \leq m$ for bridge rules of the form (1). This is necessary as we assume that false beliefs are annotated with $0_\mathcal{K}$, thus no annotations exist for such negations.

We first fix the commutative semiring for bridge rules.

Definition 6. *The commutative semiring for bridge rules $\mathcal{BR}$ is defined as $PosBool[V_*]$, for $\wedge, \vee \in \Sigma_*$, with idempotent meet ($\wedge$) and join ($\vee$), absorption on $\vee$, and logical consequence as natural order, i.e., $k_1 \preceq_{\mathcal{BR}} k_2$ iff $k_1 \models k_2$.*

We can now define when a bridge rule is applicable in a belief state, namely when the beliefs in the rule body hold true for positive elements and false for negative elements.

Definition 7. *Let $M = \langle C_1, \ldots, C_n \rangle$ be a pMCS and π an L_i-bridge rule over L of form (1). Then π is applicable in a belief state S, denoted $S \models B(\pi)$, iff*

(1) for $1 \leq k \leq j$, $S_{r_k}(p_k) = n$ for some annotation $n \neq 0$;
(2) for $j+1 \leq k \leq m$, $S_{r_k}(p_k) = 0$.

As false elements are annotated with 0, we can use the annotations corresponding to beliefs being false in the annotations of the inferred/added bridge rule heads. This allows us to define equilibria.

Definition 8. *Let $M = \langle C_1, \ldots, C_n \rangle$ be a pMCS. A belief state $S = \langle S_1, \ldots, S_n \rangle$ of M is an equilibrium if, for all i with $1 \leq i \leq n$, the following condition holds:*

$$S_i \in \mathbf{ACC}_i(kb_i \cup \{\, v@H(\pi) \mid \pi \in br_i \text{ and } S \models B(\pi) \,\})$$

where the annotation of $H(\pi)$, v, is defined over all $\pi_l \in br_i$ with $H(\pi_l) = H(\pi)$ such that $S \models B(\pi_l)$ as:

$$v = \bigvee \pi_l \wedge v_1 \wedge \ldots \wedge v_j \wedge \textbf{not } p_{j+1} \wedge \ldots \textbf{not } p_m$$

such that, for $1 \leq k \leq j$, $S_{r_k}(p_k) = v_k$.

Hence, a belief state S is an equilibrium if, for each context, the corresponding annotated belief set is acceptable for the knowledge base of the context enhanced with the heads of those bridge rules of the context that are admissible in S. The corresponding annotations for bridge rule heads are constructed as representations of the alternative provenance information (via disjunction) resulting from different bridge rules with the same head. Before we explain the reason for that, we consider an example without bridge rules with the same head.

Example 3. Consider M from Example 2. Since C_1 does not contain bridge rules, S_1 is fully determined in Example 2. Then, by the first rule in br_3, we have that $S_3(n) = c_1 \wedge d_1^2$. If the other rule in br_3 is not applicable, then $S_3(l) = r_1 \times_3 (c_1 \wedge d_1^2)$ holds. In this case, the only bridge rule in br_2 is not applicable, thus $B(w)$ cannot be inferred from C_2 which ensures that the second rule in br_3 is not applicable. In fact, together with S_2 mapping every atomic inference to 0, we obtain an equilibrium.

We next provide an example showing that absorption on disjunctions is necessary to ensure the existence of equilibria.

Example 4. Consider $M = \langle C_1 \rangle$ with $L_1 = L_{lp}$, $kb_1 = \{n@q\}$, $br_1 = \{r_1@p \leftarrow (1:p), r_2@p \leftarrow (1:q)\}$. Then, $S = \langle S_1 \rangle$ with $S_1(q) = n$ and $S_1(p) = r_2 \times_1 n$ is an equilibrium of M. Note that both bridge rules are applicable in S, so without absorption, v would be $(r_2 \times_1 n) \vee (r_1 \times_1 r_2 \times_1 n)$ and no equilibrium would exist.

One could argue that this problem can be avoided by not joining disjunctively the provenance information for bridge rules with the same head and by passing several bridge rule heads with differing provenance information. But this requires that absorption be present in the target context's provenance notion, and since this cannot be guaranteed, nor do we want to impose it as an additional restriction, we deem the solution where absorption is resolved on the level of bridge rules the most suitable one.

We also illustrate that idempotency of $\wedge$ is required.

Example 5. Take $M = \langle C_1 \rangle$ with $L_1 = L_{lp}$, $kb_1 = \{\}$, $br_1 = \{r@p \leftarrow (1:p)\}$. Then, $S = \langle S_1 \rangle$ with $S_1(p) = 0$ and $S' = \langle S_1 \rangle$ with $S_1(p) = r \times_1 p$ are equilibria of M. Note that r is applicable in S' and without idempotency of $\wedge$, v would be $r \times_1 r \times_1 p$, i.e., S' would not be an equilibrium.

One may wonder whether S' indeed should be an equilibrium, since the truth of p relies on self-support using the bridge rule, i.e., we would be interested in minimal equilibria. Formally, an equilibrium S is *minimal* if there is no equilibrium $S' = \langle S'_1, \ldots, S'_n \rangle$ such that $S'_i \preceq_{\mathcal{K}_i} S_i$ for all i with $1 \leq i \leq n$ and $S'_j \prec_{\mathcal{K}_j} S_j$ for some j with $1 \leq j \leq n$. However, it has been shown [3] that equilibria in MCSs are not necessarily minimal due to cyclic dependencies as in Example 5, and this carries over to pMCSs.

Still, we can show that equilibria of pMCSs are faithful with equilibria of MCSs as well as the provenance annotations in individual formalisms in the following sense.

Proposition 1. *Let $M = \langle C_1, \ldots, C_n \rangle$ be a pMCS and M' the MCS obtained from M by omitting all semirings $\mathcal{K}$ and all annotations from M, and, in each logic, replace the annotated belief sets by the set of beliefs not mapped to 0.*

- *For context C_i in M with $br_i = \emptyset$ and equilibrium S of M, $S_i \in \mathbf{ACC}_i(kb_i)$.*
- *If S is an equilibrium of M, then S' is an equilibrium of M' with $S'_i = \{b \mid S_i(b) \neq 0\}$.*

The converse of 2. does not hold in general because we require a method to determine the provenance annotations corresponding to equilibria of MCSs. In the next section, we investigate how and under which conditions such equilibria together with their provenance information can be effectively determined.

4   Grounded Equilibria

Building on material developed for MCSs [3], we introduce a restriction of pMCSs, called reducible pMCSs, for which minimal equilibria can be computed. To this end, we first consider definite pMCSs, a further restriction similar in spirit to definite logic programs, where reasoning is monotonic and where a unique minimal equilibrium exists.

We start with monotonic logics, where $\mathbf{ACC}$ is deterministic and monotonic. Formally, a logic $L = (\mathcal{K}, \mathbf{KB}, \mathbf{BS}, \mathbf{ACC})$ is *monotonic* if (1) $\mathbf{ACC}(kb)$ is a singleton set for each $kb \in \mathbf{KB}$, and (2) $S \preceq_{\mathcal{K}} S'$ whenever $kb \subseteq kb'$, $\mathbf{ACC}(kb) = \{S\}$, and $\mathbf{ACC}(kb') = \{S'\}$.

This excludes non-monotonic logics, but many of them are *reducible*, namely, if for some $\mathbf{KB}^* \subseteq \mathbf{KB}$ and some reduction function $red : \mathbf{KB} \times \mathbf{BS} \to \mathbf{KB}^*$:

(1) the restriction of L to $\mathbf{KB}^*$ is monotonic, and
(2) for each $kb \in \mathbf{KB}$, and all $S, S' \in \mathbf{BS}$:
  (a) $red(kb, S) = kb$ whenever $kb \in \mathbf{KB}^*$,
  (b) $red(kb, S) \subseteq red(kb, S')$ whenever $S' \preceq S$, and
  (c) $S \in \mathbf{ACC}(kb)$ iff $\mathbf{ACC}(red(kb, S)) = \{S\}$.

This is adapted from MCSs, and inspired by the Gelfond-Lifschitz reduction for logic programs, indicating that (a) reduced *kbs* do not need to be reduced any further, (b) *red* is antitonic, and (c) acceptable annotated belief sets can be checked based on *red*. Note that the latter condition implies that the annotations are determined based on the reduced knowledge base.

This is generalized to contexts that are reducible, namely, if their logic is reducible, and if the reduction function is not affected by the addition of annotated bridge rule heads. Formally, a context $C_i = (L_i, kb_i, br_i)$ is *reducible* if

- its logic L_i is reducible and,
- for all belief sets S_i and all $H \subseteq \{ v@H(\pi) \mid \pi \in br_i, v \in V_i \}$: $red(kb_i \cup H, S_i) = red(kb_i, S_i) \cup H$.

A pMCS is *reducible* if all of its contexts are.

It has been argued that a wide variety of logics is reducible [3]. Thus, reducible pMCSs admit the integration of a wide variety of logical formalisms provided the provenance notion fits or can be adjusted to the semiring requirements in Definition 2 and annotations can be determined based on reduced kbs, which arguably is the case for many KR formalisms.

We can now determine definite pMCSs as follows. A reducible pMCS $M = \langle C_1, \ldots, C_n \rangle$ is *definite* if

1. all bridge rules in all contexts are monotonic,
2. for all i and all $S \in \mathbf{BS}_i$, $kb_i = red_i(kb_i, S)$.

Thus, in definite pMCSs, bridge rules are monotonic and knowledge bases are already in reduced form. Therefore, its logics are monotonic, $\mathbf{ACC}_i(kb_i)$ is a singleton set, and the $\mathbf{ACC}_i$ themselves are monotonic. Hence, reasoning is montonic, and a unique minimal equilibrium exists.

Definition 9. *Let M be a definite pMCS. A belief state S of M is the* grounded equilibrium *of M, denoted by $\mathbf{GE}(M)$, if S is the unique minimal equilibrium of M.*

This unique equilibrium of a pMCS $M = \langle C_1, \ldots, C_n \rangle$ can be computed as follows. For $1 \leq i \leq n$, $kb_i^0 = kb_i$ and for each sucessor ordinal $\alpha + 1$,

$$kb_i^{\alpha+1} = kb_i^\alpha \cup \{v@H(\pi) | \pi \in br_i \wedge E^\alpha \models B(\pi)\}$$

where $E^\alpha = (E_1^\alpha, \ldots, E_n^\alpha)$, $\mathbf{ACC}_i(kb_i^\alpha) = \{E_i^\alpha\}$; and v defined as in Definition 8, and for limit ordinal α, $kb_i^\alpha = \bigcup_{\beta \leq \alpha} kb_i^\beta$. Furthermore, let $kb_i^\infty = \bigcup_{\alpha > 0} kb_i^\alpha$.

Essentially, we start with the set of given knowledge bases and E^0 corresponds to the belief state resulting from M without the bridge rules. The iteration then stepwise checks based on the current belief state which bridge rules are applicable, enhancing the knowledge bases which in turn increases the annotated belief sets in the iteration of E^α, based on which further bridge rules become applicable, until a fixpoint is reached. This indeed yields the unique grounded equilibrium.

Proposition 2. *Let M be a definite pMCS. Then, belief state $S = (S_1, \ldots, S_n)$ is the grounded equilibrium of M iff $\mathbf{ACC}_i(kb_i^\infty) = \{S_i\}$, for $1 \leq i \leq n$.*

Note that this construction not only allows us to iteratively determine what is true (with annotation $\neq 0$)/can be inferred as in MCSs, it also allows us to simultaneously calculate what are the actual corresponding annotations.

Example 6. Consider M from Example 2 with $br_2 = \emptyset$ and kb reduced to $\{r_1@l \leftarrow n\}$, i.e., such M is definite. We can verify that the computed grounded equilibrium is $S = \langle S_1, S_2, S_3 \rangle$ with S_1 and S_2 defined as in Example 2 and S_3 s.t. $S_3(l) = r_1 \times_3 (c_1 \wedge d_1^2)$ and $S_3(n) = c_1 \wedge d_1^2$. Here, S_1 is determined based on kb_1^0, whereas $S_3(n)$ results from the applicable bridge rule, and $S_3(l)$ from that and rule r_1.

In the more general case of reducible pMCSs, we introduce a reduct taking into account the provenance information.

Definition 10. *Let* $M = \langle C_1, \ldots, C_n \rangle$ *be a reducible pMCS s.t.* $C_i = (L_i, kb_i, br_i)$, *and* $S = \langle S_1, \ldots, S_n \rangle$ *a belief state of* M. *The S-reduct of* M *is defined as* $M^S = \langle C_1^S, \ldots, C_n^S \rangle$, *where, for* $1 \leq i \leq n$, $C_i^S = (L_i, red_i(kb_i, S_i), br_i^S)$, *and*

$$br_i^S = \{v@s \leftarrow (r_1 : p_1), \ldots, (r_j : p_j) \mid \pi \in br_i \text{ of the form (1) such that}$$
$$S_{r_i}(p_i) = 0 \text{ for all } j+1 \leq i \leq m, \text{ and } v = \pi \wedge \mathbf{not}\, p_{j+1} \wedge \ldots \mathbf{not}\, p_m\}.$$

Thus, in the reduct, knowledge bases are reduced w.r.t. the considered belief state, and bridge rules are either omitted if there is a $\mathbf{not}\,(r_k : p_k)$ in the bridge rule such that p_k is true in S_{r_i}, i.e., with annotation different from 0, or maintained in the reduct with the negated elements, just adapting the annotation v to take these negated elements into account in the annotation.

The resulting S-reduct of M is definite and we can check whether S is a grounded equilibrium in the usual manner.

Definition 11. *Let M be a reducible pMCS. A belief state S of M is a* grounded equilibrium *of M if $S = \mathbf{GE}(M^S)$.*

We can show that such grounded equilibria are minimal equilibria.

Proposition 3. *Every grounded equilibrium of a reducible pMCS M is a minimal equilibrium of M.*

Thus, for grounded equilibria, the converse of 2. (Prop. 1) can be obtained, and pMCSs indeed provide provenance annotations for grounded equilibria in MCSs.

Example 7. Consider M from Example 2. Note that M is reducible using the usual Gelfond-Lifschitz reduct for C_3 and since C_1 and C_2 are monotonic. We obtain one grounded equilibrium S as specified in Example 6 because b_1 in br_2 and c_2 in br_3 are not applicable in S. There is a second grounded equilibrium $S' = \langle S_1', S_2', S_3' \rangle$ with $S_1' = S_1$ for S_1 from Example 6, S_2' with $S_2'(A(w)) = b_1 \wedge \mathbf{not}\, l$ and $S_2'(B(w)) = o_1 \times_2 (b_1 \wedge \mathbf{not}\, l)$, and S_3' with $S_3'(m) = c_2 \wedge o_1 \times_2 (b_1 \wedge \mathbf{not}\, l)$ and $S_3'(n) = c_1 \wedge d_1^2$.

We observe that the resulting annotations concisely represent the formulas required to obtain an inference, and that this information modularily preserves

the characteristics of the semirings used in individual contexts, e.g., the annotation of n in S_3' contains that d_1 is used twice (in the database context), even
though in C_3 such repetition would be omitted due to idempotent $\times$.

We close the section with considerations on the computational complexity
where we assume familiarity with basic notions including the polynomial hierarchy. First, we recall that output-projected equilibria have been considered in the
context of MCSs [11] as a means to facilitate consistency checking, by restricting
the focus to the beliefs that occur in the bridge rules, showing in particular that
for each output-projected equilibrium there exists a corresponding equilibrium.
Then, consistency of an MCS, whose size, for fixed logics, is measured in the
size of the knowledge bases and the size of the bridge rules, can be determined
by guessing an output-projected belief state S and checking for each context
whether it accepts the guessed S w.r.t. the active bridge rule heads. The complexity of the latter step, called context complexity, influences the complexity
of consistency checking and has been determined for a number of logics [11].
Then, the context complexity of an MCS M, $CC(M)$, can be determined based
on upper and lower context complexities, which allows one to study the complexity of problems such as the existence of equilibria w.r.t. context complexity
of MCSs.

Now, for pMCSs, we have to take the anotations into account, and it turns out
that this increases the computational complexity in general. As argued in the case
of DL $\mathcal{ELH}^r$, where standard reasoning problems are polynomial, annotations
may be exponential in size [2], and similar problems can be observed for other
logics. Still, for definite pMCSs, we can take advantage of the deterministic way
to compute the unique grounded equilibrium and show that we can avoid this
exponential size of annotations when solving the problem of whether there is a
grounded equilibrium such that the annotation of belief p is n, i.e., $S_i(p) = n$.
The essential idea is to take advantage of the bound on the size of annotations
imposed by n, and limit the computation to the relevant part of the equilibrium,
and adapt at the same time the notion of $CC(M)$ from MCSs to take size of the
monomials in the individual context into account.

Proposition 4. *Let M be a definite pMCS with context complexity $CC(M)$ and
S its unique grounded equilibrium. The problem of determining whether $S_i(p) =
n$ for $p \in B_{L_i}$ and $n \in V_i$, is in $\mathcal{C}$ if $CC(M) = \mathcal{C}$ for $\mathcal{C} \supseteq \mathbf{P}$.*

It turns out that this result does not hold in the general case, because verifying
whether some belief state is an equilibrium requires the computation of the entire
belief state, thus subject to the exponential size of annotations in general.

5   Conclusions

We have introduced provenance multi-context systems as the first approach for
provenance in heterogeneous knowledge bases, allowing us to obtain annotations
for the inferences in the models of the integrating formalism. We have shown
how these models with annotations, equilibria, can be computed and, given the

generality of the approach, under which conditions this is possible, showing that the approach is viable for the integration of a wide variety of formalisms.

For future work, we will investigate the usage of power series for dealing with provenance approaches that use infinite semirings [18], as well as consider the application of semiring provenance for fixed-point logic [9].

Acknowledgment. We thank the anonymous reviewers for their comments and FCT projects RIVER (PTDC/CCI-COM/30952/2017), FORGET (PTDC/CCI-INF/32219/2017), and NOVA LINCS (UIDB/04516/2020) for partial support.

References

1. Baader, F., Calvanese, D., McGuinness, D.L., Nardi, D., Patel-Schneider, P.F. (eds.) The Description Logic Handbook. Cambridge University Press (2007)
2. Bourgaux, C., Ozaki, A., Peñaloza, R., Predoiu, L.: Provenance for the description logic $\mathcal{ELH}^r$. In: IJCAI, pp. 1862–1869. ijcai.org (2020)
3. Brewka, G., Eiter, T.: Equilibria in heterogeneous nonmonotonic multi-context systems. In: Proceedings of AAAI, pp. 385–390. AAAI Press (2007)
4. Brewka, G., Eiter, T., Truszczynski, M.: Answer set programming at a glance. Commun. ACM **54**(12), 92–103 (2011)
5. Buneman, P.: The providence of provenance. In: Gottlob, G., Grasso, G., Olteanu, D., Schallhart, C. (eds.) BNCOD 2013. LNCS, vol. 7968, pp. 7–12. Springer, Heidelberg (2013). https://doi.org/10.1007/978-3-642-39467-6_3
6. Calvanese, D., Lanti, D., Ozaki, A., Peñaloza, R., Xiao, G.: Enriching ontology-based data access with provenance. In: IJCAI, pp. 1616–1623. ijcai.org (2019)
7. Damásio, C.V., Analyti, A., Antoniou, G.: Provenance for SPARQL queries. In: Cudré-Mauroux, P., et al. (eds.) ISWC 2012. LNCS, vol. 7649, pp. 625–640. Springer, Heidelberg (2012). https://doi.org/10.1007/978-3-642-35176-1_39
8. Viegas Damásio, C., Analyti, A., Antoniou, G.: Justifications for logic programming. In: Cabalar, P., Son, T.C. (eds.) LPNMR 2013. LNCS (LNAI), vol. 8148, pp. 530–542. Springer, Heidelberg (2013). https://doi.org/10.1007/978-3-642-40564-8_53
9. Dannert, K.M., Grädel, E., Naaf, M., Tannen, V.: Semiring provenance for fixed-point logic. In: CSL, LIPIcs, vol. 183, pp. 17:1–17:22 (2021)
10. Dividino, R.Q., Schenk, S., Sizov, S., Staab, S.: Provenance, trust, explanations - and all that other meta knowledge. KI **23**(2), 24–30 (2009)
11. Eiter, T., Fink, M., Schüller, P., Weinzierl, A.: Finding explanations of inconsistency in multi-context systems. Artif. Intell. **216**, 233–274 (2014)
12. Eiter, T., Ianni, G., Lukasiewicz, T., Schindlauer, R., Tompits, H.: Combining answer set programming with description logics for the semantic web. Artif. Intell. **172**(12–13), 1495–1539 (2008)
13. Fandinno, J., Schulz, C.: Answering the "why" in answer set programming - a survey of explanation approaches. TPLP **19**(2), 114–203 (2019)
14. Geerts, F., Poggi, A.: On database query languages for k-relations. J. Appl. Log. **8**(2), 173–185 (2010)
15. Glavic, B.: Data provenance. Found. Trends Datab. **9**(3–4), 209–441 (2021)
16. Glavic, B., Esmaili, K.S., Fischer, P.M., Tatbul, N.: Ariadne: managing fine-grained provenance on data streams. In: Proceedings of DEBS, pp. 39–50. ACM (2013)

17. Grädel, E., Tannen, V.: Semiring provenance for first-order model checking. arXiv preprint arXiv:1712.01980 (2017)
18. Green, T.J., Karvounarakis, G., Tannen, V.: Provenance semirings. In: Proceedings of PODS, pp. 31–40. ACM (2007)
19. Green, T.J., Tannen, V.: The semiring framework for database provenance. In: Proceedings of PODS, pp. 93–99. ACM (2017)
20. Horridge, M., Parsia, B., Sattler, U.: Laconic and precise justifications in OWL. In: Sheth, A., et al. (eds.) ISWC 2008. LNCS, vol. 5318, pp. 323–338. Springer, Heidelberg (2008). https://doi.org/10.1007/978-3-540-88564-1_21
21. Knorr, M., Alferes, J.J., Hitzler, P.: Local closed world reasoning with description logics under the well-founded semantics. Artif. Intell. **175**(9–10), 1528–1554 (2011)
22. Knorr, M., Slota, M., Leite, J., Homola, M.: What if no hybrid reasoner is available? hybrid MKNF in multi-context systems. J. Log. Comput. **24**(6), 1279–1311 (2014)
23. Lukumbuzya, S., Ortiz, M., Simkus, M.: Resilient logic programs: answer set programs challenged by ontologies. In: AAAI, pp. 2917–2924. AAAI Press (2020)
24. Motik, B., Rosati, R.: Reconciling description logics and rules. J. ACM **57**(5), 93–154 (2010)
25. Tannen, V.: Provenance analysis for FOL model checking. ACM SIGLOG News **4**(1), 24–36 (2017)

Computing Smallest MUSes of Quantified Boolean Formulas

Andreas Niskanen, Jere Mustonen, Jeremias Berg, and Matti Järvisalo[✉]

HIIT, Department of Computer Science, University of Helsinki, Helsinki, Finland
{andreas.niskanen,matti.jarvisalo}@helsinki.fi

Abstract. Computing small (subset-minimal or smallest) explanations is a computationally challenging task for various logics and non-monotonic formalisms. Arguably the most progress in practical algorithms for computing explanations has been made for propositional logic in terms of minimal unsatisfiable subsets (MUSes) of conjunctive normal form formulas. In this work, we propose an approach to computing *smallest* MUSes of *quantified* Boolean formulas (QBFs), building on the so-called implicit hitting set approach and modern QBF solving techniques. Connecting to non-monotonic formalisms, our approach finds applications in the realm of abstract argumentation in computing smallest strong explanations of acceptance and rejection. Justifying our approach, we pinpoint the complexity of deciding the existence of small MUSes for QBFs with any fixed number of quantifier alternations. We empirically evaluate the approach on computing strong explanations in abstract argumentation frameworks as well as benchmarks from recent QBF Evaluations.

Keywords: Quantified boolean formulas · Minimum unsatisfiability · Abstract argumentation · Strong explanations

1 Introduction

Explaining inconsistency in different logics is a central problem setting with a range of applications. Finding small explanations for inconsistency is intrinsically a computationally even more challenging task than deciding satisfiability. What comes to practical algorithms for computing small explanations, arguably the most progress has been made in the realm of classical logic, in particular in propositional satisfiability where algorithms for computing minimal unsatisfiable subsets (MUSes) of conjunctive normal form formulas have been developed [4,7,8,25]. Extensions to computing smallest MUSes [17,21] and, on the other hand, to computing MUSes of quantified Boolean formulas (QBF) [16,17] have also been proposed. Recently, it has been shown that the notion of so-called strong inconsistency [10,36] provides for non-monotonic reasoning a natural counterpart of the

Work financially supported by Academy of Finland under grants 322869, 328718, 342145 and 347588. The authors thank the Finnish Computing Competence Infrastructure (FCCI) for computational and data storage resources.

G. Gottlob et al. (Eds.): LPNMR 2022, LNAI 13416, pp. 301–314, 2022.
https://doi.org/10.1007/978-3-031-15707-3_23

inconsistency notion studied in the classical setting, satisfying the well-known hitting set duality between explanations and diagnoses [30]. The general notion of strong inconsistency has already been instantiated for computing explanations in the non-monotonic formalisms of answer set programming [11,26] and abstract argumentation [27,34,35,37].

We propose an approach to computing *smallest* MUSes of *quantified* Boolean formulas (QBFs), building on the so-called implicit hitting set approach [12,17, 31,32] and modern QBF solving techniques [18,22,23]. Our approach generalizes an implicit hitting set approach [17] and a quantified MaxSAT approach [16] to computing smallest MUSes of propositional formulas to general QBFs. Justifying our approach, we pinpoint the computational complexity of deciding the existence of small MUSes for QBFs with any fixed number of quantifier alternations, generalizing and supplementing earlier complexity results related to MUSes [10,20,29]. While our approach is generic, a central motivation for developing the approach comes from the realm of abstract argumentation [13], in particular for explaining acceptance [1,5,15,37] and rejection [27,33,34] of arguments. As we will detail, computation of *smallest* strong explanations [27,34,37] in abstract argumentation frameworks can naturally be viewed as the task of computing smallest MUSes of quantified formulas. While there is work on practical procedures for computing strong explanations for credulous *rejection* in abstract argumentation [27,34], even the task of verifying a minimal strong explanation for credulous *acceptance* under admissible and stable semantics is by complexity arguments presumably beyond the reach of the earlier-proposed approaches [37]. The approach developed in this work hence provides a first practical approach to computing smallest strong explanations in particular for credulous acceptance and skeptical rejection in abstract argumentation frameworks.

Empirically, the approach scales favorably towards computing smallest strong explanations in abstract argumentation for ICCMA competition instances, despite the fact that this task is presumably considerably more challenging than the standard tasks of deciding acceptance considered in the ICCMA competitions. We also show that the approach allows for computing smallest MUSes for small unsatisfiable benchmarks from QBF Evaluation solver competitions.

2   Preliminaries

Quantified Boolean Formulas (QBFs). We consider closed QBFs in prenex normal form $\Phi = Q_1 X_1 \cdots Q_k X_k.\varphi$, where $Q_i \in \{\exists, \forall\}$ are alternating quantifiers, $X_1, \ldots, X_k$ are pairwise disjoint nonempty sets of variables, and φ is a Boolean formula over the variables $\bigcup_{i=1}^{k} X_i$ and the truth constants 1 and 0 (true and false). The sequence of quantifier blocks $Q_1 X_1 \cdots Q_k X_k$ is called the prefix and φ the matrix of Φ. We denote an arbitrary prefix of k alternating quantifier blocks by $\overrightarrow{Q}_k$. For a truth assignment $\tau \colon X \to \{0,1\}$, the formula $\varphi[\tau]$ is obtained by replacing, for each $x \in X$, all occurrences of x in φ by $\tau(x)$. As convenient, we interchangeably view assignments as either sets of non-contradictory literals or as functions mapping variables to truth values. The QBF $\Phi^\exists = \exists X \overrightarrow{Q}_k.\varphi$ is true iff there exists a truth assignment $\tau \colon X \to \{0,1\}$ for which

$\overrightarrow{Q}_k.\varphi\,[\tau]$ is true. In this case we call τ a solution to $\Phi^\exists$. The QBF $\Phi^\forall = \forall X\,\overrightarrow{Q}_k.\varphi$ is true iff for all truth assignments $\tau\colon X \to \{0,1\}$, the QBF $\overrightarrow{Q}_k.\varphi\,[\tau]$ is true. If this is not the case, that is, there is a truth assignment τ for which $\overrightarrow{Q}_k.\varphi\,[\tau]$ is false, we call τ a counterexample to $\Phi^\forall$.

Smallest MUSes of QBF Formulas. Consider a QBF $\Phi = \exists S\,\overrightarrow{Q}_k.\varphi$. A set $S^\star \subset S$ is a (an unsatisfiable) core of Φ if $\exists S\,\overrightarrow{Q}_k.\varphi\,[S^\star]$ is false. The smallest minimal unsatisfiable subsets (SMUSes) are smallest-cardinality cores: $S^\star$ is a SMUS iff $|S^\star| \le |S'|$ holds for all cores S' of Φ. A set $cs \subset S$ is a correction set (CS) if the QBF $\exists S\,\overrightarrow{Q}_k.\varphi\,[S \setminus cs]$ is true. Note that these definitions are in line with conjunctive forms: for a QBF $\overrightarrow{Q}_k.\bigwedge_{j=1}^{m}\varphi_j$, where φ_j are formulas, unsatisfiable subsets (resp. correction sets) over $\{\varphi_1,\dots,\varphi_m\}$ can be computed as cores (resp. correction sets) of $\exists S\,\overrightarrow{Q}_k.\bigwedge_{j=1}^{m}(s_j \to \varphi_j)$ with $S = \{s_1,\dots,s_m\}$.

Important to our approach is a relationship between correction sets and SMUSes of QBFs: lower bounds on the size of SMUSes of a QBF are obtained via the minimum-cost hitting sets over *any* sets of its correction sets. A set $hs \subset S$ is a hitting set over a collection $\mathcal{C}$ of correction sets if it intersects with each $cs \in \mathcal{C}$. A hitting set hs is minimum-cost if $|hs| \le |hs'|$ for all hitting sets hs'.

Proposition 1. *Let $\mathcal{C}$ be a set of correction sets of the QBF $\Phi = \exists S\,\overrightarrow{Q}_k.\varphi$, hs a minimum-cost hitting set over $\mathcal{C}$, and $S^\star$ a SMUS of Φ. Then $|hs| \le |S^\star|$.*

Proof. (Sketch) We show that $S^\star$ is also a hitting set over $\mathcal{C}$. The claim follows by observing that hs is minimum-cost. Assume for a contradiction that $S^\star \cap cs = \emptyset$ for some $cs \in \mathcal{C}$. Then $S^\star \subset S \setminus cs$. Since $\exists S\,\overrightarrow{Q}_k.\varphi\,[S \setminus cs]$ is true, so is $\exists S\,\overrightarrow{Q}_k.\varphi\,[S^\star]$, contradicting the fact that $S^\star$ is a core. $\square$

Abstract Argumentation. An argumentation framework (AF) [13] $F = (A, R)$ consists of a (finite) set of arguments A is and an attack relation $R \subseteq A \times A$. Argument b attacks argument a if $(b, a) \in R$. A $S \subseteq A$ is conflict-free in $F = (A, R)$ if $b \notin S$ or $a \notin S$ for each $(b, a) \in R$. The set of conflict-free sets in F is denoted by $cf(F)$. An AF semantics σ maps each AF to a collection $\sigma(F)$ of jointly acceptable subsets of arguments, i.e., extensions. A conflict-free set $S \in cf(F)$ is admissible if for each attack $(b, a) \in R$ with $a \in S$ there is an attack $(c, b) \in R$ with $c \in S$, i.e., for each attack on S there is a counterattack from S. A conflict-free set $S \in cf(F)$ is stable if for each argument $a \in A \setminus S$ there is an attack $(b, a) \in R$ with $b \in S$, i.e., all arguments outside S are attacked by S. The sets of admissible and stable extensions in F are denoted by $adm(F)$ and $stb(F)$, resp. An argument $q \in A$ is credulously accepted in F under semantics σ if there is an $E \in \sigma(F)$ with $q \in E$, and skeptically accepted in F under σ if $q \in E$ for all $E \in \sigma(F)$. Given an AF $F = (A, R)$ and $S \subseteq A$, the subframework induced by S is $F[S] = (S, R \cap (S \times S))$.

Computational Complexity. We assume familiarity with standard complexity classes of the polynomial hierarchy, namely $\Sigma_0^p = \Pi_0^p = \mathrm{P}$, $\Sigma_{k+1}^p = \mathrm{NP}^{\Sigma_k^p}$, $\Pi_{k+1}^p = \mathrm{coNP}^{\Sigma_k^p}$ and $D_k^p = \{L_1 \cap L_2 \mid L_1 \in \Sigma_k^p, L_2 \in \Pi_k^p\}$, and the concepts of hardness and completeness [28].

3   Smallest Strong Explanations

Computing smallest MUSes of QBF formulas is motivated by the fact that it captures smallest strong explanations for credulous acceptance [37] under admissible and stable semantics and skeptical rejection under stable semantics in the realm of abstract argumentation. Let $F = (A, R)$ be an AF and $Q \subseteq A$ be a set of arguments. Following [37], a set $S \subseteq A$ is a strong explanation for credulously accepting Q under σ if for each $S \subseteq A' \subseteq A$ and $F' = F[A']$ there exists $E \in \sigma(F')$ with $Q \subseteq E$. Similarly, explanations for skeptically rejecting $Q \subseteq A$ under σ are sets $S \subseteq A$ for which, for all $S \subseteq A' \subseteq A$ and $F' = F[A']$, there exists $E \in \sigma(F')$ with $Q \nsubseteq E$.

We focus on smallest-cardinality strong explanations. Our approach builds on the line of work on employing propositional SMUS extractors for computing smallest strong explanations for credulous rejection [27]. We similarly declare Boolean variables x_a and y_a for each argument $a \in A$, interpreting $x_a = 1$ as argument a being included in an extension, and $y_a = 1$ as argument a being included in a subframework. We denote $Y = \{y_a \mid a \in A\}$ and $X = \{x_a \mid a \in A\}$. We define the propositional formula $\varphi_{cf}(F) = \bigwedge_{(a,b) \in R}((y_a \wedge y_b) \to (\neg x_a \vee \neg x_b))$ for conflict-free sets, and formulas $\varphi_{adm}(F) = \varphi_{cf}(F) \wedge \bigwedge_{(b,a) \in R}\left((y_a \wedge y_b \wedge x_a) \to \bigvee_{(c,b) \in R}(y_c \wedge x_c)\right)$ and $\varphi_{stb}(F) = \varphi_{cf}(F) \wedge \bigwedge_{a \in A}\left((y_a \wedge \neg x_a) \to \bigvee_{(b,a) \in R}(y_b \wedge x_b)\right)$ encoding admissible and stable semantics. That is, for any assignment τ_Y over Y, the satisfying assignments over X of the formula $\varphi_\sigma(F)[\tau_Y]$ correspond exactly to $\sigma(F[A'])$ with $A' = \{a \in A \mid \tau(y_a) = 1\}$, since $\varphi_\sigma(F)[\tau_Y]$ reduces to a standard SAT encoding of semantics σ for which this result is well-known [9].

For extracting a smallest strong explanation for credulous acceptance and skeptical rejection, it suffices to compute a SMUS of a 2-QBF formula.[1]

Proposition 2. *Given an AF $F = (A, R)$, $Q \subseteq A$, and semantics $\sigma \in \{adm, stb\}$. Let $S^* \subseteq A$. It holds that $Y[S^*] = \{y_a \mid a \in S\}$ is a SMUS of*

a) $\Phi_\sigma^{CA}(F, Q) = \exists Y \forall X(\varphi_\sigma(F) \to \bigvee_{q \in Q} \neg x_q)$ if and only if S^* is a smallest strong explanation for credulously accepting Q in F under σ,

b) $\Phi_{stb}^{SR}(F, Q) = \exists Y \forall X(\varphi_{stb}(F) \to \bigwedge_{q \in Q} x_q)$ if and only if S^* is a smallest strong explanation for skeptically rejecting Q in F under stb.

Proof. Case a): Suppose S^* is a strong explanation for credulously accepting Q in F under σ, that is, for all $S^* \subseteq A' \subseteq A$ there is an extension $E \in \sigma(F[A'])$ containing Q. Equivalently, for all assignments τ_Y over Y which set $\tau_Y(y_a) = 1$ for $a \in S^*$, there is an assignment τ_X over X which satisfies $\varphi_\sigma(F)[\tau_Y]$ and sets $\tau_X(x_q) = 1$ for all $q \in Q$. This means that the QBF $\forall Y \exists X \left(\varphi_\sigma(F)[Y[S^*]] \wedge \bigwedge_{q \in Q} x_q\right)$ is true, which in turn means that $\Phi_\sigma^{CA}(F, Q)[Y[S^*]]$ is false. That is, $Y[S^*]$ is a core of

---

[1] The proposition also holds when considering subset-minimal strong explanations and MUSes of the corresponding 2-QBF.

$\Phi_\sigma^{CA}(F,Q)$. By applying the same steps in the other direction, we obtain a one-to-one mapping between strong explanations for credulous acceptance in F and cores of $\Phi_\sigma^{CA}(F,Q)$. The reasoning is similar for case b) and skeptical rejection. The claims follow.   □

The SMUSes of a 2-QBF $\Phi_{com}^{SR}(F,Q)$ with a subformula $\varphi_{com}(F)$ for complete semantics (see e.g. [6]) capture strong explanations for skeptical rejection under complete, which in turn coincides with (credulous and skeptical) rejection under grounded semantics. Further, QBF encodings for second-level-complete argumentation semantics [2,14] allow for similarly capturing strong explanations for, e.g., skeptical rejection under preferred semantics as SMUSes of 3-QBFs. In terms of computational complexity, *verifying* that a given subset of arguments is a *minimal* strong explanation for credulous acceptance is already D_2^p-complete under admissible and stable semantics [37]. In contrast, for credulous rejection this task is D_1^p-complete, and deciding whether a small strong explanation exists is Σ_2^p-complete [27]. By Proposition 2, the complexity of computing a smallest strong explanation for credulous acceptance and skeptical rejection is bounded by the complexity of computing a SMUS of a given 2-QBF formula. We find it likely that for credulous acceptance this task is complete for the third level of the polynomial hierarchy, namely, that deciding whether a small strong explanation exists is Σ_3^p-complete. This would be in line with the complexity of deciding whether a 2-QBF has a small unsatisfiable subset, detailed next.

4   On Complexity of Computing Smallest MUSes of QBFs

In the context of propositional logic, verification of a MUS is D_1^p-complete [29], and deciding the existence of MUS of small size is Σ_2^p-complete [20]. Further, verifying whether a given QBF with $k \geq 2$ alternating quantifiers is minimally unsatisfiable is D_k^p-complete [10]. However, to the best of our knowledge, the complexity of deciding whether a QBF has a small–of size at most a given integer–unsatisfiable subset has not been established so far. We show that the problem is Σ_{k+1}^p-complete for k-QBFs when the leading quantified is existential.

Theorem 1. *Consider a QBF* $\exists X_1 \forall X_2 \cdots Q_k X_k. \bigwedge_{j=1}^m \varphi_j$, *where* φ_j *are propositional formulas over* $\bigcup_{i=1}^k X_i$. *Deciding whether there is an unsatisfiable subset* $\varphi^* \subseteq \{\varphi_j \mid j = 1,\ldots,m\}$ *with* $|\varphi^*| \leq p$ *is* Σ_{k+1}^p-complete.

Proof. (Sketch) For membership, guess a subset φ^* and verify using a Π_k^p-oracle that $\exists X_1 \forall X_2 \cdots Q_k X_k.\varphi^*$ is false. For hardness, we reduce from the Σ_{k+1}^p-complete problem of deciding whether a QBF $\Psi = \exists X_1 \forall X_2 \cdots Q_{k+1} X_{k+1}.\psi$ is true. We may assume w.l.o.g. that ψ is in conjunctive normal form (CNF) if k is even ($Q_{k+1} = \exists$), and in disjunctive normal form (DNF) if k is odd ($Q_{k+1} = \forall$). For our reduction, we adapt (and simplify) the reduction for the propositional case [20]. Let $X_1 = \{x_1,\ldots,x_n\}$ and declare variables $P = \{p_i \mid i = 1,\ldots,n\}$ and $N = \{n_i \mid i = 1,\ldots,n\}$. Let ψ' be the formula obtained from ψ by replacing each literal x_i with p_i and $\neg x_i$ with n_i. Finally, consider $\varphi = \bigwedge_{i=1}^n (p_i \lor n_i) \to \neg \psi'$.

It holds that $\Phi = \exists (P \cup N \cup X_2)\forall X_3 \cdots Q_{k+1}X_{k+1}.\varphi \wedge \bigwedge_{i=1}^{n} p_i \wedge \bigwedge_{i=1}^{n} n_i$ has an unsatisfiable subset of size at most $n + 1$ iff Ψ is true. Intuitively, a solution of Ψ gives rise to an unsatisfiable subset of Φ containing φ and exactly one p_i or n_i for each $i = 1, \ldots, n$. On the other hand, all unsatisfiable subsets of Φ must contain φ, and due to the bound $n + 1$, exactly one p_i or n_i for each $i = 1, \ldots, n$, which simulates a truth assignment which is a solution of Ψ. □

Note that for even (resp. odd) k, the reduction gives hardness for k-QBFs of form $\exists X \overrightarrow{Q}_{k-1}.\varphi \wedge S$ where $S \subset X$ and φ is in DNF (resp. CNF—to see this, consider additional variables for each disjunct $p_i \vee n_i$ in φ). This is in line with SMUSes of QBFs being subsets of the first existential quantifier block. Interestingly, there is a difference between the complexity of computing a SMUS in the case $Q_1 = \forall$ and in the case $Q_1 = \exists$. For $Q_1 = \forall$ the problem turns out to be merely Σ_k^p-complete. This is because a nondeterministic guess may contain both an unsatisfiable subset candidate and a counterexample assignment.

Proposition 3. *Consider a QBF $\forall X_1 \exists X_2 \cdots Q_k X_k . \bigwedge_{j=1}^{m} \varphi_j$, where φ_j are propositional formulas over $\bigcup_{i=1}^{k} X_i$. Deciding whether there is an unsatisfiable subset $\varphi^* \subseteq \{\varphi_j \mid j = 1, \ldots, m\}$ with $|\varphi^*| \leq p$ is Σ_k^p-complete.*

Proof. For membership, guess a subset φ^* and a counterexample τ to the QBF. Verify using a Π_{k-1}^p oracle that $\exists X_2 \cdots Q_k X_k.\varphi^*[\tau]$ is false. Hardness follows by a reduction from the Σ_k^p-complete problem of deciding whether a QBF $\exists X_1 \forall X_2 \cdots Q_k X_k.\varphi$ is true (consider the negation). □

5 Computing Smallest MUSes via Implicit Hitting Sets

SMUS-IHS, the implicit-hitting set based approach for computing a SMUS of a given QBF $\Phi = \exists S \overrightarrow{Q}_k.\varphi$ is detailed in Algorithm 1. The algorithm works by

```
1 SMUS-IHS
      Input: A QBF Φ = ∃S Q⃗ₖ.φ
      Output: A SMUS S* ⊂ S of Φ
2     (τ, true?) ← QBF-Solve(Φ, S);
3     if true? then
4      |  return "no cores";
5     UB ← |S|; LB ← 0;
6     S* ← S; C ← ∅;
7     while TRUE do
8      |  (hs, opt?) ← Min-Hs(C, S, UB);
9      |  if opt? then LB ← |hs|;
10     |  if LB = UB then break;
11     |  C ←
       |     C ∪ Extract-MCS(S*, UB, Φ, S);
12     |  if LB = UB then break;
13     return S*;
Algorithm 1: Computing a QBF SMUS
```

Min-Hs($\mathcal{C}, S, UB$):

minimize: $\sum_{s \in S} s$

subject to:

$\sum_{s \in cs} s \geq 1 \quad \forall cs \in \mathcal{C}$

$s \in \{0, 1\} \quad \forall s \in S$

return:

$\{s \mid s \text{ set to 1 in opt. soln}\}$

Fig. 1. Hitting set IP

```
1 Extract-MCS(S*, hs, UB, Φ, S)
2 │   A = hs, Cn = ∅;
3 │   while TRUE do
4 │   │   (τ, true?) ←
    │   │       QBF-Solve(Φ, A);
5 │   │   if not true? then
6 │   │   │   if |A| < UB then
7 │   │   │   │   UB ← |A|; S* ← A;
8 │   │   │   return Cn;
9 │   │   else
10│   │   │   cs ←
    │   │   │       MinCS(τ, UB, S*, Φ, S);
11│   │   │   Cn ← Cn ∪ {cs};
12│   │   │   A ← A ∪ {cs};
```

```
1 MinCS(τ, UB, S*, Φ, S)
2 │   A = {s ∈ S | τ(s) = 1};
3 │   for s ∈ S \ A do
4 │   │   if s ∈ A then continue;
5 │   │   (τ, true?) ←
    │   │       QBF-Solve(Φ, A ∪ {s});
6 │   │   if not true? then
7 │   │   │   if |A| + 1 < UB then
8 │   │   │   │   UB ← |A| + 1;
9 │   │   │   │   S* ← A ∪ {s};
10│   │   else
11│   │   │   A ← {s ∈ S | τ(s) = 1};
12│   return S \ A;
```

Fig. 2. Extracting (left) and minimizing (right) correction sets of a QBF.

iteratively refining a lower and upper bound LB and UB on the size of the SMUSes of Φ. The lower bounds are obtained by extracting an increasing collection $\mathcal{C}$ of correction sets of Φ with a QBF oracle in the Extract-MCS subroutine, and computing hitting sets hs over them with an integer programming solver, in the Min-Hs subroutine. The correction set extraction subroutine also obtains unsatisfiable cores of Φ, the smallest core found at any point is stored in S^* and the upper bound UB set to $UB = |S^*|$. The search terminates when $UB = LB$ and returns S^* which at that point is known to be a SMUS.[2]

We abstract the use of a QBF oracle into the function QBF-Solve. Given a subset $S_s \subset S$, the call QBF-Solve(Φ, S_s) returns a tuple $(\tau, true?)$ where $true?$ is true iff $\exists S \vec{Q}_k.\varphi[S_s]$ is true. In the affirmative case the oracle returns a solution τ to Φ that sets $\tau(s) = 1$ for all $s \in S_s$. A useful intuition here is that if the QBF oracle returns true, then the set $cs = (S \setminus \{s \mid \tau(s) = 1\}) \supset (S \setminus S_s)$ is a correction set of Φ. Similarly, if the result is false, then S_s is a core of Φ and $|S_s|$ an upper bound on the size of the SMUSes.

More specifically, given an input QBF $\Phi = \exists S \vec{Q}_k.\varphi$, SMUS-IHS begins by checking that the QBF has no solutions by invoking QBF-Solve(Φ, S) on Line 2. If the result is true, then there are no cores (and as such no SMUSes) of Φ so the search terminates on Line 4. Otherwise, S is a core of Φ, so the upper bound UB is set to $|S|$, the smallest known core S^* to S, the set $\mathcal{C}$ of correction sets to $\emptyset$, and the lower bound LB on the size of the SMUSes to 0 (Lines 5 and 6).

Each iteration of the main search loop (Lines 7–12) starts by computing a hitting set hs over the collection $\mathcal{C}$ of correction sets extracted so far. The procedure Min-Hs on Line 8 computes an incumbent solution hs to the integer program representation of the hitting set problem detailed in Fig. 1. The solution either (a) is optimal, i.e., represents a minimum-cost hitting set or

---

[2] Note that by employing integer programming our approach also allows for computing weighted SMUSes, i.e., cores with smallest total weight over their elements.

(b) has $|hs| < UB$. In addition to hs, the procedure returns an indicator *opt?* on whether hs is minimum-cost. If it is, then by Proposition 1 $|hs|$ is a lower bound on the size of the SMUSes, so the LB is updated on Line 9 and the termination criterion ($UB = LB$) checked on Line 10. If $UB > LB$, the procedure Extract-MCS next extracts correction sets of Φ that do not intersect with hs. In addition to new correction sets, the procedure will also compute new unsatisfiable cores of the instance, thereby potentially tightening the upper bound UB, which is why the termination criterion is checked again on Line 12 before the loop is reiterated. An important note here is that no correction sets are ever removed from $\mathcal{C}$ so the sequence of LB values will be increasing.

The procedure Extract-MCS (Fig. 2, left) computes MCSes that do not intersect with hs by using a QBF oracle. The procedure maintains a subset $\mathcal{A} \subset S$ (initialized to hs) and iteratively invokes the QBF oracle by calling QBF-Solve($\Phi, \mathcal{A}$). If the result is false, the set $\mathcal{A}$ is a core of Φ, so the procedure checks whether the upper bound can be improved before terminating and returning the set $\mathcal{C}_n$ of new corrections sets extracted. Otherwise (i.e., if the result is true) the oracle also returns a solution τ to Φ that sets $\tau(s) = 1$ for each $s \in \mathcal{A}$. Since $hs \subset \mathcal{A}$ holds in each iteration of Extract-MCS, the set $S \setminus \{s \mid \tau(s) = 1\}$ is a correction set of Φ that does not intersect with hs. The correction set is then minimized in the MinCS procedure (Fig. 2, right) by repeated queries to the QBF oracle, each asking for a solution that sets at least one more variable in $S \setminus \{s \mid \tau(s) = 1\}$ to true. The minimization procedure ends when the oracle reports false. Then a new core of Φ is also obtained, potentially allowing the upper bound to be tightened. The minimized cs is added to the set $\mathcal{C}_n$ of new correction sets and to $\mathcal{A}$ to prevent it from being rediscovered.

The following proposition establishes the correctness of SMUS-IHS.

Proposition 4. *On input $\Phi = \exists S \overrightarrow{Q}_k.\varphi$, SMUS-IHS terminates and returns a SMUS $S^\star$ of Φ.*

Proof. Subject to termination, $S^\star$ is a subset of S for which $\exists S \overrightarrow{Q}_k.\varphi\,[S^\star]$ is false (since the set $S^\star$ is only updated after the QBF oracle reports false) and $|S^\star| = |hs|$ for some minimum-cost hitting set hs over a set of correction sets of Φ. Termination follows by the finite number of correction sets of Φ and the fact that each hitting set hs is computed at most twice during the execution of the algorithm. More precisely, consider a hitting set hs returned by Min-Hs. In the next invocation of Extract-MCS either (i) a new correction set cs for which $cs \cap hs = \emptyset$ is computed, or (ii) the set hs is shown to be a core of Φ. In case (i) cs is added to $\mathcal{C}$, preventing hs from being recomputed in subsequent iterations. In case (ii) SMUS-IHS will either terminate on Line 12 if $LB = |hs|$ (i.e., we know hs is minimum-cost), or compute a new hitting set hs' that is either a minimum-cost hitting set over $\mathcal{C}$ or has $|hs'| < UB \leq |hs|$. That is, the only way in which hs can be recomputed in subsequent iterations is if it was of minimum cost in which case the algorithm terminates after computing hs for a second time.   □

The proof of Proposition 4 is similar to a correctness proof of IHS for MaxSAT [3]. Note that the correctness of SMUS-IHS does not rely on correction sets being minimal or the extraction of all disjoint correction sets at each iteration; as long as the loop on Lines 3–12 is executed at least once on each invocation of `Extract-MCS`, the algorithm will either compute a previously unseen correction set, or be able to determine that the input hitting set is a SMUS. Similarly, the minimization of the correction sets need not be exhaustive. The set $S \setminus \mathcal{A}$ will be a correction set of Φ after each iteration of the loop in `MinCS`.

Dual IHS for leading universal quantifier. A way of employing `SMUS-IHS` for computing a SMUS of $\forall X_1 \overrightarrow{Q}_{k-1}.\bigwedge_{j=1}^{m} \varphi_j$ over $\{\varphi_1, \ldots, \varphi_m\}$ is to give the $(k{+}1)$-QBF $\Phi_{k+1} = \exists S \forall X_1 \overrightarrow{Q}_{k-1}.\bigwedge_{j=1}^{m}(s_j \to \varphi_j)$ as input. For an alternative—more inline with the complexity results of Proposition 3—approach we can instead consider the k-QBF $\Phi_k = \forall S \forall X_1 \overrightarrow{Q}_{k-1}.\bigwedge_{j=1}^{m}(s_j \to \varphi_j)$. For any $S^* \subset \neg S = \{\neg s \mid s \in S\}$, $\Phi_k[S^*]$ consists of the same formulas as Φ_k except for the ones corresponding to S^*, which are essentially deactivated. Thus we may define for a QBF $\Phi = \forall S \overrightarrow{Q}_k.\varphi$ that a core is a set $S^* \subset \neg S$ for which $\forall S \overrightarrow{Q}_k.\varphi[(\neg S) \setminus S^*]$ is false, and that a correction set $cs \subset \neg S$ makes $\forall S \overrightarrow{Q}_k.\varphi[cs]$ true.

This leads to a dual IHS algorithm. First, check for the existence of a core by a call to `QBF-Solve`$(\Phi_k, \emptyset)$. If the oracle reports true, exit. Else we obtain a counterexample assignment to S, giving an upper bound as the number of variables in S set to true. Similarly to `SMUS-IHS`, we obtain lower bounds by computing minimum-cost hitting sets over collections of (now the dual notion of) correction sets. A correction set is now extracted by calling `QBF-Solve`$(\Phi_k, \neg(S \setminus hs))$. A true result implies that $\neg(S \setminus hs)$ is a correction set which is then minimized similarly as in `SMUS-IHS`. Further, some modern QBF oracles are able to provide a subset $\mathcal{A}' \subset \neg(S \setminus hs)$ used to prove the absence of a counterexample. Such $\mathcal{A}'$ can directly be used as a correction set. Upper bounds on the size of SMUSes are obtained via the oracle reporting false and providing a counterexample assignment. Note that the dual algorithm can be applied for QBFs of form $\exists X_1 \overrightarrow{Q}_{k-1} \bigwedge_{j=1}^{m} \varphi_j$ by giving $\forall S \exists X_1 \overrightarrow{Q}_{k-1}.\bigwedge_{j=1}^{m}(s_j \to \varphi_j)$ as input.

6   Empirical Evaluation

We implemented the `SMUS-IHS` algorithm; the implementation is available in open source at https://bitbucket.org/coreo-group/qbf-smuser. Since no direct competitors are available, we demonstrate the feasibility of the approach for computing smallest explanations in abstract argumentation, as well as in the more general context of extracting clausal SMUSes from QBF instances. We use CPLEX as the minimum-cost hitting set problem IP solver. As choices for the QBF solver, we consider DepQBF (version 6.0.3) [24] and RAReQS (version 1.1) [18]. DepQBF is a search-based QDPLL solver with conflict-driven clause learning and solution-driven cube learning, providing an incremental interface for extracting assignments and unsatisfiable cores and solving under user-provided assumption literals [22,23]. RAReQS is an expansion-based CEGAR solver, iteratively SAT solving and refining a propositional abstraction. We modified RAReQS to extract unsatisfiable cores from the top-level SAT solver. We consider the following variants of the `SMUS-IHS` algorithm.

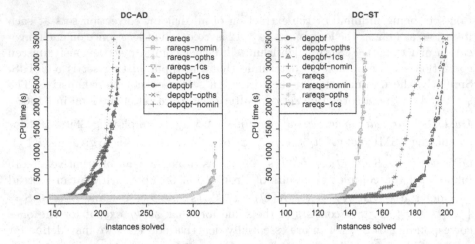

Fig. 3. Number of solved instances: strong explanations for credulous acceptance under admissible (left) and stable (right).

- S (default): S as the QBF solver, extracting all MCSes at each iteration, i.e., executing `Extract-MCS` until unsatisfiability, and calling `MinCS` in `Extract-MCS`.
- S-1CS: S, extracting at most one MCS per invocation of `Extract-MCS`.
- S-NOMIN: S without correction set minimization.
- S-OPTHS: S, computing minimum-cost hitting sets at each iteration.

Experiments were run under per-instance 3600-s time and 16-GB memory limit with Intel Xeon E5-2670 CPUs, 57-GB memory, RHEL 8.5 and GCC 8.5.0.

To obtain benchmarks for computing strong explanations in argumentation frameworks, we extended the implementation from [27] to output the negations of encodings described in Sect. 3 in QDIMACS format. The updated version is available at https://bitbucket.org/andreasniskanen/selitae/. As input AFs, we used the set of 326 AFs from ICCMA'19 (http://argumentationcompetition. org/2019/). We consider three tasks: computing smallest strong explanations for credulous acceptance under admissible and stable semantics and for skeptical rejection under stable semantics. For each AF, a query argument was picked uniformly at random from the set of credulously accepted arguments or skeptically rejected arguments. This gave 324 AF-query pairs for admissible semantics and 312 AF-query pairs for stable semantics (there were 2 AFs which have no non-empty admissible extensions and 14 AFs without a stable extension).

The runtime results for computing smallest explanations for credulous acceptance under admissible and stable are summarized in Fig. 3. On credulous admissible (left), RAReQS as the QBF solver yields clearly the best results: all algorithmic variants except for 1CS solve 324 instances under 1000 s. In contrast, using DepQBF results in solving only 221 instances using the configuration 1CS. On credulous stable (right), using RAReQS results in solving 150 instances for each

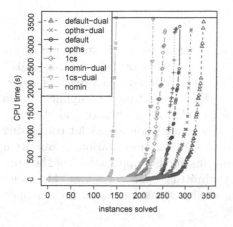 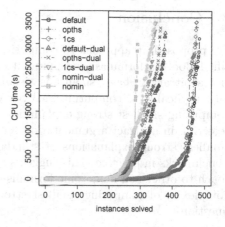

Fig. 4. Number of solved instances for different SMUS-IHS variants on 2-QBFs (left) and 3-QBFs (right) using RAReQS as the QBF oracle.

SMUS-IHS variant except 1CS. DepQBF results in clearly better performance, allowing for solving 200 instances using the default and OPTHS configurations. Interestingly, correction set minimization is an important factor for runtime efficiency when using DepQBF on these instances. The results for skeptical rejection under stable are similar: using DepQBF results in better performance, but the difference due to the choice of the QBF solver is not as drastic (with 181 solved instances using DepQBF and 156 using RAReQS).

To demonstrate more general applicability of SMUS-IHS, we also consider computing SMUSes of QBFs in CNF form, for the relatively small unsatisfiable QBFLIB (http://www.qbflib.org/) benchmarks encoding reduction finding [19] using RAReQS which has exhibited good performance for deciding satisfiability in this domain. We discarded instances for which RAReQS on its own took more than one second to decide unsatisfiability, leaving 719 2-QBF and 905 3-QBF instances. For each instance, each clause C in the matrix φ was replaced by $s_C \to C$, where s_C is a fresh variable. Finally, the quantifier QS with $S = \{s_C \mid C \in \varphi\}$ was appended as the outermost quantifier in the prefix either with $Q = \exists$ for the SMUS-IHS algorithm or with $Q = \forall$ for dual SMUS-IHS.

The results are shown in Fig. 4. For 2-QBF instances (left) we observe that the dual algorithm outperforms other solver variants if several MCSes are extracted at each iteration. The default configuration solves more instances than OPTHS-DUAL which computes minimum-cost hitting sets. Disabling either minimization (NOMIN-DUAL) or exhaustive MCS extraction (1CS-DUAL) leads to a noticeable loss in performance. The non-dual variants are not as effective, which is in line with the fact that their input is a 3-QBF. For 3-QBF instances (right) the default, OPTHS and 1CS configurations clearly outperform all other configurations, with slight performance improvements obtained by using non-optimal hitting sets and exhaustive MCS extraction. Here the dual variants are less competitive; their input is a 4-QBF, since the original 3-QBF has an $\exists\forall\exists$ prefix.

7 Conclusions

We proposed an approach to computing smallest unsatisfiable subsets of quantified Boolean formulas, and pinpointed the complexity of deciding if a k-QBF (for arbitrary k) has a small unsatisfiable subset. While the approach is generally applicable to computing SMUSes of QBFs, we detailed an application in computing smallest strong explanations for credulous acceptance and skeptical rejection in abstract argumentation. Our implementation allows for computing smallest strong explanations of standard ICCMA argumentation competition benchmarks in practice. This suggests studying further applications of the approach to other non-monotonic formalisms admitting QBF encodings. The exact complexity of computing smallest strong explanations remains a further open question.

References

1. Alfano, G., Calautti, M., Greco, S., Parisi, F., Trubitsyna, I.: Explainable acceptance in probabilistic abstract argumentation: complexity and approximation. In: KR, pp. 33–43 (2020)
2. Arieli, O., Caminada, M.W.A.: A QBF-based formalization of abstract argumentation semantics. J. Appl. Log. **11**(2), 229–252 (2013)
3. Bacchus, F., Hyttinen, A., Järvisalo, M., Saikko, P.: Reduced cost fixing in MaxSAT. In: Beck, J.C. (ed.) CP 2017. LNCS, vol. 10416, pp. 641–651. Springer, Cham (2017). https://doi.org/10.1007/978-3-319-66158-2_41
4. Bacchus, F., Katsirelos, G.: Using minimal correction sets to more efficiently compute minimal unsatisfiable sets. In: Kroening, D., Păsăreanu, C.S. (eds.) CAV 2015. LNCS, vol. 9207, pp. 70–86. Springer, Cham (2015). https://doi.org/10.1007/978-3-319-21668-3_5
5. Baumann, R., Ulbricht, M.: Choices and their consequences - explaining acceptable sets in abstract argumentation frameworks. In: KR, pp. 110–119 (2021)
6. Baumeister, D., Järvisalo, M., Neugebauer, D., Niskanen, A., Rothe, J.: Acceptance in incomplete argumentation frameworks. Artif. Intell. **295**, 103470 (2021)
7. Belov, A., Marques-Silva, J.: Accelerating MUS extraction with recursive model rotation. In: FMCAD, pp. 37–40. FMCAD Inc. (2011)
8. Bendík, J., Černá, I.: Replication-guided enumeration of minimal unsatisfiable subsets. In: Simonis, H. (ed.) CP 2020. LNCS, vol. 12333, pp. 37–54. Springer, Cham (2020). https://doi.org/10.1007/978-3-030-58475-7_3
9. Besnard, P., Doutre, S.: Checking the acceptability of a set of arguments. In: NMR, pp. 59–64 (2004)
10. Brewka, G., Thimm, M., Ulbricht, M.: Strong inconsistency. Artif. Intell. **267**, 78–117 (2019)
11. Brewka, G., Ulbricht, M.: Strong explanations for nonmonotonic reasoning. In: Lutz, C., Sattler, U., Tinelli, C., Turhan, A.-Y., Wolter, F. (eds.) Description Logic, Theory Combination, and All That. LNCS, vol. 11560, pp. 135–146. Springer, Cham (2019). https://doi.org/10.1007/978-3-030-22102-7_6
12. Delisle, E., Bacchus, F.: Solving weighted CSPs by successive relaxations. In: Schulte, C. (ed.) CP 2013. LNCS, vol. 8124, pp. 273–281. Springer, Heidelberg (2013). https://doi.org/10.1007/978-3-642-40627-0_23

13. Dung, P.M.: On the acceptability of arguments and its fundamental role in non-monotonic reasoning, logic programming and n-person games. Artif. Intell. **77**(2), 321–358 (1995)
14. Egly, U., Woltran, S.: Reasoning in argumentation frameworks using quantified boolean formulas. In: COMMA. FAIA, vol. 144, pp. 133–144. IOS Press (2006)
15. Fan, X., Toni, F.: On computing explanations in argumentation. In: AAAI, pp. 1496–1502. AAAI Press (2015)
16. Ignatiev, A., Janota, M., Marques-Silva, J.: Quantified maximum satisfiability. Constraints **21**(2), 277–302 (2015). https://doi.org/10.1007/s10601-015-9195-9
17. Ignatiev, A., Previti, A., Liffiton, M., Marques-Silva, J.: Smallest MUS extraction with minimal hitting set dualization. In: Pesant, G. (ed.) CP 2015. LNCS, vol. 9255, pp. 173–182. Springer, Cham (2015). https://doi.org/10.1007/978-3-319-23219-5_13
18. Janota, M., Klieber, W., Marques-Silva, J., Clarke, E.M.: Solving QBF with counterexample guided refinement. Artif. Intell. **234**, 1–25 (2016)
19. Jordan, C., Kaiser, L.: Experiments with reduction finding. In: Järvisalo, M., Van Gelder, A. (eds.) SAT 2013. LNCS, vol. 7962, pp. 192–207. Springer, Heidelberg (2013). https://doi.org/10.1007/978-3-642-39071-5_15
20. Liberatore, P.: Redundancy in logic I: CNF propositional formulae. Artif. Intell. **163**(2), 203–232 (2005)
21. Liffiton, M.H., Mneimneh, M.N., Lynce, I., Andraus, Z.S., Marques-Silva, J., Sakallah, K.A.: A branch and bound algorithm for extracting smallest minimal unsatisfiable subformulas. Constraints **14**(4), 415–442 (2009)
22. Lonsing, F., Egly, U.: Incremental QBF solving. In: O'Sullivan, B. (ed.) CP 2014. LNCS, vol. 8656, pp. 514–530. Springer, Cham (2014). https://doi.org/10.1007/978-3-319-10428-7_38
23. Lonsing, F., Egly, U.: Incrementally computing minimal unsatisfiable cores of QBFs via a clause group solver API. In: Heule, M., Weaver, S. (eds.) SAT 2015. LNCS, vol. 9340, pp. 191–198. Springer, Cham (2015). https://doi.org/10.1007/978-3-319-24318-4_14
24. Lonsing, F., Egly, U.: DepQBF 6.0: a search-based QBF solver beyond traditional QCDCL. In: de Moura, L. (ed.) CADE 2017. LNCS (LNAI), vol. 10395, pp. 371–384. Springer, Cham (2017). https://doi.org/10.1007/978-3-319-63046-5_23
25. Marques-Silva, J., Mencía, C.: Reasoning about inconsistent formulas. In: IJCAI, pp. 4899–4906. ijcai.org (2020)
26. Mencía, C., Marques-Silva, J.: Reasoning about strong inconsistency in ASP. In: Pulina, L., Seidl, M. (eds.) SAT 2020. LNCS, vol. 12178, pp. 332–342. Springer, Cham (2020). https://doi.org/10.1007/978-3-030-51825-7_24
27. Niskanen, A., Järvisalo, M.: Smallest explanations and diagnoses of rejection in abstract argumentation. In: KR, pp. 667–671 (2020)
28. Papadimitriou, C.H.: Computational Complexity. Addison-Wesley (1994)
29. Papadimitriou, C.H., Wolfe, D.: The complexity of facets resolved. J. Comput. Syst. Sci. **37**(1), 2–13 (1988)
30. Reiter, R.: A theory of diagnosis from first principles. Artif. Intell. **32**(1), 57–95 (1987)
31. Saikko, P., Dodaro, C., Alviano, M., Järvisalo, M.: A hybrid approach to optimization in answer set programming. In: KR, pp. 32–41. AAAI Press (2018)
32. Saikko, P., Wallner, J.P., Järvisalo, M.: Implicit hitting set algorithms for reasoning beyond NP. In: KR, pp. 104–113. AAAI Press (2016)
33. Sakama, C.: Abduction in argumentation frameworks. J. Appl. Non Class. Logics **28**(2–3), 218–239 (2018)

34. Saribatur, Z.G., Wallner, J.P., Woltran, S.: Explaining non-acceptability in abstract argumentation. In: ECAI, FAIA, vol. 325, pp. 881–888. IOS Press (2020)
35. Ulbricht, M., Baumann, R.: If nothing is accepted - repairing argumentation frameworks. J. Artif. Intell. Res. **66**, 1099–1145 (2019)
36. Ulbricht, M., Thimm, M., Brewka, G.: Handling and measuring inconsistency in non-monotonic logics. Artif. Intell. **286**, 103344 (2020)
37. Ulbricht, M., Wallner, J.P.: Strong explanations in abstract argumentation. In: AAAI, pp. 6496–6504. AAAI Press (2021)

Pinpointing Axioms in Ontologies via ASP

Rafael Peñaloza[1] and Francesco Ricca[2]([⊠])

[1] University of Milano-Bicocca, Milan, Italy
rafael.penaloza@unimib.it
[2] University of Calabria, Rende, Italy
francesco.ricca@unical.it

Abstract. Axiom pinpointing is the task of identifying the axiomatic causes for a consequence to follow from an ontology. Different approaches have been proposed in the literature for finding one or all the subset-minimal subontologies that preserve a description logic consequence. We propose an approach that leverages the capabilities of answer set programming for transparent axiom pinpointing. We show how other associated tasks can be modelled without much additional effort.

Keywords: Axiom-pinpointing · Non-standard reasoning · ASP

1 Introduction

Axiom pinpointing [16] is the task of identifying the axioms in an ontology that are responsible for a consequence to follow. It has been extensively studied in description logics (DLs) and, under different names, in other areas [11,13]. To-date, the most successful approach to axiom pinpointing which does not rely on repeated (black-box) calls to a reasoner is a reduction to MUS enumeration on a propositional formula [1,17]. The main disadvantage of this approach is that it requires, as a pre-processing step, the construction of a huge formula, which makes the reasoning steps explicit. It is also limited to enumerating one or all so-called justifications.

We propose a novel approach based on a translation to Answer Set Programming (ASP) [7,12]. The approach is general, and can be applied to any ontology language which allows a "modular" ASP representation in the sense that each axiom is translatable to a set of rules. We instantiate it to deal with the simple DL $\mathcal{HL}$ and the more expressive $\mathcal{EL}$. In addition to finding one or all justifications, we show that justifications of minimal cardinality and the intersection of all justifications can be easily computed through standard ASP constructs and reasoning tasks.

This work was partially supported by MUR under PRIN project PINPOINT Prot. 2020FNEB27, CUP H23C22000280006 and H45E21000210001.

G. Gottlob et al. (Eds.): LPNMR 2022, LNAI 13416, pp. 315–321, 2022.
https://doi.org/10.1007/978-3-031-15707-3_24

2   Preliminaries

We assume that the reader is familiar with the basic terminology and structure of answer set programming (ASP) [5,7]. Here, we recall the basic ideas of description logics (DLs) [3], with a particular focus on the lightweight DL $\mathcal{EL}$ [2], and of axiom pinpointing [15].

Description Logics. Description logics (DLs) are a family of knowledge representation formalisms characterised by a clear syntax and a formal unambiguous semantics based on first-order logic. The main building blocks of all DLs are *concepts* (corresponding to unary predicates) and *roles* (binary predicates). The knowledge of an application domain is encoded in an *ontology*, which restricts the class of relevant interpretations of the terms, thus encoding relationships between them. Among the many existing DLs, a prominent example is the lightweight DL $\mathcal{EL}$. $\mathcal{EL}$ has a very limited expressivity, but allows for efficient (standard) reasoning tasks. For the scope of this paper, we use $\mathcal{EL}$ as a prototypical example, following the fact that most work on axiom pinpointing has focused on this logic as well. Other DLs are characterised by a different notion of concepts and a larger class of axioms.

Definition 1 ($\mathcal{EL}$). *Let N_C and N_R be two disjoint sets of* concept names *and* role names, respectively. $\mathcal{EL}$ -concepts are built through the grammar rule

$$C ::= A \mid \top \mid C \sqcap C \mid \exists r.C,$$

where $A \in N_C, r \in N_R$, and $\top$ is a distinguished top concept.
    An interpretation is a pair $\mathcal{I} = (\Delta^{\mathcal{I}}, \cdot^{\mathcal{I}})$ where $\Delta^{\mathcal{I}}$ is a non-empty set called the domain and $\cdot^{\mathcal{I}}$ is the interpretation function which maps every $A \in N_C$ to a set $A^{\mathcal{I}} \subseteq \Delta^{\mathcal{I}}$ and every $r \in N_R$ to a binary relation $r^{\mathcal{I}} \subseteq \Delta^{\mathcal{I}} \times \Delta^{\mathcal{I}}$. This interpretation is extended to $\mathcal{EL}$-concepts setting $\top^{\mathcal{I}} := \Delta^{\mathcal{I}}$, $(C \sqcap D)^{\mathcal{I}} := C^{\mathcal{I}} \cap D^{\mathcal{I}}$, and $(\exists r.C)^{\mathcal{I}} := \{\delta \mid \exists \eta \in C^{\mathcal{I}}.(\delta, \eta) \in r^{\mathcal{I}}\}$.*

Ontologies are finite sets of *general concept inclusions* (GCIs), which specify the relationships between concepts.

Definition 2 (ontology). *A GCI is an expression of the form $C \sqsubseteq D$ where C, D are two concepts. An* ontology *is a finite set of GCIs. The interpretation $\mathcal{I}$ satisfies the GCI α iff $C^{\mathcal{I}} \subseteq D^{\mathcal{I}}$. It is a* model *of the ontology $\mathcal{O}$ iff it satisfies all GCIs in $\mathcal{O}$. We often call GCIs axioms.*
    The ontology $\mathcal{O}$ entails the GCI α ($\mathcal{O} \models \alpha$) iff every model of $\mathcal{O}$ satisfies α. In this case we say that α is a consequence *of $\mathcal{O}$.*

Although many reasoning tasks can be considered, along with an ample selection of axioms in the ontologies, we focus on the problem of deciding whether α is a consequence of an ontology. For simplicity, we will consider only *atomic* subsumption relations $A \sqsubseteq B$ where $A, B \in N_C$. It is well known that this problem can be solved in polynomial time through a completion algorithm [2].

In a nutshell, the algorithm runs in two phases. First, the original GCIs are decomposed into a set of GCIs in *normal form*; that is, having only the shapes

$$A_1 \sqsubseteq B, \quad A_1 \sqcap A_2 \sqsubseteq B, \quad A_1 \sqsubseteq \exists r.B, \quad \exists r.A_1 \sqsubseteq B$$

where $r \in N_R$ and $A, B \in N_C \cup \{\top\}$. These axioms are then combined through *completion rules* to make consequences explicit (more details in Sect. 3). The method is sound and complete for all atomic subsumptions over the concept names appearing in the original ontology.

As an additional example of a logic, we consider the sublanguage $\mathcal{HL}$ of $\mathcal{EL}$, which uses only concept names and the conjunction ($\sqcap$) constructor. It can be seen that $\mathcal{HL}$ is a syntactic variant of directed hypergraphs. Specifically, a GCI $A_1 \sqcap \cdots \sqcap A_m \sqsubseteq B_1 \sqcap \cdots \sqcap B_n$ represents a directed hypergraph connecting nodes $A_1, \ldots, A_m$ with nodes $B_1, \ldots, B_n$, and the entailment problem is nothing more than reachability in this hypergraph.

Axiom Pinpointing. Beyond standard reasoning, it is sometimes important to understand which axioms are responsible for a consequence to follow from an ontology. This goal is interpreted as the task of identifying *justifications*.

Definition 3. *A* justification *for a consequence α w.r.t. the ontology $\mathcal{O}$ is a set $\mathcal{M} \subseteq \mathcal{O}$ such that (i) $\mathcal{M} \models \alpha$ and (ii) for every $\mathcal{N} \subset \mathcal{M}$, $\mathcal{N} \not\models \alpha$.*

In words, a justification is a subset-minimal subontology that still entails the consequence. Most work focuses on computing one or all justifications. While the former problem remains polynomial in $\mathcal{EL}$, the latter necessarily needs exponential time, as the number of justifications may be exponential on the size of the ontology. Despite some potential uses, which have been identified for non standard reasoning [6], only very recently have specific algorithms for computing the unions and intersection of justifications been developed [9,14]. To the best of our knowledge, no previous work has considered computing the justifications of *minimal cardinality* directly.

3 Reasoning Through Rules

Before presenting our approach to axiom pinpointing using ASP, we briefly describe how to reduce reasoning in $\mathcal{EL}$ to ASP. The approach simulates the completion algorithm sketched in Sect. 2 through a small set of rules, while the ontology axioms (in normal form) are represented through facts.

Consider an ontology $\mathcal{O}$ in normal form, and let $\mathcal{C}(\mathcal{O})$ and $\mathcal{R}(\mathcal{O})$ be the sets of concept names and role names appearing in $\mathcal{O}$, respectively. For each $A \in \mathcal{C}(\mathcal{O})$ we use a constant a, and for each $r \in \mathcal{R}(\mathcal{O})$ we use a constant r. We identify the four shapes of normal form axioms via a predicate. Hence, s1(a,b) stands for the GCI $A \sqsubseteq B$ and analogously for the expressions s2(a1,a2,b), s3(a,r,b), and s4(r,a,b). For each axiom in normal form appearing in $\mathcal{O}$, we write the associated fact. As previously mentioned, the reasoning process is simulated through rules. In the specific case of $\mathcal{EL}$, these rules are shown in Fig. 1

```
s1(X,Y) :- s1(X,Z), s1(Z,Y).
s1(X,Y) :- s1(X,Z1), s1(X,Z2), s2(Z1,Z2,Y).
s3(X,R,Y) :- s1(X,Z), s3(Z,R,W), s1(W,Y).
s1(X,Y) :- s3(X,R,Z), s4(R,Z,Y).
```

```
gi :- a1, ..., am
b1 :- gi
  .
  .
  .
bn :- gi
```

Fig. 1. The rules for $\mathcal{EL}$ reasoning (left) and the translation of $\mathcal{HL}$ GCIs (right).

(left). To decide whether the atomic subsumption $A \sqsubseteq B$ is a consequence of the ontology, we need only ask the query $s1(a,b)$. Since the original ontology may not be in normal form, the facts obtained this way are the result of the normalisation step over the original GCIs. In the case of $\mathcal{HL}$, one can produce a more direct reduction, which takes into account the hyperedges without the need for normalisation or general derivation rules. We again represent each concept name A through a constant a, and associate a new constant gi for each GCI in $\mathcal{O}$. Then the GCI $A_1 \sqcap \cdots \sqcap A_m \sqsubseteq B_1 \sqcap \cdots \sqcap B_n$ is translated to the set of rules in Fig. 1 (right). To decide whether $A \sqsubseteq B$ is a consequence, we add the fact a. and verify the query b. The correctness of the approach follows from the results in [8,15].

4   Axiom Pinpointing Through ASP

We present a general approach for solving axiom pinpointing tasks through an ASP solver. The approach is applicable to any logic (including other DLs) with a *modular* ASP encoding. Roughly, an encoding is modular if each axiom in $\mathcal{O}$ translates to a set of rules, such that an ASP encoding $\Pi_{\mathcal{O}}$ of $\mathcal{O}$ is obtained by the union of the encodings of its axioms, possibly together with some additional rules (independent of the axioms in $\mathcal{O}$) needed to simulate reasoning in ASP.

Definition 4. *An encoding in ASP $\Pi_{\mathcal{O}}$ of the ontology $\mathcal{O}$ is modular iff (i) for each $\alpha \in \mathcal{O}$ there is an ASP program Π_{α}, and (ii) there is a (possibly empty) set of rules R such that $\Pi_{\mathcal{O}} = \bigcup_{\alpha \in \mathcal{O}} \Pi_{\alpha} \cup R$*

The encodings from Sect. 3 for $\mathcal{EL}$ and $\mathcal{HL}$ are both modular. In the former case, R is exactly the set of rules in Fig. 1 (left), while in the latter $R = \emptyset$.

We now formulate the problem of computing justifications in ASP. First, we apply an *adornment* step, which allows to identify and keep track of the rules of a module corresponding to a given axiom.

Definition 5. *Let P be an ASP program, and δ be an atom not occurring in P. The δ-adornment for P is the program $\Delta(P) = \{r_{\delta} : r \in P\}$, where r_{δ} is s.t. $head(r_{\delta}) = head(r)$, and $body(r_{\delta}) = body(r) \cup \delta$.*

In words, the δ-adornment adds a new identifying atom δ to the body of each rule of the program. This guarantees that the rules *trigger* only when δ is true.

Definition 6. *The adorned ASP encoding of the ontology $\mathcal{O}$ is the program*

$$\delta(\Pi_{\mathcal{O}}) = \bigcup_{\alpha \in \mathcal{O}} \Delta_{\alpha}(\Pi_{\alpha}) \cup R \cup C$$

where for each $\alpha \in \mathcal{O}$, δ_{α} is a fresh atom not occurring in $\Pi(\mathcal{O})$, and C is the ASP program containing a choice rule $\{\delta_{\alpha}\}$ for each $\alpha \in \mathcal{O}$.

In the case of $\mathcal{EL}$, the adornment will change each fact (corresponding to a GCI in normal form) `si(...)`. into the rule `si(...)  :- xj`, where `xj` is the chosen constant for the original axiom α_j. Importantly, this approach handles the original axioms in the ontology, and not those already normalised as done e.g. in [4].

We now describe an ASP program that can be used for axiom pinpointing. Given the ontology $\mathcal{O}$ and consequence c, we identify the justifications for c through the following property.

Proposition 1. *Let $\mathcal{O}$ be an ontology, c an atom modelling a consequence of $\mathcal{O}$, and P the program $P = \delta(\Pi_{\mathcal{O}}) \cup \{\leftarrow not\ c\}$. $\mathcal{M} \subseteq \mathcal{O}$ is a justification for c iff there is an answer set A of P that is minimal w.r.t. $\{\delta_{\alpha} \mid \alpha \in \mathcal{O}\}$ and $\{\delta_{\alpha} \mid \alpha \in \mathcal{M}\} \subseteq A$.*

Justifications that are cardinality minimal (and thus also subset minimal) can be directly computed using an ASP program with weak constraints.

Proposition 2. *Let $\mathcal{O}$ be an ontology, c an atom modelling a consequence of $\mathcal{O}$, and P the program $P = \delta(\Pi_{\mathcal{O}}) \cup \{:- not\ c\} \cup \{:\sim \delta_{\alpha} : \alpha \in \mathcal{O}\}$. $\mathcal{M} \subseteq \mathcal{O}$ is a justification for c iff there exists an optimal answer set A of P such that $\{\delta_{\alpha} \mid \alpha \in \mathcal{M}\} \subseteq A$.*

Before concluding, we note that the translation permits computing the *intersection* of all justifications, and consequences derived from it, through the application of *cautious reasoning* [5]. In ASP, a cautious consequence is one that holds in every answer set. Since the program P from Proposition 1 provides a one-to-one correspondence between answer sets and sub-ontologies deriving a consequence, cautious reasoning refers to reasoning over the intersection of all those sub-ontologies, and in particular over the subset-minimal ones; that is, over the justifications. Unfortunately, an analogous result does not exist for the *union* of all justifications. Indeed, every axiom would be available for *brave reasoning* (consequences which hold in at least one answer set) [5] over the same program P, but not all axioms belong to some justification.

5   Conclusions

We presented a general approach for axiom pinpointing based on a reduction to ASP. As a proof of concept, we have shown how the reduction works for the light-weight DL $\mathcal{HL}$ and the more expressive $\mathcal{EL}$. The same approach works for any logic with a modular translation to ASP, for instance any DL with a consequence-based reasoning algorithm [10,18] should enjoy such a translation. Compared to existing approaches [1,17], ours is more general and does not require the construction of a specific propositional formula encoding the reasoning task.

In future work we will extend the translation to $\mathcal{ALC}$ and more expressive DLs, and test the efficiency of our method on ASP solvers. We will also study the implementation of other axiom pinpointing services based on ASP constructs.

References

1. Arif, M.F., Mencía, C., Ignatiev, A., Manthey, N., Peñaloza, R., Marques-Silva, J.: BEACON: an efficient SAT-based tool for debugging $\mathcal{EL}^+$ ontologies. In: Creignou, N., Le Berre, D. (eds.) SAT 2016. LNCS, vol. 9710, pp. 521–530. Springer, Cham (2016). https://doi.org/10.1007/978-3-319-40970-2_32
2. Baader, F., Brandt, S., Lutz, C.: Pushing the $\mathcal{EL}$ envelope. In: Proceedings of IJCAI 2005, pp. 364–369. Professional Book Center (2005)
3. Baader, F., Calvanese, D., McGuinness, D., Nardi, D., Patel-Schneider, P. (eds.) The Description Logic Handbook: Theory, Implementation, and Applications, 2nd edn. Cambridge University Press (2007)
4. Baader, F., Peñaloza, R., Suntisrivaraporn, B.: Pinpointing in the description logic $\mathcal{EL}^+$. In: Hertzberg, J., Beetz, M., Englert, R. (eds.) KI 2007. LNCS (LNAI), vol. 4667, pp. 52–67. Springer, Heidelberg (2007). https://doi.org/10.1007/978-3-540-74565-5_7
5. Baral, C.: Knowledge Representation, Reasoning and Declarative Problem Solving. Cambridge University Press (2010)
6. Bienvenu, M., Rosati, R.: Tractable approximations of consistent query answering for robust ontology-based data access. In: Rossi, F. (ed.) Proceedings of IJCAI 2013, pp. 775–781. AAAI Press/IJCAI (2013)
7. Brewka, G., Eiter, T., Truszczynski, M.: Answer set programming at a glance. Commun. ACM 54(12), 92–103 (2011)
8. Ceylan, İ.İ., Mendez, J., Peñaloza, R.: The bayesian ontology reasoner is born! In: Proceedings of (ORE-2015). CEUR Workshop Proceedings, vol. 1387, pp. 8–14. CEUR-WS.org (2015)
9. Chen, J., Ma, Y., Peñaloza, R., Yang, H.: Union and intersection of all justifications. In: Proceedings of ESWC 2022. LNCS, vol. 13261, pp. 56–73. Springer, Cham (2022). https://doi.org/10.1007/978-3-031-06981-9_4
10. Cucala, D.T., Grau, B.C., Horrocks, I.: Consequence-based reasoning for description logics with disjunction, inverse roles, and nominals. In: Proceedings of DL 2017, Montpellier, France, 18–21 July 2017 (2017)
11. Kalyanpur, A., Parsia, B., Sirin, E., Hendler, J.A.: Debugging unsatisfiable classes in OWL ontologies. J. Web Semant. 3(4), 268–293 (2005)
12. Lifschitz, V.: Answer set planning. In: Schreye, D.D. (ed.) Logic Programming: The 1999 International Conference, pp. 23–37. MIT Press (1999)
13. Peñaloza Nyssen, R.: Axiom pinpointing in description logics and beyond. Ph.D. thesis, Technische Universität Dresden, Germany (2009). http://nbn-resolving.de/urn:nbn:de:bsz:14-qucosa-24743
14. Peñaloza, R., Mencía, C., Ignatiev, A., Marques-Silva, J.: Lean Kernels in description logics. In: Blomqvist, E., Maynard, D., Gangemi, A., Hoekstra, R., Hitzler, P., Hartig, O. (eds.) ESWC 2017. LNCS, vol. 10249, pp. 518–533. Springer, Cham (2017). https://doi.org/10.1007/978-3-319-58068-5_32

15. Peñaloza, R., Sertkaya, B.: Understanding the complexity of axiom pinpointing in lightweight description logics. Artif. Intell. **250**, 80–104 (2017)
16. Schlobach, S., Cornet, R.: Non-standard reasoning services for the debugging of description logic terminologies. In: Proceedings of IJCAI 2003, pp. 355–360. Morgan Kaufmann Publishers Inc. (2003)
17. Sebastiani, R., Vescovi, M.: Axiom pinpointing in large EL+ ontologies via SAT and SMT techniques. Disi technical report, University of Trento (2015)
18. Simančík, F., Kazakov, Y., Horrocks, I.: Consequence-based reasoning beyond Horn ontologies. In: Proceedings of the IJCAI 2011, pp. 1093–1098. AAAI Press (2011)

Interlinking Logic Programs and Argumentation Frameworks

Chiaki Sakama[1]([✉]) and Tran Cao Son[2]

[1] Wakayama University, 930 Sakaedani, Wakayama 640-8510, Japan
sakama@wakayama-u.ac.jp
[2] New Mexico State University, Las Cruces, NM 88003, USA
tson@cs.nmsu.edu

Abstract. *Logic programs* (LPs) and *argumentation frameworks* (AFs) are two declarative knowledge representation (KR) formalisms used for different reasoning tasks. The purpose of this study is interlinking two different reasoning components. To this end, we introduce two frameworks: *LPAF* and *AFLP*. The former enables to use the result of argumentation in AF for reasoning in LP, while the latter enables to use the result of reasoning in LP for arguing in AF. These frameworks are extended to *bidirectional frameworks* in which AF and LP can exchange information with each other. We also investigate their connection to several general KR frameworks from the literature.

1 Introduction

A *logic program* (LP) represents declarative knowledge as a set of rules and realizes commonsense reasoning as logical inference. An *argumentation framework* (AF), on the other hand, represents arguments and an attack relation over them, and defines acceptable arguments under various semantics. The two frameworks specify different types of knowledge and realize different types of reasoning. In our daily life, however, we often use two modes of reasoning interchangeably. For instance, consider a logic program $LP = \{\, get\_vaccine \leftarrow safe \wedge effective,\ \neg get\_vaccine \leftarrow not\, safe \,\}$ which says that we get a vaccine if it is safe and effective, and we do not get it if it is not safe. To see whether a vaccine is safe and effective, we refer to an expert opinion. It is often the case, however, that multiple experts have different opinions. In this case, we observe argumentation among experts and take it into account to make a decision. In other words, the truth value of *safe* is determined by an external argumentation framework such as $AF = (\{s,d\}, \{(s,d),(d,s)\})$ in its most condensed form where s represents safe and d represents dangerous. A credulous reasoner will accept *safe* under the stable semantics, while a skeptical reasoner will not accept it under the grounded semantics. A reasoner determines acceptable arguments under chosen semantics and makes a decision using his/her own LP. For another example, consider a debate on whether global warming is occurring. Scientists and politicians make different claims based on evidence and scientific knowledge. An argumentation framework is used for representing the debate, while

---

The second author has been partial supported by NSF grants 1914635, 1757207, 1812628.

G. Gottlob et al. (Eds.): LPNMR 2022, LNAI 13416, pp. 322–335, 2022.
https://doi.org/10.1007/978-3-031-15707-3_25

arguments appearing in the argumentation graph are generated as results of reasoning from the background knowledge of participants represented by LPs.

In these examples, we can encode reasoners' private knowledge as LPs and argumentation in the public space as AFs. It is natural to distinguish two different types of knowledge and interlink them with each other. In the first example, an agent has a private knowledge base that refers to opinions in a public argumentation framework. In the second example, on the other hand, agents participating in a debate have their private knowledge bases supporting their individual claims.

Logic programs and argumentation frameworks are mutually transformed with each other. Dung [6] provides a transformation from LPs to AFs and shows that stable models [11] (resp. the well-founded model [16]) of a logic program correspond to stable extensions (resp. the grounded extension) of a transformed argumentation framework. He also introduces a converse transformation from AFs to LPs, and shows that the semantic correspondences still hold. The results are extended to equivalences of LPs and AFs under different semantics (e.g. [5]). Using such transformational approaches, an LP and an AF can be combined and one could perform both argumentative reasoning and commonsense reasoning in a single framework. One of the limitations of this approach is that in order to combine an LP and an AF into a single framework, the two frameworks must have the corresponding semantics. For instance, suppose that an agent has a knowledge base LP and refers to an AF. If the agent uses the stable model semantics of LP, then to combine LP with AF using a transformation proposed in [5,6] AF must use the stable extension semantics. Argumentation can have an internal structure in *structured argumentation*. In *assumption based argumentation* (ABA) [7], for instance, an argument for a claim c is supported by a set of assumptions S if c is deduced from S using a set of LP rules ($S \vdash c$). A structured argumentation has a knowledge base inside an argument and provides reasons that support particular claims. An argument is represented as a tree and an attack relation is introduced between trees. However, merging argumentation and knowledge bases into a single framework would produce a huge argumentation structure that is complicated and hard to manage.

In this paper, we introduce new frameworks, called $LPAF$ and $AFLP$, for interlinking LPs and AFs. The $LPAF$ uses the result of argumentation in AFs for reasoning in LPs. In contrast, the $AFLP$ uses the result of reasoning in LPs for arguing in AFs. These frameworks are extended to *bidirectional frameworks* in which AFs and LPs can exchange information with each other. We address applications of the proposed framework and investigate connections to existing KR frameworks. The rest of this paper is organized as follows. Section 2 reviews basic notions of logic programming and argumentation frameworks. Section 3 introduces several frameworks for interlinking LPs and AFs. Section 4 presents applications to several KR frameworks. Section 5 discusses complexity issues and Sect. 6 summarizes the paper. Due to space limitation, proofs of propositions are omitted in this paper. They are available in the longer version [15].

2 Preliminaries

We consider a language that contains a finite set $\mathscr{L}$ of propositional variables.

Definition 1. A *(disjunctive) logic program* (LP) is a finite set of *rules* of the form:

$$p_1 \vee \cdots \vee p_\ell \leftarrow q_1, \ldots, q_m, not \, q_{m+1}, \ldots, not \, q_n \quad (\ell, m, n \geq 0)$$

where p_i and q_j are propositional variables in $\mathscr{L}$ and *not* is *negation as failure* (NAF).

The left-hand side of $\leftarrow$ is the *head* and the right-hand side is the *body*. For each rule r of the above form, $head(r)$, $body^+(r)$, and $body^-(r)$ respectively denote the sets of atoms $\{p_1, \ldots, p_\ell\}$, $\{q_1, \ldots, q_m\}$, and $\{q_{m+1}, \ldots, q_n\}$, and $body(r) = body^+(r) \cup body^-(r)$. A *(disjunctive) fact* is a rule r with $body(r) = \varnothing$. A fact is a *non-disjunctive fact* if $\ell = 1$. An LP is a *normal logic program* if $| head(r) | \leq 1$ for any rule r in the program. Given a logic program LP, put $Head(LP) = \bigcup_{r \in LP} head(r)$ and $Body(LP) = \bigcup_{r \in LP} body(r)$. Throughout the paper, a program means a propositional/ground logic program and $\mathscr{B}_{LP}$ is the set of ground atoms appearing in a program LP (called the *Herbrand base*).

A program LP under the μ semantics is denoted by LP_μ. The semantics of LP_μ is defined as the set $\mathscr{M}_{LP}^\mu \subseteq 2^{\mathscr{B}_{LP}}$ (or simply $\mathscr{M}^\mu$) of μ models of LP. If a ground atom p is included in every μ model of LP, we write $LP_\mu \models p$. LP_μ is simply written as LP if the semantics is clear in the context. A logic programming semantics μ is *universal* if every LP has a μ model. The stable model semantics is not universal, while the *well-founded semantics* of normal logic programs is universal. A logic program LP under the stable model semantics (resp. well-founded semantics) is written as LP_{stb} (resp. LP_{wf}).

Definition 2. An *argumentation framework* (AF) is a pair (A, R) where $A \subseteq \mathscr{L}$ is a finite set of *arguments* and $R \subseteq A \times A$ is an *attack relation*.

For an AF (A, R), we say that an argument a *attacks* an argument b if $(a, b) \in R$. A set S of arguments *attacks* an argument a iff there is an argument $b \in S$ that attacks a; S is *conflict-free* if there are no arguments $a, b \in S$ such that a attacks b. S *defends* an argument a if S attacks every argument that attacks a. We write $D(S) = \{a \mid S \text{ defends } a\}$.

The semantics of AF is defined as the set of designated *extensions* [6]. Given $AF = (A, R)$, a conflict-free set of arguments $S \subseteq A$ is a *complete extension* iff $S = D(S)$; a *stable extension* iff S attacks each argument in $A \setminus S$; a *preferred extension* iff S is a maximal complete extension of AF (wrt $\subseteq$); a *grounded extension* iff S is the minimal complete extension of AF (wrt $\subseteq$). An argumentation framework AF under the ω semantics is denoted by AF_ω. The semantics of AF_ω is defined as the set $\mathscr{E}_{AF}^\omega$ (or simply $\mathscr{E}^\omega$) of ω extensions of AF. We abbreviate the above four semantics of AF as AF_{com}, AF_{stb}, AF_{prf} and AF_{grd}, respectively. AF_ω is simply written as AF if the semantics is clear in the context. Among the four semantics, the following relations hold: for any AF, $\mathscr{E}_{AF}^{stb} \subseteq \mathscr{E}_{AF}^{prf} \subseteq \mathscr{E}_{AF}^{com}$ and $\mathscr{E}_{AF}^{grd} \subseteq \mathscr{E}_{AF}^{com}$. $\mathscr{E}_{AF}^{stb}$ is possibly empty, while others are not. In particular, $\mathscr{E}_{AF}^{grd}$ is a singleton set. An argumentation semantics ω is *universal* if every AF has an ω extension. The stable semantics is not universal, while the other three semantics presented above are universal. [1]

---

[1] We assume readers familiarity with the stable model semantics [11], [14] and the well-founded semantics [16]

3   Linking LP and AF

3.1   From AF to LP

We first introduce a framework that can use the result of argumentation in AFs for reasoning in LPs. In this subsection, we assume that $Head(LP) \cap A = \varnothing$ for a program LP and $AF = (A,R)$, that is, no rule in a logic program has an argument in its head.

Definition 3. Given an LP and $AF = (A,R)$, define $LP^{+A} = \{r \in LP \mid body(r) \cap A \neq \varnothing\}$ and $LP^{-A} = \{r \in LP \mid body(r) \cap A = \varnothing\}$. We say that each rule in LP^{+A} (resp. LP^{-A}) *refers to* arguments (resp. is *free from* arguments). An argument $a \in A$ is *referred to* in LP if a appears in LP. Define $A\,|_{LP} = \{a \in A \mid a$ is referred to in $LP\}$.

By definition, an LP is partitioned into $LP = LP^{+A} \cup LP^{-A}$.

Definition 4. Given an LP and $AF = (A,R)$, a μ *model of LP extended by* $\mathscr{A} \subseteq 2^A$ is a μ model of $LP \cup \{a \leftarrow \mid a \in E \cap A\,|_{LP}\}$ for some $E \in \mathscr{A}$ if $\mathscr{A} \neq \varnothing$; otherwise, it is a μ model of LP^{-A}.

Definition 5. A *simple LPAF framework* is a pair $\langle LP_\mu, AF_\omega \rangle$, where LP_μ is a program under the μ semantics and AF_ω is an argumentation framework under the ω semantics.

Definition 6. Let $\varphi = \langle LP_\mu, AF_\omega \rangle$ be a simple LPAF framework. Suppose that AF has the set of ω extensions: $\mathscr{E}^\omega = \{E_1, \ldots, E_k\}$ ($k \geq 0$). Then an *LPAF model* of φ is defined as a μ model of LP_μ extended by $\mathscr{E}^\omega$. The set of LPAF models of φ is denoted by $\mathbf{M}_\varphi$.

By definition, an LPAF model is defined as a μ model of the program LP by introducing arguments that are referred to in LP and are acceptable under the ω semantics of AF. If the AF part has no ω extension ($\mathscr{E}^\omega = \varnothing$), on the other hand, AF provides no justification for arguments referred to by LP. In this case, we do not take the consequences that are derived using arguments in AF. Then an LPAF model is constructed by rules that are free from arguments in AF.

Example 1. Consider $\varphi_1 = \langle LP_{stb}, AF_{stb} \rangle$ where $LP_{stb} = \{p \leftarrow a, \quad q \leftarrow not\,a\}$ and $AF_{stb} = (\{a,b\}, \{(a,b),(b,a)\})$. As AF_{stb} has two stable extensions $\{a\}$ and $\{b\}$, φ_1 has two LPAF models $\{p,a\}$ and $\{q\}$. On the other hand, if we use $\omega = grounded$ then AF_{grd} has the single extension $\varnothing$. Then $\langle LP_{stb}, AF_{grd} \rangle$ has the single LPAF model $\{q\}$.[2] Next, consider $\varphi_2 = \langle LP_{stb}, AF_{stb} \rangle$ where $LP_{stb} = \{p \leftarrow not\,a, \quad q \leftarrow not\,p\}$ and $AF_{stb} = (\{a,b\}, \{(a,b),(a,a)\})$. As AF_{stb} has no stable extension and the second rule in LP_{stb} is free from arguments, φ_2 has the single LPAF model $\{q\}$. Note that if we keep the first rule then a different conclusion p is obtained from LP_{stb}. We do not consider the conclusion justified because AF_{stb} provides no information on whether the argument a is acceptable or not.

Proposition 1. Let $\varphi_1 = \langle LP_\mu, AF_{\omega_1}^1 \rangle$ and $\varphi_2 = \langle LP_\mu, AF_{\omega_2}^2 \rangle$ be two LPAFs such that $\mathscr{E}_{AF^1}^{\omega_1} \neq \varnothing$. If $\mathscr{E}_{AF^1}^{\omega_1} \subseteq \mathscr{E}_{AF^2}^{\omega_2}$, then $\mathbf{M}_{\varphi_1} \subseteq \mathbf{M}_{\varphi_2}$.

---

[2] Note that an AF extension represents whether an argument is accepted or not. If an argument a is not in an extension E, a is not accepted in E. Then *not a* in LP becomes true by NAF.

Proposition 1 implies the inclusion relations with the same AF under different semantics: $\mathbf{M}_{\varphi_1} \subseteq \mathbf{M}_{\varphi_2}$ holds for $\varphi_1 = \langle LP_\mu, AF_{prf} \rangle$ and $\varphi_2 = \langle LP_\mu, AF_{com} \rangle$; $\varphi_1 = \langle LP_\mu, AF_{stb} \rangle$ and $\varphi_2 = \langle LP_\mu, AF_{prf} \rangle$; or $\varphi_1 = \langle LP_\mu, AF_{grd} \rangle$ and $\varphi_2 = \langle LP_\mu, AF_{com} \rangle$.

Two programs LP_μ^1 and LP_μ^2 are *uniformly equivalent relative to A* (denoted $LP_\mu^1 \equiv_u^A LP_\mu^2$) if for any set of non-disjunctive facts $F \subseteq A$, the programs $LP_\mu^1 \cup F$ and $LP_\mu^2 \cup F$ have the same set of μ models [10]. The equivalence of two simple LPAF frameworks is then characterized as follows.

Proposition 2. *Let* $\varphi_1 = \langle LP_\mu^1, AF_\omega \rangle$ *and* $\varphi_2 = \langle LP_\mu^2, AF_\omega \rangle$ *be two LPAFs such that* $\mathcal{E}^\omega \neq \varnothing$. *Then,* $\mathbf{M}_{\varphi_1} = \mathbf{M}_{\varphi_2}$ *if* $LP_\mu^1 \equiv_u^A LP_\mu^2$ *and* $A|_{LP_\mu^1} = A|_{LP_\mu^2}$ *where* $AF_\omega = (A,R)$.

A simple LPAF framework $\varphi = \langle LP_\mu, AF_\omega \rangle$ is *consistent* if φ has an LPAF model. The consistency of φ depends on the chosen semantics μ. In particular, a simple LPAF framework $\varphi = \langle LP_\mu, AF_\omega \rangle$ is consistent if μ is universal. $\varphi = \langle LP_\mu, AF_\omega \rangle$ may have an LPAF model even if $\mathcal{M}_{LP}^\mu = \mathcal{E}_{AF}^\omega = \varnothing$.

Example 2. Consider $\varphi = \langle LP_{stb}, AF_{stb} \rangle$ where $LP_{stb} = \{ p \leftarrow not\, a, not\, p, \quad q \leftarrow \}$ and $AF_{stb} = (\{a\}, \{(a,a)\})$. Then $\mathcal{M}_{LP}^{stb} = \mathcal{E}_{AF}^{stb} = \varnothing$, but φ has the LPAF model $\{q\}$.

A simple LPAF consists of a single LP and an AF, which is generalized to a framework that consists of multiple LPs and AFs.

Definition 7. A *general LPAF framework* is defined as a tuple $\langle \mathbb{LP}^m, \mathbb{AF}^n \rangle$ where $\mathbb{LP}^m = (LP_{\mu_1}^1, \ldots, LP_{\mu_m}^m)$ and $\mathbb{AF}^n = (AF_{\omega_1}^1, \ldots, AF_{\omega_n}^n)$. Each $LP_{\mu_i}^i$ $(1 \leq i \leq m)$ is a logic program LP^i under the μ_i semantics and each $AF_{\omega_j}^j$ $(1 \leq j \leq n)$ is an argumentation framework AF^j under the ω_j semantics.

A general LPAF framework is used in a situation where multiple agents have individual LPs as their private knowledge bases and each agent possibly refers to the results of argumentation of open AFs. The semantics of a general LPAF is defined as an extension of a simple LPAF framework.

Definition 8. Let $\varphi = \langle \mathbb{LP}^m, \mathbb{AF}^n \rangle$ be a general LPAF framework. The *LPAF state* of φ is defined as a tuple $(\Sigma_1, \ldots, \Sigma_m)$ where $\Sigma_i = (\mathbf{M}_1^i, \ldots, \mathbf{M}_n^i)$ $(1 \leq i \leq m)$ and $\mathbf{M}_j^i$ $(1 \leq j \leq n)$ is the set of LPAF models of $\langle LP_{\mu_i}^i, AF_{\omega_j}^j \rangle$.

By definition, an LPAF state consists of a collection of LPAF models such that each model is obtained by combining a program $LP_{\mu_i}^i$ and an argumentation framework $AF_{\omega_j}^j$.

Example 3. Consider $\varphi = \langle (LP_{stb}, LP_{wf}), (AF_{stb}, AF_{grd}) \rangle$ where $LP_{stb} = LP_{wf} = \{ p \leftarrow a, not\, q, \quad q \leftarrow a, not\, p \}$ and $AF_{stb} = AF_{grd} = (\{a,b\}, \{(a,b),(b,a)\})$. In this case, $\langle LP_{stb}, AF_{stb} \rangle$ has three LPAF models: $\{p,a\}$, $\{q,a\}$ and $\varnothing$; $\langle LP_{stb}, AF_{grd} \rangle$ has the single LPAF model: $\varnothing$; $\langle LP_{wf}, AF_{stb} \rangle$ has two LPAF models:[3] $\{a\}$ and $\varnothing$; $\langle LP_{wf}, AF_{grd} \rangle$ has the single LPAF model: $\varnothing$. Then φ has the LPAF state (Σ_1, Σ_2) where $\Sigma_1 = (\{\{p,a\}, \{q,a\}, \varnothing\}, \{\varnothing\})$ and $\Sigma_2 = (\{\{a\}, \varnothing\}, \{\varnothing\})$.

---

[3] We consider the well-founded model as the set of true atoms under the well-founded semantics.

The above example shows that a general LPAF is used for comparing the results of combination between LP and AF under different semantics. Given tuples $(S_1, \ldots, S_k)$ and $(T_1, \ldots, T_\ell)$ $(k, \ell \geq 1)$, define $(S_1, \ldots, S_k) \oplus (T_1, \ldots, T_\ell) = (S_1, \ldots, S_k, T_1, \ldots, T_\ell)$.

Proposition 3. *Let* $\varphi = \langle \mathrm{LP}^m, \mathrm{AF}^n \rangle$ *be a general LPAF framework. Then the LPAF state* $(\Sigma_1, \ldots, \Sigma_m)$ *of* φ *is obtained by* $(\Sigma_1, \ldots, \Sigma_k) \oplus (\Sigma_{k+1}, \ldots, \Sigma_m)$ $(1 \leq k \leq m - 1)$ *where* $(\Sigma_1, \ldots, \Sigma_k)$ *is the LPAF state of* $\varphi_1 = \langle \mathrm{LP}^k, \mathrm{AF}^n \rangle$ *and* $(\Sigma_{k+1}, \ldots, \Sigma_m)$ *is the LPAF state of* $\varphi_2 = \langle \mathrm{LP}^m_{k+1}, \mathrm{AF}^n \rangle$ *where* $\mathrm{LP}^m_{k+1} = (LP^{k+1}_{\mu_{k+1}}, \ldots, LP^m_{\mu_m})$.

Proposition 3 presents that a general LPAF has the modularity property; φ is partitioned into smaller φ_1 and φ_2, and the introduction of new LPs to φ is done incrementally.

3.2 From LP to AF

We next introduce a framework that can use the result of reasoning in LPs for arguing in AFs. In this subsection, we assume that $Body(LP) \cap A = \varnothing$ for a program LP and $AF = (A, R)$, that is, no rule in a logic program has an argument in its body.

Definition 9. Let $AF = (A, R)$ and $M \subseteq \mathscr{L}$. Then AF *with support* M is defined as $AF^M = (A, R')$ where $R' = R \setminus \{(x, a) \mid x \in A \text{ and } a \in A \cap M\}$.

By definition, AF^M is an argumentation framework in which every tuple attacking $a \in M$ is removed from R. As a result, every argument included in M is accepted in AF^M.

Definition 10. Let $AF = (A, R)$ and $\mathscr{M} \subseteq 2^{\mathscr{B}_{LP}}$. An ω *extension of* AF *supported by* $\mathscr{M}$ is an ω extension of AF^M for some $M \in \mathscr{M}$ if $\mathscr{M} \neq \varnothing$; otherwise, it is an ω extension of (A', R') where $A' = A \setminus \mathscr{B}_{LP}$ and $R' = R \cap (A' \times A')$.

Definition 11. A *simple AFLP framework* is a pair $\langle AF_\omega, LP_\mu \rangle$ where AF_ω is an argumentation framework under the ω semantics and LP_μ is a program under μ semantics.

Definition 12. Let $\psi = \langle AF_\omega, LP_\mu \rangle$ be a simple AFLP framework and $\mathscr{M}^\mu \subseteq 2^{\mathscr{B}_{LP}}$ be the set of μ models of LP. An *AFLP extension* of ψ is defined as an ω extension of AF_ω supported by $\mathscr{M}^\mu$. $\mathbf{E}_\psi$ denotes the set of AFLP extensions of ψ.

By definition, an AFLP extension is defined as an ω extension of AF^M_ω that takes into account support information in a μ model M of LP. If the LP part has no μ model ($\mathscr{M}^\mu = \varnothing$), on the other hand, LP provides no ground for arguments in $A \cap \mathscr{B}_{LP}$. In this case, we do not use those arguments that rely on LP. Then an AFLP extension is constructed using arguments that do not appear in LP.

Example 4. Consider $\psi_1 = \langle AF_{stb}, LP_{stb} \rangle$ where $AF_{stb} = (\{a, b\}, \{(a, b), (b, a)\})$ and $LP_{stb} = \{a \leftarrow p, \ p \leftarrow not\, q, \ q \leftarrow not\, p\}$. LP_{stb} has two stable models $M_1 = \{a, p\}$ and $M_2 = \{q\}$, then $AF^{M_1}_{stb} = (\{a, b\}, \{(a, b)\})$ and $AF^{M_2}_{stb} = AF_{stb}$. Hence, ψ_1 has two AFLP extensions $\{a\}$ and $\{b\}$. On the other hand, if we use $\omega = grounded$, then $\langle AF_{grd}, LP_{stb} \rangle$ has two AFLP extensions $\{a\}$ and $\varnothing$. Next, consider $\psi_2 = \langle AF_{grd}, LP_{stb} \rangle$ where $AF_{grd} = (\{a, b, c\}, \{(a, b), (b, c)\})$ and $LP_{stb} = \{a \leftarrow p, \ p \leftarrow not\, p\}$. As LP_{stb} has no stable model, ψ_2 has the AFLP extension $\{b\}$ as the grounded extension of $(\{b, c\}, \{(b, c)\})$.

Proposition 4. *Let* $\psi_1 = \langle AF_\omega, LP_{\mu_1}^1 \rangle$ *and* $\psi_2 = \langle AF_\omega, LP_{\mu_2}^2 \rangle$ *be two AFLPs such that* $\mathcal{M}_{LP^1}^{\mu_1} \neq \varnothing$. *If* $\mathcal{M}_{LP^1}^{\mu_1} \subseteq \mathcal{M}_{LP^2}^{\mu_2}$, *then* $\mathbf{E}_{\psi_1} \subseteq \mathbf{E}_{\psi_2}$.

Baumann [1] introduces equivalence relations of AFs with respect to deletion of arguments and attacks. For two $AF_\omega^1 = (A_1, R_1)$ and $AF_\omega^2 = (A_2, R_2)$, AF_ω^1 and AF_ω^2 are *normal deletion equivalent* (denoted by $AF_\omega^1 \equiv_{nd} AF_\omega^2$) if for any set A of arguments $(A_1', R_1 \cap (A_1' \times A_1'))$ and $(A_2', R_2 \cap (A_2' \times A_2'))$ have the same set of ω extensions where $A_1' = A_1 \setminus A$ and $A_2' = A_2 \setminus A$. In contrast, AF_ω^1 and AF_ω^2 are *local deletion equivalent* (denoted by $AF_\omega^1 \equiv_{ld} AF_\omega^2$) if for any set R of attacks $(A_1, R_1 \setminus R)$ and $(A_2, R_2 \setminus R)$ have the same set of ω extensions. By definition, we have the next result.

Proposition 5. *Let* $\psi_1 = \langle AF_\omega^1, LP_\mu \rangle$ *and* $\psi_2 = \langle AF_\omega^2, LP_\mu \rangle$ *be two AFLPs. Then,* $\mathbf{E}_{\psi_1} = \mathbf{E}_{\psi_2}$ *if (i)* $\mathcal{M}^\mu = \varnothing$ *and* $AF_\omega^1 \equiv_{nd} AF_\omega^2$; *or (ii)* $\mathcal{M}^\mu \neq \varnothing$ *and* $AF_\omega^1 \equiv_{ld} AF_\omega^2$.

Baumann shows that $AF_\omega^1 \equiv_{ld} AF_\omega^2$ if and only if $AF_\omega^1 = AF_\omega^2$ for any $\omega = \{com, stb, prf, grd\}$. In contrast, necessary or sufficient conditions for $AF_\omega^1 \equiv_{nd} AF_\omega^2$ are given by the structure of argumentation graphs and they differ from the chosen semantics in general.

A simple AFLP framework $\psi = \langle AF_\omega, LP_\mu \rangle$ is *consistent* if ψ has an AFLP extension. By definition, a simple AFLP framework $\psi = \langle AF_\omega, LP_\mu \rangle$ is consistent if ω is universal. A simple AFLP consists of a single AF and an LP, which is generalized to a framework that consists of multiple AFs and LPs.

Definition 13. A *general AFLP framework* is defined as a tuple $\langle \mathbb{AF}^n, \mathbb{LP}^m \rangle$ where $\mathbb{AF}^n = (AF_{\omega_1}^1, \dots, AF_{\omega_n}^n)$ and $\mathbb{LP}^m = (LP_{\mu_1}^1, \dots, LP_{\mu_m}^m)$. Each $AF_{\omega_j}^j$ $(1 \leq j \leq n)$ is an argumentation framework AF^j under the ω_j semantics and each $LP_{\mu_i}^i$ $(1 \leq i \leq m)$ is a logic program LP^i under the μ_i semantics.

A general AFLP framework is used in a situation such that argumentative dialogues consult LPs as information sources. The semantics of a general AFLP is defined as an extension of a simple AFLP framework.

Definition 14. Let $\psi = \langle \mathbb{AF}^n, \mathbb{LP}^m \rangle$ be a general AFLP framework. The *AFLP state* of ψ is defined as a tuple $(\Gamma_1, \dots, \Gamma_n)$ where $\Gamma_j = (\mathbf{E}_1^j, \dots, \mathbf{E}_m^j)$ $(1 \leq j \leq n)$ and $\mathbf{E}_i^j$ $(1 \leq i \leq m)$ is the set of AFLP extensions of $\langle AF_{\omega_j}^j, LP_{\mu_i}^i \rangle$.

By definition, an AFLP state consists of a collection of AFLP extensions such that each extension is obtained by combining $AF_{\omega_j}^j$ and $LP_{\mu_i}^i$.

Example 5. Consider $\psi = \langle (AF_{grd}), (LP_{stb}^1, LP_{stb}^2) \rangle$ where $AF_{grd} = (\{a, b\}, \{(a, b)\})$, $LP_{stb}^1 = \{a \leftarrow p, \quad p \leftarrow\}$, and $LP_{stb}^2 = \{b \leftarrow q, \quad q \leftarrow\}$. Then, $\langle AF_{grd}, LP_{stb}^1 \rangle$ has the AFLP extension $\{a\}$, while $\langle AF_{grd}, LP_{stb}^2 \rangle$ has the AFLP extension $\{a, b\}$. Then the AFLP state of ψ is (Γ_1) where $\Gamma_1 = (\{\{a\}\}, \{\{a, b\}\})$.

A general AFLP has the modularity property. The operation $\oplus$ is defined in Sect. 3.1.

Proposition 6. *Let* $\psi = \langle \mathbb{AF}^n, \mathbb{LP}^m \rangle$ *be a general AFLP framework. Then the AFLP state* $(\Gamma_1, \dots, \Gamma_n)$ *of* ψ *is obtained by* $(\Gamma_1, \dots, \Gamma_k) \oplus (\Gamma_{k+1}, \dots, \Gamma_n)$ $(1 \leq k \leq n - 1)$ *where* $(\Gamma_1, \dots, \Gamma_k)$ *is the AFLP state of* $\psi_1 = \langle \mathbb{AF}^k, \mathbb{LP}^m \rangle$ *and* $(\Gamma_{k+1}, \dots, \Gamma_n)$ *is the AFLP state of* $\psi_2 = \langle \mathbb{AF}_{k+1}^n, \mathbb{LP}^m \rangle$ *where* $\mathbb{AF}_{k+1}^n = (AF_{\omega_{k+1}}^{k+1}, \dots, AF_{\omega_n}^n)$.

3.3 Bidirectional Framework

In Sects. 3.1 and 3.2 we provided frameworks in which given LPs and AFs one refers the other in one direction. This subsection provides a framework such that LPs and AFs interact with each other. Such a situation happens in social media, for instance, where a person posts his/her opinion to an Internet forum, which arises public discussion on the topic, then the person revises his/her belief by the result of discussion. In this subsection, we assume that any rule in LP could contain arguments in its head or body.

Definition 15. A *simple bidirectional LPAF framework* is defined as a pair $\langle\langle LP_\mu, AF_\omega \rangle\rangle$ where LP_μ is a logic program and AF_ω is an argumentation framework.

Definition 16. Let $\zeta = \langle\langle LP_\mu, AF_\omega \rangle\rangle$ be a simple bidirectional LPAF framework. Suppose that a simple AFLP framework $\psi = \langle AF_\omega, LP_\mu \rangle$ has the set of AFLP extensions $\mathbf{E}_\psi$. Then a *BDLPAF model* of ζ is defined as a μ model of LP_μ extended by $\mathbf{E}_\psi$.

BDLPAF models reduce to LPAF models if $\mathbf{E}_\psi$ coincides with $\mathscr{E}_{AF}^\omega$. In the bidirectional framework, an LP can refer to arguments in AF and AF can get a support from the LP.

Example 6. Consider $\zeta = \langle\langle LP_{stb}, AF_{stb} \rangle\rangle$ where $LP_{stb} = \{u \leftarrow not\, p, \quad q \leftarrow c\}$ and $AF_{stb} = (\{a,b,c\}, \{(a,b),(b,a),(b,c)\})$. The simple AFLP framework $\langle AF_{stb}, LP_{stb} \rangle$ has the AFLP extension $E = \{a,c\}$. So, the BDLPAF model of ζ becomes $\{a,c,q\}$.

Similarly, we can make a simple AFLP bidirectional.

Definition 17. A *simple bidirectional AFLP framework* is defined as a pair $\langle\langle AF_\omega, LP_\mu \rangle\rangle$ where AF_ω is an argumentation framework and LP_μ is a logic program.

Definition 18. Let $\eta = \langle\langle AF_\omega, LP_\mu \rangle\rangle$ be a simple bidirectional AFLP framework. Suppose that a simple LPAF framework $\varphi = \langle LP_\mu, AF_\omega \rangle$ has the set of LPAF models $\mathbf{M}_\varphi$. Then a *BDAFLP extension* of η is defined as an ω extension of AF_ω supported by $\mathbf{M}_\varphi$.

Example 7. Consider $\eta = \langle\langle AF_{grd}, LP_{stb} \rangle\rangle$ where $AF_{grd} = (\{a,b\}, \{(a,b),(b,a)\})$ and $LP_{stb} = \{p \leftarrow a, \quad q \leftarrow not\, a, \quad b \leftarrow q\}$. The simple LPAF framework $\langle LP_{stb}, AF_{grd} \rangle$ has the single LPAF model $M = \{b,q\}$. So, the BDAFLP extension of η becomes $\{b\}$.

Given AF_ω and LP_μ, a series of BDLPAF models (or BDAFLP extensions) can be built by repeatedly referring to each other. Starting with the AFLP extensions $\mathbf{E}_\psi^0$, the BDLPAF models $\mathbf{M}_\varphi^1$ extended by $\mathbf{E}_\psi^0$ are produced, then the BDAFLP extensions $\mathbf{E}_\psi^1$ supported by $\mathbf{M}_\varphi^1$ are produced, which in turn produce the BDLPAF models $\mathbf{M}_\varphi^2$ extended by $\mathbf{E}_\psi^1$, and so on. Likewise, starting with the LPAF models $\mathbf{M}_\varphi^0$, the sets $\mathbf{E}_\psi^1$, $\mathbf{M}_\varphi^1$, $\mathbf{E}_\psi^2$, …, are produced. We write the sequences of BDLPAF models and BDAFLP extensions as $[\mathbf{M}_\varphi^1, \mathbf{M}_\varphi^2, \ldots]$ and $[\mathbf{E}_\psi^1, \mathbf{E}_\psi^2, \ldots]$, respectively.

Proposition 7. Let $[\mathbf{M}_\varphi^1, \mathbf{M}_\varphi^2, \ldots]$ and $[\mathbf{E}_\psi^1, \mathbf{E}_\psi^2, \ldots]$ be sequences defined as above. Then, $\mathbf{M}_\varphi^i = \mathbf{M}_\varphi^{i+1}$ and $\mathbf{E}_\psi^j = \mathbf{E}_\psi^{j+1}$ for some $i, j \geq 1$.

4   Applications

4.1   Deductive Argumentation

A *structured argumentation* is a framework such that there is an internal structure to an argument. In structured argumentation, knowledge is represented using a formal language and each argument is constructed from that knowledge. Given a logical language $\mathscr{L}$ and a consequence relation $\vdash$ in $\mathscr{L}$, a *deductive argument* [2] is a pair $\langle \mathscr{F}, c \rangle$ where $\mathscr{F}$ is a set of formulas in $\mathscr{L}$ and c is a (ground) atom such that $\mathscr{F} \vdash c$. $\mathscr{F}$ is called the *support* of the argument and c is the *claim*. A *counterargument* is an argument that attacks another argument. It is defined in terms of logical contradiction between the claim of a counterargument and the premises of the claim of an attacked argument.

An AFLP framework is captured as a kind of deductive arguments in the sense that *LP* can support an argument a appearing in *AF*. There is an important difference, however. In an AFLP, argumentative reasoning in AF and deductive reasoning in LP are separated. The AF part is kept at the abstract level and the LP part represents reasons for supporting particular arguments. As such, an AFLP provides a middle ground between abstract argumentation and structured argumentation. Such a separation keeps the whole structure compact and makes it easy to update AF or LP without changing the other part. Thus, AFLP/LPAF supports an elaboration tolerant development of knowledge bases. This allows us to characterize deductive argumentation in AFLP as follows.

Definition 19. Let $\psi = \langle \mathbb{AF}^n, \mathbb{LP}^m \rangle$ be a general AFLP framework s.t. $AF_{\omega_i}^i = (A^i, R^i)$ $(1 \leq i \leq n)$. (i) $a \in A^i$ is *supported* in $LP_{\mu_j}^j$ for some $1 \leq j \leq m$ (written $(LP_{\mu_j}^j, a)$) if $LP_{\mu_j}^j \models a$; (ii) $(LP_{\mu_j}^j, a)$ and $(LP_{\mu_k}^k, b)$ *rebut* each other if $\{(a, b), (b, a)\} \subseteq R^i$ for some i; (iii) $(LP_{\mu_j}^j, a)$ *undercuts* $(LP_{\mu_k}^k, b)$ if $LP_{\mu_k}^k \cup \{a\} \not\models b$.

Example 8. ([2]) (a) There is an argument that the government should cut spending because of a budget deficit. On the other hand, there is a counterargument that the government should not cut spending because the economy is weak. These arguments are respectively represented using deductive arguments as: $A1 = \langle \{deficit, \ deficit \rightarrow cut\}, \ cut \rangle$ and $A2 = \langle \{weak, \ weak \rightarrow \neg cut\}, \ \neg cut \rangle$ where $A1$ and $A2$ rebut each other. The situation is represented using the AFLP $\langle (AF_{stb}), (LP_{stb}^1, LP_{stb}^2) \rangle$ such that $AF_{stb} = (\{cut, no\text{-}cut\}, \{(cut, no\text{-}cut), (no\text{-}cut, cut)\})$; $LP_{stb}^1 = \{cut \leftarrow deficit, \ deficit \leftarrow \}$; $LP_{stb}^2 = \{no\text{-}cut \leftarrow weak, \ weak \leftarrow \}$. Then (LP_{stb}^1, cut) and $(LP_{stb}^2, no\text{-}cut)$ rebut each other.

(b) There is an argument that the metro is an efficient (*eff*) form of transport, so one can use it. On the other hand, there is a counterargument that the metro is inefficient (*ineff*) because of a strike. These arguments are respectively represented using deductive arguments as: $A1 = \langle \{eff, \ eff \rightarrow use\}, \ use \rangle$ and $A2 = \langle \{strike, \ strike \rightarrow \neg eff\}, \ \neg eff \rangle$ where $A2$ undercuts $A1$. The situation is represented using an AFLP $\langle (AF_{stb}), (LP_{stb}^1, LP_{stb}^2) \rangle$ such that $AF_{stb} = (\{eff, ineff\}, \{(eff, ineff), (ineff, eff)\})$; $LP_{stb}^1 = \{use \leftarrow eff, \ eff \leftarrow not\, ineff\}$; $LP_{stb}^2 = \{ineff \leftarrow strike, \ strike \leftarrow \}$. Then $(LP_{stb}^2, ineff)$ undercuts (LP_{stb}^1, use).

4.2   Argument Aggregation

Argument aggregation or *collective argumentation* [3] considers a situation in which multiple agents may have different arguments and/or opinions. The problems are then what and how to aggregate arguments. In abstract argumentation, the problem is formulated as follows. Given several AFs having different arguments and attacks, find acceptable arguments among those AFs. In the *argument-wise aggregation*, individually supported arguments are aggregated by some voting mechanism.

Example 9. ([3]) Suppose three agents deciding which among three arguments a, b, and c, are collectively acceptable. Each agent has a subjective evaluation of the interaction among those arguments, leading to three different individual AFs: $AF_1 = (\{a,b,c\}, \{(a,b),(b,c)\})$, $AF_2 = (\{a,b,c\}, \{(a,b)\})$, and $AF_3 = (\{a,b,c\}, \{(b,c)\})$. Three AFs have the grounded extensions $\{a,c\}$, $\{a,c\}$, and $\{a,b\}$, respectively. By majority voting, $\{a,c\}$ is obtained as the collective extension.

In Example 9, however, how an agent performs a subjective evaluation is left as a black-box. The situation is represented using a general AFLP ψ where $\psi = \langle (AF_{grd}), (LP_{stb}^1, LP_{stb}^2, LP_{stb}^3) \rangle$ with $AF_{grd} = (\{a,b,c\}, \{(a,b),(b,c)\})$, $LP_{stb}^1 = \{p \leftarrow not\, q\}$, $LP_{stb}^2 = \{c \leftarrow p, \quad p \leftarrow\}$, and $LP_{stb}^3 = \{b \leftarrow not\, q\}$. Then (AF_{grd}, LP_{stb}^1) has the AFLP extension $\{a,c\}$; (AF_{grd}, LP_{stb}^2) has the AFLP extension $\{a,c\}$; (AF_{grd}, LP_{stb}^3) has the AFLP extension $\{a,b\}$. In this case, the AFLP state of ψ is (Γ) with $\Gamma = (\{\{a,c\}\}, \{\{a,c\}\}, \{\{a,b\}\})$. As such, three agents evaluate the common AF based on their private knowledge base, which results in three individual sets of extensions in the AFLP state. Observe that in this case, the private knowledge of the agents are related to p and q, and only the third agent is *influenced* by his private knowledge base in drawing the conclusion.

When multiple agents argue on the common AF, argument-wise aggregation is characterized using AFLP as follows. Suppose $\Gamma = (T_1, \ldots, T_k)$ $(k \geq 1)$ with $T_i \subseteq 2^A$ where A is the set of arguments of AF. For any $E \subseteq A$, let $\mathscr{F}_\Gamma(E) = h$ where h is the number of occurrences of E in $T_1, \ldots, T_k$. Define $max\mathscr{F}_\Gamma = \{E \mid \mathscr{F}_\Gamma(E) \text{ is maximal}\}$.

Definition 20. Let $\psi = \langle \mathbb{AF}^1, \mathbb{LP}^m \rangle$ $(m \geq 1)$ be a general AFLP that consists of a single AF and multiple LPs. When ψ has the AFLP state (Γ) with $\Gamma = (T_1, \ldots, T_m)$, the *collective extension* by majority voting is any extension in $max\mathscr{F}_\Gamma$.

Applying it to the above example, $max\mathscr{F}_\Gamma = \{\{a,c\}\}$. In Definition 20, if there is $E \subseteq A$ such that $\mathscr{F}_\Gamma(E) = m$, then E is included in every T_i $(1 \leq i \leq m)$. In this case, all agents *agree on E*.

4.3   Multi-context System

Multi-context system (MCS) has been introduced as a general formalism for integrating heterogeneous knowledge bases [4]. An MCS $M = (C_1, \ldots, C_n)$ consists of contexts $C_i = (L_i, kb_i, br_i)$ $(1 \leq i \leq n)$, where $L_i = (KB_i, BS_i, ACC_i)$ is a logic, $kb_i \in KB_i$ is a knowledge base of L_i, BS_i is the set of possible belief sets, $ACC_i : KB_i \mapsto 2^{BS_i}$ is a semantic function of L_i, and br_i is a set of L_i-bridge rules of the form:

$$s \leftarrow (c_1:p_1), \dots, (c_j:p_j), not(c_{j+1}:p_{j+1}), \dots, not(c_m:p_m)$$

where, for each $1 \leq k \leq m$, we have that: $1 \leq c_k \leq n$, p_k is an element of some belief set of L_{c_k}, and $kb_i \cup \{s\} \in KB_i$. Intuitively, a bridge rule allows us to add s to a context, depending on the beliefs in the other contexts. Given a rule r of the above form, we denote $head(r) = s$. The semantics of an MCS is described by the notion of belief states. A *belief state* of an MCS $M = (C_1, \dots, C_n)$ is a tuple $S = (S_1, \dots, S_n)$ where $S_i \in BS_i$ $(1 \leq i \leq n)$. Given a belief state S and a bridge rule r of the above form, r is *applicable* in S if $p_\ell \in S_{c_\ell}$ for each $1 \leq \ell \leq j$ and $p_k \notin S_{c_k}$ for each $j+1 \leq k \leq m$. By $app(B, S)$ we denote the set of the bridge rules $r \in B$ that are applicable in S. A belief state S of M is an *equilibrium* if $S_i \in ACC_i(kb_i \cup \{head(r) \mid r \in app(br_i, S)\})$ for any i $(1 \leq i \leq n)$.

Given an LPAF $\varphi = \langle LP_\mu, AF_\omega \rangle$, the *corresponding MCS* of φ is defined by $\varphi_{mcs} = (C_1, C_2)$ where $C_1 = (L_1, LP_\mu, br_1)$ in which L_1 is the logic of LP under the μ semantics and $br_1 = \{a \leftarrow (c_2 : a) \mid a \in A \mid_{LP}\}$; and $C_2 = (L_2, AF_\omega, \varnothing)$ where L_2 is the logic of AF under the ω semantics. Intuitively, the bridge rules transfer the acceptability of arguments in AF_ω to LP_μ.

Proposition 8. *Let* $\varphi = \langle LP_\mu, AF_\omega \rangle$ *be an LPAF framework and* φ_{mcs} *the corresponding MCS of* φ. *If* AF_ω *is consistent then* (S_1, S_2) *is an equilibrium of* φ_{mcs} *iff* S_1 *is an LPAF model of* φ *and* S_2 *is an* ω *extension of* AF_ω.

Let $\psi = \langle AF_\omega, LP_\mu \rangle$ be an AFLP framework with $AF_\omega = (A, R)$. The *corresponding MCS* of ψ is defined by $\psi_{mcs} = (C_1, C_2)$ where $C_1 = (L_1, AF_\omega, br_1)$ in which L_1 is the logic of AF under the ω semantics, and $br_1 = \{(y, x) \leftarrow (c_2 : a) \mid \exists a \exists x [a \in A \cap \mathscr{B}_{LP} \text{ and } (x, a) \in R]\}$ where $y(\notin A)$ is a new argument; $C_2 = (L_2, LP_\mu, \varnothing)$ where L_2 is the logic of LP under the μ semantics. As with LPAF, the bridge rules transfer the acceptability of arguments from LP_μ to AF_ω. We assume that new arguments and attacks introduced by the bridge rules br_1 are respectively added to the set of arguments and attacks of AF.

Proposition 9. *Let* $\psi = \langle AF_\omega, LP_\mu \rangle$ *be an AFLP framework and* ψ_{mcs} *the corresponding MCS of* ψ. *If* LP_μ *is consistent then* (S_1, S_2) *is an equilibrium of* ψ_{mcs} *iff* $S_1 \setminus Y$ *is an AFLP extension of* ψ *and* S_2 *is a* μ *model of* LP_μ, *where* Y *is the set of new arguments introduced by* br_1.

A general LPAF $\varphi = \langle \mathbb{LP}_m, \mathbb{AF}_n \rangle$ can be viewed as a collection of MCS. Let C_i^j be the corresponding MCS of $\langle LP_{\mu_i}^i, AF_{\omega_j}^j \rangle$. It is easy to see that by Proposition 8, $(C_i^1, \dots, C_i^n)$ can be used to characterize the i-th element Σ_i of the LPAF state $(\Sigma_1, \dots, \Sigma_m)$ of φ. A similar characterization of an AFLP state using MCS could be derived by Proposition 9. A simple LPAF/AFLP is captured as an MCS with a restriction of two systems (Propositions 8 and 9). However, φ_{mcs} (resp. ψ_{mcs}) is well-defined only if its submodule AF_ω (resp. LP_μ) is *consistent*. This is because an MCS assumes that each context is consistent. By contrast, LPAF/AFLP just neglects rules/arguments relying on information that comes from inconsistent AF/LP. As such, LPAF/AFLP shares a view similar to MCS while it is *different* from MCS in general.

4.4 Constrained Argumentation Frameworks

Constrained argumentation frameworks (CAF) [13] could be viewed as another attempt to extend AF with a logical component. A CAF is of the form $\langle A,R,C \rangle$ where (A,R) is an AF and C is a propositional formula over A. A set of arguments S satisfies C if $S \cup \{\neg a \mid a \in A \setminus S\} \models C$. For a semantics ω, an ω *C-extension* of $\langle A,R,C \rangle$ is an ω extension of (A,R) that satisfies C, i.e., the constraint C is used to eliminate undesirable extensions. Therefore, a CAF can be viewed as an LPAF (LP_μ, AF_ω) where AF_ω is the original AF of the CAF and LP_μ is used to verify the condition C.

Consider a CAF $\delta = \langle A,R,C \rangle$. For simplicity of the presentation, assume that C is in DNF. For $a \in A$, let na be a unique new atom associated with a, denoting that a is not acceptable. Let $\top$ be a special atom denoting *true*. Define the logic program $LP(C)$ as: $LP(C) = \{ \top \leftarrow l_1', \dots, l_n' \mid$ a conjunct $l_1 \wedge \cdots \wedge l_n$ is in C and $l_i' = a$ if $l_i = a$, and $l_i' = not\ a$ if $l_i = \neg a\} \cup \{na \leftarrow not\ a, \ \leftarrow a, na \mid a \in A\} \cup \{\leftarrow not\ \top\}$. We can easily verify that a set of arguments S satisfies C iff $S \cup \{na \mid a \in A \setminus S\} \cup \{\top\}$ is a stable model of $LP(C)$. The next proposition highlights the flexibility of LPAF in that it can also be used to express preferences among extensions of AF.

Proposition 10. *Let* $\delta = \langle A,R,C \rangle$ *be a CAF. Then,* $(LP(C)_{stb}, AF_\omega)$ *has an LPAF model* M *iff* $M \setminus (\{na \mid a \in A\} \cup \{\top\})$ *is an* ω *C-extension of* δ.

5 Complexity

The complexity of LPAF/AFLP depends on the complexities of LP and AF. Let us consider the *model existence problem* of simple LPAF frameworks, denoted by $\texttt{Exists}^M$, which is defined as: "*given an LPAF framework* φ*, determine whether* φ *has an LPAF model.*" For a simple LPAF framework $\varphi = \langle LP_\mu, AF_\omega \rangle$, the existence of an LPAF model of φ depends on μ and ω. For example, if $\mu = $ *well-founded* and $\omega = $ *grounded* then φ has a unique LPAF model which can be computed in polynomial time (if LP is a normal logic program); on the other hand, if $\mu = $ *stable* and $\omega = $ *stable* then the existence of an LPAF model of φ is not guaranteed. Generally, the next result holds.

Proposition 11. *Let* $\varphi = \langle LP_\mu, AF_\omega \rangle$ *be a simple LPAF framework such that* μ *is not universal. Also, let* C_μ *and* C_ω *be the complexity classes of* LP_μ *and* AF_ω *in the polynomial hierarchy, respectively, and* $\max(C_\mu, C_\omega)$ *the higher complexity class among* C_μ *and* C_ω*. Then the model existence problem of* φ *belongs to the complexity class* $\max(C_\mu, C_\omega)$.

Intuitively, the result follows from the observation that we can guess a pair (X,Y) and check whether Y is an ω extension of AF_ω and X is a μ model of $LP_\mu \cup \{a \leftarrow \mid a \in Y \cap A \mid_{LP}\}$. A similar argument is done for a simple AFLP framework. As an example, the existence of a stable model of a propositional disjunctive LP is in Σ_2^P [9] while the existence of extensions in AF is generally in NP or trivial [8], then $\texttt{Exists}^M$ for LPAF/AFLP involving $\mu = $ *stable* is in Σ_2^P where ω is one of the semantics of AF considered in this paper. Other semantics of AF (e.g. semi-stable, ideal, etc.) or LP (e.g. supported, possible models, etc.) can be easily adapted.

The model existence problem of simple LPAF/AFLP can be generalized to the state existence problem of general LPAF/AFLP frameworks, and it can be shown that it is the highest complexity class among all complexity classes involved in the general framework. Similar arguments can be used to determine the complexity class of credulous or skeptical reasoning in LPAF/AFLP. For example, the skeptical entailment in LPAF, i.e., checking whether an atom a belongs to every LPAF model of $\varphi = \langle LP_{stb}, AF_\omega \rangle$ is in Π_2^P. We omit detailed discussion for space limitation.

6   Concluding Remarks

Several studies have attempted to integrate LP and AF–translating from one into the other (e.g. [5,6]), or incorporating rule bases into an AF in the context of structured argumentation (e.g. [2,7]). An approach taken in this paper is completely different from those approaches. We do not merge LP and AF while interlinking two components in different manners. LPAF and AFLP enable to combine different reasoning tasks while keeping independence of each knowledge representation. Separation of two frameworks also has an advantage of flexibility in dynamic environments, and several LPs and AFs are freely combined in general LPAF/AFLP frameworks under arbitrary semantics. In addition, it supports an elaboration tolerant use of various knowledge representation frameworks. The potential of the proposed framework is shown by several applications to existing KR frameworks. LPAF or AFLP is realized by linking solvers of LP and AF.

In the proposed framework, LP imports ω extensions from AF in LPAF, while AF imports μ models from LP in AFLP. We can also consider frameworks such that LP (resp. AF) imports *skeptical/credulous consequences* from AF_ω (resp. LP_μ). Such frameworks are realized by importing the intersection/union of ω extensions of AF to LP (or μ models of LP to AF). In this paper we considered extension based semantics of AF. If we consider the *labelling based semantics* of AF, each argument has three different justification states, *in*, *out*, or *undecided*. In this case, LPAF/AFLP is defined in a similar manner by selecting a 3-valued semantics of logic programs. The current framework can be further extended and applied in several ways. For instance, we can extend it to allow a single LP/AF to refer to multiple AFs/LPs. If AF_ω is coupled with a *probabilistic logic program* LP_μ, an AFLP (AF_ω, LP_μ) could be used for computing probabilities of arguments in LP_μ and realizing *probabilistic argumentation* in AF_ω [12]. As such, the proposed framework has potential for rich applications in AI.

References

1. Baumann, R.: Context-free and context-sensitive kernels: update and deletion equivalence in abstract argumentation. In: Proceedings of the ECAI 2014, pp. 63–68. IOS Press (2014)
2. Besnard, P., Hunter, A.: Constructing argument graphs with deductive arguments: a tutorial. Argum. Comput. 5(1), 5–30 (2014)
3. Bodanza, G., Tohmé, F., Auday, M.: Collective argumentation: a survey of aggregation issues around argumentation frameworks. Argum. Comput. 8(1), 1–34 (2017)
4. Brewka, G., Eiter, T.: Equilibria in heterogeneous nonmonotonic multi-context systems. In: AAAI'07, pp. 385–390 (2007)

5. Caminada, M., Sá, S., Alcântara, J., Dvořák, W.: On the equivalence between logic programming semantics and argumentation semantics. J. Approx. Reason. **58**, 87–111 (2015)
6. Dung, P.M.: On the acceptability of arguments and its fundamental role in nonmonotonic reasoning, logic programming and n-person games. Artif. Intell. **77**, 321–357 (1995)
7. Dung, P.M., Kowalski, R.A., Toni, F.: Assumption-based argumentation. In: Rahwan, I., Simari, G.R. (Eds.) Argumentation in Artificial Intelligence, pp. 199–218. Springer, Boston (2009). https://doi.org/10.1007/978-0-387-98197-0_10
8. Dvořák, W., Dunne, P.E.: Computational problems in formal argumentation and their complexity. In: Handbook of Formal Argumentation, pp. 631–688. College Publications (2018)
9. Eiter, T., Leone, N., Saccá, D.: Expressive power and complexity of partial models for disjunctive deductive databases. Theor. Comput. Sci. **206**, 181–218 (1998)
10. Eiter, T., Fink, M., Woltran, S.: Semantical characterizations and complexity of equivalences in answer set programming. ACM TOCL **8**(3), 17 (2007)
11. Gelfond, M., Lifschitz, V.: The stable model semantics for logic programming. In: Proceedings of the JICSLP, pp. 1070–1080. MIT Press (1988)
12. Hunter, A.: A probabilistic approach to modelling uncertain logical arguments. J. Approx. Reason. **54**, 47–81 (2013)
13. Coste-Marquis, S., Devred, C., Marquis, P.: Constrained argumentation frameworks. In: Proceedings of the KR'06, pp. 112–122 (2006)
14. Przymusinski, T.C.: Stable semantics for disjunctive programs. New Gen. Comput. **9**, 401–424 (1991)
15. Sakama, C., Son, T.C.: Interlinking logic programs and argumentation frameworks. In: Proceeding of the NMR-2021, pp. 305–314 (2021). https://sites.google.com/view/nmr2021/home
16. Van Gelder, A., Ross, K., Schlipf, J.S.: The well-founded semantics for general logic programs. J. ACM **38**, 620–650 (1991)

Gradient-Based Supported Model Computation in Vector Spaces

Akihiro Takemura[1,2(✉)] and Katsumi Inoue[1,2]

[1] Department of Informatics, The Graduate University for Advanced Studies,
SOKENDAI, Tokyo, Japan
[2] National Institute of Informatics, Tokyo, Japan
{atakemura,inoue}@nii.ac.jp

Abstract. We propose a method for computing supported models of normal logic programs in vector spaces using gradient information. First, the program is translated into a definite program and embedded into a matrix representing the program. We introduce a loss function based on the implementation of the immediate consequence operator T_P by matrix-vector multiplication with a suitable thresholding function, and we incorporate regularization terms into the loss function to avoid undesirable results. The proposed thresholding operation is an almost everywhere differentiable alternative to the non-linear thresholding operation. We report the results of several experiments where our method shows promising performance when used with adaptive gradient update.

Keywords: Logic Programming · Supported Model Computation · Differentiable Logic Programming

1 Introduction

With the recent interest in neuro-symbolic approaches, performing logical inference with linear algebraic methods has been studied as an attractive alternative to symbolic methods [2,9]. Prior implementations of neuro-symbolic systems provided interfaces for the symbolic reasoning engines to handle the outputs from the neural networks as neural predicates [6,12]. However, more direct realization of logic programming in continuous domain remains an open challenge.

Matrix representations of normal logic programs and a linear algebraic method for computing the stable models were proposed by Sakama et al. [9]. Using an alternative matrix representation, Sato et al. computed supported models in vector spaces via 3-valued completion models of normal logic programs [11]. While the aforementioned methods would allow one to compute models under non-monotonic semantics in vector spaces, they use non-differentiable operations that do not use gradient-information. More recently, gradient-based search methods have been proposed for SAT [10], supported and stable model computation [2]. Aspis et al.'s method uses a matrix representation of the program reduct, the Newton's method for root finding to find fixed points, and a parameterized

© The Author(s), under exclusive license to Springer Nature Switzerland AG 2022
G. Gottlob et al. (Eds.): LPNMR 2022, LNAI 13416, pp. 336–349, 2022.
https://doi.org/10.1007/978-3-031-15707-3_26

sigmoid function for thresholding. Compared to symbolic local search methods that flip one atom at a time [4], matrix- and gradient-based methods update all assignments simultaneously in continuous domain, which may reduce the number of restarts compared to discrete value search.

In the context of gradient-based search, many variations are possible for each component. In this paper, we build upon previous works [2,10] by presenting an alternative differentiable method for efficiently computing supported models of normal logic programs in continuous vector spaces. Our main contributions are:

- Presenting an alternative method for embedding logic programs into matrices, and designing an almost everywhere differentiable thresholding function.
- Introducing a loss function with regularization terms for computing supported models, and integrating various gradient update strategies.
- Demonstrating with a help of systematic performance evaluation on a range of programs, that by selecting appropriate components, it is possible to achieve much higher performance and stability than the existing method.

The structure of this paper is as follows: Sect. 2 covers the necessary background and definitions. Section 3 presents a method for representing logic programs with matrices. Section 4 introduces the thresholding function, loss function, and the gradient-based search algorithm for supported models. Section 5 presents the results of experiments designed to test the ability of the algorithm. Finally, Sect. 6 presents the conclusion.

2 Background

We consider a language $\mathcal{L}$ that contains a finite set of propositional variables defined over a finite alphabet and the logical connectives $\neg$, $\wedge$, $\vee$ and $\leftarrow$. The *Herbrand base*, B_P, is the set of all propositional variables in a logic program P.

A *definite program* is a set of *rules* of the form (1) or (2), where h and b_i are propositional variables (*atoms*) in $\mathcal{L}$. We refer to (2) as an *OR-rule*, which is a shorthand for m rules: $h \leftarrow b_1, h \leftarrow b_2, \ldots, h \leftarrow b_m$. For each rule r we define $head(r) = h$ and $body(r) = \{b_1, \ldots, b_m\}$. A rule r is a *fact* if $body(r) = \emptyset$.

$$h \leftarrow b_1 \wedge b_2 \wedge \cdots \wedge b_m (m \geq 0) \tag{1}$$

$$h \leftarrow b_1 \vee b_2 \vee \cdots \vee b_m (m \geq 0) \tag{2}$$

A *normal program* is a set of rules of the form (3) where h and b_i are propositional variables in $\mathcal{L}$.

$$h \leftarrow b_1 \wedge b_2 \wedge \cdots \wedge b_l \wedge \neg b_{l+1} \wedge \neg b_{l+2} \wedge \cdots \wedge \neg b_m (m \geq l \geq 0) \tag{3}$$

We refer to the positive and negative occurrences of atoms in the body as $body^+(r) = \{b_1, \ldots, b_l\}$ and $body^-(r) = \{b_{l+1}, \ldots, b_m\}$, respectively. A normal program is a definite program if $body^-(r) = \emptyset$ for every rule $r \in P$.

An *Herbrand interpretation* I, of a normal program P is a subset of B_P. A *model* M of P is an interpretation of P where for every rule $r \in P$ of the form

(3), $body^+(r) \subseteq M$ and $body^-(r) \cap M = \emptyset$ imply $h \in M$. A program is called *consistent* if it has a model. A *supported model* M is a model of P where for every $p \in M$ there exists a rule $r \in P$ such that $p = h$, $body^+(r) \subseteq M$ and $body^-(r) \cap M = \emptyset$ [1,7].

As we shall show later, in this paper we transform normal logic programs into definite programs for searching supported models. Thus, we use the following definition of the immediate consequence operator T_P. $T_P : 2^{B_P} \to 2^{B_P}$ is a function on Herbrand interpretations. For a definite program P, we have: $T_P(I) = \{h | h \leftarrow b_1 \wedge \cdots \wedge b_m \in P \text{ and } \{b_1, \ldots, b_m\} \subseteq I\} \cup \{h | h \leftarrow b_1 \vee \cdots \vee b_m \in P \text{ and } \{b_1, \ldots, b_m\} \cap I \neq \emptyset\}$. It is known that a supported model M of a program P is a fixed point of T_P, i.e. $T_P(M) = M$ [7].

Definition 1 (Singly-Defined (SD) Program). *A normal program P is an SD-program if $head(r_1) \neq head(r_2)$ for any two rules r_1 and r_2 $(r_1 \neq r_2)$ in P.*

Any normal program P can be converted into an SD-program P' in the following manner. If there are more than one rule with the same head $\{h \leftarrow body(r_1), \ldots, h \leftarrow body(r_k)\}$, where $k > 1$, then replace them with a set of new rules including an OR-rule of the form (2) $\{h \leftarrow b_1 \vee \ldots \vee b_k, b_1 \leftarrow body(r_1), \ldots, b_k \leftarrow body(r_k)\}$ containing new atoms $\{b_1, \ldots, b_k\}$. This is a stricter condition than the *multiple definitions condition* (*MD-condition*) [9]: for any two rules r_1 and r_2 in P, (i) $head(r_1) = head(r_2)$ implies $|body^+(r_1)| \leq 1$ and $|body^+(r_2)| \leq 1$, and (ii) $body^-(r_1) \cap body^-(r_2) \neq \emptyset$ implies $|body^+(r_1)| \leq 1$ and $|body^+(r_2)| \leq 1$. All SD-programs satisfy the MD condition. We shall assume all programs in this paper are SD-programs.

Given a normal program P, it is transformed into a definite program by replacing the negated literals in rules of the form (3) and rewriting:

$$h \leftarrow b_1 \wedge b_2 \wedge \cdots \wedge b_l \wedge \overline{b}_{l+1} \wedge \overline{b}_{l+2} \wedge \cdots \wedge \overline{b}_m (m \geq l \geq 0) \qquad (4)$$

where $\overline{b}_i$ are new atoms associated with the negated b_i. A collection of rules of the form (4) is referred to as the *positive form* P^+ where $B_{P^+} = B_P \cup \{\overline{a} \mid a \in B_P\}$. For transformed rules of the form (4), we refer to $\{b_1, \ldots, b_l\}$ as the *positive part* and $\{\overline{b}_{l+1}, \ldots, \overline{b}_m\}$ as the *negative part*. After transformation, the program should contain rules of the forms (1), (2), or (4). By an interpretation I^+ of P^+, we mean any set of atoms $I^+ \subseteq B_{P^+}$ that satisfies the condition for any atom $a \in B_{P^+}$, precisely one of either a or $\overline{a}$ belongs to I^+.

3 Representing Logic Programs with Matrices

3.1 Relationship Between Positive Forms and Supported Models

Consider a program $p \leftarrow \neg p$, and its positive form $p \leftarrow \overline{p}$. P^+ is a definite program, but it has no supported models in this case due to the restriction we place on the interpretation: if $p \in I^+$ then $\overline{p} \notin I^+$ and vice versa. Then in this case, the implication is that there are no fixed points of T_{P^+} for P^+ that satisfy the condition $p \in I^+$ iff $\overline{p} \notin I^+$. On the other hand, when a model M of P exists, we can show that the corresponding M^+ is a model of P^+.

Proposition 1. *Let P be a normal program, and let P^+ be its positive form. If M is a model of P, then $M' = M \cup \{\bar{a} \,|\, a \in B_{P+} \setminus M\}$ is a model of P^+. Conversely, if M^+ is a model of P^+, then $M^+ \cap B_P$ is a model of P.*

Proof. Follows from the definition of M' and M^+. Consider M'. Since $a \notin M'$ if $\bar{a} \in M'$ and vice versa, for each rule $r \in P^+$, $body(r) \subseteq M'$ implies $head(r) = a \in M'$. Thus, M' is a model of P^+. Now consider M^+. Let $K = M^+ \cap B_P$ such that $a \in K$ if $a \in M^+$. Given that M^+ is a model of P^+, for each rule $r \in P$, $body^+(r) \subseteq K$ and $body^-(r) \cap K = \emptyset$ implies $head(r) = a \in K$. Thus, K is a model of P.

Proposition 2. *Let M be a supported model of P, and put $M' = M \cup \{\bar{a} \,|\, a \in B_{P+} \setminus M\}$. Then, $T_{P+}(M') = M$.*

Proof. Suppose $a \in M$. Since M is a supported model, there exists a rule $r \in P$ such that $head(r) = a$, $body^+(r) \subseteq M$ and $body^-(r) \cap M = \emptyset$. Correspondingly, there exists a rule $r' \in P^+$ such that $head(r') = a$, $body^+(r') \subseteq M'$ and $body^-(r') \subseteq M'$. That is, $a \in T_{P+}(M')$. Hence, $M \subseteq T_{P+}(M')$.

Conversely, suppose $a \in T_{P+}(M')$. Then, there exists a rule $r' \in P^+$ such that $head(r') = a$ and $body(r') \subseteq M'$. Since M' is a model of P^+ by Proposition 1, $body(r') \subseteq M'$ implies $head(r') = a \in M'$. Because a is a positive literal, $a \in M$ holds. Hence, $T_{P+}(M') \subseteq M$. Therefore, $M = T_{P+}(M')$.

Proposition 3. *Let M' be an interpretation of P^+. If $T_{P+}(M^+) = M^+ \cap B_P$ holds, then $M = M^+ \cap B_P$ is a supported model of P.*

Proof. Suppose $T_{P+}(M^+) = M^+ \cap B_P$. Because $M^+ \cap B_P$ recovers the positive literals from M^+, for each $a \in (M^+ \cap B_P)$, there exists a rule $r \in P$ such that $head(r) = a$, $body^+(r) \subseteq (M^+ \cap B_P)$ and $body^-(r) \cap (M^+ \cap B_P) = \emptyset$. Thus, $M = M^+ \cap B_P$ is a supported model of P.

3.2   Matrix Encoding of Logic Programs

In subsequent sections we shall use the following notations: matrices and vectors are represented as bold upper-case, $\mathbf{M}$, and lower-case letters, $\mathbf{v}$, respectively. A 1-vector with length N is represented by $\mathbf{1}_N$. The indices of the entries of matrices and vectors appear in the subscript, for example, $\mathbf{M}_{ij}$ refers to the element at i-th row and j-th column of a matrix $\mathbf{M}$ and $\mathbf{v}_i$ refers to the i-th element of a column vector $\mathbf{v}$. Let $\mathbf{M}_{i:}$ and $\mathbf{M}_{:j}$ denote the i-th row slice and j-th column slice of $\mathbf{M}$, respectively. We denote the horizontal concatenation of matrices $\mathbf{M}_1$ and $\mathbf{M}_2$ as $[\mathbf{M}_1\,\mathbf{M}_2]$, and denote the vertical concatenation of column vectors $\mathbf{v}_1$ and $\mathbf{v}_2$ as $[\mathbf{v}_1; \mathbf{v}_2]$.

Let P be a normal program with size $|B_P| = N$, P^+ its positive form and B_{P+} the Herbrand base of P^+. Then we have $|B_{P+}| = 2N$ since for every $b \in B_P$ we add its negated version $\bar{b}$. We encode atoms appearing in the bodies of the rules $\in P^+$ into a binary program matrix $\mathbf{Q} \in \mathbb{Z}^{N \times 2N}$.

Definition 2 (Program Matrix). *Let P be a normal program with $|B_P| = N$ and P^+ its positive form with $|B_{P+}| = 2N$. Then P^+ is represented by a matrix $\mathbf{Q} \in \mathbb{Z}^{N \times 2N}$ such that for each element $\mathbf{Q}_{ij}(1 \leq i \leq N, 1 \leq j \leq 2N)$ in $\mathbf{Q}$,*

- *$\mathbf{Q}_{ij} = 1$ if atom $a_j \in B_{P+}(1 \leq j \leq 2N)$ appears in the body of the rule $r_i(1 \leq i \leq N)$;*
- *$\mathbf{Q}_{ij} = 0$, otherwise.*

The i-th row of $\mathbf{Q}$ corresponds to the atom a_i appearing in the head of the rule r_i, and the j-th column corresponds to the atom $a_j(1 \leq j \leq 2N)$ appearing in the body of the rules $r_i(1 \leq i \leq N)$. Atoms that do not appear in the head of any of the rules in P^+ are encoded as zero-only row vectors in $\mathbf{Q}$.

This definition is different from the previous works [2,9], in that we do not explicitly include $\top$ and $\bot$ in the program matrix, and we do not use fractional values to encode long rules. In fact, our encoding method is similar to that of [11], except that we do not use $(2N \times 2N)$ space for the program matrix since we do not encode rules with $\bar{b} \in B_{P+}$ in the head.

Definition 3 (Interpretation Vector). *Let P be a definite program and $B_P = \{a_1, \ldots, a_N\}$. Then an interpretation $I \subseteq B_P$ is represented by a vector $\mathbf{v} = (\mathbf{v}_1, \ldots, \mathbf{v}_N)^\mathsf{T} \in \mathbb{Z}^N$ where each element $\mathbf{v}_i (1 \leq i \leq N)$ represents the truth value of the proposition a_i such that $\mathbf{v}_i = 1$ if $a_i \in I$, otherwise $\mathbf{v}_i = 0$. We assume propositional variables share the common index such that $\mathbf{v}_i$ corresponds to a_i, and we write $\mathrm{var}(\mathbf{v}_i) = a_i$.*

Recall that the positive form P^+ of a normal program is a definite program, and all negated literals in the body are replaced by new atoms, e.g. in (4) $\neg b_{l+1}$ is replaced by $\bar{b}_{l+1}$. We now extend the definition of interpretation vectors to include relations between the positive and negative occurrences of atoms, to maintain whenever we have $b_1 \in I$, $\bar{b}_{l+1} \notin I$ and vice versa.

Definition 4 (Companion Vector). *Let $B_{P+}^P \subseteq B_{P+}$ denote the positive part of P, $B_{P+}^N \subseteq B_{P+}$ denote the negative part of P, with size $|B_{P+}^P| = |B_{P+}^N| = N$. Let $\mathbf{v}^P \in \mathbb{Z}^N$ be a vector representing truth assignments for $a_i \in B_{P+}^P$ such that $\mathbf{v}_i^P = 1$ if $a_i \in I$ and $\mathbf{v}_i^P = 0$ otherwise. Define a companion vector $\mathbf{w} \in \mathbb{Z}^{2N}$ representing an interpretation $I^+ \subseteq B_{P+}$ as follows: $\mathbf{w} = [\mathbf{v}^P; \mathbf{1}_N - \mathbf{v}^P]$.*

4   Gradient Descent for Computing Supported Models

4.1   Computing the T_P Operator in Vector Spaces

Sakama et al. [9] showed that the T_P operator can be computed in vector spaces using θ-*thresholding*. Here we modify θ-thresholding to accommodate our program encoding method as well as the differentiability requirement.

In previous works [8,9], the information about the nature of the rules was also stored in the program matrix $\mathbf{Q}$ alongside the atom occurrences; conjunctive rules with $|body(r_i)| > 1$ had fractional values $\mathbf{Q}_{ij} = 1/|body(r_i)|$ and disjunctive bodies had integer values $\mathbf{Q}_{ij} = 1$. Instead, we only store the atom occurrence in $\mathbf{Q}$, and keep supplementary information in the parameter vector $\mathbf{t}$.

Definition 5 (Parameter Vector t). *A set of parameters to the θ-thresholding is a column vector $\mathbf{t} \in \mathbb{Z}^N$ such that for each element $\mathbf{t}_i (1 \leq i \leq N)$ in $\mathbf{t}$,*

- *$\mathbf{t}_i = |body(r_i)|$ if the rule $r_i \in P^+$ is a conjunctive rule, e.g. (1), (4);*
- *$\mathbf{t}_i = 1$ if the rule $r_i \in P^+$ is a disjunctive rule e.g. (2);*
- *$\mathbf{t}_i = 0$, otherwise.*

Definition 6 (Parameterized θ-thresholding). *Let $\mathbf{w} \in \mathbb{Z}^{2N}$ be a companion vector representing $I^+ \subseteq B_{P^+}$. Given a parameter vector $\mathbf{t} \in \mathbb{Z}^N$, a program matrix $\mathbf{Q} \in \mathbb{Z}^{N \times 2N}$, and a vector $\mathbf{y} = \mathbf{Qw}$ where $\mathbf{y} \in \mathbb{Z}^N$, we apply the thresholding function element-wise as follows:*

$$\theta_{\mathbf{t}}(\mathbf{y}_i) = \begin{cases} \min(\max(0, \mathbf{y}_i - (\mathbf{t}_i - 1)), 1) & (\mathbf{t}_i \geq 1) \\ 0 & (\mathbf{t}_i < 1) \end{cases} \tag{5}$$

This thresholding function resembles *hardtanh* which is an activation function developed for use in natural language processing [3]. In the original *hardtanh* function, the range of the linear region is $[-1, 1]$, but here we define the linear region between $[\mathbf{t}_i - 1, \mathbf{t}_i]$. This function is almost everywhere differentiable except at $\mathbf{y}_i = \mathbf{t}_i - 1$ and $\mathbf{y}_i = \mathbf{t}_i$. The special case $\mathbf{t}_i < 1$ in Eq. (5) corresponds to the case $\mathbf{t}_i = 0$ where the head does not appear in the program P^+ and is assumed to be *false*.

Intuitively, for the head of a conjunctive rule to be *true* it is sufficient to check whether all literals in the body hold; otherwise the rule evaluates to *false*. Similarly, for a disjunctive rule, it is sufficient to check whether at least one of the literals in the body holds for the head to hold.

Proposition 4 (Thresholded T_P Operator). *Let P^+ be the positive form of a normal program P and $\mathbf{Q} \in \mathbb{Z}^{N \times 2N}$ its matrix representation. Suppose that $I^P \subseteq B_{P^+}^P$ is the positive part of an interpretation of P^+, and let $\mathbf{v}$ be its corresponding vector, i.e., $v_i = 1$ iff $a_i \in I^P$ and $v_i = 0$ otherwise, for $i = 1, ..., N$. Let $\mathbf{w} \in \mathbb{Z}^{2N}$ be the companion vector to $\mathbf{v}$. Then $\mathbf{z} = [\mathbf{u}; 1 - \mathbf{u}] \in \mathbb{Z}^{2N}$ is the vector representing $J = T_P(I)$ satisfying the condition $(a \in J$ iff $\overline{a} \notin J)$, iff $\mathbf{u} = \theta_{\mathbf{t}}(\mathbf{Qw})$.*

Proof. Consider $\mathbf{u} = \theta_{\mathbf{t}}(\mathbf{Qw})$. For $\mathbf{u} = (\mathbf{u}_1, ..., \mathbf{u}_N)^{\mathsf{T}}$, by the definition of the thresholding function, $\mathbf{u}_k = 1 (1 \leq k \leq N)$ iff $\mathbf{u}'_k \geq \mathbf{t}_k$ in $\mathbf{u}' = \mathbf{Qw}$. Take a row slice $\mathbf{Q}_{k:}$, then $\mathbf{u}'_k = \mathbf{Q}_{k:}\mathbf{w} = \mathbf{Q}_{k1}\mathbf{w}_1 + \cdots + \mathbf{Q}_{k2N}\mathbf{w}_{2N}$, and $\mathbf{u}_k = 1$ iff $\mathbf{u}'_k \geq \mathbf{t}_k$. Both $\mathbf{Q}_{k:}$ and $\mathbf{w}$ are 0-1 vectors, then it follows that there are at least $\mathbf{t}_k$ elements where $\mathbf{Q}_{kj} = \mathbf{w}_j = 1 (1 \leq j \leq 2N)$. The first N elements of $\mathbf{w}$ represent $a_i \in I^P \subseteq B_{P^+}^P$ if $\mathbf{w}_i = 1$, and if $a_i \in I^P$ then $\overline{a}_i \notin I^N \subseteq B_{P^+}^N$ which is maintained through the definition of the companion vector $\mathbf{w}$. 1) For a conjunctive rule $a_k \leftarrow a_1 \wedge \cdots \wedge a_m (1 \leq m \leq 2N)$, $\{a_1, ..., a_{2N}\} \in I$ implies $a_k \in T_P(I)$. 2) For an OR-rule $a_k \leftarrow a_1 \vee \cdots \vee a_m (1 \leq m \leq 2N)$, $\{a_1, ..., a_{2N}\} \subseteq I$ implies $a_k \in T_P(I)$. $a_m \in I$ is represented by $\mathbf{z}_m = 1 (1 \leq m \leq 2N)$. Then by putting $J = \{\text{var}(\mathbf{z}_m) | \mathbf{z}_m = 1\}$, $J = T_P(I)$ holds.

Consider $J = T_P(I)$. For $\mathbf{v} = (\mathbf{v}_1, ..., \mathbf{v}_N)^{\mathsf{T}}$ representing $I^P \subseteq B_{P^+}^P$, $\mathbf{w} = (\mathbf{v}_1, ..., \mathbf{v}_N, 1 - \mathbf{v}_1, ..., 1 - \mathbf{v}_N)^{\mathsf{T}}$ is a vector representing $I \subseteq B_{P^+}$ if we set

$I = \{\text{var}(\mathbf{w}_i)|\mathbf{w}_i = 1\}$. $\mathbf{u}' = \mathbf{Q}\mathbf{w}$ is a vector such that $\mathbf{u}'_k \geq \mathbf{t}_k \, (1 \leq k \leq N)$ iff $\text{var}(\mathbf{u}'_k) \in T_P(I)$. Define $\mathbf{u} = (\mathbf{u}_1, \ldots, \mathbf{u}_N)^{\mathsf{T}}$ such that $\mathbf{u}_k = 1 \, (1 \leq k \leq N)$ iff $\mathbf{u}'_k \geq \mathbf{t}_k$ in $\mathbf{Q}\mathbf{w}$, and $\mathbf{u}_k = 0$ otherwise. Define an interpretation $J \subseteq B_{P+}$ such that it can be partitioned into subsets of positive and negative occurrences of atoms $(J^P \cup J^N) = J \subseteq B_{P+}$. Since only positive atoms occur in the head, $\mathbf{u}$ represents a positive subset of interpretation $J^P \subseteq J \subseteq B_{P+}$ by setting $J^P = \{\text{var}(\mathbf{u}_i)|\mathbf{u}_i = 1\} \, (1 \leq i \leq N)$. If $a_i \in T_P(I)$ then $\mathbf{u}_i = 1$, and $\bar{a}_i \notin T_P(I)$ is represented by $1 - \mathbf{u}_i = 0$. Conversely, if $a_i \notin T_P(I)$ then $\mathbf{u}_i = 0$, and $1 - \mathbf{u}_i = 1$ represents $\bar{a}_i \in T_P(I)$. Thus $1 - \mathbf{u}$ represents $J^N \subseteq J \subseteq B_{P+}$. $\mathbf{z} = [\mathbf{u}; 1 - \mathbf{u}]$ is then a vector representing $J^P \cup J^N = J$ if we set $J = \{\text{var}(\mathbf{z}_m)|\mathbf{z}_m = 1\} \, (1 \leq m \leq 2N)$. Thus $\mathbf{z} = [\mathbf{u}; 1 - \mathbf{u}]$ represents $J = T_P(I)$ if $\mathbf{u} = \theta_{\mathbf{t}}(\mathbf{Q}\mathbf{w})$.

Example 1. Consider the following program:

$$
\begin{aligned}
p &\leftarrow q \\
q &\leftarrow p \wedge r \\
r &\leftarrow \neg p
\end{aligned}
\tag{6}
$$

This program has one supported (stable) model: $\{r\}$. We have $B_P = \{p, q, r\}$, $B_{P+} = \{p, q, r, \bar{p}, \bar{q}, \bar{r}\}$, the matrix representation $\mathbf{Q}$ and parameter vector $\mathbf{t}$ are:

$$
\mathbf{Q} = \begin{array}{c} \\ p \\ q \\ r \end{array}
\begin{array}{c} \begin{array}{cccccc} p & q & r & \bar{p} & \bar{q} & \bar{r} \end{array} \\
\begin{pmatrix} 0 & 1 & 0 & 0 & 0 & 0 \\ 1 & 0 & 1 & 0 & 0 & 0 \\ 0 & 0 & 0 & 1 & 0 & 0 \end{pmatrix} \end{array}
\quad
\mathbf{t} = \begin{array}{c} p \\ q \\ r \end{array} \begin{pmatrix} 1 \\ 2 \\ 1 \end{pmatrix}
\tag{7}
$$

Suppose an assignment $\mathbf{v}^{\{r\}} = (0\,0\,1)^{\mathsf{T}}$ is given. The companion vector $\mathbf{w}$ is:

$$
\mathbf{w} = [\mathbf{v}^{\{r\}}; \mathbf{1}_3 - \mathbf{v}^{\{r\}}] = (0\,0\,1\,1\,1\,0)^{\mathsf{T}}
\tag{8}
$$

Compute the matrix multiplication product $\mathbf{Q}\mathbf{w}$ and apply the thresholding:

$$
\mathbf{u} = \theta_{\mathbf{t}}(\mathbf{Q}\mathbf{w}) = \theta_{\mathbf{t}}((0\,1\,1)^{\mathsf{T}}) = (0\,0\,1)^{\mathsf{T}} = \mathbf{v}^{\{r\}}
\tag{9}
$$

Let $\mathbf{z}$ be a companion vector to $\mathbf{u}$, i.e. $\mathbf{z} = [\mathbf{u}; 1 - \mathbf{u}]$, then we have

$$
\mathbf{z} = (0\,0\,1\,1\,1\,0)^{\mathsf{T}}
\tag{10}
$$

Define $J = \{\text{var}(\mathbf{z}_m)|\mathbf{z}_m = 1\}$, then we have $J = \{r, \bar{p}, \bar{q}\}$, and $J \cap B_P = \{r\}$.

Proposition 5 (Supported Model Computation with Thresholded T_P)
    Let $\mathbf{v} \in \mathbb{Z}^N$ be a 0-1 vector representing a subset of interpretation $I^P \subseteq I \subseteq B_{P+}$, and $\mathbf{z} = [\mathbf{v}; \mathbf{1}_N - \mathbf{v}]$ be its companion vector representing $I \subseteq B_{P+}$ satisfying $(a \in I$ iff $\bar{a} \notin I)$. Given a program matrix $\mathbf{Q}$ representing a program P^+ and a thresholding function $\theta_{\mathbf{t}}$ parameterized by a vector $\mathbf{t}$, the fixed points of P^+ are represented by 0-1 binary vectors $\mathbf{z}^{FP} = [\mathbf{v}^{FP}; \mathbf{1}_N - \mathbf{v}^{FP}] \in \mathbb{Z}^{2N}$ where $\mathbf{v}^{FP} = \theta_{\mathbf{t}}(\mathbf{Q}\mathbf{z}^{FP})$. Then $\mathbf{z}^{FP}$ are vectors representing models M^+ of P^+ satisfying $(a \in M^+$ iff $\bar{a} \notin M^+)$ iff $\theta_{\mathbf{t}}(\mathbf{Q}\mathbf{z}^{FP}) = \mathbf{v}^{FP}$. When such 0-1 binary vector $\mathbf{z}^{FP}$ exists, $M^+ \cap B_P = M$ is a supported model of P.

Proof. Let $I \subseteq B_{P+}$ be a model of P^+, represented by $\mathbf{z}^{FP}$. Consider two cases (i) $T_P(I) = I$ and (ii) $\mathbf{v}^{FP} = \theta_t(\mathbf{Q}\mathbf{z}^{FP})$. In both cases, by Propositions 2, 3 and 4, if a supported model of P exists, the results hold.

4.2   Loss Function for Computing Supported Models

By the fixed point definition of supported models, a supported model M satisfies $\mathbf{v}^{M^P} = \theta_t(\mathbf{Q}[\mathbf{v}^{M^P}; \mathbf{1}_N - \mathbf{v}^{M^P}])$. We now use this definition to design a loss function which can be minimized using gradient descent. Gradient descent is a method for minimizing an objective function by updating the parameters in the opposite direction of the gradient with respect to the parameters. The size of the update is determined by the gradient and the step size α.

We define a vector $\mathbf{f} \in \mathbb{Z}^N$ which stores information about occurrences of facts in the program P^+. This vector will be used later during the minimization step to ensure that facts are not forgotten.

Definition 7 (Fact Vector f). *The set of facts in the program P^+ is represented by a column vector $\mathbf{f} \in \mathbb{Z}^N$, such that for each element $\mathbf{f}_i (1 \leq i \leq N)$,*

- $\mathbf{f}_i = 1$ *if the rule r_i is a fact: $a \leftarrow$*
- $\mathbf{f}_i = 0$ *otherwise.*

Definition 8 (Loss Function). *Given a program matrix $\mathbf{Q}$, a candidate vector $\mathbf{x}$, thresholding function θ_t, and constants λ_1 and λ_2, define the loss function as follows:*

$$L(\mathbf{x}) = \frac{1}{2}\left(\|\theta_t(\mathbf{Q}[\mathbf{x}; \mathbf{1}_N - \mathbf{x}]) - \mathbf{x}\|_F^2 + \lambda_1 \|\mathbf{x} \odot (\mathbf{x} - \mathbf{1}_N)\|_F^2 + \lambda_2 \|\mathbf{f} - (\mathbf{x} \odot \mathbf{f})\|_F^2\right) \quad (11)$$

where $\|\mathbf{x}\|_F$ denotes the Frobenius norm and $\odot$ denotes the element-wise product.

The first term is derived directly from the fixed point definition of supported models, and should be 0 if $\mathbf{x}$ is a supported model of P^+. The second term, which resembles a regularization term often used in the machine learning literature, is added to penalize candidate vectors $\mathbf{x}$ that contain fractional values, and is 0 if and only if $\mathbf{x}$ is a 0-1 vector. The third term will be 0 if and only if the facts are preserved, and will be positive non-zero if any part of the assignment is lost, i.e. by assigning 0 (*false*) to a fact where $\mathbf{f}_i = 1$.

We introduce submatrices of $\mathbf{Q}$, $\mathbf{Q}_p \in \mathbb{Z}^{N \times N}$ and $\mathbf{Q}_n \in \mathbb{Z}^{N \times N}$ that correspond to the positive bodies and negative bodies of the matrix, respectively, such that $\mathbf{Q} = [\mathbf{Q}_p \, \mathbf{Q}_n]$ (horizontal concatenation of submatrices).

Definition 9 (Gradient of the Loss Function). *The gradient of the loss function with respect to $\mathbf{x}$ is given by:*

$$\frac{\partial L(\mathbf{x})}{\partial \mathbf{x}} = \left((\mathbf{Q}_p - \mathbf{Q}_n)^T \cdot \theta_t(\mathbf{Q}\mathbf{z}_\mathbf{x}) \odot \frac{\partial \theta_t(\mathbf{Q}\mathbf{z}_\mathbf{x})}{\partial \mathbf{x}}\right) - \theta_t(\mathbf{Q}\mathbf{z}_\mathbf{x} - \mathbf{x})$$
$$+ \lambda_1(\mathbf{x} \odot (\mathbf{1}_N - \mathbf{x}) \odot (\mathbf{1}_N - 2\mathbf{x})) + \lambda_2(\mathbf{x} \odot \mathbf{f} - \mathbf{f}) \quad (12)$$

where $\mathbf{z_x} \in \mathbb{R}^{2N} = [\mathbf{x}; \mathbf{1}_N - \mathbf{x}]$ *and*

$$\frac{\partial \theta_\mathbf{t}(\mathbf{w}_i)}{\partial \mathbf{x}_i} = \begin{cases} 1 & \text{if } (\mathbf{t}_i \geq 1) \text{ and } (\mathbf{t}_i - 1) \leq \mathbf{w}_i \leq \mathbf{t}_i \\ 0 & \text{otherwise} \end{cases} \tag{13}$$

We can update $\mathbf{x}$ iteratively using, for example, gradient descent or quasi-Newton's method, to reduce the loss to zero. Here we show an example of update rule for gradient descent. Let α be the step size, then the gradient descent update rule is given by:

$$\mathbf{x}_{\text{new}} \leftarrow \mathbf{x} - \alpha \frac{\partial L(\mathbf{x})}{\partial \mathbf{x}} \tag{14}$$

Using this update rule we can design an algorithm to find supported models, as shown in Algorithm 1. Moreover, this formulation allows us to use other gradient update methods like Newton update [10] or more advanced optimizers like Adam [5], as we show later in the experiment section.

The convergence characteristics of the gradient descent algorithm are well-known. Assuming at least one 0-1 vector representing a supported model exists for $\mathbf{Q}$, all we require for Algorithm 1 to converge to the supported model is that the initial vector $\mathbf{x}$ to be in the region surrounding the supported model where the slope points towards the model. When there are multiple supported models, we expect the algorithm to converge to different models depending on the choice of initial vector. However, it is often not known *apriori* which particular values or regions of $\mathbf{x}$ lead to which models. Thus, we implement a uniform initialization strategy, where the initial values are drawn from the uniform distribution $\mathcal{U}(0, 1)$.

Depending on the program, an optimal 0-1 vector interpretation may not exist, so we limit the number of iterations to max_iter before assuming non-convergence. With gradient descent, it is often time-consuming to reduce the loss function completely to zero. We therefore implement a "peeking at a solution" heuristic, similar to the one presented in [10], where while updating $\mathbf{x}$ we round $\mathbf{x}$ to a 0-1 vector to see whether the resulting $\mathbf{x}_r$ is a solution (Lines 6–8). The output is sensitive to the choice of initial vector $\mathbf{x}$, and a poor choice may result in non-convergence to optimal solutions. We alleviate this dependency on the initial vector by introducing the max_retry parameter and changing the initial vector on each try. This algorithm declares failure to find any supported models (returns FALSE, Line 12) when both max_retry and max_iter are exhausted.

5   Experiments

All experiments in this section were performed on a desktop machine with the following specifications: Python 3.7, Intel Core i9-9900K and 64 GB RAM.

5.1 N-negative Loops

Aspis et al. [2] encode the program reduct into a matrix and employ the Newton's method for root finding to find fixed points of the program. Their matrix

Algorithm 1. Gradient descent search of supported models

Input: Program matrix $\mathbf{Q}$, thresholding parameter $\mathbf{t}$, max_retry ≥ 1, max_iter ≥ 1,
  $\epsilon > 0$, step size $\alpha > 0$, $\lambda_1 > 0$, $\lambda_2 > 0$
Output: Supported model $\mathbf{x}$ or FALSE
 1: **for** n_try $\leftarrow$ 1 **to** max_retry **do**
 2:     $\mathbf{x} \leftarrow$ vector sampled from $\mathcal{U}(0, 1)$
 3:     **for** n_iter $\leftarrow$ 1 **to** max_iter **do**
 4:         $\mathbf{x}_r \leftarrow$ round$(\mathbf{x})$ ▷ Rounding heuristic
 5:         loss $\leftarrow L(\mathbf{x}_r)$ ▷ Loss function, see Definition (8)
 6:         **if** (loss $\leq \epsilon$) **then**
 7:             $\mathbf{x} \leftarrow \mathbf{x}_r$
 8:             **return** $\mathbf{x}$
 9:         **else**
10:             gradient $\leftarrow \frac{\partial L(\mathbf{x})}{\partial \mathbf{x}}$ ▷ Gradient, see Definition (9)
11:             $\mathbf{x} \leftarrow \mathbf{x} - \alpha \cdot$ gradient   ▷ Gradient update
12: **return** FALSE

---

encoding assumes the MD condition, whereas ours assumes the SD condition. The gradient is calculated by the Jacobian matrix, and the thresholding operator is a parameterized sigmoid. They present two types of sampling methods for setting the initial vector; *uniform sampling*, similarly to our method, where the values are sampled uniformly from $[0, 1]$, and *semantic sampling*[1], where the values are sampled uniformly from $[0, \gamma^\perp] \cup [\gamma^\top, 1]$.

Firstly, we consider the "N-negative loops" programs, which involves programs in the following form: for $1 \leq i \leq N$,

$$p_i \leftarrow \text{not } q_i$$
$$q_i \leftarrow \text{not } p_i \tag{15}$$

For our algorithm, we use the following parameters: max_iter $= 10^3$, $\epsilon = 10^{-4}$, $\lambda_1 = \lambda_2 = 1$, $\alpha = 10^{-1}$. For comparison, we also implemented Aspis et al.'s algorithm, and we used the following settings: max_iter $= 10^3$, $\epsilon = 10^{-4}$. Both algorithms were allowed to restart from a new random vector up to 100 times, in case the iteration fails to find a model. We generated programs of the form (15) with N up to 100, applied the algorithms on each program 10 times, then measured the rate of success of converging to supported models and the number of restarts attempted by the algorithms (Fig. 1).

From Fig. 1a, one can observe that our method, except for the Newton update at around $N = 98$, could find the correct supported models regardless of the gradient update method. The gradient descent and Adam updates can solve this task with the least number of restarts, and in fact, they found the models on their first attempts (Fig. 1b). On the other hand, we see a gradual increase in the number of restarts required for the Newton update method, and the MD method requires more than 100 restarts past $N = 40$ to solve.

---

[1] $\gamma^\perp$ is an upper bound on false values that variables can take, and $\gamma^\top$ is a lower bound on true values. $\gamma = \frac{n}{n+1}$ where n is the length of the longest positive part in the rules, and τ was estimated as described [2].

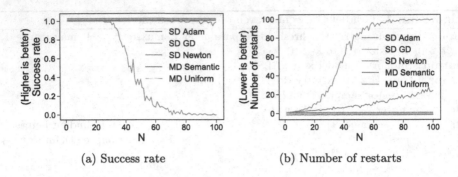

(a) Success rate   (b) Number of restarts

Fig. 1. N-negative loops. SD: Ours, MD: see Aspis et al. [2].

The design of the loss function (Sect. 4.2) also contributes to the high success rate of our method. The second term results in the loss function having non-zero values at local minima where the interpretation vector is non-binary, and drives the optimizers away from local minima. The root finding method described in [2] without this penalty term is prone to the presence of local minima, as shown by the low success rates.

5.2   Choose 1 Out of N

Secondly, we consider the "choose 1 out of N" task, where the task is to choose exactly 1 out of N options. The programs in this class have the following form:

$$
\begin{aligned}
p_1 &\leftarrow \text{not}\, p_2,\, \text{not}\, p_3,\, ...,\, \text{not}\, p_N \\
p_2 &\leftarrow \text{not}\, p_1,\, \text{not}\, p_3,\, ...,\, \text{not}\, p_N \\
&\ \ \vdots \\
p_N &\leftarrow \text{not}\, p_1,\, \text{not}\, p_2,\, ...,\, \text{not}\, p_{N-1}
\end{aligned}
\tag{16}
$$

We generated programs for N between 2 and 14, and applied the algorithms using the same parameters as the "N-negative loops" task, and repeated the process for 10 times for each N.

In contrast to the previous case, the Newton update turned out to be the most stable, followed closely by Adam and gradient descent (Fig. 2). Moreover, for gradient descent, we observe a steeper increase in the number of restarts past $N = 10$ compared to Adam (Fig. 2b). This suggests that adaptive gradient methods may be better suited for more complex programs.

5.3   Random Programs

We generated random programs by changing (a) number of atoms $[10, 50, 100]$ (b) number of rules, as a multiplier on the number of atoms $[1, 1.2, 1.4, ..., 2, 2.5, 3]$ and (c) % chance of literals in the body being negative $[0, 10, 30, ..., 90]$, and

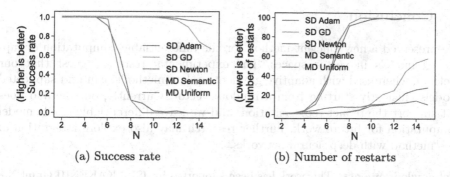

Fig. 2. Choose 1 out of N. SD: Ours, MD: see Aspis et al. [2].

generated 10 instances for each set of parameters (1,440 instances). Compared to previous works that focused on phase transition programs [13], these generated programs cover a wider range of body length and ratio of negated literals in the body. During the evaluation, it became apparent that running the MD methods on programs containing long rules with negation was very time-consuming. Thus, we created a second set of randomly generated programs, where the number of atoms was restricted to [10, 15] (960 instances). We applied the algorithms once to each of the instances with max_try = 10 and max_iter = 100, and recorded success when the algorithm declared convergence.

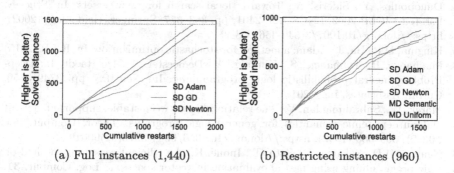

Fig. 3. Randomly generated programs. SD: Ours, MD: see Aspis et al. [2].

In Fig. 3, the dashed lines indicate the 'perfect score', which is achievable if the algorithm could find the model successfully on the first try for all instances. Thus, the closer an algorithm is to this point, the more efficient it is in finding the correct models. Overall, we see that the Newton update performs the best, followed by Adam. On smaller datasets, we found that gradient descent was less efficient than the MD method in terms of number of restarts; however, we may be able to improve the result by simply increasing the step size.

6   Conclusion

We presented a new efficient method for the differentiable computation of supported models in vector spaces. The experimental results suggest that our method, when used with adaptive gradient update methods, can find supported models efficiently starting from a random vector. Currently, our method does not support the reduct representation, and we leave differentiable stable model computation for future work. Further research may also explore integration of this method with deep neural networks.

Acknowledgements. This work has been supported by JSPS KAKENHI Grant No. JP21H04905.

References

1. Apt, K.R., Blair, H.A., Walker, A.: Towards a theory of declarative knowledge. In: Foundations of Deductive Databases and Logic Programming, pp. 89–148. Elsevier (1988)
2. Aspis, Y., Broda, K., Russo, A., Lobo, J.: Stable and supported semantics in continuous vector spaces. In: KR, pp. 59–68 (2020). https://doi.org/10.24963/kr.2020/7
3. Collobert, R., Weston, J., Bottou, L., Karlen, M., Kavukcuoglu, K., Kuksa, P.: Natural language processing (almost) from scratch. J. Mach. Learn. Res. **12**(76), 2493–2537 (2011)
4. Dimopoulos, Y., Sideris, A.: Towards local search for answer sets. In: Stuckey, P.J. (ed.) ICLP 2002. LNCS, vol. 2401, pp. 363–377. Springer, Heidelberg (2002). https://doi.org/10.1007/3-540-45619-8_25
5. Kingma, D.P., Ba, J.: Adam: a method for stochastic optimization. In: ICLR (2015)
6. Manhaeve, R., Dumancic, S., Kimmig, A., Demeester, T., De Raedt, L.: DeepProbLog: neural probabilistic logic programming. In: NeurIPS, pp. 3749–3759. Curran Associates, Inc. (2018)
7. Marek, W., Subrahmanian, V.: The relationship between stable, supported, default and autoepistemic semantics for general logic programs. Theor. Comput. Sci. **103**(2), 365–386 (1992). https://doi.org/10.1016/0304-3975(92)90019-C
8. Nguyen, H.D., Sakama, C., Sato, T., Inoue, K.: An efficient reasoning method on logic programming using partial evaluation in vector spaces. J. Log. Comput. **31**, 1298–1316 (2021). https://doi.org/10.1093/logcom/exab010
9. Sakama, C., Inoue, K., Sato, T.: Linear algebraic characterization of logic programs. In: Li, G., Ge, Y., Zhang, Z., Jin, Z., Blumenstein, M. (eds.) KSEM 2017. LNCS (LNAI), vol. 10412, pp. 520–533. Springer, Cham (2017). https://doi.org/10.1007/978-3-319-63558-3_44
10. Sato, T., Kojima, R.: Logical inference as cost minimization in vector spaces. In: El Fallah Seghrouchni, A., Sarne, D. (eds.) IJCAI 2019. LNCS (LNAI), vol. 12158, pp. 239–255. Springer, Cham (2020). https://doi.org/10.1007/978-3-030-56150-5_12
11. Sato, T., Sakama, C., Inoue, K.: From 3-valued semantics to supported model computation for logic programs in vector spaces. In: ICAART, pp. 758–765 (2020)

12. Yang, Z., Ishay, A., Lee, J.: NeurASP: embracing neural networks into answer set programming. In: IJCAI-PRICAI 2020, pp. 1755–1762 (2020). https://doi.org/10.24963/ijcai.2020/243

13. Zhao, Y., Lin, F.: Answer set programming phase transition: a study on randomly generated programs. In: Palamidessi, C. (ed.) ICLP 2003. LNCS, vol. 2916, pp. 239–253. Springer, Heidelberg (2003). https://doi.org/10.1007/978-3-540-24599-5_17

Towards Causality-Based Conflict Resolution in Answer Set Programs

Andre Thevapalan[✉] [iD], Konstantin Haupt, and Gabriele Kern-Isberner[iD]

Technische Universität Dortmund, 44227 Dortmund, Germany
{andre.thevapalan,konstantin.haupt,
gabriele.kern-isberner}@cs.tu-dortmund.de

Abstract. Using answer set programming in real-world applications requires that the answer set program is correct and adequately represents knowledge. In this paper, we present strategies to resolve unintended contradictory statements resulting from modelling gaps and other flaws by modifying the program without manipulating the actual conflicting rules (inconsistency-causing rules with complementary head literals). We show how *latent conflicts* can be detected to prevent further conflicts during the resolution process or after subsequent modifications in the future. The presented approach is another step towards a general framework where professional experts who are not necessarily familiar with ASP can repair existing answer set programs and independently resolve conflicts resulting from contradictory statements in an informative way. In such a framework, conflict resolution strategies allow for generating possible solutions that consist of informative extensions and modifications of the program. In interaction with the professional expert, these solution options can then be used to obtain the solution that represents the underlying knowledge best.

Keywords: Answer Set Programming · Conflicts · Consistency · Contradictions · Interactive Conflict Resolution

1 Introduction

In order to use answer set programming in real-world applications, the utilized answer set programs must be modelled correctly and represent professionally adequate knowledge. Especially in large programs, unintended contradictory statements due to modelling gaps and other flaws are hard to detect, and repairing a knowledge base can require both a professional expert and a technical expert. Approaches as in [1,2] rewrite an updated program using the *causal rejection principle* [2] such that in case of contradictory derivations, newer knowledge is preferred. These approaches, however, are actually "workarounds" that change the program in an automated fashion and do not guarantee that the underlying cause of the inconsistency is eliminated. In practice, such a solution may not always be desirable, e. g. when inconsistencies hint at outdated information or modelling flaws. Instead, one may wish to resolve the actual conflicting statements in the program. In [10], it is shown how rules directly involved in a *conflict*

G. Gottlob et al. (Eds.): LPNMR 2022, LNAI 13416, pp. 350–362, 2022.
https://doi.org/10.1007/978-3-031-15707-3_27

can be modified to achieve a consistent program. In this paper, we extend this approach by showing how conflicts can be resolved by modifying rules other than the conflicting ones in case the conflicting rules themselves are thought to be adequate. For that, we first outline the general relations between a conflict rule and the rest of the program. Based on these results, we exemplarily showcase two different strategies that utilize the different rule dependencies to prevent conflicting rules from being simultaneously satisfiable. In place of exploiting technical devices like causal rejection, the presented strategies, as in [10], produce informative solution options from which a professional expert can then choose the most suitable one, where informative means that modifications of rules make use of the given program language. Another aspect we cover is *latent conflicts*. We show that even consistent programs can contain contradictory knowledge that "hides" behind consistent answer sets due to the nature of answer set semantics that chooses only consistent answer sets, ignoring the inconsistent fixpoints. Accordingly, such latent conflicts should also be resolved in the process to achieve robust consistency. This way, it is guaranteed that every implemented modification to establish consistency conclusively leads to a program that adequately reflects professional knowledge.

After presenting the necessary theoretical preliminaries in Sect. 2, we introduce the notion of latent conflicts and causality-based conflict resolution in Sect. 3 that allows us to resolve conflicts without manipulating the conflicting rules themselves. In Sect. 4, we examine the general conditions for conflicting rules to become simultaneously derivable. Using these results and the definitions of the prior section, we present two exemplary strategies that follow the causality-based conflict resolution approach. After presenting a brief overview over related work in Sect. 5, the paper concludes with Sect. 6, giving a short summary and discussion of open issues and further work.

2 Preliminaries

In this paper, we look at non-disjunctive *extended logic programs* (ELPs) [6]. An ELP is a finite set of rules over a set $\mathcal{A}$ of propositional atoms. A (classical) literal L is either an atom A (*positive literal*) or a negated atom $\neg A$ (*negative literal*). For a literal L, the *strongly complementary* literal $\overline{L}$ is $\neg A$ if $L = A$ and A otherwise. A *default-negated literal* L, called *default literal*, is written as $\sim L$. A set S of literals is *consistent* iff S does not contain strongly complementary literals. A *rule* r is of the form $L_0 \leftarrow L_1, \ldots, L_m, \sim L_{m+1}, \ldots, \sim L_n.$, with literals $L_0, \ldots, L_n$ and $0 \le m \le n$. The literal L_0 is the *head* of r, denoted by $H(r)$, and $\{L_1, \ldots L_m, \sim L_{m+1}, \ldots \sim L_n\}$ is the *body* of r, denoted by $B(r)$. Furthermore, $\{L_1, \ldots, L_m\}$ is denoted by $B^+(r)$ and $\{L_{m+1}, \ldots, L_n\}$ by $B^-(r)$. A rule r with $B(r) = \emptyset$ is called a *fact*, and r is called a *constraint* if it has an empty head. An *extended logic program (ELP)* $\mathcal{P}$ is a set of rules.

Given a set S of literals, we say S *satisfies* L iff $L \in S$, and S *satisfies* $\sim L$ iff $L \notin S$. S *satisfies a rule body* $B(r)$ iff for all $L \in B^+(r)$, S satisfies L, and for all $L \in B^-(r)$, S satisfies $\sim L$. S *satisfies a rule* r iff S satisfies $H(r)$ whenever S

satisfies $B(r)$. In case r is a constraint, S satisfies r iff S does not satisfy $B(r)$. A rule body $B(r)$ is *satisfiable* if there exists a set S of literals such that S satisfies $B(r)$. Given a set $\mathcal{R}$ of rules, S *satisfies* $\mathcal{R}$ if S satisfies all $r \in \mathcal{R}$ simultaneously. S is a *pre-model of* $\mathcal{P}$ if S satisfies $\mathcal{P}$. A pre-model S of $\mathcal{P}$ is a *model of* $\mathcal{P}$ if S is consistent. A rule r is *active under* S iff S satisfies $B(r)$. The set of all rules in $\mathcal{P}$ that are active under S is denoted by $act^S(\mathcal{P})$. Given a literal L, H_L denotes the set of rules in $\mathcal{P}$ with the rule head L, i.e. $H_L = \{r \in \mathcal{P} \mid H(r) = L\}$. Given two rules $r, r' \in \mathcal{P}$, r is *supported (resp. opposed) by* r' iff there exists a literal $L \in B^+(r)$ (resp. $L \in B^-(r)$) such that $L = H(r')$. Then, r' is a *supporting (resp. opposing) rule of* r.

In the following, we extend the basic idea of answer sets to inconsistent sets of literals. Given an ELP $\mathcal{P}$ without default negation, the *pre-answer set of* $\mathcal{P}$ is a set S of literals such that S satisfies $\mathcal{P}$ and S is $\subseteq$-minimal. In general, an *answer set* of an ELP $\mathcal{P}$ is determined by its reduct. The *reduct* $\mathcal{P}^S$ of a program $\mathcal{P}$ relative to a set S of literals is defined by

$$\mathcal{P}^S = \{H(r) \leftarrow B^+(r). \mid r \in \mathcal{P}, B^-(r) \cap S = \emptyset\}.$$

A set S of literals is a *pre-answer set* of $\mathcal{P}$ if it is the pre-answer set of $\mathcal{P}^S$ [6]. A pre-answer set S is a *(classical) answer set* of $\mathcal{P}$ if S is consistent, otherwise, we call S a *pseudo answer set*. The set of all pseudo answer sets of a program $\mathcal{P}$ is denoted by $AS^\perp(\mathcal{P})$, the set of all (classical) answer set by $AS(\mathcal{P})$, and the set of all pre-answer sets $AS^\perp(\mathcal{P}) \cup AS(\mathcal{P})$ by $AS^{pre}(\mathcal{P})$. Note that $AS(\mathcal{P})$ aligns with the set of answer sets under usual definitions, e.g. [6].

For every literal of a pre-answer set S, there must exist a rule $r \in \mathcal{P}$ with $H(r) = L$ s.t. $r \in act^S(\mathcal{P})$. This is in complete analogue to answer sets [4].

Example 1. Let $\mathcal{P}_1$ be the ELP of our running example in this paper:

r_1: $drugA \leftarrow condW.$ r_2: $\overline{drugA} \leftarrow sympT.$

r_3: $treatmZ \leftarrow drugC, \sim drugD.$ r_4: $\overline{treatmZ} \leftarrow sympQ, \sim drugD, \sim sympR.$

r_5: $condW \leftarrow sympU.$ r_6: $drugC \leftarrow \sim drugD, \sim sympR.$

r_7: $drugD \leftarrow \sim drugC.$ r_8: $sympQ.$ r_9: $sympT.$ r_{10}: $sympU.$

$\mathcal{P}_1$ models a knowledge base regarding the conditions for prescribing a drug A and a treatment Z, as well as the conditions when they must not be prescribed. For example, r_3 represents the condition that treatment Z may only be recommended if the patient is already taking drug C and drug D is not known to be applied, while r_4 says that patients must not be treated with Z if they currently show symptom Q, drug D is not known to be applied, and symptom R does not seem to be developed.

$\mathcal{P}_1$ has the pre-answer sets $S_1 = \{condW, drugA, \overline{drugA}, drugD, sympQ, sympT, sympU\}$ and $S_2 = \{condW, drugA, \overline{drugA}, drugC, sympQ, sympT, sympU, treatmZ, \overline{treatmZ}\}$. Both answer sets are pseudo answer sets as they contain complementary literals. $\square$

To formalize modification operations on programs, we introduce suitable modification operations:

Definition 1 (Rule Modification Operation). *Let $\mathcal{P}$ be an ELP with a rule $r \in \mathcal{P}$ and X a set of literals and default literals where either $X \subseteq B(r)$ or $X \cap B(r) = \emptyset$. We define the rule modification operation $rmod(r, X)$ as follows:*

$$rmod(r, X) = \begin{cases} H(r) \leftarrow B(r) \backslash X & \text{if } X \subseteq B(r) \\ H(r) \leftarrow B(r) \cup X & \text{if } X \cap B(r) = \emptyset \end{cases}$$

In the following, a *program modification operation* $\mathcal{P} \diamond r^\star$ is either the addition of a new rule $r^\star$ to $\mathcal{P}$, i.e. $\mathcal{P} \cup \{r^\star\}$ or the replacement of a rule $r \in \mathcal{P}$ by a modification $r^\star = rmod(r, X)$ of r, i.e. $\mathcal{P} \backslash \{r\} \cup \{r^\star\}$. We express a set of modifications that shall be applied to $\mathcal{P}$ by simply listing the new rules and rule modifications, i.e. $R^\star = \{r_1^\star, \ldots, r_n^\star\}$ denotes a set of modification elements, where $r_i^\star$ $(1 \leq i \leq n)$ is either a new rule for $\mathcal{P}$ or a modification $rmod(r, X)$ with $r \in \mathcal{P}$ and a set of (default) literals X. Given a set $R^\star = \{r_1^\star, \ldots, r_n^\star\}$ of rule modifications and new rules for $\mathcal{P}$, the consecutive application of each element onto $\mathcal{P}$ is denoted by $\mathcal{P} \diamond R^\star$, i.e. $\mathcal{P} \diamond R^\star = (((\mathcal{P} \diamond r_1^\star) \diamond r_2^\star) \diamond \ldots \diamond r_n^\star)$.

Example 2 (Example 1 contd.). Suppose studies have shown that condition W always presents with a symptom V. The addition of a literal $symp V$ to r_5 can then be written as $rmod(r_5, \{symp V\})$, resulting in a rule $r_5^\star$: $cond W \leftarrow symp U, symp V$. Replacing r_5 in $\mathcal{P}_1$ by $r_5^\star$ can then be expressed by $\mathcal{P}_1 \diamond rmod(r_5, \{symp V\})$. □

3   Causality-Based Conflict Resolution

In this section, we introduce the notion of *derivable conflicts* and outline a method named *causality-based conflict resolution* that can be used to describe how to modify an inconsistent program to achieve consistency. During the resolution process, for every derivable conflict, a set of modifications is applied to $\mathcal{P}$. Every set of changes leads to the resolution of the respective conflict where the modifications are built from elements of the underlying language of $\mathcal{P}$.

3.1   Conflicts and Inconsistency

In this paper, we show strategies to resolve inconsistencies that are caused by rules with complementary head literals by constructing informative program modifications. To that end, we first specify the type of inconsistency that our strategies aim to resolve.

Definition 2 (Consistency, Contradictory Program). *An ELP $\mathcal{P}$ is called consistent iff $AS(\mathcal{P}) \neq \emptyset$. $\mathcal{P}$ is contradictory iff $AS(\mathcal{P}) = \emptyset$ and $AS^\perp(\mathcal{P}) \neq \emptyset$.*

This paper solely deals with programs that are inconsistent due to contradictions.

Example 3 (Example 1 contd.). Program $\mathcal{P}_1$ is inconsistent as the two existing pre-answer sets are pseudo answer sets. □

Definition 3 (Conflicting Rules, Conflict (cf. [10])). *Two rules r_1, r_2 in an ELP $\mathcal{P}$ are conflicting if $H(r_1)$ and $H(r_2)$ are strongly complementary and there exists a consistent set S of literals such that $B(r_1)$ and $B(r_2)$ are satisfied by S. A conflict is a set $\mathcal{C} = \{r_1, r_2\}$ of rules such that r_1 and r_2 are conflicting. We denote the set of all conflicts $\{r_1, r_2\}$ in an ELP $\mathcal{P}$ by Conflicts($\mathcal{P}$).*

A program that contains conflicts is not necessarily inconsistent. A conflict $\{r_1, r_2\}$ in $\mathcal{P}$ is only a potential cause of inconsistency whenever the body literals of both $B(r_1)$ and $B(r_2)$ can be simultaneously derived in $\mathcal{P}$. The program's pseudo answer sets can be used to determine whether the body literals of conflicting rules are derivable and which rules are causing inconsistency.

Definition 4 (Derivably Conflicting Rules). *Given an ELP $\mathcal{P}$ over $\mathcal{A}$, a conflict $\{r_1, r_2\} \in$ Conflicts($\mathcal{P}$) is derivable[1] in $\mathcal{P}$ iff there exists a pseudo answer set $S \in AS^{\perp}(\mathcal{P})$ s.t. r_1 and r_2 are active under S. Otherwise, a conflict is nonderivable. The set of all derivable conflicts in $\mathcal{P}$ is denoted by Conflicts$^{dv}(\mathcal{P})$.*

However, a conflict is only (co-)responsible for inconsistency if the conflict is derivable. Thus, a program is consistent if it does not possess derivable conflicts.

Proposition 1. *Let $\mathcal{P}$ be an ELP with Conflicts($\mathcal{P}$) $\neq \emptyset$. $\mathcal{P}$ is consistent if every conflict in Conflicts($\mathcal{P}$) is nonderivable, i.e. Conflicts$^{dv}(\mathcal{P}) = \emptyset$.*

Proof. Let $\mathcal{P}$ be an ELP with Conflicts($\mathcal{P}$) $\neq \emptyset$ and Conflicts$^{dv}(\mathcal{P}) = \emptyset$. Suppose $\mathcal{P}$ is inconsistent. Then there exists a pseudo answer set $S \in AS^{\perp}(\mathcal{P})$, which in turn implies that there exist two conflicting rules r_1 and r_2 that are active under S. By definition, $\{r_1, r_2\}$ is a derivable conflict which contradicts our initial assumption that Conflicts$^{dv}(\mathcal{P}) = \emptyset$. □

Example 4 (Example 1 contd.). $\mathcal{P}_1$ has two conflicts $\mathcal{C}_1 = \{r_1, r_2\}$ and $\mathcal{C}_2 = \{r_3, r_4\}$. Its answer sets show that both conflicts are derivable since the complementary literals in the answer sets can only originate from the rules in $\mathcal{C}_1$ and $\mathcal{C}_2$. Answer set S_1 shows that to achieve a consistent program, it suffices to make either $drugA$ or $\overline{drugA}$ nonderivable as r_1 and r_2 are the only conflicting rules that are active under S_1. Let $\mathcal{P}_4$ be $\mathcal{P}_1$ where the body of r_5 is extended by a literal $sympV$, i.e. $\mathcal{P}_4 = \mathcal{P}_1 \diamond rmod(r_5, \{sympV\})$. $\mathcal{P}_4$ now has the pre-answer sets $S_{4,1} = \{drugA, drugD, sympQ, \underline{sympT}, sympU\}$, and $S_{4,2} = \{\overline{drugA}, drugC, sympQ, sympT, sympU, treatmZ, \overline{treatmZ}\}$. Since $S_{4,1}$ is not a pseudo answer set, $\mathcal{P}_4$ is consistent. □

Example 4 depicts the relationship between derivable conflicts and consistency.

Depending on the actual program modifications, further inconsistency-causing conflicts, so called *latent conflicts*, can be revealed. These conflicts should therefore be handled correspondingly to ensure that after resolving all conflicts, the program is indeed consistent.

---

[1] Note that literals are classified as derivable once they appear in a pre-answer set and not only in a (classical) answer set.

Definition 5 (Latent Conflict). *Let $\mathcal{P}$ be an ELP with a conflict $\mathcal{C}$. $\mathcal{C}$ is a latent conflict if $\mathcal{C}$ is a derivable conflict and $AS(\mathcal{P}) \neq \emptyset$.*

Example 5 (Example 4 contd.). In $\mathcal{P}_4$, conflict $\mathcal{C}_2 = \{r_3, r_4\}$ is a latent conflict as its rules are active under $S_{4,2}$ but not in the (consistent) answer $S_{4,1}$. Suppose that it was prescribed that in order to take drug D, the patient also has to show symptom V. Thus, program $\mathcal{P}_4$ has to be modified to a program $\mathcal{P}_5$ by adding the literal $symp V$ to the body of r_7, i.e. $\mathcal{P}_5 = \mathcal{P}_4 \diamond rmod(r_7, \{symp V\})$. $\mathcal{P}_5$ is now inconsistent as its only pre-answer set is the pseudo answer set $S_{4,2}$ from Example 4 in which the rules of $\mathcal{C}_2$ are active. □

Given the goal of solely "repairing" an inconsistent knowledge base, modifying the corresponding inconsistent program until one gets at least one answer set seems appropriate (see Example 4). Considering Example 5, one can easily imagine that in the process of resolving conflicts, other previously latent conflicts can become effective, meaning they can cause inconsistency.

3.2 Conflict Resolution

In this paper, we want to present strategies to explicitly "resolve" all derivable conflicts (which include latent conflicts) in a knowledge base in an informative way, that is, every change made to obtain a consistent program is based on the underlying language. Therefore, each such strategy modifies the program so that every (derivable) conflict becomes nonderivable, which as a consequence also ensures the resolution of latent conflicts. We now outline, given a derivable conflict $\mathcal{C}$ in an ELP $\mathcal{P}$, how one can modify $\mathcal{P}$ to a program $\mathcal{P}^*$ such that $\mathcal{C}$ becomes nonderivable in $\mathcal{P}^*$ without manipulating the conflicting rules themselves. We call this approach *causality-based conflict resolution*. There, in each step, a conflict is resolved by applying suitable program modifications to $\mathcal{P}$. The resolution process results in a modified program $\mathcal{P}^*$ that is free of derivable conflicts and thereby consistent.

Definition 6 (Causality-Based Conflict Resolution Step and Process). *Let $\mathcal{P}$ be an ELP with $Conflicts^{dv}(\mathcal{P}) \neq \emptyset$. Given a conflict $\mathcal{C} = \{r_1, r_2\} \in Conflicts^{dv}(\mathcal{P})$, a causality-based conflict resolution step in $\mathcal{P}$ w.r.t. $\mathcal{C}$ is the modification of $\mathcal{P}$ to $\mathcal{P}^*$ such that r_1 and r_2 are not derivably conflicting in $\mathcal{P}^*$. A causality-based conflict resolution process w.r.t. $\mathcal{P}$ is a sequence $\langle \mathcal{P}_0, \mathcal{P}_1, \ldots, \mathcal{P}_n \rangle$ where $\mathcal{P}_0 = \mathcal{P}$ and for each $\mathcal{P}_i, \mathcal{P}_{i+1}(0 \leq i < n)$, $\mathcal{P}_{i+1}$ is the result of a causality-based conflict resolution step in $\mathcal{P}_i$, and $\mathcal{P}_n$ contains no derivable conflicts, i.e. $Conflicts^{dv}(\mathcal{P}_n) = \emptyset$.*

The following example illustrates a causality-based resolution process consisting of a single conflict resolution step.

Example 6 (Example 5 contd.). Let $\mathcal{P}_6$ be the following program that extends $\mathcal{P}_5$ from Example 5 by the following two additional rules:

$$r_{11}: drugC \leftarrow sympT, \sim drugD. \qquad r_{12}: drugC \leftarrow \overline{sympQ}, sympR.$$

Here, conflict $C_2 = \{r_3, r_4\}$ is the only derivable conflict, hence a single conflict resolution step suffices. One possible set of modifications is $R^\star = \{r_6^\star, r_{11}^\star\}$ with $r_6^\star = rmod(r_6, \{\sim sympT\})$ and $r_{11}^\star = rmod(r_{11}, \{sympV\})$. Program $\mathcal{P}_6 \diamond R^\star$ has the unique answer set $\{\overline{drugA}, sympQ, sympT, sympU, \overline{treatmZ}\}$.   □

Ergo, in each conflict resolution step, a derivable conflict becomes nonderivable after applying a suitable set of modifications to the program. We now present two concrete strategies to build suitable program modifications for a conflict.

4   Strategies for Conflict Resolution

After describing the general properties that have to be satisfied in order for two rules to be not simultaneously satisfiable, we present two explicit strategies to resolve derivable conflicts. While in [10], the conflicting rules themselves are modified during a conflict resolution step, the demonstrated strategies yield conflict-preventing sets that do not involve the conflicting rules by using causality-based conflict resolution. As in [10], the inconsistent program is modified using informative extensions, i. e. the modifications are based on the underlying language rather than inventing technical workarounds. The following section presents some technical considerations and results that will prove useful for the strategies.

4.1   General Satisfaction Interdependencies

We propose strategies for manipulating $\mathcal{P}$ to a consistent program $\mathcal{P}^\star$ such that $AS^\perp(\mathcal{P}^\star) = \emptyset$ where for every conflict $C = \{r_1, r_2\}$ in $\mathcal{P}^\star$ and $S \in AS^{pre}(\mathcal{P}^\star)$, it holds that if S satisfies $B(r_1)$, then S does not satisfy $B(r_2)$. In other words, whenever r_1 is active under a pre-answer set, r_2 cannot become active.

Proposition 2. *Let $\mathcal{P}$ be an ELP with Conflicts$(\mathcal{P}) \neq \emptyset$. $\mathcal{P}$ is consistent if there exists at least one pre-answer set S in $\mathcal{P}$ such that for every conflict $C = \{r_1, r_2\} \in$ Conflicts$(\mathcal{P})$, the following holds:*

$$S \text{ satisfies } B(r_1) \implies S \text{ does not satisfy } B(r_2) \tag{1}$$

Proof. Let S be a pre-answer set such that (1) holds for all conflicts $C = \{r_1, r_2\}$ in *Conflicts*$(\mathcal{P})$. Assume S is inconsistent. Then there exists at least one conflict $C \in$ *Conflicts*$(\mathcal{P})$ such that S satisfies both $B(r_1)$ and $B(r_2)$, which contradicts the initial specification of S. Thus, every pre-answer set of $\mathcal{P}$ where (1) holds for every conflict in *Conflicts*$(\mathcal{P})$ is an answer set.   □

Regarding the non-satisfiability of a body, we derive the following assertion:

Proposition 3. *Given a pre-answer set S of an ELP $\mathcal{P}$ and a rule $r \in \mathcal{P}$, the following holds (where sat. stands for satisfies/satisfy):*

$$S \text{ not sat. } B(r) \quad \text{iff } \exists L \in B^-(r) \text{ s.t. } L \in S \text{ or} \\ \exists L \in B^+(r) \text{ s.t. } L \notin S, \tag{2}$$

$$\text{iff } \exists r' \in H_L, L \in B^-(r) \text{ s.t. } S \text{ sat. } B(r') \text{ or} \\ \forall r' \in H_L, L \in B^+(r) \text{ s.t. } S \text{ not sat. } B(r'). \tag{3}$$

Proof. Let S be a pre-answer set for an ELP $\mathcal{P}$ and $r \in \mathcal{P}$ a rule in $\mathcal{P}$. Equation (2) follows directly from the definition of the satisfaction of rule bodies in Sect. 2. Equation (3) can be shown by using the properties of pre-answer sets: Since pre-answer sets are defined as minimal sets of literals that satisfy all rules in a program, each contained literal has to be derived by at least one rule whose body is satisfied and therefore adds its head literal to the pre-answer set. If there is at least one rule $r' \in H_L$ such that $L \in B^-(r)$ and S satisfies $B(r')$, the head literal $H(r') = L$ has to be contained in S. Therefore, (2) is fulfilled, and $B(r)$ is not satisfied by S. Analogously, if for every rule $r' \in H_L$ with $L \in B^+(r)$, S does not satisfy $B(r')$, L cannot be contained in S due to the minimality of pre-answer sets. Again, (2) demands that $B(r)$ is not satisfied by S.   □

The interdependencies illustrated in Proposition 3 can be used to define different strategies to modify a program such that a conflict rule becomes nonderivable without changing the conflicting rules. Basically, (3) demands that any set of literals that satisfies $B(r_2)$ for a conflict $C = \{r_1, r_2\}$ should satisfy an opposing rule of r_1 or that there exists a positive body literal $L \in B^+(r_1)$ such that every supporting rule of r_1 w.r.t. to L is not satisfied by S. Proposition 3 also illustrates the recursive nature of (non-)satisfiability of rules in logic programs, as the second case in (3) implies (2) with r replaced by each r'.

The proposed strategies focus on manipulating the answer sets in such a way that the conflicting rules can still be active if the other conflicting rule is not active under an answer set. The proposed strategies can therefore be seen as a switch that prevents a conflicting rule from becoming active whenever the other conflict rule is active under an answer set. Thereby, the approach in Sect. 4.2 exploits the rule dependencies of negative body literals while the alternative strategy in Sect. 4.3 exploits the rule dependencies of positive body literals.

4.2   Blocking Rules Using Opposing Rules

Our first approach to prevent the derivability of conflicting rules are so-called *blocking rules*. A blocking rule adds a specific literal to each pseudo answer set in which one of the conflicting rules is active. In particular, this specific literal is part of the negative body of the other conflicting rule, which therefore gets "blocked". Thus, no pre-answer set can contain the complementary (head) literals of the conflicting rules at the same time. As a blocking rule exploits the negative body literals of a conflicting rule, this approach is only applicable for conflicts of the form $C = \{r_1, r_2\}$ with $B^-(r_1) \backslash B^-(r_2) \neq \emptyset$.

Definition 7 (Blocking Rule). *Let $\mathcal{P}$ be an ELP with a conflict $C = \{r_1, r_2\}$ for which $B^-(r_1) \backslash B^-(r_2) \neq \emptyset$ holds. Then, a blocking rule $r^\star$ for C is a rule*

$$r^\star\colon E \leftarrow B(r_2)., \text{ where } E \in B^-(r_1) \backslash B^-(r_2).$$

Definition 7 demands that the bodies of $r^\star$ and r_2 are identical. As the goal is to assure that $r^\star$ becomes active under a set of literals whenever r_2 is active, it would suffice that $B(r^\star) \subseteq B(r_2)$ holds. This, however, can lead to unwanted side effects as $r^\star$ can become active in cases where r_2 is not, which then again could lead to additional (latent) conflicts.

Proposition 4. *Let $\mathcal{P}$ be an ELP with a derivable conflict $\mathcal{C} = \{r_1, r_2\}$ and $r^\star$ a blocking rule for $\mathcal{C}$. Then, it holds that $\mathcal{C}$ becomes nonderivable in $\mathcal{P} \diamond r^\star = \mathcal{P} \cup r^\star$, i. e. for every pre-answer set $S \in AS^{pre}(\mathcal{P} \diamond r^\star)$, $r_1, r_2 \notin act^S(\mathcal{P} \diamond r^\star)$ is true.*

Proof. Let $\mathcal{C} = \{r_1, r_2\}$ be a derivable conflict in $\mathcal{P}$ s.t. $B^-(r_1) \backslash B^-(r_2) \neq \emptyset$ and $r^\star$ a blocking rule for $\mathcal{C}$ which is meant to block r_1, i.e. $H(r^\star) \in B^-(r_1) \backslash B^-(r_2)$ and $B(r^\star) = B(r_2)$. If $\mathcal{C}$ was derivable in $\mathcal{P}^\star = \mathcal{P} \diamond r^\star$, there would have to exist a pseudo answer set $S \in AS^\perp(\mathcal{P}^\star)$ with $r_1, r_2 \in act^S(\mathcal{P}^\star)$. As $r_2 \in act^S(\mathcal{P}^\star)$ is assumed, $r^\star \in act^S(\mathcal{P}^\star)$ holds (due to $B(r^\star) = B(r_2)$). Thus, $H(r^\star) \in S$ is true. But, as $H(r^\star) \in B^-(r_1)$, r_1 cannot be active under S, which contradicts the assumption of r_1 and r_2 being simultaneously active under S. Thus, there cannot be any pseudo answer set $S \in AS^\perp(\mathcal{P}^\star)$ under which r_1 and r_2 are active. As due to the definition of answer sets, r_1 and r_2 can also not be active under any answer set of $AS(\mathcal{P}^\star)$, $\mathcal{C}$ is nonderivable in all pre-answer sets of $\mathcal{P}^\star$. $\square$

Example 7 (Example 6 contd.). To make the conflict $\mathcal{C}_2 = \{r_3, r_4\}$ in $\mathcal{P}_6$ non-derivable, the blocking rule $r_{13}^\star$: $sympR \leftarrow drugC, \sim drugD$. can be constructed according to Proposition 4. The head literal of $r_{13}^\star$ is referring to the negative body literal $sympR \in B^-(r_4) \backslash B^-(r_3)$. Because the body of the blocking rule $r_{13}^\star$ equals the body of r_3, $r_{13}^\star$ is guaranteed to be active whenever r_3 is active. The blocking rule $r_{13}^\star$ leads to $\mathcal{C}_2$ being nonderivable in the program $\mathcal{P}_6 \diamond r_{13}^\star$ (Proposition 4). Note that no blocking rule can be constructed for r_3 because $B^-(r_3) \backslash B^-(r_4) = \emptyset$. $\square$

Example 7 implies that there can exist multiple possible solutions for a single conflict. In a corresponding framework, the professional expert has the possibility to interactively determine the most suitable solution for each conflict. This step is also reflected in Algorithm 1, where the complete strategy is summarized.

Algorithm 1: Blocking rules using opposing rules

Input: Program $\mathcal{P}$, Conflict $\mathcal{C} = \{r_1, r_2\} \in Conflicts^{dv}(\mathcal{P})$
Output: Modified program $\mathcal{P}^\star$ with $\mathcal{C} \notin Conflicts^{dv}(\mathcal{P}^\star)$ or $\emptyset$
1 Initialize $\mathcal{R}^\star := \emptyset$;
2 **foreach** $E \in B^-(r_1) \backslash B^-(r_2)$ **do**
3   ⌊ $\mathcal{R}^\star := \mathcal{R}^\star \cup \{E \leftarrow B(r_2).\}$;
4 **foreach** $E \in B^-(r_2) \backslash B^-(r_1)$ **do**
5   ⌊ $\mathcal{R}^\star := \mathcal{R}^\star \cup \{E \leftarrow B(r_1).\}$;
6 **if** $\mathcal{R}^\star = \emptyset$ **then return** $\emptyset$;   /* no resolution found */
7 $R^\star := ChooseSuggestion(\mathcal{R}^\star)$;   /* expert chooses suitable $R^\star \in \mathcal{R}^\star$ */
8 **return** $\mathcal{P} \diamond R^\star$;

4.3   Relevant Rule Modification

Instead of adding new rules such as the blocking rules presented in Proposition 4, which represent new opposing rules for conflicting rules, another possibility to resolve conflicts would be to modify the existing supporting rules of conflicting rules. We use the notion of rule modification as presented in [10], but instead of modifying the conflicting rules directly, we focus on the rules that are primarily responsible for the bodies of the conflicting rules to be true in the pseudo answer sets of $\mathcal{P}$. Within the rules H_L w.r.t. a literal $L \in B^+(r)$ of a rule $r \in \mathcal{P}$, we can distinguish between rules that are *relevant* for the conflict resolution, i. e. rules that can potentially be simultaneously active with both conflicting rules and *irrelevant* rules, which cannot become simultaneously active with at least one conflicting rule.

Definition 8 (Relevant Rule). *Let $\mathcal{P}$ be an ELP with a conflict $\mathcal{C} = \{r_1, r_2\}$ and H_L with $L \in B^+(r_1) \cup B^+(r_2)$. A rule $r' \in H_L$ is relevant for the conflict resolution of $\mathcal{C}$ if there exists a consistent set of literals S with $r_1, r_2, r' \in act^S(\mathcal{P})$. Otherwise, r' is irrelevant for the resolution of $\mathcal{C}$.*

Example 8 (Example 6 contd.). In $\mathcal{P}_6$, r_{12} is not relevant for the resolution of $\mathcal{C}_2 = \{r_3, r_4\}$. As $B^+(r_4) \cup B^+(r_{12}) = \{sympQ, \overline{sympQ}, sympR\}$ contains complementary literals and $B^-(r_4) \cap B^+(r_{12}) \neq \emptyset$ (as well as $B^-(r_3) \cap B^+(r_{12}) \neq \emptyset$), the three rules cannot be satisfied simultaneously by a consistent set of literals. Therefore, r_{12} cannot be responsible for the derivation of $drugC$ when the conflicting rules are simultaneously satisfied in a pseudo answer set.   □

The following definition extends the modification used in [10] and guarantees that at least one body literal of a conflicting rule is not satisfied if the other conflicting rule is active under a pre-answer set, i. e. every relevant rule of the body literal is modified in a way so that it becomes irrelevant for conflict resolution. The application of this method is illustrated in the ensuing example.

Definition 9 (Relevant rule modification). *Let $\mathcal{C} = \{r_1, r_2\}$ be a conflict in an ELP $\mathcal{P}$ s. t. $B^+(r_1) \backslash B^+(r_2) \neq \emptyset$ holds. Furthermore, suppose an arbitrary literal $L \in B^+(r_1) \backslash B^+(r_2)$ and a rule $r' \in H_L$. Then, $Pot(\mathbf{M}_{r'}) = \{M \mid M \subseteq \mathbf{M}_{r'}\}$ with $\mathbf{M}_{r'} = B(r_2) \backslash B(r')$ implies the powerset of possible modifications for r'. For each $M_{r'} \in Pot(\mathbf{M}_{r'})$ and $\widetilde{M}_{r'} = \{\sim a \mid a \in M_{r'}\}$, each rule modification $r^\star$ of r' of the form $rmod(r', \widetilde{M}_{r'})$ defines a relevant rule modification of r', i. e.*

$$r^\star\colon H(r') \leftarrow B(r'), \widetilde{M}_{r'}.$$

Example 9 (Example 6 contd.). If conflict $\mathcal{C}_2$ in $\mathcal{P}_6$ should be resolved in such a way that r_4 is preferred over r_3, we can manipulate the relevant rules of literals in $B^+(r_3) \backslash B^+(r_4)$. As $drugC$ is the only literal in $B^+(r_3) \backslash B^+(r_4)$, the rules $H_{drugC} = \{r_6, r_{11}, r_{12}\}$ have to be considered. As shown in Example 8, rule r_{12} is not relevant for the resolution of $\mathcal{C}_2$, so that only r_6 and r_{11} have to be modified. According to Definition 9, the following relevant rule modifications can be constructed for r_6 and r_{11}:

$$r_6^\star\colon drugC \leftarrow {\sim}drugD, {\sim}sympR, {\sim}sympQ.$$

$$r_{11,1}^\star\colon drugC \leftarrow sympT, {\sim}drugD, {\sim}sympQ.$$

$$r_{11,2}^\star\colon drugC \leftarrow sympR, sympT, {\sim}drugD.$$

$$r_{11,3}^\star\colon drugC \leftarrow sympR, sympT, {\sim}drugD, {\sim}sympQ. \qquad \Box$$

Since we require every rule in $\mathcal{P}$ to be satisfiable, any set $M_{r'}$ is also satisfiable. Furthermore, by definition, $M_{r'}$ has no common literal with $B(r')$. Thus, for any set $\widetilde{M}_{r'}$, it holds that $B(r') \cup \widetilde{M}_{r'}$ is also satisfiable.

Proposition 5. *Let* $\mathcal{P}$ *be an ELP with a derivable conflict* $\mathcal{C} = \{r_1, r_2\}$ *and* $B^+(r_1)\backslash B^+(r_2) \neq \emptyset$. *After applying relevant rule modifications* $R^\star = \{r_1^\star, \ldots, r_n^\star\}$ *for all relevant rules* $r_1', \ldots, r_n'$ *of a set* H_L *with* $L \in B^+(r_1)\backslash B^+(r_2)$ *as defined in Definition 9,* $\mathcal{C}$ *becomes nonderivable in the resulting program* $\mathcal{P}^\star = \mathcal{P} \diamond R^\star = ((\mathcal{P} \diamond rmod(r_1', \widetilde{M}_{r_1'})) \diamond \ldots \diamond rmod(r_n', \widetilde{M}_{r_n'}))$.

Proof. Let $\mathcal{P}$ be an ELP with a conflict $\mathcal{C} = \{r_1, r_2\}$ and $B^+(r_1)\backslash B^+(r_2) \neq \emptyset$ as well as $L \in B^+(r_1)\backslash B^+(r_2)$. Furthermore, let $\mathcal{P}^\star$ be a program that results from relevant rule modifications of every relevant rule for $\mathcal{C}$. The proof of this proposition is done by contradiction: If $\mathcal{C}$ would still be derivable in $\mathcal{P}^\star$, there would have to be at least one pseudo answer set $S \in AS^{\perp}(\mathcal{P}^\star)$ with $r_1, r_2 \in act^S(\mathcal{P}^\star)$. Then, by the definition of active rules, S satisfies both $B^+(r_1)$ and $B^+(r_2)$ and L in particular since $L \in B^+(r_1)\backslash B^+(r_2)$. Consequently, there has to be at least one rule $r_i \in act^S(\mathcal{P}^\star)$ with $H(r_i) = L$, which is, by definition, also included in H_L. If this rule is not relevant for the conflict resolution, r_i was not modified but could not be active under S in the first place as we already assume $r_1, r_2 \in act^S(\mathcal{P}^\star)$. If r_i is relevant, it was transformed to a modified rule $r_i^\star$ as shown in Definition 9. Then $B^+(r_i^\star) \cap B^-(r_2) \neq \emptyset$ or $B^-(r_i^\star) \cap B^+(r_2) \neq \emptyset$ holds. In either case, $r_i^\star$ cannot be active under S (i.e. $r_i^\star \notin act^S(\mathcal{P}^\star)$). This contradicts the assumption $r_i^\star \in act^S(\mathcal{P}^\star)$. As there cannot be any active rule $r_i \in H_L$ under S, S does not satisfy $B^+(r_1)$, hence $\mathcal{C}$ has to be nonderivable in $\mathcal{P}^\star$. $\Box$

Algorithm 2 summarizes the relevant rule modification strategy. The application of this strategy is illustrated in Example 10.

Example 10 (Example 9 contd.). By extending the bodies of all relevant rules of H_{drugC} with ${\sim}sympQ$, $sympR$, or both, all rules in H_{drugC} are now irrelevant for the conflict resolution of $\mathcal{C}_2$, and it is ensured that $drugC$ cannot be derived in any answer set in which r_4 is active. Therefore, r_3 and r_4 cannot become active simultaneously in any answer set. As each combination of modifications, viz. $R_1^\star = \{r_6^\star, r_{11,1}^\star\}$, $R_2^\star = \{r_6^\star, r_{11,2}^\star\}$, and $R_3^\star = \{r_6^\star, r_{11,3}^\star\}$, constitute a possible way to resolve $\mathcal{C}_2$, $\mathcal{P}_6 \diamond R_1^\star$, $\mathcal{P}_6 \diamond R_2^\star$ and $\mathcal{P}_6 \diamond R_3^\star$ describe three different resolution possibilities for $\mathcal{C}_2$ that use relevant rule modifications. $\Box$

Algorithm 2: Relevant rule modification

Input: Program $\mathcal{P}$, Conflict $\mathcal{C} = \{r_1, r_2\} \in Conflicts^{dv}(\mathcal{P})$
Output: Modified program $\mathcal{P}^*$ with $\mathcal{C} \notin Conflicts^{dv}(\mathcal{P}^*)$ or $\emptyset$
1   Initialize $\mathcal{R}^* := \emptyset$; $X := (B^+(r_1) \backslash B^+(r_2)) \cup (B^+(r_2) \backslash B^+(r_1))$;
2   **foreach** $L \in X$ **do**
3     $\mathcal{Y} := \emptyset$;
4   **foreach** *relevant rule* $r_i' \in H_L$ **do**
5       $Y_i :=$ all possible modifications $rmod(r_i', \widetilde{M}_{r_i'})$;
6       $\mathcal{Y} := \mathcal{Y} \cup Y_i$;
7     $\mathcal{R}^* := \mathcal{R}^* \cup \{\{r_1^*, \ldots, r_{|\mathcal{Y}|}^*\} \mid r_i^* \in Y_i, 1 \leq i \leq |\mathcal{Y}|\}$
8   **if** $\mathcal{R}^* = \emptyset$ **then return** $\emptyset$;   /* no resolution found */
9   $R^* := ChooseSuggestion(\mathcal{R}^*)$;   /* expert chooses suitable $R^* \in \mathcal{R}^*$ */
10 **return** $\mathcal{P} \diamond R^*$;

---

5   Related Work

The presented approach is related to methods developed and investigated in the area of *ASP debugging*. Essentially, debugging approaches as in [5,8] aim to modify knowledge bases of any (not necessarily inconsistent) logic programs in order to remedy a mismatch between the actual semantics of the program and the semantics intended by the modeller. In general, the ability to identify errors in a given program and compute suggestions crucially depends on information by the expert that is given on top of the original program. Alternatively, with the approaches in [3,7], the expert can analyze the program step by step in order to detect error causes. Our approach, however, focuses on a specific subclass of erronous programs where the original program is by itself sufficient to identify the problem and generate suitable solution suggestions. Once possible solutions are available, both the presented method as well as debugging approaches like those based on the meta-programming technique [5] can be used to successively obtain the most suitable solution in interaction with the user.

6   Conclusion and Future Work

We have shown how consistency in an inconsistent program can be achieved without modifying the de facto conflicting rules to improve the usability of answer set programs in practice. The presented causality-based resolution approach is obligatory if the conflicting rules themselves must not be altered. By examining the dependencies between rules, we have shown how the satisfaction of conflicting rules can be prevented. For that, we defined two strategies which can be used to generate informative solutions for a professional expert. The expert can choose the most suitable solution for each conflict to achieve consistency. We have also introduced the notion of latent conflicts that can cause inconsistency either during the conflict resolution process or after subsequent modifications.

The recursive nature of rule dependencies allows for the application of the strategies not only to supporting rules of the conflicting rules, but also to their supporting rules (*transitive conflict resolution*). That leads to even more possibilities to repair a program, such that even small programs can lead to a vast amount of possible solutions for a professional expert to scan through. It is therefore critical that a framework as proposed in [9,10] incorporates different workflows and procedures to efficiently find the most fitting solution for each conflict. Such workflows imply suitable interactions with the professional expert to gather relevant background information with the goal to reduce the amount of solutions which in turn can reduce the overall complexity of such conflict resolution approaches.

In future work, we want to extend the presented approach to cover transitive conflict resolution using established methods from argumentation theory. Moreover, we want to develop methods to resolve multiple conflicts simultaneously.

References

1. Alferes, J.J., Leite, J.A., Pereira, L.M., Przymusinska, H., Przymusinski, T.C.: Dynamic logic programming. In: Freire-Nistal, J.L., Falaschi, M., Ferro, M.V. (eds.) 1998 Joint Conference on Declarative Programming, APPIA-GULP-PRODE 1998, A Coruña, Spain, 20–23 July 1998, pp. 393–408 (1998)
2. Eiter, T., Fink, M., Sabbatini, G., Tompits, H.: On properties of update sequences based on causal rejection. Theory Pract. Log. Program. **2**, 711–767 (2002)
3. Fichte, J.K., Gaggl, S.A., Rusovac, D.: Rushing and strolling among answer sets - navigation made easy. CoRR abs/2112.07596 (2021)
4. Gebser, M., Kaminski, R., Kaufmann, B., Schaub, T.: Answer Set Solving in Practice. Synthesis Lectures on Artificial Intelligence and Machine Learning. Morgan & Claypool Publishers (2012)
5. Gebser, M., Pührer, J., Schaub, T., Tompits, H.: A meta-programming technique for debugging answer-set programs. In: Fox, D., Gomes, C.P. (eds.) Proceedings of the Twenty-Third AAAI Conference on Artificial Intelligence, AAAI 2008, Chicago, Illinois, USA, 13–17 July 2008, pp. 448–453. AAAI Press (2008)
6. Gelfond, M., Lifschitz, V.: Classical negation in logic programs and disjunctive databases. New Gener. Comput. **9**(3/4), 365–386 (1991)
7. Oetsch, J., Pührer, J., Tompits, H.: Stepwise debugging of answer-set programs. Theory Pract. Log. Program. **18**(1), 30–80 (2018)
8. Shchekotykhin, K.M.: Interactive query-based debugging of ASP programs. In: Bonet, B., Koenig, S. (eds.) Proceedings of the Twenty-Ninth AAAI Conference on Artificial Intelligence, 25–30 January 2015, Austin, Texas, USA, pp. 1597–1603. AAAI Press (2015)
9. Thevapalan, A., Heyninck, J., Kern-Isberner, G.: Establish coherence in logic programs modelling expert knowledge via argumentation. In: Workshop on Causal Reasoning and Explanation in Logic Programming (CAUSAL 2021) (2021)
10. Thevapalan, A., Kern-Isberner, G.: Towards interactive conflict resolution in ASP programs. In: Martínez, M.V., Varzinczak, I. (eds.) Proceedings of the 18th International Workshop on Non-Monotonic Reasoning, NMR 2020, pp. 29–36, September 2020

xASP: An Explanation Generation System for Answer Set Programming

Ly Ly Trieu[1(✉)], Tran Cao Son[1], and Marcello Balduccini[2]

[1] New Mexico State University, New Mexico, USA
lytrieu@nmsu.edu, tson@cs.nmsu.edu
[2] Saint Joseph's University, Pennsylvania, USA
mbalducc@sju.edu

Abstract. In this paper, we present a system, called xASP, for generating explanations that explain *why* an atom belongs to (or does not belong to) an answer set of a given program. The system can generate all possible explanations for a query without the need to simplify the program before computing explanations, i.e., it works with non-ground programs. These properties distinguish xASP from existing systems such as xClingo, DiscASP, $exp(ASP^c)$, and $s(CASP)$, which also generate explanations for queries to logic programs under the answer set semantics but simplify and ground the programs (the three systems xClingo, DiscASP, $exp(ASP^c)$) or do not always generate all possible explanations (the system $s(CASP)$). In addition, the output of xASP is insensitive to syntactic variations such as the order conditions and the order of rules, which is also different from the output of $s(CASP)$.

Keywords: Explainable AI · Logic Programming · Answer Set Programming

1 Introduction

Recent interest in explainable artificial intelligence provided the impulse for the development of several systems capable of generating explanations for queries posed to a logic program under the answer set semantics such as xClingo [2], DiscASP [4], $exp(ASP^c)$ [7], and $s(CASP)$ [1]. These systems can be characterized by three dimensions: (*i*) the strategy for computing the explanation (grounding vs. non-grounding), (*ii*) the types of queries that can be posed to the system (true atoms and false atoms), and (*iii*) the representation of the answers. Among these systems, only $s(CASP)$ does not ground the program before computing the answers; both $s(CASP)$ and $exp(ASP^c)$ generate explanations for atoms in an answer set (true atoms) and atoms not in an answer set (false atoms); while xClingo is not applicable to false atoms; and DiscASP currently only works for propositional answer set programs. $s(CASP)$ generates a partial answer set supporting a query while others generate a full justification, represented by an explanation graph, given an answer set.

Partially supported by NSF grants 1914635, 1757207, 1812628. This contribution was also made possible in part through the support of NIST via cooperative agreement 70NANB21H167.

Grounding a program before computing an explanation comes at some costs. One of the most significant problems is that the grounding simplification techniques applied by answer set solvers tend to remove various pieces of information, resulting in explanations that are no longer faithful to the original program, or unable to even provide an explanation. This is illustrated in the next example.

Example 1 (Limitation of Current Approaches). Let P be a program:

$$d :- b(X), a(X). \qquad b(1). \qquad a(4).$$

This program has a unique answer set $\{a(1), b(4)\}$. d is false in this answer set. Suppose that we are interested in the question *"why is d false?"*

Among the four systems mentioned earlier, only $s(CASP)$ is able to provide an explanation for this query. For other systems, no explanation for a false atom is provided, either by design or by the simplification process. $exp(ASP^c)$ does not return an explanation graph for d because d is eliminated by the solver during the grounding phase.

In the above example, $s(CASP)$ generates the following justification[1]

```
not d :- not b(Var0 | {Var0 \= 1}), b(1), not a(1).
```

This says that there is an answer set containing $b(1)$, that does not contain $a(1)$ and does not contain any other atom of the form $b(x)$ such that $x \neq 1$.

When we switch the position of $b(X)$ and $a(X)$ in the first rule, we receive a different justification:

```
not d :- not a(Var0 | {Var0 \= 4}),   a(4), not b(4).
```

The above example highlights the shortcomings of existing systems. For $s(CASP)$, even though both answers are correct, it is not ideal that a slight semantics-preserving change in the input results in a different justification.

In this work, we describe xASP, a system capable of computing the explanation graphs of a ground atom a w.r.t. an answer set A of a non-ground program P. By working directly with programs including variables, xASP generates explanation graphs that are faithful to the program, thus distinguishing itself from xClingo, DiscASP, and $exp(ASP^c)$, which simplify the program before computing an explanation. Different from $s(CASP)$, it generates all full explanation graphs for an atom given an answer set and its behavior is not affected by semantics-preserving changes in the program. To work with programs including variables, xASP uses the given atom and answer set to dynamically identify relevant ground rules for the construction of the answers. Again, the main purpose of xASP is to help respond to the need for explainable AI. However, by presenting the applicable rules, facts, and assumptions used in the derivation of a given atom, xASP could be useful for debugging as well. For example, if an atom a is supposed to be false in all answer sets of a program P but appears in some answer set A, the explanation graph of a could be useful in figuring out which rule must not be applicable, etc.

---

[1] $p(V \mid V \neq v)$ represents the set of all atoms of the form $p(x)$ except for the atom $p(v)$.

2   The xASP System

xASP generates explanation graphs under the stable model semantics [3]. It deals with normal logic programs, which are collections of rules of the form $h \leftarrow b$ where h is an atom and $b = p_1, \ldots, p_m,\ not\ n_1, \ldots,\ not\ n_s$, p_i and n_j are atoms, and not is the default negation operator. For a rule r, r^+ and r^- denote the set of positive atoms $\{p_1, \ldots, p_m\}$ and the set of negative atoms $\{n_1, \ldots, n_s\}$, respectively. xASP utilizes the notions of supported set and derivation path [7,8] and the concept of explanation graph [5] which are illustrated using the program P_1 consisting of the following rules:

(r_1) m   :- l(X), not d, not h(X).
(r_2) d   :- b(X), a(X). (r_3) h(X) :- k(X), p.
(r_4) b(1). (r_5) a(4). (r_6) l(1). (r_7) k(6).

Given the answer set $A_1 = \{l(1), m, a(4), b(1), k(6)\}$, the explanation graphs of m are shown in Fig. 1. Both indicate that m is true in A_1 because of the existence of the rule r_1 and the following dependencies:

- m depends positively on $l(1)$, which is a fact;
- m depends negatively on $h(1)$, which is false, because there is only one instance of the rule r_3 with the head $h(1)$. In that instance, $h(1)$ depends positively on $k(1)$ (left) or p (right) and both are false because there is no rule for deriving them;
- m depends negatively on d, which is false. That is because there are two instances of rule r_2 supporting the derivation of d, but none of them is applicable in the given answer set. In fact, both $a(1)$ and $b(4)$ are false because there are no rules for deriving them.

In general, for a node x in an explanation graph G, if x is an atom a then the set of nodes directly connected to a— the nodes y such that $(a, y, \_)$ is an edge in G—represents the body of a rule whose head is x and whose body is satisfied by A. If x is $\sim a$ for some atom a, then the set of nodes directly connected to $\sim a$ represents a set of atoms whose truth values in A are such to make each rule whose head is a unsatisfied by A. In other words, the direct connections with a node represent the *support* [7] for the node being in (or not in) the answer set under consideration.

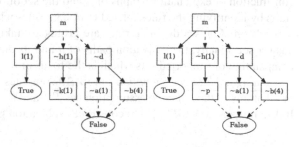

Fig. 1. Explanation graph of m

The three types of links connecting a node x (corresponding to an atom a) to a node y (for an atom b) in explanation graphs are as follows:

- + (represented by a solid link) demonstrates that the truth value of a depends *positively* on the truth value of b w.r.t. A. If node y is $\top$ ($True$), atom a is a fact.

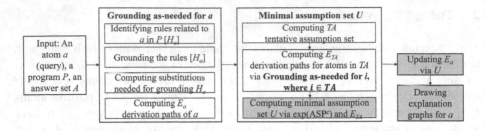

Fig. 2. The overview of xASP system

- − − (represented by a `dashed link`) demonstrates that the truth value of a depends *negatively* on the truth value of b w.r.t. A. If node y is $\bot$ (*False*), it means that atom a is always false. Note that in our prior system $exp(ASP^c)$, this link does not exist because the atoms, that are always false, have been simplified during the grounding process of `clingo`.
- − ∘ (represented by a `dotted link`) is used in the case in which node y is *assume*, which means that atom a is assumed to be false (see in examples in [5,7]).

2.1 Overview of xASP

Figure 2 shows the overview of xASP. The large two boxes represent the two main phases of xASP, *grounding as-needed* and *computing a minimal assumption set*. The grey boxes are implemented via $exp(ASP^c)$.

Grounding as-needed: xASP computes the set of ground rules that are necessary for the construction of explanation graphs of a and the set of derivation paths of a given A. It starts by identifying the rules related to a, e.g., rules whose head is a or an atom that a depends on. Afterwards, these rules are grounded, taking into consideration the given answer set. Finally, the derivation paths of a and its dependencies are obtained via the computation of supported sets which is the focus of this paper (Sect. 2.2).

Computing a minimal assumption set: xASP computes E_{TA}, the set of derivation paths of all atoms in the tentative assumption set TA and a minimal assumption set U of A. It then utilizes $exp(ASP^c)$ [7] to construct explanation graphs for a.

2.2 Computing Derivation Paths of a

This section presents a key algorithm for computing E_a, an *associative array* whose keys are a or atoms that a depends on, directly or indirectly, as defined via the dependency graph [6]. $E_a.keys()$ denotes the set of keys in E_a. For each $x \in E_a.keys()$, $E_a[x]$ is the value associated with x in E_a and contains the supported sets of x [7].

Given two atoms $a = p(t_1, t_2, .., t_n)$ and $b = q(t_1', t_2', .., t_m')$, we write $pu(a, b)$ to denote that a and b have the same predicates $(p = q)$ and arities $(n = m)$, i.e., a and b are possibly unifiable.

Algorithm 1: $PartialGrounding(a, P, A)$

  Input: a-a ground atom; P-program; A-an answer set
  Output: E_a - set of derivation paths of a and a's dependencies
1 Let $E_a[a] = []$ if $a \in A$ or let $E_a[\sim a] = []$ if $a \notin A$
2 Let $H_a = \{(h, r^+, r^-) \mid r = h \leftarrow b \in P \wedge pu(a, h)\}$
3 **for** $(h, r^+, r^-) \in H_a$ **do**
4   **if** $\exists! \theta$ such that θ be the unifier of $\{a, h\}$ **then**
5         $L = \{p \mid p \in r^+ \wedge p\theta \text{ is not ground}\}$
6   **for** $\theta' \in \omega(L, A)$ **do**
7             $\theta' \leftarrow \theta' \circ \theta$ // Composition of substitutions
8             $D \leftarrow \{d\theta' \mid d \in r^+\}, N \leftarrow \{n\theta' \mid n \in r^-\}$
9   **if** $a \in A$ **then**
10                 $T \leftarrow \{D \cup \{\sim n \mid n \in N\} \mid D \subseteq A, N \cap A = \emptyset\}$
11   Append T to $E_a[a]$
12   **else**
13                 $T \leftarrow \{\{d\} \mid d \in A \cap N\} \cup \{\{\sim n\} \mid n \in D \setminus A\}$
14                 $E_a[\sim a] \leftarrow [X \cup L \mid X \in E_a[\sim a], L \in T]$
15 $E_a[\sim a] \leftarrow [\{\bot\}] \mid \nexists(h, r^+, r^-) \in H_a$ such that a is unifiable with h
16 $PartialGrounding(c, P, A)$ where either $c \in C$ or $\sim c \in C, C \in E_a[a] \cup E_a[\sim a]$
17 **return** E_a

Algorithm 1 takes a grounded atom a and an answer set A of program P as inputs and computes E_a for the construction of the explanation graph for $a \in A$ (true atom) or $a \notin A$ (false atom). E_a is initialized with the empty array (line 1). Only rules in H_a whose head could be unified with a are involved in the partial grounding process (lines 2-14). For each $(h, r^+, r^-) \in H_a$, the grounding process starts with a unifier θ of a and h (line 4). L is the set of positive atoms that are not grounded after substituting with θ. $p\theta$ denotes that variables in atom p are substituted by elements in θ. Due to the restriction that

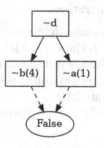

Fig. 3. Explanation graph of d

variables occurring in negative atoms must appear in positive atoms, ground substitutions of atoms in r^+ are ground substitutions for the negative atoms in r^-. We define $\omega(L, A)$ as the set of potential substitutions for variables in L given A, in which each element θ' of $\omega(L, A)$ is a set of substitutions of the form v/t such that for some $x \in L$ and $x\theta' \in A$, and $\{v \mid v/t \in \theta'\} = V$ where V is the set of variables in L. Note that θ' must be composed to a valid substitution for variables in L, e.g., it must not specify two different values for a variable (called conflict in the variable). In addition, some atoms in L cannot be unified with any atoms in A and hence are false w.r.t. A. Therefore, those atoms are not grounded (see Sect. 2.3). If $L = \emptyset$, $\omega(L, A)$ is empty. After obtaining substitutions, the positive and negative atoms are grounded via θ' (line 7) and supported sets of a are computed which depend on the truth value of a in A (lines 6-14). Note that, in line 10, if $D = \emptyset$ and $N = \emptyset$, then $T = \{\top\}$, denoting that atom a is a fact. Observe that if there are no rules whose head can be unified with a, then the atom is false (no rule in P supports a). As such, $E_a[\sim a]$ is set to $[\{\bot\}]$, i.e. atom a is false in P (line 15). Unlike $exp(ASP^c)$, Algorithm 1 is recursively called only on atoms in supported set of a (line 16).

Example 2. Let us reconsider program P_1 and compute the derivation paths for m. Given a ground atom m, there is only rule r_1 whose head is unifiable with m where $\theta = \emptyset$. θ is not a ground substitution for positive atoms in r_1. Thus, answer set A_1 is utilized to obtain a unifier $\{X/1\}$ to substitute for atoms in the body of r_1, resulting in $E_m[m] = \{l(1), \sim d, \sim h(1)\}$. Algorithm 1 is called recursively on atoms $l(1)$, d and $h(1)$.

- $E_m[l(1)] = [\{\top\}]$ because of rule r_6.
- Similar to m, unifier $\theta = \emptyset$ for atom d is not a ground substitution for positive atoms in r_2. However, given A_1, we can conclude that there are two possible substitutions, $\{X/1\}$ and $\{X/4\}$, for r_2. We have $E_m[\sim d] = [\{\sim a(1), \sim b(4)\}]$. Algorithm 1 is then called for atoms $a(1)$ and $b(4)$.
  - Although the head of rule r_5 has the same predicate and arity as $a(1)$, $a(1)$ and $a(4)$ are not unifiable. Thus, $E_m[\sim a(1)] = [\{\bot\}]$. Similar to $a(1)$, $E_m[\sim b(4)] = [\{\bot\}]$.
- Similaly, we have $E_m[\sim h(1)] = [\{\sim k(1)\}, \{\sim p\}]$, $E_m[\sim k(1)] = [\{\bot\}]$ and $E_m[\sim p] = [\{\bot\}]$.

2.3 Illustrations

Figure 3 shows the explanation graph for d in the case of Example 1. Unlike $s(CASP)$, in xASP the explanation for d being false is that all possible ground rules whose head is d have an unsatisfied body, in this case because $a(1)$ and $b(4)$ are false.

Consider another program P' containing the rules:

$(r_1)\,\texttt{m}\quad\quad\texttt{:-}\;\;not\;\texttt{q.}\quad\quad\quad(r_2)\,\texttt{q}\quad\quad\texttt{:-}\;\texttt{d(X).}$
$(r_3)\,\texttt{d(X)}\;\texttt{:-}\;\texttt{a(X), 1.}\quad\;(r_4)\,\texttt{a(1).}$

An explanation graph of m w.r.t. P' and answer set $A' = \{m, a(1)\}$ is shown in Fig. 4. It contains non-ground atom $d(X)$ because no atoms formed by $d/1$ occur in A'.

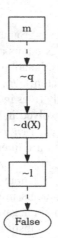

Fig. 4. Explanation graph of m

3 Conclusion

We presented xASP, a system for computing explanation graphs of true and false atoms w.r.t. an answer set of a program. xASP does not simplify the program before finding the explanations, thus providing faithful explanations for the truth value of the given atom. This is important to form a correct understanding of programs. Future work includes testing xASP on realistic debugging tasks and supporting the full language of clingo.

References

1. Arias, J., Carro, M., Chen, Z., Gupta, G.: Justifications for goal-directed constraint answer set programming. Electron. Proc. Theor. Comput. Sci. **325**, 59–72 (2020)
2. Cabalar, P., Fandinno, J., Muñiz, B.: A system for explainable answer set programming. Electron. Proc. Theor. Comput. Sci. **325**, 124–136 (2020)
3. Gelfond, M., Lifschitz, V.: The stable model semantics for logic programming. In: Kowalski, R., Bowen, K. (eds.) Logic Programming: Proceedings of the Fifth International Conference and Symposium, pp. 1070–1080 (1988)
4. Li, F., Wang, H., Basu, K., Salazar, E., Gupta, G.: Discasp: a graph-based asp system for finding relevant consistent concepts with applications to conversational socialbots. arXiv preprint arXiv:2109.08297 (2021)
5. Pontelli, E., Son, T., El-Khatib, O.: Justifications for logic programs under answer set semantics. TPLP **9**(1), 1–56 (2009)
6. Przymusinski, T.C.: On the declarative semantics of deductive databases and logic programs. In: Foundations of Deductive Databases and Logic Programming (1988)
7. Trieu, L.L., Son, T.C., Balduccini, M.: exp(aspc): explaining asp programs with choice atoms and constraint rules. Electron. Proc. Theor. Comput. Sci. **345**, 155–161 (2021)
8. Trieu, L.L., Son, T.C., Pontelli, F., Balduccini, M.: Generating explanations for answer set programming applications. In: Artificial Intelligence and Machine Learning for Multi-domain Operations Applications III, pp. 390–403. International Society for Optics and Photonics, SPIE (2021). https://doi.org/10.1117/12.2587517

Systems

Solving Problems in the Polynomial Hierarchy with ASP(Q)

Giovanni Amendola[1], Bernardo Cuteri[1], Francesco Ricca[1(✉)],
and Mirek Truszczynski[2]

[1] University of Calabria, Rende, Italy
{amendola,cuteri,ricca}@mat.unical.it
[2] University of Kentuky, Lexington, USA
mirek@cs.uky.edu

Abstract. Answer Set Programming with Quantifiers ASP(Q) is a recent extension of Answer Set Programming (ASP) that allows one to model problems from the entire polynomial hierarchy. Earlier work focused on demonstrating modeling capabilities of ASP(Q). In this paper, we propose a modular ASP(Q) solver that translates a quantified ASP program together with a given data instance into a Quantified Boolean Formula (QBF) to be solved by any QBF solver. We evaluate the performance of our solver on several instances and with different back-end QBF solvers, demonstrating the efficacy of ASP(Q) as a tool for rapid modeling and solving of complex combinatorial problems. The benchmark problems we use include two new ones, *Argumentation Coherence* and *Para-coherent ASP*, for which we develop elegant ASP(Q) encodings.

Keywords: Answer Set Programming · Quantifiers · QBF

1 Introduction

Answer Set Programming (ASP) [7,20] is a logic programming formalism for modeling and solving search and optimization problems. It is especially effective in modeling and solving search and optimization variants of decision problems in the class NP (the first level of the polynomial hierarchy) [19]. The success of ASP is due to two factors. First, problems in NP (and their search and optimization variants) can be expressed as compact and well-structured programs by following a simple programming methodology known as generate-define-test [22]. Second, solvers such as *clasp* [18], and *wasp* [1], were shown to be effective in processing programs for industrial-grade problems [11,16].

Modeling problems beyond the class NP with ASP is possible when one uses the full language of ASP that allows for disjunctions in the head of rules. In the full ASP language one can express problems whose decision variants are in the class Σ_2^P [10]. However, modeling problems beyond NP with ASP is complicated. The generate-define-test approach is insufficient, and commonly used techniques such as *saturation* [10,15] are hardly intuitive as they often introduce rules that have no direct relation to constraints of the problem being modeled.

G. Gottlob et al. (Eds.): LPNMR 2022, LNAI 13416, pp. 373–386, 2022.
https://doi.org/10.1007/978-3-031-15707-3_29

These shortcomings of ASP motivated recent research on extending ASP with quantifiers over answer sets of programs. In particular, following the way in which Quantified Boolean formulas (QBFs) add quantifiers over sets of interpretations to the language of propositional logic, we introduced the language *ASP with Quantifiers* or ASP(Q), for short [4]. The language expands ASP with quantifiers over answer sets of ASP programs; its elements are called *quantified programs*. We showed that ASP(Q) (just as QBFs) can express all decision problems forming the polynomial hierarchy [4]; we also presented quantified programs for four problems: *QBF evaluation* (spans the polynomial hierarchy), *Minmax Clique* (Π_2^P-complete), *Pebbling Number* (Π_2^P-complete) and *Vapnik-Chervonenkis Dimension* (Σ_3^P-complete).

These results notwithstanding, the ultimate adoption of ASP(Q) as a knowledge representation formalism depends on the availability of effective solvers for quantified programs. In this paper, we address this issue.

Contribution. Our primary contribution is the first ASP(Q) solver. It translates a quantified program together with a given data instance into a QBF. This QBF can be solved by any of the available QBF solvers. We study the performance of the solver on the QBF evaluation and the Minmax Clique problems [4], and on two additional problems, *Argumentation Coherence* (Π_2^P-complete) and *Paracoherent ASP* under the semi-stable semantics (Σ_2^P-complete), for which we show elegant encodings further showing the modeling efficiency of ASP(Q).

Related Work. To the best of our knowledge, this paper presents the first solver implementing the *ASP(Q)* language. Hence, no other ASP(Q) solvers are available for direct comparisons. However, some earlier works in the literature can be related to ASP(Q). The most closely-related formalisms are stable-unstable semantics [6] and quantified answer set semantics (QASP) [17]. For an exhaustive comparison of ASP(Q) with alternative formalisms we refer the reader to [4,14,17]. From the perspective of implementations, our approach builds on QBF solvers as existing ASP solvers build on SAT. Similarly to our approach, the quantified answer set semantics [23] was implemented by a translation to QBF and SAT-based ASP solving tools [17]. However, the differences in the semantics of quantifiers give rise to different encodings in QBF for the two formalisms. Translations from QASP to ASP(Q) and back were proposed by [17] but they have not been implemented. The stable-unstable semantics was implemented in a proof of concept prototype [6] and recently implemented via rewriting in ASP [21] that can only handle problems at the second level of the PH.

2   Answer Set Programming with Quantifiers

We assume familiarity with basic concepts of ASP and, in particular, ASP with variables extended with aggregates. For an answer set program P, we write H_P for the Herbrand base of P and $AS(P)$ for the collection of answer sets of P.

An *ASP with Quantifiers* (ASP(Q)) program Π is an expression of the form:

$$\Box_1 P_1 \ \Box_2 P_2 \ \cdots \ \Box_n P_n : C, \tag{1}$$

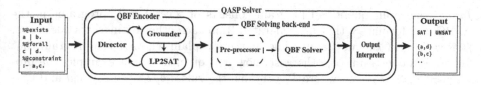

Fig. 1. System architecture

where, for each $i = 1, \ldots, n$, $\Box_i \in \{\exists^{st}, \forall^{st}\}$, P_i is an ASP program, and C is a stratified normal ASP program. An ASP(Q) program Π of the form (1) is *existential* (*universal*, respectively) if $\Box_1 = \exists^{st}$ ($= \forall^{st}$, respectively).

Given a logic program P, an interpretation I over the Herbrand base B_P of P, and an ASP(Q) program Π of the form (1), we denote by $fix_P(I)$ the set of facts and constraints $\{a \mid a \in I\} \cup \{\leftarrow a \mid a \in B_P \setminus I\}$, and by $\Pi_{P,I}$ the ASP(Q) program of the form (1), where P_1 is replaced by $P_1 \cup fix_P(I)$, that is,

$$\Pi_{P,I} = \Box_1(P_1 \cup fix_P(I)) \Box_2 P_2 \cdots \Box_n P_n : C.$$

Coherence of ASP(Q) programs is defined by induction as follows:

- $\exists^{st} P : C$ is coherent, if there exists $M \in AS(P)$ such that $C \cup fix_P(M)$ is coherent;
- $\forall^{st} P : C$ is coherent, if for every $M \in AS(P)$, $C \cup fix_P(M)$ is coherent;
- $\exists^{st} P\ \Pi$ is coherent, if there exists $M \in AS(P)$ such that $\Pi_{P,M}$ is coherent;
- $\forall^{st} P\ \Pi$ is coherent, if for every $M \in AS(P)$, $\Pi_{P,M}$ is coherent.

"Unwinding" the definition for a quantified program

$$\Pi = \exists^{st} P_1 \forall^{st} P_2 \cdots \exists^{st} P_{n-1} \forall^{st} P_n : C$$

yields that Π is coherent if there exists an answer set M_1 of P_1' such that for each answer set M_2 of P_2' there is an answer set M_3 of $P_3', \ldots$, there is an answer set M_{n-1} of P_{n-1}' such that for each answer set M_n of P_n', there is an answer set of $C \cup fix_{P_n'}(M_n)$, where $P_1' = P_1$, and $P_i' = P_i \cup fix_{P_{i-1}'}(M_{i-1})$, if $i \geq 2$.

For an ASP(Q) program Π of the form (1) such that $\Box_1 = \exists^{st}$, $M \in AS(P_1)$ is a *quantified answer set* of Π, if $(\Box_2 P_2 \cdots \Box_n P_n : C)_{P_1,M}$ is coherent. We denote by $QAS(\Pi)$ the set of all quantified answer sets of Π.

3   The ASP(Q) Solver

System Description. The architecture of the system is shown in Fig. 1. The input program Π is taken by the *QBF Encoder* module. It produces a QBF formula $\Phi(\Pi)$ such that $\Phi(\Pi)$ is true *iff* Π is coherent. The QBF $\Phi(\Pi)$ is then processed by the *QBF Solving back-end* that determines whether $\Phi(\Pi)$ is true. The *Output Interpreter* presents to the user the output in a standardized format. The modules are discussed in detail below.

Input. The input quantified program consists of several ASP programs in the ASPCore 2 format [8] that are separated from each other by markers `%@exists`, `%@forall`, and `%@constraint`. The markers explain whether the program that follows is a constraint or, otherwise, how it is quantified. For example, the program $\exists^{st} P_1 \forall^{st} P_2 : C$, where P_1 contains the rule $a|b$, P_2 the rule $c|d$ and C is the constraint $\leftarrow a, c$ is written in the input syntax in Fig. 1 the Input box.

QBF Encoder. The module translates the input program Π of the form (1) into a QBF formula $\Phi(\Pi)$. This process is driven by a *Director* submodule that analyzes the program structure to identify the quantifiers and the subprograms $P_1, ..., P_n$, and C. The subprograms P_i, $i = 1, \ldots, n$, are augmented with choice rules for ground atoms involving predicates occurring in earlier subprograms. In this way, ground atoms fixed by answer sets of earlier programs can be combined with the current program, implementing the use of the *fix* mapping described in the formal definition of the semantics. Each subprogram is then instantiated by the *Grounder* submodule that computes its propositional counterpart and converts it into a propositional formula in Conjunctive Normal Form (CNF) by *LP2SAT* module. The resulting CNF formulas are assembled together into a QBF $\Phi(\Pi)$ that is true precisely when Π is coherent. During this process the *Director* collects information that allows it to combine outputs of internal procedures. This information is also used by the *Output Interpreter* to print the results, in particular, an answer set of Π when available. We now provide a more formal account of the *QBF Encoder*.

For an ASP program P, we denote by $G(P)$ its grounding, by $pred(P)$ the set of predicates occurring in P, and by $at(P, p)$ the set of ground atoms built on predicate p from P. Given two programs P and P', we denote by $Int(P, P')$ the set $pred(P) \cap pred(P')$. Given a set of propositional atoms A, we denote by $ch(A)$ the program $\{\{a\}|a \in A\}$ made of choice rules over atoms in A. For two programs P and P', the choice interface program $CH(P, P')$ is defined as $ch(\bigcup_{p \in Int(P,P')} at(G(P), p))$. For a propositional formula Φ, $var(\Phi)$ denotes the variables occurring in Φ.

Given an input quantified program Π of the form (1), the intermediate groundings G_i of its sub-programs, and the QBF $\Phi(P)$ encoding Π are:

$$G_i = \begin{cases} G(P_1) & i = 1 \\ G(P_i \cup CH(P_{i-1}, P_i)) & i \in [2..n] \\ G(C \cup CH(P_n, C)) & i = n+1 \end{cases}$$

$$\Phi(\Pi) = \boxplus_1 \cdots \boxplus_{n+1} \left(\bigwedge_{i=1}^{n+1} (\phi_i \leftrightarrow CNF(G_i)) \right) \wedge \phi_c,$$

where $CNF(P)$ is a CNF formula encoding the ground program P (produced by *LP2SAT*); $\phi_1, \ldots, \phi_{n+1}$ are fresh propositional variables; $\boxplus_i = \exists x_i$ if either $\square_i = \exists^{st}$ or $i = n+1$, and $\boxplus_i = \forall x_i$ otherwise, $x_i = var(\phi_i \leftrightarrow CNF(G_i))$ for $i = 1, \cdots, n+1$, and ϕ_c is the formula

$$\phi_c = \phi_1' \odot_1 (\phi_2' \odot_2 (\cdots \phi_n' \odot_n (\phi_{n+1}) \cdots))$$

where $\odot_i = \vee$ if $\square_i = \forall^{st}$, and $\odot_i = \wedge$ otherwise, and $\phi_i' = \neg\phi_i$ if $\square_i = \forall^{st}$, and $\phi_i' = \phi_i$ otherwise. Intuitively, there is a direct correspondence between the quantifiers in Π and $\Phi(\Pi)$; moreover, each subprogram of Π (i.e., $P_1, \cdots, P_n, C$) is grounded taking care of the interface with preceding subprograms (i.e., of propositional atoms in common) and converted into an equivalent CNF formula; finally, the formula ϕ_c is built to constrain the variable assignments corresponding to the stable models of each subprogram so that they behave as required by the semantics of ASP(Q).

Theorem 1. *Let Π be a quantified program. Then $\Phi(\Pi)$ is true iff Π is coherent.*

Note that $\Phi(\Pi)$ is not in the normal form, thus the *QBF Encoder* outputs it in the QCIR format developed for such formulas.

QBF Solving Back-End. The QBF formula produced by the *QBF Encoder* is processed by a QBF solver of choice. To facilitate a broader range of applicable solvers and to improve solver performance, the *Pre-processor* submodule uses tools that convert the formula $\Phi(\Pi)$ to a format compatible with the solver (e.g., converting from QCIR to QDIMACS) or simplify a formula (e.g., eliminating some variables and quantifiers).

Output Interpreter. The output of the QBF back-end is parsed and printed by the *Output Interpreter*. When Π starts with an existential quantifier, and the QBF back-end is designed to provide a satisfying assignment to the corresponding existentially quantified variables, there is an option to print out the corresponding quantified answer set.

Additional Details. QASP is *modular*. That is, it might be configured with alternative grounders, ASP-to-SAT translators, and QBF solving pipelines. In current configuration, QASP is distributed as a jar package embedding all the internal components that are executed as external processes. It is made of $\geq 2k$ lines of Java code, compliant with Java 8 (or higher), requires Python 3, and runs under Linux.

4   Modeling Hard Problems with ASP(Q)

In this section, we present quantified programs encoding the Argumentation Coherence problem and the Semi-stable Semantics problem, the latter concerned with paracoherence in ASP. Both problems belong to the second level of the polynomial hierarchy.

Argumentation Coherence. Argumentation frameworks (AFs) of [12] form a powerful abstraction for several types of argumentation. To recall, an AF F is a directed graph (Ar, att), where Ar is a finite set of *arguments*, and $att \subseteq Ar \times Ar$ is a set of *attacks*: if $(a,b) \in att$ then we say that a attacks b. For a set $A \subseteq Ar$ of arguments, we denote by A^+ the set of all arguments in Ar attacked by an argument in A, i.e. $A^+ = \{b \in Ar \mid (a,b) \in att, \text{ and } a \in A\}$. We say that

$\{inA(X) : arg(X)\}$

$arg(a)$ for each $a \in Ar$
$att(a,b)$ for each $(a,b) \in Att$
$\{inS(X) : arg(X)\}$
$attackedByS(Y) \leftarrow arg(Y), inS(X), att(X,Y)$
$\quad \leftarrow inS(X), att(Y,X), not\ attackedByS(Y)$
$\quad \leftarrow inS(X), inS(Y), att(X,Y)$
$unstb \leftarrow arg(X), not\ inS(X), not\ attackedByS(X)$
$\quad \leftarrow not\ unstb.$

$attackedByA(Y) \leftarrow arg(Y), inA(X), att(X,Y)$
$\quad \leftarrow inA(X), att(Y,X), not\ attackedByA(Y)$
$\quad \leftarrow inA(X), inA(Y), att(X,Y)$

(b) Program P_2

(a) Program P_1

$nonPreferred \leftarrow inA(X), not\ inS(X)$
$\quad \leftarrow inS(X), not\ inA(X)$
$\quad \leftarrow not\ nonPreferred.$

(c) Constraint C

Fig. 2. Argumentation Coherence in ASP(Q).

A is *conflict-free* if for each $a, b \in A$, $(a, b) \notin att$. Further, A is *admissible* if A is conflict-free and if for every $a \in A$ and every $b \in Ar$ with $(b, a) \in att$, there is $c \in A$ such that $(c, b) \in att$ (a is *defended* by A in F). The *stable* and *preferred* semantics of argumentation frameworks play a prominent role in abstract argumentation. We define A to be a *stable extension* if $A^+ = Ar \setminus A$ (i.e., A is conflict-free, and for each $a \in Ar \setminus A$, there is $b \in A$, such that $(b, a) \in att$). We define A to be a *preferred extension* if A is a maximal admissible set (w.r.t. set-inclusion). Given an AF F, we denote by $stb(F)$ and $pref(F)$ the sets of all stable and preferred extensions of F, respectively.

The *Argumentation Coherence* (AC) problem consists of deciding whether for a given AF F, $stb(F) = pref(F)$. The problem is known to be Π_2^P-complete [13]. Since every stable extension is preferred, the AC problem is equivalent to checking that *for each* admissible and non-stable extension A of F, *there exists* an admissible extension A' of F, such that $A \subset A'$ (proper inclusion), thus showing that such sets A are not preferred extensions. This simple characterization leads to an encoding of an AF $F = (Ar, att)$ by an ASP(Q) program Π_F of the form $\forall^{st} P_1 \exists^{st} P_2 : C$. In Π_F, the program P_1 is given by the set of facts and rules in Fig. 2(a). The first two lines encode the input AF, using a unary predicate arg and a binary predicate att. The third line is a choice rule modeling a guess of a subset of the arguments, that are selected into the predicate inS. The fourth and fifth lines encode admissibility. The fourth rule states that $attackedByS(Y)$ must hold whenever an argument Y is attacked by an argument X from the selected set; the fifth rule (the constraint) ensures every element in the selected set is defended by the selected set. The next constraint ensures the selected set is conflict-free. Finally, the last two rules guarantee that the selected set is not stable. Indeed, the last but one rule derives an atom $unstb$ whenever the selected set is not stable, and the last rule forces $unstb$ to be derived. In other words, answer sets of P_1 correspond to admissible extensions of F that are not stable.

The program P_2 is reported in Fig. 2(b). Note that program P_2 is very similar to program P_1. It uses the predicate inA (instead of inS) to collect a guessed admissible extension. Thus, an answer set of P_2 corresponds to an admissible extension of F. Finally, the program C is reported in Fig. 2(c). Program C

ensures that a set S is a proper subset of A, therefore, not a preferred extension. It follows that Π_F is coherent if and only if for every answer set S of P_1 (an admissible extension that is not stable), there is an answer set A of P_2 (an admissible extension) such that A is a proper superset of S, thus showing that no admissible extension that is not stable is preferred or, in other words, demonstrating that for the given AF F, $stb(F) = pref(F)$. More formally:

Theorem 2. *Let* $F = (Ar, att)$ *be an AF. Then,* $stb(F) = pref(F)$ *iff the ASP(Q) program* Π_F *is coherent.*

Paracoherent ASP—Semi-stable Semantics. Paracoherent ASP is concerned with assigning a meaningful semantics to answer set programs that have no answer sets due to negative cycles [3]. One of the earliest proposed paracoherent semantics for ASP is the semantics of *semi-stable models* (the SST semantics) [24]. As required for every paracoherent semantics for ASP, the SST semantics coincides with the answer-set semantics, whenever a program has answer sets, and has *paracoherent* models, whenever the program has a classical model.

The SST semantics can be defined in terms of a certain epistemic transformation of ASP programs [2]. First, for every atom a in P, we introduce a fresh "gap" atom $gap(a)$. Then, for each rule $r \in P$, we construct a rule r' by adding to the body of r the literal *not* $gap(c)$, for every literal *not* c occurring in the body of r. The *externally supported program* of P, or P^s, in symbols, is the program obtained from all rules r', where $r \in P$, and all choice rules $\{gap(c)\}$, for all new gap atoms $gap(c)$.

It is known that if P has a classical model, then P^s has an answer set. Given a set A of atoms of P^s, we set $gap(A) = \{gap(a) | gap(a) \in A\}$. We now define A to be an *SST model* of P if A is an answer set of P^s such that for every *other* answer set A' of P^s, $gap(A') \not\subseteq gap(A)$. In other words, an *SST model* of P is an answer set of P^s that is minimal with respect to gap atoms.

The *Paracoherent ASP* problem is the functional problem to compute an SST model of a given answer set program P. If P is head-cycle-free, the Paracoherent ASP problem is in $F\Sigma_2^p$ [2]. We consider the problem under this restriction and, for a head-cycle-free program P, we construct program $\Pi_P = \exists^{st} P_1 \forall^{st} P_2 : C$ whose quantified answer sets correspond to SST models of P.

To this end, we define $P_1 = P^s$ and $P_2 = P'^s$, where P' is obtained from P by replacing each atom p occurring in P with a fresh atom p'. Finally, the program C is as follows:

$$\begin{aligned}
noSubsetGap &\leftarrow gap(X), not\ gap'(X). \\
noSupersetGap &\leftarrow not\ gap(X), gap'(X). \\
&\leftarrow noSubsetGap, not\ noSupersetGap.
\end{aligned}$$

Consider an answer set A_1 of P_1 and any answer set A_2 of P_2 extended with the facts from A_1. The first rule of C infers atom $noSubsetGap$ whenever some atom X is in the gap of A_1 but not in the gap of A_2. This means that $gap(A_1) \not\subseteq gap(A_2)$. Similarly, the second rule infers atom $noSupersetGap$ whenever some atom X is in the gap of A_2 but not in the gap of A_1. This means that $gap(A_1) \not\supseteq$

$gap(A_2)$. Whenever *noSupersetGap* is not inferred, then each atom in the gap of A_2 is also in the gap of A_1, i.e., $gap(A_2) \subseteq gap(A_1)$. Finally, the last constraint says that that it is impossible that $gap(A_1) \not\subseteq gap(A_2)$ (*noSubsetGap* is true) and $gap(A_2) \subseteq gap(A_1)$ (*noSupersetGap* is false). So, it means that it is not possible that $gap(A_2) \subset gap(A_1)$. Therefore, Π_P is coherent if and only if there exists an answer set, say A_1, of P_1 (i.e., an answer set of P^s) such that for each answer set, say A_2, of P_2 (i.e., another answer set of P'^s), $gap(A_2)$ is not strictly contained into $gap(A_1)$. Hence, $gap(A_1)$ is subset minimal and A_1 is a semi-stable model of P. This leads to the following formal result.

Theorem 3. *Let P be an ASP program. Then, A is a semi-stable model of P iff A is a quantified answer set of Π_P.*

5   Experiments

In the experiments we aim to: (i) assess the performance of the system on well-known hard benchmarks, also providing as reference dedicated state-of-the-art solvers; (ii) show the system can compute in reasonable time solutions to several problems modeled in ASP(Q); (iii) compare on the paracoherence problem our approach (modeling in ASP(Q) and solving with our tool) with the approach based on direct ASP modeling using saturation; (iv) analyze the impact of the QBF encoder and different back-ends on QBF solving.

Experimental Setup. We consider four problems: Quantified Boolean Formulas (QBF); Argumentation Coherence (AC); Minmax Clique (MMC); Paracoherent ASP (PAR). The QBF evaluation is a natural choice when studying tools for solving hard problems in the PH. The problem has been studied extensively and many instances for assessing the performance of QBF solvers are available in QBF competition archives or can be randomly generated [5]. For our study, we randomly selected *993* hard instances from QBF Lib (https://www.qbflib.org/) and generated *2049* instances using the random generator by Amendola et al. [5]. (generator setting: 32 instances per sample with 72 universal variables 36 existential variables, number of clauses per sample varying from 72 to 192 with a step of 4, and number of components set to both 1 and 2). The instances from the QBF competitions allowed us to assess our tool on a well-known benchmark set containing instances of real-world problems form the PH; the random instances allowed us to assess the system on both easy and hard instances. QBF instances have been encoded in ASP(Q) using the encoding by Amendola et al. [4]. This benchmark contributes to goals (i) and (iv) of the study.

Argumentation Coherence (AC) was discussed earlier in the paper. To the best of our knowledge there are no dedicated solvers for this problem. This benchmark contributes to goal (ii). We consider all *326* instances of the argumentation competition ICCMA 2019 (http://argumentationcompetition.org/2019).

The *Minmax Clique* (MMC) problem [9] is a well-studied Π_2^p-complete problem. An ASP(Q) encoding was proposed by Amendola et al. [4]. Evaluating our solver on this problem supports goal (ii). The instances we considered are the 45 graphs used in the ASP Competitions [19] for the graph coloring benchmark.

The Paracoherent ASP problem (PAR) consists of computing the *semi-stable* models of ASP programs [24]. We presented a ASP(Q) encoding of the problem in the previous section. A direct ASP encoding using saturation was proposed by Amendola et al. [2]. We compare the performance of QASP run on our ASP(Q) encoding with that of WASP [1] run on the saturation-based direct ASP encoding. This supports the objective (iii) of our study. We consider the instances from the ASP competition used in earlier work [2]; we also generate a new set of random instances modeling 3-SAT formulas around the phase transition. Again, the random set contains both easy and hard instances of the problem (generator setting: 20 instances per sample with 300 variables, clauses varying from 850 to 1850, so that the ratio of clauses to variables is around the threshold of 4.25).

Compared Methods. We consider four variants of our system QASP:

- QASP ^{RQS}: The pre-processor calls *qcir-conv.py* to transform QCIR to GQ, then the *RareQS* QBF solver is called.
- QASP ^{DEPS} The pre-processor calls *qcir-conv.py* and *fmla* to convert the formula from QCIR to QDIMACS. The resulting formula is then further simplified by *bloqqer*, then the QBF solver *DepQBF* is called.
- QASP ^{QBS}: No pre-processor; QBF solver is *Quabs*.

To meet goals (i) and (iii) of our experiment, we run the back-end QBF solvers on original QDIMACS instances, and WASP ASP solver on ASP inputs:

- RAREQS: the input in QDIMACS format is converted in GQ using *qcir-conv.py* and then *Quabs* is called.
- DEPQBF: the input in QDIMACS format is pre-processed by *bloqqer* and then fed in input to *DepQBF*.
- QUABS: the input in QDIMACS format is converted in QCIR using *qcir-conv.py* and then *Quabs* is called.
- WASP: the combination of *gringo* with *WASP* [1] for PAR benchmark in the same setting as that used by Amendola et al. [2].

All solvers were run in their default configurations. In a preliminary experiment (with few instances per each domain) we run several (up to 11) variants of the back-ends, where we considered different combinations of QCIR to QDIMACS/GQ converters and pre-processors, and selected the best combination for each considered QBF solver. We stress that we did not aim at comparing back-end solver performance, instead our goals were to demonstrate the feasibility and efficacy of our implementation and to get insights into the impact of selecting different back-ends. Any advancement in QBF solving techniques can be capitalized on to yield improvements in our system.

Experiment Setup. Experiments were run on a system with 2.30 GHz Intel Xeon(R) E7-8880 v4 CPUs and 512 GB of RAM with GNU/Linux Debian 4.9.272-2 (2021-07-19) x86_64, kernel 4.9.0-16-amd64 #1 SMP. Execution time

Table 1. QBF benchmark: Sided with ad hoc solvers.

	QBF Competition			Random QBF		
	# Sol.	TO	MO	# Sol.	TO	MO
QASP ^{DEPS}	**606**	0	387	**1935**	114	0
QASP ^{QBS}	521	10	462	1630	419	0
QASP ^{RQS}	339	0	654	1360	689	0
DEPQBF	**727**	0	266	1935	114	0
QUABS	665	1	327	**2049**	0	0
RAREQS	448	1	544	2048	0	1

Table 2. AC and MMC Benchmarks.

	AC			Minmax Clique		
	# Sol.	TO	MO	# Sol.	TO	MO
QASP ^{DEPS}	119	0	207	21	24	0
QASP ^{QBS}	99	18	209	**45**	0	0
QASP ^{RQS}	**177**	0	149	23	22	0

and memory were limited to 1200 s (of CPU time, i.e., user+system) and 12 GB, respectively. Each system was limited run in a single core. A package containing QASP is available online at www.mat.unical.it/ricca/downloads/qasp-0.1.2.jar.

5.1 Results

QBF. The results obtained running the three variants of our QASP on QBF instances are summarized in Table 1. We report there the number of solved instances within the timeout (#sol), the number of timeouts (TO) and the number of memory outs (MO). In this benchmark QASP ^{DEPS} seems to be the best variant, followed by QASP ^{QBS} and QASP ^{DEPS}, respectively. We also report there the results obtained by running the back-end QBF solvers on the original instances in the QDIMACS format. The QBF solvers can solve more instances than the corresponding variant of QASP. Although we tried to keep the comparison as fair as possible, there are some obvious technical reasons that make this result expected. First, the original instances in the QDIMACS format are smaller in size, since they are encoded in the numeric format, whereas ASP(Q) instances are human-readable and, thus, more verbose and slower to read. Second, ASP(Q) instances are first encoded in QCIR and have to be transformed in a different format (for RAREQS and DEPQBF). Pre-processing causes the formula to be heavily rearranged and often "inflated" with extra variables and clauses w.r.t the original QDIMACS instance. This causes all the QASP versions to be interrupted more often than QBF counterparts because they exceed the memory limit. Especially on QBF competition instances, which are larger in size, this has more impact. Nonetheless, the difference in performance (varying from about 5% to 20%) remains acceptable, and the best QASP version (QASP ^{DEPS}) compares very well with QUABS and RAREQS.

AC and MMC. AC and Minmax Clique are benchmarks assessing our implementation on hard problems. In both cases, a rather intuitive encoding in ASP(Q) was provided, and we are not aware of the existence of any specialized systems. The results obtained running the three variants of our QASP on AC and MMC are summarized in Table 2. It reports the number of solved instances within the timeout (%sol), the number of timeouts (TO) and the number of memory outs (MO) in both benchmarks. We observe that QASP ^{RQS} is the best performing variant in AC, solving 177 instances of the ICCMA Competition, which is more

Table 3. PAR Benchmark: comparison with saturation.

	PAR - ASP Comp.			PAR - Random		
	# Sol.	TO	MO	# Sol.	TO	MO
QASP ^{DEPS}	0	0	73	68	373	0
QASP ^{QBS}	0	4	69	0	441	0
QASP ^{RQS}	1	0	72	441	0	0
WASP	0	0	73	166	276	0

Table 4. Encoding performance.

Benchmark	# Sol.	avg(T)	σ^2(T)	TO	MO	Imp.
AC	326	35.3	71.1	0	0	17%
QBF Rnd	2049	2.4	0.7	0	0	15%
QBF Com.	965	49.9	176.2	0	27	50%
MMC	45	6.7	6.1	0	0	25%
PAR ASP	68	90.1	177.4	5	0	50%
PAR Rnd	441	5.0	0.9	0	0	1%

than one half of the entire set. Concerning MMC, the best performing variant is QASP ^{QBS}, solving all the 45 instances available. These results confirm that QASP is effective as a tool for modeling and solving hard problems.

PAR. This benchmark was considered to compare ASP(Q) with an alternative solution based on a plain ASP encoding exploiting saturation. The results obtained running the three variants of our QASP and WASP (on plain ASP) are summarized in Table 3. The table reports the number of solved instances within the timeout (%sol), the number of timeouts (TO) and the number of memory outs (MO) in both benchmarks. First of all we observe that QASP ^{RQS} is the only implementation that is able to solve one of the very-hard instances form the ASP competition. The rewriting in QBF are indeed very large and often cause memory outs in all QASP variants. WASP evaluating a saturation-based encoding timed out in all the instances. ASP competition instances are very hard to draw a conclusion, but on random benchmarks the picture becomes more clear. QASP ^{RQS} confirms to be very effective on PAR Random benchmark solving all the 441 instances in the set, whereas WASP could solve only 166. We can thus conclude that ASP(Q) can be a better option problems in the second level of the PH than ASP with saturation. Indeed, the ASP(Q) encoding are more intuitive and the QASP is more effective.

Impact of Main Modules. From the results we have obtained it is clear that the back-end used for solving has an impact on QASP performance. On the one hand, different back-end solvers perform better on different benchmarks, and this is just another confirmation of the "no free lunch" theorem. On the other hand, it is interesting to analyze the impact of the QBF Encoder module to better understand the behavior of the QASP. In Table 4 we report for all considered benchmarks: the number of successfully-encoded instances within the timeout (%sol), the average execution time (avg(T)), standard deviation (σ^2(T)) on successfully-encoded instances, the number of timeouts (TO), and the number of memory outs (MO), as well as an indicative measure of the average impact of the QBF encoding phase on successfully-encoded instances (Imp.). The impact is computed as the ratio of the the average encoding time divided by average execution time of the best QASP variant, and is expressed in percentage. This measure is rough, but helps identifying the benchmarks in which the encoding phase had more impact. This is the case of both QBF competition instances and ASP competition instances for the PAR experiment. In these cases the encoding took a considerable amount of resources, causing 27 memory outs in QBF competition instances. However, for most instances this was not the case and the system spent most of the time in the back-end solver phase. Finally, note that there is a high variability on encoding times (compare variance with average), this means that in the same benchmark set some instances are easily encoded, whereas some others (the larger in size) require more time. On the positive side, we observe there are many cases in which the QBF encoding has negligible impact (cf., PAR Random), and the performance is acceptable in most cases, cf. AC, QBF Random, and MMC.

Final Remark. We do not provide empirical comparisons with related formalisms mentioned in the introduction (e.g., stable-unstable or QASP). First, our goal is not to show that ASP(Q) is the best option for solving problems in the PH (it is unlikely any formalism or solver can be uniformly *best*). Rather, we aim to show that the language and the tool presented here provide both convenient modeling capability and promising performance. Second, our set of benchmarks contains problems for which there are no declarative implementations in the literature. Third, although it is straightforward to compare our system with QBF solvers on their benchmarks, the converse is not obvious. For example, devising an effective encoding of PAR in QBF is tougher than developing a QBF-based ASP solver; it would require to overcome many nontrivial issues: grounding, recursive definitions, stability checking and gap minimization. This argument alone showcases the benefits of ASP(Q) solving. Fourth, there are no tools to translate efficiently between the formalisms discussed above. Finally, a comparison with tools specialized for the second level would not be fair, since our tool is more general. In a nutshell, devising a *fair comparison* among heterogeneous languages and tools (ASP, ASP(Q), QASP, QBF, QCSP, etc.) on common benchmarks is a challenging task that is outside the scope of this work.

6   Conclusion

Modeling and solving problems on the polynomial hierarchy is needed in many areas of AI, especially for knowledge representation and reasoning. The ASP(Q) was proposed by [4] as a convenient formalism for that task, as it lifts ASP modeling capabilities to all the PH. This paper provides a modular implementation of ASP(Q) called QASP, that is based on an encoding in QBF, and resorts to effective solvers for QBFs. QASP is a fundamental contribution for the ultimate adoption of ASP(Q) as a concrete tool for knowledge representation and reasoning. We have evaluated the performance of the solver on several benchmark problems. The benchmarks include first ASP(Q) encodings of two new problems, the argumentation coherence and the semi-stable model computation, offering further evidence of modeling effectiveness of ASP(Q). The experimental study confirms that QASP is a viable solver for tackling hard problems in the PH.

For the future work, we plan to further extend the application of ASP(Q) to model hard AI problems, and improve the efficiency of the QBF encoder.

References

1. Alviano, M., Dodaro, C., Leone, N., Ricca, F.: Advances in WASP. In: Calimeri, F., Ianni, G., Truszczynski, M. (eds.) LPNMR 2015. LNCS (LNAI), vol. 9345, pp. 40–54. Springer, Cham (2015). https://doi.org/10.1007/978-3-319-23264-5_5
2. Amendola, G., Dodaro, C., Faber, W., Ricca, F.: Paracoherent answer set computation. Artif. Intell. **299**, 103519 (2021)
3. Amendola, G., Eiter, T., Fink, M., Leone, N., Moura, J.: Semi-equilibrium models for paracoherent answer set programs. Artif. Intell. **234**, 219–271 (2016)
4. Amendola, G., Ricca, F., Truszczynski, M.: Beyond NP: quantifying over answer sets. Theory Pract. Log. Program. **19**(5–6), 705–721 (2019)
5. Amendola, G., Ricca, F., Truszczynski, M.: New models for generating hard random boolean formulas and disjunctive logic programs. Artif. Intell. **279**, 103185 (2020)
6. Bogaerts, B., Janhunen, T., Tasharrofi, S.: Stable-unstable semantics: beyond NP with normal logic programs. Theory Pract. Log. Program. **16**(5–6), 570–586 (2016)
7. Brewka, G., Eiter, T., Truszczynski, M.: Answer set programming at a glance. Commun. ACM **54**(12), 92–103 (2011)
8. Calimeri, F., et al.: ASP-Core-2 input language format. Theory Pract. Log. Program. **20**(2), 294–309 (2020)
9. Cao, F., Du, D.Z., Gao, B., Wan, P.J., Pardalos, P.M.: Minimax problems in combinatorial optimization. In: Du, DZ., Pardalos, P.M. (eds.) Minimax and Applications. Nonconvex Optimization and Its Applications, vol. 4, pp. 269–292. Springer, Cham (1995). https://doi.org/10.1007/978-1-4613-3557-3_18
10. Dantsin, E., Eiter, T., Gottlob, G., Voronkov, A.: Complexity and expressive power of logic programming. ACM Comput. Surv. **33**(3), 374–425 (2001)
11. Dodaro, C., Galatà, G., Khan, M.K., Maratea, M., Porro, I.: Operating room (re)scheduling with bed management via ASP. Theory Pract. Log. Program. **22**(2), 229–253 (2022)
12. Dung, P.M.: On the acceptability of arguments and its fundamental role in nonmonotonic reasoning, logic programming and n-person games. Artif. Intell. **77**(2), 321–358 (1995)
13. Dunne, P.E., Bench-Capon, T.J.M.: Coherence in finite argument systems. Artif. Intell. **141**(1/2), 187–203 (2002)
14. Egly, U., Eiter, T., Tompits, H., Woltran, S.: Solving advanced reasoning tasks using quantified boolean formulas. In: Proceedings of IAAI 2000, pp. 417–422. AAAI Press/The MIT Press (2000)
15. Eiter, T., Gottlob, G.: On the computational cost of disjunctive logic programming: propositional case. Ann. Math. Artif. Intell. **15**(3–4), 289–323 (1995)
16. Erdem, E., Gelfond, M., Leone, N.: Applications of answer set programming. AI Mag. **37**(3), 53–68 (2016)
17. Fandinno, J., Laferrière, F., Romero, J., Schaub, T., Son, T.C.: Planning with incomplete information in quantified answer set programming. Theory Pract. Log. Program. **21**(5), 663–679 (2021)
18. Gebser, M., Kaminski, R., Kaufmann, B., Romero, J., Schaub, T.: Progress in *clasp* Series 3. In: Calimeri, F., Ianni, G., Truszczynski, M. (eds.) LPNMR 2015. LNCS (LNAI), vol. 9345, pp. 368–383. Springer, Cham (2015). https://doi.org/10.1007/978-3-319-23264-5_31
19. Gebser, M., Maratea, M., Ricca, F.: The sixth answer set programming competition. J. Artif. Intell. Res. **60**, 41–95 (2017)

20. Gelfond, M., Lifschitz, V.: Classical negation in logic programs and disjunctive databases. New Generation Comput. **9**(3/4), 365–386 (1991)
21. Janhunen, T.: Implementing stable-unstable semantics with ASPTOOLS and Clingo. In: Cheney, J., Perri, S. (eds.) PADL 2022. LNCS, vol. 13165, pp. 135–153. Springer, Cham (2022). https://doi.org/10.1007/978-3-030-94479-7_9
22. Lifschitz, V.: Answer set programming and plan generation. Artif. Intell. **138**(1–2), 39–54 (2002)
23. Romero, J., Schaub, T., Son, T.C.: Generalized answer set planning with incomplete information. In: ASPOCP@LPNMR, vol. 1868 of CEUR WS, CEUR-WS.org (2017)
24. Sakama, C., Inoue, K.: Paraconsistent stable semantics for extended disjunctive programs. J. Log. Comput. **5**(3), 265–285 (1995)

A Practical Account into Counting Dung's Extensions by Dynamic Programming

Ridhwan Dewoprabowo[1], Johannes Klaus Fichte[2]([✉]), Piotr Jerzy Gorczyca[1],
and Markus Hecher[2]

[1] TU Dresden, Dresden, Germany
piotr.gorczyca@tu-dresden.de
[2] TU Wien, Vienna, Austria
{johannes.fichte,markus.hecher}@tuwien.ac.at

Abstract. Abstract argumentation and Dung's framework are popular for modeling and evaluating arguments in artificial intelligence. We consider various counting problems in abstract argumentation under practical aspects. We revisit algorithms and establish a framework that employs dynamic programming on tree decompositions for counting extensions of abstract argumentation frameworks under admissible, stable, and complete semantics. We provide an empirical evaluation and investigate conditions under which our approach is useful.

1 Introduction

Abstract argumentation (Dung's framework) is a concept for modeling and evaluating arguments in AI and reasoning [3,8,24]. For finding so-called extensions to *abstract argumentation frameworks (AFs)*, a variety of solvers are available and frequently evaluated in competitions, e.g., ASPARTIX, ConArg, μ-toksia, and PYGLAF. Lately, interest in counting increased due to a variety of applications in probabilistic reasoning, reasoning about uncertainty, and verification. For example, abstract argumentation allows to establish cognitive computational models for human reasoning for which counting enables quantitative reasoning [7]. The recent 2021 ICCMA competition also asked for counting [22] despite being #P-hard. In propositional model counting, a system called DPDB [18] allows to effectively implement counting algorithms that exploit low primal treewidth of the input and proved competitive regardless of theoretical worst-case limitations. In fact, various problems in abstract argumentation can also be solved efficiently using dynamic programming on tree decompositions if the input has low treewidth[10]. Here, we consider various counting problems in abstract argumentation under practical aspects. Our main contributions are as follows.

1. We revisit theoretical algorithms and formulate abstract argumentation problems in relational algebra, which form the basis for our solver A-DPDB[1].

---

[1] System and supplement are available on github:gorczyca/dp_on_dbs and Zenodo.

G. Gottlob et al. (Eds.): LPNMR 2022, LNAI 13416, pp. 387–400, 2022.
https://doi.org/10.1007/978-3-031-15707-3_30

Fig. 1. An AF with the given attack relation (left) and a TD of the framework (right).

2. We establish a dedicated counting solver for counting extensions of AFs under admissible, stable, and complete semantics.
3. We provide an empirical evaluation and illustrate that A-DPDB works fine if combined with existing solvers.

2 Preliminaries

For a function f that maps from a set S to a set D, we let $\mathsf{dom}(f) := S$ be the *domain of f*. An *argumentation framework* [8] is a pair $F = \langle A, R \rangle$ where A is a set of arguments and $R \subseteq A \times A$ is an attack relation, representing attacks among arguments. We write $a \rightarrowtail b$ to denote an attack $(a, b) \in R$. In addition, for $S \subseteq A$, we denote $S \rightarrowtail a$ if there exists $b \in S$ such that $b \rightarrowtail a$; and $a \rightarrowtail S$ if $a \rightarrowtail b$, respectively. Further, for $S' \subseteq A$, we write $S \rightarrowtail S'$ if $S \rightarrowtail b'$ for some $b' \in S'$. Let $F = \langle A, R \rangle$ be an AF. A set $S \subseteq A$ is *conflict-free* (in F) if there are no $a, b \in S$, such that $a \rightarrowtail b$. An argument a is *defended* by S in F if for each $b \in A$ with $b \rightarrowtail a$ there exists a $c \in S$ such that $c \rightarrowtail b$. The semantics of our main interest are: (i) S is *admissible* if it is conflict-free in F and each $a \in S$ is defended by S in F. (ii) S is *stable* if it is conflict-free in F and for each $a \in A \setminus S$, there exists a $b \in S$, such that $b \rightarrowtail a$. (iii) S is *complete* if it is admissible in F and each $a \in A$ that is defended by S in F is contained in S.

Example 1. *Consider the AF from Fig. 1. We observe that $\{a, c\}$ and $\{b, d\}$ are admissible, stable, and complete sets. Further, $\emptyset$ is complete (admissible).* ◁

Tree Decompositions and Treewidth. We assume that the reader is familiar with basic graph terminology. We define the *tree decomposition, TD for short,* of a graph G as a pair $\mathcal{T} = (T, \chi)$, where T is a rooted tree and χ a function that assigns to each node $t \in V(T)$ a set $\chi(t) \subseteq V(G)$, called *bag*, such that (i) $V(G) = \bigcup_{t \in V(T)} \chi(t)$, (ii) $E(G) \subseteq \{\{u, v\} \mid t \in V(T), \{u, v\} \subseteq \chi(t)\}$, and (iii) for each $r, s, t \in V(T)$, such that s is a node in the path from r to t, we have $\chi(r) \cap \chi(t) \subseteq \chi(s)$. We let $width(\mathcal{T}) := max_{t \in V(T)} |\chi(t)| - 1$ and define the *treewidth* $tw(G)$ of G as the minimum $width(\mathcal{T})$ over every TD $\mathcal{T}$ of G.

Example 2. *Consider the AF from Example 1. We can construct a TD illustrated in Fig. 1. Since the largest bag is of size 3, the TD has width 2.* ◁

To simplify case distinctions in the algorithms for sake of presentation, we assume *nice TDs* as given below. Our implementation does neither make an assumption on TDs being nice nor converts TDs into nice TDs. For a node $t \in V(T)$, $type(t)$

is defined as follows: *leaf* t has no children and $\chi(t) = \emptyset$; *join* if t has children t' and t'' with $t' \neq t''$ and $\chi(t) = \chi(t') = \chi(t'')$; *intr* ("introduce") if t has a single child t', $\chi(t') \subseteq \chi(t)$ and $|\chi(t)| = |\chi(t')| + 1$; and *forget* ("forget") if t has a single child t', $\chi(t') \supseteq \chi(t)$ and $|\chi(t')| = |\chi(t)| + 1$. A tree decomposition is *nice* if for every node $t \in V(T)$, $type(t) \in \{leaf, join, intr, forget\}$. It is folklore, that a nice TD can be computed from a given TD $\mathcal{T}$ in linear time without increasing the width, assuming the width of $\mathcal{T}$ is fixed. Let $\mathcal{T} = (T, \chi)$ be a tree decomposition of an AF F and let $t \in T$. For a subtree of T that is rooted in t we define $X_{\geq t}$ as the union of all bags within this subtree. Moreover, $X_{>t}$ denotes $X_{\geq t} \setminus \chi(t)$. We also have the sub-framework in t, denoted by $F|_{\chi(t)}$ or F_t, consists of all arguments $x \in \chi(t)$ and the attack relations (x_1, x_2) where $x_1 \in \chi(t)$, $x_2 \in \chi(t)$ and $(x_1, x_2) \in R$ [10].

Relational Algebra. Our algorithms operate on sets of records, which can simply be seen as tables. It is well-known that operations on tables can consisely be described by relational algebra [6] forming the basis of *SQL (Structured Query Language)* [25]. We briefly recall basic definitions. A *column* a is of a certain finite *domain* $dom(a)$. Then, a *row* r over set $col(r)$ of columns is a set of pairs of the form (a, v) with $a \in col(r)$, $v \in dom(a)$ such that for each $a \in col(r)$, there is exactly one $v \in dom(a)$ with $(a, v) \in r$. To *access* the value v of an attribute a in a row r, we sometimes write $r.a$, which returns the unique value v with $(a, v) \in r$. A *table* τ is a finite set of rows r over set $col(\tau) := col(r)$ of columns, using domain $dom(\tau) := \bigcup_{a \in col(\tau)} dom(a)$. We define *renaming* of τ, given a set A of columns and a bijective mapping $m : col(\tau) \to A$ with $dom(a) = dom(m(a))$ for $a \in col(\tau)$, by $\rho_m(\tau) := \{(m(a), v) \mid (a, v) \in \tau\}$. In SQL, renaming can be achieved via the AS keyword. *Selection* of rows in τ according to a given equality formula φ over term variables $col(\tau)$ is defined by $\sigma_\varphi(\tau) := \{r \mid r \in \tau, \varphi$ is satisfied under the induced assignment $r\}$. We abbreviate for binary $v \in col(\tau)$ with $dom(v) = \{0, 1\}$, $v=1$ by v and $v=0$ by $\neg v$. Selection in SQL is specified using keyword WHERE. Given a relation τ' with $col(\tau') \cap col(\tau) = \emptyset$. Then, we refer to the *cross-join* by $\tau \times \tau' := \{r \cup r' \mid r \in \tau, r' \in \tau'\}$. Further, a θ-*join* according to φ corresponds to $\tau \bowtie_\varphi \tau' := \sigma_\varphi(\tau \times \tau')$. In SQL a θ-join can be achieved by specifying the two tables (cross-join) and the selection φ by means of WHERE. Assume a set $A \subseteq col(\tau)$ of columns. Then, we let table τ *projected to* A be given by $\Pi_A(\tau) := \{r_A \mid r \in \tau\}$, where $r_A := \{(a, v) \mid (a, v) \in r, a \in A\}$. This can be lifted to *extended projection* $\dot\Pi_{A,S}$, additionally given a set S of expressions of the form $a \leftarrow f$, such that $a \in col(\tau) \setminus A$, f is an arithmetic function that takes a row $r \in \tau$, and there is at most one such expression for each $a \in col(\tau) \setminus A$ in S. Formally, we define $\dot\Pi_{A,S}(\tau) := \{r_A \cup r^S \mid r \in \tau\}$ with $r^S := \{(a, f(r)) \mid a \in col(r), (a \leftarrow f) \in S\}$. SQL allows to specify projection directly after the keyword SELECT. Later, we use *aggregation by grouping* $_A G_{(a \leftarrow g)}$, where $a \in col(\tau) \setminus A$ and a so-called *aggregate function* $g : 2^\tau \to dom(a)$, which intuitively takes a table of (grouped) rows. Therefore, we let $_A G_{(a \leftarrow g)}(\tau) := \{r \cup \{(a, g(\tau[r]))\} \mid r \in \Pi_A(\tau)\}$, where $\tau[r] := \{r' \mid r' \in \tau, r \subseteq r'\}$. Therefore, we use for a set S of integers the function $g = $ SUM for summing up values in S. SQL uses projection (SELECT) to specify A and the function g, distinguished via the keyword GROUP BY.

Dynamic Programming on TDs. A solver based on *dynamic programming (DP)* evaluates a given input instance $\mathcal{I}$ in parts along a given TD of a graph representation G of the input. Therefore, the TD is traversed bottom up, i.e., in post-order. For each node t of the TD, the intermediate results are stored in a set τ_t of records, *table* for short. The tables are obtained by a local algorithm, which depends on the graph representation. The algorithm stores results of problem parts of $\mathcal{I}$ in τ_t, while considering only tables $\tau_{t'}$ for child nodes t' of t. Various solvers that use dynamic programming have been implemented in the past for SAT, ASP, or ELP. Tools that allow for meta techniques using ASP for the description of the DP algorithm including various semantics for abstract argumentation exist. However, these tools are not competitive and do not support counting problems. DPDB [18] is a tool that utilizes database management systems (DBMS) to efficiently perform table manipulation operations needed during DP, which otherwise need tedious manual implementation. Its successor NestHDB [21] uses abstractions and a different graph representation.

3   Utilizing Treewidth for AFs

First, we revisit existing DP algorithms for counting extensions of AFs under stable and admissible semantics [10]. From there, we formulate different cases of the DP algorithm in relational algebra and extend it to counting. Later, we illustrate that we can instantiate these relational algebras as SQL queries, which are however created dynamically. In a way, our algorithms present a concise generator for SQL queries. Above, we already described the main idea on traversing a TD and constructing tables. Below, we only provide the *table algorithms* that are executed in each step during the traversal depending on the semantics.

Stable Semantics. We start with the algorithm for stable semantics, which is less elaborate than the other semantics and hence easier to understand. We follow standard definitions [8].We start from describing "local solutions". An extension of an argumentation framework is a set $S \subseteq A$, which satisfies the conditions for stable semantics. When traversing the TD, the algorithm constructs partial extensions to the input framework according to the vertices that occur in the bag currently considered. Formally, we are interested in B-restricted stable sets. Therefore, assume that an argumentation framework $F = \langle A, R \rangle$ and the set $B \subseteq A$ of arguments are given. A set $S \subseteq A$ is a B-*restricted stable set* for F, if S is conflict-free in F and S attacks all $a \in B \setminus S$. Then, a partial extension can simply be that a vertex is known not to be in the set (in), not in the set (def) due to being defeated by the set, or potentially not in the set (out). More formally, a *(stable) coloring* at t for an $X_{>t}$-restricted stable set S is a mapping $C : \chi(t) \rightarrow \{\text{in}, \text{def}, \text{out}\}$ such that (i) $C(a) = \text{in}$ if $a \in S$; (ii) $C(a) = \text{def}$ if $S \rightarrowtail a$; and (iii) $C(a) = \text{out}$ if $S \not\rightarrowtail a$ and $a \notin S$. Next, we briefly describe the table algorithm. In order to concisely present and to restrict the number of case distinctions, we assume that the algorithm runs along a nice TD. In practice, we need to interleave the cases to obtain competitive runtime behavior. Otherwise, unnecessary copying operations would make the implementation practically

---

Listing 1: Table algorithm $\mathbb{S}(t, \chi(t), F_t, \langle \tau_1, \ldots, \tau_\ell \rangle)$ for stable semantics on TDs.

In: Node t, bag $\chi(t)$, AF F_t, sequence $\langle \tau_1, \ldots, \tau_\ell \rangle$ of child tables. **Out:** Table τ_t.

1 **if** type$(t) = leaf$ **then** $\tau_t := \{\langle \emptyset, 1 \rangle\}$

2 **else if** type$(t) = intr$, and $a \in \chi(t)$ is introduced **then**

3 $\left| \tau_t := \{\langle J \sqcup \{b \mapsto \text{def} \mid b \in J^{\text{out}}, J^{\text{in}} \rightarrowtail b\}, c \rangle \mid \langle I, c \rangle \in \tau_1, \right.$
$$J \in \{I^+_{a \mapsto \text{in}}, I^+_{a \mapsto \text{out}}\}, J^{\text{in}} \not\rightarrowtail J^{\text{in}}\}$$

4 **else if** type$(t) = forget$, and $a \notin \chi(t)$ is removed **then**

5 $\left| \tau_t := \{\langle I^-_a, \Sigma_{\langle J, c \rangle \in \tau_1 : I^-_a = J^-_a, a \notin J^{\text{out}}} c \rangle \mid \langle I, \cdot \rangle \in \tau_1, a \notin I^{\text{out}}\} \right.$

6 **else if** type$(t) = join$ **then**

7 $\left| \tau_t := \{\langle I_1 \sqcup \{b \mapsto \text{def} \mid b \in I^{\text{def}}_2\}, c_1 \cdot c_2 \rangle \mid \langle I_1, c_1 \rangle \in \tau_1, \langle I_2, c_2 \rangle \in \tau_2, I^{\text{in}}_1 = I^{\text{in}}_2\} \right.$

$S^-_s := S \setminus \{s \mapsto \text{in}, s \mapsto \text{def}, s \mapsto \text{out}\}$, $S^l := \{s \mid S(s) = l\}$, $S^+_s := S \cup \{s\}$,
$S \sqcup D := \bigcup_{s \in \text{dom}(S) \setminus \text{dom}(D)} \{s \mapsto S(s)\} \cup D$.

infeasible. Table algorithm $\mathbb{S}$, as presented in Listing 1, details all cases needed for the stable semantics. Parts of tuples that talk about extensions are illustrated red and counters in green. Each table τ_t consist of rows of the form $\langle I, c \rangle$, where I is a *coloring at* t and c is an integer forming a *counter* storing the number of extensions. Leaf node t consist of an empty mapping (coloring) and counter 1. For an introduce node t with introduced variable $a \in \chi(t)$, we extend each coloring I of the child table to a coloring J that additionally includes a in its domain. Therefore, we guess colors for a and keep only well-defined colorings that are obtained after ensuring conflict-freeness and setting arguments to def accordingly. When forgetting an atom a at node t, the colorings of child tables are projected to $\chi(t)$ and counters summed up of colorings that are the same after projection. However, it is important to not consider colorings, where a is set to out in order to compute $X_{>t}$-restricted stable sets. For join nodes, we update def colorings (behaves like a logical "or") and multiply the counters of extensions that are colored "in" and coincide in terms of arguments.

Listing 2 naturally introduces the algorithm for stable semantics using relational algebra instead of set theory. For each node t, tables τ_t are pictured as relations, where τ_t distinguishes for each argument $x \in \chi(t)$ unique attributes x and d_x, also just called columns, with additional attributes depending on the problem at hand. So these two columns a and d_a are of type BOOLEAN for every argument $a \in \chi(t)$, where for columns (a, d_a) we have that $(0, 0)$ represents out, $(0, 1)$ represents def, and $(1, -)$ represents in where "$-$" refers to not setting the value at all. For leaf nodes t, we create a fresh empty table τ_t, cf., Line 1. When an argument a is introduced, we perform a Cartesian product with the previously computed table and guess for argument a whether it is in the extension or not. We ensure only well-defined colorings, i.e., conflict-freeness and we potentially update color def for all bag arguments. Further, for nodes t with type$(t) = forget$, we ensure that the removed argument is not colored out, we project out the removed argument, and perform grouping in order to maintain the counter, since several rows of τ_1 might have the exact same coloring after projection in τ_t. For a join node t, we use extended projection and θ-joins, where

Listing 2: Table algorithm $\mathbb{S}(t, \chi(t), F_t, \langle \tau_1, \ldots, \tau_\ell \rangle)$ for stable semantics.

In: Node t, bag $\chi(t)$, framework $F_t = (A_t, R_t)$, sequence $\langle \tau_1, \ldots, \tau_\ell \rangle$ of child tables. **Out:** Table τ_t.

1 **if** type(t) = *leaf* **then** $\tau_t := \{\{(\mathrm{cnt}, 1)\}\}$

2 **else if** type(t) = *intr, and $a \in \chi(t)$ is introduced* **then**

3 $\quad \left| \tau_t := \dot{\Pi}_{\chi(t), \bigcup\{d_b \leftarrow d_b \vee (\neg b \wedge [\bigvee_{(c,b) \in R_t} c])\}} \atop {b \in \chi(t)} (\tau_1 \bowtie_{\bigwedge_{(b,c) \in R_t} \neg b \vee \neg c} \{\{(a, 1), (d_a, 0)\}, \{(a, 0), (d_a, 0)\}\}) \right.$

4 **else if** type(t) = *forget, and $a \notin \chi(t)$ is removed* **then**

5 $\quad \left| \tau_t := {}_{\{b, d_b | b \in \chi(t)\}} G_{\mathrm{cnt} \leftarrow \mathrm{SUM(cnt)}} (\Pi_{\mathrm{col}(\tau_1) \setminus \{a, d_a\}} (\sigma_{a \vee \neg d_a} (\tau_1))) \right.$

6 **else if** type(t) = *join* **then**

7 $\quad \left| \tau_t := \dot{\Pi}_{\chi(t), \bigcup\{\mathrm{cnt} \leftarrow \mathrm{cnt} \cdot \mathrm{cnt'}, d_b \leftarrow d_b \vee d_b'\} \atop {b \in \chi(t)}} (\tau_1 \bowtie_{\bigwedge b = b'} \rho_{\bigcup\{x \mapsto x'\} \atop x \in \mathrm{col}(\tau_2)} \tau_2) \right.$

---

we join on the coloring agreeing on those arguments in the extension, update defeated colors, and multiply the corresponding counters, accordingly.

Example 3 illustrates a resulting SQL query at an introduce node of the TD, where we interleave cases and drop the requirement on nice TDs.

Example 3. *Consider the TD from Example 2 at node h_1, which is both an introduce and forget node. Following Listing 2 for stable semantics, we obtain the SQL query below.*

```
1   SELECT a, b, d, d_a, d_b, d_d,
2          sum(cnt) AS cnt
3   FROM (WITH introduce AS
4       (SELECT true val UNION SELECT false)
5    SELECT i_a.val AS a, i_b.val AS b,
6           i_d.val AS d, a AS d_a,
7           a AS d_b, false AS d_d, 1 AS cnt
8    FROM introduce i_a, /*introduce a,b,d*/
9     introduce i_b, introduce i_d) AS cand
10   WHERE (a OR d_a) AND /*forget a*/
11    (NOT a OR NOT b) AND /*conflict-free*/
12    (NOT d OR NOT a)
13   GROUP BY a, b, d, d_a, d_b, d_d
```

$\lhd$

Admissible Semantics. In the following subsection, we extend the algorithm presented above. We present colorings for the admissible semantics following earlier work [10]. Given an argumentation framework $\langle A, R \rangle$ and a set $B \subseteq A$ of arguments. A set $S \subseteq A$ is a B-*restricted admissible set* for F, if S is conflict-free in F and S defends itself in F against all $a \in B$. Based on this definition, we construct colorings that locally satisfy certain conditions allowing to extend them to a coloring of the entire framework, which in turn can then be used to construct an admissible set of arguments. To this end, assume for an argumentation framework F a TD $\mathcal{T} = (T, \chi)$ and a node t of T. Formally, an *(admissible) coloring* at t for an $X_{>t}$-restricted admissible set S is a mapping $C : \chi(t) \to \{\mathrm{in}, \mathrm{def}, \mathrm{out}, \mathrm{att}\}$ such that for each $a \in \chi(t)$: (i) $C(a) = \mathrm{in}$ if

---

Listing 3: Table algorithm $\mathbb{A}(t, \chi(t), F_t, \langle \tau_1, \ldots, \tau_\ell \rangle)$ for admissible semantics.

In: Node t, bag $\chi(t)$, framework $F_t = (A_t, R_t)$, sequence $\langle \tau_1, \ldots, \tau_\ell \rangle$ of child tables. **Out:** Table τ_t.

1 **if** $\text{type}(t) = leaf$ **then** $\tau_t := \{\{(\text{cnt}, 1)\}\}$

2 **else if** $\text{type}(t) = intr,$ and $a \in \chi(t)$ is introduced **then**

3 $\quad \tau_t := \dot{\Pi}_{\chi(t), \bigcup_{b \in \chi(t)} \{d_b \leftarrow \text{df}_t(d_b, b)\}} (\tau_1 \bowtie_{\bigwedge_{(b,c) \in R_t} \neg b \vee \neg c} \{\{(a,1), (d_a, 0)\}, \{(a,0), (d_a, 0)\}\})$

4 **else if** $\text{type}(t) = forget,$ and $a \notin \chi(t)$ is removed **then**

5 $\quad \tau_t := {}_{\{b, d_b | b \in \chi(t)\}} G_{\text{cnt} \leftarrow \text{SUM}(\text{cnt})} (\Pi_{\text{col}(\tau_1) \setminus \{a, d_a\}} (\sigma_{a \vee d_a = 1}(\tau_1)))$

6 **else if** $\text{type}(t) = join$ **then**

7 $\quad \tau_t := \dot{\Pi}_{\chi(t), \bigcup_{b \in \chi(t)} \{\text{cnt} \leftarrow \text{cnt} \cdot \text{cnt}', d_b \leftarrow \text{jn}(d_b, d_b')\}} (\tau_1 \bowtie_{\bigwedge_{b \in \chi(t)} b = b'} \rho_{\bigcup_{x \in \text{col}(\tau_2)} \{x \mapsto x'\}} \tau_2)$

Let $\text{jn}(d, e) := 2$ if $d=2$ or $e=2$; else 1 if $d=1$ or $e=1$; else 0, and $\text{df}_t(d, b) := \text{jn}(d, 2$ if $(\bigvee_{(c,b) \in R_t} c)$; else 1 if $(\bigvee_{(b,c) \in R_t} c)$; else 0).

$a \in S$; (ii) $C(a) = \text{def}$ if $S \rightarrowtail a$; (iii) $C(a) = \text{att}$ if $S \not\rightarrowtail a$ and $a \rightarrowtail S$; and (iv) $C(a) = \text{out}$ if $S \not\rightarrowtail a$ and $a \not\rightarrowtail S$.

The algorithm to compute the admissible semantics extends the algorithm for stable semantics, as presented above. Intuitively, those arguments colored att need to become def eventually in order to obtain A-restricted admissible sets. In our implementation, we represent the range for the colorings in a database table with a BOOLEAN column a and a SMALLINT column d_a for every argument $a \in \chi(t)$. Then, $(0, 0)$ represents out, $(0, 1)$ represents att, $(0, 2)$ represents def, and $(1, -)$ represents in. Alternatively, one can also exploit the NULL value in SQL, which reduces preallocated memory for the d_a columns as we can use the more compact data type BOOLEAN instead of SMALLINT. There, we have $(0, \text{NULL})$ represents out, $(0, 0)$ represents att, $(0, 1)$ represents def, and $(1, -)$ represents in (as before). The following example illustrates a query that we obtain at node h_1 of our running example similar to the used definition in relational algebra of Listing 2.

Example 4. *Consider the TD and introduce/forget node h_1 of our running Example 2. We construct a query for admissible extensions as follows.*

```
1   SELECT a, b, d, d_a, d_b, d_d, sum(cnt) AS cnt
2   FROM (WITH introduce AS
3       (SELECT true val UNION SELECT false)
4     SELECT i_a.val AS a, i_b.val AS b, i_d.val AS d,
5       CASE WHEN i_d.val THEN 2/*coloring*/
6         WHEN i_b.val THEN 1 ELSE 0 END AS d_a,
7       CASE WHEN i_a.val THEN 2 ELSE 0 END AS d_b,
8       CASE WHEN i_a.val THEN 1 ELSE 0 END AS d_d, 1 AS cnt
9     FROM introduce i_a, /*introduce a,b,d*/
10    introduce i_b, introduce i_d) AS cand
11  WHERE (a OR d_a = 1) AND /*forget a*/
12    (NOT a OR NOT b) AND /*conflict-free*/
13    (NOT d OR NOT a)
14  GROUP BY a, b, d, d_a, d_b, d_d
```

◁

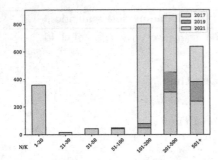

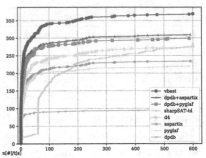

(a) Distribution of heuristically computed widths. The x-axis lists intervals into which the heuristically computed width of a TD falls (K). The y-axis states the number (N) of instances.

(b) Runtime of various solvers for admissible semantics. The x-axis depicts the runtime sorted in ascending order for each solver individually and the y-axis refers to the number of instances.

Fig. 2. Illustration of results on ICCMA competitions '17, '19, and '21. Distribution of upper bounds on treewidth (left) and runtime results for admissible semantics (right).

Complete Semantics. Subsequently, we turn our attention to complete semantics. We provide definitions for colorings that can be used to construct solutions by dynamic programming and when its satisfying all conditions for the complete semantics [5]. Given an AF $F = \langle A, R \rangle$ and a set $B \subseteq A$ of arguments. A labeling $\mathcal{L} = \langle \mathcal{L}_{\text{in}}, \mathcal{L}_{\text{def}}, \mathcal{L}_{\text{out}} \rangle$ where $\mathcal{L}_{\text{in}}, \mathcal{L}_{\text{def}}, \mathcal{L}_{\text{out}} \subseteq A$ for F is a *B-restricted complete labeling* for F if $\mathcal{L}_{\text{in}}$ is conflict-free, $\mathcal{L}_{\text{in}} \nrightarrow \mathcal{L}_{\text{out}}$, $\mathcal{L}_{\text{out}} \nrightarrow \mathcal{L}_{\text{in}}$, and for each $a \in B$ we have (i) $a \in \mathcal{L}_{\text{in}}$ if and only if $\{b \mid (b, a) \in R\} \subseteq \mathcal{L}_{\text{def}}$; (ii) $a \in \mathcal{L}_{\text{def}}$ if and only if $\mathcal{L}_{\text{in}} \rightarrowtail a$; (iii) $a \in \mathcal{L}_{\text{out}}$ if and only if $\mathcal{L}_{\text{in}} \nrightarrow a$ and $\mathcal{L}_{\text{out}} \rightarrowtail a$. Let $\mathcal{T} = (T, \chi)$ be a TD of F and t be a node of T. A *(complete) coloring at t* is a function $C_t : \chi(t) \rightarrow \{\text{in}, \text{def}, \text{defp}, \text{out}, \text{outp}\}$ such that for each $a \in \chi(t)$: (i) $C(a) = \text{in}$ if $a \in \mathcal{L}_{\text{in}}$; (ii) $C(a) = \text{def}$ if $a \in \mathcal{L}_{\text{def}}$ and $\mathcal{L}_{\text{in}} \rightarrowtail a$; (iii) $C(a) = \text{defp}$ if $a \in \mathcal{L}_{\text{def}}$ and $\mathcal{L}_{\text{in}} \nrightarrow a$; (iv) $C(a) = \text{out}$ if $a \in \mathcal{L}_{\text{out}}$, $\mathcal{L}_{\text{in}} \nrightarrow a$, $a \nrightarrow \mathcal{L}_{\text{in}}$, and $\mathcal{L}_{\text{out}} \rightarrowtail a$; and (iv) $C(a) = \text{outp}$ if $a \in \mathcal{L}_{\text{out}}$, $\mathcal{L}_{\text{in}} \nrightarrow a$, $a \nrightarrow \mathcal{L}_{\text{in}}$, and $\mathcal{L}_{\text{out}} \nrightarrow a$.

Intuitively, colors defp and outp are used to mark candidates for def and out. For such candidates, required properties need to be "proven" eventually. We further extended the algorithm of Listing 3 and implemented the handling of complete colorings. In our implementation, we represent the values for colorings in an SQL database table with a `SMALLINT` column a and a `BOOLEAN` column p_a for the "provability of the color of a", as follows: $(0, 1)$ represents out, $(0, 0)$ represents outp, $(1, -)$ stands for in, $(2, 1)$ represents def, and $(2, 0)$ states defp.

4 Preliminary Empirical Evaluation

In order to draw conclusions concerning the efficiency of our approach, we conducted a series of experiments. **Design of Experiment:** We draw a small experiment to study the following questions: (Q1.1) What are upper bounds on the treewidth for common instances in abstract argumentation? (Q1.2) Are there instances on which we can expect that solvers exploiting treewidth perform well? (Q2.1) Does the parameterized algorithm perform well on instances of low treewidth? (Q2.2) Is there a certain characteristic on the instances where our solver performs better than others? (Q2.3) Is the system competitive on its own with other solvers or can it be useful in a solving portfolio? **Instances:** We considered sets of instances from the International Competitions on Computational Models of Argumentation ICCMA'17, '19, and '21. Since the hard instances of the 2019 competition are partially contained in the ICCMA'21 set, we omit the 2019 instances. In the following, we refer by '19 to the hard instances of the 2019 competition contained in the '21 competition and by '21 to the new instances of the '21 competition. The instances originate from various domains. Details can be found online [22]. **Constructing TDs:** To construct TDs, we use the decomposer that heuristically outputs tree decompositions. The outputted TDs are correct, but are not necessarily of smallest width, i.e., the width of the resulting TD can be larger than the treewidth. Note that computing the treewidth is itself an NP-complete problem. We do not require a tree decomposition of smallest width. Larger width w increases the runtime of our implementation, since the runtime is in 2^w. There is no effect on correctness with respect to the problem statement from taking decompositions of larger width. In practice, we favor a fast heuristic, namely, htd, over decomposers such as Flow-Cutter or TCS-Meiji that provide slightly smaller width, but require longer running times.

Treewidth Classification of the Instances. Towards answering (Q1.1) and (Q1.2), we investigate whether the considered instances are relevant and solvable for an approach where the runtime already theoretically depends on the width of the heuristically computed TDs. In Fig. 2a, we present the distribution of upper bounds on the treewidth in intervals of the considered instances by competition. Decompositions of smaller width can be primarily found in the '17 instances. Recall that our parameterized algorithms have single or double exponential runtime bounds in the treewidth [10]. Hence, we immediately see that the '19 and '21 instances are theoretically out of reach for A-DPDB. For the '19 and '21 instances, we are currently unable to state a detailed picture as high width might also originate in unreliable heuristics. It is well-known that certain heuristics cannot provide a small width on very large instances even if a much smaller width is possible. Still there is a notable number of instances in the 2017 competition, which seem within reach answering Questions (Q1.1) and (Q1.2). Quite a number of instances have width beyond 100. There, we have no hope to solve them by a treewidth-based approach without preprocessing or using abstractions instead of the primal graph. Still, quite a number of instances have relatively small treewidth and the instances of high treewidth mostly originate in random generators.

Performance Comparison and Solvers. In order to address a performance analysis of A-DPDB itself and in comparison to other argumentation solvers, we run a more detailed experiment. Counts are represented with arbitrary precision for all solvers. For comparison, we evaluate leading solvers of the ICCMA'21 competition. Namely, μ-toksia [23], aspartix [9], and pyglaf [1]. The solvers

μ-toksia, aspartix, pyglaf performed well during ICCMA'17, '19, and '21. In addition, we can employ state-of-the-art propositional model counters such as the model counting competition 2021 winner SharpSAT-td or d4 on encodings of the argumentation semantics of interest. Therefore, we can use the ASP encoding from aspartix[2] directly by lp2normal and lp2sat, which translates the ground ASP instance into a SAT formula. There is only a minimal overhead between a direct CNF encoding and an ASP encoding translated into CNF in case of the relevant encodings. In more detail, most ASP encodings here are tight and therefore *do not need additional constraints* to handle cyclic dependencies of the resulting programs as one might fear from translations into CNF. SharpSAT-td employs TDs of small width, but only as in a process to speed up its internal selection heuristic, which is in stark contrast to our approach that provides strict theoretical guarantees. SharpSAT-td implements dedicated preprocessing techniques for model counting from which a translation profits. To our knowledge dedicated preprocessing for argumentation is missing. In addition, SharpSAT-td uses FlowCutter as heuristic. Both techniques make the solver incomparable to ours. We did not consider NestHDB as the translation to SAT is not treewidth-aware. All solvers including A-DPDB support complete and stable semantics. Admissible semantics is not always available to the user even though implemented, e.g., μ-toksia. We refrained from modifying the solver.

Enhancing Existing Solvers. From the results above on our instance classification with respect to treewidth and our theoretical knowledge about the implemented parameterized algorithm, we must expect clear practical limitations of A-DPDB. Still, it might solve instances that existing techniques cannot solve. Therefore, we also consider A-DPDB together with other solvers, which is usually referred to as *portfolio solver*. However, classical solving portfolios are oftentimes detected based on machine-learning techniques that train for specific instances. Our setting is different, we can simply enhance an existing solver by using DP if a heuristically computed decomposition is below 19. We obtained this threshold experimentally from simple considerations on memory consumption. Our new solvers named A-DPDB+X consist of $X \in \{\texttt{aspartix}, \mu\text{-toksia}, \texttt{pyglaf}\}$.

Hardware, Measure, and Restrictions. All solvers ran on a cluster consisting of 12 nodes equipped with two Intel Xeon E-2650 v4 CPUs running at 2.2 GHz. We follow standard guidelines for empirical evaluations [20] and measure runtime using perf. Details on the hardware will be made available in the supplemental material. We mainly compare wall clock time and follow the setup of the International Competition on Computational Models of Argumentation (ICCMA). Run times larger than 600 s count as timeout and main memory (RAM) was restricted to 64 GB. In contrast to dedicated counting competitions the runtime in the setup of the ICCMA competition is much smaller, which is also far more resource friendly. Solvers were executed sequentially without any parallel execution of other runs, i.e., we jobs run exclusively on one machine.

---

[2] μ-toksia does not have encodings readily accessible as it is tightly coupled to a SAT solver. This would require extraction from source code or implementing it ourselves.

Table 1. Overview on solved instances (left) as well as observed counts (right).

solver	adm.	complete	stable
aspartix	236	362	469
... /d4[2]	347	406	483
... /sharpSAT-td[2]	*368*	*410*	*487*
dpdb	96	100	113
...+aspartix	**311**	**379**	475
...+μ-toksia21	95	367	468
...+pyglaf	300	372	**478**
μ-toksia21	–	299	446
pyglaf	221	336	463
sharpSAT-td	284	350	387
vbest	371	411	505

(a) Number of solved instances of various solvers. "–" indicates that the solver does not support the semantics. Bold entries indicate the best result, italic entries refer to the best result among non-portfolio solvers.
[2] selects solvers also based on treewidth.

	adm.	complete	stable
median	2.9	0.5	0.0
mean	11.6	8.3	3.8
max	512.6	487.7	498.2
aspartix	7.9	8.3	8.7
dpdb	154.6	119.9	75.0
mu_toksia21	–	5.1	5.2
pyglaf	6.1	6.5	5.8
sharpSAT-td	512.6	487.7	498.2

(b) Observed counts. The lower part states the maximum count observed for the respective solver. Counts are stated in $\log_{10}$ format, meaning that 2.9 represents a count of about $0.794 \cdot 10^3$ whereas 516.6 represents about $3.98107 \cdot 10^{516}$.

Experimental Results. Table 1a lists the number of solved instances for various solvers, considered semantics, and over '17, '19, '21 competition instances. In addition, Fig. 2b visualizes the runtime behavior of various solvers for the admissible semantics. Table 1b illustrates the observed counts on the instances in terms of average and median of the computed count per semantics as well as the maximum count of an instance solved by solver. Notably, A–DPDB solved instances for which the decomposer constructed a TD of up to width 19 for complete, 35 for admissible, and 50 for stable semantics. For stable, few instances were solved where the heuristic computed TDs of width 99 containing few bags.

Discussion. When taking a more detailed look into the results, we observe that `aspartix`, μ-`toksia`, and `pyglaf` mostly solve instances that have a small number of solutions and perform overall quite well when the count is fairly low. This is not surprising, since each of the three solvers works by enumerating extensions, which can be quite expensive in practice. For all semantics, A–DPDB alone solves the least instances, but is perfectly suitable for enhancing existing solvers A–DPDB+`aspartix` and A–DPDB+`pyglaf`, respectively, solve the most instances. The solvers d4 and `sharpSAT-td` can easily be used to solve abstract argumentation instances for various semantics. In fact, we see a reasonable performance on instances even if counts are larger. For admissible semantics, `sharpSAT-td` solves more instances than `aspartix` and A–DPDB, but much less instances than our system A–DPDB+`aspartix`. More precisely, A–DPDB+`aspartix` solves $\approx$24% instances more than `aspartix` and $\approx$10% more than `sharpSAT-td`. When considering a virtual configuration that takes the best result of `sharpSAT-td` and `aspartix` (`sharpSAT-td/aspartix`), we obtain the best result. It solves 22% and 35% more instances than `sharpSAT-td` and `aspartix` alone. Note this combination is a virtual best configuration, not a solving portfolio. For complete, we see an improvement of about 4%, 8%, and 21% more solved instances over `aspartix`, `sharpSAT-td`, and μ-`toksia`, respectively. d4 and μ-`toksia` solve a similar number of instances, however the former solves also instances that have high counts. For stable, we observe only 2% improvement of the portfolio, but it solves 30% more instances than d4 and 21% more than sharpSAT-td.

Summary. In summary, A-DPDB alone has a very limited performance. The behavior was quite well expected from the results in the first part of our experimental evaluation. We expect this behavior, since DP profits significantly from preprocessing, which has to our knowledge not been investigated for argumentation. Our results show that estimating treewidth can provide useful insights into constructing a solving portfolio – regardless of the used solvers. In contrast to machine learning-based heuristics, which are commonly used in the automated reasoning community, we can statically decide which "subsolver" we take without a training phase on a subset of the existing instances. We expect that tightly coupling a #SAT solver into an argumentation solver would be successful.

5   Conclusion and Future Work

We present a practical approach to counting in abstract argumentation. Counting allows to take quantitative aspects of extensions into account. This enables us to quantify on extensions and comprehend also semantics that are sometimes considered problematic, e.g., admissible sets. Beyond, it facilitates reasoning stronger than brave and skeptical decisions [4,13,14,19]. We can ask for the relationship between total possible extensions and observed extensions (plausibility), which also forms the basis for probabilistic tasks. Our implementation A-DPDB is based on dynamic programming on TDs showing competitive behavior in a system that combines existing solvers with A-DPDB. While existing solvers can be used to count solutions by enumeration, we provide an approach that works by a compact representation and systematically splitting the search space. We also illustrate translating argumentation problems into propositional model counting showing notable performance. Since these solvers also implement dedicated simplification techniques for propositional counting, it opens the question whether argumentation semantics can benefit from argumentation specific preprocessing.

We expect that our work opens a variety of further directions. First, A-DPDB forms the basis for using more general graph representations (NestHDB), which showed notable performance gains in the propositional case also over established model counters [21]. In principle, DP works for problems on any level of the PH. While theoretical lower-bounds (under the exponential-time-hypothesis) suggest high runtime (depending on the level of the hierarchy) [12,15], parameters that combine treewidth with other approaches might be fruitful, e.g., [11]. Besides, counting might help to improve the reliability of existing systems [2,17]. From the performance of propositional model counters, which also include preprocessing, we expect notable speed up for argumentation specific preprocessing. Even though we executed A-DPDB sequentially, parallel execution is possible in principle, which could improve on larger instances of low treewidth [16].

Acknowledgements. Research was funded by the DFG through the Collaborative Research Center, Grant TRR 248 project ID 389792660, the BMBF, Grant 01IS20056_NAVAS, the Vienna Science and Technology Fund (WWTF) grant ICT19-065, and the Austrian Science Fund (FWF) grants P32830 and Y698.

References

1. Alviano, M.: The PYGLAF argumentation reasoner. In: ICLP 2017 (Technical Communications). OASICS, vol. 58, pp. 2:1–2:3, Dagstuhl (2017)
2. Alviano, M., Dodaro, C., Fichte, J.K., Hecher, M., Philipp, T., Rath, J.: Inconsistency proofs for ASP: the ASP - DRUPE format. TPLP **19**(5–6), 891–907 (2019)
3. Amgoud, L., Prade, H.: Using arguments for making and explaining decisions. AIJ **173**(3–4), 413–436 (2009)
4. Besin, V., Hecher, M., Woltran, S.: Utilizing treewidth for quantitative reasoning on epistemic logic programs. TPLP **21**(5), 575–592 (2021)
5. Charwat, G.: Tree-decomposition based algorithms for abstract argumentation framework. Master's thesis, TU Wien, Vienna, Austria (2012)
6. Codd, E.F.: A relational model of data for large shared data banks. Commun. ACM **13**(6), 377–387 (1970)
7. Dietz, E., Fichte, J.K., Hamiti, F.: A quantitative symbolic approach to individual human reasoning. In: Proceedings of CogSci 2022 (2022, to appear)
8. Dung, P.M.: On the acceptability of arguments and its fundamental role in non-monotonic reasoning, logic programming and n-person games. AIJ **77**(2), 321–357 (1995)
9. Dvořák, W., Rapberger, A., Wallner, J.P., Woltran, S.: ASPARTIX-V19 - an answer-set programming based system for abstract argumentation. In: Herzig, A., Kontinen, J. (eds.) FoIKS 2020. LNCS, vol. 12012, pp. 79–89. Springer, Cham (2020). https://doi.org/10.1007/978-3-030-39951-1_5
10. Dvořák, W., Pichler, R., Woltran, S.: Towards fixed-parameter tractable algorithms for abstract argumentation. AIJ **186**, 1–37 (2012)
11. Fandinno, J., Hecher, M.: Treewidth-aware complexity in ASP: not all positive cycles are equally hard. In: AAAI 2021, pp. 6312–6320. AAAI Press (2021)
12. Fichte, J.K., Hecher, M., Kieler, M.F.I.: Treewidth-aware quantifier elimination and expansion for QCSP. In: Simonis, H. (ed.) CP 2020. LNCS, vol. 12333, pp. 248–266. Springer, Cham (2020). https://doi.org/10.1007/978-3-030-58475-7_15
13. Fichte, J.K., Hecher, M., Meier, A.: Knowledge-base degrees of inconsistency: complexity and counting. In: AAA 2021, pp. 6349–6357. No. 7, The AAAI Press (2021)
14. Fichte, J.K., Hecher, M., Nadeem, M.A.: Plausibility reasoning via projected answer set counting–a hybrid approach. In: IJCAI 2022 (2022, to appear)
15. Fichte, J.K., Hecher, M., Pfandler, A.: Lower bounds for QBFs of bounded treewidth. In: LICS 2020, pp. 410–424. Associating for Computing Machinery, New York (2020)
16. Fichte, J.K., Hecher, M., Roland, V.: Parallel model counting with CUDA: algorithm engineering for efficient hardware utilization. In: CP 2021, pp. 24:1–24:20 (2021)
17. Fichte, J.K., Hecher, M., Roland, V.: Proofs for propositional model counting. In: SAT 2022 (2022, to appear)
18. Fichte, J.K., Hecher, M., Thier, P., Woltran, S.: Exploiting database management systems and treewidth for counting. TPLP **22**(1), 128–157 (2022)

19. Fichte, J.K., Gaggl, S.A., Rusovac, D.: Rushing and strolling among answer sets - navigation made easy. In: Proceedings of the 36th AAAI Conference on Artificial Intelligence (AAAI 2022). The AAAI Press (2022, to appear)
20. Fichte, J.K., Hecher, M., McCreesh, C., Shahab, A.: Complications for computational experiments from modern processors. In: CP 2021, pp. 25:1–25:21 (2021)
21. Hecher, M., Thier, P., Woltran, S.: Taming high treewidth with abstraction, nested dynamic programming, and database technology. In: Pulina, L., Seidl, M. (eds.) SAT 2020. LNCS, vol. 12178, pp. 343–360. Springer, Cham (2020). https://doi.org/10.1007/978-3-030-51825-7_25
22. Lagniez, J., Lonca, E., Mailly, J., Rossit, J.: Design and results of ICCMA 2021. CoRR abs/2109.08884 (2021). https://arxiv.org/abs/2109.08884
23. Niskanen, A., Järvisalo, M.: μ-toksia: an efficient abstract argumentation reasoner. In: KR 2020, pp. 800–804 (2020)
24. Rago, A., Cocarascu, O., Toni, F.: Argumentation-based recommendations: fantastic explanations and how to find them. In: IJCAI 2018, pp. 1949–1955 (2018)
25. Ullman, J.D.: Principles of Database and Knowledge-Base Systems, vol. II. Computer Science Press, New York (1989)

Clingraph: ASP-Based Visualization

Susana Hahn[1,2,3], Orkunt Sabuncu[1,2,3], Torsten Schaub[1,2,3(✉)],
and Tobias Stolzmann[1,2,3]

[1] University of Potsdam, Potsdam, Germany
`torsten@cs.uni-potsdam.de`
[2] TED University, Ankara, Turkey
[3] Potassco Solutions, Potsdam, Germany

Abstract. We present the ASP-based visualization tool *clingraph*, which aims at visualizing ASP by means of ASP itself. This idea traces back to the *aspviz* tool and *clingraph* redevelops and extends it in the context of modern ASP systems. More precisely, *clingraph* takes graph specifications in terms of ASP facts and hands them over to the graph visualization system *graphviz*. The use of ASP provides a great interface between logic programs and/or answer sets and their visualization. Also, *clingraph* offers a Python API that extends this ease of interfacing to *clingo*'s API, and in turn to connect and monitor various aspects of the solving process.

1 Introduction

With the advance of Answer Set Programming (ASP; [7]) into more and more complex application domains, also the need for inspecting problems as well as their solution increases significantly. The intrinsic difficulty lies in the fact that ASP constitutes a general problem solving paradigm, whereas the wide spectrum of applications rather calls for customized presentations.

We address this by taking up the basic idea of *aspviz* [3], to visualize ASP by means of ASP itself, and extend it in the context of modern ASP systems. The resulting system is called *clingraph* (v1.0.0).[1,2] The common idea is to specify a visualization in terms of a logic program that defines special atoms capturing graphic elements. This allows us to customize the presentation of an application domain by means of ASP, and thus to easily connect with the problem specification and its solutions.

The visualization in *clingraph* rests upon graph structures that are passed on to the graph layout system *graphviz*.[3] To this end, *clingraph* takes—in its basic setting—a set of facts over predicates `graph/1`, `node/1`, `edge/1`, and `attr/4` as input, and produces an output visualizing the induced graph structure.

As a simple example, consider the graph coloring problem in Listing 1.1.

---

[1] https://github.com/potassco/clingraph.
[2] https://clingraph.readthedocs.io.
[3] https://graphviz.org.

G. Gottlob et al. (Eds.): LPNMR 2022, LNAI 13416, pp. 401–414, 2022.
https://doi.org/10.1007/978-3-031-15707-3_31

```
1    node(1..6).
2    edge(1,2). edge(1,3). edge(1,4). edge(2,4). edge(2,5).
3    edge(2,6). edge(3,4). edge(3,5). edge(5,6).
4    color(red; green; blue).

6    { assign(N, C) : color(C) } = 1 :- node(N).
7    :- edge(N, M), assign(N, C), assign(M, C).

9    #show node/1.
10   #show edge((N,M)) : edge(N, M).
11   #show attr(graph_nodes, default, style, filled).
12   #show attr(node, N, color, C) : assign(N, C).
```

Listing 1.1. Graph coloring instance, encoding and display (`color.lp`)

The actual problem instance and encoding are given in Lines 1–4 and 6–7, respectively. However, of particular interest are Lines 9–12 that use `#show` directives to translate the resulting graph colorings into *clingraph*'s input format. While Line 9 and 10 account for the underlying graph, the two remaining lines comprise instructions to *graphviz*. Line 11 fixes the layout of graph nodes. More interestingly, Line 12 translates the obtained graph coloring to layout instructions for *graphviz*. Our omission of an atom over `graph/1` groups all entities under a default graph labeled `default` (which can be changed via an option; similarly, graphs are taken to be undirected unless changed by option `--type`).

Launching *clingo* so that only the resulting stable model is obtained as a set of facts allows us to visualize the result via *clingraph*:

```
clingo --outf=0 -V0 --out-atomf=%s. color.lp | head -n1 | \
clingraph --out=render --format=png
```

The used options suppress *clingo* output and transform atoms into facts; the intermediate UNIX command extracts the line comprising the stable model. Note that one can also use a solver other than *clingo* to generate the stable model in the expected form. The final call to *clingraph* produces a file in PNG format, shown in Fig. 1.

Fig. 1. Visualization of the (first) stable model of the logic program in Listing 1.1

Clearly, the above proceeding only reflects the very basic functionality of *clingraph*. We elaborate upon its extended functionality in the next section and present some illustrative cases studies in Sect. 3. We summarize our approach and relate it to others' in Sect. 5.

2   *Clingraph*

In its most basic setting, *clingraph* can be regarded as a front-end to *graphviz* that relies on the fact format sketched above. In fact, the full-fledged version of the fact format allows for specifying multiple graphs as well as subgraphs. The former is done by supplying several instances of predicate `graph/1` whose only argument provides an identifier for regrouping all elements belonging to the graph at hand. To that effect, there are also binary versions of predicates `node` and `edge`, whose second argument refers to the encompassing graph. For example, the following facts describe n graphs, each with one edge connecting two nodes.

```
1  id(1..n).
2  graph(g(X)) :- id(X).
3  node(n((a;b), X),g(X)) :- id(X).
4  edge((n(a,X),n(b,X)),g(X)) :- id(X).
```

Multiple graphs are of particular interest when visualizing dynamic domains, as in planning, where each graph may represent a state of the world. We illustrate this in Sect. 3 and show how the solution to a planning problem can be turned into an animation.

Subgraphs[4] are specified by the binary version of `graph/2`, whose second argument indicates the super-ordinate graph. For instance, replacing Line 2 above by the following two rules makes g(X) a subgraph of g(X+1) for X=1..n-1.

```
graph(g(X))           :- id(X), not id(X+1).
graph(g(X),g(X+1)) :- id(X),      id(X+1).
```

Clingraph allows for selecting designated graphs by supplying their identifier to option `--select-graph`; several ones are selected by repeating the option with the respective identifiers on the command line.

As mentioned, the quaternary predicate `attr/4` describes properties of graph elements; this includes all attributes of *graphviz*. The first argument fixes the type of the element, namely, `graph`, `node`, and `edge`, along with keywords `graph_nodes` and `graph_edges` to refer to all nodes and edges of a graph. The second argument gives the identifier of the element, and the last two provide the name and value of the *graphviz* attribute. Some attributes, mainly labels, are often constructed by concatenating multiple values. We simplify this by treating attribute values as a list of strings and by providing the option of using a tuple as the attribute name. Then, the first argument of the tuple is the name of the attribute and the second is the position in the list in which the value of `attr/4` is placed (see e.g., Line 37 to 40 in Table 1). We give further examples in Sect. 3 and refer to the documentation for details.

---

[4] Subgraphs correspond to clusters in *graphviz*.

In order to avoid name clashes, *clingraph* offers the option `--prefix` to change all graph-oriented predicates by prepending a common prefix. For instance, `--prefix='viz-'` changes the dedicated predicate names to `viz-graph`, `viz-node`, `viz-edge`, and `viz-attr` while maintaining their arities.

The more interesting use-cases emerge by using *visualization encodings*. While in our introductory example, the latter was mimicked by `#show` statements, in general, a visualization encoding can be an arbitrary logic program producing atoms over the four graph-oriented predicates. Obviously, when it comes to visualization, a given problem encoding can then be supplemented with a dedicated visualization encoding, whose output is then visualized by *clingraph* as shown in the introductory section.

In practice, however, it turns out that this joint approach often results in a significant deceleration of the solving process. Rather, it is often advantageous to resort to a sequential approach, in which the stable models of the problem encoding are passed to a visualization encoding. This use-case is supported by *clingraph* with extra functionality when using the ASP system *clingo*. More precisely, this functionality relies upon the *clingo* feature to combine the output of a run, possibly comprising various stable models, in a single `json` object.[5] To this end, *clingraph* offers the option `--select-model` to select one or multiple stable models from the `json` object. Multiple models are selected by repeating the option with the respective number.

To illustrate this, let us replace Line 1 above by

```
{ id(1..n) } = 1.
```

to produce n stable models with one graph each, rather than a single model with n graphs as above. The handover of all stable models of the resulting logic program in `multiple.lp` to *clingraph* can then be done by the following command:

```
clingo --outf=2 -c n=10 0 multiple.lp | \
clingraph --out=tex --select-model=0 --select-model=9
```

The option `--outf=2` instructs *clingo* to produce a single `json` object as output. We request all 10 stable models via '`-c n=10 0`'. Then, *clingraph* produces a LaTeX file depicting the graphs described in the first and tenth stable model.

In the quite frequent case that the stable models are produced exclusively by the problem encoding, an explicit visualization encoding can be supplied via option `--viz-encoding` to make *clingraph* internally produce the graphic representation from the given stable models employing the *clingo* API. To ease the development of visualization encodings, *clingraph* also provides a set of external Python functions (see Sect. 3 for an example).

Just like *clingraph*'s input, also its output may consist of one or several graph representations. The specific representation is controlled by option `--out` that can take the following values:

- `facts` produces the facts obtained after preprocessing (default)
- `dot` produces graph representations in the language DOT

---

[5] https://www.json.org.

- **render** generates images with the rendering method of *graphviz*
- **animate** generates a GIF after rendering
- **tex** produces a L^AT_EX file

The default option **facts** allows us to inspect the processed input to *clingraph* in fact format. This involves the elimination of atoms irrelevant to *clingraph* as well as the normalization of the graph representation (e.g., turning unary predicates **node** and **edge** into binary ones, etc.). Options **dot** and **tex** result in text-based descriptions of graphs in the languages DOT and L^AT_EX. These formats allows for further post-processing and editing upon document integration. The L^AT_EX file is produced with *dot2tex*.[6] Arguments to *dot2tex* can be passed through *clingraph* via **--tex-param**. At long last, the options **render** and **animate** synthesize images for the graphs at hand. While the former aims at generating one image per graph, the latter allows us to combine several graphs in an animation. The format of a rendered graph is determined by option **--format**; it defaults to PDF and alternative formats include PNG and SVG. Animation results in a GIF file. It is supported by options **--fps** to fix number of frames per second and **--sort** to fix the order of the graphs' images in the resulting animation. The latter provides a handful of alternatives to describe the order in terms of the graph identifiers.

Also, it is worth mentioning that *clingraph*'s option **--engine** allows us to choose among the eight layout engines of *graphviz*;[7] it defaults to **dot** which is optimized for drawing directed graphs.

Last but not least, *clingraph* also offers an application programming interface (API) for Python. Besides *graphviz*, it heavily relies on *clorm*,[8] a Python library providing an Object Relational Mapping (ORM) interface to *clingo*. Accordingly, the major components of *clingraph*'s API are its **Factbase** class, providing functionality for manipulating sets of facts via *clorm*, and the **Graphviz** package, gathering functionality for interfacing to *graphviz*. We refer the interested reader to the API documentation for further details.[9] In conjunction with *clingo*, the API can be used for visualizing the solving process. Two natural interfaces for this are provided by the **on_model** callback of *clingo*'s **solve** method as well *clingo*'s **Propagator** class. For example, the former would allow for visualizing the intermediate stable models obtained when converging to an optimal model during optimization. The latter provides an even more fine-grained approach that allows for monitoring the search process by visualizing partial assignments.

3   Case Studies

As a first example, consider the encoding of the Queens puzzle in Listing 1.2.[10] The idea is to place n queens on an $n \times n$ chessboard so that no two queens

---

[6] https://dot2tex.readthedocs.io.
[7] http://www.graphviz.org/docs/layouts.
[8] https://github.com/potassco/clorm.
[9] https://clingraph.readthedocs.io/en/latest/clingraph/api.html.
[10] https://github.com/potassco/clingraph/tree/master/examples/queens.

attack one another. A solution is captured by atoms over predicate `queen/2`. The one comprised in the first stable model of `queens.lp` for n=5 is depicted in Fig. 2. First of all, we note that the actual graph is laid out as a 5×5 grid of white and gray squares. Each atom `queen(x,y)` is then represented by putting the symbol ♛ on the square with coordinate (x, y). All other squares are simply labeled with their actual coordinate.

```
1   1 { queen(I,1..n) } 1 :- I = 1..n.
2   1 { queen(1..n,J) } 1 :- J = 1..n.
3     :- 2 { queen(D-J,J) }, D = 2..2*n.
4     :- 2 { queen(D+J,J) }, D = 1-n..n-1.

6   cell(1..n,1..n).
```

Listing 1.2. Queens puzzle (`queens.lp`)

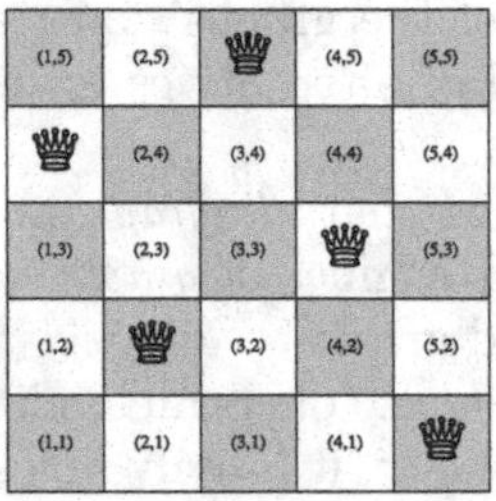

Fig. 2. Visualization of (first) stable model of the logic program in Listing 1.2

The visualization encoding producing the chessboard in Fig. 2 is given in Listing 1.3; it is used to generate the PDF in Fig. 2 in the following way.

```
clingo queens.lp -c n=5 --outf=2 | \
clingraph --viz-encoding=viz.lp --out=render --engine=neato
```

To better understand the visualization encoding, it is important to realize that we use *neato* as layout engine, since it is well-suited for dealing with coordinates.

Let us now have a closer look at the encoding in Listing 1.3. Interestingly, our graph consists of nodes only; no edges are provided. This is because nodes are explicitly positioned and no edges are needed to connect them. More precisely, one node is introduced in Line 1 for each cell of the chessboard.[11] The remainder of the encoding is concerned with the layout and positioning of each individual node, as reflected by the first and second argument of all remaining

---

[11] Strictly speaking, the definition of predicate `cell/2` belongs to the visualization encoding. Nonetheless, we add it to the problem encoding since the dimension of the board, viz. n, is unavailable in the visualization encoding. This is a drawback of the sequential approach: information must be shared via the stable models.

```
1   node((X,Y)) :- cell(X,Y).

3   attr(node,(X,Y),width,1) :- cell(X,Y).
4   attr(node,(X,Y),shape,square) :- cell(X,Y).
5   attr(node,(X,Y),style,filled) :- cell(X,Y).
6   attr(node,(X,Y),fillcolor,gray) :- cell(X,Y),(X+Y)\2 = 0.
7   attr(node,(X,Y),fillcolor,white) :- cell(X,Y),(X+Y)\2 != 0.
8   attr(node,(X,Y),fontsize,"50") :- queen(X,Y).
9   attr(node,(X,Y),label,"♛") :- queen(X,Y).
10  attr(node,(X,Y),pos,@pos(X,Y)) :- cell(X,Y).
```

Listing 1.3. Visualization encoding for Queens puzzle (`viz.lp`)

atoms over `attr/4`. This is done in a straightforward way in Lines 3 to 5 to fix the `width`, `shape`, and `style` of each node. Line 7 and 6 care about the alternating coloration of nodes, depending on whether the sum of their coordinates is even or odd. The next two lines deal with cells occupied by queens. Unlike the previous rules that only refer to the problem instance, here the derived attributes depend on the obtained solution. That is, for each atom `queen(x,y)`, Line 8 fixes the `fontsize` of the label ♛ attributed to node (x,y) in Line 9. Whenever no `label` is given to a node, its name is used instead, as witnessed by Fig. 2. Finally, Line 10 handles the positioning of nodes. In *neato*, positions are formatted by two comma-separated numbers and entered in a node's `pos` attribute. If an exclamation mark '!' is given as a suffix, the node is also pinned down. The necessary transformation from pairs of terms is implemented by the external Python function `pos(x,y)` provided by *clingraph*. This function turns a node identifier (x,y) into a string of form `"x,y!"`. For each node, the result is then inserted as the fourth argument of predicate `attr/4` in Line 10.

As a second example, let us look at a dynamic problem whose solutions can be visualized in terms of animations. To this end, we have chosen a robotic intra-logistics scenario from the *asprilo* framework [4]. This scenario amounts to an extended multi-agent path finding problem having robots transport shelves to picking stations and back somewhere. The goal is to satisfy a batch of orders by transporting shelves covering all requested products to the picking station. For brevity, we do not reproduce the actual problem encoding here[12] and rather restrict our attention to the input to the visualization encoding. The input consists of action and fluent atoms accounting for a solution and how it progresses the problem scenario over time, namely,

- `move(robot(r),(dx,dy),t)` [13] and
- `position(o,(x,y),t)` for o among `robot(r)`, `shelf(s)`, and `station(p)`.

A `move` atom indicates that a robot r moves in the cardinal direction (d_x,d_y) at time step t (for $d_x,d_y \in \{-1,0,1\}$ such that $|d_x+d_y|=1$). A `position` atom

---

[12] https://github.com/potassco/asprilo-encodings.
[13] We refrain from visualizing pickup and putdown actions, and rather represent them implicitly.

tells us that object o is at position (x,y) at time step t. All atoms sharing a common time step capture a state induced by the resulting plan.

The idea of the visualization encoding is now to depict a sequence of such states by combining the visualizations of individual states in an animation. Each state is represented by a graph that lays out the grid structure of a warehouse. We use consecutive time steps to identify and to order these graphs. This results in an atom $\mathtt{graph}(t)$ for each time step t. Similarly, we identify nodes with their coordinate along with a time stamp. This is necessary because nodes require a unique identifier across all (sub)graphs. As well, we use edges indexed by time steps to trace (the last) movements.

- $\mathtt{node}(((x,y),t),t)$
- $\mathtt{edge}((((x',y'),t),((x'+d_x,y'+d_y),t)),t)$

The first atom expresses that node $((x,y),t)$ belongs to graph t. Similarly, the second one tells us that the edge from node $((x',y'),t)$ to node $((x'+d_x,y'+d_y),t)$ belongs to graph t. It is induced by an action $\mathtt{move}(\mathtt{robot}(r),(d_x,d_y),t)$ and its precondition $\mathtt{position}(\mathtt{robot}(r),(x',y'),t-1)$.

Having settled the representation of graphs along with their nodes and edges, the rest of the visualization encoding mainly deals with setting their attributes. To see this, consider Table 1, giving excerpts of the actual visualization encoding (using line numbers in the full encoding; lines in between have been dropped for brevity).[14] The definition of graphs, nodes, and edges is given in Line 19, Line 27,

Table 1. Selected lines from the visualization encoding for an *asprilo* scenario (viz-asprilo.lp)

```
10    free(P,T) :- not position(_,P,T), position(P), step(T).

12    occo(P,T,robot(R)) :- position(robot(R),P,T),
13                          not position(station(_),P,T),
14                          not position(shelf(_),P,T).

19    graph(T) :- step(T).

27    node((P,T),T) :- position(P), step(T).

30    edge(((((X,Y),T),((X+DX,Y+DY),T)),T) :- move(robot(R),(DX,DY),T),
31                          position(robot(R),(X,Y),T-1).

37    attr(node,(P,T),(label,0),"R") :- position(robot(R),P,T).
38    attr(node,(P,T),(label,1),R) :- position(robot(R),P,T).
39    attr(node,(P,T),(label,2),"S") :- position(shelf(S),P,T).
40    attr(node,(P,T),(label,3),S) :- position(shelf(S),P,T).

43    attr(node,(P,T),shape,"point") :- free(P,T).

46    attr(node,(P,T),shape,"circle") :- occo(P,T,robot(_)).

49    attr(node,(P,T),color,white) :- free(P,T).

55    attr(node,(P,T),colorscheme,"blues9") :- occo(P,T,robot(_)).
56    attr(node,(P,T),fillcolor,R) :- occo(P,T,robot(R)).
```

---

[14] https://github.com/potassco/clingraph/tree/master/examples/asprilo.

and Line 30–31. Let us discuss the remaining lines of interest of `viz-asprilo.lp` by inspecting some features of a visualization, produced as follows.

```
clingo asprilo.lp instance.lp -c horizon=19 --outf=2    | \
clingraph --viz-encoding=viz-asprilo.lp --engine=neato  | \
          --out=animate  --sort=asc-int                 | \
          --select-model=0 --type=digraph
```

The initial call to *clingo* takes the problem encoding and instance and yields a plan of length 19, executed on a 7×7 grid with three robots, three shelves, and one picking station. The individual 20 images underlying the resulting animation are given in Fig. 3. At the beginning, robots are represented by solid blue circles, shelves by solid orange squares, and the only picking station by a solid green circle. This layout changes in the course of the plan.

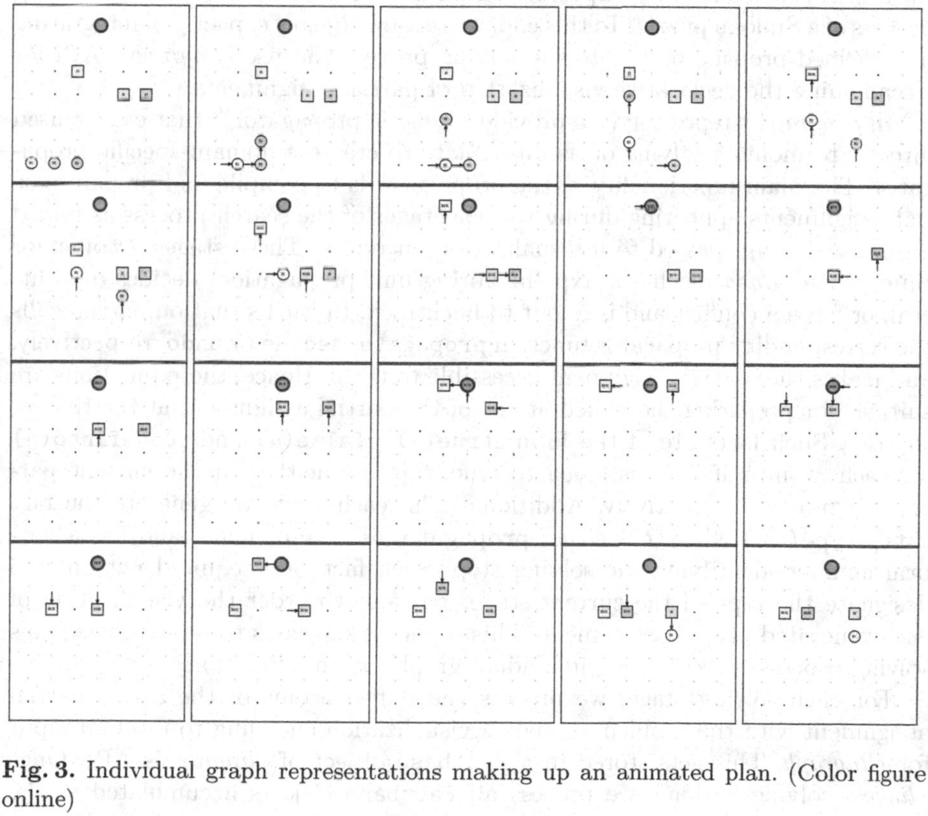

Fig. 3. Individual graph representations making up an animated plan. (Color figure online)

Let us explain how this works by focusing on unoccupied nodes and robots; shelves and picking stations are treated analogously. An unoccupied position p at a time step t is captured by `free(p,t)` in Line 10. Similarly, `occo(p,t,robot(r))` tells us that robot r is the only object on position p at a time step t. This is thus neither derivable when a robot is under a shelf, carrying one, or at a picking station. With this in mind, we see that Line 43 and 49 depict a position as a circle on a white node (plus omitted details) whenever the position is free. And analogously, Line 46, 55, and 56 represent solitary robots by solid blue circles. Once a robot shares a position with a shelf or picking station, the graphical representation changes (and instead the robot adopts the one of the shelf or picking station).

Moreover, a robot's label changes whenever it is under a shelf or carries one. This is handled in Line 37 to 40. Whenever a robot with identifier i is on a node, the label's node starts with "R" followed by "i", as indicated by the number following `label` in Line 37 to 38. Once the robots carries a shelf, it shares its position, and the label is extended with "S" and the shelf's identifier.

Up to now, all case studies take answer sets as input for visualization. For the next example, however, we visualize partial assignments appearing during the search process of *clingo*. Specifically, we discuss a visualization of the solving process of a Sudoku puzzle. To this end, we rely on *clingo*'s capacity of integrating user-defined propagators[15] into the solving process and use *clingraph*'s API for streamlining the declarative visualization of partial assignments.

In *clingraph*'s repository, we provide a generic propagator[16] that can be used directly to monitor solving or as a template to create a domain-specific propagator. The main functionality of the propagator is to compile and prepare partial assignments appearing during various stages of the search process as reified atoms, which are passed to a visualization encoding. These stages account for times when *clingo* reaches a fixpoint during unit propagation; decides on a literal; or faces a conflict and is about to backtrack. In each situation, *clingo* calls the corresponding propagator function `propagate`, `decide` or `undo`, respectively, and makes the partial assignment accessible to them. Hence, these functions are suitable for preparing the reified atoms of the partial assignment at the time of the call. Such facts are of the form `_true(a)`, `_false(a)` and `_undefined(a)` for each atom a if it is assigned to true, false or neither in the current partial assignment, respectively. Additionally, in each stage we generate the fact `_step_type(t,i)` where t is either `propagate`, `decide` or `undo`, and i is a natural number identifying the solving step. Such facts are required not only to designate the type of the current stage, but also to order the visualization of each generated partial assignment. This ordering allows us to represent *clingo*'s solving process by combining individual graphs as an animation.

For each solving stage, we process the reified atoms of the active partial assignment with the problem domain's visualization encoding to form an input for *clingraph*. This gets stored in a `Factbase` object of *clingraph*'s API. Once *clingo*'s solving is done, we process all `Factbase` objects accumulated in the propagator using *clingraph* to generate individual graphs for each of the partial assignments. Finally, we combine these graphs to generate an animation of *clingo*'s solving process. Unlike the previous example, we rely on *clingraph*'s API functions (e.g., `compute_graphs` and `save_gif`) to carry out these tasks.

---

[15] https://potassco.org/clingo/python-api/current.
[16] https://github.com/potassco/clingraph/tree/master/examples/propagator.

To illustrate the process described above, we use the Sudoku puzzle from *clingraph*'s examples folder. In this encoding, we use predicate `sudoku(x,y,v)` to represent a cell with coordinates (x,y) in a 9×9 grid with an assigned digit v from 1 to 9. A cell can have an initial value defined in the instance by predicate `initial(x,y,v)` or it can be empty if no such predicate appears. Then, the problem encoding and instance are handed to *clingo*'s solving process which is observed by our propagator. Partial assignments accumulated by the propagator are passed to the visualization encoding, which is only partially shown in Table 2 due to space constraints. Additionally, Fig. 4 depicts the resulting animation's key frames visualizing the partial assignments reached during solving.

Table 2. Selected lines from the encoding visualizing Sudoku solving

```
47  attr(node,pos(X,Y),(label,3),L) :-
48    _true(sudoku(X,Y,V)), not _true(initial(X,Y,_)),
49    opacity(sudoku(X,Y,V),0), border(sudoku(X,Y,V),B),
50    L=@concat("<td BGCOLOR='",green,0,"' BORDER='",B,"'>",V,"</td>").

52  attr(node,pos(X,Y),(label,P),L) :-
53    _undefined(sudoku(X,Y,V)), not _decide(sudoku(X,Y,V),_),
54    opacity(sudoku(X,Y,V),0), border(sudoku(X,Y,V),B), table_pos(V,P),
55    L=@concat("<td BGCOLOR='",yellow,0,"' BORDER='",B,"'>",V,"</td>").
```

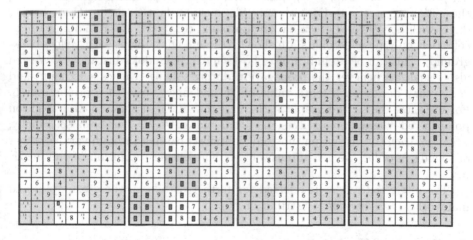

Fig. 4. Visualizations of stages of solving a Sudoku puzzle. (Color figure online)

Let us now examine how the frames from Fig. 4 are constructed. Each cell with an initial value is visualized by filling the cells with the corresponding digit as label and using a relatively larger font size. For each node of an empty cell, we construct an HTML-like label (supported by *graphviz*) as a 3×3 table allowing a slot for each digit from 1 to 9. Our aim is to visualize digits that can possibly appear in such a cell in this tabular form. Moreover, HTML-like labels allow us to use rich visual elements like borders and background colors. The rule in

Lines 47–50 from Table 2 fires whenever *clingo* reasons during propagation that an initially empty cell (captured by the body literal `not_true(initial(X,Y,_))`) must be filled with a specific digit (`_true(sudoku(X,Y,V))`). In Line 50, a partial label *L* representing an HTML table cell is constructed by concatenating the constituent strings using the `concat` external function provided by *clingraph*. Border lines and variations in the background color are controlled by the `opacity` and `border` predicates (Line 49)—which are defined based on reified `_change` facts of the partial assignment—to highlight the differences from the last assignment. Such a rule is exemplified in top leftmost graph by the cells with border lines and a dark green background. Note that the same cells in the next graph to the right still contain the same number but with no borders and a light green background, which designates that *clingo* filled them in an earlier propagation step. Additionally, *clingo* may be undecided on an empty cell's value at a particular solving stage. For instance, the top leftmost graph shows that either 2, 5 or 8 can be placed in the first cell. The rule in Lines 52–55 is responsible for visualizing these undecided digits with yellow background, where the body literal `_undefined(sudoku(X,Y,V))` states that `sudoku(X,Y,V)` is neither true nor false. Auxiliary predicate `table_pos` helps to place the constituent HTML tag in the right place of the HTML table label via the label tuple.

Ultimately, our animation allows us to analyze different aspects of the solving process of the Sudoku. For instance, the first graph illustrates that during the initial propagation *clingo* already fills many cells with digits (those having digits with borders and green background) and constrains the remaining empty cells that only possible digits are shown (those having digits with yellow background). This can be an indicator of how simple the Sudoku instance is. We can also visualize whenever the propagation during solving reaches a fixpoint, and *clingo* may decide on a truth value of an undefined atom to continue search. For instance, the second graph in the first row of Fig. 4 shows such a decision point in red where *clingo* selects the atom `sudoku(4,2,5)` to be false. Finally, when we reach the last graph (bottom rightmost) passing through various stages of solving in order, we get an answer set representing a solution of the puzzle instance.

The interested reader is referred for further details on these examples and many others to *clingraph*'s distribution.[17]

4   Related Work

Many aspects of *clingraph* are inspired by previous systems described in the literature. The basic goal—to visualize answer sets by mapping special atoms to graphic elements—traces back to *aspviz* [3], a command-line application written in Java using the Standard Widget Toolkit (SWT) for rendering. It is capable of rendering two-dimensional graphics with absolute coordinates but does neither allow relative positioning nor graph structures. These features were introduced by *kara* [5], a plugin written for the SeaLion IDE. The alternative of using

---

[17] https://github.com/potassco/clingraph/tree/master/examples.

graphviz as a backend was first mentioned by the authors of *aspviz*, and followed up with a rather basic implementation in *lonsdaleite*[18]. Another visualizer for answer sets is *idpdraw*[19], although it seems to be discontinued.

The idea of visualizing the solving process was first explored for the *nomore* system [1] which uses a graph-oriented computational model. For *dlv*, there exists a graphical tool for developing and testing logic programs [8] as well as a visual tracer [2]. In the realms of *clingo*, visualizing the solving process has been explored using a tweaked version of *clasp* [6].

Our system not only integrates ideas from the literature and makes them available for modern ASP systems, but also has some features that have—to the best of our knowledge—never been implemented before. There is a powerful API which makes it easy to include *clingraph* in custom projects, a multitude of different output formats including LaTeX and animated GIF, and the capacity of integrating a propagator for visualizing the solving process of *clingo*.

5 Discussion

Clingraph provides essentially an ASP-based front-end to the graph visualization software *graphviz*. In doing so, it takes up the early approach of *aspviz* [3] and extends it in the context of modern ASP technology. The advantage of *clingraph* is that one does not have to resort to foreign programming languages for visualization but rather remains within the realm of ASP. This provides users with an easy interface among logic programs and/or answer sets and their visualization. Moreover, *clingraph* offers a Python API that extends this ease of interfacing to *clingo*'s API, and in turn to connect and monitor various aspects of the solving process. The fact-based interface of *clingraph* makes it readily applicable to any ASP system. For more advanced features, like json output and API functionality, *clingraph* depends on *clingo*. *Clingraph* is open source software and freely available at https://github.com/potassco/clingraph.

Acknowledgments. This work was supported by DFG grants SCHA 550/11 and 15.

References

1. Bösel, A., Linke, T., Schaub, T.: Profiling answer set programming: the visualization component of the noMoRe system. In: Proceedings of the JELIA 2004, pp. 702–705. Springer, Heidelberg (2004). https://doi.org/10.1007/978-3-540-30227-8_61
2. Calimeri, F., Leone, N., Ricca, F., Veltri, P.: A visual tracer for DLV. In: Proceedings of the SEA 2009, pp. 79–93. CEUR (2009)
3. Cliffe, O., De Vos, M., Brain, M., Padget, J.: ASPVIZ: declarative visualisation and animation using answer set programming. In: Garcia de la Banda, M., Pontelli, E. (eds.) ICLP 2008. LNCS, vol. 5366, pp. 724–728. Springer, Heidelberg (2008). https://doi.org/10.1007/978-3-540-89982-2_65

---

[18] https://github.com/rndmcnlly/Lonsdaleite.

[19] https://dtai.cs.kuleuven.be/krr/files/bib/manuals/IDPDraw-manual.pdf.

4. Gebser, M., et al.: Experimenting with robotic intra-logistics domains. TPLP **18**(3–4), 502–519 (2018)
5. Kloimüllner, C., Oetsch, J., Pührer, J., Tompits, H.: Kara: a system for visualising and visual editing of interpretations for answer-set programs. In: Proceedings of the INAP 2011, pp. 325–344 (2011)
6. König, A., Schaub, T.: Monitoring and visualizing answer set solving. TPLP Suppl. **13**, 4–5 (2013)
7. Lifschitz, V.: Answer Set Programming. Springer, Cham (2019). https://doi.org/10.1007/978-3-030-24658-7
8. Perri, S., Ricca, F., Terracina, G., Cianni, D., Veltri, P.: An integrated graphic tool for developing and testing dlv programs. In: Proceedings of the SEA 2007, pp. 86–100. CEUR (2007)

A Machine Learning System to Improve the Performance of ASP Solving Based on Encoding Selection

Liu Liu[1], Mirek Truszczynski[1(✉)], and Yuliya Lierler[2]

[1] University of Kentucky, Lexington, KY 40506, USA
{liu.liu,mirek}@uky.edu
[2] University of Nebraska at Omaha, Omaha, NE 68182, USA
ylierler@unomaha.edu

Abstract. *Answer set programming* (ASP) has long been used for modeling and solving hard search problems. Experience shows that the performance of ASP tools on different ASP encodings of the same problem may vary greatly from instance to instance and it is rarely the case that one encoding outperforms all others. We describe a system and its implementation that given a set of encodings and a training set of instances, builds performance models for the encodings, predicts the execution time of these encodings on new instances, and uses these predictions to select an encoding for solving.

Keywords: answer set programming · encoding selection · machine learning

1 Introduction

Answer set programming (ASP) is a declarative programming paradigm designed primarily for solving decision problems in NP (in particular, problems that are NP-complete), and their search and optimization variants [2,4]. In ASP, an answer-set program (*AS program*) encoding a problem at hand is separate from the data. The latter is represented as a set of facts and forms a special AS program referred to as an instance. To solve the problem for a particular data instance, one combines the problem encoding with the instance into a single AS program. That program is then processed by answer set programming tools, typically a *grounder* and a *solver* such as, for instance, grounder *gringo* [6] and solver *clasp* [7].

As in other programming systems, a problem specification can be encoded in several ways in ASP. Often, this gives rise to numerous equivalent AS programs encoding the same problem. Extensive experience with ASP accumulated in the past two decades suggests that different AS programs for a given problem may differ significantly in their performance. Namely, it is rarely the case that the same encoding performs best (under a selected grounder-solver tool) across all data instances to the problem.

G. Gottlob et al. (Eds.): LPNMR 2022, LNAI 13416, pp. 415–428, 2022.
https://doi.org/10.1007/978-3-031-15707-3_32

This suggests that the availability of multiple encodings can be turned into an asset that might improve the efficiency of ASP.

Efforts were made to understand how the performance of ASP tools depends on ways AS programs encode the constraints of the problem. Automated encoding rewriting tools [1] were proposed based on tree decomposition techniques on the level of a grounder, some with Machine Learning models [18] to guide the rewriting directions that grounders may follow to produce smaller grounding. Researchers also explored the possibility of exploiting multiple solving algorithms, both outside of ASP and in ASP. *Portfolio solving* and *algorithm selection* [5,10,15,19] emerged from these efforts. The idea that we propose and explore here is to extend the scope of these approaches by taking advantage of multiple equivalent encodings for a problem, not necessarily arranged to minimize the size of the ground program. Specifically, we present a system that supports what we name *encoding portfolio* or *encoding selection* (in the last section, we also briefly discuss *encoding scheduling*). We call this encoding selection platform an ESP. The ESP system exploits collections of equivalent ASP encodings for a problem supplied by the user and can also generate additional encodings by applying simple rewritings to the encodings supplied. Thus, we provide programmers with a tool that automates systematic navigation through available encodings for the problem targeting performance improvements.

The remainder of the paper is organized as follows. Section 2 describes the architecture of the ESP, Sect. 3 presents a case study to illustrate how it works, and Sect. 4 concludes with a discussion of future work. Throughout the paper, we list insights and conclusions we arrived at while developing and using ESP. They offer practical tips on utilizing the ESP by ASP practitioners. In our discussion, we use the *hamiltonian cycle* (HC) problem to illustrate functions of the components of the ESP and their operation.

2   The Encoding Selection Platform ESP

Figure 1 shows the architecture and processes involved in the ESP encoding selection platform. The word *Input* in the flowchart indicates input data and parameters to be supplied by the user. In particular, the user provides encodings for a problem to be solved, instances of this problem, and problem specific features, if available. Components shown inside boxes denote processes implemented with the ESP. These include encoding rewriting, performance data collection, encoding candidate generation, feature extraction, machine learning modeling, per-instance encoding selection, and solving. Other annotations point at outcomes of different processes or tools utilized by the system. The ESP uses such tools as encoding rewriting system *AAgg* [3] and feature generator *claspre* [5](*claspre* is a sub-component of portfolio answer set solver *claspfolio*; it is available as a stand alone tool at https://potassco.org/labs/claspre/).

The ESP, a description of the system requirements, and instructions on how to use it are available at http://www.cs.uky.edu/ASPEncodingOptimization/esp/. Although the platform consists of several components, each part can be executed separately. Thus, users can upload encodings and instances and run all the processes, or only run some selected ones.

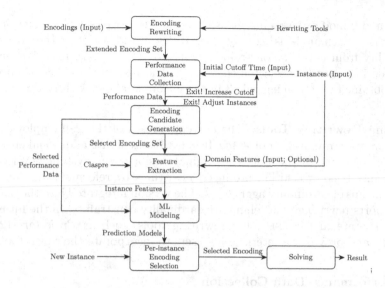

Fig. 1. A flowchart to the encoding selection platform

The ESP exploits the availability of multiple encodings of a problem to assist the user in obtaining performance improvements of ASP-based solutions to the problem. Improved performance means an increased number of instances solved for an application and decreased time spent on these instances. The platform is general purpose and can be applied to arbitrary problems solved by ASP. However, any specific use of the ESP tool assumes a concrete problem at hand. In what follows we often use the letter P to refer to that problem.

2.1 Encoding Rewriting

Encodings. The ESP expects a user to supply at least one AS program for a given problem P. However, in most cases, the user will provide several encodings for the problem. The supplied encodings are rewritten by the encoding rewriting tool available in ESP. The *extended set of encodings* is the basis for further processing that aims to select a subset of "promising" encodings to be used when solving new instances of problem P. We comment on how performance data guides the selection process implemented in ESP later in the paper.

To show examples of possible input encodings that the user might supply to the ESP, we consider a well-known Hamiltonian cycle problem. The first encoding for the HC problem follows

```
1  { hpath(X,Y) : link(X,Y) } =1:-node(X).
2  { hpath(X,Y) : link(X,Y) } =1:-node(Y).
3  reach(X) :- hpath(1,X).
4  reach(Y) :- reach(X),hpath(X,Y).
5  :- not reach(X),node(X).
```

Rules 1 and 2 model the requirement that the number of selected edges leaving and entering each node is exactly one. Rules 3 and 4 define the concept of reachability from node 1. Constraint 5 guarantees that every node is reachable from node 1 by means of selected edges only. Another (but equivalent) encoding can be obtained by replacing rule 3 in the encoding above with rule `reach(1)`.

Encoding Rewriting Tools. The current version of the ESP employs a non-ground program rewriting tool *AAgg*. It is used to generate additional encodings from those provided by the user. The original version of this system, developed by Dingess and Truszczynski [3], produced rewritings by reformulating applicable rules by means of cardinality aggregates. The version integrated into the platform also supports rewritings that eliminate cardinality constraints. In the future, we will incorporate in the ESP other rewriting tools, such as *Projector* [12] and *Lpopt* [1], and provide an interface for users to incorporate their own tools.

2.2 Performance Data Collection

Instances. Benchmark instances must be provided by the user. They are used to extract data on the performance of a solver on each of the selected encodings, to support feature extraction, and to form the training set used by machine learning tools to build encoding performance models. When a solver finds a solution to an instance in a short amount of time no matter what encoding is used, or when the solver times out no matter what encoding is used, the instance offers no insights that could inform encoding selection. Only instances that are not too easy and not too hard are meaningful. We call such instances *reasonably hard*.

More specifically, reasonably hard instances are determined by the time T_e specifying when the execution time is long enough not to view an instance as easy, and the time T_{max} specifying the cutoff time. At present, the user inputs only the cutoff time T_{max}; the system then sets $T_e = T_{max}/7$. How to select the initial value of T_{max} depends on the available computing resources, as well as the time budget for solving incoming instances of the problem at hand.

Once a user provides the ESP with the initial set of instances, and the parameter T_{max}, and the extended set of encodings is produced by rewriting, the ESP computes the *performance data* while automatically adjusting cutoff time T_{max} two times, each time doubling it, if too many time-outs occur. The ESP continues with the next step when the collected performance data suggests that the current instance set contains a sufficient proportion of reasonably hard instances. More specifically, the platform selects randomly a subset of $\min(\max(20, \min(size/10, 100)), size)$ instances to test the hardness (here *size* denotes the size of the entire input set of instances, which is expected to be greater than 500). All encodings are then run with each selected instance. An instance is easy when all encodings solve it within time T_e. An instance is too hard when it is not solved by any encoding within the cutoff time T_{max}. All other instances are *reasonably hard*. If at least 30% of instances in the selected subset

Table 1. Runtime of valid structured dataset for the HC problem

Instance_id	ham1	ham2	ham3	ham4	ham5	ham6
insttri200_33_1	114.96	0.61	200.00	12.52	2.89	2.14
insttri200_41_2	15.22	49.10	200.00	200.00	0.65	0.49
insttri200_49_1	13.22	0.16	200.00	0.23	200.00	0.62
insttri200_57_1	47.86	200.00	0.45	7.85	200.00	200.00
insttri200_57_2	41.98	200.00	59.55	53.86	0.24	1.08
insttri200_65_2	15.61	1.02	200.00	26.42	45.46	25.65
insttri200_71_10	1.22	200.00	139.17	14.84	200.00	200.00
insttri200_81_8	200.00	38.08	200.00	32.40	200.00	200.00
insttri200_91_5	200.00	74.90	116.11	1.45	40.20	200.00
insttri200_131_10	8.31	132.25	2.85	22.46	42.22	58.86

are reasonably hard, the entire input data set is *valid*. If not and also no more than 30% of instances time out on each encoding, the ESP exits and declares the original input instance set "too easy." Otherwise, the selected subset is "too hard" and the system increases T_{max} by doubling it (and adjusting T_e accordingly). After doubling, the ESP again runs all encodings with all instances. If, with the new values for T_{max} and T_e, the number of reasonably hard instances becomes 30% or more, the ESP stops and declares the original input instance set as valid. Otherwise, the ESP doubles T_{max} one more time and repeats. The possible outcomes are then: "too easy", "too hard," and valid. In the first two cases, the user is informed and asked to adjust T_{max} and the hardness of the input instances accordingly. In the last case, the ESP checks if there are at least 500 reasonably hard instances in the entire input set. If not, the ESP exits and returns to the user the numbers of instances in the set that are easy, hard and reasonably hard, and requests that the user updates the input instance set. (The first phase of the process aims to save time, if the input instance set is too hard, with a high probability the ESP will return this decision without having to process the entire data set.)

We now provide insights into the instance generation/selection process by focusing on the HC domain. Table 1 shows performance data collected by running the *gringo/clasp* tools with six encodings of the HC problem on several instances of that problem, that is, directed graphs. All graphs are generated randomly from a certain space or *model* of graphs. Graphs in the model used in this example are built by removing directed edges from *triangle grid* graphs. Nodes of those graphs are arranged in layers, the first layer has one node, the next two nodes, and so on. The external nodes form a triangle; each internal node is connected by two-directional edges with two neighboring nodes in its own layer, two neighboring nodes in the layer above and two more in the layer below. Such graphs have Hamiltonian cycles. Graphs in our example are subgraphs of a 19-layer triangle grid with 190 nodes. When the number of removed edges is small, the graphs have Hamiltonian cycles with a probability close to 1. As the number of removed edges grows, we reach the point (known as the phase transition [20]), when this probability drops quickly and becomes close to 0. The phase transition region contains graphs with and without a Hamiltonian cycle with, roughly, the same probability. Moreover, the solving time becomes significant.

Table 1 shows a selection of instances that are reasonably hard (we took $T_{max} = 200$ s as the cutoff, and set $T_e = T_{max}/7 = 28.57$ s). Building a set of reasonably hard instances (with respect to T_e and T_{max}) may still yield a data set that is relatively easy (when execution times, while greater than T_e do not come close to the cutoff time). An additional requirement one might want to impose on a "good" set of instances is that each encoding must time out on at least some instances in the set. This is the case for the set of instances in Table 1. In addition to a consideration of hardness, a valid instance set must evince complementary performance from the selected encodings. That is, no encoding must be uniformly better than others, in fact, *each* encoding must have its area of strength where it performs better than others. This is the case of the set of instances in Table 1. For example, on the instances *insttri*200_33_1 and *insttri*200_57_1 the *ham 2* and *ham 3* exhibit "opposite" performance: *ham 2* is the winner on the first instance while *ham 3* is the winner on the second one. We can observe that each instance has its own best encoding and the order of per-instance best encodings in the table are 2, 6, 2, 3, 5, 2, 1, 4, 4, 3. In particular, each encoding is the winner on at least one instance. If a dominant encoding exists (performs best on all instances), encoding selection in such case is meaningless. The ESP will inform the user about it.

Building meaningful sets of reasonably hard instances is difficult. They can be derived from the instances submitted to the past ASP competitions [8,9] in the NP category, or can be obtained by building random models of instances (as in our running example above) and finding the right settings for the model's parameters. Incorporating some structure in the model (as in the running example) offers a better chance for meaningful instances as purely random instances without any structure are often quite easy. Finally we note that to support encoding selection a large data set with at least 500 instances is needed.

The concept of an oracle helps evaluate the potential for performance improvements by encoding selection. An *oracle* is a non-deterministic algorithm that always selects the best encoding to run with a given instance. Typically, oracle's performance is much better than the performance of any individual encoding. This is the case for the data set in Table 1. Thus, the task of selecting correct encodings on a per-instance basis becomes meaningful.

Cutoff Time Penalization. Performance data represents the effectiveness of different encodings under a chosen ASP solving tool. It is obtained by processing all encodings with all instances, using a selected solver (such as the *gringo* grounder and the *clasp* solver in some selected configuration). Each individual run should be limited to the selected cutoff time, since some encodings combined with some instances may take a large amount of time before terminating.

To assess the quality of an encoding, one must account for timeouts. When an instance reaches timeout, the ESP considers the number of encodings reaching timeout for the instance, and a penalized runtime is given. The ESP uses an approach we call PARX, which takes for the runtime of a timeout instance the cutoff time multiplied by X, where X is the number of encodings that time out on this instance. For example, when this method is used, for the instances in Table 1, the penalized runtime for *insttri200_33_1* is 200.00 for *ham3*, and for *insttri200_41_2* is 400.00 for both *ham3* and *ham4*.

2.3 Encoding Candidate Selection and Feature Extraction

In this stage of the process, the ESP analyzes the performance data obtained for the extended set of encodings. The system selects a subset of the extended encoding set that consists of encodings that are most effective and that together demonstrate *run-time diversity*. At least two and no more than six encodings are selected.

To estimate the effectiveness of the encoding, we assign it a score. The score is affected by the percentage of the solved instances, the number of instances for which the encoding provided the fastest solution, and the average running time on all solved instances.

The selected encodings are organized into groups. Specifically, we consider as a group the entire set of selected encodings, if only two or three encodings were selected. Otherwise, the set of selected encodings has i encodings, where $i = 4, 5$ or 6, and we consider the group of three top-scoring encodings (the scoring is discussed in an earlier section), four top-scoring encodings etc., for the total of $i - 3$ groups (two groups if $i = 4$, three groups if $i = 5$ and four groups if $i = 6$).

To support machine learning of performance prediction models for the selected encodings, we identify instances of problem P with their *feature vectors*. In other words, each instance-encoding pair is mapped into an abstraction captured by a number of properties/features that hold for this pair. Our system relies on two sets of features. First, it exploits features that can be defined based on the generic structure of the propositional program obtained by grounding a given instance-encoding pair. To this end, we take advantage of the system *claspre* [5]. Second, the platform uses domain specific features related to problem P supplied by the user.

Claspre Features. *Claspre* is a system designed to extract features of ground ASP programs. The extracted features fall into two groups: static and dynamic. Static ones contain features about atoms, rules, and constraints. For instance, they include such program properties as the number of rules, unary rules, choice rules, normal rules, weight rules, negative body rules, binary rules, ternary rules, etc. In total, *claspre* computes 38 static features. To extract dynamic features for a ground program, *claspre* runs *clasp* on it for some short amount of time. *Clasp* returns the information about the solving process. This information is then turned into (dynamic) features of the program. The ESP uses these features for the instance-encoding pair that defined the program processed by *claspre*. These features are based on information collected after each restart performed by *clasp*, with the number of restarts being a parameter of the process. Allowing for more restarts result in features that are usually more accurate to represent a problem, but the process requires extra runtime. Overall, *claspre* computes 25 dynamic features per each restart and the platform uses features for two restarts. However, extremely easy instances have no claspre features since they are solved during the feature extraction process, and no much information can be collected for them.

Domain Features. *Claspre* features are oblivious to the nature of given problem P represented by the specific instance-encoding pair. Domain features relevant to the nature of P, expressed by properties of an instance to P often provide additional useful characteristics of the instance (note that these features are independent of properties of a particular encoding). For example, if instances for problem P are graphs, possible features may include the number of nodes in a graph, the number of edges, the minimum and maximum degrees, as well as measures reflecting connectivity and reachability properties. Availability of domain features often improves the performance of the platform. The ESP framework provides an interface for the user to supply domain features for their problems at hand. Obviously, the ultimate selection of such features as input to the platform depends on the problem being solved. Indeed, different features may be relevant to, say, problems of graph colorability and Hamiltonian Cycle. In the HC problem, the existence of long paths plays a role, and several features related to this property may be derived from running the depth-first search on the instance. Sample domain specific features for the HC problem [17] follow

- numOfNodes: the number of nodes in a graph;
- avgOutDegree: the average of outdegree of nodes;
- depthDfs1stBackJump: run depth-first search from node 1, return the depth of the first backjump, where the algorithm discovers no new nodes;
- depthBacktoRoot: run depth-first search from node 1, return the depth of a node that has a back edge to node 1;
- minDepthBfs: run breadth-first search from node 1, return the depth of the first node that has no outward edges to new nodes.

We used these features in our running example of the case study of the use of the ESP for tuning performance within the HC domain.

The output of this phase is a table whose rows correspond to instance-encoding pairs and contain the values of all its features.

2.4   Machine Learning Modeling and Solving

The goal of machine learning techniques within this project is to build encoding performance predictors based on performance data and features explained above. Once these predictors are constructed for a problem P at hand, they can be used to select the most promising encoding for processing an input instance of P. To build machine learning models, one can use regression or classification approaches. The former predicts each encoding's performance expressed as the running time, and then selects the most promising one by comparing the predicted performance. The latter method builds a multi-class machine learning model and directly selects the most promising encoding from a collection of candidate encodings. Our earlier experimental analysis (outside of the scope of this paper) indicates that regression approaches work better than classification. As a result, at present the ESP supports the construction of regression models only.

The set of selected encodings (at least two and at most six arranged into one to four groups, as discussed in Sect. 2.3) is the basis for machine learning algorithms currently used by the ESP. The ESP performs learning for each of the group based on instance features and instance performance data restricted to encodings in the group. Supervised ML techniques that we use here are trained on ⟨instance features, instance performance⟩ pairs for each encoding in the group. Once a model is trained it yields a mapping from instance features to the estimated performance of a targeted encoding. The ESP builds runtime prediction models for each encoding and selects the encoding with the minimum predicted runtime. We now explain the detailed design below.

Features Selection. *Claspre* features are collected for instance-encoding pairs. The features representing an instance consist of the features of that instance when paired with all encodings in the group being considered (88 features for each instance-encoding pair possible within the group) and the domain specific features of the instance. This is a large number of features that may cause the poor computational performance of machine learning algorithms. To address this issue, the ESP reduces the number of features by further processing. For *claspre* features, the ESP first performs feature selection inside features related to one encoding. All subsets (from 40% to 70%) of features are selected for each encoding based on standard deviation reduction [11]. These subsets of selected features are trained and validated on different data splits from the whole dataset, and validation results are compared. The subset with the lowest average mean squared error is selected as the selected features for the instance-encoding pair. When the validation results for all encodings within the group are compared, the best subset is selected as the claspre features of the group. A subset of domain specific features is selected separately and then combined with selected claspre features to form the final set of features.

Hyper-parameters Tuning. At present, the ESP supports three well-known machine learning algorithms: k-Nearest Neighbors (kNN), Decision Tree (for the review of these two methods see, for instance [21]), and Random Forest [13]. In each case, the performance of the algorithm depends on the choice of hyper-parameters (for instance, the number k of nearest neighbors to consider for the kNN method). Hyper-parameters tuning is an important step within training process of machine learning. We implemented the grid-search method for hyper-parameter searching in the ESP and combined it with the 10-fold cross-validation (for the description of k-fold cross validation method see, for instance, [16]) to improve the generalization of the obtained model.

Assessment of Learned Models. The result of the learning (for each group) is the collection of performance models obtained by applying each of the machine learning methods implemented in the ESP. These models are compared by evaluating their performance on the 5-fold cross validation approach. For each round, the platform trains models on the training set, predicts the runtime of the corresponding encoding for instances on the validation set, and selects the most promising encoding on a per-instance basis. Average solving percentage (primary criteria) and average solved time (secondary criteria, for the case of a tie) for multiply runs are compared for all learned models of all groups, and the best model among them is selected as the solution of the ESP.

Per-instance Encoding Selection and Solving. Once the platform computes and selects the model based on the performance of cross-validation results, it will use this model to solve problems provided as new instances. That is, given a new instance, it will apply the encoding selected by the model computed and selected in the machine learning phase. Specifically, the platform extracts features of the instance that are relevant to (are used by) the model, applies the model to select the encoding (the one with the lowest estimated run time is selected), and applies the solver to the instance combined with the selected encoding.

3   Experimental Analysis

We tested the performance of the ESP using the Hamiltonian Cycle problem. We now describe the experimental setup and results.

Experimental Setup. All our experiments were performed on a computer with Intel(R) Core(TM) i7-7700 CPU and 16 GB Memory, running on Linux 5.4.0-91-generic x86_64. The input to the platform consists of *six* HC encodings and *one thousand* structured graph instances. The instance set consists of graphs from four different structures used in our previous work on the HC problem [17]. The cutoff time is initially set to 200 CPU seconds. The system decided that the original cutoff time was appropriate and the cutoff time was not increased.

Each encoding was run on all instances and runtime was recorded. All instances were grounded with *gringo* version 5.2.2 and solved by *clasp* version 3.3.3 with default configurations. Only solving time was counted as runtime, while grounding time was not counted. It took ten days to collect the performance data for all six encodings. Six encodings are ranked according to their performance. They give rise to four encoding groups (top three, top four, top five and top six). For all the instances, *claspre* features are extracted and graph

Table 2. Performance of individual encoding, oracle, system solution, and other solutions

	solving%	avg_solved_t		solving%	avg_solved_t
Individual performance			Other solutions		
ham1	61.93	34.09	DTgroup4	85.16	39.14
ham2	74.83	54.31	RFgroup4	87.09	40.80
ham3	74.19	55.37	kNNgroup4	80.00	40.88
ham4	58.06	35.63	DTgroup3	87.09	36.84
ham5	**78.70**	**71.35**	KNNgroup3	80.00	41.68
ham6	68.38	45.80	DTgroup2	73.54	57.74
Oracle performance			RFgroup2	78.06	60.81
			KNNgroup2	77.41	52.54
Oracle	**95.48**	**21.64**	DTgroup1	78.06	61.74
system solution			RFgroup1	79.35	56.72
RFgroup3	**88.38**	**40.81**	KNNgroup1	76.77	57.11

specific features are provided. Out of 1000 originally provided graph instances, the ESP platform determined 775 to be reasonably hard.

The data set is split into the training and the validation set (80% of instances) and the test set (20% of instances). The former is used by the ESP to build models and select the best one. The test set is used in the experiments to evaluate the performance of the platform.

Experimental Results. The test results are shown in Table 2. Instances from the test set (in other words, instances that ESP has never seen before) are used to compile this table. The assessment of the kind is part of the platform.

The first part of the left table shows the performance of individual encodings: solving percentage (solving%) and average solved runtime (avg_solved_t) are reported. The solving percentage records the percentage of instances each encoding can solve, and the average solved time counts the average runtime for solving these instances. The average solved runtime does not accounts for unsolved instances, because different penalty methods may result in different average overall runtime. The second part reports the oracle performance, which selects the best encoding for each instance, representing the *upper bound* on what is possible with the encoding selection method. The third part shows the result for the method selected by the ESP. The right part shows the performance of other solutions (intermediate performance models), which are obtained by the system, but not selected as the best solution by ESP. The individual performance shows that the best individual encoding *ham5* can solve 78.70% of all instances. Thus, we can use the performance of this encoding as the *baseline* performance. Even though *ham5* solves the most instances, it does not have the lowest average solved running time. In fact, it has the largest average solved runtime. The encoding *ham1* is the fastest in terms of average solved runtime, but it only solves 61.93% of instances. The oracle results point at the fact that there is a huge performance gain by selecting the best encoding for each instance. It solves 95.48% of instances, with an average solving time of 21.64. Compared with *ham5*, the success percentage of the always-select-best oracle is 16.78% points higher. Overall, the table shows the encodings in the test set have complementary strengths. Each of them can solve a certain fraction of instances, but when combined, they can solve much more.

The system solution with the best cross validation result is RFgroup3, the random forest model based encoding selection from encoding group 3, which consists of top five encoding candidates. When tested on the test set, it solves 88.38% of instances, 9.68% points more than the best individual encoding *ham5*, and is also the best solution among all models. This confirms that the platform is able to generate solutions that improve the performance of ASP. The results also show all other solutions generated using the platform almost overperform the individual best. For example, these machine learning based solutions built for group 4 and group 3, which consists of six and five encoding candidates respectively, all contribute better results than *ham5*. Solutions built for group 2 and group 1 are worse since they are based only on top four and top three encoding candidates. We also observe the group 3, which consists of five encoding candidates, provides better results for corresponding models than other groups.

4   Conclusion and Future Work

In this article, we described the system ESP that can automatically improve the performance of ASP through encoding rewriting and selection. Many of the processes involved can run separately. This means that one can skip over some parts of the overall process if the necessary inputs for later steps were already computed before. *We view the platform as a valuable tool for the ASP practitioners geared to assist them with performance analysis and encoding selection tasks in a systematic and principled manner.* This paper is meant to assist them in understanding its inner components. Our experiments show that for the HC problem the ESP selects encodings and builds performance prediction models that lead to improvements in ASP solving. Despite this success, the ESP requires more insights into fine-tune machine learning methods for selecting encodings and building accurate performance predicting models. Indeed, our experiments with other problems are mixed. In some cases (for instance, the graceful graph labeling[1]), the ESP performs comparably with the best individual encodings (but not better yet), in some other cases (graph coloring) it performs worse.

Our future work will aim to address the present shortcomings. First, we will expand the encoding rewriting module, where we plan to incorporate additional encoding rewriting tools, to increase the runtime diversity of the encodings the system generates. Further, we plan to develop techniques combining encoding selection with an earlier work on solver selection. In particular, we

---

[1] https://en.wikipedia.org/wiki/Graceful_labeling.

will study learning models to estimate for a given instance the performance of a pair (*clasp* configuration, problem encoding). Second, we will incorporate into the ESP techniques constructing *schedule* [14] based solutions. In this approach, several encodings are selected to be processed by ASP tools in a certain order and for the total time equal to the cutoff limit, with each encoding receiving a certain share of the time budget.

Acknowledgments. The authors acknowledge the support of the NSF grant IIS 1707371.

References

1. Bichler, M., Morak, M., Woltran, S.: lpopt: a rule optimization tool for answer set programming. Fund. Inform. **177**(3–4), 275–296 (2020). https://doi.org/10.1007/978-3-319-63139-4_7
2. Brewka, G., Eiter, T., Truszczynski, M.: Answer set programming at a glance. Commun. ACM **54**(12), 92–103 (2011). https://doi.org/10.1145/2043174.2043195
3. Dingess, M., Truszczynski, M.: Automated aggregator - rewriting with the counting aggregate. EPTCS **325**, 96–109 (2020). https://doi.org/10.4204/EPTCS.325.17
4. Erdem, E., Gelfond, M., Leone, N.: Applications of answer set programming. AI Mag. **37**(3), 53–68 (2016). https://doi.org/10.1609/aimag.v37i3.2678
5. Gebser, M., Kaminski, R., Kaufmann, B., Schaub, T., Schneider, M.T., Ziller, S.: A portfolio solver for answer set programming: preliminary report. In: Delgrande, J.P., Faber, W. (eds.) LPNMR 2011. LNCS (LNAI), vol. 6645, pp. 352–357. Springer, Heidelberg (2011). https://doi.org/10.1007/978-3-642-20895-9_40
6. Gebser, M., Kaminski, R., König, A., Schaub, T.: Advances in *gringo* series 3. In: Delgrande, J.P., Faber, W. (eds.) LPNMR 2011. LNCS (LNAI), vol. 6645, pp. 345–351. Springer, Heidelberg (2011). https://doi.org/10.1007/978-3-642-20895-9_39
7. Gebser, M., Kaufmann, B., Schaub, T.: Conflict-driven answer set solving: from theory to practice. Artif. Intell. **187**, 52–89 (2012)
8. Gebser, M., Maratea, M., Ricca, F.: The sixth answer set programming competition. J. Artif. Intell. Res. **60**, 41–95 (2017)
9. Gebser, M., Maratea, M., Ricca, F.: The seventh answer set programming competition: design and results. Theory Pract. Logic Program. **20**(2), 176–204 (2020). https://doi.org/10.1017/S1471068419000061
10. Gomes, C.P., Selman, B.: Algorithm portfolios. Artif. Intell. **126**(1–2), 43–62 (2001). https://doi.org/10.1016/S0004-3702(00)00081-3
11. Guyon, I., Elisseeff, A.: An introduction to variable and feature selection. J. Mach. Learn. Res. **3**(Mar), 1157–1182 (2003)
12. Hippen, N., Lierler, Y.: Automatic program rewriting in non-ground answer set programs. In: Alferes, J.J., Johansson, M. (eds.) PADL 2019. LNCS, vol. 11372, pp. 19–36. Springer, Cham (2019). https://doi.org/10.1007/978-3-030-05998-9_2
13. Ho, T.K.: Random decision forests. In: Proceedings of 3rd International Conference on Document Analysis and Recognition, vol. 1, pp. 278–282. IEEE (1995)
14. Hoos, H., Kaminski, R., Schaub, T., Schneider, M.: aspeed: ASP-based solver scheduling. In: Technical Communications of the 28th International Conference on Logic Programming (ICLP 2012). Schloss Dagstuhl-Leibniz-Zentrum fuer Informatik (2012)

15. Hoos, H., Lindauer, M., Schaub, T.: claspfolio 2: advances in algorithm selection for answer set programming. Theory Pract. Logic Program. **14**(4–5), 569–585 (2014)
16. Kohavi, R.: A study of cross-validation and bootstrap for accuracy estimation and model selection. IJCAI vol. 14, pp. 1137–1145 (1995)
17. Liu, L., Truszczynski, M.: Encoding selection for solving Hamiltonian cycle problems with ASP. EPTCS **306**, 302–308 (2019). https://doi.org/10.4204/EPTCS. 306.35
18. Mastria, E., Zangari, J., Perri, S., Calimeri, F.: A machine learning guided rewriting approach for asp logic programs. EPTCS **325**, 261–267 (2020). https://doi.org/10. 4204/EPTCS.325.31
19. Rice, J.R.: The algorithm selection problem. Adv. Comput. **15**, 65–118 (1976). https://doi.org/10.1016/S0065-2458(08)60520-3
20. Selman, B., Levesque, D.G.M.H.J.: Generating hard satisfiability problems. Artif. Intell. **81**(1–2), 17–29 (1996)
21. Wu, X., et al.: Top 10 algorithms in data mining. Knowl. Inf. Syst. **14**(1), 1–37 (2008)

QMaxSATpb: A Certified MaxSAT Solver

Dieter Vandesande$^{(\boxtimes)}$ [iD], Wolf De Wulf [iD], and Bart Bogaerts [iD]

Artificial Intelligence Laboratory, Vrije Universiteit Brussel,
Pleinlaan 9, 1050 Brussel, Belgium
{dieter.vandesande,wolf.de.wulf,bart.bogaerts}@vub.be

Abstract. While certification has been successful in the context of sat-isfiablity solving, with most state-of-the-art solvers now able to provide proofs of unsatisfiability, in maximum satisfiability, such techniques are not yet widespread. In this paper, we present QMaxSATpb, an extension of QMaxSAT that can produce proofs of optimality in the VeriPB proof format, which itself builds on the well-known cutting planes proof system. Our experiments demonstrate that proof logging is possible without much overhead.

Keywords: Boolean satisfiability · maximum satisfiability · optimization · certification · proofs

1 Introduction

As the area of combinatorial search and optimization matures, we observe a strong increase in applications, as well as in highly optimized solving technology. Since some of these applications involve high-value and life-affecting decision-making processes (e.g., verifying software that drives our transportation infras-tructure [44], or matching donors and recipients for Kidney transplants [34]), it is of utmost importance that the answers produced by the solvers be completely reliable. Unfortunately, the reality is different: the constant need for more effi-cient and advanced algorithms forms an excellent breeding ground for bugs, resulting in numerous reports of solvers outputting faulty answers [1,9,11,20].

There are multiple ways to deal with this issue. One possibility is to formally verify correctness of the solvers. While there have lately been promising advances in this direction (e.g., [18]), formally verifying advanced reasoning methods used in modern-day solvers turns out to be challenging. Another approach is *certifi-cation* or *proof logging*. The idea here is that a solver should not just produce an answer, but also an efficiently verifiable *certificate* or *proof* showing that the answer is correct [2,38]. This certificate can then subsequently be verified by an independent tool (often referred to as a *verifier* or *proof checker*) of much lesser complexity. In Boolean satisfiability (SAT) [36], this approach has been successfully applied, with numerous proof formats and verifiers, including even some formally verified verifiers [6,13,14,26–28,43]. Moreover, for several years, it has been a requirement of the (main track of the) SAT competition that solvers provide certificates of their answers.

In the domain of Maximum Satisfiabilty (MaxSAT), the optimization variant of SAT, certification has not yet had its breakthrough moment. A couple of proof systems and tools have been developed to certify MaxSAT solutions [8,33,39,40]. However, none of them can truly be called a general-purpose proof system for MaxSAT, either because they are built to certify only specific MaxSAT algorithms, or because of a limited expressivity, such as for instance a lack of support for rules introducing new variables, which is common in several pre- and inprocessing techniques. For this reason, we expect that richer proof systems will be needed to handle the full range of MaxSAT solving techniques.

One promising proof format to fill this gap is VeriPB [17,22,24,25], a proof format for pseudo-Boolean satisfiability, that was recently extended to *pseudo-Boolean optimization* [7], which generalizes MaxSAT. VeriPB builds on top of the *cutting planes* proof system [12], and extends it with a generalization of the *Resolution Asymmetric Tautology* (RAT) rule that lies at the basis of the most successful proof formats for SAT. VeriPB naturally facilitates proof logging for advanced techniques such as XOR and cardinality reasoning [25] and symmetry breaking [7] that have been largely out of reach of other proof formats for SAT.

In this paper, we present QMaxSATpb, an extension of the MaxSAT solver QMaxSAT with capabilities to output proofs in the VeriPB format. In brief, QMaxSAT works as follows. First, the input CNF is augmented by a *totalizer circuit* [5]. The purpose of this circuit is to count the number of falsified clauses. Next, it iteratively calls MINISAT [16], asking for a solution in which strictly more clauses are satisfied, until no better solution can be found. The biggest challenge to obtain VeriPB-compatible proofs, was to deduce a native pseudo-Boolean encoding of the variables involved in the totalizer circuit. Once that is in place, the rest of the algorithm can easily be forced to output VeriPB-compatible proofs. In fact, since the VeriPB format generalizes the DRAT proof system, which is the most common proof system for SAT, the MINISAT oracle could be replaced by any SAT solver that supports DRAT proofs (which in practice means, most state-of-the-art SAT solvers).

We experimentally validate our solver on benchmarks from MaxSAT challenges. Our experiments show that proof logging is generally possible with minimal overhead. While most proofs can be verified by VeriPB, we do notice that verification still takes more time than solving, and we did find some cases where VeriPB can not verify a proof within reasonable limits, thereby suggesting that the proofs generated by our new tool form an interesting new testing ground for efficiency improvements to the proof verifier.

The rest of this paper is structured as follows. In Sect. 2 we introduce the necessary preliminaries. Section 3 describes how we extended QMaxSAT with proof logging and Sect. 4 contains our experiments. We conclude in Sect. 5.

2   Preliminaries

Propositional Logic. As usual, a *Boolean variable* x ranges over the Boolean values 0 (*false*) and 1 (*true*). A *literal* is a variable x or its negation $\bar{x}$. A *clause* $C = a_1 \vee \cdots \vee a_k$ is a disjunction of literals. A *formula* (in Conjunctive Normal Form – CNF) is a conjunction of clauses. The *empty clause* is denoted $\perp$. An *assignment* α is a partial function from the set of variables to 0 or 1; it is extended to literals by $\alpha(\bar{x}) = 1 - \alpha(x)$. The assignment α *satisfies* a clause C if it assigns at least one of C's literals to 1; it satisfies a formula F, if it satisfies all the clauses of F. In that case, we also call α a *model* of F. A formula F is *satisfiable* if it has a model, and *unsatisfiable* otherwise. The *Boolean Satisfiability problem* (SAT) consists of deciding whether a formula F is satisfiable. A *partial* MaxSAT-instance[1] is a tuple (F, S) with F the hard clauses and S the soft clauses. The *Maximum Boolean Satisfiability problem* (MaxSAT) consists of finding an assignment that satisfies all clauses of F and as many clauses of S as possible. Without loss of generality, we can assume that $S = \{\bar{x}_1, \ldots, \bar{x}_n\}$; this can always be enforced by introducing so-called *relaxation variables*.

QMaxSAT. QMaxSAT [32] is an *iterative partial MaxSAT solver.* Such solvers work by repeated calls to a SAT oracle, each time requesting a better solution than the best one found so far. To express the constraint that the next solution should be better than the previous one (i.e., that fewer literals in S should be falsified), QMaxSAT uses an encoding of *cardinality constraints* in propositional logic, namely the *totalizer circuit encoding* [5]. We will review the full encoding in Sect. 3, but in order to understand the algorithm what matters is that, with $S = \{\bar{x}_1, \ldots, \bar{x}_n\}$, it introduces new variables (among those new variables are the "counting" variables $v_1, \ldots, v_n$) and introduces a formula G over the original and the new variables such that: each model α of F can uniquely be extended to a model α' of $F \cup G$; moreover, α' is such that $\alpha'(v_j)$ is true if and only if at least j of the relaxation variables x_i are true.

After adding this encoding, QMaxSAT searches for a model of $F \cup G$ (using an oracle call to a SAT solver). If a model α is found, the clauses $\overline{v_j}$ are added for all $j \geq UB$, with UB (the "upper bound") equal to the number of x_i that is true in α. These added clauses express that strictly fewer of the relaxation variables x_i are true (and hence, strictly more soft constraints are satisfied), and a new model is sought. This process repeats until no more solutions can be found. Pseudocode of the QMaxSAT algorithm can be found in Algorithm 1.

The VeriPB Proof System. We now review the rules of the VeriPB proof system we use for certification of QMaxSAT; we refer the reader to Bogaerts et al. [7] for an exposition of the full proof system. A pseudo-Boolean (PB) constraint C is a linear inequality of the form $\sum_i a_i l_i \geq A$ where a_i and A are integers, l_i are

---

[1] Since QMaxSATpb is based on QMaxSAT version 0.1 [31], which does not support weights, we do not discuss weighted (partial) MaxSAT here. Later versions of QMaxSAT do support weights, using other encodings of PB constraints in CNF.

Algorithm 1: QMaxSAT

---

1 **input**: a set of hard clauses F, a set of soft clauses $S = \{\overline{x_1}, \ldots, \overline{x_n}\}$, a SAT-solver Solver

2 $\alpha \leftarrow$ Solver.solve(F)

3 **if** $\alpha =$ *'UNSAT'* **then**

4 | return 'UNSAT'

5 $G, Y \leftarrow$ generateTotalizerClauses(R) /* with G the totalizer clauses and $v_1, \ldots v_n \in Y$ the output variables meaning that at least i variables x_i are satisfied.   */

6 $F \leftarrow F \cup G$

7 **while** *true*

8 | $UB \leftarrow \#\{i \mid \alpha(x_i) = 1\}$

9 | $F \leftarrow F \cup \{\overline{v_j} \mid j \geqslant UB\}$

10 | $\alpha \leftarrow$ Solver.solve(F)

11 | **if** $\alpha =$ *'UNSAT'* **then**

12 | | **return** UB

---

literals. We call $\sum_i a_i l_i$ a *linear term*; the value of this term in a total assignment α is $\sum_i a_i \alpha(l_i)$. The constraint C is true in α if $\sum_i a_i \alpha(l_i) \geq A$. Without loss of generality it can be assumed that PB constraints are *normalized*: that all literals l_i are over distinct variables and the coefficients a_i and A are non-negative. The negation of C is a PB constraint as well, namely $\overline{C} = \sum_i -a_i l_i \geq -A + 1$. A PB formula or theory is a conjunction of PB constraints. Clearly, a clause $l_1 \vee \cdots \vee l_k$ is equivalent to the PB constraint $l_1 + \cdots + l_k \geq 1$. Hence, SAT formulas (in CNF) are special cases of PB formulas. An instance of a *pseudo-Boolean optimization problem* is a tuple (F, f) with F a PB formula and f a linear term to be minimized, referred to as the *objective function*. A solution for (F, f) is a model of F, for which there does not exist another model of F with a smaller objective function value. A partial MaxSAT problem (F, S) can also be seen as a pseudo-Boolean optimization problem $(F, \sum_{s \in S} s)$.[2]

For an instance (F, f), the VeriPB proof system keeps track of a *proof configuration* $(\mathcal{C}, v^*)$ with $\mathcal{C}$ a set of constraints (initialized as F) and v^* an integer or ∞ representing the best value for f found so far (initialized as ∞). It allows updating this configuration $(\mathcal{C}, v^*)$ using the cutting planes proof system [12]:

Literal Axioms: For any literal, we can add $l_i \geq 0$ to $\mathcal{C}$.

Linear Combination: Given two PB constraints C_1 and C_2 in $\mathcal{C}$, we can add a linear combination of C_1 and C_2 to $\mathcal{C}$.

Division: Given the normalized PB constraint $\sum_i a_i l_i \geq A$ in $\mathcal{C}$ and an integer c, we can add the constraint $\sum_i \lceil a_i/c \rceil l_i \geq \lceil A/c \rceil$ to $\mathcal{C}$.

Saturation: Given the normalized PB constraint $\sum_i a_i l_i \geq A$ in $\mathcal{C}$, we can add $\sum_i b_i l_i \geq A$ with $b_i = \min(a_i, A)$ for each i, to $\mathcal{C}$.

Additionally, VeriPB allows for rules for dealing with optimization statements:

---

[2] Here, we use the fact that we can assume that $S = \{\overline{x_1}, \ldots, \overline{x_n}\}$, but our proof logging and verification also work with an arbitrary set of soft clauses.

Objective Bound Update: Given a model α of F, we can update v^* to $\alpha(f)$.
Objective Improvement: We can always add the constraint $f < v^*$ to $\mathcal{C}$.

The first of these rules updates the objective value, given a solution; the second represents that once a solution is found, we search for strictly better solutions. VeriPB also has a rule for **deleting** constraints (in a way that guarantees that no better-than-optimal values can be found). Finally, VeriPB allows deriving non-implied constraints with a generalization of the RAT rule (which is common in proof systems for SAT). This rule makes use of a *substitution*, which maps every variable to 0, 1, or a literal. Applying a substitution ρ on a constraint C results in the constraint $C\!\restriction_\rho$ obtained from C by replacing each x by $\rho(x)$.

Redundance-based strengthening: In case $\mathcal{C} \wedge \overline{C} \vdash f\!\restriction_\rho \leq f \wedge (\mathcal{C} \cup C)\!\restriction_\rho$, we can add C to $\mathcal{C}$.

Intuitively, this rule can be used to show that ρ, when applied to assignments instead of formulas, maps any solution of $\mathcal{C}$ that does not satisfy C to a solution of $\mathcal{C}$ that does satisfy C and that has an objective value that is at least as good. Importantly, in many cases, it is not required to show precisely why a constraint can be derived, but the verifier can figure it out itself (by means of so-called *reverse unit propagation* [26]).

In case the proof system ends in a state $(\mathcal{C}, v^*)$, with $\bot \in \mathcal{C}$, we know that v^* is the value of the optimal solution of (F, f). If $v^* = \infty$, then F is unsatisfiable.

3 QMaxSATpb

We now explain how we extended QMaxSAT with proof logging capabilities, resulting in QMaxSATpb. The overall idea is that whenever the upper bound is updated (Line 8 in Algorithm 1), we have a model of F and can use the bound update rule to update v^* accordingly. In the rest of the algorithm, we make sure that every clause that is added, can be derived in the VeriPB proof system. There are three different places where new clauses are derived:

- Clauses derived by the SAT solver (Lines 2 and 10).
- Clauses representing the totalizer encoding (Line 5).
- Clauses for strengthening the theory to match the new upper bound (Line 9).

We will discuss them in this order. All the **clauses derived by the SAT solver** used by QMaxSAT (which is MINISAT), are in fact reverse unit propagation (RUP) clauses, meaning that they are implied by the cutting planes proof system. VeriPB can check itself that they are indeed implied; simply claiming they are RUP suffices to yield a valid proof. It is important to note here that our approach does not hinge on all clauses being RUP. If the solver is replaced by any other modern SAT solver with proof logging capabilities, only minor syntactic modifications are needed to make it VeriPB-compatible. Indeed, as mentioned before, redundance-based strengthening generalizes the well-known RAT rule, and moreover, VeriPB can additionally handle symmetry breaking, cardinality reasoning and XOR reasoning [7,25].

Let us now turn our attention to proofs for the **totalizer encoding**. First, we observe that cardinality definitions can easily be derived by redundancy-based strengthening.

Proposition 1. *Let* $(\mathcal{C}, v^*)$ *be a proof configuration,* X *a set of variables,* $j \leq |X| + 1$ *an integer and* v_j^X *a variable not occurring in* $\mathcal{C}$. *The following two constraints can be derived by redundancy-based-strengthening:*

$$P_{1,j}^X := \sum_{x \in X} \overline{x} + (|X| - j + 1) \cdot v_j^X \geq |X| - j + 1$$

$$P_{2,j}^X := \sum_{x \in X} x + j \cdot \overline{v_j^X} \geq j$$

The first of these constraints expresses that v_j^X is true if at least j of the variables in X are true. The second expresses that v_j^X is false if it is not the case that at least j of the variables in X are true.

Proof. The variable v_j^X is a fresh variable; the constraints enforce it to be true if and only if $\sum_{x \in X} \overline{x} \geq j$. Gocht and Nordström [25] have shown how these defining constraints can be derived using redundancy-based strengthening.[3] We include a full proof here to make the paper self-contained. To prove that a constraint $P_{i,j}^X$ can be derived by redundancy-based strengthening, we need to show that a substitution ρ exists such that $\mathcal{C} \wedge \overline{P_{i,j}^X} \vdash f\!\restriction_\rho \leq f \wedge (\mathcal{C} \cup P_{i,j}^X)\!\restriction_\rho$.

We start by proving this for $P_{1,j}^X$. Let ρ_1 be the substitution that maps v_j^X to 1 (and every other variable to itself). Since v_j^X is not used in $\mathcal{C}$ nor f, $\mathcal{C}$ clearly entails $f\!\restriction_\rho \leq f \wedge \mathcal{C}\!\restriction_{\rho_1}$. Since ρ_1 maps v_j^X to 1, $(\mathcal{C} \cup P_{i,j}^X)\!\restriction_\rho$ is trivially true.

We now have to prove that we can derive $P_{2,j}^X$ from $\mathcal{C} \cup P_{1,j}^X$, since $P_{1,j}^X$ was derived before $P_{2,j}^X$. Let ρ_2 be the substitution that maps v_j^X to 0. Since ρ_2 does not change $\mathcal{C}$ nor f and since $P_{2,j}^X\!\restriction_{\rho_2}$ is trivially satisfied, it suffices to show that $P_{1,j}^X \wedge \overline{P_{2,j}^X} \vdash P_{1,j}^X\!\restriction_\rho$. Now, whenever $\overline{P_{2,j}^X}$ holds, it must be that v_j^X is true and $\sum_{x \in X} x < j$ and therefore $\sum_{x \in X} \overline{x} \geq |X| - j + 1$. I.e., $P_{1,j}^X$ must then be satisfied independently of v_j^X and hence also $P_{1,j}^X\!\restriction_\rho$ is entailed.   □

Now, the totalizer encoding does not consist of the constraints $P_{i,j}^X$ above but of clauses encoding the same information. We will show that these clauses can be derived by cutting planes derivations from the PB constraints $P_{i,j}^X$. As such, the way we implemented proof logging in QMaxSATpb consists of first deriving the constraints in PB form, and subsequently extracting the clauses used in the totalizer encoding. Also when adding the strengthening constraints below, will we make use of the PB encoding of these variables.

---

[3] There, this rule was called *substitution redundancy*.

Definition 1 (Totalizer encoding [5]). *Let X be a set of variables and T a binary tree of which the leaves are the variables in X. For every node η of T, let $vars(\eta)$ denote the leaves of T that are descendants of η. For each internal node η, the totalizer encoding introduces variables $v_j^{vars(\eta)}$ with $0 \le j \le |vars(n)| + 1$ with intended meaning that $v_j^{vars(\eta)}$ holds if at least j variables of $vars(\eta)$ are true. For each leaf node x, we write $v_0^x = 1$, $v_1^x = x$, and $v_2^x = 1$. For each internal node η with children η_1 and η_2, the encoding consists of the clauses*

$$C_1^\eta(\alpha, \beta, \sigma) = \overline{v_\alpha^{E_l}} \vee \overline{v_\beta^{E_k}} \vee v_\sigma^{E_j} \tag{1}$$

$$C_2^\eta(\alpha, \beta, \sigma) = v_{\alpha+1}^{E_l} \vee v_{\beta+1}^{E_k} \vee \overline{v_{\sigma+1}^{E_j}} \tag{2}$$

for all combinations of $0 \le \alpha \le |vars(\eta_1)|$, $0 \le \beta \le |vars(\eta_2)|$, $0 \le \sigma \le |vars(\eta)|$, with $\alpha + \beta = \sigma$.

This encoding can be simplified by replacing v_0^η by 1 and $v_{|\eta|+1}^\eta$ by 0 for each η. QMaxSATpb adds such a totalizer encoding for the set of relaxation variables $R := \{x \mid \overline{x} \in S\}$. The next theorem shows that it can indeed be derived in the cutting planes proof system.

Theorem 1. *Let X be a set of variables and T a binary tree of which the leaves are the variables in X. Let η be an internal node of T with children η_1 and η_2. The totalizer encoding clauses $C_1^\eta(\alpha, \beta, \sigma)$ and $C_2^\eta(\alpha, \beta, \sigma)$ can be derived by a cutting planes derivation from the PB constraints*

$$P_{i,j}^\eta \cup P_{i,j}^{\eta_1} \cup P_{i,j}^{\eta_2}$$

Proof. Let η be an internal node with children η_1 and η_2 and define $X_1 = vars(\eta_1)$ and $X_2 = vars(\eta_2)$. Assume $\alpha + \beta = \sigma$ with $0 \le \alpha \le |X_1|$, $0 \le \beta \le |X_2|$, $0 \le \sigma \le |X|$.

Summation of $P_{2,\alpha}^{X_1}$, $P_{2,\beta}^{X_2}$ and $P_{1,\sigma}^X$ results in:

$$\left(\sum_{x_i \in X_1} x_i\right) + \alpha\overline{v_\alpha^{X_1}} + \left(\sum_{x_j \in X_2} x_j\right) + \beta\overline{v_\beta^{X_2}} + \left(\sum_{x \in X} \overline{x}\right) + (|X| - \sigma + 1)v_\sigma^X$$
$$\ge \alpha + \beta + |X| - \sigma + 1$$

We can rewrite the left hand side because $X_1 \cap X_2 = \emptyset$ and $X_1 \cup X_2 = X$. The right hand side can be rewritten because $\alpha + \beta - \sigma = 0$. This results in:

$$\left(\sum_{x \in X} \overline{x}\right) + \left(\sum_{x \in X} x\right) + \alpha\overline{v_\alpha^{X_1}} + \beta\overline{v_\beta^{X_2}} + (|X| - \sigma + 1)v_\sigma^X \ge |X| + 1$$

Because of the opposite signs, the first two terms simplify to $|X|$; after a saturation step, this results in:

$$\overline{v_\alpha^{X_1}} + \overline{v_\beta^{X_2}} + v_\sigma^X \ge 1$$

This is exactly $C_1^\eta(\alpha, \beta, \sigma)$ from the totalizer encoding.

A similar pattern is followed in the proof for the $C_2^\eta(\alpha, \beta, \sigma)$ constraints. First, summation of $P_{2,\sigma+1}^X$, $P_{1,\alpha+1}^{X_1}$ and $P_{1,\beta+1}^{X_2}$ gives:

$$\left(\sum_{x \in X} x \right) + (\sigma + 1)\overline{v_{\sigma+1}^X} + \left(\sum_{x_i \in X_1} \overline{x_i} \right) + (|X_1| - \alpha)v_{\alpha+1}^{X_1}$$

$$+ \left(\sum_{x_j \in X_2} \overline{x_j} \right) + (|X_2| - \beta)v_{\beta+1}^{X_2} \geq \sigma + 1 + |X_1| - \alpha + |X_2| - \beta$$

Because $X_1 \cap X_2 = \emptyset$ and $X_1 \cup X_2 = X$, the left hand side can be rewritten. The right hand side can be rewritten because $|X_1| + |X_2| = |X|$ and $\sigma - \alpha - \beta = 0$. This results in:

$$\sum_{x \in X} x + \sum_{x \in X} \overline{x} + (\sigma + 1)\overline{v_{\sigma+1}^X} + (|X_1| - \alpha)v_{\alpha+1}^{X_1} + (|X_2| - \beta)v_{\beta+1}^{X_2} \geq 1 + |X|$$

Because of the opposite signs in the first two terms, this is equivalent to:

$$(\sigma + 1)\overline{v_{\sigma+1}^X} + (|X_1| - \alpha)v_{\alpha+1}^{X_1} + (|X_2| - \beta)v_{\beta+1}^{X_2} \geq 1$$

After a saturation step, this becomes equivalent to the $C_2^\eta(\alpha, \beta, \sigma)$ constraints from the totalizer encoding. □

The next theorem shows that the unit clauses to constrain the next solutions to better ones can be derived in the VeriPB proof system as well.

Theorem 2. *Let $(\mathcal{C}, v^*)$ be a proof configuration and $Y = \{v_1^R, ...v_{|R|}^R\}$ be the set of counting variables on the set $R := \{x \mid \overline{x} \in S\}$. For any $j \geq v^*$, the unit clause $\overline{v_j^R}$ can be derived if $\mathcal{C}$ contains the pseudo-Boolean constraint $P_{2,j}^R$.*

Proof. Let $n \geq v^*$. Because of the Objective Improvement rule, VeriPB can derive the constraint:

$$\sum_{x_i \in R} \overline{x_i} \geq |R| - v^* + 1$$

Summation with $P_{2,j}^R$ results in:

$$\left(\sum_{x_i \in R} \overline{x_i} \right) + \left(\sum_{x_i \in R} x_i \right) + n\overline{v_j^S} \geq |R| - v^* + 1 + n$$

Because of the opposite signs of the first two terms, they can be dropped, resulting in:

$$n\overline{v_j^S} \geq n - v^* + 1$$

Division by $n - v^* + 1$ followed by a saturation step results in:

$$\overline{v_j^S} \geq 1$$

These are exactly the unit clauses added by QMaxSAT. □

Therefore, given an upper bound UB, QMaxSAT can derive the constraints $\overline{v_j^Y}$ for all $j \geq UB$ and call MiniSAT to find a better solution.

4 Implementation and Experiments

In order to test our work, we extend QMaxSAT (version 0.1 [31]) with proof logging as described above. The extensions amount to the following:

- All learned clauses are written to the proof file using VeriPB's RUP notation.
- All performed clause deletions (internally in the SAT solver) are written to the proof file.
- Each time a new objective value is found, it is written to the proof file using VeriPB's objective bound update notation.
- Before QMaxSAT builds its totalizer circuit, redundancy-based strengthening is used to derive a pseudo-Boolean encoding of the cardinality constraints.
- The original procedure for generating the totalizer encoding now also writes the cutting planes derivations for these clauses to the proof file.
- The unit clauses that constrain the objective function and their cutting planes derivations are written to the proof file as well.

The QMaxSAT patch as well as the source code and all necessary scripts to run the experiments, are available on GitHub [41, 42].

We experimentally validate QMaxSATpb using benchmarks from the 2021 MaxSAT evaluation [10]. All benchmarks were ran on the VUB Hydra cluster. Each solver call was assigned a single core on a 20-core INTEL Xeon Gold 6148 (skylake) processor with a time limit of 60 min and a memory limit of 32 GB, matching the resource limits used in the evaluation. Preliminary tests suggested that verification using VeriPB (commit **0e61617**) requires substantially more memory and time than solving. For this reason, we assigned veripb 600 min of computation time and 64 GB of memory.

For all instances that QMaxSAT could solve within the set limits, we plot the time taken to solve the instance using QMaxSAT and using QMaxSATpb in Fig. 1. We observe that for the majority of the instances, the overhead induced by proof logging is negligible. In fact, there are only four instances that QMaxSATpb could not solve within the limits when QMaxSAT could.

When comparing the time needed to solve instances and the time needed to verify the produced proofs (see Fig. 2), we notice that VeriPB typically needs more time to validate a proof than QMaxSATpb needs to solve the corresponding instance. Moreover, VeriPB could not verify 10.2% of the solved instances within the time limits and 2.4% within the memory limits. This suggests that VeriPB might benefit from performance and memory optimisation.

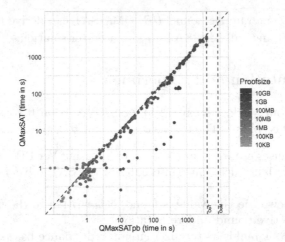

Fig. 1. Performance overhead induced by proof logging: for each instance, this plot contains a comparison between the time needed to solve it with and without proof logging.

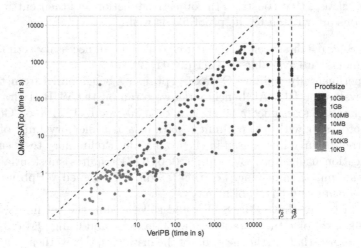

Fig. 2. Performance of proof verification: for each instance the time needed to solve the instance with proof logging enabled is compared to the time needed to verify the produced proof.

5   Conclusion

In this paper, we presented QMaxSATpb, an extension to QMaxSAT with proofs of optimality of the computed solutions. To verify solutions we used the VeriPB proof system, which is based on the cutting planes proof system. We experimentally validated our approach and found that proof logging itself requires minimal overhead. Furthermore, we find that while verification can generally happen in reasonable time, for some instances with relatively large proofs, the verifier struggles to finish in time.

Together with ongoing research on certified translations of pseudo-Boolean constraints into CNF clauses [21], this work takes an important step towards certification of state-of-the-art MaxSAT solvers. Indeed, one important contribution of our paper is to show very precisely how totalizer encodings can be added in a certified way such that the semantics of each newly introduced variable is explicitly expressed as a pseudo-Boolean formula. Such totalizer encodings lie at the heart of so-called *core-guided* MaxSAT algorithms (e.g., [4,29,30,37]). In future work we want to extend this class of solvers with proof-logging capabilities as well.

While our paper focusses on SAT and MaxSAT, the VeriPB proof system has also been used to provide proof logging for certifying solvers in richer domains [23]. We believe it can also play an important role for the field of answer set programming [35], where all modern solvers [3,15,19] support pseudo-Boolean constraints, and are based on search and optimization algorithms that are similar to those from SAT and MaxSAT.

Acknowledgement. The authors are grateful to Jeremias Berg, Stephan Gocht, Ciaran McCreesh, and Jakob Nordström for fruitful discussions on proof logging and feedback on previous versions of this manuscript. This work was partially supported by Fonds Wetenschappelijk Onderzoek – Vlaanderen (FWO) (project G070521N); computational resources and services were provided by the VSC (Flemish Supercomputer Center), funded by FWO and the Flemish Government.

References

1. Akgün, Ö., Gent, I.P., Jefferson, C., Miguel, I., Nightingale, P.: Metamorphic testing of constraint solvers. In: Proceedings of the 24th International Conference on Principles and Practice of Constraint Programming (CP 2018), pp. 727–736 (2018)
2. Alkassar, E., Böhme, S., Mehlhorn, K., Rizkallah, C., Schweitzer, P.: An introduction to certifying algorithms. it - Information Technology Methoden und innovative Anwendungen der Informatik und Informationstechnik **53**(6), 287–293 (2011)
3. Alviano, M., Dodaro, C., Faber, W., Leone, N., Ricca, F.: WASP: a native ASP solver based on constraint learning. In: Cabalar, P., Son, T.C. (eds.) LPNMR 2013. LNCS (LNAI), vol. 8148, pp. 54–66. Springer, Heidelberg (2013). https://doi.org/10.1007/978-3-642-40564-8_6
4. Avellaneda, F.: A short description of the solver EvalMaxSAT. In: MaxSAT Evaluation Solver and Benchmark Descriptions, pp. 10–11 (2021)
5. Bailleux, O., Boufkhad, Y.: Efficient CNF encoding of Boolean cardinality constraints. In: Rossi, F. (ed.) CP 2003. LNCS, vol. 2833, pp. 108–122. Springer, Heidelberg (2003). https://doi.org/10.1007/978-3-540-45193-8_8
6. Biere, A.: Tracecheck (2006). http://fmv.jku.at/tracecheck/. Accessed 19 Mar 2021
7. Bogaerts, B., Gocht, S., McCreesh, C., Nordström, J.: Certified symmetry and dominance breaking for combinatorial optimisation. In: Thirty-Sixth AAAI Conference on Artificial Intelligence, AAAI 2022, pp. 3698–3707. AAAI Press (2022). https://doi.org/10.1609/aaai.v36i4.20283

8. Bonet, M.L., Levy, J., Manyà, F.: Resolution for Max-SAT. Artif. Intell. **171**(8–9), 606–618 (2007)
9. Brummayer, R., Lonsing, F., Biere, A.: Automated testing and debugging of SAT and QBF solvers. In: Strichman, O., Szeider, S. (eds.) SAT 2010. LNCS, vol. 6175, pp. 44–57. Springer, Heidelberg (2010). https://doi.org/10.1007/978-3-642-14186-7_6
10. Carnegie Mellon University, University of Helsinki, University of Toronto: The 2021 MaxSAT Evaluation (MSE 2021). https://maxsat-evaluations.github.io/2021/. Accessed June 2022
11. Cook, W., Koch, T., Steffy, D.E., Wolter, K.: A hybrid branch-and-bound approach for exact rational mixed-integer programming. Math. Program. Comput. **5**(3), 305–344 (2013)
12. Cook, W.J., Coullard, C.R., Turán, G.: On the complexity of cutting-plane proofs. Discret. Appl. Math. **18**(1), 25–38 (1987)
13. Cruz-Filipe, L., Heule, M.J.H., Hunt, W.A., Kaufmann, M., Schneider-Kamp, P.: Efficient certified RAT verification. In: de Moura, L. (ed.) CADE 2017. LNCS (LNAI), vol. 10395, pp. 220–236. Springer, Cham (2017). https://doi.org/10.1007/978-3-319-63046-5_14
14. Cruz-Filipe, L., Marques-Silva, J., Schneider-Kamp, P.: Efficient certified resolution proof checking. In: Legay, A., Margaria, T. (eds.) TACAS 2017. LNCS, vol. 10205, pp. 118–135. Springer, Heidelberg (2017). https://doi.org/10.1007/978-3-662-54577-5_7
15. De Cat, B., Bogaerts, B., Devriendt, J., Denecker, M.: Model expansion in the presence of function symbols using constraint programming. In: 2013 IEEE 25th International Conference on Tools with Artificial Intelligence (ICTAI 2013), pp. 1068–1075 (2013)
16. Eén, N., Sörensson, N.: An extensible SAT-solver. In: Giunchiglia, E., Tacchella, A. (eds.) SAT 2003. LNCS, vol. 2919, pp. 502–518. Springer, Heidelberg (2004). https://doi.org/10.1007/978-3-540-24605-3_37
17. Elffers, J., Gocht, S., McCreesh, C., Nordström, J.: Justifying all differences using pseudo-Boolean reasoning. In: Proceedings of the 34th AAAI Conference on Artificial Intelligence (AAAI 2020), pp. 1486–1494 (2020)
18. Fleury, M.: Formalization of logical calculi in Isabelle/HOL. Ph.D. thesis, Saarland University, Saarbrücken, Germany (2020)
19. Gebser, M., Kaufmann, B., Schaub, T.: Conflict-driven answer set solving: from theory to practice. Artif. Intell. **187**, 52–89 (2012)
20. Gillard, X., Schaus, P., Deville, Y.: SolverCheck: declarative testing of constraints. In: Schiex, T., de Givry, S. (eds.) CP 2019. LNCS, vol. 11802, pp. 565–582. Springer, Cham (2019). https://doi.org/10.1007/978-3-030-30048-7_33
21. Gocht, S., Martins, R., Nordström, J., Oertel, A.: Certified CNF translations for pseudo-Boolean solving. In: Meel, K.S., Strichman, O. (eds.) 25th International Conference on Theory and Applications of Satisfiability Testing, (SAT '22), pp. 16:1–16:25. Schloss Dagstuhl-Leibniz-Zentrum für Informatik (2022). https://doi.org/10.4230/LIPIcs.SAT.2022.16
22. Gocht, S., McBride, R., McCreesh, C., Nordström, J., Prosser, P., Trimble, J.: Certifying solvers for clique and maximum common (connected) subgraph problems. In: Simonis, H. (ed.) CP 2020. LNCS, vol. 12333, pp. 338–357. Springer, Cham (2020). https://doi.org/10.1007/978-3-030-58475-7_20
23. Gocht, S., McCreesh, C., Nordström, J.: An auditable constraint programming solver. In: Solnon, C. (ed.) 28th International Conference on Principles and Practice

of Constraint Programming, (CP'2022), pp. 25:1–25:18. Schloss Dagstuhl - Leibniz-Zentrum für Informatik (2022). https://doi.org/10.4230/LIPIcs.CP.2022.25

24. Gocht, S., McCreesh, C., Nordström, J.: Subgraph isomorphism meets cutting planes: solving with certified solutions. In: Proceedings of the 29th International Joint Conference on Artificial Intelligence (IJCAI 2020), pp. 1134–1140 (2020)

25. Gocht, S., Nordström, J.: Certifying parity reasoning efficiently using pseudo-Boolean proofs. In: Proceedings of the 35th AAAI Conference on Artificial Intelligence (AAAI 2021), pp. 3768–3777 (2021)

26. Goldberg, E., Novikov, Y.: Verification of proofs of unsatisfiability for CNF formulas. In: Proceedings of the Conference on Design, Automation and Test in Europe (DATE 2003), pp. 886–891 (2003)

27. Heule, M.J.H., Hunt, W.A., Jr., Wetzler, N.: Trimming while checking clausal proofs. In: Proceedings of the 13th International Conference on Formal Methods in Computer-Aided Design (FMCAD 2013), pp. 181–188 (2013)

28. Heule, M.J.H., Hunt, W.A., Wetzler, N.: Verifying refutations with extended resolution. In: Bonacina, M.P. (ed.) CADE 2013. LNCS (LNAI), vol. 7898, pp. 345–359. Springer, Heidelberg (2013). https://doi.org/10.1007/978-3-642-38574-2_24

29. Ignatiev, A., Morgado, A., Marques-Silva, J.: RC2: an efficient MaxSAT solver. J. Satisfiability Boolean Model. Comput. **11**, 53–64 (2019)

30. Jahren, E., Achá, R.A.: The MSUSorting MaxSAT solver. In: MaxSAT Evaluation Solver and Benchmark Descriptions, p. 15 (2017)

31. Koshimura, M.: QMaxSAT: Q-dai MaxSAT solver. https://sites.google.com/site/qmaxsat/. Accessed June 2022

32. Koshimura, M., Zhang, T., Fujita, H., Hasegawa, R.: QMaxSAT: a partial MaxSAT solver. J. Satisfiability Boolean Model. Comput. **8**(1–2), 95 100 (2012). https://doi.org/10.3233/SAT190091

33. Larrosa, J., Nieuwenhuis, R., Oliveras, A., Rodríguez-Carbonell, E.: A framework for certified Boolean branch-and-bound optimization. J. Autom. Reason. **46**(1), 81–102 (2011)

34. Manlove, D.F., O'Malley, G.: Paired and altruistic kidney donation in the UK: algorithms and experimentation. In: Proceedings of the 11th International Symposium on Experimental Algorithms (SEA 2012), pp. 271–282 (2012)

35. Marek, V., Truszczyński, M.: Stable models and an alternative logic programming paradigm. In: Apt, K.R., Marek, V., Truszczyński, M., Warren, D.S. (eds.) The Logic Programming Paradigm: A 25-Year Perspective, pp. 375–398. Springer, Heidelberg (1999). https://doi.org/10.1007/978-3-642-60085-2_17

36. Marques Silva, J.P., Lynce, I., Malik, S.: Conflict-driven clause learning SAT solvers. In: Handbook of Satisfiability, pp. 131–153 (2009)

37. Martins, R., Terra-Neves, M., Joshi, S., Janota, M., Manquinho, V., Lynce, I.: Open-WBO in MaxSAT evaluation 2017. In: MaxSAT Evaluation Solver and Benchmark Descriptions, p. 17 (2017)

38. McConnell, R.M., Mehlhorn, K., Näher, S., Schweitzer, P.: Certifying algorithms. Comput. Sci. Rev. **5**(2), 119–161 (2011)

39. Morgado, A., Marques-Silva, J.: On validating Boolean optimizers. In: IEEE 23rd International Conference on Tools with Artificial Intelligence, ICTAI 2011, pp. 924–926 (2011)

40. Py, M., Cherif, M.S., Habet, D.: A proof builder for Max-SAT. In: Li, C.-M., Manyà, F. (eds.) SAT 2021. LNCS, vol. 12831, pp. 488–498. Springer, Cham (2021). https://doi.org/10.1007/978-3-030-80223-3_33

41. Vandesande, D., De Wulf, W., Bogaerts, B.: QMaxSATpb: a certified MaxSAT solver. https://github.com/wulfdewolf/CertifiedMaxSAT. Accessed June 2022

42. Vandesande, D., De Wulf, W., Bogaerts, B.: QMaxSATpb: a certified MaxSAT solver: patches & benchmarks. https://github.com/wulfdewolf/CertifiedMaxSAT_benchmarks. Accessed June 2022
43. Wetzler, N., Heule, M.J.H., Hunt, W.A.: DRAT-trim: efficient checking and trimming using expressive clausal proofs. In: Sinz, C., Egly, U. (eds.) SAT 2014. LNCS, vol. 8561, pp. 422–429. Springer, Cham (2014). https://doi.org/10.1007/978-3-319-09284-3_31
44. Zhang, H.: Combinatorial designs by SAT solvers. In: Handbook of Satisfiability, pp. 533–568 (2009)

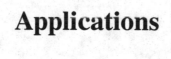

Applications

Knowledge-Based Support for Adhesive Selection

Simon Vandevelde[1,2,3](✉) ⓘ, Jeroen Jordens[4] ⓘ, Bart Van Doninck[4] ⓘ,
Maarten Witters[4] ⓘ, and Joost Vennekens[1,2,3] ⓘ

[1] Department of Computer Science, KU Leuven, De Nayer Campus,
J.-P. De Nayerlaan 5, 2860 Sint-Katelijne-Waver, Belgium
{s.vandevelde,joost.vennekens}@kuleuven.be
[2] Leuven.AI – KU Leuven institute for AI, 3000 Leuven, Belgium
[3] Flanders Make – DTAI-FET, Leuven, Belgium
[4] Flanders Make, Oude Diestersebaan 133, 3920 Lommel, Belgium
{jeroen.jordens,bart.vandoninck,maarten.witters}@flandersmake.be

Abstract. This work presents a real-life application developed to assist
adhesive experts in the selection of suitable adhesives. As the popularity
of adhesive joints in industry increases, so does the need for tools to
support the selection process. While such tools already exist, they are
either too limited in scope, or offer too little flexibility in use. In this work,
we first extract experts' knowledge about this domain and formalize it in
a Knowledge Base (KB). The IDP-Z3 reasoning system can then be used
to derive the necessary functionality from this KB. Together with a user-
friendly interactive interface, this creates an easy-to-use tool capable of
assisting the adhesive experts. The experts are positive about the tool,
stating that it will help save time and find more suitable adhesives.

1 Introduction

The Flanders Make Joining & Materials Lab (FM JML) is specialized in adhesive
bonding. They support companies in selecting the most appropriate adhesive
for their specific use case, by accounting for characteristics such as strength,
temperature resistances, adhesive durability, and more. As this selection process
requires much expert knowledge, it is performed manually by one of the *adhesive
experts* that work at FM. It is a time-consuming and labor intensive task, due
to the high number of available adhesives on the market, each with extensive
data sheets. Currently, the experts do not make use of any supporting tools to
help them perform the selection, because the current generation of tools does
not meet their requirements.

This paper describes our work on a logic-based tool which supports the
experts in the selection process. It is structured as follows. We start by describing the process of selecting an adhesive and the state-of-the-art tools in Sect. 2,
and elaborate on the logical system used in this work in Sect. 3. Next, we present
our Adhesive Selector Tool in Sect. 4, where we discuss the process of Knowledge
Acquisition, how the system handles unknown parameter values, and how the

G. Gottlob et al. (Eds.): LPNMR 2022, LNAI 13416, pp. 445–455, 2022.
https://doi.org/10.1007/978-3-031-15707-3_34

experts interface with the knowledge. We share the results of our three-fold validation in Sect. 5, and describe our lessons learned in Sect. 6. Finally, we conclude in Sect. 7 and discuss further work.

2   Adhesive Selection and Current Tools

As there is no universally applicable adhesive, the selection of an adhesive is an important process. There are many factors on which the choice of an adhesive depends: structural requirements such as bonding strength and maximum elongation, environmental factors such as temperature and humidity, economic factors, and more. Due to the complexity of the problem, there is quite a potential for tools that support this selection process. Yet, in [8] the author concludes that "there is a severe shortage of selection software, which is perplexing especially when the task of adhesive selection is so important".

Currently, when tasked with a use case, the experts work in two steps. First, they start out by trying to derive necessary requirements, such as defining the temperature ranges or calculating values for parameters like minimum strength. Based on this list of requirements, they perform the selection. This selection consists of manually looking through various data sheets, keeping track of which adhesives are suitable. In the second step, these adhesives are put to the test by performing real-life experiments in FM's lab, to ensure suitability. However, this testing step is costly and time-consuming, so it is important that the initial selection is as precise as possible. While there are tools available for this process, the FM experts do not use them because they are either too simplistic, or not sufficiently flexible.

The most straightforward selection tools are websites offering simple interfaces[1] [16]. Based on a series of questions, they provide neutral advise to support selection. However, they still require the expert to look up and process the information themselves.

There are also a number of expert systems to be found in the literature [9–13,15,17]. Here, domain knowledge is captured and formalized in the form of rules, which can be used for adhesive selection by forward chaining and often also for generating explanations by backward chaining. However, these systems have a number of downsides: they are low in both interpretability and maintainability by the expert, often not all required knowledge can be expressed, and they generally only contain a low number of adhesives or substrates. Finally, these systems typically only allow forward/backward chaining, which is not enough to provide all the functionality the experts need. For instance, a situation might arise in which an adhesive is already pre-defined (e.g., left-over from a previous gluing operation), and the selection of a second substrate is required. While this selection requires the same knowledge, the expert tools are not capable of performing this operation.

---

[1] such as www.adhesivestoolkit.com and www.adhesives.org.

3   Knowledge Base Paradigm

The core idea in the Knowledge Base Paradigm (KBP) [5] is to represent knowledge in a purely declarative way, independently of how it is to be applied. Knowledge is stored in a Knowledge Base (KB) to which different inference tasks can be applied. This approach stimulates *knowledge reuse*, as multiple inference tasks can be used to solve multiple problems with the same knowledge.

3.1   IDP

The IDP (Imperative Declarative Programming) system [4] is an implementation of the KBP. The knowledge in the KB is represented in a rich extension of First Order Logic (FOL), called $FO(\cdot)^2$. It extends FOL with types, aggregates, inductive definitions and more. $FO(\cdot)$ is an expressive and flexible knowledge representation language, capable of modeling complex domains. The knowledge in a KB is structured in three kinds of blocks: *vocabularies, structures* and *theories*.

A *vocabulary* specifies a set of symbols. A symbol is either a type, predicate, or a function. A type represents a range of values, e.g., an enumeration list of adhesives called *adhesiveType* or the domain of real numbers $\mathbb{R}$. A predicate symbol either expresses a boolean or a *relation* on one or more types, such as *BondScaling()* or *Available(adhesiveType)*. A function symbol represents a function from the Cartesian product $T_1 \times \ldots \times T_n$ of a number of types to a type T_{n+1}. For example, the function *BondStrength(adhesiveType)* $\rightarrow \mathbb{R}$ maps each adhesive on its bond strength.

A *structure* is a (partial) interpretation of a specific vocabulary. A full interpretation contains the concrete values for each symbol of the vocabulary, whereas a partial interpretation only contains values for some of them.

A *theory* contains a set of logical formulae in $FO(\cdot)$.

By itself, the KB cannot be executed: it is merely a "bag of knowledge', which contains no information on how it should be used. The latest version of the IDP system, IDP-Z3[3], supports many different inference tasks to apply this knowledge. We will briefly go over the relevant inferences for this work: **propagation, model expansion, optimization** and **explanation**. Given a partial interpretation $\mathcal{I}$ for the vocabulary of a theory T, **propagation** derives the consequences of $\mathcal{I}$ according to T, resulting in a more precise partial interpretation $\mathcal{I}'$. **Model expansion** extends a partial structure $\mathcal{I}$ to a complete interpretation I that satisfies the KB theory T ($I \models T$). **Optimization** is similar to model expansion, but looks for the model with the lowest/highest value for a given term. Finally, **explanation** will, given a structure $\mathcal{I}$ which does not satisfy the theory T ($\mathcal{I} \not\models T$), find a minimal subset of the interpretations in $\mathcal{I}$ which together explain why $\mathcal{I}$ does not satisfy the theory.

---

[2] also written as FO-dot.
[3] www.IDP-Z3.be.

3.2   Interactive Consultant

The Interactive Consultant [2] is a generic interface for IDP-Z3, which aims at facilitating interaction between a user and the system. It is a generic interface, in the sense that it is capable of generating a view for any syntactically correct KB. In short, each symbol of the KB is represented using a *symbol tile*, allowing users to set or inspect that symbol's value. Each time a value is assigned, IDP's propagation is performed, after which the interface is updated: symbols for which the value was propagated are updated accordingly, and for the other symbols the values that are no longer possible are removed. In this way, a user is *guided* towards a correct solution: it is not possible to enter a value that would make the partial structure represented by the current state of the GUI inconsistent with the theory.

At any point in time the user can ask for an explanation of a system-derived value, e.g., when the user does not understand it or questions the outcome. The system will then respond with the relevant laws and user-made assignments that lead to the derived value. In this way, the tool becomes more explainable, leading to more trust in the system.

The Interactive Consultant interface has already successfully been used in multiple applications in the past, e.g. [1,6].

4   Adhesive Selector Tool

This section outlines the creation and usage of the tool, and the main challenges that were faced in that process.

4.1   Knowledge Acquisition

The creation of the knowledge base is an important element in the development process of knowledge-based tools. It requires performing knowledge acquisition, which is traditionally the most difficult step, as the knowledge about the problem domain needs to be extracted from the domain expert to be formalized by the knowledge engineer. While knowledge acquisition comes in many shapes and forms, we applied the *Knowledge Articulation* method [7]. The central principle of this method is to formalize knowledge in a common notation for both domain expert and knowledge engineer, so that both sides actively participate in the formalization process.

We started by organizing three knowledge articulation workshops, each lasting between three and four hours. Each of these workshops was held with a group of domain experts. While typically a single domain expert would suffice for knowledge extraction, having a group present can help as an initial form of knowledge validation, as the experts discuss their personal way of working amongst themselves, before coming to a consensus. For the common notation we used Constraint Decision Model and Notation (cDMN) [18], an extension of the Decision Model and Notation (DMN) standard [14]. DMN is a user-friendly, intuitive notation for (simple) decision logic. cDMN aims to increase the expressiveness of the notation (e.g., by adding constraints) while maintaining this user-friendliness.

The first workshop consisted of identifying all relevant adhesive selection parameters and using them to create an initial structure of the knowledge in the form of DMN's Decision Requirement Diagram (DRD). This DRD is meant to give an overview of a decision model, by showing the connections between input variables (ovals) and decisions/calculations (rectangles). Figure 1 shows a fragment of the DRD constructed during the first workshop. It is structured in a bottom-to-top way, similar to how the experts would reason: they start by calculating the thermal expansions, and then work their way up to the calculation of the maximum stress.

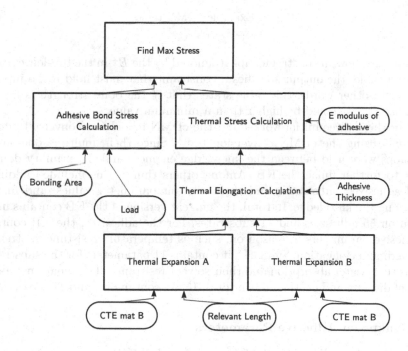

Fig. 1. Snippet of created DRD.

During the subsequent workshops, the rest of the model was fleshed out. This consists of the *decision tables* and the *constraint tables*. An example of such a decision table can be found in Fig. 2a. In such a table, the inputs (in green, left) define the outputs (in light blue, right). Each row represents a decision rule, which *fires* if the values of the input variables match the values listed in the row. If a row fires, the value of the output is set accordingly. E.g., if *Support = fixed*, then the *MinElongation* is calculated as *deltaLength/BondThickness*. The (U)nique hit policy of this table, indicated in the top left, means that the different rows must be mutually exclusive.

MinElongation		
U	Support	MinElongation
1	free	0.5 × deltaLength / BondThickness
2	fixed	deltaLength / BondThickness

(a) Calculation of MinElongation

BondStrength constraint		
E*	Strength is Known	Max Stress
1	Yes	≥ MinStrength

(b) BondStrength constraint table.

Fig. 2. Example cDMN tables

Figure 2b shows a constraint table (denoted by the E^* in the top-left corner). In such a table, the output specifies a constraint that must hold if the input is satisfied. In other words, this table states that *if* the bond strength is known, *then Max Stress* should be higher than a minimum value.

After these three initial workshops, the cDMN model was converted into an FO($\cdot$) KB using the cDMN conversion tool[4]. Since then, multiple one-on-one workshops were held between the knowledge engineer and the primary domain expert to further finish the KB. Among others things, this included adding a list of adhesives, substrates, and their relevant parameter values, and further fine-tuning the knowledge. In total, the current version of the KB contains information on 55 adhesives and 31 substrates. For the adhesives, the KB contains 21 adhesive parameters to reason on, such as temperature resistances, strength and maximum elongation. Similarly, it contains 11 parameters for the substrates, such as their water absorption and their solvent resistance. These parameters are a mix of discrete and continuous: in total, 15 are continuous, and 17 are discrete.

4.2   Unknown Adhesive Parameters

One of the main challenges in the formalization of the KB was handling unknown adhesive data. Indeed, often an adhesive's data sheet does not list all of its properties. This raises the question of how the tool should deal with this: should the adhesive be excluded, or should it simply ignore the constraints that mention unknown properties? Together with the experts we agreed on a third approach, in which we first look at the adhesive's family. Each adhesive belongs to one of 18 families, for which often some indicative parameter values are known. Whenever an adhesive's parameter is unknown, we use its family's value as an approximation. If the family's value is also unknown, then the constraint is ignored. This best corresponds to how the experts typically work.

---

[4] www.cdmn.be.

This way of reasoning is formalized in the KB. For example, the constraint that an adhesive should have a minimum required bonding strength is written as follows:

$$\forall p \in param : Known(p) \Leftrightarrow (KnownAdh(p)$$
$$\vee \, KnownFam(p))$$
$$KnownAdh(strength) \Rightarrow BondStr = StrAdh(Adh).$$
$$\neg KnownAdh(strength) \Rightarrow BondStr = StrFam(Adh).$$
$$Known(strength) \Rightarrow BondStr \geq MinBondStr.$$

with *StrAdh* and *StrFam* representing respectively the specific adhesive's and its family's bonding strength. This approach is used for all 21 adhesive parameters.

4.3   Interface

A crucial requirement of this application is that the adhesive experts are able to interactively explore the search space. To this end, our tool integrates the Interactive Consultant to facilitate interaction with the KB. This interface makes use of several functionalities of the IDP system to make interactive exploration possible: the "propagation" inference algorithm is used to show the consequences of each choice, the "explain" inference is used to help the user understand why certain propagations were made, the "optimize" inference is used to compute the best adhesive that matches all of the choices made so far.

Usage of the interface consists of filling in symbol tiles, each representing a different symbol of the KB, and having the interface compute the consequences. For example, Fig. 3a shows a segment of the interface in which a user set a minimum bond strength of 12 MPa as a requirement. The interface also shows the number of adhesives that remain feasible: after setting the earlier constraint, that drops from 55 to 12, as shown in Fig. 3b. If the user does not understand why a certain consequence was propagated, they can ask the system for an explanation, as demonstrated in Fig. 3c.

Besides generating a list of all the adhesives that meet certain requirements, the tool can also find the optimal adhesive according to a criterion, such as lowest price or highest strength.

5   Validation

We have performed three types of validation for this tool: a benchmark to measure the efficiency, a survey to measure the opinion of the adhesive experts and a discussion with the Flanders Make AI project lead.

Benchmark. In an initial benchmark, an adhesive expert was tasked with finding a suitable adhesive for an industrial use case which the company received. In total, it took the expert about three hours to find such an adhesive, after delving through multiple data sheets. We then used our tool for the same use case, and were able to find the exact same adhesive within three minutes. Interestingly, the reasoning of the tool closely mimicked that of the expert: for example, they both excluded specific families for the same reasons.

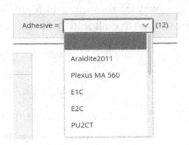

(a) Some of the symbol tiles available in the interface.

(b) List of remaining suitable adhesives during selection.

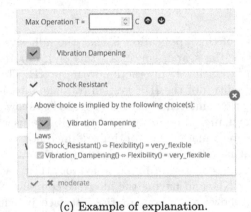

(c) Example of explanation.

Fig. 3. Screenshots of the interface.

Survey. After a demonstration of the tool to four adhesive experts, we asked them to fill out a survey to better gauge their opinion. Their answers can be summarized as follows.

- The experts find the tool most useful for finding a list of initial adhesives to start performance testing with.
- The tool will be most useful for the newer, less knowledgeable members of the lab.
- However, it is also useful for senior experts as they can discover adhesives which they have not yet used before.

The main critique of the tool given by the experts is that more adhesives should be added, to make the selection more complete.

Project Lead Discussion. As part of a discussion with Flanders Make's project lead, who oversees multiple AI-related projects, they outlined their perception of our tool. They see many advantages. Firstly, as there is not much data available on adhesive selection, and data generation is quite expensive, building a tool based on the knowledge they already have is very interesting. Secondly, by "storing" the expert knowledge formally in a KB they can retain this information, even when experts leave the company. Thirdly, having a formal representation also makes the selection process more uniform across different experts, who typically use different heuristics or rules-of-thumb. Lastly, they indicated that there is trust in the system, because the knowledge it contains is tangible. This makes it more likely that the experts will agree with the outcome of the tool.

The project lead also expressed that there is potential to maintain and extend this tool themselves, which would be a significant advantage compared to their other AI systems. However, we currently have not yet focused on this aspect.

6   Lessons Learned

Typically, knowledge acquisition is a time-consuming and difficult process. We have found that the use of DMN as a common notation can help facilitate this process. By keeping the experts in the loop with an understandable knowledge representation, they can actively participate in the formalization. This way of working is less error-prone, as it functions as a preliminary validation of the knowledge.

After our three initial workshops, we mainly held one on-one meetings with one of the experts to add information on the adhesives, and to further fine-tune the knowledge. This resulted in a tight feedback loop, which turned out to be a key element in our formalization. Indeed, thanks to thorough examinations of the tool by the expert, we were able to discover additional bugs in our KB. Here, the Interactive Consultant was of paramount importance: each time the KB was modified, the expert could immediately play around with it using the generic interface. In this way, the knowledge validation of the tool could happen directly after the modifications, allowing for a swifter detection of any errors.

Having knowledge in a declarative format, independent of how it will be used, has multiple advantages. To begin with, it allows using the knowledge for multiple purposes, even when this initially might not seem useful. Furthermore, it increases the experts' trust in the system, as it reasons on the same knowledge as they do, and is interpretable.

The main advantage of using IDP-Z3 does not lie in any one of its inference algorithms, but rather in the fact that it allows all of these functionalities that are required for interactive exploration of the search space to be performed by applying different inference algorithms to a single knowledge-base. Indeed, some of the inference tasks supported by IDP-Z3 are widely supported by other tools (e.g., model expansion), while others are unique to IDP-Z3 as far as we know (at least for a language such as FO($\cdot$)).

7   Conclusions and Future Work

This paper presents the Adhesive Selector, a tool to support adhesive selection using a knowledge-based approach. The Knowledge Base was constructed by performing several workshops and one-on-one meetings, using a combination of DMN and cDMN. Our current iteration of the tool contains sufficient knowledge to assist an expert in finding an initial list of adhesives. Compared to the state-of-the-art, it is declarative, more explainable, and more extensive. The KB is also not limited to just adhesive selection, but can also be used to perform other related tasks.

In future work, we plan on converting the entire FO($\cdot$) KB into cDMN, and evaluating its readability and maintainability from the perspective of the domain experts. Besides this, we intend to test the tool using more real-life use cases, to quantify the gain in efficiency. Additionally, we are also collaborating with an external research group to develop an AI-based tool capable of extracting adhesive information from data sheets, to efficiently add more adhesives to our KB.

Acknowledgements. This research received funding from the Flemish Government under the "Onderzoeksprogramma Artificiële Intelligentie (AI) Vlaanderen" programme and Flanders Make vzw.

References

1. Aerts, B., Deryck, M., Vennekens, J.: Knowledge-based decision support for machine component design: a case study. Exp. Syst. Appl. **187**, 115869 (2022), https://www.sciencedirect.com/science/article/pii/S0957417421012288
2. Carbonnelle, P., Aerts, B., Deryck, M., Vennekens, J., Denecker, M.: An interactive consultant. In: Proceedings of the 31st Benelux Conference on Artificial Intelligence (BNAIC 2019) and the 28th Belgian Dutch Conference on Machine Learning (BENELEARN 2019), Brussels, Belgium, 6–8 November 2019. CEUR workshop proceedings, vol. 2491. CEUR-WS.org (2019)
3. Carbonnelle, P., Vandevelde, S., Vennekens, J., Denecker, M.: IDP-Z3: a reasoning engine for FO(.) (2022). https://arxiv.org/abs/2202.00343
4. De Cat, B., Bogaerts, B., Bruynooghe, M., Janssens, G., Denecker, M.: Predicate logic as a modeling language: the IDP system. In: Kifer, M., Liu, Y.A. (eds.) Declarative Logic Programming: Theory, Systems, and Applications, pp. 279–323. ACM (September 2018). https://dl.acm.org/citation.cfm?id=3191321
5. Denecker, M., Vennekens, J.: Building a knowledge base system for an integration of logic programming and classical logic. In: Garcia de la Banda, M., Pontelli, E. (eds.) ICLP 2008. LNCS, vol. 5366, pp. 71–76. Springer, Heidelberg (2008). https://doi.org/10.1007/978-3-540-89982-2_12
6. Deryck, M., Devriendt, J., Marynissen, S., Vennekens, J.: Legislation in the knowledge base paradigm: interactive decision enactment for registration duties. In: Proceedings of the 13th IEEE Conference on Semantic Computing, pp. 174–177. IEEE (2019)
7. Deryck, M., Vennekens, J.: An integrated method for knowledge management in product configuration projects. In: Andersen, A.-L., et al. (eds.) CARV/MCPC -2021. LNME, pp. 860–868. Springer, Cham (2022). https://doi.org/10.1007/978-3-030-90700-6_98
8. Kellar, E.J.C.: Key issues in selecting the right adhesive. In: Dillard, D.A. (ed.) Advances in Structural Adhesive Bonding, pp. 3–19. Woodhead Publishing in Materials, Woodhead Publishing (2010). https://www.sciencedirect.com/science/article/pii/B9781845694357500018

9. Kannan, T., Prabu, S.S.: Expert system for selection of adhesives. In: Proceedings of the Recent Developments in Materials Processing Conference (2004)
10. Lammel, C., Dilger, K.: Software for a rule-based adhesive-selection system. Adhes. Sealants Ind. **9**(5), 42–43 (2002)
11. Lees, W., Selby, P.: The PAL program mark II. Int. J. Adhes. Adhes. **13**(2), 120–125 (1993)
12. Meyler, K.L., Brescia, J.A.: Design of a computer expert system for adhesive selection using artificial intelligence techniques. Technical report, Army armament research development and engineering center Picatinny Arsenal (1993)
13. Moseley, L., Cartwright, M.: The development of an expert system for operational use in the selection of industrial adhesives. Eng. Appl. Artif. Intell. **5**(4), 319–328 (1992)
14. Object Modelling Group: Decision model and notation v1.3 (2021). http://www.omg.org/spec/DMN/
15. Rb, A., Hh, V.: Expert-system selects adhesives for composite-material joints. Adhes. Age **38**(7), 16–19 (1995)
16. da Silva, L.F.M., Öchsner, A., Adams, R.D.: Introduction to adhesive bonding technology. In: da Silva, L.F.M., Öchsner, A., Adams, R.D. (eds.) Handbook of Adhesion Technology, pp. 1–7. Springer, Cham (2018). https://doi.org/10.1007/978-3-319-55411-2_1
17. Su, Y., Srihari, K., Adriance, J.: A knowledge update mechanism for an adhesive advisor. Comput. Ind. Eng. **25**(1–4), 111–114 (1993)
18. Vandevelde, S., Aerts, B., Vennekens, J.: Tackling the DM challenges with cDMN: a tight integration of DMN and constraint reasoning. In: Theory and Practice of Logic Programming. Cambridge University Press (CUP) (2021)

ASP for Flexible Payroll Management

Benjamin Callewaert[1,2,3(✉)] and Joost Vennekens[1,2,3]

[1] Department of Computer Science, KU Leuven, De Nayer Campus,
J.-P. De Nayerlaan 5, 2860 Sint-Katelijne-Waver, Belgium
{benjamin.callewaert,joost.vennekens}@kuleuven.be
[2] Leuven.AI - KU Leuven Institute for AI, 3000 Leuven, Belgium
[3] Flanders Make - DTAI-FET, Leuven, Belgium

Abstract. Payroll management is a critical business task that is subject to a large number of rules, which vary widely between companies, sectors and countries. Moreover, the rules are often complex and change regularly. Therefore, payroll management systems must be flexible in design. In this paper, we suggest an approach based on a flexible Answer Set Programming model, and an easy-to-read tabular representation based on the DMN standard. It allows HR consultants to represent complex rules without the need for a software engineer, and to ultimately design payroll systems for diverging scenarios. We show how the multi-shot solving capabilities of the clingo ASP system can be used to reach the performance that is necessary to handle real-world instances.

Keywords: ASP · Payroll management · Decision modelling

1 Introduction

Payroll management is a critical business task that concerns the administration and management of staff financial reports, such as wages, salaries, deductions and bonuses. Manual preparation of staff's salaries is often error prone and time consuming due to the large number of relevant rules. Automated payroll management systems are therefore being used to speed up the process. The set of applicable rules can vary widely based on the sector and the country in which the company operates, and on company-specific agreements that have been made. Correctly implementing and maintaining a payroll system can thus be a challenging exercise [3]. Based on talks with the company ProTime, a market leader in the area of time registration, we have identified the following three key challenges for such a system.

1. When deploying the system for a new company or updating it for an existing customer, HR consultants are typically employed to figure out the rules that apply. If they need to communicate all their knowledge to software engineers before it can be entered into the system, this introduces a lot of overhead, delays and the risk of communication errors. Therefore, the HR consultants should be able to configure as much of the system as possible without the

G. Gottlob et al. (Eds.): LPNMR 2022, LNAI 13416, pp. 456–469, 2022.
https://doi.org/10.1007/978-3-031-15707-3_35

help of a software engineer. Due to the complexity of the rules, a simple configuration file does not suffice and a more elaborate knowledge representation language is needed. Providing such a language that is both powerful enough and easy to use for HR consultants is an important challenge.

2. There are essentially no restrictions on the kinds of rules that the HR consultants may encounter. It is therefore not possible to cover all the expressivity that the HR consultants might need up-front. Therefore, the language in which they write down the rules must not only be easy to use for them, but it should also be possible to easily extend it with new language features, without invalidating models that have been built earlier.

3. Finally, despite the required flexibility, the solution should still be computationally efficient. In particular, a single employee shift should be handled in $< 1s$. This is very challenging, as shifts may run over several days and it is necessary to determine the employee's wage at each point in time. Moreover, it is impossible to know up-front at which points in time the pay rate will change, because this can be determined by the rules in a complex way.

In this paper, we propose an approach based on a combination of multi-shot Answer Set Programming and decision tables to tackle these challenges. Throughout the paper, we use the following real-life example to illustrate our approach:

An employee receives a normal wage of 20 €per hour and an overtime premium of 20% for any work done after 8 hours of working. The employee should also receive a night premium of 25% for any work done at night or any work done in the evening that continues into the night, provided that more time was spent in the night than in the evening. Employees are also allowed to take a break, but breaks are only paid as (official) rest breaks after their shift has started for one hour.

2   Proposed Approach

We first outline our general approach to tackling the three challenges described in the introduction, before discussing each component of our solution in more detail. To tackle the first challenge, we base ourselves on the Event Calculus [12]. An EC model consists of a general theory of how properties evolve through time, complemented by a concrete list of a actions and fluents. We provide a generic implementation of a suitable variant of the EC, and the HR consultants can then represent the rules for a specific company by defining a concrete set of actions and fluents. To allow this to be done in an easy way, we make use of decision tables, as specified in the Decision Model and Notation (DMN) standard [11], to define the actions and fluents. To provide the necessary expressive power, we extend this notation using a simple temporal logic and an interval logic. To cope with the second challenge, we define the semantics of the language that is provided to the HR consultants by means of a declarative Answer Set Program [6]. Known for its flexibility and elaboration tolerance, ASP allows us to implement this language in such a way that new language features can easily be added when necessary, with minimal running risk of introducing bugs in the existing models. Due to space limitations, we refer to [2] for an introduction to ASP. One downside of using the expressive declarative ASP formalism is that the third challenge, i.e., that of computational efficiency, may be hard to meet. Indeed, as we show below, the normal ground-and-solve approach of ASP solvers falls far short of the required performance. To address this issue, we make use of the multi-shot solving capabilities [5] of the ASP solver clingo [4]. Here, the user defines a number of parameterised ASP programs and writes an imperative program, e.g. in Python, to manipulate these program. We now discuss the different components of our approach in more detail.

Event Calculus. Different variants have been proposed over the years; in this study, we made an implementation based on the Functional Event Calculus (FEC) [10]. The FEC extends the EC with non-boolean fluents. Recent work [7–9] formulated different versions of the Event Calculus in ASP. These implementations are both fast and expressive in comparison to previous SAT- or Prolog-based encodings. We implement the FEC axioms in ASP in the same way as [9] and use the clingo system recommended in [7]. Recently, the goal-directed ASP system s(CASP) [13] was also used to implement the event calculus formalism and reason about events without grounding the whole ASP program [1]. However, since the task we try to solve explicitly requires us to consider the state of the employee at each timepoint, we would not benefit from such an approach.

DMN Decision Tables. The specific part then defines which fluents and actions there actually are, and how each interval should be interpreted (e.g., as unpaid time, overtime, ...). To enable the HR consultants to construct and maintain this specification, we use the Decision Model and Notation (DMN) standard [11]. An important component of DMN are its decision tables which we use here to represent the payroll rules. As a result, HR experts can understand the logic behind the payroll system and take on most of the work of maintaining it.

Temporal Logic. Some of the domain knowledge that the consultants need to express concerns temporal properties. For instance, overtime starts after an employee has been working for 8 h. We represent such knowledge using the following simple linear time logic:

- An atomic temporal formula is of the form $f = v$, with f a fluent and v a value from the domain of f;
- If ϕ and ψ are temporal formulas, then so are $\phi \wedge \psi$ and $\neg\phi$;
- If ϕ is a temporal formula and $n \in \mathbb{N}$, then $[\geq n]\phi$ is a temporal formula, which intuitively represents that ϕ has been true for at least n time points.

Given a time line $T = (I_0, I_1, \ldots)$ and a time point $i \geq 0$, we define that a temporal formula ϕ holds in (T, i), denoted as $(T, i) \models \phi$, as follows:

- For an atomic temporal formula, $(T, i) \models f = v$ if $f^{I_i} = v$,
- For a conjunction $\phi \wedge \psi$, $(T, i) \models \phi \wedge \psi$ if $(T, i) \models \phi$ and $(T, i) \models \psi$
- For a negation $\neg\phi$, $(T, i) \models \neg\phi$ if $(T, i) \not\models \phi$

– For $[\geq n]\phi$, $(T, i) \models [\geq n]\phi$ if $i \geq n$ and for all $i - n \leq j \leq i$, $(T, j) \models \phi$.

We also introduce an abbreviation $[= n]\phi$ for the formula $[\geq n]\phi \wedge \neg[\geq n + 1]\phi$. As we will show in Sect. 3, this temporal logic is easily defined in ASP.

Interval Logic. The wage of an employee is not defined in terms of individual timepoints but in terms of **intervals**. The consultants can define which fluents are considered *relevant* for the wage of an employee. Within an interval, all the relevant fluents keep their value, i.e., the boundaries of the interval are timepoints at which the value of a relevant fluent changes. We consider half-open intervals [i,j) where i is the timepoint at which the value of a relevant fluent changes and j is the next such timepoint. An *interval property* describes a characteristic of an interval. It is either a relevant fluent f, or an aggregate function like *length*. We denote the value of an interval property p in an interval $[i, j)$ as $p^{[i,j)}$. Given a time line $T = (I_0, I_1, \ldots)$, we define this value in the following way:

– For a relevant fluent f, $f^{[i,j)} = f^{I_i}$, that is the value of fluent f at the start of the interval. Because f is relevant, this is also the value that f has in all following I_k for $k \in [i, j)$.
– For the aggregate function *length*, $length^{[i,j)} = j - i$.

Alongside interval properties, we also define *interval terms*. An interval term is an expression that refers to a specific interval. The atomic interval term *this* refers to the current interval. For an interval term t, $next(t)$ refers to the next interval, and $prev(t)$ to the previous one. Given a sequence of intervals $S = (\mathcal{I}_0, \mathcal{I}_1, \ldots)$, we define $this^{(S,i)} = \mathcal{I}_i$ and for every interval term t with $t^{(S,i)} = \mathcal{I}_j$, we define $next(t)^{(S,i)} = \mathcal{I}_{j+1}$ and $prev(t)^{(S,i)} = \mathcal{I}_{j-1}$.

An *interval value* is then of the form $[t]p$ and refers to the value of the interval property p for the interval that is indicated by the interval term t. We define this value as $[t]p = p^{t^{(S,i)}}$. We define an *atomic interval formula* as $v\theta w$ where v and w are two interval values and θ a comparison operator. Finally, we combine these atomic interval formulas with the standard boolean operators, as usual.

3   Single-Shot Implementation

First we present an implementation for use by a standard single-shot solver. Afterwards we show how a more efficient implementation can be developed that uses the multi shot solving capabilities of *clingo*.

Functional Event Calculus.(based on [9]) The timeline consists of a number of discrete timepoints 0..n, represented by the *time(T)* predicate. Each timepoint corresponds to a certain duration in clock-on-the-wall time. For the moment, we consider timepoints that are 10 min long. The *ts(Days, Hours, Minutes, Stamp)* predicate links a duration expressed in real-world *Days*, *Hours* and *Minutes* to the corresponding timepoint *Stamp*.

```
day(0..1).    hour(0..23).      minute(0..59).
ts(Days, Hours, Minutes, Stamp):-day(Days), hour(Hours),
    minute(Minutes),Stamp = (Days*24+Hours)*6+Minutes/10.
time(T):-day(Days),hour(Hours),minute(Minutes),ts(Days,Hours,Minutes,T).
maxTime(M):-M =  #max{T: time(T)}.
```

The situation of the employee at a certain time point is described by a complete set of **fluents**. Fluents have a domain of possible values. An example is the boolean fluent *present*, which indicates whether the employee is currently clocked in. At each point in time, a fluent has a certain value, as represented by the predicate *value(F,V,T)*. At timepoint 0, the fluent's value is specified by the *initially(F,V)* predicate. The *cause(F,V,T)* predicate represents that at timepoint T there is a cause for the value of F to change to V, which leads to the current value of F being terminated at $T+1$ and the value V being initiated.

```
value(F,V,0):- fluent(F),initially(F,Val),domain(F,V).
value(F,V,T+1):- fluent(F),time(T+1),value(F,V,T),not terminated(F,V,T).
value(F,Val,T+1):- fluent(F),time(T+1),initiated(F,Val,T).
initiated(F,V,T):- fluent(F),cause(F,V,T),value(F,V2,T),V2 != V.
terminated(F,V,T):- fluent(F),value(F,V,T),cause(F,V2,T),V2 != V.
```

The only reason for a fluent to change is because an **action** changes it. In general, the effect of an action may depend on the state of the world at the time the action occurs. However, for the moment, we will consider only actions that have the fixed effect of causing a *Fluent* to take on a specific *Value*, as represented by the *causes(Action,Fluent,Value)* predicate. For now, we define 2 types of actions. A **user action** is an action that is performed by the user in an intentional way (i.e., the employee). A **wall-time action** happens at specific clock-on-the-wall time. Both wall-time actions and user actions thus happen at a given absolute time, represented by the *userDoes(A,T)* and *actionTime(A,T)* predicates.

```
action(A):- userAction(A).
action(A):- walltimeAction(A).
happens(A,T):- userAction(A), userDoes(A,T),time(T).
happens(A,T):- walltimeAction(A), actionTime(A, T),time(T).
cause(F,Val,T):- action(A), happens(A,T), causes(A,F,Val,T), time(T).
```

With these concepts, we now represent the case-specific knowledge in an easy-to-read tabular representation. The case-specific knowledge for our running example is shown in Fig. 1. Each table enumerates a single predicate, e.g., the first table corresponds to the *initially(F,V)* predicate, etc.

Inertial Fluent

	Inertial Fluents	Initial value
1	present	false
2	timeOfDay	night
3	dayStarted	false
4	restBreakPossible	false
5	shifStarted	false
6	cumul	false
7	break	no

Actions effects

	Action	Affected Fluent	Action causes Fluent to
1	clockIn	present	true
2	clockout	present	false
3	nightfall	timeOfDay	night
4	morning	timeOfDay	day
5	dayStarts	dayStarted	true
6	dayEnds	dayStarted	false

Walltime Actions

	Action	Wall-time
1	nightfall	22h00
2	morning	7h00
3	dayStarts	14h00
4	dayEnds	23h00

User Actions

	Action	User does Action at
1	clockIn	13h45
2	clockOut	16h00
3	clockIn	16h30
4	clockOut	23h30

Fig. 1. Case-specific representation of a basic scenario

Conditional Effects. The effect of an action may depend on the current state of the world. We describe such a conditional effect with a *ccauses(Action, Fluent, Value, Condition)* predicate.

```
causes(Act,Fl,Val,T):-ccauses(Act,Fl,Val,Cond), holds(Cond,T).
```

Conditions are formatted in the temporal logic of Sect. 2. In the tables we use a slightly more user-friendly syntax, writing e.g., $f1 = v1 \land [= n]f2 = v2$ as $f1 = v1$ *and* $f2 = v2$ *since* n. In our ASP implementation, we represent each such condition as a set of facts. For instance, the above condition *cond1* is represented as follows:

```
and(cond1,2).    sub(cond1,0,v(f1,v1)).    sub(cond1,1,since(f2,v2,n)).
```

Here the *and(C, N)* predicate denotes that condition C is a conjunction of N sub-conditions, each represented by a *sub(C, I, SC)* fact, with $0 \le I < N$.

The *holds(Cond, T)* predicate specifies whether a condition *Cond* holds at a certain timepoint T. For *Cond* = $v(F, V)$, we just check whether Fluent F has Value V. *Cond* = *since(F, V, D)*, representing whether a fluent F has had a value V for D timepoints, is defined by two rules. The first rule states that the initiation of V for F at $T-1$ marks timepoint T as the start of a period in which F has value V. The recursive rule extends such a period with one timepoint if F still has value V at T. Finally, if *Cond* is a conjunction, we check whether the number conjuncts that hold at T matches its total number of conjuncts N.

```
holds(v(F,V),T):-value(F,V,T).
holds(since(F,V,0),T):-time(T), initiated(F,V,T-1).
holds(since(F,V,D+1),T):-time(T), value(F,V,T), holds(since(F,V,D),T-1).
holds(C,T):-and(C,N), time(T), #count{I:sub(C,I,Sub), holds(Sub,T)}=N.
```

We can now represent scenarios where these conditional effects come into play in the tabular representation. In the first table of Fig. 2, we specify that a shift starts if an employee clocks in when the workday has already started or when the day starts and the employee is already clocked in.

Conditional effects

	Action	Condition	Fluent	Action changes Fluent to if Condition holds
1	clockIn	dayStarted=true	shiftStarted	true
2	dayStarts	present=true	shiftstarted	true

Triggered Action

	Action	Condition that triggers Action
1	makeRestBreakPossible	shiftStarted=true since 1h00

Fig. 2. Case-specific representation of conditional effects and triggered actions

Automatically Triggered Actions. An action can also be automatically triggered if a certain temporal condition is fulfilled. To specify that an employee's break is paid as an (official) rest break after their shift has started for one hour, we specify an action *makeRestBreakPossible*, which causes fluent *restbreakPossible* to be *true*. Such actions are not performed by the user, but happen automatically after a certain fluent F has had a certain value V for a specific duration

D, as represented by an *after(F,V,D,A)* predicate. Figure 2 represents triggered action *makeRestBreakPossible* in our tabular form.

```
action (A):- triggeredAction (A).
happens (A,T):- holds (since (F,Val,Dur),T), after (F,Val,Dur,A), time(T).
```

Defined Fluents. To avoid repeated use of complex fluent formulas, we introduce defined fluents. The value of a defined fluent is completely determined by the values of the other fluents. Therefore, they provide no additional information about the state of the world; they simply make it easier to track its properties. The value of a defined fluent is defined by a set of *rule(F,V,C)* facts: if the condition C holds, the defined fluent F has the value V. To cover the case that no rules are applicable, each defined fluent must have a default value.

```
value (F,Val,T):- defined (F),time(T),rule (F,Val,Cond), holds (Cond,T).
value (F,Val,T):- defined (F),time(T),default (F,Val),not appliedRule (F,T).
appliedRule (Fluent ,T):- rule (Fluent ,Val,Cond),holds (Cond,T).
```

For example, to indicate whether an employee is working, we introduce the defined fluent *atWork = true* if and only if the inertial fluents *present* and *shiftStarted* are *true*. Figure 3 represents this in our tabular representation.

Defined Fluents		
	Defined Fluent	Default Value
1	atWork	false

Count Fluent		
	Count Fluent	Count Rule
1	workedHours	atWork=true

Defined Fluent		
	Defined Fluent	Rule	Value
1	atWork	present=true and shiftStarted=true	true

Fig. 3. Case-specific representation of defined and count fluents

Count Fluents. An employee receives a bonus for any overtime done after they have already worked eight hours. This can be modelled with a third type of fluents, the count fluents. Each count fluent CF is defined by a rule of the form *countRule(CF,Cond)*, that specifies that this fluent counts the timepoints at which the condition *Cond* holds.

```
value (CF,0,0):- countFluent (CF).
value (CF,S+1,T):- countFluent (CF), value (CF,S,T-1), countRule (CF,Cond),
    holds (Cond,T).
value (CF,S,T):- countFluent (CF), value (CF,S,T-1), countRule (CF,Cond),
    not holds (Cond,T).
```

In Fig. 3, we define the count fluent *workedHours*, which, at each timepoint, keeps track of how long the fluent *atWork* has been *true* up to that point.

Count fluents can also trigger actions. The predicate *when(CF,Value,A)* states that if count fluent CF reaches a certain *Value*, an action A is triggered. To make sure that an action is not triggered multiple times if the desired value is maintained for multiple timepoints, we state that the value of the count fluent in the previous timepoint should be smaller than the desired value.

```
happens (A,T):- when(CF,V,A), value (CF,V,T), value (CF,V1,T-1), V > V1.
```

For example, the overtime bonus is applied by triggering an action *cumulPremiumAction* after eight hours of work. Figure 4, adds this triggered action and its effect to the existing tables for triggered actions and effects (Figs. 2 and 1). Note that conditions specifying that a fluent F has had a value V for a duration D are translated in ASP as an $after(F, V, D, A)$ predicate and those that specify value V for a count fluent CF are translated as a $when(CF, V, A)$ predicate.

Triggered Action		
Action	Condition that triggers Action	
1	...	...
2	cumulPremium	workedHours=8h00

Actions effects		
Action	Fluent	Action causes Fluent
1	...	...	...
2	cumulPremium	cumul	true

Fig. 4. Extended case-specific representation of triggered actions and effects

Reasoning About Intervals. Up to now we have only reasoned about individual timepoints. To calculate the total wage of employees we consider intervals. As described in Sect. 2, within intervals all of the "relevant" fluents keep their value. By restricting attention to only the relevant fluents, we avoid creating too many small intervals. A relevant fluent is annotated by the *relevant(Fluent)* predicate. We denote the relevant fluents by introducing a new column in the inertial and defined fluent table (Figs. 1 and 3), as can be seen in Fig. 5.

Inertial Fluents		
Inertial Fluents	Default Value	Relevant
1	timeOfDay	night	true
2	cumul	false	true
3	...	...	...

Defined Fluent		
Defined Fluent	Default Value	Relevant
1	atWork	false	true

Fig. 5. Case-specific representation of relevant fluents

The boundaries of intervals are those timepoints at which the value of at least one relevant variables changes.

```
boundary(T):-relevant(Var), changes(Var,T).
changes(Var,T):-time(T), time(T-1), value(Var,Old,T-1),
      value(Var,New,T), Old != New.
```

To define the intervals, we assign an *id* to each boundary. The intervals will be of the form $[B(i), B(i + 1))$, where $B(i)$ denotes the boundary with id i. The *stretchesTo(Id, T)* predicate denotes that interval *Id* includes timepoint T. We model this with two rules. The first one states that if the interval includes the previous timepoint $T - 1$ and timepoint T is not a boundary then the interval includes T as well. Boundaries themselves are included in a time interval that they start. Timepoint T is thus a boundary of time interval $I + 1$ if timepoint $T - 1$ is included in the previous interval I and T is a boundary. A boundary thus denotes the start of an interval (*intervalFrom(Id,From)* predicate) and the end of the previous interval (*intervalTo(Id, To)* predicate).

```
boundary (0,0).
intervalFrom (Id ,From):− boundary (Id ,From).
intervalTo (Id ,To):− id (Id ),  boundary (Id+1,To).
boundary (I+1,T):− id (I+1),id (I ),boundary (T) ,stretchesTo (I ,T−1).
stretchesTo (I ,T):− id (I ),stretchesTo (I ,T−1),not  boundary (T).
stretchesTo (I ,T):− boundary (I ,T).
```

In principle, there could be as many interval as there are timepoints. Typically, there will be far fewer. To speed up the program, we assume an upper bound of at most 20 intervals. We include that the final interval id should not be used. If this ever happens, the upper bound should be increased. Next, as described in the interval logic of Sect. 2, we define interval terms, such as *prev(this)*.

```
id (0..20).
enoughIds:− freeId (I ).
freeId (I ):− id (I ),  maxId (M),  I > M.
maxId (M):− id (M),  M = #max{I :  usedId (I )}.
usedId (I ):− id (I ),  boundary (I ,T).
:− not  enoughIds.
refersTo (this ,Id ,Id ):− id (Id ).
refersTo (prev (I ),J−1,Id ):− id (Id ),  id (J ),  refersTo (I ,J ,Id ).
refersTo (next (I ),J+1,Id ):− id (Id ),  id (J ),  refersTo (I ,J ,Id ).
```

To clearly track the characteristics of the interval and avoid repeated use of complex interval formulas, we introduce **defined interval properties**. The value of a defined property is specified by a set of *intRule(P,V,C)* facts. If the condition C holds in the current interval, the defined property P has the value V. These conditions are formatted in the interval logic of Sect. 2. The *intHolds(Cond,Id)* predicate specifies when a condition for an interval holds. To check whether a condition holds, we define the value of the properties described in the interval logic of Sect. 2. A *valueOfProp(P,V,Id)* predicate denotes that an interval property P has value V in interval Id. If P is a relevant fluent, this is simply the case if this fluent has that value. If $P = length$, its value is the length of interval Id. The value of an interval atom $[IntTerm]P$, which we denote in ASP as *at(IntTerm, P)*, is the value of a property P in the interval that $IntTerm$ refers to. We define when two such atom values are equal, when one atom value is smaller than another and when an atom value has a certain value from its domain. Finally, a conjunction C holds in an interval, if all N of its conjuncts, specified by the *iand(C,N)* predicate, hold.

```
valueOfProp (F,V, Id ):− relevant (F) ,value (F,V,T) ,id (Id ),intervalFrom (Id ,T).
valueOfProp (length ,Value , Id ):− id (Id ),  length (Id ,Value ).
length (Id ,L):− intervalFrom (Id ,From),  intervalTo (Id ,  To),  L = To − From.
valueOfAtom (at (IntTerm ,Prop ),Val , Id ):− refersTo (IntTerm ,Int ,Id ),
     valueOfProp (Prop ,Val ,Int ).
intHolds (equals (A1,A2) ,Id ):− valueOfAtom (A1,V,Id ),  valueOfAtom (A2,V,Id ).
intHolds (hasValue (Atom ,V) ,Id ):− valueOfAtom (Atom ,V,Id ).
intHolds (less (A1,A2) ,Id ):− valueOfAtom (A1,V1,Id ) ,valueOfAtom (A2,V2,Id ),
     V1 < V2.
intHolds (C, Id ):− iand (C,N) ,id (Id ),#count{I : isub (C,I ,S) ,intHolds (S,Id )}=N.
definedProp (Prop ,V, Id ):− id (Id ),  intRule (Prop ,V,Cond ),  intHolds (Cond ,Id ).
```

In Fig. 6, to specify the wage in a certain interval, we introduce some defined properties. The *normalwage* property is 20 euros if an employee is working, and 0 if they are not. They receive a *nightpremium* of 20% for any interval in the night or in the day if the interval precedes an interval in the night, provided that the night interval is larger. Finally the employee receives an *cumulPremium* of 25%. Note that compared to the interval logic of 2 we omit the interval term *this* in our tables to improve readability.

Defined properties	
Defined property	Default Value
1	normalwage	0
2	nightpremium	0
3	cumulpremium	0
4	totalWage	= normalwage × (1 + nigtpremium + cumulpremium)

Defined property rules		
Defined property	Rule	Value
1	normalwage	atWork=true	20
2	nightPremium	timeOfDay=day and [next]timeOfDay=night and length < [next]length	0.20
3	nightPremium	timeOfDay=Night	0.20
4	cumulPremium	cumul=true	0.25

Fig. 6. Case-specific representation of relevant fluents and output

Calculating the Total Wage. In general, our goal is to compute a single wage as a sum $\sum_{interval\ i} totalWage(i)$ with the *totalWage* property determining the hourly wage in each interval. We translate this to an ASP sum as follows:

```
totalWage(S):-S=#sum{T:definedProp(totalWage,W,I),length(I,L),T=W*L/60}.
```

In total, an HR consultant thus only needs 10 tables to specify the specific rules. A concrete scenario can be represented as the single user action table.

4 Multi-shot Implementation

In the previous section, we presented a model for use by a standard single-shot ASP solving. This model may produce large groundings, which form a bottleneck for realistic instances. Indeed, to handle a scenario of two days with an accuracy of one minute, for instance, we need 60×48 timepoints. Because the grounding size is quadratic in the number of timepoints, this is problematic. In this section, we show how we can use *multi-shot solving* to drastically reduce the grounding size, by restricting attention to only those timepoints at which the state of the world actually changes. We refer to these timepoints as **changepoints**. Our multi-shot model is purely an optimised version of the single-shot model: functionally, it is still the same, and it still allows the HR consultant to represent his knowledge in the same user-friendly way. It consists of 3 parts: a static part, a dynamic part, and an interval part.

Static Code. The static part of the code contains the non-temporal information, which consists of rules that contain no predicates with a timepoint argument. For example, in the last code listing of the Functional Event Calculus paragraph in Sect. 3, the first two lines, which state that *user actions* and *walltime actions* are two kinds of actions, are included in the static part, while the last two rules, which define *at which timepoints* such actions actually happen, does not. We collect the static code in a subprogram #*static()*, that takes no parameters.

Dynamic Code. The dynamic program defines the current state of the world in term of the previous state. It therefore takes two changepoints as parameters.

The program first asserts that the current changepoint cp is a new timepoint, which follows the previous changepoint pp. In addition to this, the dynamic program also contains all rules that include predicates that take a timepoint as argument. These rules typically define the value of some dynamic predicate at $T + 1$ in terms of the values of dynamic predicates at timepoint T. Such rules now undergo a minor syntactic change, where we replace all such terms $T + 1$ by the parameter cp of the program and the terms T by its parameter pp. In effect, this change is what allow to "skip ahead" to the next changepoint, instead of having to go through each timepoint individually. This necessitates a number of other small changes in the code, which we will not describe in detail.

Multi-shot Solving Algorithm. Algorithm 1 shows how the static and dynamic program can be used to implement the desired behavior, by means of clingo's multi-shot solving. This algorithm uses the following notations: For a program $P(x_1, \ldots x_n)$ with parameters x_i and constants $c_1, \ldots, c_n$, we denote by $AnswerSet(P(c_1, .., c_n))$ the unique answer set of $P(c_1, \ldots, c_n)$. For a predicate P, we denote by P^X the set of all tuples $\vec{c}$ such that $P(\vec{c}) \in X$. On line 1, the static program P_{static}, is solved. Its answer set provides the upper-bound max of the timeline and the list $upfrontPoints$ of all changepoints that are already known up-front, i.e., all the time points at which wall-time actions or user actions happen. We also include the greatest time point max in this list, to ensure termination of the $while$-loop (line 6). In each iteration, this loop instantiates the dynamic program $P_{dynamic}$ for the next changepoint. The if-test (line 8) distinguishes two cases: either the next changepoint comes from the list $upfrontPoints$, or else it corresponds to a $triggered$ action. The next timepoints at which such a triggered action occurs is not known up-front, but is computed in each iteration of this loop by the function $searchNext$. The $searchNext$ algorithm (Algorithm 2) considers both actions that are triggered by a fluent maintaining its value for a certain time, represented by the $after$-predicate (line 3), and those triggered by a count fluent reaching a certain value, represented by the $when$-predicate (line 8). The result of the algorithm is the smallest timepoint $next > current$ at which such an action happens (or ∞ if no such timepoint exists). Once the main $while$-loop of Algorithm 1 ends, the program $P_{dynamic}$ has been grounded for all changepoints. The predicate $boundary$ now identifies all the timepoints that delineate an interval. The for-loop in line 16 the introduces an identifier i for each such interval $[b_i, b_{i+1})$. Finally, these intervals are then passed to the program $\#intervals$, which gathers all the rules concerning intervals, unchanged from our single-shot implementation.

Algorithm 1. Solve algorithm

1: $X = AnswerSet(P_{static}())$
2: max = the unique t such that $(t) \in maxTime^X$
3: $current = 0$
4: $upfrontPoints$ = sorted list of all t where $t = max$ or $\exists a : (a, t) \in happens^X$
5: $i = 0$ ▷ i is the counter for action points list
6: **while** $current < max$ **do**
7:      $triggered$ = searchNext($current, X$)
8:      **if** $triggered < upfrontPoints[i]$ **then**
9:          $next = triggered$
10:     **else**
11:         $next = upfrontPoints[i]$
12:         $i += 1$
13:     $X = $ AnswerSet($P_{dynamic}(current, next) \cup X$)
14:     $current = next$
15: $(b_1, \ldots, b_n)$ = sorted list of all t such that $(t) \in boundary^X$
16: **for** i in $1, \ldots, n - 1$ **do**
17:     $X = X \cup \{intervalFrom(i, b_i), intervalTo(i, b_{i+1})\}$
18: $X = $ AnswerSet($P_{intervals}() \cup X$)

Algorithm 2. searchNext algorithm

1: **procedure** SEARCHNEXT($current, X$)
2:      $next = \infty$
3:      **for** (f, v, d, a) in $after^X$ **do**
4:          **if** $\exists t' = $ the unique t'' such that $(f, v, t'', current) \in sameSince^X$ **then**
5:              $possible = t' + d$
6:              **if** $current < possible < next$ **then**
7:                  $next = possible$
8:      **for** (cf, cv, a) in $when^X$ **do**
9:          $cond = $ the unique c such that $(cf, c) \in countRule^X$
10:         **if** $(cond, current) \in holds^X$ **then**
11:             $cv' = $ the unique cv'' such that $(cf, cv'', current) \in value^X$
12:             $possible = current + (cv - cv')$
13:             **if** $current < possible < next$ **then**
14:                 $next = possible$
15:     **return** $next$

---

5   Experimental Results and Discussion

As discussed before, the grounding size of the single-shot implementation is quadratic in the number of timepoints. Consequently, the number of timepoints has a large effect on the computational performance of this approach. Figure 7 shows how the duration of a single timepoint affects the computation time for a two-day scenario, the minimum for a realistic scenario. The company we collaborated with would like a single scenario to be handled in under a second of computation time. At the same time, a granularity in which a single time point is more than five minutes in length is unacceptable for them. The left-hand side of Fig. 7 therefore clearly shows that the single-shot implementation is feasible.

The multi-shot approach drastically reduces the impact of the total number of timepoints on the computation time. Indeed, the main parameter is now the number of *changepoints*, which means that the run-time is mainly determined by the scenario that needs to be handled, rather than by the granularity of the timepoints. The right-hand side of Fig. 7 shows how the computation time of our multi-shot implementation depends on the number of changepoints. In a realistic two-day scenario, the number of changepoints is typically around twenty, so here the performance is acceptable. Note also that even for sixty changepoints, the run-time remains well under that of the single-shot implementation for all but the coarsest granularities of times. We also implemented scenarios stretching over a week using our multi-shot implementation. Although there is a small increase in run-time compared to a two-day scenario with the same number of changepoints (probably due to the grounding size of the static part of the code), we can still conclude that the run-time indeed depends on the number of changepoints instead of the total number of timepoints. In both graphs, Fig. 7 shows the average computation time per scenario over 5 runs on an Intel i5-8265U CPU. A repository containing all used scenarios is available online[1].

In order to use the system in practice, the continuous timeline needs to be split up into a number of independent scenarios. Typically this can be done by a single rule, e.g. in our example the end of a scenario coincides with the end of the shift of an employee, happening when they are absent for more than 4 h.

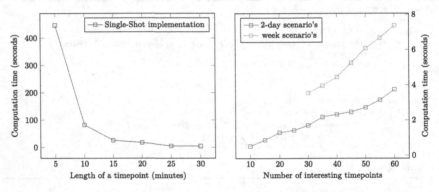

Fig. 7. Computation time of single-shot and multi-shot implementation

6 Conclusion

In this paper, we have presented an approach for payroll management. We identified three key challenges for a payroll management system. HR consultants should be able to configure as much of the system as possible and the language in which they write down the rules must not only be easy to use for them, but it should also be possible to easily extend it with new language features. Finally, despite the required flexibility, the solution should still be computationally efficient. To tackle these challenges, we have split up the model in a generic event-calculus-based ASP program, and a decision-table-based model of the specific rules that apply in one particular set of circumstances. When used with a standard single-shot ASP solver, the computational performance does not meet the computational requirements, due to the large number of timepoints that

---

[1] https://gitlab.com/EAVISE/bca/asp-for-flexible-payroll-management.

must be considered. We also present a multi-shot approach that eliminates this dependency on the absolute number of timepoints, by only considering those timepoints at which the state of the world actually changes. This multi-shot approach does reach the required performance.

References

1. Arias, J., Chen, Z., Carro, M., Gupta, G.: Modeling and reasoning in event calculus using goal-directed constraint answer set programming. In: International Symposium on Logic-Based Program Synthesis and Transformation (2019)
2. Brewka, G., Eiter, T., Truszczyński, M.: Answer set programming at a glance. Commun. ACM **54**(12), 92–103 (2011)
3. Doody, R.J., et al.: Report on the payroll system. In: More: Management Operations Review & Evaluation (1982)
4. Gebser, M., Kaminski, R., Kaufmann, B., Schaub, T.: Clingo= asp+ control: preliminary report. arXiv preprint arXiv:1405.3694 (2014)
5. Gebser, M., Kaminski, R., Kaufmann, B., Schaub, T.: Multi-shot asp solving with clingo. Theory Pract. Logic Prog. **19**(1), 27–82 (2019)
6. Gelfond, M., Lifschitz, V.: The stable model semantics for logic programming (1988)
7. Kim, T.W., Lee, J., Palla, R.: Circumscriptive event calculus as answer set programming. In: Twenty-First International Joint Conference on AI (2009)
8. Lee, J., Palla, R.: Reformulating the situation calculus and the event calculus in the general theory of stable models and in answer set programming (2012)
9. Ma, J., Miller, R., Morgenstern, L., Patkos, T.: An epistemic event calculus for asp-based reasoning about knowledge of the past, present and future. EPiC Ser. Comput. **26**, 75–87 (2014)
10. Miller, R., Shanahan, M.: Some alternative formulations of the event calculus. In: Kakas, A.C., Sadri, F. (eds.) Computational Logic: Logic Programming and Beyond. LNCS (LNAI), vol. 2408, pp. 452–490. Springer, Heidelberg (2002). https://doi.org/10.1007/3-540-45632-5_17
11. Object Management Group. Decision model and notation v1.3 (2021). http://www.omg.org/spec/DMN/
12. Shanahan, M.: The event calculus explained. Artif. Intell. Today (1999)
13. Wielemaker, J., Arias, J., Gupta, G.: s(casp) for swi-prolog. In: 2021 International Conference on Logic Programming Workshops (2021)

Analysis of Cyclic Fault Propagation via ASP

Marco Bozzano[1], Alessandro Cimatti[1], Alberto Griggio[1],
Martin Jonáš[1](✉), and Greg Kimberly[2]

[1] Fondazione Bruno Kessler, Trento, Italy
{bozzano,cimatti,griggio,mjonas}@fbk.eu
[2] The Boeing Company, Seattle, USA
greg.kimberly@boeing.com

Abstract. Analyzing the propagation of faults is part of the preliminary safety assessment for complex safety-critical systems. A recent work proposes an SMT-based approach to deal with propagation of faults in presence of circular dependencies. The set of all the fault configurations that cause the violation of a property, also referred to as the set of minimal cut sets, is computed by means of repeated calls to the SMT solver, hence enumerating all minimal models of an SMT formula. Circularity is dealt with by imposing a strict temporal order, using the theory of difference logic.

In this paper, we explore the use of Answer-Set Programming to tackle the same problem. We propose two encodings, leveraging the notion of stable model. The first approach deals with cycles in the encoding, while the second relies on ASP Modulo Acyclicity (ASPMA).

We experimentally evaluate the three approaches on a comprehensive set of benchmarks. The first ASP-based encoding significantly outperforms the SMT-based approach; the ASPMA-based encoding, on the other hand, does not yield the expected performance gains.

Keywords: Fault propagation · SMT · ASP modulo acyclicity · Minimal models

1 Introduction

Analyzing the propagation of faults is an important step of the preliminary safety assessment for complex safety-critical systems. When a physical component fails, its faults can propagate to the other components and compromise their behaviour. Fault propagation is often mitigated by adopting suitable architectures based on redundancy and voting. In order to analyze such architectures, the challenge is to compute the set of all minimal cut sets (MCS), i.e., minimal fault configurations that can compromise a given function under investigation. Since the behavior of the systems in question is usually monotone, i.e., adding more faults does not fix the compromised function, the *minimal* cut sets are

G. Gottlob et al. (Eds.): LPNMR 2022, LNAI 13416, pp. 470–483, 2022.
https://doi.org/10.1007/978-3-031-15707-3_36

sufficient to succinctly represent the set of *all* cut sets, which might be exponentially larger. From the set of all minimal cut sets it is thus possible to extract important artifacts such as fault trees and reliability measures (e.g., overall system failure probability). For this reason, the main focus of this paper is on the task of enumerating all minimal cut sets of the given system.

MCS enumeration is particularly challenging when dealing with cyclic dependencies. Consider, for example, the case of an electrically-controlled hydraulic system. Its fault may compromise power generation; on the other hand, the failure of power generation may compromise the hydraulic operation. This circularity makes it difficult to model fault propagation in form of simple logical implications because self-supporting, unjustified models arise. A recent work [4] shows how the inherent sequential nature of the problem can be reduced to an approach based on Satisfiability Modulo Theories (SMT). The set of minimal cut sets is computed by means of repeated calls to the SMT solver, hence enumerating all minimal models of an SMT formula. The key idea in dealing with circularity is to impose a strict temporal ordering on the propagation of events, using the theory of difference logic. The results presented in [3] and in [4] show that the SMT approach is able to deal with realistically-sized redundancy architectures.

In this paper, we explore an alternative approach to minimal cut set enumeration, based on the use of Answer-Set Programming (ASP). The intuition is to leverage the fact that in ASP clauses are interpreted as (directed) rules rather than implications, thus limiting the search based on the notion of stable model.

We propose two approaches. The first one is a direct encoding into ASP. It deals with cycles in the encoding by requiring that the failure of a component must be justified either by a local fault or by the justified failure of neighboring components (or their combination). Default negation is used to model the justifications of the propagation.

The second encoding relies on the idea of ASP Modulo Acyclicity (ASPMA) [2], where models can be required to be acyclic with directives to an extended solver. Acyclicity is then enforced at run-time by means of a dedicated, graph-based data-structure preventing circular dependencies. Although not all ASP solvers deal with a built-in "modulo acyclicity" feature, we expected that this could lead to additional performance boost.

We carried out an extensive experimental evaluation, on all Boolean (real-world and random scalable) fault propagation benchmarks from [4] and [3]. The benchmark suite includes both acyclic and cyclic problems. We contrasted the SMT approach with the ASP and ASPMA approaches proposed in this paper. On acyclic benchmarks, the ASP encodings demonstrate better scalability than the SMT-based cut set enumeration. On the cyclic benchmarks, the ASP encoding dominates over the SMT-based encoding. Quite surprisingly, the ASPMA encoding does not scale as well, and it is outperformed, especially on the hardest benchmarks, both by the ASP-based and SMT-based encodings.

The paper is structured as follows. Section 2 presents the logical preliminaries. Section 3 describes fault propagation graphs and the SMT-based encoding. Section 4 presents the ASP-based and ASPMA-based encodings. Section 5 discusses the issue of minimality. Section 6 presents the experimental evaluation. Section 7 draws conclusions and outlines directions for future works.

2   Preliminaries

2.1   Logic and Notation

We assume that the reader is familiar with standard first-order logic and the basic ideas of Satisfiability Modulo Theories (SMT), as presented, e.g., in [1]. We use the standard notions of interpretation, theory, assignment, model, and satisfiability.

Given a quantifier-free formula $\varphi(B, R)$ in real arithmetic defined over a set of Boolean variables B and of real variables R, a *model* of φ is an assignment μ that maps each $b \in B$ to a truth value $\mu(b) \in \mathbb{B}$ ($\top$ for true and $\bot$ for false) and each $x \in R$ to a real number $\mu(x) \in \mathbb{R}$, such that φ evaluates to true on μ. We denote this with $\mu \models \varphi$. If φ is a formula and μ is an assignment that maps each variable of φ to a value of the corresponding sort, $[\![\varphi]\!]_\mu$ denotes the result of the evaluation of φ under this assignment. If $B' \subseteq B$ is a subset of the Boolean variables of φ, μ is called its *minimal model with respect to* B' if μ is a model of φ and there is no model $\mu' \models \varphi$ such that $\{b \in B' \mid \mu'(b) = \top\} \subsetneq \{b \in B' \mid \mu(b) = \top\}$.

2.2   Answer Set Programming

This subsection briefly introduces the syntax and semantics of disjunctive Answer-Set Programs and ASP modulo acyclicity, based on [8] and [2], respectively.

Rules. A disjunctive rule r is an expression of the form

$$p_1 \vee \ldots \vee p_l \leftarrow p_{l+1}, \ldots, p_m, \sim p_{m+1}, \ldots, \sim p_n,$$

where $0 \leq l \leq m \leq n$ and $p_1, \ldots, p_n$ are propositional atoms. The *head* of r is defined as $hd(r) = \{p_1, \ldots p_l\}$ and the *body* of r is defined as $bd(r) = \{p_{l+1}, \ldots, p_m, \sim p_{m+1}, \ldots, \sim p_n\}$. For any set $L = \{p_{l+1}, \ldots, p_m, \sim p_{m+1}, \ldots, \sim p_n\}$, let $L^+ = \{p_{l+1}, \ldots, p_m\}$ and $L^- = \{p_{m+1}, \ldots, p_n\}$. A rule r is said to be *applicable* with respect to a set of propositional atoms X if the set X contains all the positive atoms from $bd(r)$ and no negative atoms from $bd(r)$, i.e., $bd(r)^+ \subseteq X$ and $bd(r)^- \cap X = \emptyset$. The rule r is said to be *satisfied* with respect to X if its body implies its head, i.e., the rule is not applicable or $hd(r) \cap X \neq \emptyset$. The rules with $bd(r) = \emptyset$ are called *facts* and are written as $p_1 \vee \ldots \vee p_l$. The rules with $hd(r) = \emptyset$ are called *integrity constraints*, are written as $\leftarrow p_{l+1}, \ldots, p_m, \sim p_{m+1}, \ldots, \sim p_n$, and are satisfied only if they are not applicable, i.e., if at least one of the atoms in the body is not satisfied.

Answer Set Programs. A disjunctive answer set program P is a set of rules. A set of atoms that occur in the program P is denoted as $\text{At}(P)$. A set of atoms X is called a *model* of P if all rules $r \in P$ are satisfied with respect to X. The *reduct of P with respect to the set of atoms X* is defined as $P^X = \{hd(r) \leftarrow bd(r)^+ \mid r \in P, bd(r)^- \cap X = \emptyset\}$. A model X of P is called an *answer set of P* or a *stable model of P* if X is a minimal model of P^X, i.e., there is no $Y \subsetneq X$ such that Y is a model of P^X.

ASP modulo acyclicity. An *acyclicity extension* of a program P is a pair (V, e) where V is a set of nodes and $e\colon \text{At}(P) \to V \times V$ is a partial function that assigns edges between vertices of V to atoms of P. A program together with its acyclicity extension is called an *acyclicity program.*

A set of atoms X is called a *stable model of the acyclicity program P subject to the acyclicity extension (V, e)* if X is a stable model of P and the graph $(V, \{e(p) \mid p \in X\})$ induced by the set of atoms X is acyclic.

3 Fault Propagation Graphs

In this section we briefly introduce the formalism of *(symbolic) fault propagation graphs* (FPGs). Intuitively, FPGs describe how failures of some components of a given system can cause the failure of other components of the system. In an explicit graph representation, nodes correspond to components, and edges model their dependencies, with the meaning that an edge from c_1 to c_2 states that the failure of c_1 can cause the failure (propagation) of c_2. Here, we adopt a symbolic representation, in which components are modeled as Boolean variables (where $\bot$ means "not failed" and $\top$ means "failed"), and the failure dependencies are encoded as formulae $\mathsf{canFail}(c)$, which describe the conditions that may cause a failure of c. The basic concepts are formalized in the following definitions, which are simplified definitions from [3] and [4]. The original paper [4] also defines FPGs with multiple failure modes with arbitrary orderings. We do not treat these features here to simplify the presentation, but we note that the approach of this paper can be extended to accommodate them in the same way as in [4].

Definition 1 (Fault propagation graph [3]). *A (symbolic) fault propagation graph (*FPG*) is a pair $(C, \mathsf{canFail})$, where C is a finite set of* system components *and $\mathsf{canFail}$ is a function that assigns to each component c a Boolean formula $\mathsf{canFail}(c)$ over the set of variables C.*

We assume that all the $\mathsf{canFail}(c)$ formulas are *positive*, i.e., they can contain only conjunctions, disjunctions, and variables. Moreover, without loss of generality, we assume that all the $\mathsf{canFail}(c)$ formulas are in disjunctive normal form, i.e., they are of the form $\bigvee_{D \in F} \bigwedge_{d \in D} d$ for some set F of *cubes* of dependencies.

Definition 2 (Trace of FPG [3]). *Let G be an* FPG *$(C, \mathsf{canFail})$. A* state of *G is a function from C to $\mathbb{B}$. A* trace of *G is a (potentially infinite) sequence of states $\pi = \pi_0 \pi_1 \ldots$ such that all $i > 0$ and $c \in C$ satisfy (i) $\pi_i(c) = \pi_{i-1}(c)$ or (ii) $\pi_{i-1}(c) = \bot$ and $\pi_i(c) = [\![\mathsf{canFail}(c)]\!]_{\pi_{i-1}}$.*

Example 1 ([3]). Consider a system with components *control on ground* (G), *hydraulic control* (H), and *electric control* (E) such that G can fail if both H and E have failed, H can fail if E has failed, and E can fail if H has failed. This system can be modeled by a fault propagation graph ({G, H, E}, canFail), where canFail(G) = H ∧ E, canFail(H) = E, and canFail(E) = H.

One of the traces of this system is {G ↦ ⊥, H ↦ T, E ↦ ⊥}{G ↦ ⊥, H ↦ T, E ↦ T}{G ↦ T, H ↦ T, E ↦ T}, where H is failed initially, which causes failure of E in the second step, and the failures of H and E together cause a failure of G in the third step.

Definition 3 (Cut set [3]). *Let G be an* FPG *G = (C, canFail) and φ a positive Boolean formula, called* top level event. *The assignment cs: C → B is called a* cut set *of G for φ if there is a trace π of G that starts in the state cs and there is some k ≥ 0 such that $\pi_k \models \varphi$. A cut set cs is called* minimal *if there is no other cut set cs′ such that {c ∈ C | cs′(c) = T} ⊊ {c ∈ C | cs(c) = T}.*

Without loss of generality, we assume in the rest of the paper that the top level event φ consists only of one variable, i.e., φ = c for some c ∈ C. For brevity, when talking about cut sets, we often mention only the components that are set to T by the cut set.

Example 2 ([3]). The minimal cut sets of the FPG from Example 1 for the top level event φ = G are {G}, {H}, and {E}. These three cut sets are witnessed by the following traces:

1. {G ↦ T, H ↦ ⊥, E ↦ ⊥},
2. {G ↦ ⊥, H ↦ T, E ↦ ⊥}{G ↦ ⊥, H ↦ T, E ↦ T}{G ↦ T, H ↦ T, E ↦ T},
3. {G ↦ ⊥, H ↦ ⊥, E ↦ T}{G ↦ ⊥, H ↦ T, E ↦ T}{G ↦ T, H ↦ T, E ↦ T}.

Note that the FPG has also other cut sets, such as {G, E}, {H, E}, and {G, H, E}, which are not minimal.

3.1 SMT-Based Encoding of Fault Propagation

In our previous work [4], we have shown that MCS enumeration of cyclic FPGs can be reduced to enumeration of projected minimal models of a certain SMT formula over the difference logic fragment of linear real arithmetic. The arithmetic is used to enforce causality ordering between the propagated failures, which would otherwise cause spurious self-supported propagations.

In particular, for each FPG *G = (C, canFail)*, the paper defines a formula that contains two Boolean variables I_c and F_c and one real variable o_c for each component c. The variables have the following intuitive meaning: I_c denotes that the component c is failed in the initial state, F_c denotes that the component c is failed at some point during the propagation, and o_c is a so called *time stamp* variable, which intuitively denotes the time when the component c failed.

These variables are then used to construct a formula φ_{prop}, which describes fault propagations. The formula contains the following constraints for each c ∈ C with canFail(c) = $\bigvee_{D \in F} \bigwedge_{d \in D} d$:

- $I_c \rightarrow F_c$, i.e., if the component is failed initially, it is failed at some point during the propagation,
- $F_c \rightarrow (I_c \vee \bigvee_{D \in F} \bigwedge_{d \in D}(F_d \wedge o_d < o_c))$, i.e., if component c fails at some point during the propagation, it is failed either initially or as a result of a propagation from its failed dependencies *that failed before c*.

Insisting that a failure of a variable can be caused only by failures that occurred before it is a crucial point to preserve causality and prohibit self-supporting cyclic propagations where a component causes its own failure.

4 Encoding in Disjunctive ASP

In this section we present our novel encodings of fault propagation in ASP. In the rest of the section, let $G = (C, \mathsf{canFail})$ be a fixed FPG and $c_{tle} \in C$ a top level event.

4.1 Encoding Propagations

The encoding uses the following variables for each component $c \in C$ with $\mathsf{canFail}(c) = \bigvee_{D \in F} \bigwedge_{d \in D} d$ and $F = \{D_1, \ldots, D_n\}$:

- $\mathtt{fail}(c)$, which will denote that $\pi_i(c) = \top$ for some $i \geq 0$,
- $\mathtt{fail\_local}(c)$, which will denote that $\pi_0(c) = \top$, i.e., the component c is initially failed,
- $\mathtt{fail\_ext}(c)$, which will denote that $\pi_0(c) \neq \top$ and $\pi_i(c) = \top$ for some $i > 0$, i.e., the component c is failed as a result of fault propagation.
- $\mathtt{fail\_dep}(c,j)$ for each $1 \leq j \leq n$, which will denote that $\pi_i \models \bigwedge_{d \in D_j} d$ for some $i \geq 0$, i.e., the conditions of a propagated failure of c are satisfied thanks to the j-th disjunct of $\mathsf{canFail}(c)$.

Using these variables, we construct an answer set program that contains the fact

$$\mathtt{fail}(c_{tle}) \tag{1}$$

and the following rules for each component $c \in C$:

$$\mathtt{fail\_local}(c) \vee \mathtt{fail\_ext}(c) \leftarrow \mathtt{fail}(c), \tag{2}$$

$$\mathtt{fail\_dep}(c,1) \vee \ldots \vee \mathtt{fail\_dep}(c,n) \leftarrow \mathtt{fail\_ext}(c), \tag{3}$$

$$\mathtt{fail}(d) \leftarrow \mathtt{fail\_dep}(c,j) \text{ for each } 1 \leq j \leq n, d \in D_j. \tag{4}$$

The rules have the following meaning: (1) states that the TLE must be satisfied; (2) that if a component is failed, it has to be failed either initially or as a result of a propagation; (3) that if a component is failed as a result of a propagation, one of the disjuncts in $\mathsf{canFail}(c)$ must be satisfied; and (4) that if the j-th disjunct of $\mathsf{canFail}(c)$ is satisfied, all the components that it depends on must be failed.

However, similarly to a naive SMT encoding, this encoding allows spurious propagations in presence of cycles. Given the FPG from Example 1, the encoding has a stable model $\{\texttt{fail}(c), \texttt{fail\_ext}(c), \texttt{fail\_dep}(c, 1) \mid c \in \{\text{G}, \text{H}, \text{E}\}\}$, where none of the components is failed initially, yet all are failed in the end. This model does not correspond to any real fault propagation and relies on the impossible propagation where H fails because of E, which in turn fails because of H. We now show two possible extensions of the encoding that solve this problem.

4.2   Enforcing Causality by ASP

To solve the problem with self-supporting circular propagations, we introduce new variables that will encode that a failure is *justified*, i.e., it is supported by sufficient initial faults. Intuitively, a failure of component c is justified if it is due to an initial fault of component c. Moreover, a failure of component c is justified if it is due to a propagation from a dependency D_j (the j-th disjunct of $\mathsf{canFail}(c)$) such that all $d \in D_j$ are in turn failed and justified.

Therefore, we introduce the following additional variables for each component $c \in C$ with $\mathsf{canFail}(c) = \bigvee_{D \in F} \bigwedge_{d \in D} d$ and $F = \{D_1, \ldots, D_n\}$:

- $\texttt{justified}(c)$, which will denote that the failure of c is justified,
- $\texttt{justified\_dep}(c, j)$ for each $1 \leq j \leq n$, which will denote that the failure of c is justified by the j-th disjunct of $\mathsf{canFail}(c)$.

We then define the program P_{asp} as a union of the rules from the previous subsection and the additional *causality rules*:

$$\leftarrow \texttt{fail}(c), \sim\texttt{justified}(c) \tag{5}$$

$$\texttt{justified}(c) \leftarrow \texttt{fail\_local}(c) \tag{6}$$

$$\texttt{justified}(c) \leftarrow \texttt{justified\_dep}(c, j), \texttt{fail\_dep}(c, j) \text{ for all } 1 \leq j \leq n \tag{7}$$

$$\leftarrow \texttt{fail\_dep}(c, j), \sim\texttt{justified\_dep}(c, j) \text{ for all } 1 \leq j \leq n \tag{8}$$

$$\texttt{justified\_dep}(c, j) \leftarrow \texttt{justified}(d_1), \ldots, \texttt{justified}(d_m) \text{ where } d_i \in D_j \tag{9}$$

The rules have the following intuitive meaning: (5) states that it is not possible that the component c is failed without a justification for the failure; (6) that the local failure is enough to justify the failure of the component; (7) that if the j-th disjunct is justified and satisfied, the failure of c is justified; (8) that it is not possible that the j-th disjunct of the component c is satisfied without a justification; and (9) that if all dependencies of the j-th disjunct are justified, the j-th disjunct itself is justified.

Observe how we use integrity constraints and default negation to impose that failed components/dependencies must be justified. This prohibits the spurious cyclic propagations and gives the following correctness result:

Theorem 1. *Let $X \subseteq \mathrm{At}(P_{asp})$ be a set of atoms. If X is a stable model of P_{asp} then $\{c \in C \mid \mathit{fail\_local}(c) \in X\}$ is a cut set of G for c_{tle}. Conversely, if $\{c \in C \mid \mathit{fail\_local}(c) \in X\}$ is a minimal cut set of G then X is a stable model of P_{asp}.*

Note that due to the stable model semantics, the program P_{asp} does not represent all cut sets of G, because some non-minimal cut sets are prohibited. Nevertheless, it represents all *minimal* cut sets, in which we are mainly interested.

4.3   Enforcing Causality by ASP Modulo Acyclicity

In this subsection, we present a second encoding of fault propagation. In contrast to the encoding from the previous subsection, which uses justification rules to break self-supporting cyclic propagations, this encoding relies on ASP modulo acyclicity. This makes the encoding simpler, easier to implement, and might offer better performance due to dedicated implementation of acyclicity propagation in ASP solvers. On the other hand, it restricts the set of usable ASP solvers as not all ASP solvers support acyclicity constraints.

The encoding uses the variables $\mathtt{fail}(c)$, $\mathtt{fail\_local}(c)$, $\mathtt{fail\_ext}(c)$, and $\mathtt{fail\_dep}(c, j)$ with the same intuitive meaning as in the previous encoding. Moreover, for every pair of components $c, d \in C$ it uses a variable $\mathtt{caused\_by}(c, d)$ with the intuitive meaning that the failure of c was directly caused by the failure (initial or propagated) of d.

Using these variables, we construct the program P_{aspma} that contains rule (1), for each component $c \in C$ contains the rules (2),(3),(4), and for each $c \in C$, $1 \leq j \leq n$ and $d \in D_j$ also the rule $\mathtt{caused\_by}(c, d) \leftarrow \mathtt{fail\_dep}(c, j)$. The rules state that if the j-th disjunct of $\mathsf{canFail}(c)$ is satisfied, the failure of c is caused by failures of all the components in the disjunct. We then define the acyclicity extension (C, e), where $c(\mathtt{caused\_by}(c, d)) = (c, d)$ and e is undefined for the remaining variables. This ensures that there are no causal cycles among the propagated failures and therefore no component can cause its own failure. As a result, an analogue of Theorem 1 holds also for P_{aspma}.

5   Minimality of the Cut Sets

As was shown in the previous section, both the introduced ASP encodings contain stable models for all MCSs of the given FPG. Although the stable-model semantics is able to rule out some non-minimal cut sets thanks to the condition that the model X must be a *minimal* model of P^X, the programs still admit some stable models that correspond to *non-minimal* cut sets. This can be seen in the following example. Note that the FPG in question is acyclic, and therefore there is no need of encoding the causality constraints.

Example 3. Consider an FPG $(C, \mathsf{canFail})$ with $C = \{c_1, c_2, c_3\}$ and $\mathsf{canFail}(c_1) = c_2 \wedge c_3$, $\mathsf{canFail}(c_2) = c_3$, $\mathsf{canFail}(c_3) = \bot$ with the top level event c_1. The ASP encodings from the previous section produce the following program P:

```
fail(c₁).
fail_local(c₁) ∨ fail_ext(c₁) ← fail(c₁).
fail_local(c₂) ∨ fail_ext(c₂) ← fail(c₂).
fail_local(c₃) ∨ fail_ext(c₃) ← fail(c₃).
fail_dep(c₁, 1) ← fail_ext(c₁).
fail_dep(c₂, 1) ← fail_ext(c₂).
← fail_ext(c₃).
fail(c₂) ← fail_dep(c₁, 1).
fail(c₃) ← fail_dep(c₁, 1).
fail(c₃) ← fail_dep(c₂, 1).
```

This program has a stable model $M = \{$fail(c_1), fail(c_2), fail(c_3), fail_ext(c_1), fail_local(c_2), fail_local(c_3), fail_dep$(c_1, 1)\}$, which corresponds to a non-minimal cut set $\{c_2, c_3\}$. The reason for this is that in order to obtain a model for the minimal cut set $\{c_3\}$, the model M would have to be extended with fail_ext(c_2) and fail_dep$(c_2, 1)$ before removing fail_local(c_2). □

Non-minimal cut sets arise because the minimality of the cut set is defined with respect to the local faults, while the minimality of the model is defined with respect to all atoms, which also include the atoms used for propagation. Fortunately, ASP solvers offer *optimization* facilities for enumerating stable models that are minimal according to a given criterion. In particular, it is possible to enumerate minimal stable models with respect to a given subset of atoms, either by using subset preference [5] or modified branching heuristics [9]. Our preliminary experiments shown that the latter option provides vastly superior performance. Moreover, as each minimal cut set is identified only by values of atoms $FailLocal = \{$fail_local$(c) \mid c \in C\}$, it is sufficient to enumerate the minimal models w.r.t $FailLocal$, projected to the set of atoms $FailLocal$.[1]

Note that the enumeration of *minimal* models is more expensive. It prevents the solver to perform enumeration based only on backtracking: it either forces the solver to minimize each model and possibly enumerate a single minimal model multiple times, or it forces the solver to remember *all* already enumerated models, which can increase the space complexity of the search. However, the technique based on branching heuristics is also successfully used for MCS enumeration in the original SMT-based approach.

6   Experimental Evaluation

6.1   Implementation and Setup

We implemented the encodings proposed in Sect. 4 in a simple Python script. In the following experiments, these two encodings are denoted as asp and aspma. To enumerate their minimal stable models, we have used the state-of-the-art ASP solver Clingo [7] in version 5.5.1, which supports both ASP modulo acyclicity and also Boolean model minimization by modified branching heuristics.

For comparison, we used the SMT-based MCS enumerator SMT-PGFDS [4], which is implemented as a Python tool that produces the SMT encoding of the FPG and uses the SMT solver MathSAT 5 [6] to enumerate its minimal models. In the experiments below, the approach is denoted as smt.

We used several families of FPG benchmarks, which are described in §6.2. We ran all the experiments on a cluster of 13 nodes with Intel Xeon CPU E5520 @ 2.27GHz CPUs. We used a 30 min timeout and 8 GiB of RAM. All the measured times are wall-times. Additional data for the experiments are available from https://es-static.fbk.eu/people/griggio/papers/lpnmr2022.html.

---

[1] This can be achieved, e.g., by adding a directive #show fail_local/1. and calling clingo --project --heuristic=Domain --dom-mod=5,16 --enum-mod=domRec 0.

6.2 Benchmarks

We compared the three encodings (asp, aspma, smt) on various FPG benchmarks from the literature. We do not restrict the evaluation only to cyclic FPGs, where the three encodings differ, but also use benchmarks without cycles, which do not require the causality constraints and can thus be encoded in a purely Boolean way. This allows us to compare the performance of the underlying solvers (i.e., Clingo, MathSAT 5) for purely Boolean search.

Acyclic. We used *acyclic* benchmarks that result from encoding acyclic redundancy architectures extended by triple modular redundancy (TMR) with voters [3]. In particular, these benchmarks consist of families linear, rectangular, and redarch-random-acycl. The linear benchmark family consists of linear-shaped architectures of sizes between 1 and 200, extended by one to three voters; each architecture of size n corresponds to a FPG with $3n + (\#voters \cdot n)$ components. Similarly, rectangular benchmarks come from encoding of rectangular-shaped redundancy architectures of sizes between 1 and 200 and one to three voters and yield FPGs with $6n + 2 \cdot (\#voters \cdot n)$ components. Family redarch-random-acycl consists of FPG encodings of randomly generated acyclic TMR architectures.

Cyclic. As *cyclic* benchmarks, we first used the benchmark family cav21, which is an extension of a benchmark set used to evaluate the performance of the SMT-based FPG analysis. It is generated exactly the same way as in the original paper [4] and consists of randomly generated FPGs of size between 500 and 1500, which have similar distribution of degrees as our proprietary industrial systems.

Second, we also use cyclic benchmarks that result from encoding cyclic redundancy architectures [3]. In particular, these benchmarks consist of three families: ladder, radiator, and redarch-random-cycl. Ladder-shaped benchmarks come from architectures of size between 1 and 200 and radiator-shaped benchmarks come from architectures of size between 1 and 50. Both these architecture shapes of size n yield an FPG with $6n + 2 \cdot (\#voters \cdot n)$ components. However, the redundancy architectures differ in the shape of the dependency graph; whereas ladder benchmarks contain a linear number of cycles, radiator benchmarks contain an exponential number of cycles. Finally, redarch-random-cycl family consists of FPG encodings of randomly generated cyclic TMR architectures.

6.3 Results

This subsection presents MCS enumeration times for the compared encodings on the benchmarks. Note that all plots show times on a logarithmic scale.

Acyclic. The MCS enumeration times for the smt and asp encodings for linear and rectangular benchmarks are shown in Fig. 1a. The plot does not show the runtimes of aspma encoding, because for benchmarks without cycles, it is

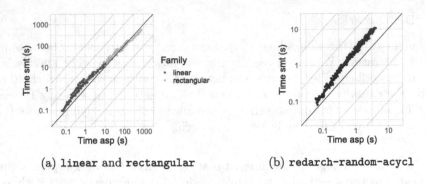

(a) linear and rectangular   (b) redarch-random-acycl

Fig. 1. Scatter plots of solving time on acyclic benchmarks.

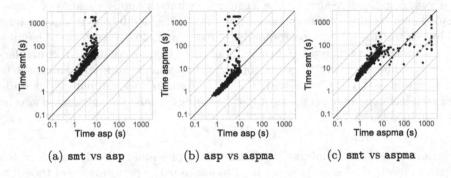

(a) smt vs asp   (b) asp vs aspma   (c) smt vs aspma

Fig. 2. Scatter plots of solving time on cav21 cyclic benchmarks.

identical to asp. For the simple benchmarks, ASP-based enumeration performs slightly better, but the difference vanishes with the increasing hardness of the benchmarks, i.e., going to rectangular structure or adding voters.

The comparison of MCS enumeration times of smt and asp encodings for redarch-random-acycl benchmarks is shown in Fig. 1b. For FPGs coming from random redundancy architectures, asp provides 2 to 3-times better performance.

Cyclic. The comparison of MCS enumeration times of all three encodings for cav21 benchmarks is shown in Fig. 2. The ASP-based breaking of self-supporting propagation cycles is beneficial in comparison to the previously proposed SMT-based encoding; for some benchmarks, the ASP-based techniques provide 10-times and even better performance. The performance of aspma is significantly worse than the purely ASP-based one on a non-trivial number of the benchmarks.

Figures 3 and 4 show the performance of the three approaches on the ladder and radiator benchmarks. On the ladder-shaped benchmarks, the ASP-based approach provides substantial speedup with respect to the SMT-based approach. Interestingly, the ASPMA approach performs worse than the purely ASP-based approach and even comparable to the SMT-based one for the more complicated systems with more voters.

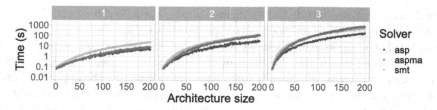

Fig. 3. Solving time on ladder-shaped cyclic benchmarks. Divided according to the number of voters per one reference module.

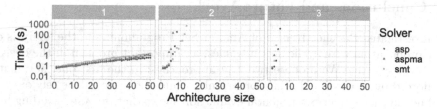

Fig. 4. Solving time on radiator-shaped cyclic benchmarks. Divided according to the number of voters per one reference module.

The situation is more interesting on radiator benchmarks, which are substantially harder as they contain a larger number of cycles. While the SMT-based approach provides a better performance for architectures with two voters, the ASP-based approach provides a better performance for even harder architectures with three voters. Nevertheless, the benchmarks with two and three voters are difficult for all of the approaches and pose a good target for future research.

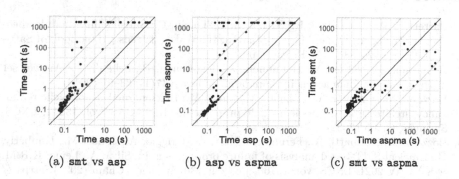

(a) smt vs asp   (b) asp vs aspma   (c) smt vs aspma

Fig. 5. Scatter plots of solving time on redarch-random-cycl cyclic benchmarks.

Finally, Fig. 5 compares the three approaches on the family of benchmarks redarch-random-cycl. The purely ASP-based encoding provides significantly better performance both than smt and aspma. The difference can be even in several orders of magnitude. Nevertheless, there are a few benchmarks where the SMT-based encoding provides better performance.

In total, the approach based on ASP, which we introduced in this paper, provides better performance for most of the benchmarks used; the difference is sometimes even in several orders of magnitude. Interestingly, the approach based on ASPMA, which uses a dedicated acyclicity solver, does not bring a significant benefit in comparison to the previously introduced solver based on SMT and is mostly inferior to our purely ASP-based encoding.

7   Conclusions and Future Work

We investigated the effectiveness of Answer Set Programming in the analysis of fault propagation with cyclic dependencies, an important problem in the design of critical systems. We propose two ASP approaches: in the first one, acyclicity is enforced by means of encoding constraints, while in the second we rely on ASP modulo acyclicity. The experimental evaluation shows that the ASP encoding has significant advantages over the state-of-the-art SMT encoding. We also see that, quite surprisingly, ASP modulo acyclicity does not yield the expected results.

In the future we will investigate in detail why the ASP-based encoding is superior to the SMT-based one and whether the observation can be leveraged to improve performance of SMT solvers. We will also investigate precise computational complexity of decision problems related to fault propagation analysis. Finally, we will explore extensions of the ASP approach to deal with fault propagation under timing constrains, partial observability, and with dynamic fault degradation structures with recovery.

References

1. Barrett, C.W., Sebastiani, R., Seshia, S.A., Tinelli, C.: Satisfiability modulo theories. In: Biere, A., Heule, M., van Maaren, H., Walsh, T. (eds.) Handbook of Satisfiability, pp. 825–885. IOS Press (2009)
2. Bomanson, J., Gebser, M., Janhunen, T., Kaufmann, B., Schaub, T.: Answer set programming modulo acyclicity. Fundam. Inform. **147**(1), 63–91 (2016)
3. Bozzano, M., Cimatti, A., Griggio, A., Jonáš, M.: Efficient analysis of cyclic redundancy architectures via boolean fault propagation. In TACAS, vol. 13244, LNCS, Springer, Cham (2022)
4. Bozzano, M., Cimatti, A., Fernandes Pires, A., Griggio, A., Jonáš, M., Kimberly, G.: Efficient SMT-based analysis of failure propagation. In: Silva, A., Leino, K.R.M. (eds.) CAV 2021. LNCS, vol. 12760, pp. 209–230. Springer, Cham (2021). https://doi.org/10.1007/978-3-030-81688-9_10
5. Brewka, G., Delgrande, J.,Romero, J., Schaub, T.: asprin: Customizing answer set preferences without a headache. In: AAAI, pp. 1467–1474, AAAI, Press (2015)
6. Cimatti, A., Griggio, A., Schaafsma, B.J., Sebastiani, R.: The MathSAT5 SMT solver. In: Piterman, N., Smolka, S.A. (eds.) TACAS 2013. LNCS, vol. 7795, pp. 93–107. Springer, Heidelberg (2013). https://doi.org/10.1007/978-3-642-36742-7_7
7. Gebser, M., Kaminski, R., Kaufmann, B., Schaub, T.: Multi-shot ASP solving with clingo. CoRR, abs/1705.09811 (2017)

8. Gebser, M., Kaufmann, B., Schaub, T.: Advanced conflict-driven disjunctive answer set solving. In: IJCAI (2013)
9. Di Rosa, E., Giunchiglia, E., Maratea, M.: Solving satisfiability problems with preferences. Constraints An Int. J. **15**(4), 485–515 (2010)

Learning to Rank the Distinctiveness of Behaviour in Serial Offending

Mark Law[1][(✉)], Theophile Sautory[2], Ludovico Mitchener[3], Kari Davies[4], Matthew Tonkin[5], Jessica Woodhams[6], and Dalal Alrajeh[3]

[1] ILASP Limited, Grantham, UK
mark@ilasp.com
[2] University of California Berkeley, Berkeley, USA
[3] Imperial College London, London, UK
[4] University of Bournemouth, Bournemouth, UK
[5] University of Leicester, Leicester, UK
[6] University of Birmingham, Birmingham, UK

Abstract. Comparative Case Analysis is an analytical process used to detect serial offending. It focuses on identifying distinctive behaviour that an offender displays consistently when committing their crimes. In practice, crime analysts consider the context in which each behaviour occurs to determine its distinctiveness, which subsequently impacts on their determination of whether crimes are committed by the same person or not. Existing algorithms do not currently consider context in this way when generating linkage predictions.

This paper presents the first learning-based approach aimed at identifying contexts within which behaviour may be considered more distinctive. We show how this problem can be modelled as that of learning preferences (in answer set programming) from examples of ordered pairs of contexts in which a behaviour was observed. In this setting, a context is preferred to another context if the behaviour is rarer in the first context. We make novel use of odds ratios to determine which examples are used for learning. Our approach has been applied to a real dataset of serious sexual offences provided by the UK National Crime Agency. The approach provides (i) a systematic methodology for selecting examples from which to learn preferences; (ii) novel insights for practitioners into the contexts under which an exhibited behaviour is more rare.

Keywords: Crime Linkage · Answer Set Programming · Inductive Logic Programming

1 Introduction

Comparative case analysis (CCA) is an analytical process that involves searching for offences that share distinctive behavioural similarities [28]. It is used

This work was undertaken while Theophile Sautory was at Imperial College London and Kari Davies was at the University of Birmingham.

to detect serial offending of many kinds (e.g. serial sex offending, serial burglary, serial robbery) and it can also be used to attribute crimes to an identified offender. The latter tends to occur where an offender has been identified for one or more crimes and further unsolved crimes are attributed to them through this analytical process [8,12]. Importantly, CCA focuses on the behaviour that an offender displays when committing their crimes to make predictions that the same individual is responsible for two or more crimes.

In practice, to identify crimes linked to a particular offence, crime analysts consider which of the behaviour an offender exhibits at the crime scene is distinctive (and hence particularly characteristic behaviour of that offender) and use this information to search their databases for crimes sharing similar behaviours [5]. The underlying principle is the behaviour of one offender must be distinguishable from other offenders' in order for crimes to be attributed accurately to an offender [2]. The distinctiveness of a behaviour depends on the context [5,8,27]. For example, wearing gloves in summer is a more distinctive feature (owing to the offender's forensic awareness) than exhibiting the same behaviour in the winter, where it is more common due to the cold weather. Hence, it is important to understand when and why a behaviour is distinctive for effective CCA.

Little research has considered the relative distinctiveness of behaviours seen in sexual offences. Some studies have calculated the base rates (frequencies) for individual crime scene behaviours and reported these in papers of descriptive analyses of sexual offender behaviour (e.g. [24,26]). However, none to date have considered the relative rarity of a behaviour, given the context in which it is expressed. Understanding the context under which a behaviour observed is more rare than another can provide a means for including or excluding offences as a potentially linked series based on the distinctiveness of observed behaviour.

This work focuses on an important task for supporting CCA in practice: comparative rarity analysis. Given two offence descriptions we aim to learn to predict whether a given behaviour is rarer in one than in the other. This corresponds to learning a ranking over the set of offence descriptions, where one offence description is ranked lower than another if the behaviour is rarer in the first. To learn this ranking, we use Inductive Logic Programming (ILP) [19].

The Learning from Answer Sets family of systems [14–16] are aimed at learning Answer Set Programs (ASP) [4]. ASP can model orderings using *weak constraints*, which induce an ordering over the answer sets of a program. Although weak constraints are usually used to capture preference orderings, they can also capture the rarity orderings learn in this paper. To learn weak constraints, we need pairwise examples of which answer sets should be ranked lower than others. In our case, we need to generate examples of pairs of offence descriptions such that a given behaviour is rarer in the first than in the second. In practice, the datasets of past offences are likely to be partial (e.g., due to lack of witness recall) or noisy (e.g., as a result of inconsistency in some offender's behavior). This means it is necessary to consider whether the evidence we have for each example pair is statistically significant and hence can be used to infer some general patterns about the contexts in which a behaviour is deemed rarer.

This paper introduces a novel approach to decide this, based on odds ratios and Fisher's Exact test. This approach also allows us to generate weights for the examples, which can be given to the ILP system as a measure of the confidence in each example. Of the two main Learning from Answer Set systems, ILASP [15] is capable of learning weak constraints, whereas FastLAS [14] is not. On the other hand, FastLAS is much more scalable than ILASP w.r.t. the size of the search space. Therefore, due to the size of the domain in this paper, we extended FastLAS to enable it to learn weak constraints.

Our approach is applied to a unique dataset provided for the purpose of this research by the UK National Crime Agency describing serious sexual offences committed by strangers in the UK. Through our evaluation, we demonstrate that our approach is able to learn to accurately predict the ranking. One of the hyper-parameters is the p-value threshold used to determine whether an example is statistically significant. For lower thresholds, fewer examples are given to the learner, but as these examples are less likely to be noisy, our evaluation shows that the learner achieves a higher precision. Thus, our approach provides a systematic way of handling noise in such probability ranking tasks. The main contributions of the paper are: (i) an interdisciplinary approach that combines ILP, statistical analysis and forensic psychology; (ii) a novel application to a real dataset; (iii) a general technique for noise-tolerant probability ranking.

2   Comparative Case Analysis

Over the last two decades, a growing body of research has developed and tested algorithmic approaches to CCA, with a range of methodological approaches. One key difference in methodological approaches is whether researchers are using algorithms to distinguish between linked and unlinked pairs (e.g. see [3], for a review of such studies) or whether they are using them to assign a given crime to a particular series, e.g. [23]. These correspond to different CCA scenarios. The first methodological approach attempts to develop algorithms that help to determine whether two offences were committed by the same person (linked pairs) or not (unlinked pairs). The second methodological approach attempts to develop algorithms that can help to predict to which series/offender a single crime is most likely to belong.

In both methodological scenarios, a range of algorithmic techniques have been tested, including, but not limited to, discriminant function analysis, logistic regression, Bayesian-based algorithms and classification trees. In the literature analysing criminal behaviour, context (a.k.a. a situation) is defined as a collection of situational factors that trigger behaviour through the activation of mental representation-behaviour pathways (see [28]'s interpretation of Mischel and Shoda's Cognitive Affective Personality System [18]). A situational factor can be external to the offender (e.g. a witness arriving on the scene, the degree of lighting) or internal (e.g. consumption of alcohol by the offender, mood). It also includes the victim's behaviour - in psychological theories, the partner's behaviour creates part of the situation [18]. Hence examples of context in a crime may be "the crime scene is poorly lit", or "close to a public thorough-fare with potential for witnesses", or even "the victim is heavily intoxicated and subdued".

A general limitation of the linkage literature is the way in which the various algorithms have been applied. While these algorithms have utilised contextual variables in the past, they have not utilised these variables in a way that accounts for the interaction between context and behaviour. That is, contextual factors change/impact on the behaviour demonstrated by an offender (e.g. victim resistance impacts on the likelihood of an offender being physically violent during an offence). These inter-dependencies have not been incorporated in previous algorithmic approaches to CCA developed by researchers.

An exception to this is the work presented in [27] where the authors investigated whether context could impact on offender behaviour and whether greater behavioural consistency was seen for serial sex offenders in offences which were characterised as being more situationally similar. The approach, however, only considered victim behaviour as a situational factor, yet we know that situational influence extends far beyond victim behaviour. In addition, while it investigated if(victim behaviour)-then(offender behaviour) contingencies, it only considered the victim behaviour immediately preceding an offender behaviour, and due to the small sample size, it only investigated the three most common victim behaviours as situational factors. In contrast, our work aims to learn which contexts to prioritise for offender behaviour to be considered distinctive.

In summary, contextual factors have a significant impact on offender behaviour and should be factored into the crime linkage decision-making process [6]. Despite this, existing algorithmic approaches do not yet recognise or account for the importance of context in crime linkage. This work attempts to provide a first step towards filling this important gap in the literature. The approach presented in the rest of this paper aims to solve an important problem, which can be used to support CCA; specifically, we present an approach that learns to rank contexts by the distinctiveness of a given behaviour. These rankings are encoded as sets of weak constraints in ASP.

3   Background

Answer Set Programming. Given any atoms $h, b_1, \ldots, b_n, c_1, \ldots, c_m$, a *normal rule* is $h \text{:-} b_1, \ldots, b_n, \text{not } c_1, \ldots, \text{not } c_m$. The head (resp. body) of a rule R is denoted $head(R)$ (resp. $body(R)$). In this paper, we assume an ASP program to be a set of normal rules. Given a program P and an interpretation $I \subseteq HB_P$, the *reduct* P^I is constructed from the grounding of P by removing rules whose bodies contain the negation of an atom in I and removing negative literals from the remaining rules. A set of ground atoms I is an *answer set* of P iff it is the minimal model of P^I. The set of all answer sets of P is denoted $AS(P)$. In addition to normal rules, modern ASP solvers support *weak constraints*, which can be used to create an ordering over $AS(P)$. A *weak constraint* is of the form $\text{:} \sim b_1, \ldots, b_n, \text{not } c_1, \ldots, \text{not } c_m.[\text{w@l}, t_1, \ldots, t_k]$ where

$b_1, \ldots, b_n, c_1, \ldots, c_m$ are atoms, w and l are terms specifying the *weight* and the *level*, and $t_1, \ldots, t_k$ are terms. A weak constraint W is *safe* if every variable in W occurs in at least one positive literal in the body of W. At each *priority level* l, the aim is to discard any answer set which does not minimise the sum of the weights of the ground weak constraints (with level l) whose bodies are true. The higher levels are minimised first. Terms specify which ground weak constraints should be considered unique. For any program P and $A \in AS(P)$, $weak(P, A)$ is the set of tuples $(w, l, t_1, \ldots, t_k)$ for which there is some :~ $b_1, \ldots, b_n$, not $c_1, \ldots$, not $c_m.[w@l, t_1, \ldots, t_k]$ in the grounding of P such that A satisfies $b_1, \ldots, b_n$, not $c_1, \ldots$, not c_m. For each level l, $P_A^l = \sum_{(w,l,t_1,\ldots,t_k)\in weak(P,A)} w$. For $A_1, A_2 \in AS(P)$, A_1 *dominates* A_2 (written $A_1 \succ_P A_2$) iff $\exists l$ such that $P_{A_1}^l < P_{A_2}^l$ and $\forall m > l, P_{A_1}^m = P_{A_2}^m$. An answer set $A \in AS(P)$ is *optimal* if it is not dominated by any $A_2 \in AS(P)$.

Learning from Ordered Answer Sets. In this paper, we aim to learn to rank contexts by their distinctiveness. While weak constraints in ASP are usually used to represent preference orderings, they can in principle be used to represent an arbitrary ranking. In this work, we aim to learn a set of weak constraints[1] representing a ranking over contexts (by distinctiveness of a given behaviour). To the best of our knowledge, the *Learning from Ordered Answer Sets* (LOAS) framework [16] is the only current ILP framework designed to learn ASP programs that include weak constraints. The full LOAS setting is more expressive than is necessary for this paper. To avoid burdening the reader with unnecessary background material, we now present a simplified version of the framework. Examples in this setting are *weighted orderings* of the form $\langle C_1, C_2, pen \rangle$, where C_1 and C_2 are sets of normal rules (usually sets of facts) and *pen* is either ∞ or a positive integer representing the *penalty* that must be paid if the example is not covered. An infinite penalty represents that the example *must* be covered.

Many ILP systems (e.g. [15,25]) use mode declarations as a form of language bias to specify hypothesis spaces. A *mode bias* is defined as a tuple $M = \langle M_o, M_W, M_L \rangle$, where M_o is a set of mode declarations, $W \subseteq \mathbb{Z}$ and L is a set of positive integers. For simplicity of presentation, we only use propositional mode declarations (i.e. M_o is a set of propositional literals) in this paper, but our implementation supports first-order mode declarations in the style of FastLAS [14] and learning first-order rules. Given a mode bias $M = \langle M_o, M_W, M_L \rangle$, a weak constraint :~ body.$[w@l, \text{terms}]$ is in the search space S_M iff body $\subseteq M_o$, terms is the set of variables that occur in body, $w \in M_W$ and $l \in M_L$.

The following definition formalises the simplified setting used in this paper. For the full LOAS approach supported by ILASP, we refer the reader to [13].

Definition 1. *A* Simplified Learning from Ordered Answer Sets *task is a tuple* $T = \langle B, M, O^b \rangle$ *where B is an ASP program, M is a mode bias and O^b is a finite set of simplified ordering examples. For any hypothesis $H \subseteq S_M$:*

---

[1] We learn these weak constraints using a modified version of the FastLAS [14] system, called FastLOAS.

- For any $o = \langle C_1, C_2, pen \rangle \in O^b$, H covers o iff there is a pair of answer sets A_1 and A_2 of $B \cup C_1$ and $B \cup C_2$ (respectively), such that $A_1 \succ_H A_2$.
- The score of H, $\mathcal{S}_{len}(H,T)$ is the number of literals in H, written $|H|$, plus the penalty of each example in O^b which is not covered by H.
- H is an optimal solution of T iff $\mathcal{S}_{len}(H,T)$ is finite and there is no $H' \subseteq S_M$ s.t. $\mathcal{S}_{len}(H',T) < \mathcal{S}_{len}(H,T)$.

Odds Ratios and Fisher's Exact Test The odds of an event is a measure of how likely that event is to occur, and can be defined as $\frac{p}{1-p}$, where p is the probability of the event occurring. The *odds ratio* can be used to measure the association between two events; if we have two events e_1 and e_2, we can observe the number of times the two events occur separately and together, leading to a contingency table, such as the one below.

	e_1	$\neg c_1$
e_2	c_1	c_2
$\neg e_2$	c_3	c_4

The odds ratio is defined as $\frac{c_1 \times c_4}{c_2 \times c_3}$, which is the odds of e_1 given e_2 over the odds of e_1 given $\neg e_2$ (or equivalently, the odds of e_2 given e_1 over the odds of e_2 given $\neg e_1$). An odds ratio of 1 would indicate that the two events are independent (i.e. there is no association between them). An odds ratio of less than (resp. greater than) 1 indicates that the odds of e_1 are lower (resp. higher) if e_2 is observed. Fisher's Exact test is designed to test the statistical significance of such a statement. The two-tailed Fisher test yields a p-value used to test whether the null hypothesis "there is no association between e_1 and e_2" can be rejected. One-tailed Fisher tests can be used to assess whether we can reject the null hypotheses "the odds ratio is less than or equal to 1" and "the odds ratio is greater than or equal to 1". We use $Fisher(<, [[c_1, c_2], [c_3, c_4]])$ to denote the p-value yielded by applying a one-sided Fisher test on the above contingency table with a null hypothesis that the odds ratio is greater or equal to one. If this p-value is below a given threshold, we can claim that there is enough evidence to reject the null hypothesis and state that the odds of e_1 is lower if e_2 is observed.

4 Domain

We focus our application of comparative rarity analysis on serial sexual offences. Sexual offending imposes a significant human and economic impact on society. The overall costs to the UK society for all sexual offending per year is £12.2bn [9]. With public confidence in the criminal justice response to rape is at an all-time low (e.g. [10]), it is of paramount importance to provide decision-support mechanisms that can help tackle the adverse effects of sexual offending, including on health, education and employment [29].

Dataset. The dataset used in this paper was taken from the Violent Crime Linkage Analysis System (ViCLAS), which is a database management system, used by the Serious Crime Analysis Section (SCAS) of the UK's National Crime Agency. The system is designed to hold information about sexual offences (victim, scene, vehicle, weapon, and other variables specific to the actual offence) with which analysts can search for potential behavioural links between offences [11, 22]. The dataset we obtained contains details of 1482 single-offender, single-victim sexual offences that occurred in the UK between 1966 and 2013. The dataset contains 493 series of an average length of 3.1. To focus our analysis (and avoid temporal dependencies within lengthy offences), we consider a subset of 817 offences, each of which occurred in a single location. The ViCLAS variables deemed most relevant to the project were selected for inclusion, and were provided to the researchers as binary codes, with 1 indicating that an attribute was observed, and 0 indicating it was not observed or recorded.

Behavioural and Situational Factors. To support reasoning about context, we split the attributes into *behavioural factors* exhibited by the offender and *situational factors*, which describe the context in which the offence took place. The dataset does not make any explicit distinction between situational factors and behavioural factors. To this end, we pre-processed the data in two steps. In the first, our aim was to identify all situational factors in the dataset. We conducted an extensive review of the forensic psychology and criminology literature (2,372 articles were screened), ran two focus groups with analysts in the SCAS unit, and re-analysed 11 existing transcripts of interviews that were conducted by some of the authors with SCAS analysts [5]. This resulted in a list of 28 situational factors. The second step aimed at reducing the dimensionality of the dataset, owing to the large number of behavioural factors in the dataset. A review of literature allowed us to propose various themes for offender and victim behaviours in sexual assaults. The behavioural themes are the following: Aggressive, Criminal, Sexual, Approach and Verbal Themes. From these higher-level themes, we group selections of ViCLAS variables and create new behavioural features. In a similar way to the mapping of situational factors, some granularity was removed from the ViCLAS data. The resulting mapping was reviewed by experts in forensic and behavioural psychology, as well as analysts in SCAS. This resulted in 33 behavioural factors such as the types of sex acts committed and the precautions taken by the offender to avoid detection. We are not able to share the mappings developed as they are governed a by confidentiality agreement with the Agency.

After pre-processing, examples are of the form $\langle B, C \rangle$, where B is a set of behaviours that occurred and C is the *context* in which the offence took place (i.e. a subset of the situational factors). A single context can occur multiple times in the dataset with a different set of behaviours. For our analysis, we consider each behavioural variable b in isolation, since we are concerned with ranking the rarity of individual behaviour, independent of the occurrence of others. Therefore, for each behaviour b, we consider examples of the form $\langle C, t, f \rangle$, where C is a context and t (resp. f) is the number of examples $\langle B, C \rangle$ in which $b \in B$ (resp. $b \notin B$).

5 Probability Ranking

In this section, we describe a general approach to learn to rank contexts by the probability of a given observation. The aim of this work is to learn a set of weak constraints W which yields a ranking $\succ_W$ over contexts such that $C_1 \succ_W C_2$ implies that the probability of observing a behaviour in C_1 is lower than the probability of observing the same behaviour in C_2. We assume for each context C, the probability of observing the behaviour B in the context C is modelled by an independent Bernoulli distribution, with parameter p_C. We are, therefore, aiming to learn a ranking such that $C_1 \succ_W C_2$ if and only if $p_{C_1} < p_{C_2}$. To do so, we count the number of times a behaviour is present/absent in each context.

Definition 2. *A probability ranking task is of the form $\langle M, E \rangle$, where M is a mode bias and E is a set of examples of the form $\langle C, t, f \rangle$ s.t. $C \subseteq M_o$, $t, f \in \mathbb{N}$ and no C occurs more than once. A hypothesis $H \subseteq S_M$ covers a pair $\langle \langle C_1, t_1, f_1 \rangle, \langle C_2, t_2, f_2 \rangle \rangle \in E \times E$ if either: (i) $\frac{t_1}{t_1+f_1} < \frac{t_2}{t_2+f_2}$ and $C_1 \succ_H C_2$; (ii) $\frac{t_1}{t_1+f_1} > \frac{t_2}{t_2+f_2}$ and $C_2 \succ_H C_1$; or (iii) $\frac{t_1}{t_1+f_1} = \frac{t_2}{t_2+f_2}$, $C_1 \not\succ_H C_2$ and $C_2 \not\succ_H C_1$.*

Example 1. For the purpose of illustration, we consider the very small mode bias: $M_o = \{\, \mathtt{outdoors}, \mathtt{daylight}, \mathtt{darkness} \,\}$, $M_w = \{1, -1\}$, $M_l = \{1, \ldots, 3\}$ (the mode biases in the evaluation section are significantly larger). Consider the two examples $e_1 = \langle C_1 = \{\mathtt{outdoors}, \mathtt{darkness}\}, 4, 1 \rangle$ and $e_2 = \langle C_2 = \{\mathtt{outdoors}, \mathtt{daylight}\}, 1, 7 \rangle$, for the behaviour $\mathtt{violence\_unprovoked}$. This example represents that "unprovoked violence" was present in 4 of the cases where the context C_1 applies and absent in 1. For C_2 "unprovoked violence" is present and absent in 1 and 7 cases (respectively). As $\frac{4}{4+1} > \frac{1}{1+7}$, for the pair of examples $\langle e_1, e_2 \rangle$ to be covered by a hypothesis H, it must be the case that $\{\mathtt{outdoors}, \mathtt{daylight}\} \succ_H \{\mathtt{outdoors}, \mathtt{darkness}\}$. Given the mode bias above, there are many H's satisfying this condition; for example, $\{: \sim \mathtt{daylight}.[-1@1]\}$ or $\{: \sim \mathtt{outdoors}, \mathtt{darkness}.[1@1]\}$, which mean that "unprovoked violence" is rarer in daylight and more common outdoors in darkness.

5.1 Using Fisher's Exact Test to Decide Example Significance

Although it may be technically possible to find a set of weak constraints that will cover all examples, this is often impractical (it depends on having enough distinct priority levels) and it may not be desirable – the observed fraction for an example $\frac{t}{t+f}$ may not reflect the true probability, meaning that some of the orderings are essentially *noisy examples*. In this section, we describe a method to find a set of pairs of examples $\langle \langle C_1, t_1, f_1 \rangle, \langle C_2, t_2, f_2 \rangle \rangle$ for which the evidence that the probability of observing the behaviour in the context of C_1 is lower than the probability of observing the behaviour in the context of C_2 is statistically significant. By selecting those pairs for which there is statistically significant evidence, we eliminate the pairs that are most likely to be noisy.

Our method for determining statistical significance relies on Fisher's Exact test and the odds ratio. First, note that the probability of observing a behaviour monotonically increases with the odds of observing a behaviour b, meaning that an equivalent task would be to rank the contexts by the odds of observing the behaviours. Hence, the (observed) probability of b is lower in the context of C_1 than in the context of C_2 iff $\frac{t_1}{f_1} < \frac{t_2}{f_2}$, which is the case iff $\frac{t_1 \times f_2}{t_2 \times f_1} < 1$. This is equivalent to checking that the odds ratio of b and C_1, given $C_1 \vee C_2,$[2] is less than 1. Hence, we can establish the statistical significance of the statement "the probability of b is lower in the context of C_1 than in the context of C_2" by checking the statistical significance of the odds ratio being strictly lower than 1. This can be checked using a one-sided Fisher test with the null hypothesis that the odds ratio is greater of equal to 1.

Definition 3. *Given examples $\langle C_1, t_1, f_1 \rangle$ and $\langle C_2, t_2, f_2 \rangle$, the p-value of $C_1 < C_2$ is the p-value Fisher($<, [[t_1, f_1], [t_2, f_2]]$). Given a p-value threshold $\alpha \in (0, 1]$, $C_1 < C_2$ is statistically significant if the p-value of $C_1 < C_2$ is less than α.*

Example 2. Consider the pair of examples from Example 1. In order to test whether the ordering $C_1 < C2$ is statistically significant w.r.t. $\alpha = 0.1$, we must check that the p-value *Fisher*($<, [[4, 1], [1, 7]]$) is less than 0.1. In this case, the p-value is 0.99, so the ordering is not statistically significant. If we check the converse order ($C_2 < C_1$), the p-value is 0.03, meaning that the ordering is statistically significant. Hence, we can reject the null hypothesis and assert that the probability of observing b in the context of C_2 is lower than the probability of observing b in the context of C_2.

Weighting Examples by p-Values. Even when we use Fisher's Exact test to select those orderings which are statistically significant, it may not be possible to cover all the examples, given a particular search space (e.g. owing to the inconsistent nature of offending behaviour). One approach in ILP (e.g. [14,17]) is to give each example a weight and minimise the total weight of uncovered examples. In this paper, we define the weight of the ordering $C_1 < C_2$, written $w(C_1, C_2)$, to be $100/max(\{0.001, p\})$, where p is the p-value of $C_1 < C_2$. The motivation is that this function gives higher weight to those orderings that are more statistically significant. Note that the *max* function is used to put an upper bound on the weight of the examples (of 100000), as tiny p-values can otherwise lead to weights that are larger than the maximum allowed by the ILP system.

Example 3. Again, reconsider the pair of examples from Example 1. Example 2 demonstrated that the evidence for $C_1 < C_2$ is not statistically significant. On the other hand, the ordering $C_2 < C_1$ is statistically significant (at threshold $\alpha = 0.1$) with a p-value of ~ 0.03. In this case, the weight is equal to $\frac{100}{0.03} = 3139$.

5.2   Encoding a Probability Ranking Task as a LOAS Task

Now that we have defined the subset of orderings that are statistically significant, and the weight of such orderings, the search for an optimal solution to the task

---

[2] As C_1 and C_2 are mutually exclusive, if we consider only the cases where $C_1 \vee C_2$, then $\neg C_1$ holds iff C_2 holds.

(i.e. one which minimises the weight of all uncovered statistically significant orderings plus the number of literals in the learned weak constraints) can be encoded as a simplified LOAS task. This is captured by the following definition.

Definition 4. *Let $T = \langle M, E \rangle$ be a probability ranking task and α be a threshold. The simplified LOAS encoding of T is $\langle \emptyset, S_M, O \rangle$, where $O = \{\langle C_i, C_j, w(C_i, C_j) \rangle \mid \langle C_i, t_i, f_i \rangle, \langle C_j, t_j, f_j \rangle \in E, Fisher(<, [[t_i, f_i], [t_j, f_j]]) < \alpha\}$.*

6 Evaluation

In this section, we present the result of running our probability ranking approach with various parameters. Our initial experiments showed that for many of the learning tasks we were solving, ILASP was unable to provide a solution in a reasonable time, due to the size of the hypothesis space. The reason for this is that the first step of ILASP's algorithm is always to compute the hypothesis space in full.[3] In recent years the FastLAS systems [14] have been developed to solve restricted versions of ILASP's learning task without the need to compute the full hypothesis space. Until now, FastLAS has not been able to learn weak constraints. As part of this work, we extended the FastLAS system to enable it to solve the simplified LOAS tasks introduced in Definition 1,[4] yielding a new system – FastLOAS. While this extension was not particularly complicated, describing it would require recalling the inner-workings of the FastLAS algorithm and explaining how each of the steps was tweaked. As the focus of this paper is on our new probability ranking approach and its application to CCA using the ViCLAS dataset, the description of FastLOAS is out of scope. For full details

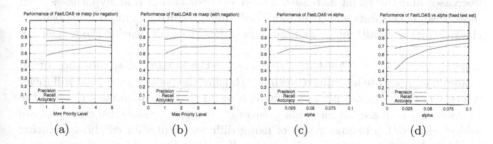

(a)   (b)   (c)   (d)

Fig. 1. (a) and (b) show how the performance of the approach varies with the maximum priority level (i.e. the maximum number of weak constraints that can be learned; (c) and (d) show how the performance varies with the p-value threshold α.

---

[3] Note that this is not the solution space; it is the set of all rules that can appear in a hypothesis. The solution space is the power set of the hypothesis space.

[4] This extension is restricted to the case where for each context C, $B \cup C$ has a single answer set, but is otherwise as general as Definition 1, and can solve tasks including first order ASP and negation as failure.

of FastLOAS, including the source code and some example tasks, please see https://spike-imperial.github.io/FastLAS/fastloas.html.

We divided the 817 cases into a training set of 408 examples (50% of the dataset) and a test set consisting of the remaining 409 examples (again, 50% of the dataset). In each experiment, FastLOAS was run on the training set and the learned hypothesis was then evaluated on the test set. In each case, we evaluated the learned hypothesis by measuring the proportion of statistically significant ordered pairs in the test set (using the same p-value threshold as in training) that are correctly/incorrectly ordered by the learned hypothesis. Note that in some cases, none of the learned weak constraints apply to either of the pair of contexts being analysed, meaning that no ordering is given.

Varying the Language Bias. One of the main factors in the performance of an ILP system is the set of mode declarations it is given (i.e. the language bias). A language bias that is too restrictive may result in poor performance, as the best performing solutions are not in the search space; on the other hand, a language bias that is too general can result in the learner being able to overfit the data (although this can be somewhat ameliorated by using an appropriate scoring function), and can also result in the computation time being significantly longer. We experimented by varying the maximum priority level allowed (i.e. the maximum number of weak constraints that could appear in a hypothesis) and by running experiments both allowing and not allowing negation as failure (NAF). The results in Figs. 1(a) and (b) show that the performance with NAF are better than those without. This is because some concepts in the search space with NAF are not available in the search space without NAF. Notably, increasing the maximum number of weak constraints has a mixed effect, both with and without NAF. The overall accuracy stays fairly constant in both cases, but the precision decreases and the recall increases. The reason for this is that hypotheses with more weak constraints will cover more orderings, resulting in more true positives (increasing the recall), but also in more false positives (decreasing the precision).

Varying the p-Value Threshold. To measure the statistical significance of an example pair, we use a p-value threshold. Raising the p-value threshold will mean a larger number of examples, but will also mean that the amount of noise in the dataset may increase (as there is a greater chance that mislabelled examples are added). Figure 1 (c) shows result of using different values for α, and evaluating on the test set generated using the same α. This experiment is important because it shows how accurately the learner can learn to predict comparative rarity at a given p-value threshold. It is also important to compare the results of training with different α's and evaluating on the same test set. Figure 1(d) shows the results of training with different α's and evaluating on the test set generated using $\alpha = 0.05$. In both cases, the precision is higher with a lower α, while the recall increases as α increases. The increase in recall can be explained by the larger number of examples. The drop in precision can be explained by the increased amount of noise. Interestingly, the precision rises slightly after $\alpha = 0.05$ in Fig. 1, which indicates that the number of extra examples has more of an effect than the increased noise – note also that the weight of these examples is inversely proportional to their p-value, meaning that the extra examples are only likely to have an effect if a large number of them show a clear pattern.

7   Related Work

The general notion of learning an ordering is an instance of preference learning called *learning to rank* [7]. Relatively little work has been conducted on Inductive Logic Programming methods for preference learning, with the exception of the ILASP systems [15,16] and the work in [20], which used the Aleph system to learn rankings. In [13], ILASP was shown to outperform [20] in terms of predictive accuracy. Compared to ILASP, the FastLOAS system used in this paper is limited in that it can *only* learn weak constraints; whereas ILASP is capable of learning general programs including weak constraints, but also including other constructs, such as normal rules, choice rules and disjunctive rules. Furthermore, it only supports what ILASP calls *brave ordering examples* in which the pair of examples have to be covered by at least one pair of answer sets; whereas, ILASP also supports *cautious ordering examples*. On the other hand, unlike FastLOAS, ILASP generates every weak constraint that is compatible with the mode declarations, meaning that it does not scale w.r.t. the size of the search space, so is not capable of handling the domain in this paper.

As the notion that we are ranking – rarity – in linked to the probability of observing a behaviour in a given context, our approach is also related to *Probabilistic Inductive Logic Programming* (PILP) methods, which aim to learn probabilistic theories (e.g. [1,21]). The key difference between our approach and PILP methods is that we do not aim to learn probabilities directly. Instead, we are essentially learning a "less likely than" relation (captured by a set of weak constraints). Given this, the search space of possible solutions is significantly smaller than if we had tried to encode the same problem as a PILP task.

8   Conclusion

This paper has demonstrated that it is possible to learn to rank contexts by the rarity of a behaviour. In particular, we have shown that the FastLOAS ILP system is capable of learning weak constraints that can accurately rank an unseen set of contexts by the situational factors present/absent in those contexts. Due to the limitations of the dataset we have, the learned constraints are ground, and each condition is either satisfied entirely, or not satisfied at all. The FastLOAS/ILASP systems do not have such restrictions, so in future work it would be interesting to investigate datasets that allow first order weak constraints to be learned. Such datasets would also enable the FastLOAS system to learn concepts such as minimising or maximising a particular quantity. Our approach is not limited to the domain in this paper, but instead provides a general noise-tolerant method for ranking the likelihood of an event across contexts.

References

1. Bellodi, E., Riguzzi, F.: Structure learning of probabilistic logic programs by searching the clause space. TPLP **15**(2), 169–212 (2015)
2. Bennell, C., Canter, D.V.: Linking commercial burglaries by modus operandi: tests using regression and roc analysis. Sci. Just. **42**(3), 153–164 (2002)
3. Bennell, C., Mugford, R., Ellingwood, H., Woodhams, J.: Linking crimes using behavioural clues: current levels of linking accuracy and strategies for moving forward. J. Investig. Psychol. Offend. Profil. **11**(1), 29–56 (2014)
4. Brewka, G., Eiter, T., Truszczyński, M.: Answer set programming at a glance. Commun. ACM **54**(12), 92–103 (2011)
5. Davies, K., Alrajeh, D., Woodhams, J.: An investigation into the process of comparative case analysis conducted by analysts working in the serious crime analysis section in the united kingdom. In: Official report for the Serious Crime Analysis Section (2018)
6. Davies, K.: The practice of crime linkage. Ph.D. thesis, University of Birmingham (2018)
7. Fürnkranz, J., Hüllermeier, E.: Pairwise preference learning and ranking. In: Lavrač, N., Gamberger, D., Blockeel, H., Todorovski, L. (eds.) ECML 2003. LNCS (LNAI), vol. 2837, pp. 145–156. Springer, Heidelberg (2003). https://doi.org/10.1007/978-3-540-39857-8_15
8. Hazelwood, R.R., Warren, J.I.: Linkage analysis: modus operandi, ritual, and signature in serial sexual crime. Aggress. Violent Behav. **8**(6), 587–598 (2003)
9. Home Office. The Economic and Social Costs of Crime, 2nd edn (2018)
10. Home Office. The End-to-End Rape Review Report on Findings and Actions (2021)
11. Johnson, G.: Viclas: violent crime linkage analysis system. Gazette **56**, 9–13 (1994)
12. Labuschagne, G.N.: The use of a linkage analysis as evidence in the conviction of the Newcastle serial murderer, South Africa. Investig. Psychol. Offend. Profil. **3**(3), 183–191 (2006)
13. Law, M.: Inductive learning of answer set programs. PhD thesis, Imperial College London (2018)
14. Law, M., Russo, A., Bertino, E., Broda, K., Lobo, J.: FastLAS: scalable inductive logic programming incorporating domain-specific optimisation criteria. In: AAAI, Association for the Advancement of Artificial Intelligence (2020)
15. Law, M., Russo, A., Broda, K.: The ILASP system for learning answer set programs (2015). https://www.ilasp.com
16. Law, M., Russo, A., Broda, K.: Learning weak constraints in answer set programming. TPLP **15**(4–5), 511–525 (2015)
17. Law, M., Russo, A., Broda, K.: Inductive learning of answer set programs from noisy examples. Adv. Cognit. Syst. (2018)
18. Mischel, W., Shoda, Y.: A cognitive-affective system theory of personality: reconceptualizing situations, dispositions, dynamics, and invariance in personality structure. Psychol. Rev. **102**(2), 246 (1995)
19. Muggleton, S.: Inductive logic programming. New Gen. Comput. **8**(4), 295–318 (1991)
20. Qomariyah, N.N., Kazakov, D.: Learning binary preference relations. In: Proceedings of the 4th Joint Workshop on Interfaces and Human Decision Making for Recommender Systems (IntRS), p. 30. (2017)
21. De Raedt, L., Thon, I.: Probabilistic rule learning. In: Frasconi, P., Lisi, F.A. (eds.) ILP 2010. LNCS (LNAI), vol. 6489, pp. 47–58. Springer, Heidelberg (2011). https://doi.org/10.1007/978-3-642-21295-6_9

22. Royal Canadian Mounted Police. Violent crime linkage analysis system. https://www.rcmp-grc.gc.ca/en/violent-crime-linkage-analysis-system. Accessed 28 Apr 2022
23. Santtila, P., Junkkila, J., Sandnabba, N.K.: Behavioural linking of stranger rapes. J. Investig. Psychol. Offend. Profil. **2**(2), 87–103 (2005)
24. Sea, J., Beauregard, E., Martineau, M.: A cross-cultural comparison of Canadian and Korean sexual homicide. Int. J. Offend. Therapy Comparat. Criminol. **63**(9), 1538–1556 (2019)
25. Srinivasan, A.: The Aleph Manual. Machine Learning at the Computing Laboratory. Oxford University (2001)
26. Woodhamns, J., Labuschagne, G.N.: A test of crime linkage principles with solved and unsolved serial rapes. J. Police Criminal Psychol. **27**(11), 85–98 (2012)
27. Woodhams, J., Hollin, C., Bull, R.: Incorporating context in linking crimes: an exploratory study of situational similarity and if-then contingencies. J. Investig. Psychol. Offend. Profil. **5**(1–2), 1–23 (2008)
28. Woodhams, J., Bennell, C. (eds.) Crime Linkage: Theory, Research, and Practice. Routledgey (2014)
29. World Health Organization. World Health Statistics 2010 (2010)

Optimising Business Process Discovery Using Answer Set Programming

Federico Chesani[1], Chiara Di Francescomarino[2], Chiara Ghidini[2],
Giulia Grundler[1], Daniela Loreti[1], Fabrizio Maria Maggi[3], Paola Mello[1],
Marco Montali[3], and Sergio Tessaris[3(✉)]

[1] DISI - University of Bologna, Bologna, Italy
[2] Fondazione Bruno Kessler, Trento, Italy
[3] Free University of Bozen/Bolzano, Bolzano, Italy
`tessaris@inf.unibz.it`

Abstract. Declarative business process discovery aims at identifying sets of constraints, from a given formal language, that characterise a workflow by using pre-recorded activity logs. Since the provided logs represent a fraction of all the consistent evolution of a process, and the fact that many sets of constraints covering those examples can be selected, empirical criteria should be employed to identify the "best" candidates. In our work we frame the process discovery as an optimisation problem, where we want to identify optimal sets of constraints according to preference criteria. Declarative constraints for processes are usually characterised via temporal logics, so different solutions can be semantically equivalent. For this reason, it is difficult to use an arbitrary finite domain constraints solvers for the optimisation. The use of Answer Set Programming enables the combination of deduction rules within the optimisation algorithm, in order to take into account not only the user preferences but also the implicit semantics of the formal language. In this paper we show how we encoded the process discovery problem using the ASPrin framework for qualitative and quantitative optimisation in ASP, and the results of our experiments.

Keywords: Preferences · Answer set programming · Optimisation · Process mining · Process discovery · Declarative process models

1 Introduction

Process discovery is one of the most investigated process mining techniques [13]. It deals with the automatic learning of a process model from a given set of logged traces, each one representing the digital footprint of a specific execution of the process. Our work develops in the context of *binary* process discovery, in which the model-extraction is seen as a two-class supervised task (see [2,7,8,11]), where log traces are partitioned into two sets according to some business or domain-related criteria (the so-called *positive* and *negative* – i.e., undesired – traces).

© The Author(s), under exclusive license to Springer Nature Switzerland AG 2022
G. Gottlob et al. (Eds.): LPNMR 2022, LNAI 13416, pp. 498–504, 2022.
https://doi.org/10.1007/978-3-031-15707-3_38

The target of the learning process is a model that discriminates one set from the other.

Process discovery algorithms are also classified according to the language they employ to represent the output model: procedural and declarative. Techniques of the first kind envisage the process model as a synthetic description of all possible sequences of actions that the process accepts from an initial to an ending state. In declarative discovery—the focus of this work—models are sets of constraints, characterised by a declarative, logic-based semantics. Both approaches have their strengths and weaknesses depending on the characteristics of the considered process. Procedural techniques may generate hard to understand "spaghetti"-like models, and in these cases declarative-based approaches might be preferable [5]. A problem that remains unsolved in process discovery, is the need to select, among all possible discovered models, the ones that best fit the expectations of the user. This problem is manifesting in techniques that rely only on one set of traces (the positive); where the risk is to generate overfitting models. Therefore, mechanisms are introduced to "select" specific behaviours; e.g., the frequency of a certain element (e.g., an activity or a path), or the presence of certain modelling patterns. In spite of the possibility of exploiting the negative information, binary discovery techniques are also affected by the same problem. As recently shown in [11], perfect binary miners (able to discover models that accept all positive examples and none of the negative examples) do not necessarily exist; many suboptimal models can be identified by the discovery process, leading to the issue of identifying criteria for preferring one model. In most of the techniques in literature, the criteria are built in the discovery process, leaving small room for dedicated user-driven preferences. In [2] we introduced a novel algorithm that splits the discovery process in two stages: first, the set of all candidate constraints are identified, and then the selection of the model is framed as an optimisation problem selecting one (or more) subsets according to given preferences. Its implementation (NegDis) is available in [12]. In this short paper we focus on the optimisation stage, showing how we used Answer Set Programming Optimisation to encode and solve the second stage.

2   Declarative Process Discovery

The discovery approach we introduce in this paper is based on Declare, a language for describing declarative process models first introduced in [10]. A Declare model consists of a set of constraints on a finite set of (atomic) activities. Constraints are ground instantiation from a given set of abstract parametrised patterns (*templates*); where parameters are substituted with activities. Templates have a graphical representation and their semantics can be formalised using different logics, the main one being linear temporal logic (LTL) over finite traces, making them verifiable and executable. The major benefit of using templates – e.g., instead of LTL – is that analysts do not have to be aware of the underlying logic-based formalisation to understand the models. Table 1 summaries some common Declare templates. The reader can refer to [10] for a full description of the language. It is important to emphasise that Declare is a *family* of languages defined by a set of templates.

Table 1. Example of Declare templates

Template	Explanation
existence(A)	A occurs at least once
init(A)	A is the *first* to occur
response(A, B)	If A occurs, then B occurs after A
alternate_response(A, B)	Each time A occurs, then B occurs afterwards, before A recurs
precedence(A, B)	B occurs only if preceded by A
co_existence(A, B)	If B occurs, then A occurs, and vice versa
not_succession(A, B)	A never occurs before B

Given a finite set of Declare templates D and a finite set of activities A, we indicate with $D[A]$ all possible groundings of templates in D w.r.t. A, i.e., all the constraints that can be built using activities from A. Traces—i.e., finite sequences of activities from A—can be understood as (logical) models for constraints, and we say that $M \subseteq D[A]$ *accepts* a trace t iff, for each constraint $c \in M$, $t \models c$ w.r.t. its semantics [10]. The semantics of Declare introduces a natural notion of *generality* between process models; i.e. a model M is more general than M' ($M' \preceq M$) if the latter accepts all the traces accepted by M. In [3], templates are organised into a *subsumption* hierarchy, and this relation (between constraints) is used as a preference for guiding the discovery process. We generalise this notion by introducing the *deductive closure operator* based on a given set R of (correct) deduction rules,[1] as a function $cl_R : \mathcal{P}(D[A]) \rightarrow \mathcal{P}(D[A])$ that associates any set $M \in D[A]$ with all the constraints that can be logically derived from M by applying one or more deduction rules in R. For brevity, in the rest of the paper we will omit the set R, and we will simply write $cl(M)$ to indicate the deductive closure of M. The complete set deduction rules that we considered, including those introduced in [3], is available in the source code [12].[2] All the rules we analysed in the literature can be encoded as Normal Logic Program rules (more on this in Sect. 3).

Although NegDis takes as input the set of templates and deduction rules, for the sake of simplicity, in the rest of the paper we assume that they are fixed and input consists on the sets of positive and negative examples (denoted by L^+ and L^-). Candidate solutions for the discovery task are any set of constraints $S \subseteq D[A]$ s.t. *(i)* $\forall t \in L^+$ we have $t \models S$; *(ii)* S maximizes the set $\{t \in L^- \mid t \not\models S\}$.

In the first stage of the algorithm, NegDis builds a function (*sheriffs*) that associates each trace in L^- with the set of constraints, chosen from those accepting all traces in L^+, that reject it:

$$sheriffs(t) = \{c \in D[A] \mid t \not\models c \land \forall t' \in L^+ . t' \models c\} \quad (1)$$

---

[1] Identifying whether there is a complete set of rules for a specific set of templates is an open problem outside the scope of this work.

[2] The file declare_rules.txt in the data directory.

Note that, due to the fact that not all the pairs of negative and positive sets of traces can be perfectly separated using Declare [11], there can be traces t in L^- for which $sheriffs(t)$ is empty, meaning that those traces cannot be excluded by any model that guarantees the acceptance of all the positive ones. The actual implementation of the first stage is outside the scope of this paper and the reader is referred to [2]. Based on $sheriffs$, the space of all solutions can be defined as

$$\mathcal{Z} = \{M \subseteq \bigcup_{t \in L^-} sheriffs(t) \mid \forall t \in L^- \ t \not\models M \vee sheriffs(t) = \emptyset\} \qquad (2)$$

That is, the subsets of the set of all constraints in $sheriffs(t)$ that reject all the negative traces (excluding those that cannot be rejected, i.e., $sheriffs(t) = \emptyset$). In the next section we show how we use an ASP optimisation system to order $\mathcal{Z}$ and select the "best" process models.

3   ASP Encoding and Evaluation

For our experiments we used the *Clingo* system [6] because it supports *function* terms, and an advanced optimisation frontend (*ASPrin* [1]), enabling the declarative specification of preferences. The encoding of the optimisation stage in ASP follows the common Guess/Check/Optimise (GCO) ASP paradigm [9]: the *guessing* part selects subsets of $\bigcup_{t \in L^-} sheriffs(t)$ using a *choice rule* [6], the *checking* part selects only (ASP) models that "reject" the negative traces, while the *optimisation* part depends on selected preferences.

The *sheriffs* input is encoded as a binary predicate choice/2 where the first argument is a trace ID (an integer) and the second a constraint that "rejects" the trace. The "output" predicate, identifying the selected constraints, is the unary predicate selected/1.[3] We decided to encode constraints as function terms in order to avoid the ad-hoc handling of the number of template parameters (e.g., terms like decl(init,a)), so the fact that the constraint init(a) rejects the third trace is encoded by the fact choice(3,decl(init,a)).

The *guessing* part is composed by a single choice rule

```
{ selected(C) : choice(_,C) }.
```

The *checking* part must take into account not only the selected constraints, but also their closure, since it affects the optimisation preferences. To this end we introduced a derived/1 predicate, and the checking is encoded as

```
derived(C) :- selected(C).
rejected(T) :- choice(T,C), derived(C).
:- choice(T,_), not rejected(T).
```

The *guessing* and *checking* parts above enables the generation of all models corresponding to the sets in $\mathcal{Z}$ (Eq. 2). Deduction rules are encoded using the derived/1 predicate; e.g., the rule init(A) → precedence(A, B) is encoded as

---

[3] In the actual code the predicate names are slightly different to avoid potential clashes with names used by *ASPrin*, and they can be parametrised.

derived(decl(precedence,X,Y)) :− derived(decl(init,X)), action(Y).

Assuming a finite number of activities, Declare deduction rules studied in literature can be encoded as *full tuple-generating dependencies* [4]. Therefore, for any subset of $\bigcup_{t \in L^-}$ *sheriffs*(t), the extension of derived/1 is unique. Moreover, since each constraint in *sheriffs* accepts all traces in L^+, any subset of $\bigcup_{t \in L^-}$ *sheriffs*(t) is consistent.

Enumerating all models is too expensive, and doesn't provide any guide to select the most suitable (from the user point of view). For the *optimisation* part we started experimenting with cardinality preferences over the deductive closure and selection; which can be simply implemented via *Clingo* minimisation statements (grounding macros for *weak constraints* [6]):

```
#minimize{1@2,C: derived(C)}.
#minimize{1@1,C: selected(C)}.
```

Specifying more elaborate preferences require complex encodings and ASP techniques, which are difficult to manage and error-prone to non ASP experts. To simplify the specification we exploit the *ASPrin Clingo* frontend [1], which provides a general framework for optimising qualitative and quantitative preferences in ASP. For example, "subset" optimality can be encoded using

```
#preference(p1,subset){ derived(C) : constraint(C) }.
#preference(p2,less(cardinality)){ selected(C) : choice(_, C) }.
#preference(p10,lexico){ 1::**p2; 2::**p1 }.
#optimize(p10).
```

which prefers models with a (subset) smaller closure, and (cardinality) smaller selected in case of ties. The built-in directives of *ASPrin* can be used to specify also preferences of specific properties of the models; e.g., to prefer models with specific templates:

```
not_nice_model :− selected(C), template_name(C,not_succession).
nice_model :− not not_nice_model.
#preference(p1,aso){ nice_model >> not_nice_model }.
#preference(p2,subset){ derived(C) : constraint(C) }.
#preference(p10,lexico){ 1::**p2; 2::**p1 }.
#optimize(p10).
```

The encoding has been evaluated in the context of the discovery process using both synthetic and real datasets. For the description of the datasets and details on the results the reader is referred to [2]. In this paper we focus on the optimisation stage, considering the size and structure of the *sheriffs* input: the number of traces and the average number of "rejecting" constraints per trace. Table 2

Table 2. Running time

Dataset	*sheriffs* input		CPU time (sec)		
	size	avg	*sheriffs*	subset	card
SYNT$_a$	25600	32.2491	113.06	15.085	11.559
SYNT$_b$	10240	9.40303	97.47	1.377	1.201
CERV$_{compl}$	102	10.402	0.33	0.065	0.045
SEPSIS$_{mean}$	9	2.44444	1.04	0.039	0.035
SEPSIS$_{median}$	141	24.0851	1.05	0.2	0.087
BPIC12$_{mean}$	70	8.84286	31	0.096	0.066
BPIC12$_{median}$	2394	9.15748	37.63	359.164	43.846

shows the optimisation time, for the "subset" and "cardinality" criteria above, compared to the time spent to calculate the *sheriffs* input. By considering the whole discovery problem, in most of the datasets, the runtime of the optimisation is an order of magnitude smaller than the first stage, and it seems to be correlated with the size of the minimal (process) model discovered.

4 Conclusions

In this paper we demonstrate the use of ASP optimisation to encode preferences in complex domains where the optimisation criteria cannot be fixed beforehand; e.g., in our case process models can be preferred because of the presence of some patterns which are domain dependent. The flexibility of a rule-based system enables the handling of complex interactions between the components of a solution and its optimisation. In our domain, because of the need to take into account the deductive dependency between `Declare` constraints, we cannot use traditional finite domain solvers. Our empirical evaluation shows that the *Clingo* solver can efficiently handle the optimisation stage for the preferences we selected. We plan to investigate whether the system can be pushed further with more complex preferences; e.g., interaction between different templates or activities.

References

1. Brewka, G., Delgrande, J.P., Romero, J., Schaub, T.: asprin: customizing answer set preferences without a headache. In: AAAI, pp. 1467–1474. AAAI Press (2015)
2. Chesani, F., et al.: Process discovery on deviant traces and other stranger things. arXiv preprint arXiv:2109.14883 (2021)
3. Di Ciccio, C., Maggi, F.M., Montali, M., Mendling, J.: Resolving inconsistencies and redundancies in declarative process models. Inf. Syst. **64**, 425–446 (2017)
4. Fagin, R.: Tuple-generating dependencies. In: Liu, L., Özsu, M.T. (eds.) Encyclopedia of Database Systems, pp. 3201–3202. Springer, Boston (2009). https://doi.org/10.1007/978-1-4614-8265-9_1274
5. Fahland, D., et al.: Declarative versus imperative process modeling languages: the issue of understandability. In: Halpin, T., et al. (eds.) BPMDS/EMMSAD -2009. LNBIP, vol. 29, pp. 353–366. Springer, Heidelberg (2009). https://doi.org/10.1007/978-3-642-01862-6_29
6. Gebser, M., Kaminski, R., Kauffman, B., Schaub, T.: Multi-shot asp solving with clingo. Theory Practice Logic Prog. **19**(1), 27–82 (2019)
7. Goedertier, S., Martens, D., Vanthienen, J., Baesens, B.: Robust process discovery with artificial negative events. J. Mach. Learn. Res. **10**, 1305–1340 (2009)
8. de León, H.P., Nardelli, L., Carmona, J., vanden Broucke, S.K.L.M.: Incorporating negative information to process discovery of complex systems. Inf. Sci. **422**, 480–496 (2018)
9. Leone, N., et al.: The DLV system for knowledge representation and reasoning. ACM Trans. Computat. Logic **7**(3), 499–562 (2006)
10. Pesic, M., Schonenberg, H., van der Aalst, W.M.P.: DECLARE: full support for loosely-structured processes. In: 11th IEEE International Enterprise Distributed Object Computing Conference (EDOC 2007), pp. 287–300 (2007)

11. Slaats, T., Debois, S., Back, C.O.: Weighing the pros and cons: process discovery with negative examples. In: Polyvyanyy, A., Wynn, M.T., Van Looy, A., Reichert, M. (eds.) BPM 2021. LNCS, vol. 12875, pp. 47–64. Springer, Cham (2021). https://doi.org/10.1007/978-3-030-85469-0_6

12. Tessaris, S., Di Francescomarino, C., Chesani, F.: Negdis: code for the experiments (2022). https://doi.org/10.5281/zenodo.6396859

13. van der Aalst, W., et al.: Process mining manifesto. In: Daniel, F., Barkaoui, K., Dustdar, S. (eds.) BPM 2011. LNBIP, vol. 99, pp. 169–194. Springer, Heidelberg (2012). https://doi.org/10.1007/978-3-642-28108-2_19

DeduDeep: An Extensible Framework for Combining Deep Learning and ASP-Based Models

Pierangela Bruno$^{(\boxtimes)}$ (ID), Francesco Calimeri$^{(\boxtimes)}$ (ID), and Cinzia Marte$^{(\boxtimes)}$ (ID)

Department of Mathematics and Computer Science,
University of Calabria, Rende, Italy
{bruno,calimeri,marte}@mat.unical.it

Abstract. In the last decades, Deep Learning (DL)-based approaches have been fruitfully employed in many tasks, such as providing valuable support to computer-aided diagnosis and medicine. However, DL-based approaches are known to suffer from some limitations; for instance, they lack of proper means for providing clear explanations and interpretations of the results, or explicitly including available knowledge to drive decisions. In this work, we present DeduDeep, the prototypical implementation of a framework explicitly conceived with the aim of tackling such limitations by making use of deductive declarative formalisms. In particular, the framework aims at enabling the declarative encoding of explicit knowledge, and, by relying on the use of Answer Set Programming (ASP), taking advantage of it for driving decisions taken by neural networks and refining the output. The framework has been tested using different artificial neural networks tailored to semantic segmentation tasks over Laryngeal Endoscopic Images and Freiburg Sitting People Images.

Keywords: Answer Set Programming · Knowledge Representation and Reasoning · Non-monotonic reasoning · Deep Learning · Semantic Segmentation · Inductive-deductive coupling

1 Introduction

In the field of Artificial Intelligence (AI), Deep Learning (DL)-based approaches have been successfully employed in several application domains, for example, in performing an automatic diagnosis [2] or in analyzing medical images [5]. However, despite their clear advantages, these approaches suffer from some limitations; for instance, there are no satisfactory standard means for (i) providing a proper explanation and interpretation of the decisions taken by the network to produce a specif output, or (ii) explicitly including available pieces of knowledge in order to "steer" decisions made by the network.

In this work, we present DeduDeep, the prototype of a training system implementing a framework designed to steer neural networks decisions and refine

© The Author(s), under exclusive license to Springer Nature Switzerland AG 2022
G. Gottlob et al. (Eds.): LPNMR 2022, LNAI 13416, pp. 505–510, 2022.
https://doi.org/10.1007/978-3-031-15707-3_39

the predicted output via the integration of the deductive declarative formalism
Answer Set Programming (ASP) [1,4,6]. The design of DeduDeep relies on the
seminal work appeared in [3]; even if explainability is not expressly tackled yet,
it aims at contributing on the road towards an integration between inductive and
deductive approaches to Artificial Intelligence. While some proposals have been
presented in the state-of-the-art for "guiding" ASP via ML/DL techniques, the
one herein presented is among the less common proposals for doing the opposite:
a combination of DL and ASP that makes use of the latter for fine-tuning loss
functions and post-processing phases. Such framework has been very recently
proposed in [3] and it was tested using different artificial neural networks (i.e.,
DeepLab-v3, SegNet, U-Net) to perform semantic segmentation over Laryngeal
Endoscopic Images [7].

The DeduDeep framework is conceived for easing the design of ad-hoc application in practice; for this reason, a platform has been designed for supporting
the user in selecting proper tuning parameters, managing the knowledge base,
including explicit additional knowledge in the model. We point out that, at
present, the platform has been used for our experimental activities aimed at
assessing the framework, but it will be released in the near future. Indeed, we
present here a new experimental campaign, based on the Freiburg Sitting People
dataset [8].

The remainder of the paper is structured as follows. In Sect. 2 we describe our
approach; then, we report about a careful experimental activity that is discussed
in Sect. 3; finally, we draw our conclusions in Sect. 4.

2   DeduDeep: Proposed Approach

The herein proposed framework relies on the use of ASP for supporting DL-based
approaches in the task of semantic segmentation. Specifically, we design a standard methodology to construct a proper rule-based model that represents prior
knowledge and network prediction into ASP rules, and to convert the output of
ASP computation into values "understandable" by the network.

As shown in Fig. 1, our framework is designed to:

- *Drive the network's learning and penalize misclassification.* We quantify a
  penalty value using an ASP-based model that compares the network's prediction to ground truth segmentation, prior knowledge and rational insight of
  evident truths. The penalty value, which expresses "how wrong" the classification is, takes part in defining the loss function. Specifically, we introduce
  the penalty value in the last 250 epochs of the training to refine the network
  decisions. For more details we refer the reader to [3].
- *Improve the quality of the results.* We define an ASP-based post-processing
  to remove noise (i.e., small "islands" of misclassified pixels) and wrong predicted classes (i.e., classes which do not comply with available prior knowledge). More precisely, we first translate the network's prediction into logical
  rules and then define an ASP-based model to identify pixels that need to
  be removed; eventually, we rely on such model to re-assign misclassified pix-
  els/elements to the "more frequent" class in the neighborhood [3].

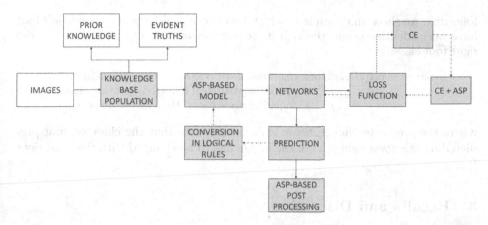

Fig. 1. Workflow of the current DeduDeep architecture. The knowledge bases are build from input raw images and used to support the training of the networks via the loss function. At each epoch, the prediction is converted into logical rules that are incorporated in the ASP-based model, and it is then refined by the post-processing phase.

ASP-Based Post Processing. The post-processing phase is designed to improve the quality of the prediction by (*i*) cleaning the image from noise (e.g., small sets of pixels that, under a certain size, can be considered as wrongly detected areas) (*ii*) removing objects that do not comply with prior knowledge or do not respect evident truth. This greatly varies depending on the specific application, and must be carefully encoded. In the herein reported scenario, we can think about medical knowledge and find that it somehow contains constraints. For instance, it is not possible that a specific class is detected in some sequence or image; furthermore, examples of evident truths include: it is not possible that the class head is detected close to the class foot or, it is not possible that there are two elements belonging to left foot class and no elements for right foot class – roughly speaking, a person can't have two left feet.

These pixels/objects are afterwards colored by either (*i*) selecting the most frequent color (i.e., class) in the neighborhood (see [3] for further details), or (*ii*) by replacing them with the logically correct classes. To take one example, if there are two objects of the left foot class and no one of the right foot class, then the rightmost object is changed into an element of the right foot class. Hence, fixed an image and a class, we recognize if there are two or more objects of the class by counting in how many different positions the object is predicted. The latter is expressed via the following rule:

$$twins(ID, CL) : - \ position\_predicted(ID, CL, \_, \_),$$
$$\#count\{X, Y : position\_predicted(ID, CL, X, Y) >= 2.$$

where the predicate *position_predicted* represents the position (X, Y) in which the element class CL is predicted in an image ID (see [3] for further details), while the predicate *twins* identifies all the classes that appear at least two times in a given image. Then, we use additional ad-hoc rules to identify the object that has been supposedly misidentified, and hence should be "changed". In the

following, we show an example in which two distinct objects of the class left foot
have been identified, and the rightmost one is changed into an element of the
right foot class:

$$change\_twins(ID, leftFoot, rightFoot, down, rigth) : -twins(ID, leftFoot),$$
$$position\_predicted(ID, leftFoot, down, rigth),$$
$$position\_predicted(ID, leftFoot, down, left).$$

where the predicate *change_twins* is used to denote that the class left foot predicted on the down right part of the image has to be changed with the class right
foot.

3   Results and Discussion

A first experimental campaign for assessing the viability of our approach has been
reported in [3]; we refer the reader to the cited work for some insights about
settings and fine-tuning description. With respect to that campaign, besides
making use of the herein presented prototype, we also tested the approach on
the Freiburg Sitting People dataset with the aim of segmenting different parts
of human body (e.g., head, arms, legs).

It is worth noting that these first prototypical implementations of the approach look to require a relevant effort in terms of computational time; nevertheless, the main purpose of the proposal and the overlying DeduDeep system showed
promising results.

In order to assess the viability of our approach we compared the results
obtained using (*i*) cross-entropy (*CE*) as loss function, (*ii*) a combination of *CE*
and a penalty value derived via ASP-based model, and (*iii*) ASP-based post-
processing phase. In general, including the ASP-based penalty in the loss function and, especially, performing post-processing phase involve an improvement
in the Intersection-over-Union *(IoU)* mean value (e.g., DeepLab-v3 (*ii*) 0.755
and (*iii*) 0.768). Further details about experiments performed on the Laryngeal
Endoscopic images are provided in [3].

As already introduced, in the present work we additionally tested DeduDeep
on the Freiburg Sitting People dataset [8], on the task of performing human part
segmentation. As previously described in Sect. 2, we automatically extracted evident truths from the dataset by considering the neighborhood of the objects and
their logical proximity. The results obtained so far over this dataset show slight,
but systematic improvements. Figure 2 shows an example of results achieved
using DeepLab-v3 network which obtained the best results using both datasets.
As illustrated in Fig. 2, ASP-based post-processing is able to remove small island
of noise and re-assign the class of the objects that do not comply with evident
truth, resulting in a relevant improvement. Indeed, in Fig. 2(c) we can see that
the network identified left foot class both on right and left side of the image
and no right foot class was predicted, similarly for the lower left leg class. Our
approach is able to identify the error and correct the misclassification as shown
in Fig. 2(d).

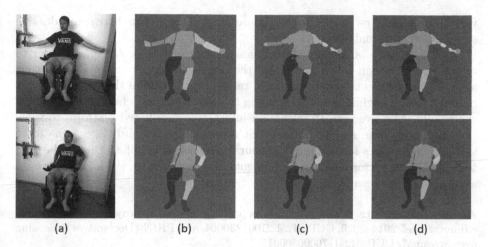

Fig. 2. Example of results obtained by DeepLab-v3. From left to right: raw image (a), ground truth segmentation (b), results achieved without post-processing (c), and the results of post-processing (d).

4   Conclusions

We presented a novel prototypical system called DeduDeep, designed to help at combining inductive and deductive approaches for tackling AI tasks. In particular, we take advantage of the potential coming from the declarative nature of ASP to steer approaches based on Deep Learning and to improve the quality of results via a proper post-processing phase. To this aim, we defined a loss function by combining the cross-entropy loss function and a penalty value, derived from the ASP-based model, that indicates the number of objects wrongly identified by the network.

The first experiments we performed in order to assess the viability of the approach and the robustness of the prototype allow to draw some considerations. First of all, it is worth noting that the approach is best suited for domains where some sort of explicit knowledge is available or obtainable somehow, so that it can be modeled in terms of ASP; furthermore, as far as the current design and implementation are concerned, the introduction of the ASP-driven tasks requires a relevant effort in terms of computational costs. Nevertheless, DeduDeep achieved promising results, proving to be able to improve the quality of the results and that there is significant room for further improvements; more importantly, it proved that the approach is viable and has some interesting potential in tackling the limitations of DL-based approach, thus contributing at the journey towards a more human-centered and more explainable AI.

It is worth noting that the approach herein presented can be in principle adapted to any scenario where some sort of explicit knowledge is available. Naturally, such knowledge vary over different domains, and new knowledge bases must be defined on a problem basis; here, the expressive and declarative modelling capabilities of ASP are of great use. Hence, the resulting framework is very flexible, and paves the way to more tight integrations between inductive and deductive formalisms.

As future work is concerned, we plan to work on the prototype in order to release it, to focus on better "tailoring" the ASP-based programs, to evaluate our approach in different domains and DL task, and to include the rule-based loss function at the beginning of the training to analyze the effects on the quality of the results. Also, we plan to release an interactive web-based platform to show the knowledge base model, add explicit additional rules and choose the most suitable parameters for training the neural network. This platform will be able to help users in performing the experiments, interacting with the knowledge base and showing the results.

Acknowledgements. This work has been partially funded by projects: PON "Ricerca e Innovazione" 2014–2020, CUP: H25F21001230004, and PRIN "Declarative Reasoning over Streams", CUP: H24I17000080001.

References

1. Brewka, G., Eiter, T., Truszczynski, M.: Answer set programming at a glance. Commun. ACM **54**(12), 92–103 (2011)
2. Bruno, P., Calimeri, F., Kitanidis, A.S., De Momi, E.: Data reduction and data visualization for automatic diagnosis using gene expression and clinical data. Artif. Intell. Med. **107**, 101884 (2020)
3. Bruno, P., Calimeri, F., Marte, C., Manna, M.: Combining deep learning and ASP-based models for the semantic segmentation of medical images. In: Moschoyiannis, S., Peñaloza, R., Vanthienen, J., Soylu, A., Roman, D. (eds.) RuleML+RR 2021. LNCS, vol. 12851, pp. 95–110. Springer, Cham (2021). https://doi.org/10.1007/978-3-030-91167-6_7
4. Calimeri, F., et al.: Asp-core-2 input language format. Theory Pract. Logic Prog. **20**(2), 294–309 (2020)
5. Chen, X., et al.: Recent advances and clinical applications of deep learning in medical image analysis. Med. Image Anal. 102444 (2022)
6. Gelfond, M., Lifschitz, V.: Classical negation in logic programs and disjunctive databases. New Gen. Comput. **9**(3–4), 365–385 (1991)
7. Laves, M.-H., Bicker, J., Kahrs, L.A., Ortmaier, T.: A dataset of laryngeal endoscopic images with comparative study on convolution neural network-based semantic segmentation. Int. J. Comput. Assist. Radiol. Surg. **14**(3), 483–492 (2019). https://doi.org/10.1007/s11548-018-01910-0
8. Oliveira, G.L., Valada, A., Bollen, C., Burgard, W., Brox, T.: Deep learning for human part discovery in images. In: 2016 IEEE International Conference on Robotics and Automation (ICRA), pp. 1634–1641. IEEE (2016)

Correction to: Logic Programming and Nonmonotonic Reasoning

Georg Gottlob⦿, Daniela Inclezan⦿, and Marco Maratea⦿

Correction to:
G. Gottlob et al. (Eds.):
Logic Programming and Nonmonotonic Reasoning,
LNAI 13416, https://doi.org/10.1007/978-3-031-15707-3

Chapters ["Statistical Statements in Probabilistic Logic Programming" and "Efficient Computation of Answer Sets via SAT Modulo Acyclicity and Vertex Elimination"] were previously published non-open access. They have now been changed to open access under a CC BY 4.0 license and the copyright holder updated to 'The Author(s)'. The book has also been updated with these changes.

The updated original version of these chapters can be found at
https://doi.org/10.1007/978-3-031-15707-3_4
https://doi.org/10.1007/978-3-031-15707-3_16

© The Author(s) 2022
G. Gottlob et al. (Eds.): LPNMR 2022, LNAI 13416, p. C1, 2022.
https://doi.org/10.1007/978-3-031-15707-3_40

Author Index

Printed in the United States
by Baker & Taylor Publisher Services